SECOND EDITION

Changing American Families

Judy Root Aulette

University of North Carolina at Charlotte

PEARSON

Boston   New York   San Francisco
Mexico City   Montreal   Toronto   London   Madrid   Munich   Paris
Hong Kong   Singapore   Tokyo   Cape Town   Sydney

Senior Series Editor: Jeff Lasser
Series Editorial Assistant: Erikka Adams
Senior Marketing Manager: Kelly May
Production Editor: Won McIntosh
Editorial Production Service: Pine Tree Composition, Inc.
Composition Buyer: Linda Cox
Manufacturing Buyer: JoAnne Sweeney
Electronic Composition: Pine Tree Composition, Inc.
Photo Researcher: Annie Pickert
Cover Administrator: Linda Knowles

For related titles and support materials, visit our online catalog at www.ablongman.com.

Between the time website information is gathered and then published, it is not unusual for some sites to have closed. Also, the transcription of URLs can result in typographical errors. The publisher would appreciate notification where these errors occur so that they may be corrected in subsequent editions.

Library of Congress Cataloging-in-Publication Data

Aulette Root, Judy.
   Changing American families / Judy Root Aulette.—2nd ed.
      p. cm.
   Includes bibliographical references and index.
   ISBN 0-205-48446-8
   1. Family—United States. 2. Family—United States—History. 3.
Family—United States—Statistics. I. Title.

   HQ536.A92 2007
   306.850973—dc22

                                    2006024264

Printed in the United States of America

10 9 8 7 6 5 4 3 2   RRD-VA   10 09 08 07

CONTENTS

PREFACE

Over the years I have observed that students come to sociology classes, and particularly family sociology classes, with a perspective that emphasizes what is up close and personal. They want to know why some families are often unhappy and why others seem to be a source of comfort and support. Students want to know why so many people are divorced and how to avoid this in their own lives. They want to know why people have children or not, how to make decisions about relationships, and how to make sense of their own lives. My interests in sociology tend to emphasize social structure and historical change in social institutions. For a long time I tried to get my students to put aside their individualistic concerns and look at the broad social context of families and large social factors like economic conditions; class, gender, and racial ethnic inequality; and social policy that shapes our lives. Finally I realized I needed to meet them in the middle and that is when I decided to write a book that brings together our microlevel experience of families with the macrolevel structures that have such a profound effect on our lives.

I decided to write a book that explicitly bridges the gap between the two levels of analysis, a book with a central focus on the interplay between the big picture—a society with its large structural features—and the everyday personal experiences of individuals interacting with one another.

My goal is to show how massive social institutions such as the economy, the government, and stratification systems are organized (and have changed historically). Like the first, this second edition of *Changing American Families* discusses the ways in which that social structure plays out in the lives of people interacting with each other in families—how their personal experiences, the way they feel about one another, and the way they treat one another—are influenced and sometimes even determined by what happens in social institutions far beyond the control of any individual or small group of people. I emphasize the space between social structure and individual social experience, addressing questions such as: How exactly did the economic system of slavery shape families in the eighteenth and nineteenth centuries? How do laws about divorce create relationships between divorcing men and women? How are our feelings about our grandparents and our children shaped by demographic change and media?

This insight, which Mills called the sociological imagination, is of course a core principle of the discipline. *Changing American Families* makes that idea the central organizing principle and consistently and explicitly integrates the concepts throughout every chapter. The idea of the sociological imagination is laid out in four components in the first chapter, and each of these components is featured in every subsequent chapter. First, the microlevel of family experience is explored. Second, the macrolevel, or social context, of families is described. Third, the effect of the macrolevel on the microlevel—the way in which the social structure affects family life—is investigated. Fourth, the effects of microlevel activity on the macrolevel—individuals interacting and sometimes organizing into social movements shaping and reshaping the larger society—is examined. Each chapter concludes with a section titled "The Micro-Macro Connection" that summarizes and reemphasizes what the chapter has revealed about these links.

The Importance of Agency

One of the comments that sociology professors often hear is "You sociologists are so critical. All I learn is how everything thing is screwed up. It's depressing." While I want students to learn how to take a critical view of their social world, my goal is not to depress them but to help them to learn to understand issues so that they can formulate changes to transform society and solve problems. Like other textbooks that stress a macrolevel approach, this book emphasizes social context and the ways in which family issues are determined by social structure or the economically and politically powerful. In addition, this book does something else—it reverses this relationship and calls the reader's attention to the way in which macrolevel social institutions are shaped, resisted, and challenged by individuals working together to seek change.

As I note in the book, Mills not only argued that the sociological imagination allows us to look at how large social institutions shape our everyday individual encounters. The sociological imagination also provides us with a tool for seeing the ways our seemingly small social interactions shape the social context in which we find ourselves. Each chapter also identifies how people resist and sometimes reconstruct social institutions that envelop families in order to address the problems they face in their families.

The title of the book, *Changing American Families,* refers to two processes. First, families are dynamic social institutions that change, sometimes, dramatically over time, and certainly our ideas and experience of families are moving through some important changes now. Second, people can and do seek to change families and the social forces that affect them. Change isn't something that just happens to us; we also create change.

Every chapter in the book is laid out according to the following formula: (1) A description of the issues related to the topic is presented. For example, how many people are married and divorced, and what happened to families during the Industrial Revolution? (2) One or two theoretical debates that exist within the field are examined. For example, is sexuality inborn or is it socially structured? And is violence in families caused by socialization, stress or patriarchy? (3) A discussion of social movements that are addressing issues related to the chapter is offered. What actions have people taken to try to cope with, resist, or change the family problems created for them by the organization of our society? What social movements have emerged, what have they done, what are their goals and what difficulties have they faced? Chapter 14 further emphasizes this theme of making change by covering the issue of family policy and the government as a critical arena of change.

A Fresh View of Families

In addition to Mills's sociological imagination, a second overarching framework for this text is the vast literature of a broad range of feminists. The book incorporates the work of scholars from many points of view but the emphasis is on those with a feminist understanding of families. Because the social organization of family is central to gender and women's lives, the development of feminist studies in the past four decades has created a large body of research and writing on issues related to families. Feminists have problematized gender—that is, they have moved beyond thinking about similarities, differences, and relationships between women and men as variables and have sought to reveal the ways in which these patterns are unacceptable and the ways in which we might alter them. Feminists have made gender the core of their work, and they have been especially conscious of the link between their ideas, research, and writing, and the ongoing political struggles for equality.

Based on this feminist model, this book is marked by its presentation of sociology of family as a political area of study about the ways in which people differ, confront, negotiate, and struggle for change. Families continue to be the center of theoretical and political debate in academia, the media, Congress, City Hall, and even the streets. My goal is to show students what ideas and information are available to help make sense of these controversies.

Organization of the Book

Each chapter opens with a vignette about a microlevel experience relating to the family topic of the chapter. These vignettes are based on sociological studies but are mostly fictional. Throughout the chapter, the characters and their dilemmas are referred to as a way of tying together the issues and of reminding students of how the research represents real lives.

At the same time that I try to reach students with the human impact of social phenomena and the human face of research findings, I also keep reminding them of the scientific and empirical base of a sociological understanding of families. A perennial student query to sociology professors is "But isn't this just a lot of opinion?' I tell my students that yes, opinion and point of view are important features of debates around families but scholars must pay careful attention to finding data to support or refute our assertions and to help us evaluate the debates. Each chapter includes much empirical data in the form of tables and graphs, as well as descriptions of research findings. In addition, the text includes boxes about research methods that provide students with insights about how to assess information by looking at the way in which research is conducted not just about what the findings are.

While feminism is the most prominent theoretical model, a wide range of analysis from a number of disciplines, such as economics, history, anthropology, and social psychology, are included. The theories are described, contrasted, and critiqued, showing the reader the diverse ways in which scholars have tried to explain and understand families.

The book is divided into five sections. The first chapter looks at recent changes in the study of families and introduces the concept of the Sociological Imagination, explaining how it is useful to understanding families.

The second section, Chapters 2 and 3, provides an historical overview of family issues in the United States from the Colonial period up to the early 1960s. These two chapters are divided by race ethnicity. Chapter 2 emphasizes Euro-Americans, and Chapter 3 focuses on the history of African Americans. Both chapters include historical information about Latinos, Asian Americans, and Native Americans.

The third section of the book explores contemporary families and the importance of social structure and social context especially the economy. Chapter 4 examines the relationships between families and the economy from the 1970s to today. Chapter 5 looks at systems of stratification by gender, race ethnicity, and social class and the way in which they affect families. Chapter 6 reviews the connections between work and families. Chapter 7 explores unpaid labor, housework in families. The fourth section of the book examines relationships and conflicts within families including love and sex in Chapter 8, marriage in Chapter 9, divorce and remarriage in Chapter 10, violence in Chapter 11, parents in Chapter 12, and children in Chapter 13.

The last chapter of the book investigates the social institution that is particularly important for those seeking change in contemporary United States—the government.

New Additions

This second edition of *Changing American Families* has retained much of the style and information of that text. But it has been substantially revised and altered. In particular, tables and figures have been updated, and new research that appeared and has become much more accessible through the Internet from sources like the U.S. Census have been incorporated. In addition, I have brought in more information on two important issues: gay and lesbian families and Latino families. These two communities are increasingly important in the United States. Latino families have grown to become the largest minority in the nation and a majority in many regions and cities. The research is beginning to pay more attention to these families and this text includes as much up-to date information as is available.

Acknowledgments

Many people have helped me write this book. My family—Albert Aulette, Anna Aulette-Root, and Elizabeth Aulette-Root—have all read chapters, offered advice, taken care of me while I worked, and helped me to see the many ways people think, feel, and act. In addition, Albert Aulette did an enormous amount of work helping me to make sense of the all the new Census data and helping me to compile tables and keep track of citations. Many others have reviewed manuscripts, helped me to find information, and taught me what I need to know to write this book. They include my sociology of family students at University of North Carolina at Charlotte and my Women's and Gender Studies students and colleagues at the University of the Western Cape in South Africa, and Harry Rahn, George Root, Ruth Root, Edith Ward, and Tracy Buege Hilton. I am also grateful to the following reviewers for their insights: Bruce Bayley, California State University at Sacramento; Jerry Cook, California State University at Sacramento; Kathy Greaves, Oregon State University; Cynthia Hancock, University of North Carolina at Charlotte; Terina Robinson, Central Piedmont Community College; and Paula Tripp, California State University at Sacramento. Finally I would like to thank the people at Allyn & Bacon for allowing me this opportunity and helping me on the way—Jeff Lasser, Erikka Adams, Rebecca Nasman, Karen Hanson, and Patty Donovan.

Judy Root Aulette

1 How to Study Families in the Twenty-First Century

We think of weddings as personal, but they are affected by an array of social forces including the economy, the government, and religious institutions. (Tracy Buege Hilton, Troy, Michigan)

Michael and Kimberly are getting married next week. They have spent the past two years getting to know each other and planning their future. They met at the E-marketing company where Michael is an accountant and Kimberly is a secretary in the front office. Michael just finished his degree in business, and he hopes that his career will go like his father's and he will move up the ladder in his company. Kimberly still has a year to go before she finishes her degree in management information systems, and she also has high expectations that she will be able to establish a career and eventually have a well-paid and secure job. They expect to have two children, but they plan to wait before they start a family because they would like to have Kimberly stay home with the new baby, at least for the first year or two. After the wedding, they will be moving into an apartment, but they are sure they will be able to save enough money in two or three years to put a down payment on a house. Michael's parents were divorced when he was in grade school, and he believes that they took the easy way out. Michael is convinced, and Kimberly agrees, that divorce is not in their future.

> This young couple has made many choices about marriage and family. But how well have Michael and Kimberly predicted their future? How has our society—for example, the media and the schools—shaped the way they think about these issues? Do such social institutions as the legal system, the government, religious institutions, and places of employment set limits on the options from which Kimberly and Michael have chosen? What might interfere with their choices, causing their lives to move in a dramatically different direction? Kimberly and Michael are very much in agreement about the choices they have made. What could happen that would cause them to discover that they had serious differences about the best way to organize their family life?

These are the kinds of questions sociologists ask. They are also important questions for people who are not sociologists. Most of you have families with whom you interact, and many of you are thinking about forming relationships or having children to begin a new generation of families. The better we understand what we expect from our families and what helps us in—or prevents us from—establishing and maintaining happy relationships, the more likely we will be to attain our goals.

Analyzing Social Life

In order to answer the questions we have posed about Michael and Kimberly's plans, we need to ensure that our information about families is accurate and that the concepts we use to make sense of that information are capable of interpreting reality. This book will provide the most accurate information possible about the reality of family organization in contemporary American society. It will attempt to make sense of that reality by analyzing it in a conscious and systematic way.

Although you may be unaware of it, you are constantly analyzing your social environment. You predict events, make assumptions, interpret behavior, correlate activities and feelings with other activities and feelings, and assign significance to relationships and interactions among people. All of these activities—predicting, assuming, interpreting, correlating, and assigning significance—are aspects of creating sociological analysis. You probably do these activities, however, without giving them much thought, and if someone were to ask you what your analysis of a social issue is, you might have a hard time answering.

This book will help you to learn a formal method for analyzing your experiences and your relationship to the social world. One tool that is especially important in this analysis is called the sociological imagination.

The Sociological Imagination: Bridging the Gap between Individuals and Society

C. Wright Mills, one of the most important twentieth-century American sociologists, called individuals' lives biographies, and he used the term histories for the "lives" of societies. He taught that the relationship between biography and history should be the focus of sociology. Mills argued that our goal as sociologists should be to examine and understand the ways in which individuals interact with one another in social activities. He maintained, at the same time, that we must also examine and understand the way in which society affects social relationships among individuals. Mills named the ability to bridge this gap between society and the individual social experience the Sociological Imagination.

Mills noted that using the Sociological Imagination demands a lot of practice. People do not naturally think like sociologists. Most people in our society, like Kimberly and Michael, believe that individuals choose their own destinies. Although it is true that individuals make choices, they make them within the limits of the society in which they live. Sociologists attempt to understand what those limitations are and how they affect individual choices.

C. Wright Mills (1959) explained this task stating:

> Neither the life of an individual nor the history of a society can be understood without understanding both. Yet men do not usually define the troubles they endure in terms of historical change and institutional contradiction. The sociological imagination enables its possessor to understand the larger historical scene in terms of its meaning for the inner life and the external career of a variety of individuals. The first fruit of this imagination—and the first lesson of the social science that embodies it—is the idea that the individual can understand his own experience and gauge his own fate only by locating himself within his period, that he can know his own chances in life only by becoming aware of those of all individuals in his circumstances. We have come to know that every individual lives, from one generation to the next, in some society; that he lives out a biography, and that he lives it out within some historical sequence. (Mills 1959, p. 3)

Like Michael and Kimberly, we all will make decisions about with whom to live and establish intimate relationships, whether to marry, whom to marry, whether to have children, and how to divide work within our households. Many people negotiating these choices with one another create a society. But beyond these individuals and their interactions is a social structure that shapes the decisions that individuals make and the experiences that individuals have. Social structure includes, for example, the laws that allow some people to marry but not others; the media messages we are sent about acceptable ways for husbands to treat wives or parents to raise children; the technology available for housework; and the pay scale for wage work. These social structural factors shape, limit, and sometimes even determine the activities and choices of individuals as they interact with one another.

Micro- and Macrolevels of Analysis

Using the Sociological Imagination means that we will analyze social experience at two levels: the micro- and macrolevels. The microlevel focuses on the family life of individual families or individual family members in face-to-face relationships. Analyzing the microlevel of social experience means we are examining society in its smallest expression. Here we would observe social life up close among people who are in contact with each other on a regular basis. This might be called the everyday life of people.

The macrolevel of analysis focuses on social structure, which includes ideologies, technologies, and social institutions such as the government, the economy, and social classes. Analyzing social life at the macrolevel means that we try to understand society, or at least a large segment of society, as a whole.

Society Is a Human Invention

C. Wright Mills observed not only that the microlevel is affected by the macrolevel, but that the macrolevel is affected by the microlevel. The society in which we live was created by individual people working together. The laws, ideas, technology, and ways of carrying out day-to-day tasks that characterize our society did not drop from the sky or emerge as a fact of nature, but were invented and implemented by humans, and they are constantly being reinvented and re-created. Mills wrote of every individual: "By the fact of his living he contributes, however minutely, to the shaping of this society and to the course of its history, even as he is made by society and by its historical push and shove" (Mills 1959, p. 11).

This statement has two important implications. First, it means that our families and the social contexts in which they are embedded are the subjects of constant debate and struggle among all the different people in our society who are either seeking to maintain or seeking to change the status quo. Second, it means that we have the opportunity to shape the course of history—our own and our society's—by entering into these disputes and the social movements that have emerged around them. In the past few decades, the contest over who should decide what a family is, what makes a family good or bad, and how best to solve the problems families face has been especially intense. If we discover that our family problems are caused by the limitations placed on us by our society and we choose to alter those limitations through social action, we will discover a flurry of activity and organizations already operating to address family issues. Activists from the political right to the left are putting forward their visions of the problems and their solutions to many questions related to families, such as child care, abortion, housing, welfare, sexuality, and violence.

For example, suppose that Michael and Kimberly have a child before they feel financially ready. Although they would prefer to have Kimberly stay home to take care of the baby, they may find themselves unable to survive without her paycheck. They will then find that day care is expensive. If they decide to become involved in political action to convince the federal government to fund day care for working parents like themselves, they would find numerous organizations already lobbying Congress. Some of those groups petitioning and rallying would be arguing for federal funding of day care, and others would be arguing that child care, including how it is paid for, is a matter that is best left to parents and that the government should not interfere.

In sum, C. Wright Mills's model for understanding the social organization of families points toward four sets of issues that we will examine:

1. The microlevel—the social experience of individuals and individual families.

   How do different family members use their time?

   How do they treat each other?

   What are the patterns of conflict?

   How do family members support and care for each other?

   How do these personal interactions change over time as family members grow older?

2. The macrolevel—the organization of our society and its major social institutions as they relate to families.

   What are the most important aspects of contemporary American society in which our families are embedded?

   How are social institutions such as our economic system, government, and class, race, and gender stratification systems organized?

3. The macrolevel affecting the microlevel—the daily experience.

   How does our society shape our family lives?

   What problems do families face in trying to survive within our society?

   What choices must families make? How are these choices necessitated by social context? How are they restricted by social institutions such as the government, the economy, or religious institutions?

   What are the varieties of families in which Michaels, Kimberlys, and others live? How do race ethnicity, social class, and historical period affect that variation?

4. Microlevel activities shaping the macrolevel organization of our society.

   How do people seeking solutions to problems their families face create change in their society?

   Since people make changes not only as individuals interacting within their own families, but as organized groups of individuals, what ideas are being promoted and what solutions are being offered by the many organizations that are concerned about family issues?

   For example:

   What are the different points of view on various welfare reform bills?

   What should the relationship of the government be to families? Are children best raised by families without government interference, or should the government help provide food and shelter for children?

   Is sexuality legitimate only for married heterosexual couples?

   How can we stop violence?

   Who is responsible for taking care of the sick, the homeless, or the elderly—their families, the government, or both?

   Who should make decisions about abortion?

Families as a Political Issue

Is the family a political institution? Not according to the popular notion of family in the United States. Families are not considered part of the politics of society. Sometimes families are even thought of as the opposite of politics—a private space away from the public world (Lasch 1977). Ernest Burgess (Burgess and Locke 1945), who is considered the father of family sociology, took this position. A basic assumption of his work is that "the family sphere is qualitatively different from the public sphere. The public and private spheres are separate social realms. The family is a psychological relief station from the public world" (quoted in Osmond 1987, p. 113). Others, however, have argued that families are very much part of the "public sphere" and the political debates that take place there and that, in addition, families are not "psychological relief stations" but often sites of power struggles themselves (Berger and Berger 1974; Ferree 1990; Thornton and Freidman 1983).

In order to address the question of whether the family is a political institution, we first need to determine what the word politics means. Politics is the expression and organization of power. Power can have many meanings, as we explore in Chapter 9 (Hartsock 1998). Jean Lipman-Blumen (1984, p. 6) defines power as "the process whereby individuals or groups gain or maintain the capacity to impose their will upon others, to have their way recurrently, despite implicit or explicit opposition through invoking or threatening punishment, as well as offering or withholding rewards." If these kinds of activities touch on families or take place within families, then families must be arenas of power and political institutions.

Families are political institutions in two ways (Pogrebin 1983). At the macrolevel, families have a political relationship to the rest of society. At the microlevel, families include political relationships within their own boundaries. Families are political configurations existing within larger political configurations.

The first type of politics of family is evident in the current debates around families and family issues such as child care, education, abortion, sexuality, and welfare rights. These are topics of great concern to the politicians, governmental agencies, and social organizations that we commonly think of as political institutions. What happens to families with respect to these issues is tightly tied to political decisions, the relationships of power, and the battles over power that underpin those decisions. Sometimes the discussions of these issues even go so far as to claim that families do not just touch on the politics of our society, but that families are at the center of the political world (Harding 1981; Pogrebin 1983).

Families: Hot Issue in the United States

During the 1992 presidential campaign, a controversy that has become known as the family values debate emerged, illustrating the political character of families (Chira 1998; Coontz 1997). The debate was part of an older polemic that can be traced back through the development of the Christian Right in the 1980s, efforts by conservative organizations in the 1970s, and the controversy surrounding the Moynihan Report in the 1960s (Hadden 1995). We look at this history and these issues more extensively, especially in Chapter 5, but the point here is that families have been and still are a central political issue in the United States and the questions surrounding families are often controversial and volatile political topics.

Three contending views dominate in the political debates surrounding families (Giele 1999). The first of these might be called the conservative position (see, e.g., Wolfe 1998). Conservatives argue that our values or beliefs about families and the ways in which we try to make our lives live up to those beliefs should follow certain prescribed patterns. They assert that families are the most important social institution. Jerry Falwell, a conservative religious leader and political activist, takes the conservative approach. He states that family "is the fundamental building block and basic unit of our society, and its continued health is a prerequisite for a healthy and prosperous nation" (Falwell 1980, p. 205).

Conservatives believe that "the way things ought to be" is for men and women to marry and raise children in families that, at least in the parenting years, have a husband as prime provider and protector and a wife as a primary nurturer (Coontz 1997; Skolnick 1991). Parents should be most responsible for their own children, with little interference from other institutions such as schools and the government, and women should focus on the role of mother (Hardacre 1994). Those who fit into the conservative category are busy financing political campaigns, lobbying for candidates and legislation, and formulating and disseminating information on their view of families. Conservatives organize against legal abortion and protection of homosexuals and lesbians from discrimination. They are in favor of policies that inhibit divorce and single motherhood. According to their point of view, policies or individual choices outside of this model should be discouraged or even prohibited.

A second point of view in this political debate might be called the liberal viewpoint (Giele 1999). Proponents of this position argue that values are not as important as the economic context in which families exist. They argue that the focus on "family values" has deflected attention from more important practical issues regarding families, such as making decent wages to support our families and ensuring that our children receive sufficient nutrition, housing, and education. According to the liberal viewpoint, we need candidates, laws, and social institutions that address the physical needs of families and communities instead of spending time making sure we have the "right" ideas.

The third point of view is articulated by Stephanie Coontz (1997), who argues that both of these positions fall short. Hers might be called a feminist perspective (Giele 1999). She contends that the conservative framework is flawed in two ways. First, its model of what ought to be is too narrow and does not encompass the varieties of ways people successfully organize families. Coontz asserts, furthermore, that the model of family proposed by conservatives seeks to subjugate women and children to men. It also implies that men are inherently irresponsible and oppressive and that only if we can offer them authority over their wives and children will they be willing to engage in family life.

Second, Coontz argues that the conservative position is also wrong because it ignores the economic context. She maintains that irreversible changes in our economy have caused changes in family organization that cannot be undone by changing our values. For example, families cannot survive on one paycheck, which means that women have become permanent, essential parts of the labor market. We cannot turn back the clock and send mothers and wives home.

Coontz also critiques the liberal viewpoint. While liberals pay attention to economic context, she believes they do not acknowledge the kinds of changes in our values that will be necessary to alter the economic context so that it supports families drowning in debt and declining wages. Coontz contends that we need to broaden our view of acceptable family forms and pay attention to the economic needs of all families. But in order to do that, we also need to alter our values. Like conservatives, Coontz believes that we need strong family values. Her family values, however, are quite different from those proposed by conservatives. For example, she suggests that one essential family value we should promote is the idea of community responsibility for children. Unlike conservatives who insist that children are primarily or even solely the responsibility of their biological or legally adoptive parents, Coontz supports the notion that "it takes a village to raise a child."

Coontz relates a story to illustrate this value. In the sixteenth and seventeenth centuries, Europeans who came to North America were impressed with the generous and egalitarian way in which Native American groups such as the Montagnais-Naskapi Indians treated one another. But the French missionaries were critical of the family values of the group. The Jesuits believed that the Montagnais-Naskapis allowed their women too much independence and failed to discipline their children strictly enough. The priests tried to convince the Indian men that they needed to better control their wives to ensure that the children they bore were really their husbands'. The men were horrified by the priest's logic, and one Naskapi man replied, "You French people love only your children; but we love all the children of our tribe" (Coontz 1997, p. 120). The debate over family values apparently has a long history. But today it is especially relevant (Gillis 1997).

You have probably heard about these debates. Family is a political hot topic. We all have opinions about what values are best and what our social institutions need to do (or not do) to help us live "the way we ought to." In this book we will be looking at several political debates that surround families. I have mentioned two prominent social institutions as they intersect with family life—the economic system and the political system. A third social institution is increasingly important in these debates—religion. The United States is one of the most religious nations in the world today. Eighty-eight percent of Americans claim that religion is very important or fairly important to them; 96 percent say they believe in God or a universal spirit; and 89 percent attend religious services at least once a month (Saad, 1996). Some religions have been active in their involvement in the political arena over family issues. Members of religious organizations decide their positions on political issues and then decide whether and how they will promote those ideas in larger contexts, such as by participating in funding lobbying efforts or campaigns and producing information and education for their membership and for the broader public. In the earlier discussion of conservatives, I mentioned Jerry Falwell, who is a religious leader as well as a political leader. Religious people and religious leaders, however, find themselves on many sides of these debates (Shibley 1996). Religious people and religious organizations are sometimes part of the conservative movement, but many others take an active role in liberal or feminist activities.

The Personal Is Political

Families are political in a second way—in their internal relationships. These relationships have to do with the relative amounts of power of various family members, the sources of power among family members, and the implementation of power. If you look back at

BOX **1.1**

Religion in the United States

All religions are concerned with issues related to families, such as birth, death, sexuality, gender relations, and marriage. Religious institutions, in addition, often handle family rituals such as weddings and funerals. Families also act as agents of religions by providing religious education and involving family members in religious activities (McGuire 1992). Religious institutions, therefore, spend a lot of time considering family issues, and they are an important source of information about ideas about families in a society (Kosmin and Lachman 1993).

Compared with other nations, religion is especially important in the United States (Bellah et al. 1985). Almost all Americans say that religion is at least fairly important to them. Most Americans are Christians, but there are a large number of different denominations and sects to which people belong..

Table 1.1 shows the distribution of different religions and the ways in which organizational affiliation varies by race ethnicity. These data show us the diversity of experience of religion. Religious organizations have at least slightly different and sometimes dramatically different views on family matters. Like many other issues we explore in this book, we need to be careful not to make assumptions about people's beliefs and behaviors just because they belong to some general category based on gender, race ethnicity, or religion.

TABLE 1.1   Denominational Affiliation for all Americans, African Americans, and Hispanic Americans

Denomination	All Americans	African Americans	Hispanic Americans
Catholic	25%	8%	72%
Baptist	22	55	5
Methodist	10	10	
Lutheran	7	1	
Presbyterian	4	1	
Jewish	2		
Episcopalian	2	1	
Protestant	19	17	18
None	7	5	5
Other	2	2	

Source: Greeley 1995, pp. 344–45.

Lipman-Blumen's (1984) definition of power, you will see that it can be applied to many of the relationships and activities that exist within families. In your own family, certain family members may have more power than others. For example, parents may have greater ability than children to offer rewards or to mete out punishment to others in the family. And you undoubtedly have been involved in power struggles within your family over issues such as who should do the dishes, who should decide how money will be spent, or which family members can use violence against others in the family. The politics of family, in both forms, will be a recurring theme in this book. We will be looking at the role family issues play in the broad political struggles within our society. We will also be examining the political relationships within families.

Recent History of the Sociology of Family

Sociology has never been a uniform discipline. A variety of contending schools of thought within the field has characterized its history, just as it does today. Critical theorists such as C. Wright Mills, symbolic interactionists such as Herbert Blumer and Erving Goffman, behavioral sociologists such as Ernest Burgess, and structural functionalists such as Talcott Parsons were all actively working to shape sociology in the 1940s and 1950s. Some scholars argue that structural functionalism dominated during this period, despite the diversity within the field (Glenn 1987). In the United States, the early 1950s was an era of social and political conservatism. The social sciences reflected the public mood, and the dominant theoretical perspective within sociology reflected the ideological climate of the times. The framework of structural functionalism adapted itself well to the cultural and political mood of conservatism (Giddens 1977; Gouldner 1970; Huaco 1986; Ritzer 1992).

Structural functionalists examine society as a whole system. They assume that each part of a society fits with the other parts to create a smoothly functioning system. Functionalists believe that society is essentially stable and beneficial for nearly all its members, and changes must take place very slowly so that they do not prove too disruptive. Functionalism has been criticized because it emphasizes social order and stability and ignores or justifies problems such as inequality.

Talcott Parsons was a key figure in the development and promotion of functionalist theory within sociology. In particular, Parsons's work was essential to the development of the sociology of family (Morgan 1975). Like conservatives in the family values debate, Parsons believed that society is best served by families that are functional units in which one male person serves the "instrumental" needs of the family members. By this he meant that men should be the rational, decision-making, money-earning public figures. Parsons thought that the ideal complement to the instrumental husband was an "expressive" wife, a woman who would be the nurturant, domestic, provider of child care. Within this framework, a woman employed outside the home was believed to be disruptive or dysfunctional for her family. In 1955, Parsons wrote, "It seems quite safe in general to say that the adult feminine role has not ceased to be anchored primarily in the internal affairs of the family, as wife, mother and manager of the household, while the role of the adult male is primarily anchored in the occupational world, in his job and through it by his status-giving and income-earning functions for the family" (pp. 14–15).

Another functionalist, Mirra Komarovsky, wrote:

> A social order can function only because the vast majority have somehow adjusted themselves to their place in society and perform the functions expected of them. Even if a parent correctly considers certain conventional attributes of the feminine role to be worthless, he creates risks for the girl in forcing her to stray too far from the accepted mores of her time.

At the present historical moment the best adjusted girl is probably one who is intelligent enough to do well in school but not so brilliant as to get all A's—capable, but not in areas relatively new to women; able to stand on her own two feet and to earn a living, but not so good a living as to compete with men. (1953, pp. 52–74)

As you can see, functionalists' ideas about families included many questionable assumptions about gender. Both men and women were given stereotyped prescriptions for their behavior with little room for individual variation. The implications for women were particularly troublesome. The structural functionalist position on families was also questionable for working-class and racial-ethnic families. The assertion that a nuclear family with a male breadwinner and a female housewife was the best type of family ignored the need for wives in working-class and many racial-ethnic families to work outside of the home. And it denied the possibility that alternative family forms could provide equally positive environments. During the 1960s, powerful social movements challenged functionalist ideas. The civil rights movement, which grew rapidly in the 1950s and 1960s in the United States, was one that disagreed with the functionalist analysis (Wiley 1979). Civil rights activists demanded that we acknowledge the diversity within our society in all social activities, including family. Many families, especially many African American families, were not organized as Parsons and Komarovsky claimed they should be. Civil rights advocates argued that we must understand racial-ethnic families in terms of their relationship to the larger society and that we should consider the positive aspects of different family forms (Billingsley 1968; Gresham 1989; Ladner 1971; Rainwater and Yancey 1967; Stack 1974). Scholars and activists whose work addresses the problem of racial ethnic inequality continue to assert these concerns (Baca Zinn 1998a, 1998b).

The gay rights movement initiated in the 1970s in the United States also reminded us that our ideas about families were too narrow and failed to include the experience of gay men and lesbians. Gay rights activists and scholars argued that our ideas about intimacy, love, and sexuality needed to be broadened beyond the assumption of heterosexuality for all (Altman 1971, 1982; Brake 1982b; Rich 1986; Rubin 1975; Weeks 1985). As the gay rights movement grew and became more visible in the 1980s and 1990s, activists and scholars concerned with addressing homophobia and establishing justice for gay people continued to debate family issues regarding partnerships, marriage, and children (Stacey 1996).

The women's movement, in particular, focused its attention on families, and it too was critical of the functionalist view (Benston 1969; Cronan 1971; Firestone 1970; Millett 1970). Some feminists argued that families like those functionalists portrayed as ideal were really prisons for women. The women's movement took as its central concerns the problems women experienced in families in dividing work, expressing their sexuality, and facing violence (Flax 1982).

Women's Liberation Movement

The battle for the right of women to vote that developed in the nineteenth century and ended with the passage of the Nineteenth Amendment on August 26, 1920, was called the First Wave women's movement. The Second Wave emerged in the 1960s and was called the

Women's Liberation Movement. By 1970, "for the first time the potential power of the feminist movement became publicly apparent" (Freeman 1975, p. 84). And throughout the decade, consciousness-raising groups, conferences, protests, speak-outs, and teach-ins abounded. In all these activities, family issues took center stage with debates on abortion, sexuality, housework, child care, battering, and marriage.

In 1963, Betty Friedan, one of the earliest feminist authors of this period and the first president of the National Organization for Women (NOW), published *The Feminine Mystique,* a book about the same white middle-class housewives Parsons had described. Friedan's depiction, however, was not of the benign, natural, functional family. Instead, she described these families as "comfortable concentration camps." According to Friedan and other feminists (Firestone 1970; Mitchell 1984), Parsons's ideal family was not functional for women because it limited their ability to be independent, active participants in their society.

In response to these social movements and sometimes as part of them, family sociology scholars began to question their work in fundamental ways (Morgan 1975). They asked:

> How do people organize their family lives, and what does that organization mean to them?
>
> Who lives with whom?
>
> Whom do we call family?
>
> Are families prisons, havens, or both for women, men, and children?

Revisioning Families

Since the 1970s, sociologists have continued to ask these kinds of questions and worked to reconceptualize the study of families (Flax 1993; Hartsock 1993; Myers, Anderson, and Risman 1998). Jessie Bernard (1989), a prominent sociologist and a founding member of Sociologists for Women in Society, named this period of scholarship "The Feminist Enlightenment" because of the important role feminists played in this revisioning.

The revisioning, however, has not been carried out by feminists alone; a variety of recent family scholars have also participated in the effort (Baca Zinn 1998a). Barrie Thorne (1992) asserts that the last quarter of the twentieth century has been a period of rethinking families—questioning myths, asking new questions, and considering alternative ideas. The following themes are drawn from Thorne's and Baca Zinn's (1995, 1998a) revisionist view of families:

1. Challenging the myth of the monolithic family. This theme includes both acknowledging and appreciating diversity as it occurs historically or within a particular historical period.
2. Observing that families are sites of a variety of different activities, including production, reproduction, socialization of children, and sex.
3. Acknowledging differences among family members within families by gender and age.
4. Asking whether families are separate from the rest of society.
5. Creating families that provide both love and individual freedom and equality.

6. Asserting that families, as well as other social institutions, need to be changed in order to meet the human needs of women, men, and children.

Challenging the Myth of the Monolithic Family

The word monolithic describes something as being totally uniform. Frequently we speak of The Family as if it were a monolith and all families were the same. But is there really one way of organizing families that is most prevalent, natural, and beneficial for humans?

The family that was described earlier by functionalist theorists and conservatives in the family values debate is one in which a husband and wife and their minor children live together. The father is a full-time worker who earns enough money to allow the mother to be a full-time housewife (at least until the children are in school). This family lives in a single-family home; the parents are not divorced; and the children are natural or adopted. Families like this do exist in the United States, but they are a tiny minority. Only about 7 percent of households in the United States are composed of a father who is in the labor force, a mother who is a housewife, and their children (U.S. Census Bureau 2005d). If we were to restrict this category further by counting only households in which the children are the natural or adopted children of the married couple—not their stepchildren—or in which the family lives in a single-family home, the proportion would become even smaller.

Table 1.2 presents data collected by the U.S. Census Bureau that shows us how people organize their households. One of the questions asked by the Census is "With whom do you live?" Answers to this question are grouped into two main categories: family and nonfamily. Family includes households where the inhabitants are related to each other by blood, marriage, or adoption. Families that fit this legal definition make up about 70 percent of the total households. The figure indicates that a little more than one-quarter of households (27 percent) are composed of a husband and wife without children under the age of eighteen and one-quarter are composed of a husband and wife with children under the age of eighteen. Many of these households do not have children under eighteen. They do, however, have adult children living in them. In 2000, 56 percent of men aged eighteen to

TABLE 1.2　Percentage Distribution of Households in the United States, 2000

Families	68.1%
Married with children under 18	24.9%
Married without children under 18	26.8%
Single mother and children	8.4%
Single father with children	2.4%
Other family	5.6%
Nonfamilies	31.9%
Women alone	14.6%
Men alone	11.2%
Other nonfamily	5.8%

Source: U.S. Census Bureau 2000c Summary File 1.

twenty-four lived at home with one or both of their parents; 43 percent of women this age lived at home (U.S. Census Bureau 2000b). Single mothers with children under eighteen account for 8.4 percent, and single fathers with children under eighteen account for 2.4 percent of households. About 6 percent are households with other family members living together, for example, two brothers.

Nonfamily households include women living alone (15%) and men living alone (11%). One important difference between the men who live alone and the women who live alone is age. On the average, men who live alone are forty-four-years-old, and women who live alone are sixty-six (Bryson and Casper 1997). About 6 percent of households are made up of people who live with at least one other person but are not considered family by the government. The category of nonfamily households, however, may hide familial relationships because they include unmarried gay or heterosexual couples who may be cohabiting, as well as unrelated people who may rent a room in a house but have no personal relationship. In 1990, for the first time, people who were living together could identify themselves in the census as either partners or roommates. Regardless of their answer, however, they are not defined as family by the government.

Some people who have been designated by the government as nonfamily might argue that even though they do not have a marriage license their relationship is an intimate one and they consider themselves family. Most people in the United States, in fact, do have a broader definition of family. A *Newsweek* poll found that about 75 percent of people defined the family as "a group of people who love and care for each other" (Seligman 1990). What is your opinion? Think about your own family and imagine that you wanted to have a family portrait taken. Who should and should not be included? Your brother's girlfriend? What if she and your brother are engaged? Your sister's husbands' children? What if your sister is a lesbian and wants to include her partner? What about her partner's children? Would it be more important to include your biological grandparents or your stepfather? Would you include your children's father (your ex-husband) or his new baby, your son's half sister? Do you agree with the *Newsweek* poll, or do you think the government has a better definition of families?

Appreciating Diversity

The real-life experience of family is so diverse that using the term The Family to suggest a wife, a husband, and their two children (a nuclear family) is not a useful way to accurately describe the way most people live. The concept of The Family is also problematic because it may imply certain assumptions about how people ought to live. If one assumes that there is such a thing as The Family, families that do not fit this mold can be labeled deviant, dysfunctional, or abnormal (Baca Zinn 1998a). This assumption is especially loathsome to scholars concerned with racism. Patricia Hill Collins writes

> the archetypal white middle-class nuclear family divides family life into two oppositional spheres: the "male" sphere of economic providing and the "female" sphere of affective nurturing. Black women's experience and those of other women of color has never fit this model. Rather than trying to explain why Black women's work and family patterns deviate from the alleged norm, a more fruitful approach lies in challenging the very constructs of work and family themselves" (1990, p. 47).

All racial ethnic groups in the United States, including whites, blacks, Latinos, Native Americans, and Asians, have substantial numbers of nonnuclear families. Regardless of race, these nonnuclear families have been subject to criticism. In particular, African American families that have not fit the mold of The Family have been accused of being chaotic, dysfunctional, and broken. In Chapter 5 we explore the organization of African American families that are not nuclear but also are not chaotic and dysfunctional. We will see the importance of extended family, shared child raising, and cooperative systems for providing shelter and food for members of the community (Stack 1974).

Collins (1990) argues that instead of using concepts such as the monolithic family that do not fit the experience of large segments of our society and tend to reinforce prejudice, we should research real families. Furthermore, we should keep our eyes open not only to the validity of differences among families but also to the potentially positive effects of diversity. "Different" families, compared with The Family, often have more effective and humane ways of organizing social life. In addition, variety in family forms in itself may be a positive characteristic of a society.

The Monolithic Family and the Denial of Historical Change

The concept of The Family sometimes reflects an assumption that one kind of family has dominated all human societies throughout history. Imagining what life was like a thousand or even a hundred years ago is hard to do, especially if we are trying to envision the ways in which people thought or the ways in which they felt about each other or treated each other. We can see the artifacts in museums that show us how people dressed, the vehicles they drove, or what tools they used. But when we try to picture a mother feeding a baby and we speculate about how she felt about the baby, or when we try to picture a woman and man being married and we wonder what was going through their minds, the task becomes more difficult. This is because we tend to imagine people wearing different clothes, using different tools in different dwellings, but thinking, feeling, and acting pretty much the same as we do.

Women have always borne children; and for many centuries, at least, men and women have married each other. But the ways in which motherhood and marriage, as well as other family relationships, have been organized have changed throughout human history. The ways in which mothers and children and husbands and wives, grandparents, aunts, and cousins treated each other and thought about each other have varied considerably through all of human history.

One does not have to go back too many years to notice historical change in families. As recently as the end of the nineteenth century, for example, children were seen in a very different light than today. Viviana Zelizer describes two legal cases that contrast how children were valued in 1896 compared with 1979:

> In 1896, the parents of a two-year-old child sued the Southern Railroad Company of Georgia for the wrongful death of their son. The court concluded that the child was "of such tender years as to be unable to have any earning capacity, and hence the defendant could not be held liable in damages." In striking contrast, in January 1979, when three-year-old William

Kennerly died from a lethal dose of fluoride at a city dental clinic, the New York State Supreme Court jury awarded $750,000 to the boy's parents. (1985, pp. 138–39)

Zelizer explains that before the early part of the twentieth century, children were valued on the basis of their ability to contribute economically. Since the passage of child labor laws at the turn of the twentieth century, children have become valued as economically useless but emotionally priceless. Making the assumption that families have always been the same blinds us to the reality of human history and limits our ability to understand who we are and where we came from. But more important, denying historical change means that we cannot see the direction in which we are heading.

If we assume that families have always been the same, we must assume that they will not change in the future or that if they do change, they can only disappear. On the other hand, if we see families as moving through history and constantly changing, we can understand the changes taking place in our own time as a part of that history, not as evidence of the collapse of The Family. Scholars are increasingly becoming aware of the need to acknowledge the diversity of family organization both in contemporary American society and throughout human history (Collier, Rosaldo, and Yanagisako 1992).

Observing That Families Are the Sites of Many Different Social Activities

Many activities take place within families. Juliet Mitchell (1984) wrote that four essential social structures are interwoven throughout society, they intersect in many modern Western families and provide examples of the variety of activities that simultaneously take place in families.

Mitchell named one structure production. This refers to the way in which families are economic institutions producing food and shelter, preparing workers to enter the wage system, and purchasing and consuming goods and services.

The second structure Mitchell describes is reproduction. Families also play a central role in the reproduction of the next generation. Women, both supported and constrained by their husbands, the church, the legal system, and physicians, frequently make decisions about fertility within their families. Birth is increasingly in a family context, with fathers and siblings attending the birth of new babies. In the United States, we also have explicit laws designating children's relationship to adults. For example, every child must be under the legal custody of a natural or adoptive parent or guardian.

Families are also sites of the socialization of these children, Mitchell's third structure. Socialization is the process by which humans learn the rules of a society—what is appropriate and what is inappropriate behavior and what one might expect if one behaves in either way. Along with other social institutions such as schools, the media, and the courts, families are a key site for the socialization of children in our society.

Finally, Mitchell reminds us that in our society sexuality is part of family organization. Although there is much sexual activity outside of marriage, the primary "legitimate" and often only legal form of sexuality is heterosexual intercourse between husbands and wives. Other expressions of sexuality and sexual relationships are always compared with this standard and are treated unequally and often critically by informal rules and formal laws. For example, gay men and lesbians are harassed and can even be imprisoned in some states for their sexual activities. And the unmarried sexual relationships of young people, heterosexual or homosexual, are publicly denounced in the government's AIDS education materials prepared for the public schools.

Sociologists who approach social phenomena from a macrolevel have claimed that these different systems within families must be recognized as separate though interlocking and must each be examined both alone and relative to each other.

All the activities that Mitchell cited—production, reproduction, socialization, and sexuality—take place both inside and outside of families. In some families, all four activities might occur, in others only one or two. Other theorists have focused on other structures not included in Mitchell's framework. For example, violence or emotions such as love might be included as activities that take place in several sites in our society, including some families. In sum, sociologists agree that families are complex social institutions in which many different kinds of activities and connections occur.

Acknowledging Differences within Families by Gender and Age

We often speak of the happy family, the good family, the violent family, or the strong family. The implication is that families are united and that the experiences of all family members are uniform. According to writer Heidi Hartmann:

> Such a view assumes the unity of interests among family members: it stresses the role of the family as a unit and tends to downplay conflicts or differences of interest among family members. I offer an alternative concept of the family as a locus of struggle. In my view, the family cannot be understood solely or even primarily as a unit shaped by affection or kinship, but must be seen as a location where production and redistribution take place. As such, it is a location where people with different activities and interest in these processes often come into conflict with one another. (1981, p. 368)

Hartmann reminds us that families are made of sets of relationships among different members. A family may be a happy place for some family members but not for others. It may be strong because of one or two members. We might call a family violent, but if we look inside that family we could find that the experience of violence is very different for different family members. One person may be a batterer, another a victim of abuse, and another a witness to it—all within the same family.

This differential experience occurs partly because every person is unique. We are all individuals and have different personalities and different experiences that we bring to our family relationships. But in many families, there are patterns of differences along the lines of gender and generation. For example, men and women do different tasks in families. Even today, housework is often divided between women and men in gendered ways. We might assume that the increasing proportion of women in the paid labor force and the visibility of the women's movement would have created equality in the way in which housework is divided. Recent studies, however, as we see in Chapter 7, show that women still do more housework and, when men pitch in, they do certain tasks such as taking out the garbage and yard work.

Furthermore, changes in families are experienced in different ways. For example, men and women emerge from divorce with different resources, a topic that is explored in Chapter 10. Generation, too, is a factor distinguishing family members. For example, violence between parents and children usually victimizes children, as discussed in Chapter 13.

Writers like Hartmann remind us that when we look inside families, we need to be careful to look at conflict and competition as well as consensus. This does not mean that we will only look at tensions and differences within families, because sometimes families work together or experience themselves as an integrated unit. For example, in Chapter 3 we observe the way in which African American sharecropping families worked together to protect their members from assault by violent landowners. In this book, we will see that families are places where people can be both allies and adversaries.

Asking Whether Families Are Separate from the Rest of Society

Sometimes the obvious truth of the many strands of our social roles and relationships is blurred by our belief that families have fixed boundaries. We believe that if we have a good family, we will be a good person or we will have a good life. We think of our families as rigid containers that insulate and separate us from the rest of society. But our family relationships and our experiences of family life are only one part of our social existence. And our family relationships and our experience of family life are constantly being shaped and reshaped by social relationships and institutions outside of families and vice versa.

If we are to understand families, we need to examine the fluid boundaries of families and the ways in which families and family members interact with other aspects of society. Imagine that you were born and raised in your present family, but that family was part of a different society. Would your life be the same? Would you be the same kind of person as you are now? What if you were born into a peasant family in Guatemala, a blue-collar family in Tokyo, or Bill Gates's family?

These families are all different from yours and from one another because they exist in different societies or in different social classes. The members of these different families would participate in different activities, think different thoughts, and experience different emotions, because not only are they part of a particular family, but also they are simultaneously part of different societies and different social classes within those societies.

Scholars who are committed to revisioning families have paid attention, in particular, to the ways in which the economy and the government are organized and how these two social institutions interact with families and individual lives (Gerstel and Gross 1987; Mitchell 1986). Work, for example, has an important influence on our family life:

> If any one statement can be said to define the most prevalent sociological position on work and family, it is the myth of separate worlds. . . . The myth goes like this: In a modern industrial society, work life and family life constitute two separate and non-overlapping worlds, with their own functions, territories, and behavioral rules. Each operates by its own laws and can be studied independently. A corollary of the myth is the assumed separation of men's and women's domains, with the family woman's place. (Kanter 1977a, pp. 16, 20)

B O X **1.2**

The Greying of America

In 1850, 2 percent of the population lived past their sixty-fifth birthday. Today 75 percent of us do. Membership in the AARP (American Association of Retired Persons) is now larger than any single religious denomination except the Roman Catholic Church (Treas and Torrecilha 1995). The proportion of older people is growing steadily. Table 1.3 shows the proportion of the total population who are aged sixty-five and older from 1900 to its projected percentage in 2050. In addition women are likely to live longer than men, and the gender gap for older Americans is expected to grow (Thompson 1992). Race ethnicity also makes a difference. Only about 4 percent of the Latino population, for example, is over sixty-five (De Anda 2004).

These changes are having significant effects on our lives (Powell, Branco, and Williamson 1996). And since this trend is so recent, we are not sure what all of those effects might be (Skolnick and Skolnick 1999). Matilda White Riley (1999) writes that one of the important effects is the proliferation of family attachments, especially intergenerational links. By this she means that as people live longer, many more generations of family will be alive at one time. Families, therefore, cannot be thought of as primarily relationships between parents and children because there are families of four or even five generations. We must think in terms of children, grandchildren, great-grandchildren, parents, grandparents, and great-grandparents. Along with these are great-aunts and great-uncles, grandnieces and grandnephews. We have more people to connect with as family. Riley also notes that besides the greater numbers of people in our families, our family relationships have longer duration. For example, instead of knowing our grandparents or great-grandparents only briefly during our childhood, they may be in our lives for many years. Multigenerational families as the experience of nearly everyone is something new.

TABLE 1.3   America's Population is Aging and is Projected to get Older

		Projections	
Year	Percent Age 65 and Over	Year	Percent Age 65 and Over
1900	4.1	2000	12.8
1910	4.3	2010	13.3
1920	4.7	2020	16.4
1930	5.5	2030	20.1
1940	6.9	2040	20.7
1950	8.1	2050	20.4
1960	9.2		
1970	9.8		
1980	11.3		
1990	12.5		

Source: U.S. Census Bureau 1975, 1993.

In the scenario with which we began the chapter, Michael and Kimberly assume that their jobs will not interfere with their family decisions and vice versa. But what if Kimberly finds that finishing her degree and building her career takes several years, and that at age thirty-five she still has not had the two children she wanted? Taking time off to have the babies, and especially taking several years off to stay home with them until they go to kindergarten, will affect her career. The gap in her résumé might prevent her from advancing in her field. On the other hand, if she delays childbirth too much longer, she may be physically unable to have children because infertility increases as women age.

Creating Families That Provide Both Love and Individual Freedom

If we call for changes in families, we need to identify goals for reconstructing families and societies in ways that provide for loving and egalitarian communities. But we also need to be careful not to maintain or create relationships that place some people at a disadvantage. Michele Hoffnung describes the dilemma between advocating for individual freedom and equality and for societies that are nurturant and collectively run:

> Mothering is done at home, outside the world of achievement, power and money. It is this aspect of motherhood—its limiting effect on women's public participation at a time when women have won access to the public world—that must inform the next stages of feminist activity for social change. It is not enough for women to be able to do men's work as well as women's; it is necessary to reconsider the value of mothering and to reorder public priorities so that caring for children counts in and adds to the lives of women and men. (1989, p. 157)

For example, we want individual women to be able to decide about their own fertility—to choose whether to have children without the interference of the government, their parents, or their husbands. On the other hand, we must recognize that bearing children is a social activity. It necessitates the interaction of at least two people, and many people have direct or indirect interest in the birth of a child.

We need to support individual women's right to make their own fertility decisions, as well as to expand opportunities for men to participate more fully in the lives of children (Ehrensaft 1987). We must also increase the responsibility of our society for children instead of leaving nurturance, or the loving care of children, in the hands of mothers, or mothers and fathers, alone.

Asserting the Need to Change Families So They Can Better Serve the Needs of Women, Men, and Children

In discussing each of these five themes, the need for change has been shown. Those who have sought to revision families have been especially interested in identifying problem areas and possible ways to address those problems. Our goal is not just to describe or understand families but also to create new visions of families and to participate in reshaping families and their social context. At the end of each chapter are some examples of people actively engaged in creating social change. Their projects are sometimes small and sometimes

BOX **1.3**

The Question of Research Methodology

The six themes suggested by Thorne (1992) and Baca Zinn (1995, 1998a) show that sociologists who are committed to revisioning the study of families have asked certain kinds of questions about the social world that were often left unasked by other scholars. They have also challenged the methodologies of social inquiry, the way in which scholars have attempted to answer their questions (Ferree and Hess 1985; Harding 1987; Renzetti 1997; D. Smith, 1974, 1979).

Social science researchers use a variety of techniques to gather and analyze data, including interviews, observation, case studies, historical documents, experiments, surveys, and content analysis (Reinharz 1992). When these techniques are used by feminist researchers and other scholar-activists, however, they are incorporated into a methodology that is characterized by three principles (DeVault 1996).

The first principle is to replace the "view from above" with the "view from below" (Mies 1983). This means that we examine the lives of people who have often been invisible, such as women, working-class people, racial ethnic people, and children. This practice provides us with a better understanding of those who have been ignored, censored, or oppressed, and it also gives us a more accurate picture of society by including them (DeVault 1996).

The second principle is to minimize harm to those who are being studied and to maximize leveling hierarchies in the research process (DeVault 1996). This means that we examine people's experience from their point of view. In many sociological investigations, the researcher alone chooses the topics, determines the questions, and explains the findings. In contrast, leveling hierarchies means that researchers seek ways to conduct research activities with the people whose lives are being examined. For example, researchers might incorporate participants into the creation and implementation of research projects and into decisions about what use should be made of the findings. In this way lines between researcher and researched become blurred.

The third principle is the integration of research and social action with the intention of changing the status quo (Reinharz 1992). Throughout this text, you will notice boxes with discussions of how the research that is reported in the book was conducted. The boxes should help you see the broad range of methodologies social scientists use. It should also help you see how important methodology is to creating information. When you read the results reported, think about how those results were obtained and how the techniques used might have influenced the findings.

---

global. Their points of view on what needs change, how best to change it, and what the changes should be are varied. Think about people you know or stories you have read about that show people making changes that relate to family life. How do they compare with the studies reported in this book? What organizations do you think might yet emerge?

The Question of Theory

Theory is an essential feature of sociological inquiry. Theory helps us understand and explain our social experience, and it also helps determine ways to resolve the problems we uncover. We cannot solve problems that we cannot explain and understand. Nancy Hartsock writes, "Our theory gives us a description of the problems we face, provides an analysis of the forces which maintain social life, defines the problems we should concentrate on, and acts as a set of criteria for evaluating the strategies we develop" (1993, p. 8). Based on her reading of Antonio Gramsci (1971), Hartsock argues that theory not only can serve as a guide to social change, but also can itself become a force for change. When people's understanding of social issues is enhanced by theory and their political activities are thereby made more efficient, theory serves as a tool for accelerating the process of social change.

This chapter has focused attention on the contrast between two theoretical frameworks that are currently important to understanding families: structural functionalism and feminism. Structural functionalism was dominant in the 1950s, and although it was challenged in the 1960s, it remains prevalent in the work of social scientists (Glenn 1987). Feminists are among a variety of social theorists who have challenged functionalism.

Feminists are a diverse group of people, and in this text we examine some of the debates that have emerged among feminist sociologists. But Janet Chafetz argues that all feminist theories share three characteristics:

1. Gender comprises a central focus or subject matter of the theory. Feminist theory seeks ultimately to understand the gendered nature of virtually all social relations, institutions, and processes.
2. Gender relations are viewed as a problem. By this I mean that feminist theory seeks to understand how gender is related to social inequities, strains, and contradictions.
3. Gender relations are not viewed as either natural or immutable. Rather, the gender-related status quo is viewed as the product of sociocultural and historical forces which have been created, and are constantly re-created by humans, and therefore can potentially be changed by human agency. (1988, p. 5)

In addition to looking at the diversity among feminists, we examine the ways in which other theorists have tried to revision our understanding of families. In every chapter, several theoretical frameworks are described and compared. For example, Chapter 4 discusses a symbolic interactionist approach to the response of families to unemployment. In Chapter 6 we look at what exchange theorists have had to say about the effect of work and family on relationships between husbands and wives. We examine the Marxist analysis of marriage in Chapter 9. In Chapters 11 and 12 we look at psychoanalytic theory and the relationship between parents and children. And in Chapter 13 we review social constructionism and its contribution to understanding socialization. Many other theories are reviewed as well, and in every case the alternative theories are examined with regard to their strengths, weaknesses, and connection to empirical evidence.

Mills's theory of the Sociological Imagination provides the overarching theoretical framework for each chapter. Each chapter in this book includes the four sets of issues proposed by Mills: the microlevel, the macrolevel, the effect of the macrolevel on the microlevel, and the effect of the microlevel on the macrolevel.

To illustrate the microlevel, the chapters open with a vignette like the story of Kimberly and Michael. These stories are based on historical documents, interviews, and other sociological research, but they may or may not be about real people. Their purpose is to capture an image of the ways in which the issues addressed in the chapter might be experienced by individuals in their everyday lives. Be careful not to fall into accepting them as the only ways the issues are experienced. Let yourself think about how they might be similar or different for you or for other people you know. For example, perhaps the story of Kimberly and Michael does not capture your experience at all because you are a single mother, a divorced person, or a gay man. What would your story sound like and how would it fit into the broader picture?

2 A History of U.S. Families with a Focus on Euro-Americans

The transition from an agriculturally based economy to an industrialized one in the nineteenth century created changes in white families that included a decline in fertility and alterations in the expectations and experience of husbands, wives, and children. (Harry Rahn, Lincoln Park, Michigan)

S̲arah was born in the late 1700s in Massachusetts. When she was a child, her mother Ruth told her stories about life in the mid-1700s on the family farm. Ruth spoke of the hard work and the self-sufficiency of the household. The family purchased very little because their own work provided nearly all the food, clothing, and shelter they needed. Sarah liked to hear Ruth talk about the many people who lived in the house—Ruth's parents, her six sisters and brothers, apprentices, servants, and frequently a youth who had run into trouble in town and whom the authorities wished to place under the stern guidance of Ruth's father. Ruth's father was the head of the household and led the family in their work, religion, and education. He even chose Ruth's husband for her. When she grew up, Sarah was glad women of her generation were able to choose their own husbands.

Sarah's mother's and grandmother's lives were controlled by hard physical work. Sarah's life is easier because she lives in Boston with her husband, a bank manager. Many of the items she uses in her household are purchased with his wages. She does not have to weave cloth, carry water, or tend animals. Sarah's job has been to raise her four children and to provide a moral and nurturing environment for them and her husband.

Although her life has been sheltered and privileged compared with the working-class women she sees on the streets of Boston, Sarah has not been entirely happy. She feels that she has been prevented from using all of her talents. When she was a child she was clever with numbers, and now she sometimes watches her husband working at home and wishes she could work at the bank.

As Sarah sits in her dining room reminiscing about her memories of her mother and about her own life, there is a knock at the door. A messenger has brought her a letter from her daughter Elaine. Elaine writes, "July 28, 1848. My dearest mother, I am writing to tell you I have decided to break off my engagement to be married. This week I have attended the Seneca Falls Convention and I intend to dedicate my energies to winning the vote for women. We have remained in the shadow of men for too long. Your loving daughter."

How much have families changed over the past few centuries?

Would these changes have been the same for Sarah and her kin if they had been from another social class?

How is Sarah's life better than her mother's? How is it more difficult?

How are the differences between Sarah and Ruth's lives related to the development of an urban, industrial economy in the nineteenth century?

What kinds of problems do you think Sarah's husband might have because of his role as the only family member able to earn money and the person who must always be in charge of the family?

The Seneca Falls Convention of 1848 is recognized as an important event in women's history. What kinds of family issues do you think the women discussed at this meeting? How might they be different from the family issues about which women speak today?

Studying the Social History of Families

Until quite recently, sociologists were unconcerned with historical change (Goode 1964). Before 1960, sociologists who were interested in the history of American families had only three or four books from which to choose. Since the 1960s, however, the field of social history and especially the social history of families has burgeoned (M. Gordon 1978).

The growth in scholarly attention to the social history of families has two sources. First, as noted in Chapter 1, sociologists who are revisioning families are concerned with acknowledging the diversity of families, including the ways in which families vary over time.

Second, the growth in the study of the social history of families is related to a change in our thinking about legitimate areas of scholarly interest (Bridenthal and Koonz 1977; Tilly and Scott 1978). Forty years ago historians tended to focus their attention on dominant figures in society. Their concern was with great men and extraordinary events. Since women and other "lesser" people such as peasants, slaves, and workers were less likely to be dominant figures, their stories were not as likely to be examined. The focus of more recent scholarship in history, however, has shifted to include the everyday life of the common person, which includes family matters.

This chapter and Chapter 3 review the family history of people in the United States from the colonial period until the mid-twentieth century. Since race ethnicity has had such a striking effect on the experience of Americans, this history is divided into two chapters, one with an emphasis on Euro-Americans and one with an emphasis on African Americans and Latinos. This chapter focuses on Euro-Americans, although Native Americans, Chinese Americans, and Japanese Americans are also included. In Chapter 4 we will further explore the concept of race ethnicity itself, including the words like Black, white, Latino, and Hispanic we use to describe ourselves.

A central theme of this chapter is that as the Industrial Revolution developed in the United States, family organization changed with it. As the economy moved through distinct stages, so did families. Along with this general pattern of macrolevel changes in the economy causing microlevel changes in the organization of families, however, there are two important variables. First, at each stage important distinctions existed among families who differed by race ethnicity and social class. Second, people like Elaine in the scenario that opened this chapter created social movements to try to change both the economy and families; the microlevel affected the macrolevel.

The chapter is organized into three major sections. The first section reviews U.S. history through a number of periods: Colonial America, industrialization, the pioneer era, the Great Depression, World War II, and the Fifties. Each of these subsections discusses the development of various families, as well as the changing relationships among men, women, and children within households. The second section discusses the technique of breaking history into periods and some of the problems with using periods as a way of understanding historical change. The third section describes the development of the women's movement that emerged in the 1900s and sought changes in family organization, as well as other aspects of American society.

Stages in the History of Euro-American Families

White middle-class families in the United States have moved though three stages from the time the Europeans first began to immigrate to North America in the 1600s until the present. The family form that characterized the first stage, called the Godly Family, lasted from the early 1600s until about the time of the Revolutionary War in 1776.

The Modern Family is the term family historians use to designate the family form like that of Sarah's in the scenario at the beginning of the chapter. This form emerged among white middle-class Americans at the end of the eighteenth century. The Modern Family consists of a breadwinning husband, a housewife, and their dependent children. Table 1.2 in Chapter 1 showed that this family form has declined in the last half of the twentieth century and is no longer the most common one (Coontz 1988; Degler 1980; Mintz and Kellogg 1988). Before its decline, the Modern Family passed through two periods: the Democratic Family, which lasted from about 1780 until the end of the nineteenth century, and the Companionate Family, which lasted from about 1900 until 1970. In the decades since 1970, family organization has moved into the third stage, the Postmodern Family (Stacey 1996). Postmodern families will be the focus of Chapters 4 through 14.

One of the critical factors in the social context of these changes in family organization has been the organization of the economy. An economy is a system by which the goods and services that people need to live are produced and distributed. The macrolevel social institution of the economy has changed as industrialization developed through the eighteenth, nineteenth, and twentieth centuries. These macrolevel changes have been accompanied by parallel developments at the microlevel of family organization.

Changes over time in the economy have shaped the history of the organization of families, as shown in Table 2.1. The first stage, the Godly Family, is associated with a preindustrial, agriculturally based economy. The second stage, the Modern Family, is associated with the development of industrialization. The third stage, the Postmodern Family, is associated with deindustrialization. This chapter focuses on the first two stages. Chapter 4 explains what deindustrialization means and how it relates to our experience of family organization today.

At the same time that macrolevel changes in the economy have had an important effect on the organization of families, activity at the microlevel among individuals and individual families has also affected the organization of the economy. For example, one of the first goals of the women's movement was to contest the laws that barred married women from owning property.

TABLE 2.1   The History of Euro-American Families in the United States

Family Form	Economic System	Time Period
1. Godly Family	Preindustrial agriculture	1620–1780
2. Modern Family	Industrial capitalism	1780–1970
a. Democratic Family		1780–1900
b. Companionate Family		1900–1970
3. Postmodern Family	Postindustrial capitalism	1970–present

The Godly Family

Colonists from Germany, Holland, Sweden, Ireland, and other European countries came to settle in the United States in the 1600s. Those from England were particularly numerous, especially in what came to be the New England states.

The twenty thousand people who emigrated from England to Massachusetts between 1620 and 1640 had a vision of a new world that included a new kind of family, one that did not exist in England. They wanted to establish a Godly Family that conformed strictly to the teachings of the Bible (Mintz and Kellogg 1988).

The Godly Family the Puritans established in the colonies was characterized by four factors:

1. The family structure was patriarchal.
2. Families were highly integrated into the community.
3. Each family was a nearly self-sufficient economic unit.
4. All social activities, including education, health care, and welfare, took place within families.

The Godly Family was patriarchal. Patriarchy literally means rule by the father. The term, however, is used in a variety of ways. Radical feminists use it to describe a broad system of oppression and control of women by men (Jagger 1983). Before the emergence of radical feminism in the 1960s, the term patriarchy was used mostly by anthropologists who defined it more narrowly as a system of control by men that was associated with a fairly specific family organization. Gayle Rubin (1975, p. 168) described this older definition of patriarchy as a family that was dominated by "one old man whose absolute power over wives, herds, children and dependents was an aspect of the institution of fatherhood." Puritan families fit both definitions.

In the religious beliefs of the Puritans, God the father ruled over his children, and they modeled their human families after this image. Puritan fathers exercised authority over large households that included their wives, children, and servants. Puritan fathers were the representatives of their families in the social and political affairs of the community; they owned most of the property; and their wives, children, and servants were required by civil and religious law to submit to the patriarch's authority.

Statutes in Connecticut, Massachusetts, and New Hampshire called for the death penalty for children who cursed or struck their fathers. Fathers had the legal right and obligation to select a spouse for their children. And even when the children were married adults, fathers could intervene in their affairs.

The role of wives was also determined by the demands of patriarchy. "Puritans believed that a wife should be submissive to her husband's demands and should exhibit toward him an attitude of 'reverence,' by which they meant a proper mixture of fear and awe" (Mintz and Kellogg 1988, p. 11). Court records show that women who did not obey their husbands were subject to fines and whippings. One of the symbols of a woman's relationship to her husband was the name she took after marriage. A married woman was not called Mary Brown or even Mrs. John Brown. In colonial society, she was called John Brown his wife (Ulrich 1991).

In addition to laws that demanded that children and wives submit to the patriarch's authority, fathers also controlled most of the property. Their ownership of the most important means of obtaining food and shelter meant that those who did not own the land had to obey the landowner's wishes. During this time, married women were not allowed to own property, and single women were not likely to inherit property. In order to survive, women had to be attached to husbands who would provide them with access to food and all the other materials they needed. Sons could legally own property once they became adults, but they rarely were able to accumulate enough capital to do so. Eventually sons were likely to obtain property through inheritance from their fathers, but the deeds were almost never passed on until the father died. This meant that adult sons worked for many years under the control of their landowning fathers (Greven 1978).

Puritans, however, did not believe that families should be isolated patriarchal kingdoms. Families were very much part of the whole community. The integration of family and community is the second characteristic of the Godly Family. Actions that today we might consider outside interference in family affairs were accepted as legitimate. For example, in the late 1600s in Massachusetts, the court appointed tithingmen to watch over ten or twelve households. Their job was to make sure that the internal affairs of the families were harmonious and proper. They sought out and punished parents who did not control their children, husbands who did not support their families, and anyone who fornicated or committed adultery. These tithingmen were devoted to their jobs and successfully identified many people who were not conducting themselves properly. Court documents show that fornication and adultery were by far the most numerous criminal cases (E. Morgan 1978). Punishments for not maintaining a proper home included fines, brandings, whippings, and occasionally the death penalty.

When children were found to be unruly, they were removed from their home and placed in the household of a patriarch whom the community believed to be a more effective disciplinarian (Mintz and Kellogg 1988). In the scenario at the beginning of the chapter, Sarah recalls the stories of her grandfather boarding one of these wayward youths.

The third characteristic of the Puritan family was that it was a self-sufficient economic unit. Puritan families were likely to be large. Nine was the average size, and many families had as many as fifteen members. This included not only children and parents, but also unrelated apprentices and servants and extended kin such as unmarried aunts.

One of the myths of the preindustrial patriarchal family is that it included several generations of kin. Households with more than two generations were rare because of the short life span. Puritan households were large not because they included several generations of people related by blood, but because they were usually composed of a nuclear family and a number of other unrelated people whose work helped make the household economically self-sufficient (Modell and Haraven 1978).

All members of the household participated in the production of nearly all the goods they needed to survive. A few people produced specialized goods, such as shoes, furniture, and leather, to be sold in distant markets. But like Ruth's family, nearly all white families in Colonial America were primarily self-sufficient agricultural units (Mintz and Kellogg 1988). The work that took place in these families was enormous. Records of the homemaking tasks of the women during this era show that work fell into four categories: mothering, meal provision, clothes provision, and nursing (Matthaei 1982).

During the colonial period, pregnancy and childbearing occupied much of a woman's life. A woman bore an average of eight children. She would see one in three of her children die before reaching the age of twenty (Matthaei 1982). Childbearing was dangerous work, and maternal deaths were also common. In Plymouth in the 1600s, records show that 20 percent of women died from causes associated with childbirth.

Providing meals was another onerous activity. A recipe from 1742 for a pork dish begins: "Cut off the head of your pig; then cut the Body asunder; bone it, and cut two Collars of each side; then lay it in Water to take out the blood" (Matthaei 1982, p. 42).

Women were also expected to provide clothes for their families. Starting from scratch meant growing the cotton and tending the sheep that provided the wool. Thread was made, cloth was woven, and finally clothes were sewn.

The fourth area of domestic work was the provision of medical care. Health care was so closely related to women's other domestic work that cookbooks included recipes for medicines, ointments, salves, and sleeping potions alongside the recipes for vegetables, pastry, and wine.

The final characteristic of Godly Families was that they were the site of social activities that today we expect to find in other institutions such as churches or schools. For example, the law required fathers to lead their households in prayer and teach all family members, servants, and apprentices reading and the principles of religion and law, as well as a trade. The family was also responsible for social service tasks we usually associate with outside agencies, such as caring for orphans, the ill, and the elderly (Demos 1970).

A striking difference between the Godly Family and its present-day counterpart is in the experience of childhood (Mintz and Kellogg 1988). By the age of seven, children were full participants in the productive work of their families, that is, farming, weaving, gardening, making soap and candles, and engaging in all the other activities of the household.

Children were strictly controlled by their families, especially by their fathers. The Puritans believed that children were born sinners and that the task of parents was to drive out that sin through religious study, physical beatings, and psychological pressure. One technique was for a family to send adolescent children to live in another household where the adults, unrestrained by parental concern, would be able to administer the proper discipline. Nearly all boys and girls of all classes were placed in other households as students, servants, or apprentices.

The Godly Family lasted for about 150 years until the late 1700s. Rising population and abundant land to the west made it increasingly difficult for fathers to use the distribution of land to their sons as a way to control them. In addition, changes in the American economy opened up new sources of income in the production of goods outside the family. Children who could earn their own money in factories and shops could also defy their parents' wishes about sexual behavior and make their own decisions about when and whom to marry. Among Euro-Americans, as the industrial economy developed and manufacturing and transportation improved, the Modern Family began to emerge as an alternative to the Godly Family.

Before moving to the next historical period, let us look at a family form that existed in North America at the same time as the Godly Family, the Iroquois family. The Iroquois family provides a significant contrast to the Godly Family.

Iroquois Families

When the Puritans arrived in North America to establish their new society and its Godly Family, between 10 and 20 million Native Americans inhabited the continent (Amott and Matthaei 1991). They represented about three hundred distinct cultures and two hundred languages (Nabakov 1991). Before their history could be documented, many of these peoples were killed by war and disease brought by the Europeans (Stiffarm and Lane 1992). We know very little about most of them. One group about whom records were kept and saved is the League of the Iroquois.

The League of the Iroquois was made up of six member nations—the Mohawk, Onondaga, Seneca, Oneida, Cayuga, and Tuscaroras, who lived in the area that is now the state of New York. It is estimated that the Seneca numbered about ten thousand when the Europeans began settling in North America (Jensen 1991).

The Seneca people lived in extended kin groups that were controlled by older women. These matrons owned the houses, the seeds, the tools, and the harvests. They supervised the work and distributed the food to the rest of the clan. The land was communally owned by all of the women in common (Brown 1977; Jensen 1991).

The matrons also wielded much social power. In 1390 the Iroquois Confederacy created a constitution called the Great Law of Peace. The constitution stated:

> Women shall be considered the progenitors of the nation. They shall own the land and the soil. Men and women shall follow the status of their mothers. You are what your mother is: the ways in which you see the world and all of the things in it are through your mother's eyes. What you learn from the father comes later and is of a different sort. Clan Mothers and their sisters select the chiefs and remove them from office when they fail the people. Clan Mothers! You gave us life—continue now to place our feet on the right path. (Amott and Matthaei 1991, p. 36)

Just as the Puritan patriarchs arranged their children's marriages, the Seneca matrons arranged for their children's marriages. Lineage was traced through the mother's line. Because the women owned the houses in which the families lived, if a wife wished to divorce her husband she could order him to leave on grounds of sterility, adultery, laziness, cruelty, or bad temper (Evans 1991). If he wanted to stay, he had to have an aunt or grandmother intervene on his behalf (L. Morgan 1965).

The governing body of the Seneca was composed of men. The men, however, were appointed by the matrons, who watched the men carefully and quickly deposed any whom they felt were not representing the women's interests. The Seneca matrons could not decide to go to war because that was the business of the male warriors. The women, however, ultimately controlled even decisions of war and peace because they could refuse to provide the warriors with such necessities as shoes and food (Randle 1951).

Both of the societies that inhabited what is now the northeastern United States, the Puritan society and the Iroquois Confederacy, were preindustrial. They both had family forms in which power was held by those who controlled the source of livelihood, the land. In the case of the Puritans, the men controlled the land, and the family form was patriarchal. Among the Seneca, the women controlled the land and the family form was matriarchal.

The Modern Family, Stage I: The Democratic Family

The Modern Family is divided into two stages. The first stage is called the Democratic Family. This term was coined by Alexis de Tocqueville, a French aristocrat who visited the United States in 1830 and wrote a book about the new society being created in North America and the new family form that was emerging among the white middle class.

The Modern Family differed from the premodern Godly Family in four ways:

1. Work was split into unpaid domestic work and paid work.
2. Individuals could freely contract marriages based on love.
3. Privacy and the separation of families from the community were promoted for middle-class families.
4. Women had fewer children, but were supposed to spend more time at their "natural" and demanding task of mothering (Stacey 1990).

The Split between Family and Work among Euro-Americans.   The rise of industrial capitalism coincided with the rise of the Modern Family (Stacey 1990). During the early 1800s, the operation of families as self-sufficient economic units began to change. In 1776, Watt perfected the invention of the steam engine, and the Industrial Revolution rapidly advanced. Family farms began to specialize in crops to sell on the market, and the production of food and clothing, soap, candles, and nearly every other commodity moved from the home of the premodern, preindustrial family into the factories of industrial capitalists.

As the jobs moved, so did the workers. A new domestic division of labor appeared to replace the old preindustrial form of women, men, and children working together in a common economic enterprise. Among the middle class, husbands were expected to follow the wage-earning jobs. Women were expected to stay home, and the occupation of housewife emerged (Mintz and Kellogg 1988). Women were supposed to use their time to take care of their families, to raise their children, and to maintain the morals of the community.

At the same time that the task of rearing children intensified in the sense that mothers were supposed to be more involved with their children's upbringing, the numbers of children born to the average woman declined. Table 2.2 shows the fertility rate for women from about the time of the emergence of the Modern Family until 2000. The data only show two racial ethnic groups, white and black, and the numbers are only available for white women until 1850. In 1800, white women had an average of 7. That number steadily declined until the late 1930s, when the average was down to 2.5. At the very end of the Modern Family era during the 1940s and 1950s, the numbers began to rise and went up to 3.8 in the late 1950s. Since then, the Postmodern family developed, and fertility had declined to 2 children for every woman on average in 2000. The figure shows that while we might describe the Modern Family as one in which women are having fewer children, that change gradually developed over a period of 150 years. The trends for black women followed the same trends although the numbers have been consistently higher for black women, and in 2000, black women still had a slightly higher number of children although the difference is small.

Another change that accompanied the transition to the Modern Family among middle-class whites was that men and women became divided from one another in their work. As industrialization developed throughout the nineteenth century, men were increas-

TABLE 2.2   Numbers of Children Born to Women from 1800 to 2000

Year	Child/Woman Ratio	
	White Women	**African American Women**
1800	7.04	
1820	6.73	
1840	6.14	
1860	5.21	7.58
1880	4.24	7.26
1900	3.56	5.61
1920	3.17	3.84
1940	2.22	2.87
1960	3.53	4.52
1980	1.77	2.18
2000	2.05	2.13

Source: Haines and Steckel 2001; Hamilton et al. 2003.

ingly brought into the paid labor force while many women were likely to remain as unpaid workers in the home. Work and family life came to be viewed as two distinct spheres, and women and men were viewed as the appropriate occupants of these two different worlds (Mintz and Kellogg 1988).

The idea that social life is ideally divided into two spheres still influences popular notions about work and family. Chapter 6 looks at the way in which the idea of a split between work and family is still part of many people's thinking, although the idea has been criticized for two reasons. First, it does not accurately depict the experience of most families (Bose 1987). In the nineteenth century, many families did not have a breadwinning husband and a housewife, especially African American families living during the periods of slavery and sharecropping, as discussed in Chapter 3.

The proportion of children in families with a father breadwinner and mother at home—a modern family—was a small proportion of all families (about 15%) from 1790 to 1850. In 1850, it began to rise steadily until 1965, when it peaked at about 55 percent and then began to decline rapidly. Today, dual-earner families and single-parent families are now the dominant groups, comprising about two-thirds of all families. Only about 22 percent of children today live in families with a father breadwinner and mother homemaker (U.S. Census Bureau 2004a).

The second reason idealizing a split between work and family has been criticized is because in families in which work is divided between a wage-earning man and a housewife, problems can occur. Because housework does not earn money, it is economically invisible, and the women who do it appear to be noncontributing members of their society. Chapter 7 describes how this problem remains even today.

In addition, with the development of an industrial economy, access to goods and services became limited to those who could purchase them. Wages emerged as essential to survival. Women who did unpaid housework and did not earn money therefore were dependent on their wage-earning husbands (Stacey 1990).

Also, the women who were left in these middle-class homes began to have other responsibilities that tied them to unrealistic and stifling roles. As the production of food and shelter moved into the factory, housework increasingly became focused on the task of providing the "proper" social environment for children and husbands. This required that women behave in carefully prescribed and restricted ways. The prescription for proper behavior for wives and mothers in the early nineteenth century has been called the "cult of true womanhood" (Welter 1978).

The Cult of True Womanhood.   Between 1820 and 1860, a new definition of womanhood emerged and was widely disseminated in popular magazines, novels, and religious literature and sermons. In the 1700s, womanhood was associated with deviousness, sexual voraciousness, emotional inconstancy, and physical and intellectual inferiority (Mintz and Kellogg 1988). This image of womanhood changed dramatically in the nineteenth century. Historian Barbara Welter (1978) coined the term "cult of true womanhood" to name the image of women she found in nineteenth-century literature.

According to advice manuals, true women were to be judged by four virtues: piety, purity, submissiveness, and domesticity. A woman who displayed these attributes was promised happiness and power. If a society was composed of women with these attributes, it was safe from damnation (Welter 1978).

Piety was argued to be the most important attribute, and women who were without religion were believed to be restless and unhappy. Physicians and scholars "spoke of religion for women as a kind of tranquilizer for the many undefined longings which swept even the most pious young girl and about which it was better to pray than to think" (Welter 1978, p. 314).

Purity was the second attribute. Women were warned that men were more sensual and prone to sin than women. Women must protect both themselves and these weak men by not giving in. A woman's greatest treasure was her virginity, which she bestowed on her husband on the single most important day of her life—her wedding day.

Books and magazines in the nineteenth century gave practical advice to women to ensure that they remained chaste. In the early 1800s, Eliza Farrar recommended, "Sit not with another in a place that is too narrow; read not out of the same book, let not your eagerness to see anything induce you to place your head close to another person's" (1837, p. 293).

The third attribute of true women was submissiveness. Women were supposed to be weak, timid, humble, and dependent. Caroline Gilman (1834, p. 122) advised brides, "Oh young and lovely bride, watch well the first moments when your will conflicts with his to whom God and society have given the control. Reverence his wishes even when you do not his opinion." One advice book went so far as to advise that "if he is abusive, never retort" (Welter 1978, p. 319).

The fourth characteristic of true women was domesticity. Women's duty was to provide a domestic life that would keep men home and out of trouble. They were to be skilled in housework, needlework, health care, and flower cultivation.

The Ideal of Real Womanhood.   The cult of true womanhood was a powerful force in the 1800s, but did everyone listen to the message and were all writers espousing it? Frances Cogan's (1989) research on the mid-nineteenth century in the United States suggests that alternative views of women were also alive during this time. She calls these alternative views "the ideal of real womanhood." "Real women," unlike "true women," were being advised to avoid the frail, helpless, dependent role and to take pride in strong bodies and minds. Some novelists, magazine short story authors, and advice writers described models of this ideal and called on women to make their needs and their strengths known in a variety of arenas.

First, real women were counseled to have "muscles like harpstrings" in this alternative literature (Cogan 1989). Physicians and others stressed physical fitness and told women to engage in active outdoor sports, to build their bodies by doing their own household work instead of hiring servants, and to avoid the horrors of corsets.

Second, women were told to extend their education in order to attract and choose good husbands and to run their households. In addition, although mentioned less often, women were reminded that they needed an education in order to take care of themselves if they were widowed or never married. Third, advice professionals told woman to be careful in their courtship, engagement, and choice of husband. These writers implied that women were in charge of their destinies and should negotiate wisely. They should not behave as passive victims but as assertive, cautious, and knowledgeable. The fourth topic about which women were advised was employment. Women's options in employment were limited, but progressive voices told them if they did not have a husband, every woman should be able to take care of herself in an acceptable occupation such as teaching. And even if she was not paid, she should participate in charity and missionary activities in the community.

Cogan's (1989) research shows that the idea of the real woman was most clearly articulated between 1840 and 1880, but before and after that, egalitarian ideas were nearly silent. In 1848, however, a fully developed women's movement emerged, perhaps at least partially from these alternative views and the debates between them and more conservative ideologies like the cult of true womanhood.

Capitalist Industrialization and the Working-Class Family

In the latter half of the nineteenth century, industrialization intensified. Millions of Europeans immigrated to the United States seeking work in the growing number of manufacturing plants. At the beginning of the 1800s, about five thousand immigrants arrived every year. By 1850, that number had risen to 2.8 million per year, and between the end of the Civil War and the beginning of World War I, 24 million immigrants arrived.

The Modern Family, consisting of a breadwinning husband, a housewife, and their children, common in the white middle class, was not an effective form for the working class. Working-class people, especially the recent European immigrants who poured into the cities, could not live on the income of one family member.

Sometimes entire families were employed in the factories. In 1828 an advertisement in a Rhode Island newspaper read, "Family Wanted. Ten or Twelve good respectable families consisting of four or five children each, from nine to sixteen years of age, are wanted to work in a cotton mill, in the vicinity of Providence" (Mintz and Kellogg 1988, p. 94).

The more typical situation, however, was for fathers and children to work for wages and wives to earn money while staying at home (Sacks 1984). One study in Massachusetts in 1875 found that 44 percent of outdoor laborers and mill operators were children (Matthaei 1982). Although boys were more likely to work than girls, girls were frequently pulled out of school to work so that their brothers could finish their education.

Young single women during this time often worked for wages. In 1890, for example, 70 percent of foreign-born single white women were in the paid labor force (Matthaei 1982). Wives who were not employed outside of the home contributed to the family by earning money taking in boarders. Only about 5 percent of today's families take in boarders, but in the 1880s in the working-class towns of Pennsylvania, nearly one-half of the homes had nonrelative boarders living in them. Women who stayed at home also earned money by making flowers, doing piecework from the clothing factories, or doing laundry.

Decisions about who would work and where were made on the basis of the collective needs of the family as a whole, rather than on the basis of individual preference. If times were hard, working-class children were expected to defer marriage or education and to remain with their parents and earn a wage (Mintz and Kellogg 1988).

The Problem of the Family Wage.   The ideology of the cult of true womanhood and its insistence that women remain in their homes as unpaid housewives did not fit the economic circumstances of the working class. Working-class men were unable to earn sufficient wages to provide for economic dependents. In some cases, as we have seen earlier, the ideology of the cult of true womanhood was set aside, and working-class women found ways to earn wages. Sometimes the ideology was used to support the demand for better wages for working-class men—a family wage.

Samuel Gompers, an early leader in the American labor movement, called for a family wage in 1898. He stated that working men must have "a minimum wage, a living wage, which when expended in an economic manner shall be sufficient to maintain an average sized family in a manner consistent with whatever the contemporary local civilization recognizes as indispensable to physical and mental health, as required by the rational respect of human beings" (Boyle 1913, p. 73).

Gompers found support for his quest for a family wage among those who were usually his adversaries, such as Henry Ford, a major industrialist. Ford strongly supported the family wage and the maintenance of families in which husbands provided for their non–income-earning wives. As a way to allow men to become the sole breadwinners in their families, Ford established the wage of $5 a day for his employees, twice that of workers in other factories at the time. These improvements for working-class men, however, were made at the expense of working-class women. In 1919, Ford fired eighty-two women from their jobs in the Ford plant in Highland Park, Michigan, when management discovered that they were married to men who had jobs.

The family wage was both a boon and a tragedy for women. Women whose husbands were able to earn a family wage, like the Ford workers, benefited from the higher pay their husbands brought home. At the same time, the policy of a family wage was used to justify pushing women out of jobs and back to their "proper place" as non–wage-earning housewives.

Martha May (1982) argues that the key problem with the family wage was that it was premised on a particular organization of family, one with a male breadwinner and his dependent wife and children. The family wage defined normal men as those who accepted their position as economic provider. The family wage endorsed the cult of true womanhood. It promoted the idea that all women could and should become economically dependent wives and, therefore, could be legitimately excluded from the labor force.

The call for a family wage, therefore, carried a mixed message for working-class people, especially for working-class women. On the one hand, the demand for a family wage was a radical one that would improve the quality of life of working-class people and free them from some of the oppression of long, grinding hours in the factories. On the other hand, the demand for a family wage was conservative because it it advocated that working-class women be more tightly controlled by and dependent on their husbands. The limited economic opportunities of working-class women were further eroded by the family wage because it legitimated the exclusion of married women from the workplace.

Pioneer Families: Leaving Friends, Facing Hardship. At the same time the eastern part of the United States was urbanizing during the nineteenth century, another social change was taking place—the westward expansion of Euro-Americans. The migration had important effects on the families that made the journey.

Under the Homestead Act of 1862, any citizen or anyone declaring an intention to become a citizen who was over the age of twenty-one could pay a fee of $10 to live on 160 acres of government-owned land. After living on the land for five years and making certain improvements, the person could file for final title to the land. From 1840 to 1870, between a quarter and a half million people moved west (Billington 1949).

Historians who have studied the diaries and journals of the people who set out on the Overland Trail have found that in nearly every case it was men who decided to take advantage of this opportunity, and that among married couples, the husband made the decision for the whole family to go. And only about 25 percent of the women who made the trip said they agreed with that decision (McNall and McNall 1983). Women's diaries and letters show that many of those women who followed their husbands felt sadness and anger at having to leave their families and friends behind.

The close ties among women during the nineteenth century and the difficulty they had in leaving their friends is shown in letters written by women to each other that reveal deep and intimate relationships. One woman, a twenty-nine-year-old wife and mother, wrote to her lifelong friend: "Dear darling Sarah, How I love you and how happy I have been! You are the joy of my life. I cannot tell you how much happiness you gave me, nor how constantly it is all in my thoughts. My darling how I long for the time when I shall see you, your Angelina" (Smith-Rosenberg 1985, p. 56).

In addition to leaving their friends, pioneer women, men, and children faced enormous physical hardship (West 1992). Anna Howard Shaw wrote:

> When my father took up his claim of three hundred and sixty acres of land in the wilderness of northern Michigan, and sent my mother and five young children to live there alone until he could join us eighteen months later, he gave no thought to the manner in which we were to struggle and survive the hardships before us. We were one hundred miles from a railroad,

forty miles from the nearest post office, and half a dozen miles from any neighbors and a creek a long distance from our house for our only source of water. (1915, p. 28)

Women's hard labor also contributed significantly to their families' cash income. In some households, women's sale of such goods as butter and milk amounted to incomes as high as $200 or $300 a year in an economy where an annual cash income of about $400 per household was typical (McNall and McNall 1983).

The Modern Family, Stage II: The Companionate Family

Table 2.1 showed the Modern Family divided into two periods, the Democratic Family, which lasted from about 1780 until 1900, and the Companionate Family, which lasted from about 1900 until 1970.

The idea of a companionate marriage emerged around the start of the twentieth century. The term companionate marriage describes marriages that are held together by mutual affection, sexual attraction, and equal rights, rather than by moral duty. In companionate marriages husbands and wives are friends and lovers, and parents and children are pals (Mintz and Kellogg 1988). Scholars do not agree about whether companionate marriage is really characteristic of our behavior, but most agree the idea emerged as a popular one in the early twentieth century.

The idea of a Companionate Family stressed the importance of sexual gratification in marriage. Husbands and wives were encouraged by the growing numbers of professionals in marriage counseling, sex education, and sex counseling to seek emotional and sexual fulfillment (Jackson 1994). The emphasis on sex created an interest in contraception (Mintz

---

BOX 2.1

Methods: Cultural Artifacts

In her investigation of women in the westward expansion, Smith-Rosenberg (1985) reviewed thousands of letters written during the 1800s. Collecting these types of data is called content analysis: studying cultural artifacts that were not originally prepared to provide information for a researcher. Smith-Rosenberg examined written records, letters, and diaries. Barbara Welter (1978) also used this technique when she studied the cult of true womanhood by reviewing narrative texts, speeches, and advice manuals for brides and wives. Similarly, Valerie Matsumoto's (1990) research on Japanese Americans who were kept in internment camps during World War II analyzed letters written by the people being held in the camps.

Harriet Martineau (1834), one of the first women sociologists, wrote in the early 1800s that the study of cultural products was a key source of information (Reinharz 1992). Modern scholars have taken her advice, arguing that especially when studying women there may be little information in official documents and the researcher must search for these informal sources of information. Shulamit Reinharz warns, however, that one of the problems with such research is that the documents that are left tend to overrepresent more privileged groups of women who were literate and whose cultural products were saved.

and Kellogg 1988), or perhaps increasing access to contraceptives helped fuel an interest in sex. In any event, the rise of the companionate marriage paralleled the political struggle to make contraceptives available in the United States.

Women and men in modern families used a variety of ways to control fertility. Births had fallen since 1800. Letters among women on the frontier show people sharing information about abortion, ovulation, pessaries (small sponges placed in the vagina as a barrier), spermicidal douches, and withdrawal (Garey 1998). But the distribution of contraceptives or even information about contraceptives was illegal in the early part of the twentieth century. In 1917, Margaret Sanger, a nurse and the founder of the birth control movement in the United States, was arrested in New York City for distributing obscene materials when she dispensed diaphragms at a health care clinic (Sanger 1931). After numerous demonstrations, jailing of movement leaders, and legislative battles, in 1936 the courts ruled that physicians could prescribe birth control for whatever reasons they saw fit (Hymowitz and Weissman 1978).

The ideal of the Companionate Family also called for changing relationships between parents and children. During this period, relationships between children and parents became more intimate and affectionate, and children were allowed greater freedom (Mintz and Kellogg 1988).

The Twentieth Century and the History of Childhood.   During the rise of the companionate marriage from the end of the nineteenth century until recently, the way that people thought about and treated children and the way in which children experienced their lives changed substantially. A key aspect in these changes was the increasing differentiation between children and adults, especially in terms of their responsibility to work (Zelizer 1985).

In 1900, one child of every six between the ages of ten and fifteen was gainfully employed, and this did not count all the children who worked for their parents in sweatshops and farms (Zelizer 1985). The contribution of these children to their household income was significant. In Philadelphia in 1880, children contributed from 28 to 46 percent of the total family labor income in two-parent families (Goldin 1981).

Making children earn a living not only was seen as economically necessary but also as morally sound. In 1924, the *Saturday Evening Post* reported, "The work of the world has to be done; and these children have their share. Why should we place the emphasis on prohibitions. We don't want to rear up a generation of non-workers, what we want is workers and more workers" (quoted in Zelizer 1985, p. 67). The role of paid work in children's lives, however, changed quickly in the late 1920s. By 1930, most children were out of the labor market. As children lost their role as economic assets, they gained sentimental value. Zelizer (1985) traces the changing social value of children from economically useful at the start of the twentieth century to economically useless but emotionally priceless by the 1930s. She examined the process of placing adoptive and foster children as an indicator of children's changing value:

> Nineteenth century foster parents took in useful children expecting them to help out with farm chores and household tasks. In this context, babies were "unmarketable," and hard to place except in foundling asylums or commercial baby farms The useful child was generally

older than ten and a boy. More than three times as many boys as girls were placed. (1985, pp. 170, 173)

Within this system, mothers of infants had to pay a surrender fee to people who agreed to take their babies. By 1920, however, the situation had reversed, and babies could be sold for $100. By 1950, babies were sold illegally for as much as $10,000 (Zelizer 1985). From 1920 on, the value of adopted children was no longer measured by the economic contribution they could make, but by emotion and sentiment.

Families during the Great Depression.   Families were affected not only by the relatively slow unfolding of economic change over the past few centuries, but also by the turning points, the great upheavals in that history. In the next two sections of this chapter, we examine two important historical events in the twentieth century, the Great Depression and World War II. In both these cases, the country underwent profound changes. These macrolevel shocks reverberated in the microlevel of the everyday experiences of families, especially in the organization of gender within those families.

In 1929, the stock market crashed, ushering in the Great Depression. Unemployment rose from 3 million that year to 12.5 million in 1932. The Depression created intense poverty for most U.S. families. It also caused changes in behavior. The birthrate, marriage rate, and divorce rate all fell dramatically (Elder 1974; Mintz and Kellogg 1988).

The Depression created other changes in family life. Women, especially wives, increased their participation in the labor force more between 1930 and 1940 than in any previous decade in the twentieth century (Milkman 1976). Many women sought to compensate for the family's lack of income when their husbands were laid off (Cavan and Ranck 1938; Komarovsky 1940).

The economic crisis also had an effect on women's family work. Women attempted to maintain their families' standard of living, despite decreases in their income, by substituting their labor for goods and services they had previously purchased. For example, they increased their activity in such tasks as canning food and sewing clothes. Women's responsibility for emotional support was also intensified as unemployment and poverty disrupted people's lives (Milkman 1976).

World War II and Families.   The Depression ended with World War II, which stimulated the economy with the new demands for war materials and ended unemployment with the draft. The boom in industry coupled with the enrollment of huge numbers of men in the armed services created a shortage of workers that could be made up only by hiring women (Milkman 1991).

The women hired at manufacturing plants during World War II were called Rosie the Riveters. According to a popular song during the war:

> Rosie's got a boyfriend Charlie;
> Charlie he's a marine.
> Rosie is protecting Charlie
> Working overtime on the riveting machine. (Kessler-Harris 1982, p. 276)

The government and businesses flooded the media with pitches to encourage women to change their ways and the organization of their families' lives (Milkman 1991). Women were told that their domestic skills could easily be translated into war work. The new message was that a sewing machine was hardly different from a punch press (Gluck 1987).

The need for women workers challenged the ideologies that defined good wives and mothers as those who did not work outside the home but rather devoted themselves to domesticity. A new image was quickly fashioned. The ideal wartime woman was one who placed her child in a day care center, found fast, efficient methods to prepare meals and clean house, tied back her hair, and went to work as a riveter, welder, or electrician.

Table 2.3 shows the change in labor force participation rates for women from 1900 to 1995. The data are divided by race. The data are most complete for African Americans and whites. Numbers are available for Hispanic and Asian Americans only in the last few decades. Black women, white women, and Hispanic women have increasingly been part of the labor force. In comparisons of white and black women over the twentieth century, the numbers show that both groups increased their labor force participation, but the change is more dramatic for white women. At the start of the twentieth century, African American women (41%) were much more likely than white women (17%) to be in the paid labor force. At the end of the twentieth century white women, Asian women, and Hispanic women were quite similar to each other and all three groups were closing the gap with black women, but black women were still most likely to be in the paid labor force. The increase in labor force participation during World War II for women was mostly the experience of white women. African American women, however, were more likely to be employed before and during this time.

World War II and Marriage. The entrance of the United States into the war had other effects on family life as well (Elder 1986). Quick marriages became the rage. "In the month after the surprise attack on Pearl Harbor the marriage rate was 60% higher than in the same month the year before" (Mintz and Kellogg 1988, p. 153). Some men married because they

TABLE 2.3   Labor Force Participation Rates of Women, 1900–2003

Year	African Americans	Whites	Asians	Hispanics
1900	41%	17%		
1920	39	18		
1940	39	23		
1960	41	33		
1980	52	51		47%
1990	58	57		53
2000	63	60	59%	58
2003	62	59	58	56

Source: Bureau of Labor Statistics 2003b.

thought they were going to die. Others married to avoid the draft. Some married because husbands received higher wages than single soldiers. The soaring marriage rate was quickly followed by a baby boom.

Figure 2.1 shows data on the rate of first marriage between 1921 and 1994. The data are reported for women between the ages of fourteen and forty-four in three-year averages. This means that every three years, the numbers are averaged and recorded in the figure rather than showing exactly how the numbers changed every year. The figure shows that 100 of every 1,000 women in this age category were marrying in 1921. The numbers declined to 90 in 1933 and then rose to 140, its peak this century, in 1945. Between 1945 and 1981, the numbers declined to 82. After 1981, the numbers edged up a little to 99.7 in 1985 and then fell to 86.3 in 1994. We can probably assume that the rate of first marriage for men is similar to women, but it might not be. An improbable but possible situation could exist where a small number of men were marrying (and divorcing) many women. The rate of first marriage for men would then be lower than the rate for women. In Chapter 9 we examine marriage rates more extensively.

World War II and Divorce.   Another change that took place throughout the twentieth century but stands out as extraordinary immediately following World War II is the increase in the divorce rate. Figure 2.2 shows changes in the divorce rate since 1860. This figure reports the number of divorces per 1,000 married women over the age of fifteen from 1860 until 1920. The numbers reported after 1920 are the number of divorces per 1,000 marriages. The figure shows that the divorce rate steadily increased from 1860 until 1940 and shot up in a peak right after World War II in the mid-1940s. In the 1960s, it fell to prewar

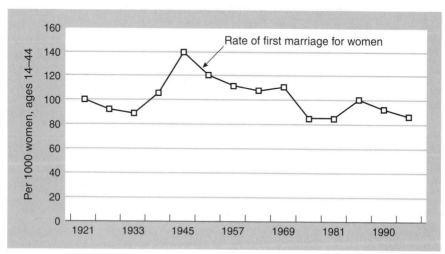

FIGURE 2.1   Rate of First Marriage for Women, 1921–1994 (in three-year averages)

Source: U.S. Census Bureau 1996, p. 104.

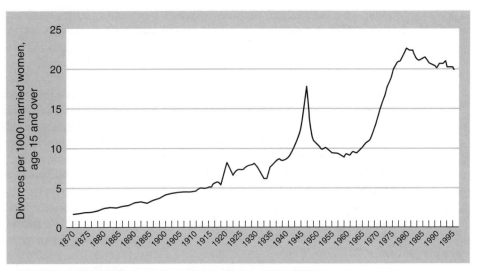

FIGURE 2.2   Annual Divorce Rate, United States 1860–1995

Note: For 1860–1920: divorces per 1,000 existing marriages; divorces per 1,000 married women aged fifteen and over.

Source: Baca Zinn & Eitzen, *Diversity in Families,* 5th ed., © 1999 by Allyn and Bacon. Adapted by permission.

rates and then began to rise rapidly in the 1970s. In the 1980s, the divorce rate leveled off and even fell a little from its all-time highs in the late 1970s. The spike in divorce in the late 1940s stands out dramatically. World War II seems to have created problems in marriages, causing them to end in divorce after the war. Long periods of separation, the stress of worrying about the future, and new opportunities for independence for women may have contributed to the high divorce rate.

In 1979, Sherna Gluck (1987) began a research project to find out how social changes during World War II affected individual Rosies. She conducted oral history interviews with women who had worked in aircraft manufacturing plants during the war. Gluck found that the war had been an important shaper of the women's work and family histories. Although most had been employed before the war, their experience during the war of taking blue-collar jobs that had previously been reserved for white men changed their thinking about what women should be. Betty Jean Boggs said, "I think it showed me that a young woman could work in different jobs other than say, an office, which you ordinarily expect a woman to be in. It really opened up another viewpoint on life in general" (Gluck 1987, p. 103).

Other women used the opportunity to make changes in their family lives. Marie Baker said she was unhappy with her marriage before the war started and that she left her husband when she heard about openings for women in the aircraft plant. She explained, "I needed a job because I was going to be very independent. I wasn't going to ask for any alimony or anything. I was just going to take care of myself" (Gluck 1987, p. 221).

Tina Miller, a black woman, pointed out that the new opportunities in the job market brought about by the war caused changes in her family life. But more significant, in her opinion, were the changes that took place in race discrimination during the war. She explained, "The war made me live better, it really did. My sister always said that Hitler was the one that got us out of the white folks' kitchen" (Gluck 1987, p. 24).

Japanese American Families during the War.   The United States entered World War II on December 7, 1941, when the Japanese bombed Pearl Harbor, Hawaii. On December 8 the financial resources of Japanese Americans and Japanese nationals who lived in the United States were frozen, and the FBI began to arrest leaders in the Japanese American community. Within two months President Roosevelt signed Executive Order 9066, which suspended all civil rights of Japanese Americans and authorized the removal of 120,000 Japanese and Japanese Americans—60 percent were American citizens—from their homes. The exclusion order was posted in neighborhoods where Japanese Americans lived. It read: "Instructions to all persons of Japanese ancestry: All Japanese persons, both alien and non-alien American citizens will be evacuated from the above designated area by 12:00 Tuesday" (Nakano 1990, p. 135). They were incarcerated in concentration camps for an average of two to three years. No formal charges were ever brought against them, and they had no opportunity for a trial of any kind (Nagata 1991).

After being forced from their homes, many of the evacuees were taken to internment camps in California. Others were first sent to sixteen temporary compounds called assembly centers which were horse stalls at racetracks, fairgrounds, and livestock exhibition halls, or tar paper–covered barracks that were built for the camps. After one to six months in the assembly centers, they were loaded onto trains and taken to desolate areas in the deserts and semideserts of Arizona, Utah, Colorado, Wyoming, and Idaho and the swampy lowlands of Arkansas (Matsumoto 1990).

People were given one week to prepare for the evacuation. They could bring to the camps only as many clothes and personal belongings as each person could carry. One man who was nineteen when his family was forced to move to a camp wrote, "For those who had small children or babies it was rough. They said you could only take their babies in their arms and maybe the little children could carry something but it was pretty limited" (Kochiyama 1998, p. 102). They were forced to either abandon their homes, businesses, and personal possessions or sell them within a few days at a fraction of their worth. By November 1942, the involuntary evacuation was complete. The camps were not closed until the end of 1945.

At the camps, people were housed in military barracks that had been subdivided into cramped apartments measuring about 20 by 20 feet, sometimes furnished with steel army cots and sometimes with gunny sacks filled with straw that served as beds (Takaki 1989). Families were often housed together. Single people were placed with smaller families so that eight people on average lived in each unit. Some families were split up and had little or no information about what had happened to their missing members.

There was no privacy. The walls to the units in the barracks did not reach the ceilings, and sounds traveled throughout the barracks. In addition, eating, showers, and toilets were all communal (Matsumoto 1990). One person remembered, "There was constant buzzing conversations, talk. Then, as the evening wore on, during the still of the night, things would get quiet, except for the occasional coughing, snoring, giggles. Then someone would get up to go to the bathroom. It was like a family of three thousand people camped out in a barn" (Takaki 1989, p. 394).

Valerie Matsumoto (1990) studied life in the internment camps by examining letters that people wrote while living there. One letter written by Shizuko Horiuchi in 1942 read, "The life here cannot be expressed. Sometimes we are resigned to it, but when we see the barbed wire fences and the sentry tower with floodlights, it gives us a feeling of being prisoners in a 'concentration camp'" (p. 373).

Every able-bodied person in the camps was required to work. The pay was the same for young and old, women and men. Most people received $16 a month; professionals such as physicians and teachers earned only slightly more—$19.

Internment in the camps had a traumatic effect on the adults and children forced to live there. In addition, the internment of their parents and grandparents continued to adversely affect the children and grandchildren who were born after the camps closed. Like victims of the Holocaust, many of the people held in the camps found it difficult to express their feelings about their imprisonment, even years after their release. Children born after the war ended observed that the experience had been painful and traumatic but were unable to obtain enough concrete information to understand their parents' reactions. Research on these children shows that the experience had a negative effect on their lives and altered their perception of their own place in U.S. society. These third-generation children whose parents had been imprisoned developed a sense of foreboding and secrecy about the internment. Compared with third-generation Japanese Americans whose parents had not been imprisoned, they also felt more vulnerable, more fearful that a future internment might occur, and more likely to prefer Japanese Americans over whites for friends (Nagata 1991).

In addition to these negative effects, some researchers have argued that there may have been some positive outcomes as well. Before the war, Japanese American parents, and especially fathers, had much authority over their children. Marriages were arranged, and decisions that were made by fathers were usually strictly followed by their children and wives. Internment changed those relationships (Pleck 1991). The paid employment of all family members and the nearly equal wages earned combined with the harsh living conditions and lack of privacy made it difficult to maintain rigid boundaries around families and the strong authority of fathers over their families. Although the internment in the camps was a horrific event, the uprooting ironically resulted in children and wives gaining more control over their lives (Matsumoto 1990).

The Fifties.   When the war ended, a new era in U.S. history began and a new era in family organization also emerged. This period was called the fifties, although it actually lasted from about 1947 to 1963. The fifties have played a particularly important role in contemporary images of families, especially the idea of a traditional family.

When people speak of a traditional family, we might wonder what they mean, since this chapter's historical review of families over the past few centuries shows that families have taken many forms over time. What many people think about when they use the term traditional family is the image of families in the 1950s, a father going off to work while his wife stays home to tend the children. But the word traditional implies something that is typical, customary, and established. Are the families of the fifties a valid standard?

Take a look at the figures we have examined in this chapter on fertility, marriage, divorce, and employment among women to see where the fifties fit into the overall trends. Table 2.2 shows how the long-standing decline in the birthrate stopped in the 1950s, and births rose sharply. A relatively small generation of parents gave birth to a large generation of babies (Cherlin 1992a). Between 1940 and 1957, the fertility rate climbed 50 percent (E. Pleck 1991). The increase in births was so remarkable it was given a special name—the postwar baby boom—and people born during the period are called baby boomers. Figure 2.1 shows that the marriage rate during the 1950s was also unusual relative to the rest of the century. The marriage rate declined to a low in the 1930s and then steadily climbed during the war. Right after the war, the rate shot up and remained high through the 1960s when it again began to decline. The 1950s had the highest rate of marriage of any generation on record: 96 percent of the women and 94 percent of the men were married. Even more remarkable were the record low ages at which women (20.2 on average) and men (22.6 on average) married in the 1950s (Levitan, Belous, and Gallo 1988).

The divorce rate peaked immediately following the war, perhaps making official the changes that had taken place in marriages during the war, but Figure 2.2 shows that during the decade of the 1950s, the divorce rate was low and stayed that way until the 1960s when it began to rapidly rise until the 1980s.

Table 2.3 shows that one trend that did not decline during the 1950s was the increasing numbers of women entering the labor force. After the war, the government and businesses began a propaganda campaign to reverse the images of working women and ideas about families that had been popularized during the war. Women were asked to give up their jobs to the returning soldiers, and many women who did not voluntarily quit were fired. In a postwar *Atlantic Monthly* article, Agnes Meyer wrote, "Women have many careers but only one vocation—motherhood. It is for women as mothers, actual or vicarious, to restore security in our insecure world" (1950, p. 32).

Although women were forced out of the "men's jobs" of the war industry, many remained employed and more women joined them in "pink-collar jobs." White married women increased their labor force participation rate from 17 percent in 1950 to 30 percent in 1960 (Evans, 1989).

The image that women were not "real" employees nevertheless permeated the media. In 1956, *Look* magazine reported, "No longer a psychological immigrant to man's world, she works casually, as a third of the U.S. labor force, and less toward a big career than as a way of filling a hope chest or buying a new home freezer. She gracefully concedes the top job rungs to men" (1956, p. 35).

In Chapters 9 and 10, we examine marriage and divorce rates more extensively. The important point about the discussion here is that the fifties was a period that was out of sync with the trends of the rest of the century. Sometimes people look at marriage and divorce rates today, compare them with the 1950s, and conclude that the years since the 1970s are somehow unusual, showing that families are in crisis. Families in the fifties were in many ways a novelty in the broad sweep of history of families in the United States. "At the end of the 1940s, all the trends characterizing the rest of the twentieth century suddenly reversed themselves: For the first time in more than one hundred years, the age for marriage and motherhood fell, fertility increased, divorce rates declined, and women's degree of educational parity with men dropped sharply" (Coontz 1992, p. 25). And in the areas such as increase in the participation of women in paid employment, the fifties were consistent with trends in the rest of the century, but the rhetoric about what women should be doing in the popular media and images of fifties women in television programs contradicted that reality.

BOX **2.2**

America Is Founded on Its Self-Reliant Families, or Is It?

The idea of self-reliant families is a cherished value in the United States, especially the legends of the frontier family and the suburban family of the 1950s (Coontz 1992). But is this idea based on reality?

One of the sources of images of the self-reliant pioneer family is the collection of *Little House on the Prairie* books, which depict an isolated family pitted against the elements, on their own, with no help from their neighbors or from their government. In reality, prairie farmers and other pioneer families owed their existence to massive federal land grants, government-funded military mobilizations that dispossessed hundreds of Native American societies and confiscated half of Mexico. It would be hard to find a Western family today or at any time in the past whose land rights, transportation options, economic existence, and even access to water were not dependent on federal funds (Coontz 1992, p. 73).

Public funds were used to purchase Louisiana ($15 million), to support three years of war with the British to obtain Florida, and to build canals in the Midwest and around the Ohio and Mississippi rivers ($150 million). The U.S. government paid $9 million for Cherokee land before forcing the Cherokees to march to Oklahoma ($6 million was then deducted from the bill as expenses for the eviction). Public money was used to finance a $97 million war against Mexico and then to allow the victorious United States to pay $15 million for Texas, California, Colorado, and parts of New Mexico and Arizona (Coontz 1992). At a more local level, pioneer families were not entirely self-sufficient. Frontier life was very much a community affair, with families sharing work, tools, products, and labor.

Like the legendary frontier family of the nineteenth century, the suburban family of the 1950s is a prevalent image in the myth of self-reliance. The surge in home ownership and other indications of a rising standard of living is believed by many to have been a result of people standing on their own two feet without government interference or community support. In fact, suburban families were the beneficiaries of enormous government subsidies. The GI Bill allowed nearly half a generation of young men to obtain a college education. Prior to World War II, banks often required a 50 percent down payment on homes. The GI Bill provided for down payments of 5 to 10 percent and guaranteed thirty-year mortgages for fixed rates of 2 or 3 percent. The Veteran's Administration asked for only one dollar down. Fixed-rate mortgages, furthermore, freed this generation from inflation—at least in their housing costs—for thirty years (Coontz 1992; Lee 1986). Even the construction of the homes was partially federally funded. The development of aluminum clapboards, prefabricated walls and ceilings, and plywood paneling all resulted from government-funded research.

The idyllic families depicted in novels, television, and movies about European American history included hardworking people. Their ability to sustain their standard of living, however, was often largely based on the government "handouts."

Periodicizing

Historians trying to understand historical change have created a variety of ways to break history into sections or periods. In this chapter, we have looked at one way to periodicize history that seems useful for understanding Euro-American families, as illustrated in Table 2.1. There are three problems, however, to keep in mind when we use these schemes of historical periods. First, periods can be arranged around any number of social issues or events. For example, some historians emphasize important political events such as wars. The system of periodicizing used in this chapter emphasizes relationships between husbands and wives, and it underscores the importance of political and economic context for family organization and experience. But these are not the only factors that could be used.

Esther Chow (1998) points out a second problem. She argues that, although the concept of periods is a good idea, scholars need to remember that not all schemes work for every racial ethnic group. She describes the way in which Chinese American family history could be periodicized into three eras: split families, family wage or family based economies, and consumption economies. From 1848 to 1882, Chinese men were recruited into the Western states and Hawaii, but women were excluded. This created split families, which we look at more carefully in Chapter 3. Most Chinese immigrants were men, and many of them left their wives behind in China. Family life was divided by thousands of miles.

In 1882, the American government passed the Chinese Exclusion Act barring all immigration of men and women from China. The Chinese Americans who were already here entered a new period of family history from 1882 to 1960. This period had two tracks. One track was a family based economy in which Chinese Americans ran small family businesses catering to the Chinese community. Running restaurants, groceries, and other shops generated money to meet the needs of families and was done in or near the home by all family members. Like the Euro-American families during the colonial period, the lines between work and family were blurred, and older men had a great deal of power over their wives, children, and other household members.

The other track was a family wage economy. This existed at the same time as the family based economy, but families were organized differently because adult men and women in the family wage economy households worked outside of the home in wage labor positions. Women and men both worked long hours at menial jobs, and women were mostly responsible for taking care of their families as well. Women, however, also benefited from this family type because it allowed them to be more independent of the social constraints of traditional Chinese family life.

The third period, consumption economy, dates from 1960 to the present. This period is marked by increased immigration, especially by women, which we examine more fully in Chapter 5. Since 1960, the family wage economy has become more predominant. An increasing number of women are in the labor market and produce fewer goods and services in the home, instead purchasing them in the marketplace with earned wages. Social class differences among Chinese families also intensified during this time. This system of periodicizing Chinese American families uses criteria similar to those used for periodicizing Euro-American families, such as political economic context and relationships between women and men in families. It also looks at these histories during similar time periods. But the dates, significant events, family forms, and transitions are quite different. In the next chapter, we look at another set of periods for African Americans, which is different from both Chinese American and European American history. Periods are a useful way to look at family history, but we need to be careful not to make assumptions that everyone's family history is the same or that every racial and ethnic group can be fit into one grand format.

The third problem with periodicizing is that it can give a false notion of history as proceeding in discrete steps, with one step rapidly transforming into another. For example, although we date the Industrial Revolution, it really took place over a long period of time. We also know that certain changes in Euro-American families became more intense with the development of the Industrial Revolution, but the seeds of those change may have emerged long before industrialization and continued to fully unfold many years after (Ulrich 1991). It is useful to think about turning points in history as breaks between periods, but real life is much more fluid.

The First-Wave Women's Movement

This overview of the history of families in the United States shows great changes over time in several features of the organization of families. One theme, however, threads through the entire history: the inequality in relationships between women and men and the struggle to make those relationships more equal.

Just as gender inequality has changed over time, so, too, has the women's movement. Many scholars divide the American women's movement into three waves. The first-wave women's movement developed in the mid-1800s. The second wave, mentioned in Chapter 1, was the women's liberation movement of the 1960s. The third wave was recognized in the 1970s and 1980s. We spend some time examining it in later chapters.

The first-wave women's movement was the first time women organized in the United States to protest for women's equality. Middle-class women in the 1800s were faced with problems as a result of the development of industrialization and the Modern Family. Although the economy provided these women with comfortable lives, the cult of true womanhood and their role in their families did not. Like Sarah in the opening scenario, many were unhappy with the limitations of their role as "true women." A feminist movement developed in response to these and other problems.

The first published works of feminist protest are dated in the early 1600s, but it was not until the middle of the 1800s that the women's movement became fully focused and organized in the United States (Lengermann and Niebrugge-Brantley 1992). July 19, 1848, marked a particularly important event in this development. On that day three hundred people, including Susan B. Anthony, Elizabeth Cady Stanton, Frederick Douglass, and Lucretia Mott, convened a Women's Rights Convention in Seneca Falls, New York. At that meeting they approved a Declaration of Sentiments and twelve resolutions (Hole and Levine 1971).

The resolutions passed by the Seneca Falls convention covered a wide range of reforms, including woman's suffrage and the right of women to work and to keep their wages. The convention even advocated changes in dress, calling on women to abandon their cinched waist and multilayered petticoats and replace them with loose-fitting bloomers.

Some of the proposals made at Seneca Falls and subsequent feminist gatherings also directly addressed issues related to family. Women demanded the right to divorce and to retain custody of their children after a divorce. They also sought the right of a married woman to retain her own property and to be safe from marital rape (Stanton 1889/1990).

The women's movement continued to press for change throughout the nineteenth and twentieth centuries. The feminists' work addressed a wide range of topics, including slavery, suffrage, and equal rights, but issues related to women's role in families were always prominent.

The Micro-Macro Connection

This chapter shows how families have changed over time in the United States. One of the major aspects of the macrolevel of society, the economy and changes in its organization, profoundly affected the microlevel, the organization of families and the everyday experience of family life. For example, the patriarchal Puritan family could not survive the development of industrial capitalism. The growth of jobs that were controlled by factory owners rather than fathers undermined the hold that the patriarchs had over their families. In Chapter 4 we continue to examine some of the relationships between the economy and families by looking at changes in today's economic system and considering some of the effects on families that might result.

The relatively constant evolution of the macrolevel of economic conditions is marked periodically by major shifts at critical turning points. These turning points are related to (1) changes in technology, for example, the Industrial Revolution; (2) the economy, for example, the Great Depression, and (3) war, for example, World War II. Shifts at the macrolevel of society alter the everyday experience of families at the microlevel.

Although the economy has been identified as an aspect of the macrolevel of society that has been especially important in shaping family life, other social institutions that make up the macrolevel of society have had an effect as well. Political institutions affect families. For example, governments that decide to go to war or that place families in internment camps create changes in gender relationships and divisions of labor within families. Government proclamations that offer huge tracts of land, like the Homestead Act, shape family decisions.

Popular media and religious institutions are another feature of the macrolevel of society that can have an effect on families. For example, we observed the activities of these two aspects of the macro-organization of our society in the creation of the cult of true womanhood and its alternative, the ideal of real womanhood.

The macrolevel, in addition to being complex and dynamic, also may affect various members of society differently. For example, the families of Ford workers faced different issues than their middle-class counterparts, and Chinese Americans faced still different problems. Although all of these groups—white middle class, white working class, and Chinese Americans—lived within the same broad social context, their experience of that context was remarkably dissimilar.

The macrolevel also affects members of families differently. The case of the family wage is an especially good example. The battle for the family wage created different problems for husbands than for wives in blue-collar families. In another example, the decision to move west implied different losses and gains for husbands compared with wives. The macrocontext includes not just an economic system or a political system that creates the same social context for everyone; it also includes systems of gender and racial ethnic inequality that affect families and family members. Chapter 5 continues this discussion by focusing attention on issues of diversity among contemporary U.S. families.

In sum, the macrolevel affects the microlevel. The economy, the government, social class, and race ethnicity influenced and sometimes determined the organization of families and the experience of people within those families. History also shows us the ways in which individual people attempted to shape their society—the effect of the micro on the macro. The birth control movement, the labor movement, the women's movement, and the reformers who fought for child labor laws all represent individuals organizing to address issues related to family life. These social movements were composed of people working together to both revise and reformulate the macro-organization of society.

3 A History of U.S. Families with a Focus on African Americans

Sharecropping was established in the cotton fields of the south after the Civil War. Work for African Americans was much the same after the end of slavery. Families, however, changed in important ways as African Americans sought to allow women to reduce their work in the fields so that they could take care of their families. (Brown Brothers)

The year is 1840. Seventeen-year-old John is a slave on a large South Carolina cotton plantation owned by a man named Franklin. When John was ten, the slaveowner on the plantation where he was born sold him and his father and brothers. John was unable to keep track of his brothers and father, knowing only that a man named Brady from Mississippi bought them. His mother stayed at the old plantation, and John was separated from all of them to go to work at Franklin's.

When John was younger, his mother used to walk to his plantation occasionally to see him. She was permitted to make the twelve-mile walk between dusk and dawn; if she came home after dawn she was beaten. John's mother died when he was thirteen, but he was not allowed to attend her funeral because she died during harvest and he had too much work to do.

John has a woman friend, Mary, whom he cares about and would like to marry, but Franklin, his owner, plans to sell her because she has already suffered a miscarriage and may be unable to bear any more children. Franklin has been talking about making John sleep with another slave woman, Caroline, because she is robust, and he believes that John and Caroline would produce strong children. John hears about a woman named Harriet Tubman who helps slaves escape. He decides to convince Mary that they should both go with her on the Underground Railroad up to Canada.

What kinds of family life were possible for African Americans under slavery?

How did the ideas and experience of family for other racial ethnic groups such as whites, Latinos, Native Americans and Chinese Americans differ from that of African Americans during slavery?

What kinds of choices did slaves have to make about family issues like marriage and children?

How does the extreme case of slavery help us see the importance of the effect of social context on families?

What happened after slavery? How did the new system of sharecropping, and later industrialization, affect family organization among African Americans?

Diversity in American Families

The United States is a nation of diversity. Many groups of people came to live here from Europe, Asia, Africa, Latin America and the rest of the world. Before European contact, there were millions of Native Americans living in dozens of different nations throughout the hemisphere. This means that the cultural roots and the history of Americans are varied and complex (Root 1996).

In addition, many groups have been exploited or oppressed in a variety of ways. Several Native American groups were completely wiped out, and others were forced to march across the country to be "resettled" on the lands of other Native American peoples. As we saw in Chapter 2, Japanese who lived in the United States during World War II were forced out of their homes and communities and held in camps. Asians, Puerto Ricans, and Chicanos have been and continue to be discriminated against and exploited as cheap labor in mines, fields, and sweatshops across the country.

These various groups have their own histories of family organization, which are different from the history of white Americans. Family sociologists, therefore, are presented with the dilemma of needing to pay close attention to diversity, but finding it impossible to cover all of the possibilities in one book.

In our examination of the historical development of families in this book, we focused in Chapter 2 on Euro-Americans during the colonization of the United States, the westward expansion, and the period of immigration and urbanization. We also explored examples of Japanese, Chinese, and Native American families. In this chapter we turn our attention to African Americans during the eighteenth, nineteenth, and twentieth centuries.

Among all the possible groups that could be examined, African American families have been chosen for special attention for several reasons. First, there is a large body of literature on African Americans and African American families (DuBois 1969/1908). Less research has been done on other groups of people, for example, Cherokees, Vietnamese Americans, or Latino Americans (Roosa et al. 2005).

Second, until the 2000 Census African Americans were the largest racial ethnic group in the United States. Table 3.1 shows how the distribution of various racial ethnic groups has changed over the centuries. Table 5.1 in Chapter 5 shows the most recent data: African Americans make up 12.8 percent of the total population, whites 67.4 percent, and Hispanics are 14.1 percent; all other groups make up the remaining 6.8 percent. Hispanics are now the largest minority group. Historically, however, African Americans have been the largest minority group. In 1860, African Americans made up 14 percent of the total U.S. population and 36.4 percent of the population in the southern states (U.S. Census Bureau 1975). In 1800, ten years after the first census, African Americans comprised almost one-third of those counted.

Third, African Americans are the only group of people who were legally enslaved for a long period of time (more than two hundred years) in the United States. They are also the only group that was legally segregated in a large region (the entire South) for a long period of time (from 1877, the end of Reconstruction, until the passage of the Civil Rights Bill in 1964). Finally, African Americans are the only group of people for whom a civil war was fought at least in part over the question of whether to end their enslavement.

In a sense, then, African Americans are a special case, and when we study their family history, we need to keep that in mind. On the other hand, examining the changes over time in the organization of African American families and their relationship to the changing social context should help us develop principles that might be tested in the cases of the many other peoples of the United States.

Throughout the chapter we will see the way in which the macrolevel of social organization affected the microlevel of everyday life for African American people. The key element in the macrolevel that we explore in this chapter is the political economy. A political economy is the manner in which a society organizes its political and economic institutions.

TABLE 3.1   **Racial and Ethnic Populations as a Proportion of Total U.S. Population, 1800–2000**

	1800	**1860**	**1900**	**1940**	**1970**	**1990**	**2000**
Whites	68.6%	85.6%	87.9%	89.8%	83.3%	75.3%	69.1%
Blacks	31.3	14.1	11.6	9.8	10.9	11.9	12.4
Hispanics	N.A.	N.A.	N.A.	N.A.	4.5	9.0	12.6
Asians/Other	N.A.	0.2	0.5	0.5	1.3	3.8	5.9

Source: U.S. Census Bureau 1975, 1990a, 2000c.

Political institutions refer to the organization and distribution of power and decision making. Economic institutions are those that produce and distribute the goods people use to survive.

Slavery, for example, was a particular type of political economy that had an enormous effect on the family lives of slaves. Our review of the macrolevel of political economy and its effect on families will show how the political economy changed and in turn created changes at the microlevel. In addition, this history will show the ways in which African Americans working in social networks at the microlevel fought back in attempts to alter both their family organization and the larger, oppressive political economy.

This chapter is organized into three major sections. The first section reviews the history of African Americans and is divided into a number of subsections that cover slavery, sharecropping, and the industrialization of the South. I discuss the relationships between African American men and women and adults and children in each of these periods and compare the organization of African American families to that of middle-class whites. The second section focuses on the central role played by issues related to families in the struggle to create equality and to end the oppression of African American people. In Chapter 5 we pick up this history again and look at recent developments in African American family history during the last half of the twentieth century and into the twenty-first.

The third major section examines the history of Latino Americans beginning with the Mexican American War which transferred a huge piece of land in North America from Mexico to the United States. Latinos comprise an increasingly larger and more important sector of the population as well. Historically they were a smaller population in the United States than African Americans. Their numbers today, however, have now surpassed African Americans, and in some states in the west and southwest, people whose families came from Latin America or whose families lived in areas formally part of Mexico are the majority. The history of the migration of Latinos to the United States and the claiming of the land that was originally Mexico and ways in which these historical forces shaped Latino families will be addressed in this chapter.

Four Periods in African American History

The history of African Americans can be traced through four historical periods, each creating a different social context for families. The four historical periods are (1) slavery, 1600 to 1865; (2) sharecropping, 1865 to 1940; (3) industrialization, 1940 to 1965; and (4) the New South or post–Civil Rights era, since 1965 (Scott 1988). In each of these periods, different family forms dominated among African Americans. As we observed in Chapter 2 among European Americans and Chinese Americans, families changed over time as the economic context evolved. The periods and the transitions, however, were quite different for African Americans compared with these other two groups. This chapter examines the first three of the periods. In the rest of the book, we will be looking at contemporary families.

Slavery

During the period of slavery, which lasted from colonial times until the end of the Civil War, the experience of most African Americans was tied to a particular region in the United States—the South. "At the end of the nineteenth century, nine out of ten Afro-Americans lived in the South" (J. Jones 1985, p. 80). Although the Southern states were part of the United States, they maintained a political and economic system that differed dramatically from that of the North. Until the end of the Civil War, the Southern states had a separate and unique political economy—the American slave system.

The political economy of slavery was characterized by segregation between whites and African Americans, the concentration of power and wealth in the hands of very few whites, and the ownership of nearly all African Americans as a form of property. The dominant economic activity in the region was the production of agricultural products, especially cotton, for export to the North and to Europe. Huge plantations covered the South, each using the labor of hundreds of slaves. The plantation economy was enormously wealthy, and production by the slave laborers created a large proportion of the total economic output of the entire nation. In the mid-1800s, 5.4 million bales of cotton a year were produced by Southern plantations, accounting for 75 percent of the total U.S. exports (J. Keller 1983).

About 90 percent of African Americans were slaves who had no civil or legal rights but were considered the property of the slave owners. The other 10 percent of the African American population during this time were not slaves. They were called freedmen, but their rights were curtailed as well. Most freedmen lived in such urban areas as Charleston and New Orleans and worked in skilled trades.

Most whites were not slaveholders and were not part of the plantation economy. About 25 percent of Southern whites owned one or more slaves, and about 15 percent owned large numbers on enormous plantations. The large slaveholders owned huge plots of land where the soil was richest. The rest of the whites (75%) had little power in political institutions and were not part of the dominant economic activity. They worked as subsistence farmers in less-productive agricultural areas.

Early in the development of the slave system in the United States, the northern states of New York, New Jersey, Delaware, Pennsylvania, Massachusetts, Connecticut, and Rhode Island had legally sanctioned slavery. In fact, in New York City in 1741 twenty-three armed slaves burned down a slaveowner's house. The incident developed into an insurrection by hundreds of African American and poor white people, two hundred of whom were eventually arrested. Thirty-one African Americans and four whites were subsequently executed (Zinn 1980).

The number of people who were enslaved in the Northern states, however, was relatively small, and the system disappeared there in the eighteenth century. In the South, in contrast, slavery was legally established in Virginia in 1640 and lasted in the states that seceded from the Union—Florida, Virginia, North Carolina, South Carolina, Georgia, Alabama, Mississippi, Louisiana, Arkansas, Texas, and Tennessee—until the Emancipation Proclamation in 1863. In the slave states that did not secede—Delaware, Kentucky, Maryland, and Missouri—slavery finally ended in 1865 with the passage of the Thirteenth Amendment.

Since the Civil War, the Southern political economy has remained somewhat different from that of other regions in the United States because segregation and discrimination were legal until the 1960s. A system of legal segregation is called de jure segregation. Those black people who moved north or west also lived segregated lives in separate neighborhoods, held different jobs, and attended separate schools, but in those areas the system of segregation usually was not stated in the laws. This is called de facto segregation because although it is not specified in the laws it nevertheless exists. Throughout the United States,

African Americans have experienced a history that was different from but highly interrelated with that of other racial ethnic groups. Family organization for African Americans, not surprisingly, has been different from that of whites and other groups of Americans.

Family Life under Slavery.   Historians are still debating about which family form was dominant among African Americans in the slave community. Some scholars argue the nuclear family was the most common family form among slaves (Gutman 1976). A nuclear family is one in which a legally married husband and wife and their children live together. Slavery interfered with this kind of family organization. Slaves could be bought and sold, seized in payment of a master's debts, and inherited. African American families under slavery, therefore, lived in constant fear of separation. Even for women and men who lived together as husbands and wives, legal marriage was not possible. Since slaves were property, they had no legal right to make a contract, including a marriage contract. The slave owner had complete legal authority over his slaves, and it was the slave owner who decided who could live with whom.

Neither was monogamy legal for slaves. Monogamy is the practice of marrying only one person at a time and remaining sexually exclusive with that person. Slave women were constantly sexually abused by white men, and they had no legal right to resist that abuse. "To oppose the rape of black women in effect meant opposing slavery. A black woman's body was not considered her own. Control over her body was passed from white person to white person along with a bill of sale" (Hymowitz and Weissman 1978, p. 51).

BOX 3.1

Sally Hemings and Thomas Jefferson

For a long time, historians have been debating whether President Thomas Jefferson had sexual relations with his slaves that produced slave children. During his presidency, a journalist named James Callender was the first to publicly make such charges. Many others have debated the issue since then. Recently, biologists have provided empirical evidence of these relationships through DNA tests. The tests conclude that at least one of Sally Hemings's seven children was fathered by Jefferson (Lander and Ellis 1998).

Sally Hemings was a slave who was owned by Jefferson. She was the half sister of his wife because Mrs. Jefferson's father had sexual relations with Hemings's mother, who was also a slave. When Jefferson first engaged in sex with Hemings, she was only about fourteen years old, thirty years younger than he was. Their sexual relationship lasted for a long time, and at least one of the children she bore was his. Jefferson never freed Hemings or his children who were born to her (Burstein, Isenberg, and Gordon-Reed 1999).

Some scholars have portrayed the relationship between Hemings and Jefferson as a love affair. Others have questioned whether a teenage slave who had no right to refuse her master's sexual advances could enter into a relationship of love or even consent. What do you think of this debate? Were slave women who were subjected to sex with their owners sometimes their lovers? Or were these encounters always a form of rape since the women could not voice their own feelings, and, regardless of their feelings, they did not have the right to refuse the slave owner?

In 1855, a nineteen-year-old slave woman was hanged because she defended herself against a rapist. Celia, who had no last name, had been repeatedly raped by her owner since she was fourteen years old. She had borne two children as a result of the rapes and had begged the rapist's two legitimate adult daughters to help her stop him, but they refused. In desperation one night she killed the master. The jury did not accept her argument that the murder had been in self-defense, and she was sentenced to be executed (McLaurin 1992).

Slave parents also had no legal rights in regard to their children (King 1995). Children could be sold away from their mother at any age: "The young of slaves stand on the same footing as any other animal" (Davis 1981, p. 7). In a famous statement Sojourner Truth, an African American woman active in the abolitionist movement and the women's movement, describes her experience as a parent under slavery: "I have borne thirteen chillun and seen 'em mos' all sold off into slavery and when I cried out with a mother's grief, none but Jesus heard" (Lowenberg and Bogin 1976, p. 235).

The threat of separation of parents and children was constantly feared. It was evident even in the play of slave children. In the 1930s, former slaves were interviewed about their lives under slavery. David Wiggins (1985) studied the play of slave children by examining these statements. He found that one of the games the slave children played was called auction. One of the children acted as the auctioneer and conducted a simulated slave sale.

Even when children were not separated from their parents, parents had little authority over them. One former slave woman, remembering her childhood, said, "When de young folks wanted to go dey didn't have to ax their mama an' papa, dey axed de white folks an ef de white folks said yes it was all right wid dem. See we b'long to de white folks, not to our mamas and papas" (Blassingame 1997, p. 644).

Worse than not having authority over their children, parents who were slaves did not have the right to protect their children. One woman who had been a slave explained, "Many a day my old mama has stood by and watched massa beat her chillun 'til dey bled an' she couldn't open her mouth" (Perdue and Barden 1976, p. 149).

At about thirteen, children were expected to work full time in the fields. Before then they performed chores like hauling water, tending gardens, fetching wood, cleaning the yard, feeding livestock, and caring for younger children (Corsaro 1997).

Like all social systems, slavery was not uniform in its expression. The laws forbade slaves to marry, and slave masters had the final say in the organization of the family lives of their slaves. Nevertheless, some slaveholders were more lenient than others and allowed some small "privileges," acknowledging slave marriages. More important, family issues such as marriage were arenas of constant struggle between slaves and slaveowners. In some cases, slaves were able to bend the rules in order to attempt to maintain relationships of parenthood and monogamous marriage.

Herbert Gutman (1976) is the most prominent of the scholars who argue that despite the legal sanctions against nuclear families, the slaves themselves maintained complex, organized systems of rules, expectations, and emotional relationships among husbands and wives and parents and children. As evidence of nuclear families, Gutman notes, for example, that slaves had their own rituals that displayed their marriages to their community. One of these rituals was called jumping the broom. The broom represents the domestic life the couple will share with one another. The bride and groom jumped over a broom handle as a symbol of their commitment to each other.

Gutman also examined historical documents that showed how slaves maintained strong family ties even when it meant risking severe punishment. In the scenario at the beginning of this chapter, John tells how his mother used to walk thirteen miles to visit him at night. This is based on the true story of Frederick Douglass, who was a slave and who wrote about his mother traveling thirteen miles to visit him after he was sold to another plantation. Gutman argues that this kind of sacrifice to preserve links between parents and children, siblings, and husbands and wives was common.

Slave men who were married to women who lived on different plantations were allowed to visit their wives, whom they called "abroadwives," but the journey was dangerous:

> The men were given passes to visit their wives on Wednesday and Saturday nights and all day Sunday. In their journey to the other plantation the black men had to deal with "Patterollers" who were patrols of whites whose task was to see that no slaves traveled about at night without the proper credentials. The Patterollers were notorious for their brutality. (Hymowitz and Weissman 1978)

If slaves visited other plantations without carrying the proper documents, they were likely to be beaten or killed. In 1712, the state of South Carolina passed "an Act for better ordering and governing of Negroes and slaves. If a slave was caught away from his or her plantation without a 'ticket' from the master's plantation, 'it is hereby declared lawful for any white person to beat, maim, or assault, and if such Negro or slave cannot otherwise be taken, to kill him'" (Act 1992).

Others tried to find their kin by running away. The most common reason people ran away was resentment over punishment. The second most common reason was to find relatives (Genovese 1972). Numerous newspaper advertisements refer to runaway slaves whom slave owners believed to be fleeing to make contact with their families. One ad describes a fourteen-year-old who was thought to have fled to Atlanta, where his mother had been sent. Another ad was for a mother who had escaped to find her children at another plantation. Husbands sought wives and wives husbands (Franklin 1988).

On plantations, slaves also preferred to organize their lives to emphasize the importance of nuclear family units. For example, sons were frequently named after their fathers, and both sons and daughters were named after blood relatives (Gutman 1976). Slave women preferred cooking for their own families to taking their meals in a communal kitchen, even when it meant additional work. In some cases, when plantation owners tried to establish communal kitchens, slaves refused them (Hymowitz and Weissman 1978). Thus, the ability to maintain control over family life and especially the right to establish nuclear families was a point of constant struggle between slaves and slaveowners.

Family Organization and Black Women's Role in a Community of Slaves. Angela Davis is an African American scholar and activist who has examined the organization of families under slavery and the relationship between African American family organization and African American women's political activity. Davis's (1981) point of view differs somewhat from Gutman's. Like W. E. B. DuBois (1969), one of the earliest scholars of African American culture, Davis argues that slaves may have aspired to live in nuclear families and may have gone to great lengths to maintain contact with their families, but slavery ultimately disrupted the nuclear family. Davis is quick to point out, however, that the difficulty of maintaining nuclear families did not mean that slaves had no families.

Gutman's work tends to emphasize those people who were successful in establishing and maintaining nuclear family organization. Davis's work tends to emphasize the alternative kinds of families that were established within the slave community. Both these scholars' research indicates that even within a system as harsh and restrictive as slavery, a variety of families existed.

Davis believes that her work shows that the dominant family organization among slaves was an extended family that consisted of both kin (people related by blood) and fictive kin (people who are not related by blood but are close personal friends). She argues that the intensity of the labor demanded of slaves and the disruption of marriages and relationships between parents and children meant that people relied on a wider circle of social contacts than a nuclear family. This wider circle included both relatives and others in the community.

When Wiggins (1985) examined the narratives of former slaves talking about the games slave children played, he found evidence of the cohesiveness of the entire community of slaves and the lack of boundaries between groups within the community. A theme that ran through all of the narratives was the absence of any games that required the elimination of players; all players stayed in all the games. He argues that this was a reaction to the possibility that members of a slave community might be sold suddenly. Keeping all players in the game shows the value placed on the maintenance of community that characterized the culture of African Americans under slavery.

One of the features of the extended community-based family was a sharing of responsibility for food and shelter. In a community made up of nuclear families, each family is an economic unit that divides the labor among its members. In the community of slaves, Davis (1981) argues, much of the domestic work of supporting the community was done communally by slave women. For example, "most infants and toddlers spent the day in a children's house, where an elderly slave was in charge" (Hymowitz and Weissman 1978, p. 47).

Davis points out that the only work that was done by slaves that contributed to the survival of the slaves themselves—as opposed to contributing only to the lives of the slave owners—was the domestic work in the community that fed and provided clothes, health care, and shelter for its members. All the other work done by slaves, in the fields and in the slave owner's house, was done for the white plantation owners and served no useful purpose for the slave community.

James Curry, a former slave, described the work of his mother, a house servant who labored both for the plantation owner and for the other slaves:

> My mother's labor was very hard. She would go to the plantation owner's house in the morning, take her pail upon her head, and go away to the cow-pen, and milk fourteen cows. She then put on the bread for the white family breakfast, and got the cream ready for churning, and set a little child to churn it, she having the care of from ten to fifteen children, whose mothers worked in the field. After clearing away the family breakfast, she got breakfast for the slaves—which was taken at twelve o'clock. In the meantime, she had beds to make, rooms to sweep and clean. Then she cooked the white family dinner. Then the slaves' dinner was to be ready at from eight to nine o'clock in the evening. At night she had the cows to milk again. This was her work day to day. Then in the course of the week, she had the wash-

---

B O X 3.2

Slave Narratives

In the 1930s, the federal government decided to conduct a massive research project to save the history of slavery from the point of view of people who had been slaves. Between 1936 and 1938, two thousand three hundred former slaves were interviewed by writers and journalists hired by the Works Project Administration's Writer's Project. These interviews exist in sound tapes and are collected in a forty-one-volume series titled *The American Slave: A Composite Autobiography* by George P. Rawick. The interviews vary in length, and some of them are colored by the prejudiced viewpoint of the writers who conducted the interviews and wrote them into narratives. The interviews as a set, however, provide a rich source of information about slavery. The interviewees talk about their daily lives as well as extraordinary events. Since slavery ended in the 1860s and the interviews were conducted in the 1930s, the interviewees were over the age of seventy. A long time had passed since they had been slaves. The memories, however, are clear. They give vivid firsthand accounts of brutality, work, family life, and religion among slaves during slavery.

---

ing and ironing to do for the master's family—and for her husband, seven children, and herself. She would not get through to go to her log cabin until nine or ten o'clock at night. She would then be so tired that she could scarcely stand; but she would find one boy with his knee out, and another with his elbow out, a patch wanting here and a stitch there, and she would sit down by her light—a wood fire, and sew and sleep alternately, often till the light began to streak in the east; and then lying down, she would catch a nap and hasten to the toil of the day. (Blassingame 1977, pp. 132–33)

Davis (1981) maintains that the critical contribution of women doing this survival labor within the slave community enhanced their value to the community. Women were essential to the community's survival. Davis also argues that the recognition of women as critical members of the community allowed them to emerge as important political leaders.

Davis found that African American women took leadership in many community activities. For example, African American women played an active role in the Underground Railroad and other forms of insurrection against the slave system. Women were likely to initiate and implement acts of sabotage, arson, and assassination as part of an ongoing battle against slavery. Sometimes domestic work itself was openly political, for example, when women fed runaway slaves, thus aiding them in their journey (Aptheker 1943).

This kind of resistance was so common that a law was passed in South Carolina requiring that plantation owners regularly search slave quarters for runaways and arms. The act read, "Be it further enacted by the authority aforesaid, that every master, mistress or overseer of a family of this Province, shall cause all his Negro houses to be searched diligently and effectually, on every fourteen days, for fugitive and runaway slaves, guns, swords, clubs and any other mischievous weapons" (Act 1992, p. 260).

The political activity of African American women was not practiced without African American men. Rather, just as the oppression and exploitation of black women was equal to that of black men, there was an equality in their struggle against the system (Davis 1981).

Davis (1981) provides much evidence that the African American family was community based as opposed to nuclear and that it included many people, kin and nonkin, working together. Why did this particular type of family occur in the slave community? Davis contends that the extended character of the families in the slave community resulted from the difficulties of establishing nuclear families (see also DuBois 1969/1908). Others (R. Hill et al. 1989; Sudarkasa 1988) take a different position on this question. They agree with Davis that the dominant form of family in the slave community was an extended kin-based network family. They argue, however, that the organization of African American families during slavery and up to the present has been influenced by the cultural roots of West African societies. In contrast to Davis scholars such as R. Hill and his colleagues (1989) and Sudarkasa (1988) maintain that extended families were not created as a survival tactic in the unique situation of slavery. Rather this form of family came from the African cultures from which African Americans had been taken.

One group of people who may have been especially important to passing down information about Africa were elderly slaves (Close 1997; King 1995). The hardships of slavery meant that few slaves lived to be elderly. For example, in one census of slaves at Kelvin Plantation in Saint Simons Island, Georgia, eighty-one slaves were listed, but only four were over the age of fifty: "Molly 60, fl hand; Robin 80,/hand; Elsy 60,/hand; and Sam 70, gardener" (King 1995, p. 18). This list shows that even elderly slaves were expected to work for the plantation owner. But elderly slaves had more time to spend with children, and during the time they cared for slave children, they passed down knowledge about their ancestors' culture through songs, games, and stories (Close 1997).

Robert Hill and his colleagues (1989) argue that one aspect of this cultural heritage was family organization. They describe West African families as differing from nuclear families in three dimensions. First, the African concept of family includes many people who may not actually live in the same household. Second, extended kin (blood relatives like grandparents and cousins) are thought of and treated as family instead of limiting family to nuclear members only. Third, Africans include as family many people who may not be related by blood. These unrelated people may be incorporated into a family through informal adoption and foster care. These characteristics were ones that Davis found typical of families in the slave community. She argues that these families were created in response to the experience of slavery. Robert Hill and his colleagues (1988) and Sudarkasa (1988) maintain that these families were part of the culture of black Americans because their ancestors came from West African cultures.

Comparing White Middle-Class Women to African American Women in the Nineteenth Century. "Third wave feminism looks critically at the tendency of work done in the 1960's and 1970's to use a generalized, monolithic concept of 'woman' as a generic category in stratification and focuses instead on the factual and theoretical implications of differences among women" (Lengermann and Niebrugge-Brantley 1992, p. 480; see also Chow 1987; Dill 1983; Hooks 1984). Jacqueline Jones (1985) is an example of a third-wave feminist. Her work allows us to make a comparison between black women and white women living in the United States during the nineteenth century.

We noted in the last chapter that during the nineteenth century, white women in middle-class and upper-class families were identified with domesticity. Jones (1985) found that in addition to the work they did for the white plantation owner, black women also performed much domestic work in the slave community. The division of labor in both Northern middle-class white families and in the Southern slave community assigned women to cooking, child care, and sewing.

As I described in the last chapter, according to the cult of true womanhood, white women were supposed to make their family work the center of their lives. Their identification with domesticity diminished white women's importance in the community, since their domestic work kept them away from activities in the economic and political world that were the seats of power. As a result, women's work was invisible, and women's attempts to have any effect on politics were discouraged or even banned.

We have seen that African American women were doing the same household work as middle-class white women, but in a very different context and with a very different effect. Black women's domestic activities performed in service to the adults and children of the slave community enhanced their importance to that community and their ability to serve the political struggle against slavery. At the same time the African American community allowed, encouraged, and even demanded that African American slave women run an Underground Railroad and burn down plantations, the white community would not even allow white women to speak before a crowd (Dill 1986).

This contrast between white women and African American women shows that the assignment of women to certain kinds of family work—cooking, child care, sewing, and the like—does not necessarily give women power nor does it diminish their power. It is the combination of the division of work in families and the relationship of families to the dominant political structure that creates opportunities for women to emerge as leaders or to be victims.

Reproduction.   Slaveowners attempted to treat women and men slaves the same way, working them all to their maximum ability and treating them all with the same ruthlessness, regardless of their sex. One problem with this strategy for the slave owners, however, was the need to replenish the numbers of slaves. Laws passed in 1807 made it illegal to import slaves from other nations, so the population of slaves could be increased only by allowing slave women to bear children. The physical demands of pregnancy, childbirth, and nursing an infant were not easily combined with starvation, brutality, and exhausting and difficult work on the plantations. The "solution" that the plantation owners developed was to divide the work between different groups of slave women. Women in the border states were forced to bear large numbers of children, and fertility levels in the upper South neared human capacity. Records show that slave women in Kentucky had high birthrates, bearing as many as twelve or thirteen children. Records also indicate that some slave owners offered the women freedom or let them stay in their marriages if they bore large numbers of children (D. White 1985). Lacking the large, lucrative cotton plantations of the Deep South, slave owners in the border areas turned the production of slaves into their dominant industry.

At the same time, the huge agricultural operations of the Deep South, which were highly productive, literally worked people to death. Women in the lower South were worked so hard that they were often unable to bear children. Slave women in Mississippi, for example, had low birthrates because of their large number of miscarriages, especially during the cotton boom years of 1830 to 1860 (J. Jones 1985).

In a nuclear family, the task of reproduction is divided between the husband and wife. The wife bears the children and frequently cares for the young infants. Under the slave system, the task of reproduction was divided among women based on where they lived and what role they played within the system as a whole.

Sharecropping

After the slave system was abolished by the Civil War, a new economic system called sharecropping was established in the South, and a different form of family developed for African Americans who lived there. The sharecropping system guaranteed that ex-slaves would continue to be available to work the land after the Civil War. Jay Mandle (1978) defines sharecropping as a crop lien system in which sharecroppers pledged their unplanted crops to landowners or local merchants, frequently at high interest rates.

The arrangements of sharecropping varied, but typically sharecroppers received the use of a house, tools, farm animals, and a plot of land in exchange for a portion of the crop they produced. The rest of the crop was due to the landowner. Regardless of how good a year it was, the landowner demanded his due. If there was drought or insect infestation, the sharecropper still owed the landowner for the tools, farm animals, and the value of the crop that would have been available in a good year. This resulted in sharecroppers being in constant debt to the landowners and, therefore, unable to leave the plantation (Mandle 1978, p. 18).

Work for African Americans was much the same after the transition from slavery to sharecropping. Families, however, changed in important ways as African Americans sought to allow women to reduce their work in the fields so that they could take care of their families.

Although the Civil War made it illegal for plantation masters to own slaves, for the most part the old slaveholders still owned the land. African American people who had lived in the region as slaves before the war now lived as sharecroppers on farms that were owned by the landholders after the war. Sharecropping was similar to slavery in other ways. Both slaves and sharecroppers worked the land for the plantation owner, had few rights, were frequently subjected to barbarous treatment at the hands of the landowner, and lived hard, impoverished lives.

In addition, sharecroppers had little opportunity to move away from the plantations. Sharecroppers were obligated to give the landowners a specific amount of salable produce regardless of the actual production of the farm. If the crops did not come in as well as the landowner stipulated they should, the sharecroppers still owed the same amount. Sharecroppers, therefore, tended to sink further and further into debt. Debtors who wished to leave the plantations were in some cases forced to remain, creating a debt peonage system backed by the local sheriff. Although the sharecroppers were no longer slaves, in a sense they were enslaved by the sharecropping system because if they tried to leave the plantation, they would be arrested for not paying their debts.

In one way, however, sharecropping was quite different from slavery—in the organization of African American families. Sharecroppers retained their ties to an extended community network, as they had under slavery. Nuclear families, however, became the dominant form of family life under the sharecropping system. At the end of the Civil War, observers described masses of black couples coming to Freedmen's Bureau offices to legalize their marriages (Giddings 1984). And by "1870, 80 percent of black households in the Cotton Belt included a male head and his wife" (J. Jones 1985, p. 62).

The macrolevel of Southern society, the political economy, changed from a system of slavery to a system of sharecropping. In some ways this transition was not as dramatic as many had hoped when they fought for the abolition of slavery. The transition, however, was significant enough to alter the organization of most families from an extended community-based form to one that was nuclear and more male dominated.

The basic unit of labor under sharecropping was the nuclear family. Under slavery the basic unit had been the individual slave, who was often kept separated from his or her nuclear family and could be sold away from kin at any time. As described earlier, this made it difficult and frequently impossible for people to maintain nuclear families. In contrast, nuclear families organized as economic teams with men as their head were the core of the sharecropping system.

Men sharecroppers were the ones who were in direct contact with the landholders, the creditors, and the people in the market who purchased the crops. Women were tied into the sharecropping system through their husbands. Wives and children worked in the fields under the direction of the father. When a landholder allowed a sharecropper to live on his land, he assumed that the sharecropper's entire family would work together on the land. If landholders suspected that all family members were not working the land, they would arm themselves and ride through sharecropping communities to make sure that women and children were doing their share by working in the fields.

Who Shall Control Women's and Children's Labor?   Jacqueline Jones (1985, p. 45) says that one of the great fears among whites after the Civil War was that "black people's desire for family autonomy, as exemplified by the 'evil of female loaferism'—the preference among wives and mothers to eschew wage work in favor of attending to their own households—threatened to subvert the free labor nonslavery experiment." The Boston cotton brokers, for example, claimed that the cotton crop of 1867–1868 was disastrous because of the decision of "growing numbers of Negro women to devote their time to their homes and children" (Giddings 1984, p. 63).

African American women in sharecropping households were not loafers. They did, however, attempt to control their own labor by considering the needs of their families. The women tried to divide their labor between housework and field work to allow them enough time for their families. Often they were not successful. "In 1870 more than four out of ten black married women listed jobs, almost all as field laborers. By contrast, fully 98.4 percent of white wives told the census taker they were 'keeping house' and had no gainful occupation" (J. Jones 1985, p. 63).

Field work was not the only work required of African American women. In the 1930s, the Commission on Race Relations interviewed African American people about their lives. A stockyard worker in Mississippi explained how women in his community were required to work for whites. He said:

> Men and women had to work in the fields. A woman was not permitted to remain at home if she felt like it. If she was found at home, some of the white people would come and ask why she was not in the field and tell her she had better get to the field or else abide by the

consequences. After the summer crops were all in, any of the white people could send for any Negro woman to come and do the family washing at 75 cents to $1 a day. If she sent word she could not come she had to send an excuse why she could not come. They were never allowed to stay at home as long as they were able to go. Had to take whatever they paid you for your work. (J. Jones 1985, p. 157)

From the point of view of the ex-slaves, freedom meant the opportunity to create autonomous independent families. Nearly every family that had an able-bodied man aspired to a division of labor that allowed African American women to take care of their own families, and during Reconstruction large numbers of women dropped out of the wage labor system and limited their fieldwork under sharecropping. "The institution of slavery had posed a constant threat to the stability of family relationships; after emancipation these relationships became solidified, though the sanctity of family life continued to come under pressure from the larger white society" (J. Jones 1985, p. 58).

Women were pressured to work in the fields and the homes of rich white people, which limited the time they had for their own families. They were also limited by the circumstances of poverty and instability that characterized the sharecroppers' lives. The women nevertheless tried to maintain "homelikeness" in the constantly moving households of the sharecroppers.

Sharecropping and tenant families frequently moved at the end of the year—in some cases hounded off a plantation by an unscrupulous employer, in other cases determined to seek out a better contract or sympathetic kinfolk down the road. They tacked brightly colored magazine pictures or calendars on the walls of bare, drafty cabins; fashioned embroidered curtains out of fertilizer sacks; and planted flowers in the front yard. (J. Jones 1989, p. 34)

Gender Equality and Changes in Families under Sharecropping.   The historical documents show that the African American family was a central arena of the struggle between the old slave masters and the ex-slaves. Former slave owners wanted to continue to dominate black people by controlling their work and their family organization. Newly emancipated people wanted to control their own labor and that of their family members.

Susan Archer Mann (1986) argues that there was another struggle being waged, the one within sharecropper families between husbands and wives. The development of the nuclear male-headed household (at least as an ideal) marks a change that was not entirely positive for women. Certainly women were greatly relieved by the abolishment of slavery, and within the sharecropping system they chose to contribute as much of their labor as possible to their families. But the equality between women and men that was present under slavery was diminished when the sharecropping system developed, placing wives under the control of their husbands (Janiewski 1983). Paula Giddings (1984, p. 61) states that "following the Civil War, men attempted to vindicate their manhood largely through asserting their authority over women."

The absorption of African American women into more nuclear households also may have pulled them away from their extrafamilial connections in the larger community, such as those Davis described as characteristic of the slave communities. Throughout the period of sharecropping and industrialization, African American women continued to try to keep

---

BOX **3.3**

Did the Abolishment of Slavery End the Involuntary Servitude of African American Children?

Just as the ratification of the Thirteenth Amendment did not guarantee the right of African American families to make choices about the activities of wives and mothers, it also did not guarantee that families could make choices about their children. Rebecca Scott (1985) found that in North Carolina after the Civil War, apprenticeships were used as a way to reenslave African American children. People under the age of twenty-one could be legally indentured to employers.

For a brief period following the Civil War, from 1865 until 1877, the former Confederate states were placed under martial law, and the Union Army attempted to make sure that Southern political leaders abided by the agreements made at the end of the war. This period in American history is called Reconstruction. One of the institutions that was established during Reconstruction was the Freedmen's Bureau, which was supposed to try to rebuild the South and to aid the 4 million former slaves. The Bureau received numerous complaints about children who were seized from their parents and taken to work on former slave owners' plantations.

Children could be legally bound if they were "base-born" (their parents were not legally married) or if their parents "did not employ them in some honest industrious occupation." An estimated ten thousand children were bound in Maryland, despite the objections of their parents (Giddings 1984, p. 57). "Often no money was specified to be given at the end of the term, children were bound without parental consent, no trades were specified, or children were bound beyond the legal age" (Scott 1985, p. 196).

The former slave owners fought hard to reestablish their system. For example, William Cole, a former slave owner of Rockingham, North Carolina, wrote to the Freedmen's Bureau in 1865, "I understand you are authorized to bind out to the former owners of slaves all those under the age of twenty-one years, under certain conditions," explaining that about thirty of his former slaves were under twenty-one and that he would like them all bound to him (Scott 1985, p. 194).

African American people fought equally hard to contest the reestablishment of slavery. One ex-slave woman named Huley Tilor wrote to the North Carolina Freedmen's Bureau about her former master:

> Dear Sir if you please to do a Good Favor for me if Pleas i have been to Mr. Tilor about my children and he will not let me have them an he say he will Beat me to deth if i cross his plantasion A Gain an so i dont now what to do About it an i wish if you pleas that you wood rite Mr. Joseph tilor a letter an let him Give me my childrin Mr. cory i want my children if you Pleas to get them for me i have bin after them an he says i shall not have them and he will not Pay me nor my children ether for thar last year work and now want let me have my childrin nother an i will close huley tilor. (Scott 1985, p. 198)

---

their commitment to the larger community, especially in their efforts to develop, support, and teach in schools for black children.

Jacqueline Jones (1985, p. 99) reminds us that our concern for the loss of equality of black women in gender relations must be tempered by the acknowledgment that under sharecropping, "black working women in the South had a more equal relationship than northern middle-class white women with their husbands in the sense that the two partners were not separated by extremes of economic power or political rights; black men and women lacked both."

She also argues that the impact of the larger political and economic context must be remembered. The maintenance of more isolated nuclear families was not for the purpose of empowering black men. The "seclusion" of women in nuclear families in which men were the heads of the households and in direct contact with white landowners and merchants was a strategy to protect women from a real threat. One ex-slave vowed "to support his family by his own efforts; never to allow his wife and daughters to be thrown in contact with Southern white men in their homes" (Lerner 1973, p. 292). When the Union troops left and Reconstruction ended, a backlash occurred, and tremendous brutality was directed against all African American people. One of the legacies of slavery was the sexual assault of African American women by white men. One way to try to prevent this was to make African American husbands the social and economic link between the family and white landowners. Minimizing the contact between white men and African American women was an attempt to hold back the constant threat of sexual violence.

Sharecropping and the formation of male-headed nuclear families for African Americans who lived under the system was, therefore, a result of several intersecting factors. African American families were contested terrain. Who would control these families, white landowners, African American men, or African American families themselves? And where would African American women fit in?

BOX 3.4

Parents and Children in Native American Families

Throughout the periods of slavery and sharecropping, African American parents were prevented from exercising authority over their children and in many instances from even being able to live with them or spend time with them. Parents and children challenged this separation by running away to be with one another and, during Reconstruction, calling on the government to assist them in keeping their families together. During the late nineteenth and early twentieth centuries, a similar battle was being waged by Native Americans.

The Revolutionary War is often thought of as one that was fought between two opposing forces seeking to control North America, the British and the Americans. A third party, Native Americans, played an equally important role. Most Native Americans fought on the side of the British, and when the war ended and the British returned home, Native Americans continued their effort to claim the right to live in their ancestral lands. Their struggle, however, was unsuccessful. The European Americans pushed westward, seeking resources and land to expand the cotton plantations (Zinn 1980).

In 1820, there were 120,000 Native Americans living east of the Mississippi River, but by 1844, fewer than 30,000 were left. This change was brought about by a government policy euphemistically called Indian Removal. Some Native American groups were forced to cede land to the U.S. government and white settlers. Those who refused were killed or run off by troops, and their property was destroyed or confiscated. Those who took refuge in the surrounding area were eventually rounded up by the army and forced to march west to states like Arkansas. Eventually they were driven even farther west to what became the reservations of Oklahoma and other Western states. Dale VanEvery (1976) wrote of one of the marches out of Arkansas in the mid-1800s: "By midwinter, the interminable, stumbling procession of more than 15,000 Creeks stretched from border to border across Arkansas. The passage of the exiles could be distinguished from afar by the howling of trailing wolf packs and the circling flocks of buzzards" (p. 142).

Once the Native Americans were removed to the isolated reservations, around 1880, the federal government sought "to obliterate the cultural heritage of Native Americans and to replace it with the values of Anglo-American society" (Trennert 1990, p. 224). The key strategy for accomplishing this was to remove children from their tribal homes and place them in boarding schools, which were located a long distance from where their families lived. Parents were required to enroll their children for a minimum of three years, and the Bureau of Indian Affairs (BIA) paid for transportation for only one round trip. During the summer most students could not afford to return home and were therefore placed in local homes to work for 50 cents to $1 a week (Littlefield 1989). Alice Littlefield reviewed student files and found that a number of parents requested that their children be sent home because of illness or economic hardship or because they believed the schools were not treating their children properly. In every case the school superintendent denied the request. Children usually did not see their parents for several years.

At the turn of the century, 17,000 Native American children were sent away to boarding schools while only 5,000 attended federal day schools (Szasz 1985). The schools were run as paramilitary institutions with rigid discipline, beatings, highly regimented daily activities, students in uniforms, marching in formation, and rising to 5:00 A.M. drills. There was little emphasis on academics. Boys were likely to be trained in a trade and girls in domestic work. Each hour of academic work was matched by three hours of industrial work, most of it unpaid (Szasz 1985). Children were not allowed to speak their native languages and at some schools were punished if they were caught doing so. Although the schools were government run and therefore nondenominational, students were required to participate in service organizations sponsored by Christian churches (Trennert 1979). In addition, children were malnourished, and crowded conditions led to widespread tuberculosis and trachoma (Szasz 1985).

Official government policy in regard to Native Americans in the late eighteenth and early nineteenth centuries sought to separate parents from children, to diminish the authority of parents over their children, and to prevent parents from passing on their cultural heritage and values to their children (Noriega 1992). The U.S. government believed that if children were removed from their families and their communities, they would be better assimilated as useful workers in the dominant white society. Children resisted by frequently running away and breaking rules, especially by pilfering food (Littlefield 1989). Parents resisted by hiding their children and not allowing government officials to send them to boarding schools (Amott and Matthaei 1991).

Industrialization

Agriculture remained the core industry in the South, with cotton as the most important crop, until after World War II. But throughout the twentieth century, the introduction of machinery displaced more and more sharecroppers. Rural Southerners whose jobs were taken over by farm equipment were forced to move to the North and into the urban areas of the South.

This period in history is known as the Great Migration because it was the largest migration of people within the United States in history. Until the start of the twentieth century, nearly all African Americans lived in the Southern states. Between 1910 and 1930, one million African American people (10% of the total black population) moved from the

South to the North. And even larger numbers moved from the rural South to Southern cities during that period (Marks 1985). This migration reversed in the 1990s when more than 368,800 African Americans left the Western, Midwestern, and Northeastern states to move to the South (Vobejda 1998).

The move was not just a geographic one; it was also economic, marking a transition of the political economy of the South. This change was not just one of black workers moving from one locale to another, but of workers moving from agricultural work to urban manufacturing and service jobs. The migration occurred simultaneously with the transition of the political economy of the South from being based on farming to being based on industry and service.

The move had different results for men and women. African American men and white people moved from agricultural work into manufacturing jobs; African American women moved from agricultural work into domestic work. "Less than 3% of all black working women were engaged in manufacturing in 1900 compared with 21% of foreign-born and 38% of native-born white working women" (J. Jones 1985, p. 166).

It is difficult to say why African American women entered domestic work rather than manufacturing. The pay in manufacturing work was slightly higher than for domestic work, and factory work often meant somewhat less degrading supervision by whites compared with what the domestic worker had to endure. For these reasons black women undoubtedly would have preferred industrial jobs to domestic service. They probably did not have that choice. There is some evidence that black women were forced into domestic work by racially discriminatory laws that barred them from factory jobs.

Even African American women who did manage to secure work in the factories had a difficult time. "Black women who fled from the degradation of domestic service only to find themselves in the hot, humid tobacco stemmers' room paid a high price in terms of their general health and well-being" (J. Jones 1985, p. 135).

African American women remained concentrated in domestic work for another five decades. Until the middle 1960s, the largest single occupation of African American women was domestic work. "By 1950, 60 percent of all African American working women (compared to 16 percent of all white working women) were concentrated in institutional and private household service jobs" (J. Jones 1985, p. 235).

African American families changed as women went to work in the homes of white people and spent long hours away from their own families. Some employers insisted that their maids "live in," which meant that domestic workers were able to see their own families only every other weekend. Once again, an African American woman's time with her own family was a battleground between herself and her white employer.

A similar battle was being waged in California during this same period. Japanese American women and men who had also immigrated from rural agricultural economies to the growing U.S. urban centers found themselves limited in their occupational choices. Large numbers of Japanese American women and men became live-in domestic employees for whites. They also would have preferred factory or shop employment, but like African Americans were barred from those jobs by race and gender discrimination.

Being on call twenty-four hours a day by an employer was intolerable for African Americans and Japanese Americans, and both fought against live-in domestic service.

African Americans resisted and defied their employers more openly than Japanese Americans, although both groups used a number of resistance strategies (Glenn 1990).

Bonnie Thornton Dill interviewed domestic workers who had been employed in the first half of the twentieth century. She found that they used several techniques to gain control of their work, including direct confrontation, threatening to quit, chicanery, and quitting (Dill 1988). Although they were not all successful, many were able to work out some degree of autonomy and gain some respect on their jobs. Ultimately, they were successful in changing domestic work from live-in to day work, which meant they could go to their own homes at night (Dill 1988; Glenn 1990).

In Chapter 7 we continue this investigation of domestic work by African American women, as well as other racial ethnic women. The important points to be remembered here are, first, that private domestic work was overwhelmingly the largest occupation for African American women in the early part of the twentieth century and, second, that work involved conflicts between maids and their employers over a maid's right to spend time with her own family.

African American Families in the Struggle for Equality

Although each of these historical periods shows different political economies and different family forms, one theme runs through them all: the centrality of family in the battle waged by African Americans for equality. Jacqueline Jones (1985, p. 4) states, "Throughout American history, the black family has been the focus of a struggle between black women and the whites who sought to profit from their labor."

During the slave period, the goal of slave owners was to use their slaves to make as much profit as possible. Slaves had very different goals. They fought to maintain their family ties, to keep their community alive, and to topple the slave system. Central issues of contention between slaveholder and slave were related to family organization, such as the right of slaves to choose a spouse, to legally marry, to live with their spouses and children, and to be free from sexual assault by plantation owners. Despite enormous difficulty, slaves often kept track of their kin and created their own rituals to recognize marriage and parenthood, regardless of the slave owners' laws.

Slaves also organized insurrections and other forms of rebellion, such as running away from the plantations. In the opening scenario, John mentions that he has decided to go north with Harriet Tubman on the Underground Railroad. The Underground Railroad was a large international network of black and white people who smuggled thousands of slaves out of the South before the Civil War.

Harriet Tubman was a "conductor" on a Underground Railroad. She was born into slavery, and after escaping she returned to the South, first to bring her husband and other family members to freedom and then to make nineteen more trips carrying more than 300 slaves to freedom. Harriet Tubman was not alone. More than 3,200 people ran the Underground Railroad, transporting 2,500 slaves a year to freedom between 1830 and 1860 (Zinn 1980).

During sharecropping, the battle over African American families continued. Landowners physically threatened women who did not work in the fields and kidnapped children to be field workers. Sharecropper families fought back by defying the landowners and often the sheriff in attempts to run away or at least to maintain some control over their lives. Sharecropper women tried to spend as much time as they could on their family work, and parents sought to retain their rights to protect their children and make decisions about when and where they would work. Sharecropper men attempted to seclude women and children away from whites to protect them from sexual assault.

In the first half of the twentieth century, the Great Migration and industrialization pulled Southerners from the rural areas into the cities. African American women who were pushed into wage labor as maids fought with their white mistresses over the time they could spend with their own families and over control of their work. Employers ignored maids' family connections and obligations, demanding that they be on call twenty-four hours a day. Maids had to defy their employers to claim even a small part of their lives for their families and themselves. Eventually the maids' protest spilled into the streets in the Montgomery Bus Boycott, which is discussed below.

During Reconstruction, an attempt was made to integrate African Americans into Southern society. African American men were allowed to vote, and many African Americans were appointed or elected to government positions. For example, in South Carolina in the years immediately following the Civil War, fifty members of the state legislature were black and only thirteen were white. But as the old plantation owners regained political power, the situation deteriorated. In 1883, the Civil Rights Act of 1875 was declared unconstitutional. In 1896, the final blow occurred with the Supreme Court decision in the case of *Plessy* v. *Ferguson.* From the end of the nineteenth century until the middle of the twentieth century, Jim Crow laws created a legal apartheid in southern United States.

Homer Plessy, a black man, rode a segregated train through Louisiana and was required to sit in a car reserved for African Americans. He sued the railroad, claiming that his constitutional rights had been violated. The Supreme Court ruled in favor of the railroad, making legal the doctrine of "separate but equal" or what were called Jim Crow laws. Much like the apartheid system in twentieth-century South Africa, the doctrine of separate but equal meant that all public facilities in the South, including restaurants, drinking fountains, public restrooms, schools, blood banks, and public transportation, could be segregated.

Black people who rode the bus were required to pay at the front of the bus, then get off, walk to the back door, and get on in the back of the bus. They were allowed to sit only in the seats in the back of the bus even if there were empty seats in the front section, which was "for whites only." If a white person got on and there were no "white seats" left, a black person was required to give up his or her seat. One evening in 1955, Rosa Parks, a black woman, refused to give up her seat. She was arrested and placed in jail. Her action sparked the Montgomery Bus Boycott, which was to become a major event in the history of the civil rights movement. Many of the riders on the city buses were African American maids who rode to work at white homes across town. The maids and other African Americans boycotted the buses for many months and eventually were successful in changing the Jim Crow laws affecting public transportation.

When we examine diversity among contemporary American families in Chapter 5, we will continue the discussion of the history of African Americans and the relationship

TABLE 3.2   **Recent Changes in Black Family Organization, 1970–2004**

Type of Family	1970	1980	1990	2000	2004
Married couples	68.3	55.5	50.2	47	44.2
Single male-headed	3.7	4.1	6.0	8	8.9
Single female-headed	28.0	40.3	43.8	44	46.9

Source: U.S. Census Bureau 1990a, 2000e, 2003b.

between changes in the macrolevel of social context and changes in the microlevel of families' everyday experiences. More than half of all African Americans now live outside the South, and most of them live in urban areas. As noted in Figure 2.2 in the last chapter, black women have continued to increase their numbers in the paid labor force. Along with these changes in the context of African American families, the organization of those families has also changed. Table 3.2 shows, for example, that a growing number of African American households are headed by single men and especially single women. As we moved into the fourth period of African American family history, the organization of the African American family continued to be controversial. These issues are examined in Chapter 5.

Latino American Family History

In Chapter 5, we sort out the question of who exactly are Latino Americans. This broad group includes people from many different nations and cultures. The largest category of Latino Americans are Mexican Americans, Chicanos. This section looks at some of the history of Mexico and Mexican Americans and the ways that history shaped family life in the late nineteenth and early twentieth centuries.

Sometimes the debate around immigrants and borders in the United States sounds as if Northern Europeans settled in North America establishing the nation called the United States, and Spanish-speaking people from nations south of the border have been trying to get in ever since. This image of American history is a myth. About one-third of the area that is currently the United States was originally settled by Spanish colonists and then later became part of Mexico. In 1847, the American military invaded northern Mexico. When the war ended in 1848, the Treaty of Guadalupe Hidalgo was signed, allowing the United States to purchase for $15 million the area we now know as Texas, Arizona, New Mexico, California, and Colorado. The people who lived in those areas (about half of Mexico) suddenly found themselves living in a new nation; And they found that family and friends on the other side of the new border were no longer fellow citizens (Acuna 2003).

Split Households among Chicanos and Chinese Americans

In Chapter 2 we explored the historical development of the relationship between work and family for working-class and middle-class Euro-Americans. The dominant ideology romanticized the split between work and family, while making it inaccessible to working-class

European American families because of low wages. For middle-class European Americans, the split between work and family was an important part of their history and has created problems, especially for women. In this chapter, we noted in the history of African American families the blurring of the lines between work and family and women's and men's work.

Two other groups of Americans experienced a sharp split between between work and family and between the work that men and women engaged in. Both Chicanos (Mexican Americans) and Chinese Americans were required to divide their households for the men to be allowed to work (Glenn 1991).

Chicano Families.   In the late nineteenth and early twentieth centuries, Chicano men were recruited to work in mining camps and on railroad gangs, which did not provide accommodations for wives and children and usually prohibited them from being there (Barerra 1979). The men were required to leave their families for long periods of time in order to earn a living. The women who were left behind worked in subsistence farming and wage labor in urban areas. They had jobs as cooks, maids, and laundry workers in hotels and other public establishments (Camarillo 1979; Garcia 1980). In addition to these tasks, Chicanas—Mexican American women—also raised their children and provided health care in communities that often had no running water or public sanitation systems.

After the start of the twentieth century, the split between work and family and women's and men's work began to decline as growers increasingly hired entire Chicano families to work as farm laborers in the large fields of the Southwest. For many Chicanos, the split between work and family disappeared as husbands, wives, and even small children and infants went to work in the fields. While these changes may have improved family life by allowing family members more contact with one another, living conditions were no better. Infant and child mortality was high, wages were low, education was nonexistent, and life expectancy was short (Glenn 1991).

Today many Latino families still work in the fields, but many other Latino families remain split. Latina women who come to the United States to work as domestic workers or nannies often must leave behind their own children. More and more women from Mexico, Honduras, Ecuador, and other Latin American countries are crossing the border as demand for their labor grows. The global trend is not new, but in Mexico and other parts of Latin America the growing numbers of mothers migrating for work without their children is leaving hundreds of families without parents. The United Nations estimates that 85 million women in the world migrated in search of work in 2000 (United Nations 2004). Researchers studying the trend say it takes a heavy toll on the emotional well-being of these migrant mothers as well as that of their children (Bhatia and Braine 2005).

Chinese American Families.   Among Chinese workers the split was more formalized. A significant number of Chinese immigrants arrived in the western United States and Hawaii during the 1800s. Chinese people were the first Asians to immigrate to the United States in significant numbers (Wong 1995). By the end of the century, Chinese people constituted 25 percent of the entire workforce in California (Takaki 1989). Nearly all these immigrants were men. Because the United States was known as Gold Mountain, the wives who were left behind were called Gold Mountain Ladies. About one-half of the Chinese men who immigrated left wives in China (Chow 1998).

There are several reasons for this (Chow 1998). First, only male workers were offered jobs, and when the men were recruited, it was with the specification that their wives and children must be left behind. Second, the men's families in China may have encouraged them to leave their wives and children behind, believing that this would increase the probability that the men would remain in contact with their relatives in China and especially that they would continue to send money home.

A third factor influencing the number of Chinese women entering the United States was immigration law. In 1882, the Chinese Exclusion Act prohibited Chinese women from entering the country even if they had husbands waiting for them. The purpose of the act was to prevent the Chinese from settling permanently after their labor was no longer needed for such major projects as building the railways (Glenn 1991). The law prohibited Chinese women from entering the United States so they would not bear children who could claim U.S. citizenship (Espiritu 1997).

Fourth, Chinese people were afraid to raise families and make their homes in the United States because of racial harassment and attacks against them (R. Daniels 1978). "From Los Angeles to Seattle and as far east as Denver and Rock Springs, Wyoming, Chinese were run out of town or beaten and killed by mobs whose members were almost never brought to justice" (Kitano and Daniels 1988, p. 22). Because of these four factors, very few Chinese women lived in the United States during the nineteenth century, and as late as 1930, the ratio of Chinese men to women was still 11:2 (Glenn 1991).

Little is known about the wives and children who were left behind in China. Their numbers, however, were significant, since about half the men who came to work in the United States were married. Many of these women never saw their husbands again. Some men were able to visit China twenty or thirty years later. Most of the wives lived with their husband's parents, where their behavior, especially their sexual behavior, was carefully monitored. Although the women rarely saw their husbands, the marriage contract held a tight rein on their lives (Glenn 1991).

Chicanos, Chinese Americans, working-class Euro-Americans, and middle-class Euro-Americans were living in the same developing industrial capitalist economy in the United States. But they all experienced a different history of changing relationships between the organization of work and family and between men's work and women's work. Each of these groups also faced problems as a result of the way in which families and work were organized throughout this period. Those problems, however, differed significantly (Dill 1986). The division of labor for African American slaves presents yet another pattern.

In Chapter 2 we noted that in the nuclear families of middle-class whites in the nineteenth century, work was divided into two spheres—paid work in the labor market for men and unpaid domestic work for women. Work and family were separate, and men's work and women's work was different. In Chinese American and Mexican American families, work and family and men's work and women's work were also separate. Under the slave system, both African American men and women labored at the same exhausting jobs for no pay. The lines between work and family and between women's work and men's work were blurred in the African American family under slavery (Dill 1986; Matthaei 1982).

Based on the experience of white middle-class women, a conceptualization of a split between work and family has been developed. This conceptualization is especially inconsistent with the experience of African Americans (Brewer 1988). Rather than attempting to explain why African American families "deviate" from this "norm," Collins (1990) suggests that we reconstruct our thinking about families based on our discovery of these kinds of diversity. The different relationship between work and family and men's and women's work, in particular, helps us see how useless definitions of The Family are. Family has many meanings depending on the social context in which a family exists.

The discovery of the contrasts in the experience of separate spheres among Euro-Americans, African Americans, Chinese Americans, and Mexican Americans teaches us a second lesson—that diversity is not just between whites and nonwhites. Diversity occurs across many lines, and we should not speak of people of color as if they were a monolithic group.

Salt of the Earth

Not all Latino families were split in this way. In the early part of the twentieth century, many Latinos lived in mining communities in the Southwest where whole families settled around the mines where men were employed. In the 1950s an important strike, which was documented in a film titled *Salt of the Earth,* took place at a zinc mine in New Mexico. Fourteen hundred men from the IUMMSW (International Union of Mill Mine and Smelter Workers) walked out in protest of conditions of work at the mine. The courts ruled that the union members could not maintain a picket line at the company gates. At first the union did not know how to respond since their inability to picket greatly reduced the pressure they could put on management in their negotiations, and the miners would not be able to prevent the company from hiring nonunion replacements (scabs). The miners, however, came up with an innovative plan. The women in the community would "man" the picket line. Since the women were not members of the union, the court could not restrict them from marching. Every day the women marched with their signs (Acuna 2003; Wilson 1977).

Their action was hailed as an heroic act in defense of the men of the community. As time passed, however, the women's activities began to alter relations in families in a way that challenged the old ideas and old ways of organizing family life that kept women subordinate to their husbands. Because the women were busy at the picket line, the men had to take over the household chores that had been women's work. The men discovered that the work the women did was difficult and time-consuming and that some of the work was made unnecessarily ardouous because it was seen as unimportant. The men had heard their wives complain for years about the lack of a plumbing system into the community, which meant they had to carry water to do their household chores. This problem, however, had not been seen as important enough to include in contract negotiations with the mine owners. But when carrying water became men's work, it was brought to the table as a critical issue in the contracts. By the time the strike had ended, women had gained respect in their community for taking over the men's action. In addition, the household work that had been women's work also gained respect and was recognized as a critical part of the total workload of the community and therefore suitable for consideration in labor negotiations (Wilson 1977).

In the discussion earlier in this chapter on domestic work done by African American women who were slaves for the slave community and especially for people attempting to walk to freedom through the Underground Railroad, we observed that domestic work became transformed into a revolutionary activity. This was in contrast to the housework done by white women which was a sign of their subordination. In the case of the Chicanas in the zinc strike, housework also was transformed. In this case it was invisible and not given much respect when work was divided between men who worked for wages in the mine and women who worked at home. But when the work began to be done by men while the women were "on strike," doing laundry, carrying water, and washing dishes emerged as important political issues and became part of the negotiations of the miners' union.

Structuration Theory and the Importance of Agency

Chapter 1 discussed C. Wright Mills's notion of the Sociological Imagination and the importance of acknowledging both the way in which the larger social context affects our everyday experiences and interactions and the way in which day-to-day social activities help shape the larger social context. The interplay between the micro- and macrolevels of society has continued to be of interest to social theorists. Anthony Giddens (1984) worked to develop sociological theory around the question of the relationship between the micro- and macrolevels of society. He has been especially intent on drawing our attention to the microlevel social activities that influence the macrolevel. He refers to this activity as agency (Ritzer 1992). Giddens writes, "Agency concerns events of which an individual is a perpetrator. Whatever happened would not have happened if that individual had not intervened" (p. 9).

Giddens was influenced by Marxism, and his work has grown from Karl Marx's observation that "men make history, but they do not make it just as they please; they do not make it under circumstances chosen by themselves, but under circumstances directly encountered, given, and transmitted from the past" (K. Marx 1869/1963, p. 15). Giddens's concept of agency fits the first clause of the sentence "men make history" (Ritzer 1992). He argues that people have agency; they act on their surroundings. He refers to the surroundings on which they act as social structure, and he asserts that social structure can be divided into four clusters: symbolic orders, political institutions, economic institutions, and laws.

1. Symbolic orders can refer to ideas, images, and words we use to think about and communicate about humans and their interactions. For example, during slavery, an important aspect of the maintenance of the system was ideas among slaveholders that slaves were less than human and therefore had less feelings and need for family. These same kinds of ideas rationalized the laws that brought Chinese American and Latino men to work while forcing them to leave their families behind.

2. Political institutions include the government and the police, any organizations that serve to maintain or alter relationships of power. Political institutions encompass written and unwritten rules about how people should conduct their affairs. They also include physical structures like the White House and the Pentagon. The sheriffs' departments that restricted sharecroppers from leaving the plantation communities and the court that blocked the miners from picketing in the zinc mine strike are examples of political institutions. The military decision to invade Mexico in order to claim the land we now know as

California, New Mexico, Arizona, and Texas are also examples of actions taken by political institutions.

3. Economic institutions include the slave market, the sharecropping plantation, and the race- and gender-segregated labor market of industrialization. These economic institutions created an important part of the social-structural context of African American family history. They also include the unions that negotiated contracts for the zinc miners.

4. Laws that made slavery and Jim Crow legal played an essential role in this history. During slavery, laws that restricted African Americans' rights to marry and prohibited parents from living with their children were especially important. During the period of share-cropping and industrialization, laws that did not allow workers to choose whom they would work for and what hours they would work were important to family life. Immigration laws restricted Chinese Americans and Mexican Americans from deciding about their work and family life.

This chapter's review of American history provides evidence of the importance of structure in the description of the dominant systems within each historical period that set the conditions under which African Americans and others lived. It also shows evidence of agency in the efforts of African Americans and others to alter, abolish, or maintain these social structures. African Americans fought against slavery and Jim Crow laws; Native Americans struggled to reclaim their children from the federal government; and Latino Americans struck to improve their working conditions. Giddens's (1984) structuration theory helps us see these two levels, structure and agency, and the constant interplay between them.

The Micro–Macro Connection

We see from this history that the macrolevel of social organization makes an enormous difference to family organization and family life. The division of labor between women and men, the political relationship between women and men, and even the reproduction of children are greatly affected by the kind of political economy in which those relationships are embedded. The startling and alien quality of the slave system provides powerful evidence of the importance of understanding the macrolevel of society, the social context, in order to understand the organization of families and the everyday experiences of family members. We would never make the mistake of saying that John and Mary, from the story at the beginning of the chapter, chose their family life without acknowledging the limitations placed on those "choices" by the slave system. Although our own society is not as grotesque as the slave society, it is equally powerful in its effect on individual lives. When we try to understand our own families, we commonly assume our social context to be something natural or inevitable, and we believe that we make free and individual choices. This history of African American families helps us see that our social surroundings profoundly affect and sometimes even determine what our lives will be like.

Once again we observe that society and families have not remained the same throughout history. The macrolevel of society is not static, but changes sometimes slowly and sometimes dramatically. The history of African Americans shows both the steady evolution and dramatic turning points of the last two centuries. It is not unusual to hear people in contemporary American society speak of "the downfall of the family," as if families had remained unchanged for centuries and have only recently deviated from some fixed form. But the Johns and Marys of the slave period led very different lives from the Johns and Marys of the sharecropping period and the Great Migration. This history, like that in Chapter 2, reminds us that change is a constant factor and that families have always been in transition.

We also see how historical change was experienced differently by African Americans compared with white, Mexican, and Chinese Americans. This suggests that when we speak of families, we must be careful to remember that families vary by race ethnicity, class, region, nation, and many other factors. These variations form stratification systems that are part of the macrolevel of society and that create significant differences in the microlevel experiences of members of various strata. In the next two chapters, we develop this discussion of stratification and the way in which it affects family life.

The two chapters on history show the ties between gender, family, and political economy. Social contexts are made of many factors and even systems of factors. Social structure itself is complex. The history of a society is really made up of many histories of many social structures.

In this history of African American society, we see that systems—family, gender, race, and political economy—make up part of the macrolevel of social structure and that these systems are interrelated. As families vary according to their social context, so do gender relations and family organization. The relative power of women and men, the tasks assigned to women and men, and the importance attached to those tasks all differ according to the time, place, and racial ethnic group in which they occur.

This chapter has described the day-to-day experience of African Americans at the microlevel. It has also described the social organization of slavery, sharecropping, migration, and industrialization at the macrolevel. And it has shown how this macro-organization affected the everyday life of African American people.

The relationship between macro- and microlevel forces is not one way. This chapter also shows the effect of the micro on the macro, of individuals working together to change the system, whether in slave insurrections, in the struggle over black families, or in the fight for equality for African Americans, Latino Americans, and for women.

4 Families and the Economic System

The Great U-turn marked a major shift in the U.S. economy, causing unemployment, poverty, and homelessness. Some families were forced on the road to try to find work. (© David Wells/The Image Works)

Jackie grew up in a blue-collar family in Miami. Her husband Al worked construction there until he was injured on the job. They have a five-year-old son called AJ. Jackie has worked on and off as a waitress in the big tourist hotels. When Al fell on a building site while working on a high rise on the beach, he broke his pelvis and required several surgeries. He now can get around with the use of a cane but still is in a lot of pain and requires medicine and physical therapy, and he will never be able to do construction work again. He thought he was covered for the accident but found out while he was in the hospital that he had to pay a deductible and a percentage of all the expenses for the hospital stay and the surgery. His health insurance also had a cap which he quickly reached. Now his expenses are all out of pocket because he is unemployed and can't find insurance that will cover pre-existing conditions plus he owes the hospital thousands of dollars and they have turned the bill over to collection. Before the accident Jackie and Al were doing pretty well and even put away some money to buy a house, but their savings are all gone now. Jackie's income has helped them to at least keep a roof over their heads, but they now live in a small trailer and even this expense will soon be beyond their means. Al has tried to get a desk job but when employers see his physical difficulties and the constant pain that afflicts him, they hesitate to take him on. Now Jackie is afraid she is pregnant, but she has no insurance since she is part time and cannot afford a doctor or an abortion. She is worried about AJ because he has asthma, but they have no insurance to help pay for his shots or visits to the doctor's office so she has been putting off finding care for him and he seems to be getting worse. To help make ends meet, Jackie has been taking lunch at a soup kitchen run by the church in her neighborhood. As she waits in line, she begins to feel sick. She sits down and cries.

> Jackie and Al's story sounds melodramatic and unreal.
>
> How extraordinary is their experience?
>
> Do you think it's true that many of us live one paycheck away from economic disaster?
>
> Are all American families facing economic hardship in these times?
>
> What are all the circumstances that bring Jackie to the final scene?
>
> How might these economic issues affect family life for Jackie and Al?
>
> What is the solution to Jackie's family's economic crisis?

The Critical Link between Families and the Economy

The most basic activity in which humans participate is providing themselves with the necessities of physical survival. Like other animals, humans must find food and shelter to keep themselves alive and able to produce the next generation. Sociologists call the organization of the production and distribution of the necessities of life the economic system. In order to understand our societies and our lives, we need to take into consideration the way in which our economic system is organized.

As we have seen in the previous two chapters and will observe throughout this book, economics is not the only important factor in the social context of families, but it is an essential one. Because economic activities are so critical to our existence, they affect all other aspects of our lives. Not surprisingly, when significant changes take place in the production and distribution of goods and services, dramatic changes occur in other parts of our society as well. New problems and new possibilities emerge. In the historical review in the preceding two chapters, we noted the way in which changes in the economy such as the development of industrialization or the transition from slavery to sharecropping had important effects on the family lives of the people living during those transitions. Now we will look at families in the contemporary economic context.

This chapter is divided into three sections. The first section describes the current economic situation and some of the problems it has created for many families. The second section looks at how families respond to economic issues by developing coping techniques or organizations to alter the economic context. The third section proposes an analytical framework for understanding today's economic picture. This last section also considers some of the potentially favorable possibilities that may emerge from the difficult changes we are witnessing.

The Contemporary Economic Scene in the United States: The Great U-Turn

The United States emerged from World War II ready to move into a leadership position in the world economy (Berberoglu 1992). Unlike Japan, the Soviet Union, and European nations, the United States suffered little damage to its industrial base during the war. Buildings and factories were left standing, and mines, roads, airports, harbors, and the energy distribution and communication systems were relatively untouched.

At the same time, the destruction in other nations created a huge market for the goods that Americans could produce. American steel, autos, tractors, food, clothes, building materials, and chemicals were needed by consumers and businesses all over the world. This combination of demand for goods and little competition for markets created an enormous boom in the U.S. economy (Tanzer 1974). Throughout the 1950s and 1960s, Americans grew to expect that each year would bring a higher standard of living, and a great number of people found their expectations realized.

But in the middle of the 1970s, this economic growth reversed (Farley 1996), and the wages of American workers began to decline. This reversal in the direction of the U.S. economy has been called the "Great U-turn" by economists Bennett Harrison and Barry Bluestone (1988). Table 4.1 illustrates the Great U-turn, showing the increase in wages from the late 1950s until they peaked in the late 1970s and then decrease until the mid 1990s. The figure shows that by 1994 average wages for production and nonsupervisory workers—about 80 percent of the workforce—had declined to below the level of the 1970s. In the middle of the 1990s, the line began to move up, and by 2003 was a little over the wages of 1978 (Bernstein and Mishel 2005). In sum, economic indicators have moved up and down in the past 30 years but overall American workers saw little or no improvement in their economic situation since the 1970s. And because their wages were depressed for many of those years they lost income over a lifetime of working.

In Table 4.1 the numbers have been adjusted for inflation. The real numbers before 2003 were lower. The buying power for all of the years, however, is comparable when the numbers are adjusted. For example, in 1960 a worker may have brought home $100 (unadjusted) per week, but in that same year he or she could buy a new car for only $2,500. One hundred dollars sounds small to us, but the buying power of that $100 was greater than it is today because of inflation. Since the prices of cars and everything else have risen over the past decades, it is more realistic to compare buying power than to compare absolute numbers. When the numbers are adjusted, the buying power can be compared.

Over the last quarter of the twentieth century, some workers received increases, but their raises were not as great as the inflation rate. At the same time prices were rising, jobs were changing, too. Newly created jobs since the 1970s are likely to be low paid. Table 4.2

**TABLE 4.1   Hourly Wage Change for
Production and Nonsupervisory Workers
(80% of Workforce), 1947–2003 (in 2003 $)**

1947	$ 8.47
1950	9.29
1955	10.65
1960	11.79
1965	13.02
1970	13.95
1975	14.25
1978	15.08
1980	14.46
1985	14.23
1990	13.91
1993	13.83 low
1995	13.95
2000	14.95
2003	15.35 peak

Source: Mishel, Bernstein, and Allegretto, 2005; Bureau
of Labor Statistics 2003a.

shows a projection of the types of new jobs that will be added to the economy. Most of these are not highly paid occupations. On the average, new jobs are likely to pay the minimum wage. The jobs that were being removed from the labor market were those that were better paid while new jobs coming into the labor market were lower paid (Mishel and Bernstein 1992; Bernstein and Mishel 2004).

Unemployment

In addition to a decline in wages from the 1980s to today, unemployment was also a problem. Unemployment rates fluctuated but inched consistently upward from the 1970s until the middle of the 1990s, then fell as the century ended. But from 2000 to 2004, the rates began to rise again, and unemployment has been especially prevalent among African Americans and Hispanic Americans (Bureau of Labor Statistics 2004b). Even those who keep their jobs are worried. Sixty-one percent of Americans say they are concerned that they might lose their job because their employer is moving jobs to another country through outsourcing (Business 2004).

Many people who lose their jobs do not show up in unemployment statistics. These are people who are currently neither working nor looking for work because they have given up. They say they are available for work and would like a job and have looked for one in the past twelve months but have not been able to find one. Unemployment statistics also do not count people who accepted part-time jobs when they would have preferred full-time employment. By April 2005, 7.7 million people were officially jobless, but the number of unemployed and underemployed was actually 13.7 million (AFL-CIO 2005).

TABLE 4.2   Occupations with the Largest Numerical Increases
in Employment, 2002–2012

Occupation	Number of New Jobs (in 1000s)
	Number of Jobs to be Added in Decade in 1000s
Registered nurses	630
Postsecondary teachers	615
Retail salesperson	600
Customer service reps	460
Food prep and service including fast food	459
Cashiers	458
Janitors	400
General and operations managers	376
Waiters and waitresses	375
Nursing aides, orderlies, and attendants	360
Truck drivers	358
Receptionists	350
Security guards	348

Source: Bureau of Labor Statistics 2004d.

Some people who lose their jobs find new jobs but at lower wages. On the average, workers who lost their jobs and found new ones have reported that the new job pays 15 percent less than their previous job. About 25 percent of those who found new jobs and were covered in their previous jobs with health care plans say their new jobs do not provide them with this benefit (Mishel, Bernstein, and Schmitt 1997). Projections reveal that in nearly all states businesses are shifting away from providing health insurance (AFL-CIO 2005), and health care costs have risen 43 percent since 2000. The scenario at the beginning of this chapter shows the devastating effect no health insurance can have on both our physical health when AJ didn't get his asthma medication, as well as our economic health when Jackie and Al found themselves falling deeper and deeper into debt as their health bills piled up.

Economic Decline and Poverty

Falling incomes and growing unemployment took their toll from the 1970s to the early 2000s. Table 4.3 shows how the percentage of poor rose sharply in the late 1970s and remained high throughout the 1980s and early 1990s. Poverty rates declined slightly in the late 1990s but are on the rise in the 2000s. In 2004, 37 million Americans had incomes below the poverty line. They comprised about 12.7 percent of the total population (U.S. Census Bureau 2005a).

Every year, the government determines the poverty income by looking at the cost of living. Table 4.4 shows the poverty threshold, the line at which the government defines dif-

TABLE 4.3   **Trends in Poverty, 1959–2004**

Year	Number Living Below 125% Poverty Level	Percent Living Below 125% Poverty Level
1959	54,942,000	31.1%
1965	46,163,000	24.1
1970	35,624,000	17.6
1975	37,182,000	17.6
1980	40,658,000	18.1
1985	44,166,000	18.7
1990	44,837,000	18.0
1995	48,761,000	18.5
2000	43,612,000	15.6
2004	49,666,000	17.1

Source: U.S. Census Bureau 2005b.

ferent households as poor depending on their income and the number of people sharing that income. Poverty was defined by the government in 2004 as income less than $14,476 for a family of three.

Poverty is not distributed evenly in the population. Race ethnicity, age, and household type influence our chances of being poor. In 2003, 24.4 percent of the black population, 22.5 percent of the Hispanic population, 11.8 percent of the Asian population, and 10.5 percent of the white population were poor (U.S. Census Bureau 2005c).

Age is also an important factor in poverty. Children are the most likely group to be poor (Lichter 1997). Child poverty fell quite dramatically from the 1950s to the late 1960s. It remained fairly low through the 1970s but began to rise in the 1980s and 1990s. The child poverty rate in 1994 was about the same as it had been in the mid-1960s. In 2003, 14.3 percent of white children under eighteen were poor, while 33.6 percent of black children,

TABLE 4.4   **Poverty Thresholds, 2004**

Size of family	Poverty Threshold
One person	
Under 65 years old	$ 9,827
65 and over	9,060
Two people	
Householder under 65	12,649
Householder 65 and over	11,418
Three people	14,476
Six people	27,025
Nine people or more	41,826

Source: U.S. Census Bureau 2005g.

12.7 percent of Asian children, and 29.7 percent of Hispanic children were poor (U.S. Census Bureau 2004f). We will return to the problem of poverty among children in Chapter 13.

Household type is a third critical factor in poverty. The poverty rate in 2003 was 12.5 percent for all people. But it was 5.4 percent for people in married couple families and 30 percent for families headed by single women (U.S. Census Bureau 2005b).

Sometimes when we see people like Jackie and Al living on the streets, we wonder what they did to become homeless. These statistics show that structural changes in the economy, not individual choices, are the most important factors in the creation of poverty and homelessness for U.S. families. Macrolevel structural changes such as plant closings, layoffs, inadequate wages, and cuts in benefits in remaining jobs are beyond the control of any individual, and they are events about which people like Jackie and Al have little choice.

More Workers per Family.   One way families have tried to cope with the problem of economic decline is by putting more people per household into the labor market. Table 4.5 shows the growing contribution wives are making to their families' income. The figure shows the change between 1970 and 2003. From 1970 to 1980, the median percent of family income that came from wives fluctuated at around 26 percent. In 1980, it began to rise, and in 2003, wives were contributing more than one-third of their families' income. Teenage children are also increasingly taking paid jobs. About 75 percent of teens have been in the paid labor force by the time they graduate from high school. In Chapter 6 we look more closely at the effect of these changes on family life.

Increased Debt and Decreased Savings.   Another way in which families have sought to counter their declining incomes is by increasing their debt. As a result, more people are in debt, and the average debt is larger than ever before. The total amount of money that U.S. consumers owe has grown steadily over the past four decades.

Table 4.6 shows the dramatic rise in household debt relative to annual income between 1949 and 2001. The table indicates that the ratio between what people earn in a

TABLE 4.5   Working Wives' Contribution to Family Income, 1970–2003

Year	Contribution to Family Income (Median Percent)
1970	26.6%
1975	26.3
1980	26.7
1985	28.3
1990	30.7
1995	31.9
2000	33.5
2003	35.2

Source: Bureau of Labor Statistics 2005d.

TABLE 4.6   **Household Debt, 1949–2001**

Year	Debt as Percent of Disposable Personal Income
1949	31.9%
1967	66.9
1973	65.2
1979	71.9
1989	84.6
1995	91.9
1999	103.0
2001	110.0

Source: Reprinted from Lawrence Mishel, Jared Bernstein, and Heather Boushey, *The State of Working America, 2002–2003.* Copyright © 2002 and 2003 by Cornell University. Used by permission of the publisher,Cornell University Press.

year and what they owe grew from about 30 percent in 1949 to about 110 percent in 2001. On the average, we now owe more than we earn per year. Not surprisingly, the debt load has been accompanied by an increase in personal bankruptcies and mortgage delinquencies. The foreclosure rate reached a record high in 1998 (Larson 1999). And almost half of American households say they have been called by a bill collector in the past year (www.responsiblelending.org/news).

Savings, not surprisingly, have been nonexistent for many households. Savings are now the lowest they have been since the Great Depression. In 2005, Americans spent $42 billion more than they earned (Thornton 2006).

Immigration.   Some families have migrated as a technique for generating income. Families in Mexico, for example, decide to risk great danger, even death, to come north looking for work. Frequently men come first, and wives and children follow. The demand for labor in the United States pulls workers across the border. Families then decide that they do not want to live apart, and entire families follow the workers (Sarmiento 2002).

Housing

The cost of housing has risen faster than wages in the past two decades. Table 4.7 shows the increase from 1970 to 2004 in the median sale price of new homes. The median price of new houses rose from $23,400 in 1970 to $221,000 in 2004. Look at Box 4.1, which shows the finances of a family of four living on one person's wages, which are at the national average. The box tells us that if they pay 25 percent of their income for housing, they have $438 a month to spend for a house payment or rent and utilities. This would not cover the cost of financing a median-priced home. In fact, the family would undoubtedly have difficulty financing a home that was half of the median price.

TABLE 4.7   Median Purchase Price of New Homes, 1970–2004

1970	$ 23,400
1976	43,340
1980	68,714
1985	90,400
1990	131,200
1995	147,700
1996	153,200
2000	169,000
2004	221,000

Source: U.S. Census Bureau 1997, p. 730;
U.S. Census Bureau 2005d.

Renters face the same problems. Rent has also risen faster than renters' incomes (Gilderbloom and Appelbaum 1988). In 2004, one-third of Americans lived in rental units, and on average they spent over one-quarter of their pretax income on rent (U.S. Census Bureau 2004j).

Families have used three strategies to try to maintain shelter in the face of the rising costs. One strategy is to pay a larger proportion of their income for housing. Economists believe that the ideal maximum amount a family should pay for housing is 25 percent of their household income. Paying over 30 percent is considered excessive (Dolbeare, Salaf and Crowley 2005). Yet researchers have found that poor families often pay 50 percent or more of their income for housing (National Center for Housing Policy 2005). Of course, this means that they have less money to spend on other necessities such as food, fuel, and health care.

A second strategy is to try to find cheaper housing. The number of low-rent housing units, however, has declined. By 1998, there was a shortage of 4.7 million affordable housing units for low-income households, the largest deficiency on record (U.S. Department of Housing and Urban Development 1998).

Third, families have looked to the government for assistance to help them meet their housing costs. In 2002, requests for assisted housing by low-income families increased in 88 percent of the cities surveyed (U.S. Conference of Mayors 2002). But there is little assistance available to them. Housing assistance programs began to be dismantled in the 1980s and continued to be cut in the 1990s (Timmer and Eitzen 1992). In 2005, budget proposals to cut housing subsidies for low-income people will provide support for only one in four of those who are eligble for the programs (Children's Defense Fund 2004).

Government subsidization of housing for the rich increased during this period. This is because the largest federal housing program is the tax deduction for mortgage interest payments and property taxes (Hope and Young 1986). In 2001, 82 percent of the mortgage interest deduction tax savings went to households with annual incomes over $75,000 (Bringing America Home Campaign 2005).

BOX 4.1

Making Ends Meet

Let us take a look at the numbers for the average household that is trying to make ends meet (D. Gordon 1996). Assume that we have a household that has one full-time breadwinner, one part-time breadwinner, and two children. The average hourly wage in 2004 was $15.77, so their total annual income at that rate would be $47,310. The average taxes on this income would leave about $39,268. If they spent one-third of their income on housing, they would be paying $1,080 a month for rent and utilities, a total of $12,958 for the year. If they spent $6 a day on food per person, their total grocery bill would amount to $8,760. They also spent $2,733 on health care for insurance, doctor's visits, dentist appointments, and prescription and nonprescription drugs; $4,751 would cover transportation—a car payment, repairs, insurance, and fuel—and $2,606 would cover clothes. At about $12.50 a week per person, they would have to save for several weeks to buy a pair of Nikes. They would be left with $7,460, an allowance of about $36 per person per week for all other expenditures, like life insurance, entertainment, education, emergencies, gifts, dog food, and newspapers. Nothing would be left for savings and in most cases families like these are spending more than they have, charging about $2,400 a year on credit cards. Remember, this is not a poverty case; it is a description of an average family.

Growing Homelessness.   The most life-threatening result of the Great U-turn is home-lessness. At the beginning of the Great U-turn, millions of people were pushed out of their homes and found themselves living on the streets. The government has had a hard time estimating the number of homeless people. The first problem encountered when trying to count homeless people is defining who they are. To overcome this problem, in 1987 Congress attempted to define homelessness more precisely:

1. An individual who lacks a fixed regular and adequate nighttime residence
2. An individual who has a primary nighttime residence that is:
    a. A supervised or publicly operated shelter designed to provide temporary living accommodations (including welfare motels, congregate shelters, and transitional housing for the mentally ill)
    b. An institution that provides a temporary residence for individuals intended to be institutionalized or
    c. A public or private place not designed for, or ordinarily used as, a regular sleeping accommodation for human beings. This would include, for example, people who live in the subways in New York, in tents in the desert in Arizona, in caves in the Midwest, in a box in Washington, D.C., in abandoned buildings and under bridges in Atlanta, and in cars in suburban shopping malls. (Committee on Health Care for People 1988, p. 2)

Despite these improved definitions, it is still difficult to determine just how many homeless there are. Every year, however, U.S. mayors meet to talk about urban problems and continue to report more and more people coming to shelters seeking a place to sleep (U.S. Conference of Mayors 2003).

The Rich Get Richer

On the average, wages declined for working Americans in the past two decades. Does that mean that everyone saw a decrease in income? Not necessarily. Although most people experienced downward mobility, some people, particularly those at the top, saw their fortunes increase. Their taxes are lower; the government is providing them with housing subsidies; and Tables 4.8 and 4.9 show the increase in their income and wealth.

When sociologists talk about financial gaps among different kinds of households, they distinguish between income and wealth. Income is the amount of money earned by an individual from wages and salary or the unearned money derived from investments. Table 4.8 compares the difference in trends for income among different sectors of our society: the very rich (top 1%), the rich (top 5%), and everyone else (bottom 90%). Table 4.8 shows that the Great U-turn describes the change in income for most but not all Americans. The vast majority of people became poorer since the mid-1970s. At the very top of the socioeconomic system, however, households made large gains in income during this period. The share of income now held by the top 1 percent is the largest since the 1920s. The average income for the top 1 percent is now 88.5 times as much as the income of the lowest 20 percent (Economic Policy Institute 2005).

Wealth refers to the assets an individual owns. These assets might include money, houses, stocks, buildings, bonds, land, or other items. Table 4.9 shows the different trends in the ownership of wealth between 1976 and 1998. Like income, wealth has increased in a few households at the top of the socioeconomic system while it has decreased for the majority of people at the bottom of the system (Wolff 2000).

Taxes have also declined for those at the top. About 53 percent of the tax cuts since 2000 have gone to the top 10 percent income bracket (Francis 2001; Johnston 2005).

Families on one side of this line face increasing difficulties in staying afloat financially or even surviving. Families on the other side of the line are becoming more wealthy. And the gap between the two groups is growing. In Chapter 5, we look at these social-class differences more closely.

TABLE 4.8   Share of National After-Tax Income, 1977–2004

	Top 1 Percent	Top 5 Percent	Bottom 90 Percent
1977	7.3%	18.7%	71.4%
1989	12.5	25.4	63.5
1998	15.7	29.3	59.8
2004	19.6	33.2	56.8

Source: Shapiro 2001; Economics Policy Institute 2005.

TABLE 4.9   Ownership of Private Wealth in the United States, 1976 and 1998

	Wealthiest 1 Percent	Next 9 Percent	Bottom 90 Percent
1976	19%	30%	51%
1998	38	33	29

Source: Wolff 1995b, 2000.

Economic Decline and U.S. Families

The statistics in this chapter show a dramatic decline in the economic fortunes of most people in the United States. One of the important results of this decline has been the creation of intense poverty. The crisis at the macrolevel of the economy has created a crisis within many families who have found themselves facing problems such as homelessness, unemployment, impoverishment, and downward mobility. In this section we examine the effect of changes in the economy and the Great U-turn on families.

Homelessness.   When the problem of homelessness first captured the public's attention, it appeared that nearly all of the new homeless were single men. Since then we find that a large and growing proportion of the homeless are families. In a recent survey, the National Conference of Mayors reported that about 41 percent of the homeless were single men, 14 percent were single women, 5 percent were unaccompanied youth, and 40 percent were families with children (U.S. Conference of Mayors 2003).

Homeless parents typically are isolated and have few if any social supports. In one survey (Wright, Rubin, and Devine 1998), homeless mothers were asked to name three persons on whom they could depend for support: 43 percent named no one or only one other person, and 25 percent named one of their children as their main source of support.

Researchers (McChesney 1986) have found that mothers have used a number of varied and creative means to stave off homelessness, such as living with friends. Often, however, homeless people have been unable to call on their parents or siblings, for three reasons: (1) their parents were dead, (2) their parents or siblings lived too far away, or (3) they were estranged from their families.

Shelters: An Inadequate Solution.   Despite the fact that families make up a large and growing proportion of homeless people, most shelters are designed for single individuals. Homeless families, therefore, must frequently break up, with the mother sent to the women's shelter, the father sent to the men's shelter, and the children placed in the custody of child welfare authorities (Committee on Health Care for Homeless People 1988; Shinn and Weitzman 1997).

The problem of the government's practice of separating children from their parents is one that appears in a number of studies of homeless people. The dilemma of wanting to ask for assistance but fearing that the Department of Social Services would place children in foster care if they found their parents were homeless is one that faces many homeless parents (Anderson and Koblinsky 1999).

In those shelters that do allow parents to stay with their children, families have other problems. A common practice is to require people to leave the shelter early in the morning and not return until evening. Parents must find a safe spot protected from the weather for their children during the day. Second, the shelters themselves are not safe. They are usually large rooms full of closely spaced cots, which allow no isolation of children from people who may have any number of physical, psychological, and social problems. Third, shelters are located away from schools, and parents often lack transportation, making school attendance erratic at best (Traveler's Aid Program and Child Welfare League 1987).

Some homeless families who receive government grants have been housed in welfare hotels as an alternative to staying in shelters. Twenty-eight states have elected to use this form of emergency assistance (U.S. Congress House Committee on Ways and Means 1987b).

Welfare hotels also have serious shortcomings. First, they do not have facilities for food storage or preparation. Cooking is not allowed in the rooms. This means that more expensive cooked food must be purchased. It also makes it difficult to provide nutritious meals for children. For example, milk, fresh fruits and vegetables, meat, cheese, and infant formula cannot be kept without refrigeration (Committee on Health Care for Homeless People 1988). When Jonathan Kozol (1988) interviewed people in the world's largest welfare hotel, the Hotel Martinique in Manhattan, a continuing complaint was hunger.

Second, although welfare hotels provide more privacy than shelters, families still must share accommodations with prostitutes and drug users. For example, homeless people have been assigned by the District of Columbia to stay in the Annex, a rooming house for prostitutes (Kozol 1988).

Third, welfare hotels are extremely costly. Massachusetts spent $16,000 per year per family for a room in a welfare hotel (Gallagher 1986). This amount would provide a spacious apartment in a good neighborhood. By law, the money is not allowed to be spent that way; it must be used to rent temporary space in a welfare hotel.

The research done on the problems with welfare hotels was done in the 1980s, but the practice continues. In 2001, New York City reported increased use of them at a cost of $3,000 per month per family, far more expensive than providing permanent apartments (Bernstein 2002).

Blue-Collar Layoffs.   Manufacturing workers are faced with declining numbers of jobs because of many factors, including automation and globalization. Those people who have been able to keep their jobs have taken pay cuts.

Researchers who have examined the effect of the economic crisis and specifically the effect of unemployment on blue-collar workers have found that it results in three problems. The first is economic difficulty (Perucci and Targ 1988).

Lillian Rubin asked working-class people in the 1990s for their reflections on current economic problems and their own layoffs. One of her interviewees described the economic difficulties her family faced when her husband was laid off:

> The scariest part about Bill being out of a job is we don't have any medical insurance anymore. My daughter got pneumonia real bad last winter and I had to borrow money from my

---

BOX 4.2

Do All People in the United States Have the Right to Bury Their Dead and Visit Family Members' Grave Sites?

While examining homelessness in New York City, Kozol (1988) looked into the question of what happens when a homeless person dies. He found that funeral and burial costs amount to about $3,500 in New York City. Until 1986, the government provided up to $250 for these expenses, and since then it has raised the amount to $900. Most homeless people who die in New York City, therefore, are buried in Potter's Field, a pauper's grave located on Hart Island.

The unembalmed bodies are taken to the grave by the truckload in rough wooden boxes, which are buried in trenches twenty to thirty at a time. This forty-five-acre site is strictly a place of disposal, not remembrance. There are no grave markers, and after thirty years the graves are bulldozed under to make room for more trenches. "Between 1981 and 1984, nearly half the children who died in New York City before their second year of life were buried at Potter's Field. Almost a third of all persons buried at Potter's Field during those years were infants" (Kozol 1988, p. 192).

Hart Island is also a prison facility, and inmates perform the burials. Because it is a prison site, no one—including family members of the deceased, even parents—is allowed to attend the burial or visit the area.

Many choices we assume should be made by families are taken from homeless families: the choice of where their children will live and with whom, the choice of who will share their close physical surroundings, and, in the case of death, the choice of where their children and other kin will be buried and whether they will be able to attend the funeral or visit the grave site.

---

sister for the doctor bill and her medicine. Just the medicine was almost $100. The doctor wanted to put her in the hospital, but we couldn't because we don't have any health insurance. (1995, p. 118)

Children were also likely to mention economic hardship as a difficult burden for them when their parents lost their jobs. One fifteen-year-old explained:

We can't afford anything anymore; and I mean anything. I don't even go to the mall with the other kids because they've got money to buy things and I don't. I haven't bought a new record since we moved here. Now my mom says I can't get new school clothes this year; I have to wear my cousin's hand-me-downs. How am I going to go to school in these ugly things. It's bad enough being in this new school but now. (Rubin 1995, pp. 123–24)

The second result researchers have identified is social-psychological difficulty. Men who have been laid off started off optimistically, thinking they will soon find another job and return to work, but as the weeks went by the real suffering began (Ferman and Blehar 1983). The layoff itself, therefore, was not as traumatic as the subsequent period. The job loss is often "only mildly traumatic compared to what follows—searching for new jobs, dashing of hopes that the old employer will call again, being rebuffed by new prospective employers. These are the events that try the patience and sanity of most workers" (Ferman and Blehar 1983, p. 590). One of Rubin's (1995, p. 110) interviewees explained:

> It's not just the income; you lose a part of yourself. It's terrible; something goes out of you. Then on top of that by staying home and not going to work and associating with people of your own level, you begin to lose the sharpness you developed at work. Everything gets slower; you move slower; your mind works slower.

The third problem area is marital relationships (Voydanoff and Donnelley 1988). Rubin found that the most intimate aspect of marriage, sex, was altered by unemployment and the anxiety produced by it. One woman described her situation:

> Sometimes when we try to do it, he can't and then he acts like it's the end of the world— depressed and moody, and I can't get near him. It's scary. He won't talk about it. But I can see it's eating at him. So I worry a lot about it. But I don't know what to do, because if I try to, you know, seduce him and it doesn't work, then it only makes things worse. (Rubin 1995, p. 120)

Not all families are affected in the same way, however. Some seem better able to cope with the difficulties of unemployment (Perucci and Targ 1988). In the section below, we will look at the reasons why differences exist among families. But first let us look at the effect of economic downturns on one more group, the middle class.

Downward Mobility in the Middle Class. Blue-collar workers were hit hard by the layoffs in the past few decades. However, nearly one in six of the displaced workers was a manager or professional and more than one in five was in a technical, sales, or administrative support position in the 1980s (Newman 1988). And these numbers increased in the 1990s and 2000s as white-collar workers were downsized.

Studies of downsizing of managers and professionals show that these job losses create long-term unemployment for many (Nulty 1987). Long-term unemployment, even among people who have had relatively good jobs before they were terminated, creates economic difficulties. Although middle-class families earn more than they did a generation ago, inflation of costs for housing, health care, education, and cars leaves them with less money to spend on other items and savings. They have no padding if breadwinners lose their income. Some scholars predict that by the end of this decade, one of every seven families with children will file for bankruptcy (Warren and Tyagi 2003). New bankruptcy laws will make it more difficult to get out of debt as most families whose incomes are above the median will now be required to pay back their debts rather than waive them (Fowles 2005).

Perhaps even more important than the economic disruption, layoffs destroy a person's self-esteem (Newman 1988). Job loss and downward mobility causes social disorientation and feelings of failure and loss of control. The personal crisis of unemployed individuals spills over onto their families. When families of managers who had been laid off describe their experience, they state that every aspect of their family's life becomes strangely different. "The ultimate victim of downward mobility is not just the breadwinner's occupational identity, nor even the checkbook and savings account, but the whole family's sense of normalcy. Nothing seems the same" (Newman 1988, p. 60).

One of the daughters of a man who lost his business described the catastrophic change brought by her family's economic collapse. She said:

> We went from one day in which we owned a business that was worth probably four or five million dollars in assets and woke up the next day to find that we were personally probably a half a million dollars in debt. Creditors called the house and started to send threatening notices. (Newman 1988, p. 96)

Initially the families responded to the economic crisis by trying to cover up their downward mobility. They tried to make it appear that nothing had changed. They created stories to account for their situation, and they held on to houses and cars to perpetuate their previous lifestyle. Eventually the pretense could no longer be maintained, and with the loss of the job and material possessions, they also lost their friends.

Friendships among these managers' families were based on participating in certain kinds of activities, such as giving dinner parties, going to dances at the country club, attending shows and symphonies, and dining at expensive restaurants. When their income declined and they were unable to sustain these luxuries, their friends began to disappear.

These social losses were accompanied by psychological distress, particularly self-blame. At first, others pointed the finger of blame at the unemployed person. One man explained how his wife was quizzed about whether he was trying hard enough to find work:

> People say to her, "With all the companies on Long Island, your husband can't find a job? Is he really trying? Maybe he likes not working." This really hurts her and it hurts me. People don't understand that you can send out 150 letters to headhunters and get 10 replies. Maybe one or two will turn into something, but there are hundreds of qualified people going after each job. (Newman 1988, p. 5)

Eventually the blame turns to self-blame. One manager described it:

> I'm beginning to wonder about my abilities to run an association, to manage and motivate people. Having been demoted has to make you think. I have to accept my firing. The people involved in it are people I respect for the most part. So I can't blame them for doing what they think is right. I have to say where have I gone wrong? (Newman 1988, p. 78)

The self-blame spilled into the next generation. Children of downwardly mobile families worried that failure was genetic and that they would become like their fathers—"losers," "friendless," and "unable to find a job," with "a life that has fallen apart" (Newman 1988).

Responding to Economic Crisis

Thus far, this chapter has focused on the way in which the macro-organization of society affects the microlevel. We have looked at the way in which massive structural changes in the economy have affected families and individuals within families. We have observed that the effects are substantial and that they differ by age, class, race, ethnicity, and occupation.

In this section, we will shift our focus to examine how individuals and families are responding. First, we will look at families that attempt to cope with economic crisis.

Unemployment, as we have seen, can be devastating. Some families respond by falling apart and others seem to adapt to the situation. What are the differences between these two groups?

There are several mediating factors in a person's response to a layoff that can make the difference in a family's ability to cope with the event (Voydanoff 1984). Mediating factors can be divided into two types: family definition of the event and family resources.

Family definition has three components. The first is the suddenness of the layoff. If the family interprets the layoff as something they had anticipated, they are better able to cope with it (Hansen and Johnson 1979). Second, family definition includes assessment of responsibility. When the worker is blamed for the job loss, coping is more difficult (Cobb and Kasl 1977). Third is a sense of failure. Even if the worker is not seen as having caused the job loss, if he or she is perceived to have failed his or her responsibility to the family as a breadwinner, difficulty with coping is intensified (Nye 1974).

The factor of family resources also has three components. First is financial resources. Savings, home ownership, and other financial resources buffer the response to the job loss (Voydanoff 1963). Second is family system characteristics. Families that are characterized by cohesion and adaptability are better at coping (McCubbin et al. 1980). Third is social support. Family support mediates the effects of the layoff for the unemployed person, and further social support from extended kin and the community contributes to the stability of the whole family (Cobb and Kasl 1977). This includes both material support like loans and food, as well as emotional support.

Family coping strategies are multifaceted combinations of all of these factors. Families that cope most successfully with unemployment develop effective coping methods, such as placing more members in the labor market to make up for the lost income, managing finances more efficiently, strengthening internal and external family support, and redefining the situation as an opportunity for positive changes, as well as a hardship (Voydanoff 1984).

Social Victims or Social Critics?

Do some workers move beyond coping with unemployment to become social critics of the society in which unemployment has become so prevalent? It may appear that this is not often the case. Many accounts in the popular media of workers who have lost jobs portray unemployed workers as passive victims—baffled, depressed, cynical, and resigned (Frisch and Watts 1980).

Frisch and Watts (1980) were curious about the validity of the image of workers they saw in the *New York Times,* so they obtained copies of the complete interviews with workers who were quoted in the newspaper articles about the economic crisis and compared the interviews with the edited quotes that were published. They found that when journalists edited the interviews for inclusion in their articles, they selected quotes that were emotive, exclamatory, ungrounded, arbitrary, and individualistic. The published quotes reflected only part of the perception of the workers they interviewed. The journalists tended to omit quotes from workers who were reflective and informed and offered a political analysis.

Ramsey Liem interviewed unemployed people in Boston to see if the workers' comments reflected helplessness and victimization as portrayed in the media or if they expressed informed social criticism. He found that they did both. Liem offers as an example of victimization the response of one man explaining what unemployment means, "It means being without power to control the things you normally like to have control over in your life like happiness, for me anyway. I lost confidence. I'm actually scared to go on a job interview" (Liem 1988, p. 143).

Workers also talk about their unemployment in ways that do not blame themselves or internalize the problem, but instead articulate an understanding of the inequities of the system as a source of their difficulties. For example, another man told Liem: "Help in finding a job wasn't available because in my opinion the corporate system from government on down is not really concerned with the plight of the unemployed person be they white collar or blue collar" (Liem 1988, p. 144).

Liem argues, in addition, that workers express their social criticism in their refusal to give up their desire to find meaningful work and decent pay. Finally, Liem's research provides evidence that workers were knowledgeable about the industry in which they had been employed and able to explain the conflict of interest between themselves and management that touched on the layoffs. For example, one assembly-line worker who had been laid off said:

> Polaroid goofed a lot of things. They overproduced and overspeculated. Some guy making $100,000 a year made a film cartridge for $27. They had to sell it by government standards for $10 and also the chemicals leaked into the camera. Suddenly making of the camera ceased and the people making that camera were higher in seniority than us so they had to get rid of the excess and we were the excess baggage. (Liem 1988, p. 147)

Altering the Social Context

Voydanoff's work shows unemployed people and their families adapting. Liem shows them criticizing. A third response exists as well. Some people have moved beyond thinking about the sources of their problems to acting collectively in a manner that can change the system (Deitch 1984).

Campaign for a Living Wage.   The development of the new economy in the late 1990s diminished the problem of unemployment. Jobs were available, but because they have continued to offer only low wages and few or no benefits to many employees, the working poor are a sign of our times. A number of unions and other activist organizations across the country have created a solution to this problem—a living wage—and have established 103 living-wage ordinances in cities, school districts, townships, and counties and campaigns continue to be underway (ACORN Living Wage Resource Center 2005). Baltimore was the site of the first living-wage campaign in 1994 initiated by the AFSCME (American Federation of State, County and Municipal Employees) union and a community grassroots organization called BUILD (Baltimoreans United in Leadership Development) (Lazarovici 1999).

In a nutshell, living-wage ordinances force employers who receive contracts or tax benefits from local governments (city councils, county commissions, school boards, etc.) to pay their employees wages a few dollars over minimum wage. The program is based on two premises. First, living-wage campaigns assert that no one who works for a living should be poor. Second, advocates point out that employers often benefit from incentives to enter a local market, such as tax breaks or opportunities to take over businesses previously handled by the local authorities (called privatization which we discuss more extensively in Chapter 14). Living-wage campaigns argue that employers who have benefited in this way should give something back to their workforce and the communities (Bernstein 1999).

Five years after the first living-wage ordinance, Jared Bernstein conducted some research in Baltimore to determine how well the program was working. He concluded:

1. Cost increase to the city was less than the rate of inflation.
2. No evidence of job loss in response to the wage increases.
3. A small decrease in the number of bids per contract. The decrease did not appear to lower competitiveness or raise contract costs.
4. Some of the increased labor costs are absorbed through efficiency gains, especially lower turnover.
5. The numbers affected (benefiting) from the raises is small.
6. Some "spillover" benefits to workers who were not previously earning minimum wage.
7. Noncompliance by employers remains a significant problem. (Bernstein 1999)

What Is Behind the Great U-Turn?

This chapter has presented much evidence that we are living through difficult economic times and that those difficulties are having serious consequences for most American families. What underlies these problems? One way of trying to answer that question is to step back for a minute and look at the current era within the broad sweep of human history. If we could see a picture of the last several thousand years of human history, we would notice that at two times in that history, revolutionary changes have taken place in the organization of the production and distribution of the necessities of life. The first was the Neolithic Agricultural Revolution about eight thousand years ago. The second was the Industrial Revolution, which began about two hundred years ago (Eitzen and Baca Zinn 1989).

Important changes are now occurring in our society. Is a third revolution in the making? If a revolution in the economy is occurring, it would certainly have an enormous effect on the rest of society, and it might cause the kinds of unsettling problems we have reviewed in this chapter. Before trying to answer the question of whether a revolutionary transition is taking place now, let us look at how transformation occurred in the two previous revolutions so that we have some sense of what these transitions look like.

The First Revolution

During the Neolithic Agricultural Revolution, humans began to control their environment by settling down, planting food to harvest, and domesticating animals to eat. This was very different from the life they had led earlier: following the herds and gathering the food that was naturally available. Throughout the agricultural period, people developed better and better tools. They invented hoes, shovels, and picks, and they invented methods of making the metals to produce these tools. They devised ways to harness the energy of animals to use them as vehicles and to plow and turn mills. Production increased enormously, and, most important, humans had greater control of that production than they had before the Agricultural Revolution (Beals, Hoijer, and Beals 1977; Childe 1948).

The effect of the Agricultural Revolution on human existence was overwhelming. Some of the features of our society that we think of as natural developed during this period. For example, nations were established, money was invented, as was the concept of government, calendars to keep track of seasons, writing, and numbering systems. The Neolithic Agricultural Revolution lasted for about ten thousand years, from roughly 8000 B.C. to the late 1700s.

The Second Revolution

The Industrial Revolution created another turning point in human history—machines were added to human and animal energy to produce the necessities of life. Once again, production increased enormously. Although machines enhanced human energy, they could not run on their own. The Industrial Revolution is marked by the pressure to put as many people as possible into manufacturing for as many hours as possible. In Chapter 2 we observed the way in which industrial capitalism developed in the United States and how factories employed entire families—men, women, and children. People were driven off the land into the cities and the factories (Beals, Hoijer, and Beals 1977).

Wages were increasingly used as a means to distribute the goods and services produced by the offices and factories. Prior to the Industrial Revolution, people used what they produced or traded what they produced for the materials they needed. As the Industrial Revolution developed, work occurred in factories, and workers who were employed in factories could not use what they produced. Instead, wages were paid to workers, who then could purchase what they needed from those who owned the factories.

The effects of the Industrial Revolution were felt in every part of society. Cities, banks, factories, world wars, international economies, and, as we saw in Chapter 2, relatively isolated mobile nuclear families, at least among the white middle class, emerged during this period. The Industrial Revolution began in the late 1700s and began to shift to a postindustrial period in the 1970s.

Postindustrial Society: A Third Revolution?

We may now be at another monumental turning point in the economic, and thus social, organization of humanity (Berberoglu 2002, 2005; Boyett and Conn 1992; Dunkerly 1996; Edwards 1993; B. Jones 1985; T. Moore 1996; Rifkin 1995). Eitzen and Baca Zinn (1989) argue that four forces have converged in the past two decades to create such a turning point. The first force is the expansion of industrial capitalism throughout the world, resulting in increased competition for U.S. business. The second force is increased investment by U.S. businesses in other countries, which moves jobs from the United States to such places as Mexico, Central America, and Asia. The third force is the shift in the economy from manufacturing to information and services, which leaves many workers unskilled to perform the jobs that are being created.

All these are important, but it is the fourth force that may be the most significant: the development of microelectronics, computers, and robotics. The microchip and its application in robotics is creating the possibility of the production of the necessities of life without human labor. Table 4.10 shows the dramatic effect this has had on manufacturing, where production has expanded enormously while the number of workers involved in that production has declined. Microelectronics may be ushering in a new era that does not yet have a name, but it might be called an Electronics Revolution (Davis, Hirschl, and Stack 1997).

Unlike industrial production, electronic production can be done with less and less human energy and ultimately, perhaps, with none at all. The key difference between this production system and an industrial one is that industrial production enhances human energy, while electronics and robotics replace human energy (B. Jones 1985). Machines can build everything we need to stay alive. Computers can guide their production. Computers were invented by humans and initially involved a lot of input from humans. But computers increasingly can learn from other computers, can program themselves and other computers, and can make decisions. Wassily Leontief (1983, p. 3), a Nobel laureate, writes, "The role of humans as the most important factor in production is bound to diminish in the same way that the role of horses in agricultural production was first diminished and then eliminated by the introduction of tractors."

There is debate over whether the trend we see in increasing automation will actually continue to develop and will continue to eliminate jobs (Block 1984). For example, some have argued that services or the need for assembling and transmitting information will simultaneously produce more jobs to make up for those lost in manufacturing (Dassbach 1986). Others contend, however, that the same technologies that have eliminated so many

TABLE 4.10   Fewer Workers while Sales Grow

Top Ten U.S. Manufacturing Companies	Employment Change 1968 to 1998	Sales Increase 1968 to 1998
General Motors	−155,731	46%
Ford Motor	−69,839	112
Exxon	−71,500	48
General Electric	−115,500	148
IBM	−38,226	145
Philip Morris	−166,496	1,668
Boeing	+92,100	254
AT&T	−752,718	−22
Mobil	−36,200	58
Hewlett Packard	+109,870	3,515

Source: Copyright © 2000 *Field Guide to the Global Economy* by Sarah Anderson and John Cavanagh with Thea Lee. Reprinted by permission of The New Press. (800) 233-4830.

manufacturing jobs are already having a significant effect on reducing the need for human labor in services and information processing (Leontief and Duchen 1986; Rifkin 1995). For example, word processors have eliminated the jobs of many secretaries who used to type multiple letters and keep elaborate filing systems of written materials in cabinets (*New York Times* 1993). Electronic mail has eliminated postal jobs through the use of computers and electronics in communications. Automatic teller machines replaced 37 percent of bank tellers between 1983 and 1993 (*Wall Street Journal* 1994). Computers have replaced library clerks (Machung 1984). Retail has been downsized by automated warehousing, scanners, and televised shopping networks (*New York Times* 1993). Computers are now in place that can understand speech, read script, repair themselves, "learn" from their mistakes, and perform more and more tasks that humans used to do (Rifkin 1995). Undoubtedly electronics will continue to be applied in ways that eliminate jobs, and the effect of automation will be significant. In short, technological changes are producing an expanded flow of goods and services with a declining amount of work per man, woman, and child (Berberoglu 2005; Block 1988; Kuznets 1971).

Like changes in each of the two previous revolutions, the changes in production in the third revolution will demand another form of distribution. In the discussion of the Industrial Revolution, I noted that wages were increasingly used during that period as the sole means to distribute the goods and services being produced. In an electronically based system of production, people are not working as many hours (if at all) to produce. Therefore, they cannot earn wages to allow them access to goods and services (Block 1988). This factor plays a key role in the problems described in this chapter (*Oxford Analytica* 1986). Workers' wages decreased because of rising unemployment, and those who held onto their jobs have seen a decrease in the buying power of their take-home pay. Consequently fewer and fewer people are able to purchase the necessities of life for themselves and their families (Aronowitz and DiFazio 1994).

Barry Jones (1985) suggests that we might resolve some of the problems of unemployment, poverty, and homelessness that are being created by the Electronics Revolution by inventing a citizen wage. A citizen wage system would distribute the goods and services to those who needed them regardless of the number of hours they worked in production (see also Block 1988; Van Til 1988). This is not a new idea. What is new about Jones's argument is the link he draws between the utopian notion of distribution based on need and the real potential of electronically based production.

The questions of whether the Electronics Revolution will develop further and what kind of distribution system will emerge from it will demand enormous efforts by large numbers of people in thinking, planning, and creating political change (Davis, Hirschl, and Stack 1997). At this point it is difficult to predict either the kind of distribution system that will work best or the further effects the changes in production and distribution will have on every aspect of our society.

If we are living through a revolution and moving toward a society in which, for the first time in human history, the necessities of life can be produced without (or with a minimal amount of) human energy, we can look forward to some wonderful possibilities (Block 1988). We could see a world in which robots and computers provide us with food and shelter and where people would be able to spend all or most of their energy doing those things that only humans can do: creating, exploring, learning, and nurturing.

Ironically, in spite of the fact that this new electronically based production system can produce more than enough for everyone, because of our system of distribution, the way in which we are currently experiencing this revolution is as a system of scarcity. Our economy seems to be running in reverse as more and more of us are unable to find subsistence. As robots and computers eliminate jobs and deskill others, we see layoffs, unemployment, lower wages, poverty, homelessness, and all of the resultant social and psychological problems of families trying to cope with those problems. Harley Shaiken writes, "The technology provides choices: what is selected depends on who does the choosing and with what purpose in mind" (1984, p. 2).

In Chapter 3, we could see that the problems that slaves faced in trying to maintain a decent life for themselves and their families could not be resolved without abolishing slavery. Today we cannot imagine anyone wanting to preserve the slavery system. The maintenance of an economic and political system that caused such human misery seems unthinkable. During the period of slavery, the microexperience was so severely constrained and dehumanized by the macro-organization of slave society, there was no choice but to make radical change.

What about the problems of poverty and homelessness we face today? Can we continue to maintain the status quo? What changes must we make? How far must we go to create a society that will allow people to live and raise their children in decency?

Chapter 3 described a social structure that existed long ago and that we now agree was completely untenable. In the current chapter, the macrolevel becomes more personal because we are speaking of our own times. We are no longer considering a society that lives only in history books. We are assessing our own society and our own history. We must be the ones to decide what should stay and what must go. Will we need to be as radical as the abolitionists were in their day?

The Micro–Macro Connection

The focus of the last three chapters has been on the relationship between the economy and families. Chapters 2 and 3 covered the historical period from the colonial era to the 1960s. This chapter brings us up to date by reviewing the past four decades. We see that throughout history and even today, economic context shapes the organization of families. While this relationship holds all the time, it becomes most apparent when a crisis occurs in the economy. Since the 1970s, a crisis occurred in the American economy that caused a Great U-turn, resulting in serious problems for most American families. As the century ended, some of the problems were alleviated as the new economy emerged, sending stocks soaring and increasing wages and lowering unemployment. Since then the economy has continued to improve, but the benefits are being felt mostly by those at the very top of the economic system while the majority of us are barely keeping up or even falling behind as wages stagnate and prices and unemployment increase. Throughout the ups and downs, we see the important effect of economics on families.

The relationship between families and the economy, however, is a two-way street. The macrolevel of social organization has affected the microlevel; the economic crisis has tossed and battered families. But in return, the microlevel has vigorously reacted. Families have responded individually by offering psychological support for their members and attempting to shuffle resources by going into debt, reducing the quality of their lives, seeking support from the government, and finally by surviving in the streets. Some people have also tried to address these problems by changing the social structure. People organizing at the microlevel have fought for changes at the macrolevel. Some have developed new ways of looking at the issues that are critical of the social structure. Others have formed organizations to make demands for stopping plant closings and aiding families whose breadwinners have lost their jobs and who have lost their homes. And through the Living Wage Campaigns they are fighting for a liveable reimbursement for their labor.

In the last part of this chapter, we saw that beyond the macrostructure of our contemporary society is an even larger social context, the whole sweep of history. Our own society is a part of that sweep and may in fact be at a particularly important turning point. The profound changes in the macrolevel of the economy are creating profound changes in other areas of our society as well. These social changes are so large and new that in these early stages it is difficult to imagine their final shape.

5 Families and the Organization of Race, Class, and Gender

Television cameras in the aftermath of Hurricane Katrina revealed shocking images of American poverty. As politicians debated about what had happened and who was to blame for the tragic events, two familiar arguments came to the fore. One group argued that poverty was caused by faulty family organizations. Another asserted that poverty was a result of problems in the social structure and that families were victims not causes of poverty. (AP Wide World Photos)

August 2005. Hurricane Katrina slammed into the Gulf Coast resulting in the worst natural disaster in American history, causing billions of dollars in damage, thousands of deaths, untold homes to be lost, and lives turned upside down as people were forced to flee from their homes with nothing more than what they could carry with them. Hospitals, schools, and businesses shut down for months, in some cases forever.

The morning after the hurricane, the people of Lousiana and and Mississippi woke up to assess the damage relieved that it wasn't worse, but another danger was building for the citizens of New Orleans as the old levees began to crack. Scientists had been warning for decades that the high walls of dirt could not sustain a major hurricane and had sent word to Washington again that the levees would burst only 48 hours before the hurricane made landfall (Treaster and Kleinfield 2005).

As the hurricane moved in, the people in New Orleans and other cities on the Gulf were told to leave. Thousands who were too poor to own transportation could not evacuate and went to emergency shelters. When the levees broke, people who had been sent to shelters to weather the storm found themselves stranded as the floodwaters rose around them. Images of dead bodies, people clinging to rooftops, and crowded into shelters like the Superdome showed the victims of the hurricane and the ruptured levees were largely black and poor. Hurricane Katrina put poverty and racism on the national agenda. News commentators, human rights organizations, and disaster relief groups from around the world began to question why the government had failed to act before the hurricane hit and why it seemingly ignored the plight of poor and black gulf residents after the disaster (Gonzalez 2005). How could the United States have people living in such dire circumstances? How could the government have ignored reports about the imminent failure of the levees? And why did the federal government act so slowly or not at all to help the victims of Katrina?

Activists from all over the country, and even the world, poured into the area to attempt to help the people who had apparently been abandoned by the U.S. government. Events seemed to show unmistakably that large social institutions like the federal, state, and local governments and agencies like FEMA (Federal Emergency Management Agency) were responsible, having failed to maintain safe standards in the levees, evacuate people efficiently, and aid those affected after the storm hit. The images of those who were left behind also seemed to point to large social issues of growing poverty, especially among African Americans, and inadequate wages for the working poor and declining job opportunties.

Soon after Katrina, however, another analysis was presented (Rosen 2005). Rich Lowry, editor of the conservative National Review said the federal government had not failed, instead he identified another cause: "the breakdown of the family." Lowry (2005) wrote, "The root of it [poverty], more than anything else, is the breakdown of the family. Roughly 60 percent of births in New Orleans are out of wedlock. If people are stripped of the most basic social support—the two-parent family—they will be more vulnerable in countless ways, especially, one assumes, in moments of crisis like that that has befallen New Orleans."

Lowry and the politicians and spokespersons who supported his assessment assert that if poor single mothers were married they would not be poor and therefore would have had been able to evacuate from New Orleans and now would be collecting their home owner's insurance and rebuilding their lives instead of living in refugee shelters scattered around the nation.

These events illustrate a debate that places family at the center of the question of what causes social inequality, poverty, and racism. From each point of view, family is important, either as cause or an effect. Lowry, a conservative spokesperson, says that improper families (children born to single unmarried mothers) are the cause of poverty and vulnerability. Activists from organizations such as Amnesty International and the NAACP say that the economy is the cause of poverty and that families are victims of an unjust and failing economic system. Furthermore in disasters such as Katrina people become victims of a government that fails to address their problems.

Does it surprise you that family could emerge as an important role in the analysis of the Katrina disaster?

Is this the first time that the family has been central in the debate over the causes of and solutions to the problem of inequality in the United States?

What is the relationship between family organization and inequality by race, class, and gender?

Do different classes and races of people have different families? Do some have "better" families?

Is gender inequality expressed in the same way in families of different classes and racial ethnic groups?

What exactly are race, class, and gender?

Systems of Stratification

In the last chapter, we looked at the broad social context of contemporary American families and noted that economic downturns are a critical factor in the declining financial situation of nearly all families. We also noted, however, that the effect of economic crisis was not the same for all families. Some suffer more than others from recessions, but a few families at the top of the socioeconomic system continue to thrive even when the economy declines. Perhaps the most significant change in the economic context of families at the start of the twenty-first century is the growing gap between those at the top of the system and the rest of us.

The situation of families within society and, therefore, their response to social forces varies because all families are not the same. This issue of diversity is the focus of this chapter.

Sociologists use the word *stratification* to describe systems of social inequality among different groups of people. Stratification is organized around many factors across human societies. For example, in some societies like those of Ireland or Israel, religion is a critical factor. In an aristocratic system like that of premodern England, bloodline is the most important issue. Today in the United States, three systems of stratification—race, class, and gender—are most important.

People in our society are classified as members of various categories according to their gender, race, and class. Each of these social markers has an important effect on individuals. Gender, race, and class affect a person's access to jobs, housing, and education.

Family experience is also affected by these systems of stratification. Our chances of marrying, divorcing, bearing children, and our health and even the cause of death are related to where we are in the stratification systems of gender, race, and class.

This chapter is divided into four major sections. The first examines the stratification systems of social class, race ethnicity, and gender. The second section looks at the way in which each of these systems affects family organization. The third section briefly sums up the observation that attempting to develop one definition of *The Family* may be a useless and impossible exercise. The fourth section looks at the contemporary political debate over efforts to define *The Family* and the various political groups that are attempting to promote their vision of good families.

What Is Social Class?

Not all societies have social classes. For most of human history, people lived in hunting and gathering societies that were not stratified by social class. Contemporary U.S. society, however, is a capitalist society, and social class is a critical feature of its organization. Our class system is a form of stratification that is characterized by four factors:

1. Class is economically based and is measured by economic variables such as occupation, income, and ownership of wealth (Giddens 1991).

2. Class is a social relationship. A society with one social class would be classless because class rests on the assumption of inequality. In order to have inequality, the system has to have at least two strata. Furthermore, social class is not just a category but is also a relationship, because class assumes that some people have a relationship of inequality with other people in the society. For example, in the contemporary United States, working-class people have less money than members of the owning class, which puts them into a different economic category. But working-class people also have a social relationship with the owning class, because working-class people work for the people who own the factories and offices (Ollman 1976; Wright 1985).

3. Class system boundaries are fluid. Unlike other systems of inequality, such as slavery, people can move in and out of the class into which they were born. Boundaries between classes are not clear-cut. Social interaction, even marriage, occurs between members of different social classes (Giddens 1991).

4. Class positions are in some part achieved. Although it is difficult to be born into a working-class family and later become a member of the owning class, for example, it is not impossible (Giddens 1991).

In the last chapter, Tables 4.5 and 4.6 showed the distribution of income and wealth in the United States. The figures showed that there is considerable inequality in their distribution. The figures also showed that the gap between rich and poor has grown in the last three decades. One economist has tried to describe just how large the gap is in the United States. He notes that if one piled up small blocks sized 1.5 square inches and each block was equal to $500, the average American would be about 5 feet off the ground and the average family about 9 feet up. The income of the very wealthiest families would be higher than Mount Everest, which is over 29,000 feet high (Samuelson and Nordhaus 1989).

Scholars have created many systems to try to conceptualize classes within this broad stretch. In this book, I distinguish among three major social classes: an owning class, a middle class, and a working class. The owning or upper class is a small elite of about 10 percent of the total population that owns 71 percent of all the wealth and receives 43.2 percent of all of the household income. Even within this small but very wealthy category, there is stratification. The top 1 percent of the population owns 44 percent of all stock (Mishel, Bernstein, and Allegretto 2005). A core of 250 families within this group have incomes of over $100 million a year (Wolff 1995a).

The middle class includes those people who are self-employed, such as small business owners and farmers, and managers and professionals. The income range of this group is large. A middle-class person could be a self-employed physician with a lucrative practice or a farmer who owns a small peach orchard and barely keeps ahead of expenses. Professionals range from wealthy attorneys to low-wage school teachers. About 25 to 30 percent of the population fits into this social class (Rothman 1998).

The definition of *social class* indicates that social class is a relationship and explains how this relationship is structured for owning-class and working-class people. Middle-class people frequently have jobs that literally put them in the middle between working-class and owning-class people. For example, a manager of a plant is a middle-class person who may have a relatively high income but little real control over the business. A manager of a plant who does not own the plant must obey the wishes of the owner. In that sense, the manager is like a working-class person in his or her relationship with the owner. On the other hand, a manager does control the workers and in that sense is like the owning class (Wright 1985, 1990).

The working class consists of those people who are not professionals or managers and who earn wages by working for someone else. Large groups of workers such as factory workers, restaurant workers, and clerical workers fall into this category. Within the working class, there is also a range of incomes from relatively well-paid skilled blue-collar workers in union shops to the cashiers at fast-food restaurants and day-labor construction workers. About 60 to 65 percent of the population fits into this category.

Race Ethnicity

Nearly every time we fill out a form, we are asked to identify our race. Most of us respond by checking one of the boxes. Every ten years, the government conducts a census that attempts to literally count everyone in the United States and then samples the population in years between the decades to see how the population is changing. Table 5.1 shows which box people in the United States checked in the census in 2004. It also shows some of the most recent list of categories used by the government. This list has changed dramatically over time (Cornell and Hartmann 1997). For example, in 1870 there were five categories: white, colored, mulatto, Chinese, and Indian. In 2004, people could choose among fifteen categories. In addition, they could check more than one box for the first time. Also notice that Hispanics can be of any race and therefore overlap with all the other categories.

TABLE 5.1   Racial Ethnic Distribution in the United States, 2004

White not Hispanic	67.4%
Black	12.8%
American Indian, Eskimo, and Aleut	1.0%
Asian or Pacific Islander	4.4%
two or more	1.5%
Hispanic	14.1% (can be any race)

Source: U.S. Census Bureau, 2004i.

Race is a widely recognized and critically important social factor in shaping our lives. What most people don't recognize, however, is that people cannot be separated into biologically different races (Lewontin, Rose, and Kamin 1984; http://raceandeconomics.ssrc.org).

For a long time, scholars attempted to develop categories of races into which all humans fit. Some came up with only a few categories; others came up with a few dozen. Around 1940, biologists were forced to abandon the concept of race among humans when they discovered that the amount of genetic variation from one individual to the next is enormously greater than any variation between so-called racial groups. Any attempt to divide people into a few "races" on the basis of genetics, or even a more superficial measure, was impossible.

The problem of using genetics to support our ideas about race is illustrated by comparing two groups of people in Africa with Japanese people. The Kikuyu of East Africa differ from the Japanese in gene frequencies, but they also differ from their neighbors, the Masai, and, although the extent of the differences might be less in one case than in the other, it is only a matter of degree. This means that the social and historical definitions of race that put the two East African tribes in the same "race" but put the Japanese in a different "race" are biologically arbitrary. In practice, "racial" categories correspond to major skin-color groups, and all the borderline cases are distributed among these or made into new races according to the whim of the scientist (Lewontin, Rose, and Kamin 1984, pp. 120, 126). But science cannot be based on whim, and geneticists have decided that distinguishing among races scientifically cannot be done.

Even if we attempt to distinguish among "races" on the basis of something more superficial than genes, like physical appearance, we run into barriers. For example, we often refer to black people as members of a race that can be designated by dark skin and dark curly hair. However, the original inhabitants of Australia have very dark skin, and their hair is wavy and sometimes blond (Giddens 1991). Where would we classify these people? Would we put them in the same category as a person from Ohio with dark skin and wavy light brown hair whose mother is African American and whose father is Euro-American?

Dividing people into biologically distinct races is impossible for three reasons: (1) there are so many varieties of groups of people; (2) there is so much variation within each group; and (3) there are so many children whose ancestors came from different groups (P. Brown 1997).

Nevertheless, people continue to check a box on the forms because race is an important *social* category. Although it is entirely "made up," we learn to overlook the irrationality of the system and to create ways in which to classify ourselves and everyone else into a few "races" (Root 1998). These classifications then have enormous repercussions for the people so classified.

In addition, we may identify with a culture we believe is related to race. These cultural distinctions are called ethnicity. For example, an African American may identify himself or herself as a member of the black community and may study African American history or become interested in African American music. A Native American may study the languages and religions of his or her "race." Ethnicity can be based on distinctions by religion, nationality, or race. Jewish, Greek, and Irish people are members of ethnic groups. These categories are related to religion and nationality. Ethnic groups based on the social category of race are called racial ethnic groups. In this book, I use the term racial ethnic to refer to socially defined categories of people.

TABLE 5.2   Subgroups within the Hispanic Population, 2000

Mexican	58.5
Central/South American	8.6%
Puerto Rican	9.6%
Other Hispanic	20.1%
Cuban	3.5%

Source: U.S. Census Bureau, 2000e, Table DP-1, p. 1.

One of the results of the fact that race is not a biologically valid category but is still a critical social factor is the problem of naming groups of people. In this book, for example, I use both African American and black. In the 1960s, the Black Power movement called for the replacement of the term Negro with the term black. In the 1980s, black people began to call for another change to African American. They argued that the name black did not fully capture the importance of culture and historical roots to the African American community. Some authors use one word; others use another. Current government documents usually use the word black. In this book, I use an eclectic mix of terms based on the use by the scholars whose work I am discussing.

Finding an appropriate name for the Latino population in the United States is even more difficult. The government uses the term Hispanic, but that is not often used by authors who are Latino or who write about Latinos because Hispanic is an English word. The word Latino is more acceptable because it is Spanish. Latino, however, is not completely accurate because the Latino population is made up of many different cultures and nationalities. For example, Latinos include Cubans, Cuban Americans, Puerto Ricans, Mexicans, Mexican Americans, Chicanos, and Central and South Americans who come from many different countries and cultures. Table 5.2 displays the subgroups within the Hispanic American community. The table shows that the largest group has ancestors from Mexico (58.5%) followed by Puerto Rico (9.6%).

Table 5.3 shows the problems sociologists can run into if they assume that all Latino subgroups have similar family experiences. The table indicates that, among five different

TABLE 5.3   Latino Household Composition

	Percent of Families with Husband and Wife				
Ethnic Group	*1960*	*1970*	*1980*	*1990*	*1999*
Mexican	75.9	70.7	66.1	60.7	69.9
Puerto Rican	71.8	62.2	48.7	44.0	56.7
Cuban	72.1	74.4	65.7	59.2	79.2
Central/South American	68.0	64.1	56.8	54.8	66.6
Other Latino	75.7	70.6	58.1	50.5	61.7

Source: Bean, Frank and Marta Tienda, 1987. *The Hispanic Population of the U.S.* New York: Russell Sage.

Latino ethnic groups, different proportions live in husband and wife households. In 1999, Cuban Americans (79%) were most likely to live in married couple households (79%) and Puerto Ricans were least likely (57%). The numbers in previous decades were more similar, so the experience of change is also different for different subgroups.

This same problem emerges in the use of the term Asian, which can include people whose ancestry is Japanese, Chinese, Korean, Vietnamese, Filipino, and from many other Asian nations and ethnic groups (Jesu 1995). Although they may share an ancestry from a

---

BOX 5.1

Matriarchies and Patriarchies in Racial Ethnic Families

At the same time the Moynihan Report was criticizing African American families for being matriarchal and proposing that African American men be encouraged to take a more dominant role in their families, another racial ethnic group—Chicanos—was being criticized for being patriarchal (Baca Zinn and Eitzen 1990). In 1966, Arthur Rubel and Celia Heller both published books on the Mexican American community that were highly critical of Chicano families. Moynihan, Rubel, and Heller used the same family pathology argument, but they made the argument for opposite characteristics of racial ethnic families.

Like Moynihan, Rubel and Heller argued that the reason Mexican Americans were not making sufficient progress in the United States and remained impoverished was because of their faulty family structure. The difference in the two arguments is that Moynihan claimed that the flaw in the African American family was their matriarchal character. Rubel and Heller blamed the poverty of Mexican Americans on their patriarchal families.

Mexican American families supposedly were characterized by an intense segregation between men and women and the nearly total dominance of Chicanas by Chicanos within their families. As a result, children were not being raised in a sufficiently modern manner so that they could successfully compete in contemporary American society. In order to lift themselves out of poverty, Chicano families were told they must adapt more modern nonpatriarchal values and ways of organizing their families.

There are three problems with this argument. First, it assumes that Chicano families are more patriarchal than white families. Studies of parenting in Chicano families indicate that they are more democratic and egalitarian than the old stereotypes suggest (Baca Zinn 1989b). Furthermore, comparisons of white men, African American men, and Chicanos conclude that there are few differences in their expression of *machismo* (Senour and Warren 1976).

Second, the argument asserts that the ideals of masculinity in Chicano families are a result of the culture of the community rather than a response to the oppression of Chicano men by a racist social structure. Baca Zinn (1989b) points out that there has been no research conducted on the effect of discrimination on the way in which men in oppressed groups express gender. Ramos (1979, p. 61) speculates that what has been called *machismo* may be a "way of feeling capable in a world that makes it difficult for Chicanos to demonstrate their capabilities."

Third, the argument assumes that family structure rather than discrimination and an inadequate economic system should be blamed for causing poverty. This assumption places both the Moynihan Report and Rubel's and Heller's work within the framework of the "culture of poverty" approach. This approach is discussed in this chapter in the section titled "Theoretical Models: The Culture of Poverty."

particular region of the world, there are enormous differences in their religions, history, cultures, languages, and social organization.

Based on pre-European religious beliefs, for example, Filipinos have a family structure that is different from many other Asians. Before the Spanish colonized the Phillipines, the indigenous religion taught that the first man and the first woman emerged simultaneously from a bamboo tube, and this image of equality has been preserved in the practice of Filipinos today who trace their ancestry through both parents. In contemporary Filipino society, in contrast to many other Asian cultures, authority and power are not as patriarchal, and husbands and wives are relatively equal to one another. Collapsing Asian Americans into one category and making assumptions about Asian American families causes us to make incorrect assessments of real people's experiences.

Table 5.4 shows the distribution of Asians and Pacific Islanders from different nations. The largest category is Chinese (23.8%) and the smallest is Japanese (8%).

Immigration

Although people have been immigrating into the United States from all over the world for many centuries, immigration is currently an especially important feature of our stratification system. Thirty years ago, Americans spoke of race ethnicity as the division between whites and nonwhites, and words like desegregation meant bringing together white and black people. But today the picture is more complex. Our communities are more diverse, and we need to rethink many social ideas, including issues that relate to families (Aguilar-San Juan 1994; Chinen et al. 1997; Donnelly 1994; Suro 1998).

Immigration was very high at the turn of the nineteenth century and then fell until the 1930s. Since then, the proportion of people living in the United States who were born in another country has risen steadily. The importance of immigration may vary depending on where you live in the United States. The Southwest has the greatest proportion of people from other countries. In 2004, Texas became the fourth "majority minority" state following Hawaii, New Mexico, California, and the District of Columbia. Five other states now have almost half (40%) minority populations: Maryland, Mississippi, Georgia, New York, and Arizona (Contreras, Kerns, and Neal-Bennett 2000).

TABLE 5.4   Asian and Pacific Islander Population, 2000

Chinese	23.8%
Filipino	18.1%
Indian	16.4%
Vietnamese	11.0%
Korean	10.5%
Japanese	8.0%
Other	12.6%

Source: U.S. Census Bureau, 2000e, p. 1.

BOX **5.2**

Who Should Be Concerned about Gender, Race, and Class?

Michael Kimmel tells a story in the book he coauthored with Michael Messner (Kimmel and Messner 1989) about overhearing a conversation between a black woman and a white woman. The white woman was trying to convince the black woman that their similarities as women were greater than their racial differences. The black woman asked the white woman, "When you look in the mirror, what do you see?" The white woman replied, "I see a woman." The black woman responded, "That is precisely what I mean. When I look in the mirror I see a black woman. For me race is visible every day because I am not privileged in this culture."

Kimmel was startled when he heard this exchange. He thought to himself as he overheard the women talking, "When I look in the mirror I see a human being, universally generalizable. The generic person" (Kimmel and Messner 1990, p. 57). His race, gender, and class were invisible to him. He had not thought about how they affected his life.

This experience led Kimmel to begin thinking about gender, race, and class and why they are so visible to some but not to others. He concluded that "there is a sociological explanation for this blind spot in our thinking: the mechanisms that afford us privilege are very often invisible to us. What makes us marginal (unempowered, oppressed) are the mechanisms that we understand because those are the ones that are most painful in our daily lives" (Kimmel and Messner 1990, p. 57).

The people who are at the bottom of the stratification systems of race, class, and gender may be the first to notice those systems, and they may be the most persistent in drawing our attention to their importance. But race is not an issue of concern only for racially oppressed people. We are all defined and influenced by our race. Class inequality is not just a question for poor people. Social class affects everyone's life. And gender is not just a problem for women. Every discussion of gender has significance for men's experience as well. We all need to see how these systems shape every individual's life.

One important difference in recent immigrants is a greater proportion of women as a result of changes in immigration law. The 1965 Immigration Act gives preference to the following categories: spouses of U.S. citizens; unmarried children (under age twenty-one) of U.S. citizens; spouses and unmarried children of permanent residents; professional scientists and artists of "exceptional ability"; married children over twenty-one of U.S. citizens; skilled and unskilled workers in short supply; and refugees (Espiritu 1997). Many people immigrating under the act are women joining their husbands (Wong 1995, Zhou 1999). Another reason women are now more likely to immigrate is because of the preference given to professionals in the 1980s. For example, the 1989 Immigrant Nurses Act offered permanent residency to incoming nurses. Since nursing and other preferred health care jobs are often held by women, more women immigrated.

Gender

Most humans can be divided into one of two categories—male or female. (For a discussion of the range of sex categories among humans and the surprising difficulty of classifying people, see Stoltenberg 1997 and Lorber 1996). This biological category is called *sex,* and it is determined by physical factors such as genes and sex organs. All known societies also create expectations about these two categories of people. The constructs a society creates about what females and males should be like, women (or girls) and men (or boys), are called gender.

These social constructs vary widely from one society to another. When Margaret Mead (1935) studied three societies in New Guinea, she found that each had an entirely different way of defining masculinity and femininity. Among the Arapesh, both women and men were gentle and passive. Their neighbors, the Mundugumor, expected both men and women to be aggressive and violent. In the third group, the Tchambuli, the women were domineering and wore no adornment, while the men were gossipy, nurturant, and artistic and spent much of their time with the children.

Gender also may vary within a society (Rogers 1978). For example, in our society, masculinity might be defined in one way among pro football players and another way among surgeons.

In some societies, gender is clearly distinguished from sex. For example, among some Native Americans in western North America and the plains, females may act "like men." They may take on the gender of masculinity in their group, even though they are biological females. These female men may dress, speak, work, and in every way behave as men are expected to behave. They may even marry another female and treat her as a wife (Blackwood 1984).

Gender and sex are collapsed into one category in the contemporary United States. In our society, many people believe mistakenly that biological sex determines gender. For example, people may believe that because someone is male, he is more interested in making money and less interested in caring for children. They may also believe that if a woman is skilled at taking care of children, it is because she is a female, not because she has been socialized to care for children or because she has chosen to learn how to care for children.

Whereas sex, for the most part, is a given, gender is not. Gender is socially defined. It comes from people's being exposed to certain ideas and expressions of gender and from their being required or choosing to participate in the categories of masculine and feminine.

Both sex and gender have an important effect on families. Even if men and women were absolutely socially identical in our society, their experience of parenting would often differ because of their sex difference. Only females can be pregnant, give birth, and breastfeed. Bearing and raising children, therefore, includes activities that make the experience different for biological mothers than for fathers. But in addition, society creates ideas and activities for parenting that differ based on gender and are entirely unrelated to biology.

Gender has an important effect on nearly every facet of families' experiences, and families play an important role in the maintenance of gender.

Social Class, Race Ethnicity, and Gender and Family Life

The stratification systems of class, race ethnicity, and gender constitute a major feature of the macrolevel of social organization in our society. They exist beyond the control of any individual and are so pervasive they sometimes become invisible. But they weave in and out of our lives, sometimes overlapping, and sometimes contradicting each other, but always defining and shaping our lives and our relationships with others.

In this section, we will examine the way in which class, race, and gender create different experiences within families. The emphasis will be on the effect that the macro-organization of our society, which includes these three systems of stratification, has on the microlevel of society, the everyday experience of families. We will also observe the ways in which families respond to the macrosystem by helping to preserve inequality, attempting to survive in spite of inequality, and creating ways in which to resist inequality and thereby alter the institutions of inequality.

This section investigates different social classes and racial ethnic groups. Gender is also covered, as the section discusses how women and men relate to each other in families in various social classes and racial ethnic groups.

Upper-Class Families: Gatekeepers

Life in an upper-class family is not often open to scrutiny by the public or by researchers. As a result, less is known about the private lives of the members of this social class than of others. Rich people, however, know a lot about each other. Their preoccupation with maintaining boundaries between themselves and others has been noted by a number of scholars who have studied the elite (Domhoff 1970; Eitzen 1985; Mills 1956). Families are a key way in which "membership" is identified. Being from a "good family" is essential and sometimes even overrides financial status. For example, when one of the "best families" loses its fortune, family members may be still counted as upper class, at least for a time, because of their ancestry (Bedard 1992).

Georg Simmel (1907/1978) wrote that "aristocrats would get to know each other better in an evening than the middle class would in a month." He meant that wealthy people identify themselves by membership and background, while middle-class people identify themselves by individual achievement. Therefore, a person who knows the meaning of various memberships and connections among the upper class can draw a complete picture of a person. An essential piece of information in determining membership is family lineage.

Families play a critical role in keeping an individual in the upper class. The most important single predictor of a son's occupational status is his father's occupational status (Braun 1991). A man born into the top 5 percent of family income had a 63 percent chance of earning over $25,000 a year in 1976 (being in the top 17.8% of family income). But a man born into the bottom 10 percent of family income had only a 1 percent chance of attaining this level. Since the 1980s the chances of moving from middle or working class into the upper class has declined, and surprisingly Americans have less social mobility than many European nations (Berube 2005).

Women in elite families play a special role in maintaining boundaries. "Women serve as gatekeepers of many of the institutions of the very rich. They launch children, serve as board members at private schools, run clubs, and facilitate marriage pools through events like debuts and charity balls" (Rapp 1982).

Families also help maintain an individual's social standing among the wealthy class by teaching family members how to maintain their class position. For example, upper-class children learn not to "spend down capital" (Millman 1991). This means that they should use only the interest, not the principal, of an inherited estate. The wealth that has been accumulated may have taken generations to acquire and is thought of as belonging to the family line, not to individuals.

Tax laws reinforce the idea that wealth belongs to all generations of a family rather than to individuals. Inheritance taxes can be reduced if the inheritance of an estate skips generations. When the inheritance is claimed only every other generation, taxes must be paid only every other generation. For example, if a wealthy person wills his or her estate to grandchildren rather than to children, one tax is paid rather than two (Millman 1991). This increases the motivation to teach children to live on the interest and not to touch the principal and that the family fortune should be shared only within a small circle of kin.

Volunteer work is an especially important activity in the production and maintenance of social status (Daniels 1988). Susan Ostrander interviewed thirty-six upper-class women about their activities "to uphold the power and privilege of their class in the social order of things" (1984, p. 3).

Marriage was one issue about which they spoke. One woman explained, "A compatible marriage first and foremost is a marriage within one's class" (Ostrander 1984, p. 86). The women talked about debuts as critical events to ensure that their children met the proper prospective mates. Social clubs were also cited as places to keep themselves away from those the women referred to as "anybodies."

Athletic games and activities were also mentioned as important. The women believed that these activities enhanced the ability of their children to stay in their class. They spoke of the lessons of "discipline, confidence, competition and a sense of control" (Ostrander 1984, p. 94).

A good education in a prestigious upper-class school was another goal because of both the academic training and the social networks it afforded their children. The women spent much time planning and orchestrating all of these activities.

Upper-class families are largely responsible for maintaining their own position within the stratification system. They pass wealth down within families. They teach their children how to maintain their position, and they bring their children into the social institutions such as elite schools and clubs that further reinforce their membership in the class. Women play a special role in maintaining the class and especially the boundaries around the class.

Along with the maintenance of individual families within the class or the maintenance of the class itself is the maintenance of the system of inequality. In a system of finite resources where some have control over a large proportion of those resources, others have control over less. Resources are not distributed equally. Families are essential to the constant work of retaining those resources and creating relationships of difference and inequality between themselves and other classes. "The family as an institution ensures the continuity of the have-nots as well as entrenching the power and privilege of the haves" (D. Morgan 1985, p. 214).

Middle-Class Families

Four factors characterize middle-class families: (1) geographic mobility resulting in residence away from kin; (2) replacement of kin with other institutions for economic support; (3) reliance on friendship rather than kinship for affective support and exchange; and (4) investment of resources lineally (Rapp 1982).

In order to maintain their income, middle-class families may have to move around. For example, people in middle-class occupations are frequently asked to move when their company needs them to work at another site. Middle-class professionals may find that to get a raise or further their career they must take a job with another company in another state.

These moves remove them from extended family ties, and when economic help is needed, middle-class people may rely on nonfamily sources. For example, a middle-class family that needs money for a down payment on a house would go to a bank for a loan. Both upper-class and working-class families might be more likely to seek assistance from their kin.

Middle-class families may also replace kin with friends in seeking emotional and social support. In the discussion of working-class families that follows, we will see how working-class people convert friends into kin in order to facilitate sharing material goods (Stack 1974). Rayna Rapp (1982) argues that middle-class people do just the opposite. She states that middle-class people refrain from sharing with extended kin and maintain friendships that do not include sharing resources. In this way, middle-class families are better able to accumulate material wealth rather than dispersing it. Middle-class families stress upward mobility based on not sharing what they have accumulated (Millman 1991).

The wealth that each relatively independent middle-class household is able to accumulate is invested lineally—between parents and children—rather than laterally among extended family and close friends, as is the case in working-class households. Investing in education for their children and in extravagant wedding gifts are examples of the ways middle-class families share lineally (Rapp 1982).

Geographic Mobility.   Americans have always been a mobile community, although today we are somewhat less mobile than in previous years. In the nineteenth century, 50 to 75 percent of the residents in any given town were likely to not be there ten years later. People born in the twentieth century were more likely to live near their birthplace than people born in the nineteenth century (Coontz 1992). Nevertheless, one of the sources of the independence and isolation of contemporary middle-class families is the geographic mobility that accompanies their occupations. Every year about 45 million Americans move. More than half of these moves are for a job. Of interstate moves, 22 percent are for a job transfer, 19 percent are for a new job, 6 percent are to look for a job, and 3 percent are for what the Census Bureau calls "unspecified employment related reasons" (Hendershott 1995).

Most researchers have looked at this issue as it exists in families where the husband needs to move because men are much more likely than women, especially married women, to move for work. The "typical" relocated corporate employee is a thirty-seven-year-old married man who owns his home, has two children, and works in sales and marketing (Hendershott 1995).

These moves are experienced differently for women and men in families. The moves enhance the career of the husband for whom the move is being made, and many men seem to feel that moving is not a problem. Almost half of the men in one survey said that family ties pose no obstacle to their possible relocation (Harrison 1991). When a man must move because his wife has found another job, however, his response is somewhat different. Research shows that a man will follow his wife only if she earns 25 percent to 40 percent more than he does (Lee 1986). Although the moves are rewarding for men and the household they support, they also create hardship for wives and children. "Very few women do not suffer some losses as the result of a family move. These may include giving up friends, community and sense of self-worth and identity, close contact with relatives and often, a job or career possibility" (Gaylord 1984). Children, especially those between the ages of three and five and the ages of fourteen and sixteen, also report emotional difficulties with moving (Seidenberg 1973).

Much of the research on the "trailing wife" and the difficulty that relocation for a man's job causes for his family was done in the 1970s and 1980s. Hendershott (1995) reviewed relocation policies and surveys of more than five hundred companies in the 1990s and found that some factors have been altered more recently. She found that moving is not without stress, but that the focus of the older research on the disruption and loss caused by relocation overshadows the ways in which mobility creates improved economic opportunities for the moving families and at times even for the trailing spouse and children. In addition to the greater opportunities of the new job, some companies offer incentives for the move itself. For example, the FBI has given 25 percent cost-of-living increases and $20,000 bonuses to agents who move (Hendershott 1995).

Hendershott (1995) also compared relocaters with "stayers," people who did not agree to relocate. She found that the stress of declining an opportunity that involved moving can be equal to the stress of accepting a move.

Another area of change Hendershott (1995) observed was an increase in the importance of elder care concerns. In a large 1993 survey of corporations, 25 percent said they believed that concern for employees about their older parents was growing in importance in decisions about relocation.

The Black Middle Class.   Black middle-class families are similar to white ones in the focus of their lives on home and family (Bedard 1992). Charles Willie's (1983) research on black middle-class families shows them to be achievement oriented, upwardly mobile, immersed in work, and with little time for leisure. Education, hard work, and thrift are perceived to be the means to achievement.

There are also some interesting differences between black middle-class and working-class families and white middle-class and working-class families. Attitudes about education are one example. Middle-class and working-class black families place an enormous amount of emphasis on education for their children because they perceive education to be the road to success and a way to overcome racial discrimination (Wilkinson 1984). Lower-middle-class black families prioritize education and encourage their daughters to choose education over marriage (Higgenbotham 1981).

In contrast working-class white families are more ambivalent and sometimes even negative about education for their children (Willie 1985). They "worry that highly educated children will no longer honor family customs and maintain cohesion with their relatives" (Anderson 1988, p. 177).

A second racial ethnic difference is the perception by black middle-class families of cultivating community responsibility:

> Middle-class black parents insist that their children get a good education not only to escape possible deprivations but to serve as symbols of achievement for the family as well as for the race. Each generation is expected to stand on the shoulders of the past generation and to do more. All achievement by members in black middle-class families is for the purpose of group advancement as well as individual enhancement. (Willie 1988, p. 183)

In contrast, white families emphasize freedom, autonomy, and individualism. The negative feature of this emphasis is that individualism can shatter family solidarity and can lead individuals to display narcissistic attitudes and hedonistic behavior (Willie 1988).

In the black middle-class family, "Individual fulfillment is seen as self-centered activity and therefore is less valued. What counts in the black middle class is how the family is faring" (Willie 1988, p. 184). The downside of the emphasis on solidarity is that it stifles experimentation. Risk taking is discouraged, and individuals may hesitate to try more experimental and creative activities.

Willie (1988) concludes that blacks and whites can learn from each other on this question. "Too much creativity has been stifled in middle-class blacks who have been trained to put family needs above personal needs. And too many individuals have drifted aimlessly in middle-class white families who have been taught to put individual freedom before collective concern" (p. 184).

The third difference concerns the question of gender equality. A number of studies have found a greater level of equality between husbands and wives in black families than in white families (Mack 1978; Middleton and Putney 1960; D. Morgan 1985; TenHouton 1970; Willie 1983, 1985, 1988). As shown in Figure 2.2 in Chapter 2, black women are more likely to have been in the labor force than white women. Egalitarian ideologies are stronger among blacks than whites (Hunter and Sellers 1998). Black men are more likely to share in housework and child care than white men (Anderson 1988). Willie (1988) asserts that gender equality is a worthy goal and that black families have been pioneers in this effort. Therefore, he concludes, "the egalitarian family form is a major contribution by blacks to American society" (1988, p. 186).

Working-Class White Families

White working-class families are characterized by three factors: (1) the ideological commitment to marry for love, not money; (2) the importance of extended kin and other networks to economic and emotional survival; and (3) the appearance of separation of work and family. Within each of these factors is a contrast between what people believe and what they really experience (Rapp 1982).

Working-class couples marry for love. Person after person in Lillian Rubin's interviews of blue-collar couples said they had married for love and that love provided a way to escape from the difficulties of their parents' homes. One young woman recalled, "We just knew right away that we were in love. We met at a school dance, and that was it. I knew who he was before. He was real popular; everybody liked him. I was so excited when he asked me to dance, I just melted" (Rubin 1976, p. 52).

In contrast, upper-class couples recognize their marriages as a way to preserve their class identity (Millman 1991). Upper-class couples may marry for love, but they are conscious that love should only occur between themselves and others of their class. Middle-class people may also marry for love, but as we saw in the earlier discussion of middle-class families, the overriding task of middle-class families is also an economic one, to enhance the earning power of the breadwinner.

Working-class people are also affected by the economic realities of their lives. Working-class families must operate as economic units. The economic tasks of families are less a part of their dreams about marriage than they are a part of the reality of their married lives. "The economic realities that so quickly confronted the young working-class couples of this study ricocheted through the marriage dominating every aspect of experience, coloring every facet of their early adjustment. The women finding their dreams disappointed felt somehow that their men had betrayed the promise implicit in their union" (Rubin 1976, p. 75).

The second characteristic of working-class families is the reliance on extended kin and others "to bridge the gap between what a household's resources really are and what a family's position is supposed to be" (Rapp 1982, p. 175). Rapp says that working-class families are normatively nuclear. By this she means that they believe that independent autonomous families are the best form and that for the most part their families are independent and autonomous.

Observations of their real behavior, however, reveal much sharing of babysitting, meals, and small amounts of money, especially among extended kin (Rubin 1976; Stacey 1990). Sometimes these extended kin relationships became problematic, and half of the women Rubin (1976) interviewed said that the struggle over who comes first, a man's wife or his mother, was a source of contention between themselves and their husbands. For example, one woman told Rubin: "He used to stop off there at his mother's house on his way home from work and that used to make me furious. On top of that they eat supper earlier than we do, so a lot of times, he'd eat with them. Then he'd come home and I'd have a nice meal fixed, and he'd say he wasn't hungry. Boy did that make me mad" (p. 88).

The third characteristic of working-class families is the appearance that work and family are completely separate. Blue-collar jobs do not include bringing work home, and one's occupation does not carry over into one's identity in the way a middle-class professional's might. But work and family are not entirely separate in the working class, where work affects family life and family affects the workplace. In Chapter 6 we examine some of the specific ways in which this interaction takes place.

Working-Class African American Families: The Moynihan Report and Its Historical Context

In Chapter 3 we reviewed black history from the days of slavery up to the middle of the twentieth century. Throughout that time, black families were a focus of the struggle of African Americans for equality. During slavery, African American people fought plantation owners and the slave system for the right to marry and live with their spouses and children. During the sharecropping period, black families struggled for the right for wives and mothers to devote time to their families instead of working for whites. As industrialization developed, African American women moved from the farms to the cities to take jobs as domestics. Here they challenged their employers for the right to work shorter hours to spend time with their husbands and children.

In the last half of the twentieth century and into the twenty-first, African American families continue to be a volatile political issue. Some have blamed African American families for a myriad of urban problems, as we saw in the opening scenario. Advocates of African American families have fought back, expressing an alternative point of view. They argue that black families have been scapegoats and are not to blame for poverty and civil unrest. Furthermore, they argue, black families have been the victims of poverty and inequality caused by structural problems.

One important event in this history was the publication of a U.S. Labor Department report titled *The Negro Family: A Case for National Action* (Moynihan 1965), commonly called the Moynihan Report after its author, Daniel Patrick Moynihan, the senator from the state of New York.

The 1950s and 1960s were an important period in American history because of one of the most significant social movements in the twentieth century, the civil rights movement, which protested the unequal treatment of African Americans in the United States. Civil rights activists argued that socially powerful institutions like the legal system, government, schools, businesses, and landlords had created poverty and injustice in the black community. In 1965, the Moynihan Report appeared with an alternative point of view.

The Moynihan Report blamed the dilapidated housing, poverty, unemployment, and inferior education experienced by African Americans on the organization of black families. Where the civil rights movement saw these same problems and found their cause in the racism of the most powerful sectors of society, Moynihan blamed the victims.

Moynihan argued that black families were disorganized and female dominated. He maintained that black men were humiliated and emasculated by domineering black women. According to Moynihan, the only hope for saving the black family and therefore the community was to reestablish black men as the rightful heads of their families (Giddings 1984). Moynihan wrote, "Ours is a society which presumes male leadership in private and public affairs, a subculture such as that of the Negro American, in which this is not the pattern, is placed at a distinct disadvantage" (quoted in Gresham 1989, p. 118). In order to overcome this disadvantage, the Moynihan Report advised "that jobs had primacy and the government should not rest until every able-bodied Negro man was working even if it meant that some women's jobs had to be redesigned to enable men to fulfill them" (Giddings 1984, p. 328).

The Moynihan Report also suggested that if black men were to take their rightful place as head of the family and community, they would need to bolster their skills in behaving in a properly masculine manner. Moynihan suggested they join the army: "There is another special quality about military service for Negro men: it is an utterly masculine world. Given the strains of the disorganized and matrifocal family life in which so many Negro youth come of age, the Armed Forces are a dramatic and desperately needed change: a world away from women, a world run by strong men of unquestioned authority" (Moynihan 1965, p. 42).

Moynihan reframed the debate around civil rights so that the opposing sides were no longer African Americans versus an unrepresentative government or poor people versus the power structure. New lines were drawn by the Moynihan Report between black men and black women over who would have access to scarce jobs and who would dominate in families.

Several scholars and the African American community in general reacted critically to the Moynihan Report. People such as Joyce Ladner (1971), Andrew Billingsley (1968), and William Ryan (1971) led the debate against Moynihan's assertions (Giddings 1984; Rainwater and Yancey 1967).

One of the most controversial features of the report concerned the so-called "black matriarchy." The term *matriarchy* means rule by the mother. At the core of Moynihan's argument was the characterization of African American women as dominant authoritarian figures, matriarchs. Robert Staples (1981) actively attacked this idea, calling black matriarchy a myth. He asked, if black women are so dominant and powerful, why do we not see great numbers of black women in Congress, and why do we continue to see black women earning less than white men and women and black men? Staples argued, furthermore, that when we see black women actively working to ensure that their children are fed and when we see black women fighting shoulder to shoulder with black men for integration, education, and civil rights, we should be proud, not critical. Staples commented, "While white women have entered the history books for making flags and engaging in social work, black women have participated in the total black liberation struggle" (p. 32).

Carol Stack (1974), an anthropologist, decided to systematically investigate Moynihan's thesis by doing fieldwork in a low-income black neighborhood she called the Flats. Her work became one of the most influential alternative views of poor black families (M. Katz 1989).

The Flats. Were African American families in the Flats disorganized matriarchies? This was the question with which Stack began her research. After two years of observing and interviewing the residents of the Flats, Stack (1974) concluded that the families there were neither nuclear nor male dominated. Nor were they disintegrating, nonexistent, or matriarchal. Instead, Stack found families that were complex organized networks characterized by five factors: (1) kin and nonkin membership, (2) swapping, (3) shared child raising, (4) fluid physical boundaries, and (5) domestic authority of women.

Networks were composed of both kin and nonkin—parents, siblings, cousins, aunts, uncles, and grandparents, as well as nonkin who became "like family" because of their extended interaction and support of network members. After living in the Flats for two years and sharing rides and child care, even Carol Stack was integrated into the network as a member of the family and began to be called sister by one of the women in the Flats. When people change friends into family, as the people in the Flats did with Carol Stack, sociologists call them fictive kin (Gittens 1998).

The stereotypical middle-class white family is bound together through blood or legal relationships of marriage and adoption. In the Flats, people recognized these ties. More important, however, familial networks in the Flats were also bound together by social relationships based on swapping.

Swapping. Swapping refers to the borrowing and trading of resources, possessions, and services. In times of need, a member of the network could rely on other members for money, food, clothes, a ride, or child care. In return the member was obligated to share what he or she had with those in need. Because resources were scarce, people in the Flats constantly redistributed them in order to survive. Stack describes an example of a swapping network. The description illustrates the many different kinds of resources that are swapped and the complex system that keeps those resources moving in an efficient and fair manner:

> Cecil (35) lives in the Flats with his mother Willie Mae, his oldest sister and her two children, and his younger brother. Cecil's younger sister Lily lives with their mother's sister Bessie. Bessie has three children and Lily has two. Cecil and his mother have part-time jobs in a cafe and Lily's children are on aid. In July of 1970 Cecil and his mother had just put together enough money to cover their rent. Lily paid her utilities, but she did not have

enough money to buy food stamps for herself and her children. Cecil and Willie Mae knew that after they paid their rent they would not have any money for food for the family. They helped Lily by buying her food stamps, and then the two households shared meals together until Willie Mae was paid two weeks later. A week later Lily received her second ADC check and Bessie got some spending money from her boyfriends. They gave some of this money to Cecil and Willie Mae to pay their rent, and gave Willie Mae money to cover her insurance and pay a small sum on a living room suite at the local furniture store. Willie Mae reciprocated later on by buying dresses for Bessie and Lily's daughters and by caring for all the children when Bessie got a temporary job. (1974, p. 37)

Bloodmothers and Other Mothers.   Child keeping is a special form of swapping in the Flats and other black communities (Collins 1990). Poverty makes it difficult for parents to care for children alone. In addition, the value of community responsibility is historically rooted in the culture of West Africa and the slave community of the South. Sharing child care in the black community is common, with various adults in addition to the parents sharing or entirely taking over the responsibility for raising a child. Sometimes child keeping may be shared among parents and other adults for a short time. In other cases it may be for an extended period of years. Sometimes the child lives with one adult at a time. In other cases the child is literally shared, staying in one residence one night and another the next, or eating with one adult and sleeping in the home of another.

Children do not see this as being without a real parent but rather as having a number of real parents. Adults, likewise, do not treat their children differently depending on whether they are their natural children or network children. Rather, among many African Americans, adults feel a sense of responsibility for all children in the community (Collins 1990).

Household and Family.   The domestic networks that comprise the families in the Flats are often spread over several addresses. On the other hand, people who are not nuclear family members may "double up" within a household. Where people sleep and eat and where they contribute money for the rent or spend their time is not necessarily concentrated in one physical location. The physical boundaries of families in the Flats are fluid. They range over several addresses; they change; and they overlap.

In middle-class nuclear families, in contrast, households and families tend to be the same. Nuclear family members live in a single family home, and other people do not live with them. A person who assumes that nuclear families are the only possible way in which to organize a family might look at families in the Flats and conclude that no family existed. A more careful examination, however, reveals that a family form does exist, although it is quite different from that of the middle-class nuclear family.

Extended Network Families in Racial Ethnic Communities.   Child sharing among an extended network family is not unique to African American communities. John Red Horse (1980) describes this kind of family organization in some Native American societies. He explains, "An Indian family, therefore, is an active kinship system inclusive of parents, children, aunts, uncles, cousins and grandparents and is accompanied by the incorporation of significant non-kin who become family members" (p. 463).

Red Horse notes that sharing in the Native American community is sometimes informal, as it is for African Americans in the Flats, but also may be formally marked by naming rituals. In naming ceremonies, which may occur immediately after birth or later in a child's life, the child is given a name, and an adult is chosen as the namesake. After the ceremony, the adult is responsible for the child and is obligated to set a good example and to help care for the child or to take over child care completely if the parent is unable to care for the child.

In the Chicano community, a similar system of shared child raising occurs, called *compadrazgo* (Dill 1986). Many parents designate nonkin, *compadres,* as godparents (*padrinos* and *madrinas*). Godparents celebrate holidays and important rites of passage like first communion and marriage with their godchildren. They are also relied on for economic and social support in times of need and to substitute in case of the death of a parent (Camarillo 1979).

Asian American families, especially those that are recent immigrants to the United States, also rely on networks of kin and nonkin (Hein 1993; Lockery 1998). John Matsuoko (1990) explains that among Vietnamese and other Southeast Asian immigrants, a quickly expanding population, extended family includes not only those who are currently alive but also ancestors and families of the future. Children are taught that their primary duty is to their family lineage. The dominant American ideology that emphasizes the individual and his or her place in a nuclear family has been problematic for Asian immigrants who believe that one's connections are much broader (Kitano and Daniels 1988). Asian families illustrate the way in which child sharing not only implies a broad range of people who are responsible for children but also a range of people to whom children are obligated.

Women's Domestic Authority.   This description of life in the Flats indicates that Moynihan's (1965) portrayal of the black community as one in which families were disrupted or chaotic was false. The families in the Flats were quite different from the stereotypical middle-class white family. But they were highly organized and provided a source of survival in an impoverished community.

Moynihan (1965) also proposed that black families were matriarchal. Stack (1974) investigated this issue as well and concluded that women in the Flats were not matriarchal.

In a matriarchal society, power over households and the community as a whole is controlled by older women. In Chapter 2, for example, we observed a matriarchal society in the Iroquois Confederacy during the colonial period of U.S. history. The Flats was not matriarchal because women were not powerful in the community. Power in the Flats was wielded by landlords, employers, and especially the government through the welfare office.

Stack (1974) found that women in the Flats also did not have matriarchal relationships with the men in their network families. Women had more authority relative to men than women in white middle-class, male-dominated nuclear families. But decisions in the Flats tended to be made by groups of people that included both women and men in the network. In more general overviews of the question of the black matriarchy, no empirical data have been shown to support its existence (McAdoo 1988).

Immigrant Families

The percentage of the population living in the United States that was born in another country was highest, about 14 percent, at the turn of the nineteenth century. It fell steadily to a low of about 4.5 percent in 1970, when it began to rise, reaching 11.1 percent in 2000 (U.S. Census

BOX **5.3**

Extended Community-Based Network Families in the 1990s

Anne Roschelle (1997) conducted research on the question of maintaining kin and nonkin networks as a family support system. She found that some changes may have taken place in the 1990s. Roschelle examined the ways in which people from four racial ethnic groups—white, black, Puerto Rican, and Chicano—shared resources and services with kin and nonkin. She asked them how often and with whom they shared babysitting, transportation, repairs to their home and car, and any other help around the house. She discovered that in the 1990s, white families were more likely than other racial ethnic groups to participate in informal support networks that included kin and fictive kin. Black people were most likely to help their relatives. Puerto Ricans were least likely to develop such networks of kin or nonkin.

Roschelle (1997) concludes that need and desire are not the only important ingredients in the development of these networks; people must also have at least some minimum amount of resources. Since the Great U-turn, black grandparents who have been so central to this activity may have become too poor to provide assistance to their neighbors and family (D. Anderson 1993).

Roschelle (1997) also argues that stability in a geographic area is critical. Chicanos who had been in the area for a longer time participated in networks about the same amount as whites, but those who were recent immigrants were less likely to have established networks. Puerto Ricans were inhibited from establishing networks because they frequently moved back and forth between the United States and Puerto Rico. This mobility made it more difficult for them to form connections and it also made them "poor investments" from the point of view of others because they might not be living in the area for long.

Bureau 2000d). Almost one quarter (22%) of children in the United States live in immigrant families. Immigrant families are an important part of our population (Capps et al. 2005).

Earlier in the century, most immigrants came from Europe. Today most come from Latin America and Asia. Mexico represents the largest source country, with 13 percent of immigrants. It is followed by the Philippines (7%), Vietnam (6%), Dominican Republic (5%), China (5%), and India (5%). Most immigrants are concentrated in the following states California: (23%), New York (18%), Florida (9%), Texas (7%), New Jersey (6%), and Illinois (5%) (Littman 1998).

Mexican Americans.   Until the middle of the nineteenth century, the areas that we now call the states of New Mexico, California, Nevada, Utah, Arizona, as well as most of Texas, half of Colorado, and a little bit of Oklahoma, Kansas, and Wyoming were part of Mexico. The Texas War of Independence and the Mexican-American War resulted in 814,145 square miles of land becoming part of the United States (Russell 1994). The people who lived in those areas included many Mexicans and Native Americans as well as Anglos who had migrated there before annexation. Since then, many Mexican people born in the currently Mexican area have migrated into the formerly Mexican area.

Table 5.1 earlier in this chapter shows the growing proportion of the U.S. population that is Hispanic. Through births and continued immigration, the proportion of the population that is Hispanic is predicted to grow from about 12.5 percent in 2000 to about 25 percent in 2050. These data include people from many other Latin American nations besides Mexico, but as Table 5.2 showed, Mexicans Americans make up a significant percentage of the total Latino population.

Immigrant families face special kinds of problems. Julia Rodriguez (1988; see also Zavella 1987) studied women who came north both to follow their husbands who were seeking work and to find jobs themselves. Their emigration from Mexico depended on their ability to obtain support from relatives and friends in Mexico who could help them obtain documents, pay for travel, and arrange for child care. In addition, some had to find child care for children they left temporarily in Mexico while they moved to the United States.

Once they arrived in the United States, the women quickly worked to become familiar with their new communities and to establish new networks to exchange goods. They also needed to establish information networks because of their special needs as new immigrants or undocumented workers so as to find employment, housing, health care, and schools in a new environment.

This kind of migration, which takes place in steps with some members following others, is called family stage migration (Hondagneu-Sotelo 1997). Hondagneu-Sotelo has found that the process of migration creates change in gender relations within families. She reviews two periods of migration: pre-1965 and post-1965. In the 1950s and 1960s, ideas about what is properly masculine gave men the authority to act autonomously to decide to migrate. Gender expectations also told men that they were supposed to be good providers and therefore had to choose to leave their families. Properly gendered women had to accept their husband's decision, remain chaste, and stay behind to take care of the children despite their fears of becoming *mujer abandonada* (an abandoned woman) or being unable to handle the financial and social burdens of raising a family alone. After the 1970s, expectations about gender changed, and women were more likely to follow their husbands rather than stay behind.

Before 1965, men had come mostly unaccompanied and had stayed for long periods of time in bachelor communities in which many men shared households. Men learned to do work that had been reserved for women, like cooking, cleaning, and shopping. One man explained

> Back in Mexico, I didn't know how to prepare food, iron a shirt or wash my clothes. I only knew how to work, how to harvest. But when I found myself with certain urgencies here, I learned how to do everything that a woman can do to keep a man comfortable. And the custom stayed with me I now know how to prepare American food and Mexican food, while back in my country I didn't know to cook at all. Necessity forced me to do things which I had previously ignored. (Hondagneu-Sotelo 1997, p. 480)

The men expressed pride in their newfound talents and continued to share these tasks when their wives joined them. At the same time, the long periods during which wives had been forced to take charge while their husbands were away changed them as well, making them more assertive and less subservient. One woman explained

> When he came here [to the United States], everything changed. It was different. It was me who took the responsibility for putting food on the table, for keeping the children clothed,

for tending the animals. I did all of these things alone, and in this way, I discovered my capacities. And do you know, these accomplishments gave me satisfaction. (Hondagneu-Sotelo 1997, p. 479)

In households where the men had migrated after 1965 and their wives had quickly joined them, these kind of gender transitions had not occurred. The pre-1965 migrants' households were strikingly more egalitarian than the post-1965 households (Hondanegeu-Sotelo 1997).

Vietnamese Immigrant Families. Vietnamese families have described similar experiences (Kibria 1996). Traditional Vietnamese families were modeled on Confucian principles that organized extended families around a patriarch. Young brides joined their husbands' households, where they had little status and were subordinate and dependent on their husbands (Kandiyoti 1988). If the wife lived long enough, however, she could expect in her old age to take her place at a higher level in the household hierarchy and enjoy deference and allegiance from younger members. This model began to change in Vietnam in the 1950s and 1960s as a result of the war.

Migration to the United States further challenged the traditional model for two reasons. First, Vietnamese women were more likely to find employment in the United States than men were, which created a shift in power that benefited women. Second, women began to organize social networks to help them survive in their new communities. They exchanged food, information, and strategies to use to negotiate institutions such as social services, hospitals, and schools. The networks also became useful ways to control men inside households. For example, if men were abusive or tried to keep their wives from working outside the home, network members would intervene by mobilizing community opinion against them.

Kibria (1996) argues that these changes altered the patriarchal relations but did not transform them. Gender inequality remained intact despite immigration, although it was renegotiated. Access to economic resources improved for women, but such resources were too limited to provide independence. In addition, women themselves often wanted to maintain the old system because it allotted authority over children to them in their old age, which they did not wish to give up.

What Is a Family?

Contrary to the negative stereotype sometimes portrayed of poor racial ethnic families, the examples in this chapter show complex, well-organized families. Most of the families, however, are not isolated, male-dominated nuclear families. This challenges classical definitions and suggests that asking how to define The Family may be an impossible and irrelevant question.

In the 1940s George Murdock offered this definition of family:

A social group characterized by common residence, economic cooperation, and reproduction. It includes adults of both sexes at least two of whom maintain a socially approved sexual relationship and one or more children, own or adopted, of the sexually cohabiting adults. (1949, p. 1)

Murdock's definition is widely cited, but it has also been roundly criticized (Gerstel and Gross 1987). The way in which people define family and certainly the way in which they live their family lives frequently vary on every one of the components suggested by Murdock.

Stack concluded her studies by offering a definition of family that fit the families in the Flats and that leaves more room for the diversity that exists in our family lives:

> Ultimately I define "family" as the smallest, organized, durable network of kin and non-kin who interact daily, providing domestic needs of children and assuring their survival. The family network is diffused over several kin-based households. An arbitrary imposition of widely accepted definitions of the family, the nuclear family or the matrifocal family blocks the way to understanding how people in the Flats describe and order the world in which they live. (1974, p. 31)

In the scenario at the beginning of the chapter, Lowry's definition of The Family is very much like Murdock's. He argues that, based on this definition, families in poor black neighborhoods have been destroyed or are nonexistent. Stack (1974) asserts that families are varied and that our definitions need to be equally diverse. How would you define family? Does your own family fit this definition? Can we define The Family? Is it necessary to do so?

Renewed Interest in Poor Families

The debate over poor black families has not abated. The 1980s and 1990s brought forth a renewed interest in poor families. And although most poor families are white, the stereotype of the poor family is of one that is headed by a black single woman.

Most poor families in the United States are white, but as we observed in Chapter 4, African Americans, Latinos, and Native Americans, especially those with children, are disproportionately likely to be poor. In 2003, 34 percent of African American children lived below the poverty level; 28 percent of Latino children lived below the poverty level; and 13 percent of white children lived below the poverty level. Table 5.5 shows how these numbers have changed over the past thirty years.

Poor families are likely to be single female-headed households. Almost 39 percent of single female-headed households with children were poor, and women and children make

TABLE 5.5   **Children Age Eighteen and Younger Below the Poverty Level, 1970–2003**

	1970	1980	1990	1995	2003
White	10.5%	13.4%	15.1%	16.2%	13.3%
Black	41.5%	42.1%	44.2%	41.9%	34.1%
Hispanic	N.A.	33.0%	39.7%	40.0%	28.4%

Source: Reprinted from Lawrence Mishel, Jared Bernstein, John Schmitt, and Economic Policy Institute, *The State of Working America, 2000–2001.* Copyright © 2001 by Cornell University. Used by permission of the publisher, Cornell University Press; U.S. Census Bureau 2003a.

up the majority of the poor. Of all the poor people in the United States, 25 percent are children. Among adults, 57 percent are women, and 43 percent are men (Census Bureau 2004b). Diana Pearce (1978) coined the term "the feminization of poverty" to describe the trend toward larger numbers of single women and children in poor households. She attributed the feminization of poverty to two factors: the responsibility of women for children and discrimination in the labor market against women. Single women are responsible for more mouths to feed than single men, but when women enter the labor force, they are paid less than men. The result is more poor single women and more poor children.

The feminization of poverty is compounded by race because race discrimination further limits access to housing, education, jobs, and good pay. Among female-headed households with children, 32 percent of those headed by whites are poor, 43 percent of those headed by blacks are poor, and 46 percent of those headed by Latinos are poor (Census Bureau 2003a). During the 1980s and 1990s, the proportion of single women heading households and the prevalence of poverty in these households increased.

The statistics above show that black and Hispanic people are more likely than white people to be poor. Black people and Hispanics, however, make up only about 12 percent of the total population. The largest proportion of poor people are white. Table 5.6 shows the proportion of poor who are white, black, Hispanic, and other.

Are poor and black single female-headed households pathological? Are they the source of the many social problems we see in our society? Or are they victims who are being scapegoated (Gresham 1989)? The debate around this question, which gained much attention in the 1960s and reemerged in the 1980s and 1990s continues to be a focus today as we saw in the response to Hurricane Katrina. The Moynihan Report came out as an alternative to the message carried by civil rights leaders during a period of social unrest over the question of equality for African Americans. Civil rights leaders blamed the system and the powerful people who worked to maintain it. Moynihan blamed the victims. In the 1990s, poverty, inequality, and urban unrest erupted into the Los Angeles rebellion. People like Congresswoman Maxine Waters claimed that the problem is the economy and the ineffective leadership of those who wish to maintain the status quo. Former Vice President Quayle argued that the victims are to blame. These two sides emerged again in the debate over what caused the Katrina disaster. The debate between these two points of view brings together the three systems of inequality we reviewed at the beginning of the chapter—gender, race, and class—and the relationship of these stratification systems to families. Those people who are at the bottom of each of these systems of inequality—poor black women and their families—are at the core of the debate.

TABLE 5.6   Most Poor People Are White

White Not Hispanic	45.9%
Black	23.5%
White Hispanic	23.8%
Other	8.0%

Source: U.S. Census Bureau 2003a.

The Culture of Poverty

The debate over the causes and effects of the problems faced by poor families and their solutions involves two opposing models for understanding the relationship between family structure and poverty. One model is cultural and the other is structural (Baca Zinn 1989a; Jarrett 1994). The cultural deficiency model claims that poor people have a different and inferior culture compared with that of middle-class and upper-class people. Baca Zinn (1989a) argues that currently the deficiency model actually has three variations: culture as villain, family as villain, and welfare as villain. The central thesis of all these variations of the cultural deficiency model is that bad culture causes poverty. Within this framework, poverty is an effect, not a cause. The Moynihan Report in the 1960s and the comments by Rich Lowry in the opening scenario are illustrations of the cultural deficiency model. They maintain that certain individuals within our society have adopted values and behaviors that make them unable to succeed economically and socially and that these bad values and behaviors are passed on within families.

The University of Michigan's Panel Study of Income Dynamics (PSID) has collected data that challenge the cultural deficiency model (Baca Zinn 1989a). First, the PSID found that people who are poor in one year are not necessarily poor in the next year. People move in and out of poverty status. This means that poor people are not members of a deviant sub-group who are always poor.

Also, the panel discovered that the values of welfare-dependent families and non–welfare-dependent families were not significantly different. These two groups share similar ideas regarding their desire to be good parents, their concern for the future, and their motivation to achieve.

A second variation of the culture of poverty argument is that the lack of a two-parent family is what causes and sustains poverty. According to this point of view, unmarried mothers and divorced single parents create a deficit in their children's lives that leads to poverty (Baca Zinn 1989a).

Being in a two-parent family, however, does not necessarily keep people out of poverty. The National Center for Children in Poverty (Koball and Douglas-Hall 2005) reports that more than one in four children with married parents is low income. The major-ity of low-income children in rural and suburban areas live with parents who are married, and most single parents were formerly married as well. The majority of married low-income parents are employed, and 41 percent of their children have two employed parents. Illness and disability are common reasons for unemployment. Low wages, lack of employee benefits, frequent moves, and low levels of education are common among these parents, and their need for public health insurance and food stamps is rising.

Poverty is a common experience regardless of family structure. The data do not sup-port the family deficit argument that single-parent families cause poverty.

The third variation of the cultural deficit model blames welfare for poverty. This argument contends that welfare makes people lazy and causes poor women to have babies and poor men to abandon these women and their children (Murray 1984).

Research comparing different welfare benefits in different states, however, shows no systematic variation in family structure (Baca Zinn 1989a). Furthermore, increases and decreases in welfare spending over time do not produce predictable changes in family organization (Danziger and Gottschalk 1985; Ellwood and Summers 1986). For example, from 1960 to 1972 welfare spending increased, and from 1972 to 1984, it declined. During both of these periods, family composition increasingly included more female-headed households. If welfare spending causes single-parent households to increase, there should have been a reversal of this trend after 1972.

Despite its popularity in the media and among conservative politicians, the cultural deficit theory is not well supported by systematic research. An alternative model for understanding the links among poverty and family organization is the social structural model.

Social Structural Model

The second model Baca Zinn (1989a) describes is a social structural model that emphasizes the trends we reviewed in Chapter 4. The transition to an electronically based economy, the accompanying decline of the industrial manufacturing sector, and the shift of jobs from the central cities of the Midwest and Northeast to the suburbs, the South, and other countries have created cycles of unemployment and a decline in wages for those left with jobs. From the perspective of the social structural model, massive changes in the structure of the American economy create poverty (Baca Zinn 1989a).

In particular, racial ethnic people have had their source of livelihood ripped from them. Many jobs have been eliminated entirely by automation, and others have been sent far away.

Shifts in the economy eliminate jobs or remove them to inaccessible sites. Unemployment then affects family organization. For example, the lack of jobs inhibits marriage. William Wilson and Kathryn Neckerman's (1986) research shows that high unemployment is a major factor in explaining the low number of marriages among young African American men.

The social structural model asserts that economic decline causes poverty, which creates changes in family structure. The decline in the number of jobs created by major shifts in the economy causes significantly greater unemployment among blacks and Latinos, which in turn causes fewer marriages and greater numbers of single-parent households. The structural model has gained much less attention in the popular media than the cultural model, but it appears to be better supported by the research evidence.

Do Families Contain the Seeds of Resistance?

Thus far, the discussion in this chapter has emphasized the way in which the macrolevel of social structure, particularly social stratification, affects the microlevel of family organization and the everyday experience of people living in families. We have also observed how families have attempted to cope with problems of poverty and inadequate housing by pooling their resources and restructuring. These responses are examples of the way in which the microlevel responds to the macrolevel by attempting to hold back the most devastating effects of inequality and oppression.

Mina Caulfield (1974) argues that families can also provide a base of operation for people attempting to challenge their governments. Families provide a vehicle of resistance in three ways. First, families aid the physical survival of their members. Second, families preserve and teach the culture of the community, thereby keeping alive not only individuals but also a point of view. Families can teach a history, a culture, and an alternative way of thinking and acting, all of which incorporate an ideology that questions the current organization of power. For example, in Chapter 13 we look at specific proposals being made by scholars to socialize children by teaching them alternative, critical points of view. Bem (1983) tells us to teach our children to be feminists. Peters (1988) tells us how to teach our children to recognize and challenge racism.

Third, families create or strengthen the organizations that struggle against the powerful (Naples 1992). For example, during the labor organizing drives in the United States at the turn of the century, workers had difficulty creating organizations that crossed lines among those who were unionized and nonunionized, skilled and unskilled, men and women. One of the ways in which these groups of workers were brought together was through their family connections. Unskilled young women meat packers were able to unite with skilled older men butchers because the women were the daughters and nieces of the men (Benenson 1985; Lembcke 1991).

The Mothers of East Los Angeles

The Mothers of East Los Angeles (MELA) is a contemporary example of a conscious organized effort by people working together at the microlevel to affect the organization of the macrolevel of society. It also is an example of women using their family networks and family roles as the basis of political action. Working to create change in one's community and using the neighborhood as a site of resistance is called "activist mothering" (Naples 1996).

MELA is a group of about four hundred Mexican American women who initially came together in the mid-1980s to protest the state's proposal to build a prison in their neighborhood. Since then, they have fought the building of a toxic waste incinerator. They have elected representatives, lobbied the state legislature, and defeated a proposal to build an oil pipeline through their community. Their goal is to bring new schools to their neighborhood instead of prisons, and safe work sites instead of hazardous industries (Pardo 1990, 1998).

The typical member of MELA is a low-income, high school educated, highly religious (Catholic), middle-aged (forty to sixty) Mexican American woman. Some scholars have identified these characteristics as "retardants" to political activism. Pardo's (1990, 1998) work shows, however, that the women in MELA have transformed their social identity from "retardant" to activist in the politics of East Los Angeles.

Pardo (1990) describes how the members of MELA have transformed their oppressed social position into a basis of empowerment. She cites five areas of this transformation. The first of these is the transformation of gender-based roles, responsibilities, and networks into a political resource (p. 2). For example, women used experiences and friends they had met in their children's school activities. Second was the transformation of "invisible" women into a focal point (p. 3). Many women literally expanded their discussion and activity from the neighborhood to the state capital. Third was the transformation of ethnic and class identity into a basis of community unity (p. 3). The women took pride in who they were and contrasted their grassroots style to the highly paid lobbyists they confronted. Fourth was the transformation or redefinition of *mother* to include militancy and political responsibility (p. 4). Fifth was the transformation of "unspoken sentiments of individual women into collective voices of community protest" (p. 5). This final transformation included personal change when they needed to take strong public positions to win their battles.

Pardo (1990, 1998) concludes that the women in MELA defy the common perception of who will become a political activist. The problems within their community have forced them to reconstruct a definition of themselves as militant fighters. Their activity reminds us to keep an open mind when we look for avenues for change and the people who might lead us there. This chapter has presented much evidence of the oppressiveness of the stratification systems of class, race, and gender. The Mothers of East Los Angeles assure us that it will take more than that to prevent people from seeking justice.

The Micro–Macro Connection

A stratification system with three major components—gender, race, and class—creates an important part of the macrolevel of our society. Each of these systems of stratification has an effect on the organization of families. Social class creates certain tasks and opportunities that impinge on families. Upper-class families are called on to maintain the system. Middle-class families work to keep themselves financially afloat. Working-class and poor families must invent creative ways to organize their families to survive.

The system of race stratification also shapes families. Gender differentiates the experience of women and men within families of all social classes and racial ethnic groups.

In addition, the three systems work together to create an especially vulnerable family type that finds itself at the bottom of the three systems—poor, black, and Latino single female-headed households. The question of whether these kinds of families are the victims or the cause of urgent problems of poverty, inequality, and civil unrest is a focus of debate among political activists on every side.

In previous chapters I emphasized the importance of the way in which the microlevel affects the macrolevel. As evidence of this we have seen examples of political movements that have been critical of the maintenance of the status quo. In this chapter I introduced the idea that there are also political activists who seek to maintain the present organization of the macrolevel, including its systems of stratification.

Upper-class women, for example, work to reproduce the social-class system and the boundaries between themselves and other classes. People like Rich Lowry today and Senator Daniel Moynihan in the past take the position that it is not the system that should be criticized and changed but rather the individuals who are unsuccessful within that system.

At the other end of the spectrum, scholars like Carol Stack and Maxine Baca Zinn write about alternative critical views. Their work at the microlevel challenges the organization of the social structure. Other people have also called for changes in the macro-organization of our society. Organizations that criticized the government for its handling of the Katrina disaster say that we need to restructure the United States to eliminate poverty and inequality. The Mothers of East Los Angeles continue their efforts to build a political organization that will address the problems that affect their families, like inadequate schools, jobs, clean environment, and housing in their community.

The macrolevel has an important effect on our families and our individual lives. Part of that effect is to differentiate families by race, class, and gender. The microlevel in turn fights back, but not in only one way. People who hold different places in the stratification system have different interests, different ways of resisting, and different goals in their efforts to shape the macrolevel of society.

CHAPTER

6 Work and Family

Work and family ideally should fit together allowing people to earn a living as well as to enjoy family life. Balancing both is a challenge we usually cannot meet depending on our partners and children alone. Like many parents, this father depends on a childcare center to help take care of his son while he works. (© Ellen Senisi/The Image Works)

Cindy and Jordan are seniors in college. They have been good friends throughout their years at the university. Both will be graduating at the end of this semester. They sit in the student union discussing where they will be in five years.

Cindy says, "I might go back to school for an MBA later, but for now I want to get out and make some money." Jordan nods his head in agreement, saying, "Yes, but what about a family? You'll probably be married with a kid by then, too."

"No," says Cindy, "I want to get established first, with a good position and a house and car before I settle down. It's too hard to do everything, and I want to use my degree. What about you and Allie?"

"We're all set to get married next fall. I don't think it will be that hard. We want to have kids, too, but we plan to share. That way we can both establish our careers and raise a family," Jordan replies. "Allie can work during the day and I can work during the evening at the bank. It's just a matter of scheduling and commitment. Having a wife and kids at home will help me keep my life more balanced and not just job, job, job."

"What if the boss wants you to entertain clients from out of town, or travel to a conference, or just work late, or what if the baby gets sick, then what?" says Cindy. "No, it's not for me, I've made my choice. Women have to make choices these days, and thank God they can."

Cindy and Jordan are at a similar juncture in their lives, finishing college, making plans for their careers, and thinking about where family will fit in. Despite their similarity, they have come to different conclusions. Cindy is convinced that she must make a choice between work and family because they would interfere too much with each other. Jordan believes he can integrate the two activities. He also thinks that family pressures will be good for his personal well-being, keeping him from being a workaholic.

> What kinds of assumptions are Cindy and Jordan making about the organization of work and family and the intersection of the two?
>
> Are their opinions based on a perception of work and family as two separate spheres, or do they see work and family holistically?
>
> How does gender affect their thinking?
>
> Are Cindy and Jordan limited in their thinking about what they can do about their social environment? Are there demands they could make on their employers or the government that might alter their possible choices?

Myth of Separate Spheres

In Chapter 2 we examined the emergence of a split between work and family among upper and middle-class whites during the development of industrialization. Many productive activities that took place within families in preindustrial society were moved to factories as society industrialized. Work that took place outside of families was separated spatially and temporally from work and other activities within some families.

Along with these developments, ideas began to change as well, and new ideas emerged about what families are like or should be like. The new ideas separated work and family into two different spheres. The new ideology also separated women from men, placing men in the public work sphere and women in the domestic family sphere.

During the nineteenth and early twentieth centuries, this familial ideology caused problems for most people. Upper-class and middle-class white women often lived in separate spheres but felt isolated and stifled in their domestic role.

African American and working-class white families found the ideology problematic because it was held up as an ideal but was often impossible for them to attain. The idea of men in the public sphere earning money and women in the domestic sphere taking care of the home did not accurately depict their lives. Work and family were not separate spheres for African Americans who as slaves and sharecroppers were all forced to work constantly.

Among white working-class families, the idea of separate spheres was also largely mythical because nearly all members of working-class families worked for wages, including wives who stayed home and did piecework or took in boarders to earn money. In these families, women were not separated from the work sphere, although their paid work and unpaid family work sometimes existed in the same physical space, the home.

As we enter the twenty-first century, the idea of separate spheres has become increasingly mythical not only for racial ethnic people and working-class whites but also for the white middle class as well. The majority (57.5%) of women in the United States are now in the labor force (Mishel, Bernstein, and Allegretto 2005). Even women who are wives and mothers in families are likely also to be in the paid labor force. In fact, mothers with children under 18 (70.4%) were more likely than other women to be in the labor force (Bureau of Labor Statistics 2005c). Furthermore, as we will discuss in this chapter, work shapes and penetrates families, and families influence and overlap work. Unlike the myth of separate spheres, work and family are inseparable in real lives (Bose 1987; Chow and Berheide 1988; Kanter 1977a; J. Kelly 1979).

This chapter is divided into four major sections. The first is a critical examination of the conceptualization of work and family as separate spheres. In the second section, we will look at the ways in which work affects family, and in the third how family affects work. Finally, we will consider the demands for changes that people are making to try to alleviate the difficult tension between work and family.

The Study of Work and Family Is Distorted by the Concept of Separate Spheres

One of the results of the conceptualization of work and family as two separate spheres—one for women and one for men—is that the study of work has been segregated into two models: a job model and a gender model (Feldberg and Glenn 1979). When men workers are studied, the job model is used to explain their behavior. The job model focuses on working conditions, opportunities, and problems in trying to understand men's behavior at work and their expectations about their jobs. This model assumes that men in the paid labor force are in their proper sphere and that their experience and obligation as members of families are unrelated to their work experience and largely irrelevant to their lives.

When women workers are studied, the gender model is used. This model ignores working conditions or job characteristics and instead focuses on personal characteristics of the worker and her family circumstances to explain her behavior and expectations at work. The gender model, furthermore, assumes that women put their families first in making decisions about work. This model proposes that women in the paid labor force are out of their "true" sphere. Women's experience at work, therefore, is determined or overshadowed by family.

These different models result in distorted interpretations of men's and women's lives. To illustrate this issue, Roslyn Feldberg and Evelyn Glenn (1979) surveyed Robert Blauner's (1964) book, *Alienation and Freedom,* a classic study of textile workers. They argue that in his research Blauner used the two different models—gender and job—to interpret women's and men's work behavior.

Blauner reported that women workers were more closely supervised than men and did more physically demanding, machine-paced work. Women workers also complained more about their work than did the men. The women said they had to work too fast, that there was too much pressure at work, and that they became tired.

When Blauner (1964) discussed why the women complained, he ignored what he had discovered about the difficult conditions of the women's work. Using a gender model to explain the women's complaints, Blauner said that they complained because compared with men, women had less physical stamina and greater home responsibilities as housewives and mothers. Blauner's explanation ignored the job-related explanation provided by his own data that the work the women did was more oppressive because it was more closely supervised and more physically challenging; it required constant motion and was machine-paced. Instead he relied on an explanation that emphasized gender and the connection between women and families.

Another example of gender bias in Blauner's work was revealed when Feldberg and Glenn reviewed his interpretation of the responses of men and women workers to their jobs. Blauner found that, in the textile mills, both women and men worked under trying conditions, yet they expressed relatively little dissatisfaction with their jobs and little aspiration to find better ones. Blauner explained that the men's lack of dissatisfaction and aspiration resulted from their low levels of education and the scarcity of alternatives in the small one-industry towns in which they lived. For the women, Blauner switched to the gender model and explained that the women were not dissatisfied because "work does not have the central importance and meaning in their lives that it does for men, since their most important roles are those of wife and mother" (Blauner 1964, p. 87).

Feldberg and Glenn (1979) concluded that both the job model and the gender model are partial explanations. When they are used alone, they distort and obscure rather than help us understand. What is needed is an integrated model that takes into consideration both work and family and the links between them for both women and men.

Young Women Speak of Work and Family in Their Future

Figuring out how work and family fit into our lives is not a problem just for scholars, of course. Everyone has ideas about how these two activities fit together and how they would like to experience them (Granrose and Kaplan 1996). And almost everyone has trouble determining what the choices are, what choices they should make, and especially how they will be able to attain those choices (Potuchek 1997). Ruth Sidel (1990) interviewed young women about their expectations for the future. Many of their responses included consideration of their future activities as employees and as wives and mothers. Based on their responses, Sidel grouped them into one of three categories: New American Dreamers, Neo-traditionalists, and Outsiders.

The New American Dreamers plan to have it all. They optimistically predict that they will be successful, affluent, and independent. They will enter professions that have been dominated by men. They will also be extraordinary wives and mothers with lots of children and a big house. But first they plan to establish their careers.

New American Dreamers speak of having careers as models, judges, and physicians. They believe that all they must do is establish their goals and work hard. One sixteen-year-old New American Dreamer told Sidel:

> It's your life. You have to live it yourself. You must decide what you want in high school, plan your college education, and from there you can basically get what you want. If you work hard enough, you will get there. You must be in control of your life and then somehow it will all work out. (1990, p. 25)

The young women whom Sidel (1990) placed in the category of New American Dreamer put work before family both in time and priority. However, they also believed that they would eventually be successful in both areas. The New American Dreamers had contemplated the ways in which work and family might affect each other in their lives, especially the ways in which work might interfere with their ability to excel as wives and mothers, or the ways in which family might interfere with their ability to reach the top at work.

In the scenario at the beginning of the chapter, Cindy is a New American Dreamer. She wants to be successful in a business career, and she believes she must choose between work and family. Her choice is to establish herself as a professional and then consider marriage and childbearing.

The second category Sidel called Neotraditionalists. These women had considered the interaction between work and family. They, too, wished to have interesting and well-paid work, but they named family as their top priority. One woman, a senior in college, explained

> I want to be smart. I want to be somebody. I want to make money. I want to be a successful lawyer but my personal life comes first. I want to be a lovely wife, do my husband's shirts, take Chinese cooking lessons and have two children. (1990, p. 37)

In the scenario at the beginning of the chapter, Jordan shares the point of view of the Neotraditionalist women. He wants to have both a career and a family. He has chosen to place priority on marriage and children. (Because Sidel interviewed only women, we have no basis for comparing young men to young women on the question of work and family. This question would be an interesting one to pursue.)

The third group of young women Sidel interviewed she named Outsiders. They felt they had little chance of success in any arena, including work and family, and they could not imagine negotiating the two. Linda, age seventeen, expresses the position: "I don't plan. I don't look to the future. I can't plan 'cause my plans never work out. They never go through" (1990, p. 67).

Where do you or the young women and men you know fit into these three models? How do the personal lives of the three types mesh with the social reality in which they live? In the next section, we will look at the reality of work and family and their intersection in order to understand where these young people's dreams fit and to determine what might need to change to allow them to successfully negotiate the choices.

Women in the Paid Labor Force

What is work? Nona Glazer (1987) suggests that when we speak of the contemporary United States, we define work as "those activities which produce goods and/or services and/or provide for the circulation of goods and services which are directly or indirectly for capitalism" (p. 240).

Much of Glazer's research has been on unpaid work such as housework. In the next chapter we examine the unpaid work that takes place in families. In this chapter we focus on paid work and its intersection with families.

Women are still largely identified with unpaid domestic activities and, in fact, women do an enormous amount of unpaid housework. One of the most significant changes in American society in this century, however, has been the steady increase of women in the paid labor force (Blau and Ehrenberg 1997). In 2004, 57.5 percent of women were in the paid labor force compared with 43.3 percent in 1970 (Mishel, Bernstein, and Schmitt 2001; Mishel, Bernstein, and Allegretto 2005).

Table 6.1 shows that while men still are more likely than women to be in the paid labor force, the majority of women are working for wages outside of their homes. Although the numbers vary some by race, within the categories of white, black, and Hispanic the majority of women are earning money.

The number of women in the labor force grew steadily throughout the last half of the twentieth century. The increases have been especially dramatic for women with children (Burris 1991). For example, in 1960 only about 19 percent of women with children under the age of six were in the labor force. By 1993, that proportion had jumped to 58 percent (Stetson 1997). Women are projected to make up 47 percent of the total labor force by 2012 compared with 38.1 percent in 1970 (Littman 1998; Bureau of Labor Statistics 2004e).

Why Have Women Increasingly Entered the Labor Force?

Explanations for why women have entered the labor force in the twentieth century can be divided into three groups: supply side, demand side, and social structural (Strober 1988). Supply-siders (Becker 1965; Mincer 1962) argue that as the twentieth century progressed, women's work at home decreased in its value. Falling birthrates and labor-saving devices for housework made unpaid domestic labor less important for the family economy. The supply of women available for paid work outside of the home thus increased, putting pressure on the labor market to open up jobs for women.

TABLE 6.1   Labor Force Participation Rates for All Adults over Age Twenty, by Race and Sex, 2005

	All	Whites	Blacks	Hispanics
Men	76.0%	76.2%	72.8%	83.7%
Women	60.4%	59.8%	64.3%	57.3%

Source: U.S. Department of Labor 2005d.

The second explanation focuses on the demand for women in the labor market. They (Oppenheimer 1969) assert that jobs that have been identified as women's occupations, such as secretary, nurse, and waitress, have increased. The demand for women to fill these positions has created a pull on women to enter the labor force .

The third explanation emphasizes the broader social structure (Vickery 1979). Improved birth control and increased life span for women are two aspects of social structure that have been identified as important factors in relation to the increasing number of women in the workforce. In addition, improved technology in factories has made it cheaper and easier to purchase goods and services than it is to produce them at home. For example, automated factories can produce clothes more cheaply and efficiently than individual seamstresses can. These structural factors, which make up the social context of women's work at home and in the labor force, have created the impetus for bringing women into paid work. This third explanation is similar to the supply-side argument. The difference between the two is that supply-siders emphasize the changes in families—fewer children, less housework. Those who focus on social structure, in contrast, emphasize the social factors outside of families, such as the development of contraceptives and microwaves, that influence these changes.

Despite the pervasiveness and strength of the forces identified in the three frameworks, the effect has not been uniform for all women. Research on Asian American women, for example, indicates that although recent immigrants have all of these pressures to place them in the labor force, they may still be impeded from entering it because of factors having to do with their immigrant status, most importantly their language skills (Stier 1991).

Supply factors, demand factors, other structural factors, the economic climate, and racial ethnic discrimination are all macrolevel features that play a role in creating the impetus for women to enter the paid labor force in increasing numbers. Let us now move to the microlevel to see how individual women make the choice to work outside the home.

How Do Women Choose to Work?

Most women work because of economic need. But women work for social rewards as well. Most employed women say they would not leave their paid employment even if they did not need the money.

Kathleen Gerson (1987) decided to investigate the question of how women choose to enter the paid labor force. She asked sixty women how they chose between work and family and found that their choice was largely the result of two influences: (1) early childhood experiences, and (2) constraints and opportunities they encountered as adults.

Twenty percent followed a traditional model in which they were prepared emotionally and practically as girls to be housewives and remained committed to that choice. Thirty percent were also socialized as children to become housewives and mothers, but as adults experienced rising aspirations to enter the labor force and increasing ambivalence about motherhood. Another 20 percent had hoped even as children to enter the paid labor force, and they retained that desire into adulthood. The last 30 percent had grown up wanting to have careers but experienced falling employment aspirations when they became adults.

Four factors tended to push women into the domestic path. First, women were influenced by their experiences within their families. A stable relationship with a male partner reinforced the idea among the women that marriage provided a safe, secure place that allowed wives to stay home. A stable marriage also frequently resulted in family decisions that prioritized the husband's career, thereby diminishing the wife's opportunities in the paid labor force.

A second factor that pushed women toward a domestic choice was their experience in the workplace. Upward mobility at work and a rewarding job tended to diminish the likelihood of their quitting work.

Third was the ability of the husband to provide an adequate income. Low wages for husbands caused an economic squeeze in the family, which pushed wives into the paid labor force.

Fourth, women considered the social rewards and costs of domesticity. Those who had neighbors and friends who devalued being full-time housewives and mothers were more likely to choose to seek paid work outside the home.

Gerson's (1987) research illustrates the interaction of work and family. It shows how girls' family experiences combine with both their family and work experiences as they become women. The combination of factors throughout their lives creates pushes and pulls into and out of the paid labor force. The tensions between work and family as well as within them provide the impetus for the decision whether to enter the paid labor force.

Chicanas and a Fifth Way of Choosing to Work for Wages

Patricia Zavella (1987) interviewed Chicanas who worked in canneries in California about the tensions between work and family in their lives and how they made the decision to get a job. The women she interviewed had been encouraged and socialized as girls to become full-time housewives and mothers. A typical pattern was to work outside the home in the early days of their marriage and quit when their first child was born. Then when it became clear that their husbands' paycheck could not adequately support the household, the women returned to work in the cannery. Choosing to work in the cannery, however, was not perceived as an alternative to their responsibilities as wives and mothers but as an extension of that role.

Gerson (1987) presents the two roles, employee and wife/mother, as two opposing possibilities. The women in Zavella's (1987) research saw them as contiguous. Gerson describes the women she interviewed as having been socialized as children to be either domestic or career-oriented. She describes their experience as adults as pushing them into or away from the domestic choice, and she develops a four-part model to summarize the possible factors.

The cannery workers fit into a fifth category in which the women seek outside employment, not because they wish to move away from their domestic role, but because they wish to be better wives and mothers. The Chicanas argue that they chose to go to work because of their obligation to their families. When Zavella asked one woman why she had sought work in the cannery, for example, she said, "I did it for my family. We needed the money, why else?" (1987, p. 88). Another woman who was asked this question responded by motioning to her child, who was carrying a large doll, and said, "That's why I work, for my daughter, so I can give her those things" (p. 134).

BOX **6.1**

Third-Wave Feminism

The term *Third-Wave feminism,* as I described in Chapter 3, refers to recent work in feminist theory that focuses on differences among women. Much of the most significant work in Third-Wave feminism is done by racial ethnic scholars (Collins 1998; Lengermann and Niebrugge-Brantley 1992).

This discussion of the contrast between the work of Gerson and Zavella shows the way in which theories based on the experience of one group of women may not sufficiently capture the experience of another group. Zavella, who is a Third-Wave feminist, offers insights from her research on Chicanas that make two contributions. First, her work reminds us once more that "Woman" is not a monolith. All women are not the same, and race ethnicity makes a significant difference in our lives. Second, Zavella's work enriches the work of scholars like Gerson because it broadens the analysis, making it not just more inclusive but also a more powerful theory.

The women in both Gerson's and Zavella's research were moved to take jobs outside the home if their husbands' wages were inadequate. The difference between the two groups was in their perception of this choice. The women in Gerson's research chose to work for wages as an alternative to staying home. Gerson describes their decision as choosing between two separate options. The women in Zavella's interviews, in contrast, insist that work and family are not two alternatives, but that working for wages is a way of fulfilling their role in family (Segura 1999).

Why Do Men Work?

Just as women have been increasing their participation in the paid labor force in recent years, men have also been experiencing changes: changes in their work experience; changes in their family roles; and changes in their gender identity (Coltrane 1996; Levine and Pettinsky 1997). As women become breadwinners, the idea that breadwinning and masculinity are closely bound has been undone. But if men cannot claim a distinctive identity as the sole or primary economic resource for their families, what is a man? Gerson (1993) interviewed men from many walks of life to see how they were negotiating this new terrain of work, family, and gender—what she calls "no man's land." She found that men traveled many different paths, but they could be grouped into three general categories. The first of these identified men who maintained their breadwinning role, sometimes with wives who stayed home and sometimes with wives who were in the labor market. Gerson says that these men reflect a "stalled revolution." They take their responsibility to provide an income for their family very seriously, and they also expect to have their economic contribution translated into authority in their homes. One man interviewed said

> There has to be a leader. And the responsibility of the leader is to be fair, not just to boss people, but to make decisions, right or wrong. I provide the money, so it's a success. There has to be a system, and that's ours. My wife loves her lifestyle; she's got it made. She drives a new car, has great clothes, her friends, no responsibilities. What the hell does she need a job for? She's got her freedom. What more could you want? (p. 86)

A second group of men took another path, choosing autonomy over parenthood. Some of these men, "the rebels," did not have children. Others, "the estranged dads," had children but had grown apart from them. One man who fit into this category explained:

> Nobody has a hold on me. I do as I wish, and if tomorrow I don't want to, I don't have to. It's very important that I never feel trapped, locked in. It leads me away from feeling angry, mad, hostile, all those sort of things. (Gerson 1993, p. 109)

The third category of men, "the involved father," works to become more integrated into the work of family life, especially the work of raising children. One man reported

> I thought I was going to be a wild and crazy guy for the rest of my life. I never thought about getting married. But the real me is what's been happening from being married on, not beforehand. Being responsible, getting married, having a child, bringing up a family, becoming responsible for our daughter. This is the real me. (Gerson 1993, p. 142)

All three of these paths are difficult. Men are faced with the dilemma of either protecting privileges of not having to come home to do housework or child care, or accepting arrangements that ease their economic burden or emotional isolation (Gerson 1993). Men who choose the breadwinner or autonomy route resist family involvement and domestic participation in order to protect their benefits. But they also face problems of having to work long hours in the paid labor force in order to single-handedly support their families, dealing with wives who may not approve of their choices, or being cut off from close relationships.

Involved fathers face difficulties, too. First, they face the dilemma of both spending time making money and spending time with their children. Second, if they want to develop in their careers, they may be asked to travel or to take classes after work, resulting in additional time crunches. Third, even if they are able to balance work and family, they still face the problem of trade-offs of freedom or commitment and their ability to find time for their personal interests in leisure activities, community involvement, or just sleeping late once in a while (Gerson 1993).

While Gerson found that few men had fully accepted complete equality with their wives, many men were moving in this direction. A recent study found that 82 percent of men ages twenty to thirty-nine said they put family time at the top of their list of priorities, ahead of money, power, or prestige (Raman 2000).

Why are these changes in men's lives occurring now, and why are there three different paths? Gerson argues that the diversity of responses—the three paths—she discovered in her research is a result of the diversity of exposure individual men have to the massive structural changes in our society that underlie the challenges men face in work, family, and gender. The first of these important structural changes is a decline in economic opportunities for men. Men can maintain the breadwinner role only if they are able to earn enough money to take care of their families. As we saw in Chapter 4, incomes have stagnated for most Americans.

A second factor is women's participation in the paid labor force. Women of every marital and parental status are taking paid jobs and establishing themselves permanently in the paid labor force, and wives' incomes contribute an increasing proportion of the total household income.

The third change underlying the shake-up in the breadwinner role for men is the expansion of alternatives to permanent marriage. As we explore more in Chapters 9 and 10, legal marriage has become one of a number of alternatives. Over the course of their lives, many adults move in and out of different arrangements through marriage, divorce, remarriage, and cohabitation.

Fourth, Gerson cites a growing separation between marriage and parenthood. Demographers estimate that about half of American children will spend at least part of their childhood in a single-parent family and many more will grow up in households with stepparents. Since many of these children will remain with their biological mothers, biological fathers will have to be creative and active if they wish to sustain their relationships with their children (Levine and Pittinsky 1997).

How Does Work Influence Families?

The relationship between work and families can be looked at in three ways: as separate spheres, as spillover from work to family, and as interactive (Chow and Berheide 1988). We have already discussed the separate spheres model and its shortcomings. The second model is one in which the connections between work and family are noted but in which attention is paid almost exclusively to the way in which work spills over into families. Within this spillover model, work is seen as more fundamental and causal, and families are seen as secondary results of work organization and experience. The third model is an interactive one in which the mutual dependence of families is emphasized. The interactive model is the one that organizes this chapter. Here we will review the way in which jobs shape and influence families and then move to issues associated with the way in which families shape the occupational experiences of workers and sometimes the organization of the workplace.

Rosabeth Moss Kanter (1977a) was one of the first scholars to examine the effect of work on family. She cites five ways in which the organization of paid work affects families:

1. Absorptiveness of an occupation—the extent to which a job draws in an employee and his or her family members.
2. Time and timing—the amount of time a job requires and when the time is demanded.
3. Income (or lack of income, e.g., if a breadwinner becomes unemployed) provided by the job.
4. Worldview—the values and ideas promoted at work that influence the employee in his or her behavior at home.
5. Emotional climate—the social-psychological influences at work that affect employees and their relationships in families.

Absorption

Different occupations demand different amounts of commitment by workers. For example, a receptionist in a physician's office may commit only the time when she is on the job to her career. When she leaves the office for the weekend, she can stop thinking about her job and can stop identifying herself by her occupation. The physician in that office, in contrast, rarely leaves the role of her occupation. She is addressed as Doctor whether she is at work or not. She probably brings work home and may be on call most of the time. Her occupation is part of her identity.

The contrast in the absorption of the workers in these two jobs will influence their families. The receptionist's family can remain unconcerned with her job, and they will rarely be called on to participate in her work. The physician's family frequently will be identified as part of the profession. They may be asked to participate in community events as a way for the doctor to maintain a proper image, or they may be asked to assist the physician in building the practice by helping to decorate the office and advertise the business.

Time and Timing

Another way in which jobs differ in their effect on families is by the demand on time placed on the employee (Eckenrode and Gore 1990). Time can be divided into three categories: (1) the number of hours of work employees perform per day or week, (2) when the work is done during the day or week, and (3) long-term time commitments. If a profession demands long hours away from family members, less time is available for participation in family activities. For example, a nurse who frequently works double shifts at the hospital will have little time for doing anything other than sleeping when she gets off work. A teacher, in contrast, may have more time to spend with his family in the afternoons and in the summer.

The amount of time is only one facet of the issue of time. Equally important is what time of the day work is scheduled. Families must organize their activities around the work schedules of employed family members. In addition, certain work schedules do not mesh with "normal" scheduling, interfering with participation in particular kinds of activities. For example, a waiter who works the weekend night shift will rarely have time to spend with his wife and friends if that is the time slot they use for their social activities (Lein et al. 1974).

We may have little choice but to work hours that are staggered and out of sync with our families. Our economy increasingly runs twenty-four hours a day seven days a week (Presser 1998). Blue-collar workers have worked three shifts for many decades, but service, retail, and professional workers are joining them in growing numbers. These changes and the fact they are trends that appear to be continuing to develop will undoubtedly have important implications for families (Epstein and Kallenberg 2004).

The third way in which time at work can affect family life is in the long-term demands of a job. For example, some jobs may demand large amounts of time for relatively short periods. The manager of a grocery store might find that he must work long hours training new personnel when the store first opens. After a few months, when the staff is in place, he is able to cut back his hours. A college professor, however, may need to spend large amounts of time on research and publishing for several years in order to receive tenure (Steiner 1972). Both would find that they had removed themselves from family activities and had caused other family members to readjust to the time required of the job. The professor might even find that the new patterns had become too entrenched for her to reintegrate herself after she is granted tenure.

B O X 6.2

The Time Bind

Employees today on average spend 44 hours a week at work—an increase of 3.5 hours since 1977. In addition, 68 percent of workers today say they must work very fast, and 88 percent say they must work very hard (Bond and Galinsky 1998). Pressures from work increasingly spill over into families. Paid work is staging a quiet takeover of life at home (Snell 1997). Trying to keep up with piled-up laundry and dirty dishes and finding quality time to spend with children make family seem like more and more work—work that cannot be done in the time left over after paid work. Some people have responded to this time bind by "escaping" to their offices (Hochschild 1997).

Arlie Hochschild (1997) followed people around, interviewing them about work and family and watching them on the job, in their homes, and running errands. Even when companies offer family friendly supports like flextime and family leave, employees often opt to spend more time at work. Although company policy officially has placed these options on the books, the culture of the office says that long hours and working hard are good and "making excuses" to spend time with family isn't good enough. Workers feel that they cannot cut back on work time without going out on a limb.

Hochshild says that, furthermore, along with feeling the pressures of workplace culture, employees also like to put in hours at work because it is enjoyable and because it takes them away from family problems largely caused by the time bind. Christopher Lasch (1977) called families "havens in a heartless world." Hochschild's interviews suggest that pressures from the heartless world have encroached so far into our families that the heartless world sometimes looks like a better place to be. She found that people spend long hours at work because they need the money and because of economic insecurity and the fear of being downsized. They also work long hours, however, because they like work and find it rewarding, sometimes more rewarding than their families. Workplaces emphasize teamwork, and colleagues and supervisors recognize and honor successful efforts. Family activities have few extrinsic rewards—plaques are not given for the most hours put in on the vacuum cleaner or even the most time spent reading books to your children. Addressing problems in families can also be lonely work, while at the office if you get into trouble there is usually someone there to help you out (Snell 1997). In many homes, family life has become "a frantic exercise in beat the clock, while work, by comparison, seems a haven of grown-up sociability, competence and relative freedom" (L. Shapiro 1997, p. 64).

Companies have speeded up their demands on employees, but they have also created an environment that offers community, friendship among coworkers, and recognition. Hochschild says the marketplace has won by creating a place for human interaction. But it has also sucked up all of the time for human interaction. We are not developing a society in which people can find emotional connection, fun, and especially time to enjoy these in a variety of settings—at home, in our neighborhoods, in community organizations, and among friends and family. Instead, we are developing a society in which the workplace is the only place where people can feel even a little bit human, while other social spaces wither away.

How can we solve the time bind? Hochschild (1998) identifies three possible solutions: cool modern, traditional, and warm modern. The cool modern solution is to continue to rationalize family work. Authors like Marjorie Schaevitz (1984) tell us that we should not try to change men, our culture, or the workplace. Instead, women should become more efficient at rationing out "quality time" with their children. Hochschild's (1997) work seems to show that families have been trying this for more than a decade since Schaevitz made her suggestions, and the problem is getting worse, not better.

(continued)

B O X **6.2** *(continued)*

The second solution is the traditional solution. Women should stay home with their families or at least enter the "mommy track" at work (see Box 6.3). Family and work should remain separate, and women should stand guard at the home. The problem with this is that married and single women have entered the labor force because they need the money. Also, how would single parents implement this solution?

Hochschild advocates the third solution, warm modern. She says we need fundamental social change: men and women who are willing to share parenting and housework; communities that value work in the home as highly as work on the job; and policy makers who demand family friendly reforms.

A Special Case of Timing: Working Parents and Their Children.   Can employed women be good mothers? Research that has examined the children of employed mothers shows mixed results. Some studies show positive effects, some negative, and some have shown no differences at all in children of employed mothers and those whose mothers are not in the paid labor force (Hoffman 1984; Mischel and Fuhr, 1988; Orenstein 2001; Ramey, Bryant and Suarez 1985). Elizabeth Harvey (1999) argues that this is because the studies are so variable in the ways they measured changes and differences and the size and kind of sample they chose. She tried to address some of the methodological problems in former studies and used a very large data set, the National Longitudinal Survey of Youth (NLSY). The NLSY is a survey of approximately 12,600 individuals who have been interviewed annually since 1979 when they were between fourteen and twenty-two years of age. Beginning in 1986, the children of women in the group were also assessed.

Harvey's research examined four employment variables: Whether the mother worked during the first three years of the child's life, how soon a mother returned to work after childbirth, how much she worked (hours per week) during the first three years of her child's life, and the discontinuity of employment (if there were any periods of unemployment during the same time frame). She compared these variables with five child outcome measures: compliance/temperment, behavior problems, cognitive development, self-esteem, and academic achievement.

The study found that children whose mothers worked during the first three years of their lives were not significantly different from children whose mothers did not work during that time frame. Only one difference showed up. Children whose mothers worked long hours had slightly lower scores on tests, which measured children's vocabulary and individual student achievement, but these differences were small and faded over time. Fathers' employment status and working hours also had no significant effects on children's development.

Two important factors that Harvey did not include in her study are the effect of different kinds of day care on the children whose parents work. Another is the mother's satisfaction with her role. Earlier research by Farel (1980) looked at mother's job satisfaction.

Farel (1980) compared children whose mothers stayed home and children whose mothers were employed. He subdivided these groups according to those who were pleased with their role and those who were not. He found that children of mothers who stayed at home and who believed that working outside the home would be detrimental for their children scored highest on several measures of social and cognitive development. Children of mothers who stayed at home but wished they had a paid job, however, scored lowest.

Teenage Workers and Their Families.   Almost all young people in the United States work sometime during their high school years (Mortimer and Finch 1996; U.S. Census Bureau 2004d). A national study found that 61 percent of tenth graders said they had worked during the previous year, and 90 percent of eleventh and twelfth graders said they had (Manning 1990). Similar numbers of boys (75 percent) and girls (73 percent) worked, but boys (47 percent) compared with girls (38 percent) were more likely to work more than twenty hours per week. How might this participation in the paid labor force affect family relationships of working teens?

The discussion above about men and women suggests that when workers spend time on the job, it may weaken their family ties. Research that has been done on teenage girls who work supports this argument. Girls who work report a decrease in feelings of closeness to their parents (Steinberg et al., 1982).

The experience for boys, however, is different. Boys who work report increased feelings of closeness to their parents (Steinberg et al. 1982). Greenberger (1987) explains this difference by calling our attention to differences in the relationships between daughters and their parents and sons and their parents. Girls generally report much greater closeness and self-disclosure to parents (especially mothers) than same-age boys (Douvan and Adelson 1966; Kandel and Lesser 1972).

Greenberger argues that work helps both girls and boys grow up and begin to take on adult roles, but because they begin with different kinds of relationships with their parents, their maturation is expressed in different ways. For girls, working increases their feelings of autonomy and self-reliance and lessens their dependence on their parents. Work helps them move away from their parents. For boys the opposite occurs. Their experience at work increases their identification with their parents, who are also workers, and brings them closer, especially to their fathers.

This research shows that work has an important effect on an individual's experience in a family. But work does not occur in isolation from other factors. Here the equally salient factor of gender combines with work to affect boys and girls in different ways.

Retirement.   Much of the discussion of work and families focuses on the period in family histories in which parents are raising young children. As we noted in Chapter 1, however, the U.S. population has a growing number of older people. We might expect, therefore, that many more of us will have to pay attention to the transition from work to retirement and its effect on families.

Many people believe that retirement is a stressful life transition and that it has a negative effect on married couples who make this passage together. In the 1960s and 1970s, research found that retirement had a negative effect on marriages (Fengler 1975; Heyman and Jeffers 1968). Women who were housewives resented having their husbands around invading their turf, and husbands who had been breadwinners felt they had lost their primary identity (Lipman 1961).

More recent research, however, has found that retirement is experienced as a relatively mild change and often has a positive effect (Atchley 1992). Robert Atchley, for example, found that 87 percent of people in his study of retired couples said that retirement had no effect on the quality of their relationship with their spouse. Most of those who said there had been a change described it as positive. One man (age sixty-three) explained, "I did not believe it was possible, but retirement has enhanced our marriage. We spend much more time together, have more time to share, more time to do for each other" (1992, p. 147). Only a few people said it had created difficulties, such as the one this woman (age sixty-six) relates, "I found it to be more confusing, being with my husband twenty-four hours a day and giving up much of my privacy and quiet times. There are more meals to cook and more housework."

Income

The third way work may affect families is through the amount of money brought into the family by the employment. This economic issue was addressed in Chapter 4, where we discussed the current economic crisis and its effects on families.

Wages can also have an effect on the internal dynamics of families, either disrupting or creating and reinforcing gender inequality. Women still tend to earn less than their husbands do. On the average, wives earn about 33 percent of the total family income (Mishel, Bernstein, and Allegretto 2005). Although this amount is significant and indispensable, it is still less than their husbands' income. In only about one-quarter of marriages do wives earn more than their husbands (U.S. Census Bureau 2004e). For most couples, the inequity in wages reinforces gender inequality both inside and outside the family. Women who earn less than their husbands are more economically dependent on their husbands than women who earn more. When a husband makes more money than his wife, the family must treat the husband's job as more important because it contributes more to the total income (Coltrane 1996; Gerstel and Gross 1987). Unequal wages between women and men can inhibit women's ability to attain equality within their families:

Marital power is higher for women who work full time than those who work part time or not at all, and it is greatest among women with the most prestigious occupations, women who are most committed to their work, and those whose salaries exceed their husbands'. Working women have more say especially in financial decisions. This tendency for employment to enhance women's power is strongest among lower income and working class couples (Moore and Sawhill 1984, p. 158).

In Phillip Blumstein and Pepper Schwartz's (1990a) interviews, one wife, Leanna, explained this connection succinctly. Leanna, who works in a delicatessen, earns less than her husband Gordon, who is a police officer. She says

Gordon still has the last word on everything. We get annoyed with each other over that, but when I start to push back, he reminds me just who supports me and the children. He gives me the final line which is something like, "If you're so smart, why don't you earn more money?" or how dumb I am 'cause if I had to go out and support myself I'd be a big fizzle. (p. 125)

Earning any wages, however, helps to move wives in the direction of greater equality. Although Leanna is unable to get as much acknowledgment of her contribution as she would like, research indicates that her situation would probably be worse if she were a full-time housewife. Women who earn wages exercise greater power in their families than women who are not employed (Baca Zinn 1980; Blumstein and Schwartz 1990a; Ybarra 1977, 1982a, 1982b).

Exchange Theory.   In order to understand the process by which having both husband and wife in the paid labor force enhances gender equality, scholars have used a theoretical framework called exchange theory. George Homans (1958) was the major figure in the early development of this theory in the 1950s (Ritzer 1992).

Exchange theorists argue that people enter into social relationships in which they exchange rewards with each other. This theory assumes that people need rewards and endeavor to enhance their self-interest. When two individuals interact, they attempt to negotiate an exchange of rewards, each trying to gain as much for himself or herself as possible through the exchange.

For example, in the case of a husband and wife, both seek from each other such rewards as status, love, control over family finances, and decision-making power. When the woman is employed, she brings to the negotiating table more chips with which to bargain because she can contribute more to the total resources available within the family. Table 4.5 in Chapter 4 shows that since the early 1970s, an increasing proportion of family income comes from wives' wages. In the early 1990s, about one-third of working wives were contributing half or more of the total family income (Hayghe 1993; Mishel, Bernstein, and Schmitt 2001; Bureau of Labor Statistics 2005d). We would expect, therefore, that wives' power is increasing in a growing number of families.

Wives or husbands who are not in the paid labor force are not entirely without power. But money is a particularly useful reward because it can be exchanged for many other rewards. Some exchange theorists (Bushnell and Burgess 1969) have argued further that money is an especially good asset to bring to an exchange because it is nearly impossible to satiate the desire for money.

Robert Blood and Donald Wolfe (1960) are important early figures in the study of power in marriage. They rely on exchange theory in their description of marital power. They write

> The sources of power in so intimate a relationship as marriage must be sought in the comparative resources which the husband and wife bring to the marriage rather than in brute force. A resource may be defined as anything that one partner may make available to the other, helping the latter satisfy his needs or attain his goals. The partner who may provide or withhold resources is in a strategic position. Hence power accrues spontaneously to the partner who has the greater resources at his or her disposal. (p. 12)

A Feminist Critique of Exchange Theory.   Some feminist scholars (England 1989; England and Kilbourne 1990; Ferber and Nelson 1993; Glenn 1987; Hartsock 1983; Risman and Ferree 1995) have been critical of exchange theory like that expressed by Blood and Wolfe (1960) because exchange theorists often assume that women and men are the same; they ignore gender. Critics of exchange theory argue that husbands and wives come to the bargaining table not just as two individuals but as gendered people. The wife has learned to act in certain "feminine" ways and is expected by her husband, herself, and almost everyone else to behave in those ways. Likewise, the husband is expected to be "masculine" (E. Rosen 1987).

The negotiating options available to the two are, therefore, different and are restricted by their gender. Paula England (1989) believes that one especially important gender difference is that, in our society and much of the Western world, to be masculine is to be independent and selfish, "a separative self." To be feminine is to be concerned for others, "an emotionally connected self" (England 1989, p. 15).

As support for this distinction, England cites the work of Carol Gilligan (1982). In examining the moral reasoning of women and men, Gilligan found that when women decide what is moral they base their beliefs on an ethic of caring and responsibility, which flows from their feeling of connection between themselves and others. Men, in contrast, base their moral decisions on "an ethic of principled noncoercion, which presumes and seeks to honor the other's separateness" (England 1989, p. 16).

Exchange theory assumes that all individuals operate from their own self-interest. Gilligan's work suggests that while this may be true for many men, it is less likely to be true for women. Furthermore, women who behave in this way are stepping out of the expectations for a properly feminine person. For example, imagine a husband and wife who are trying to decide how to spend their income tax refund. His salary is larger than hers, and he wins the argument by claiming he should, therefore, decide how the money is spent. Although she has lost the argument, they both have played their gender roles appropriately. He is masculine because he makes more money, and his selfish, independent reasoning has won the argument. She is feminine because she makes less money, and she has given in to him and also has been able to do something to make him happy.

But what if she has a larger salary and therefore wins the argument about how to spend the money? She has won the argument, but neither spouse has behaved in an "appropriate" manner. He not only lost the argument (which is unmasculine in itself) but has been openly exposed as earning less money. She has won the argument by behaving in a selfish, adversarial, "unfeminine" manner.

These imbalances mean that although exchanges may take place between husbands and wives, they are not exchanges between equals. Furthermore, given our culture's definitions of femininity and masculinity, the goal of serving one's self-interest fits men more comfortably than it does women (Hochschild 1989).

Blumstein and Schwartz (1983) conducted a study that illustrates the importance of gender in exchanges among intimate couples. They interviewed four types of cohabiting couples: married couples, unmarried heterosexuals, gay men, and lesbians. In their research they found that differences in earning caused the largest power differences in couples of gay men. Heterosexuals, married or not, fell in the middle, and power differences among lesbians were not related to their earnings at all.

England (1989) says that this shows that money and power are linked when the negotiating team includes men and that the links are strongest when the exchange is between two men. Exchange theory is valid for explaining men's behavior because the social construction of masculinity idealizes men who behave as separate selves seeking individual rewards. But for explaining relationships between two women, exchange theory has little validity. And in mixed couples its validity is diminished because women make up half of these couples and they are likely to behave in an emotionally connected way.

Worldview

According to Kanter (1977a), the fourth way in which work affects family is by bringing a worldview from the workplace to the family. Worldview is an aspect of culture. *Culture* can be defined as the values a given group holds, the norms they follow, and the material goods they create (Giddens 1991). Culture is usually associated with nations and societies, but occupations can also be said to have distinct cultures (Hughes 1958).

Occupations can create ways in which to think about the world, including oneself. They can create rules about appropriate behavior on the job and off, and they can create material goods to represent these ideas.

People who are socialized into an occupational culture may bring their beliefs and ways of doing things into their families. One way to distinguish among occupations is to divide them into two types: entrepreneurial and bureaucratic. These two occupational culture types might have very different ways of raising children (Kanter 1977a).

An entrepreneurial father who is a car salesman works in a job that demands independence from and competition with his coworkers. As a parent he would be more likely to encourage his children to develop strong self-control, independence, and an active, manipulative approach to the world. A bureaucratic mother who works in a welfare office must interact with her coworkers in a cooperative manner in order to provide all the necessary services to her clients. She would encourage her children to be accommodating and to seek direction from others. In these two examples, the context of the parents' work causes the employee to value certain attitudes and to develop certain ways of behaving. He or she then brings home these ideas to the family and uses them in raising the children.

Emotional Climate

Emotional climate is the fifth way work affects families (Kanter 1977a). Job satisfaction, tensions, and pressures at work are three areas of emotional climate that can affect an employee and his or her family (Eckenrode and Gore 1990). If a job is stressful and unsatisfying, an employee may use his or her family to compensate for the emotional rewards that do not come at work. Or employees may displace anger and frustration at home (Blau and Duncan 1967; Hoffman and Manis 1979; McKinlay 1964). Families of police officers (Norlicht 1979) and military personnel (Myers 1979) have been studied in this regard and provide evidence that these highly stressful occupations may be related to high incidences of wife and child abuse.

Emotional demands at work may also affect workers' interactions with family. Kanter (1977b) argues that people in high-interaction occupations may develop interaction fatigue and withdraw at home. The corporate wives she interviewed told her that they noticed when their husbands were training others and needed to be highly involved with the trainees, the husbands were distant and insensitive when they came home, as though they had been burned out at work.

David Halle (1984) argues that tensions in blue-collar jobs may create socializing patterns that compete with the time men have to spend with their families. He interviewed working-class men and found that friendships at work were essential to making their boring and stressful jobs tolerable. This camaraderie frequently spilled over after work and competed with wives' claims to their husbands' time. About half the men he interviewed went straight home from work, but the other half spent a good amount of time with their male friends after work. One might assume that when emotional needs are created by job pressures, people bring those needs home to be met by their families. Halle's interviews show how work can create emotional needs that can sometimes be met by social relationships on the job. But in solving that problem, husbands may create another set of problems because their friendships with work buddies pull them away from their wives, illustrating another way in which the conditions of work touch employees' interactions with their families.

The Influence of Families on Work

So far we have focused on the ways in which work affects families. But the relationship between work and families is not indirectional; families also influence work. First, families place workers into the labor force by making demands on family members for economic support (Duncan, Featherman, and Duncan 1972). For example, not surprisingly, wives whose husbands have below-average incomes have the highest rates of labor force participation (Ryscavage 1979).

Families also socialize new workers for the labor force, teaching them values and attitudes about the meaning of work and appropriate behavior on the job. For example, families teach their children communication skills and how to take advantage of educational opportunities that will allow them to obtain training for certain types of work (D. Smith 1987). The work that parents do to shape their children into acceptable members of society is further discussed in Chapter 12 on parenting and Chapter 13 on children.

Families also introduce workers to specific information about job choices (Mortimer and Kumka 1982; Spenner 1981). Fathers are especially influential in their sons' vocational choices, particularly when the father is in a prestigious occupation himself and has a close relationship with his son (Hetherington 1979; Hoffman 1961).

Bringing the Family to Work

In assessing the effect of work on family, I described the way in which work culture can be brought home to influence family life. This effect can also operate in reverse: the culture of family can be brought to work by employees. The activities and values that people express at home can be carried over to their work and become important influences in the relationships among workers and between workers and their bosses.

For example, the struggle over the conditions of work has been central to the history of industrialization, and it continues to take place. When women workers engage in conflicts with management, they sometimes bring with them to the workplace certain skills, values, and social connections that are related to their roles as wives and mothers.

Chicanas bring their family culture to work with them when they celebrate important family transitions like weddings and births with their coworkers and create familial relationships by sharing information and supporting one another on the job. In addition to making the work environment more tolerable, this kind of familial activity can also create networks and opportunities for political activity, such as union organizing.

Two "feminine" strategies that Louise Lamphere (1985) and Patricia Zavella (1987) discovered in their interviews and observations of women workers are "1) the organization of informal activities often focusing on the female life cycles such as birthday celebrations, baby and wedding showers, potlucks and retirement parties; and 2) the use of workers' common identities as women, wives and mothers in interworker communication" (Lamphere 1985, pp. 520–21). These activities, which are closely associated with women's role in families and might be described as bringing the family to work, provide a humanization of the workplace and a vehicle of support for coping with inhumane working conditions (Zavella 1987).

In addition, these activities can sometimes create or enhance a culture of resistance on the shop floor. The activities and associations create friendships, trust, and a shared understanding that can then become the basis for collective action (Benson 1978; Costello 1985; Sacks 1984; Zavella 1987).

The women come to know each other well. They keep track of who is getting married, whose daughter is having a baby, and whose husband has died. They develop ways in which to communicate across lines of race ethnicity, age, and job category. Women workers who socially interact with one another on the job can easily move from talking about family affairs to sharing ideas about the conditions of work, interpretations of events that differ from management's, and the possibility for change.

Zavella (1987) observed indirect examples of resistance. She noted the way in which the networks based on "feminine" activities served as vehicles of information distribution about how to get around rules and how to bypass steps in production. Other researchers, especially those who have focused on Chicanas (Coyle, Hershatter, and Honig 1980; Ruiz 1990), have found that the familial culture the women create at work has directly supported militant actions at work. For example, Lamphere (1985) found that those connections allowed or at least enhanced the ability of women in the apparel plant she studied to stage a successful wildcat strike.

Managing the Contradiction

In Chapter 1, I suggested that people are not just passive products of their environments. C. Wright Mills (1959) argued that social context is a human creation; people build and rebuild the societies in which they live. This theme has been illustrated in other chapters in the discussions of social movements that have formed with the intention of changing public practice in order to solve personal problems.

Sometimes instead of trying to change the social structure, people who are faced with difficult or impossible tasks create ways in which to cope with the social structure, as we saw in Chapter 4 in the discussion of families coping with unemployment. In the case of the conflict between work and family, women physicians are an example of a group that has managed to solve or at least ameliorate the contradiction between work and family by specializing in areas where there is less conflict.

Unprecedented numbers of women have entered the medical profession since 1970 (Bourne and Wikler 1982). Only 5.5 percent of physicians were women in 1960. Today about one third of physicians are women (National Committee on Bay Equity 2006; U.S. Census Bureau 1994b). The profession of physician has long been identified as a particularly masculine occupation (Hughes 1945). The women who enter the field as students and then as professionals sometimes have found it difficult to negotiate the masculine character of the field.

Medicine is a "greedy" institution for both men and women, making enormous demands on their time and attention. It appears, however, that women find it particularly problematic (Lorber 1984). Linda Grant and her colleagues (1987) looked at the differences between women and men medical students as they progressed through their training.

When asked how much time they believed they would be spending on work and family, women predicted they would be spending more hours on family, and men predicted they would be spending more hours on their practice. As the years went by at medical school, both women and men increased the number of hours they believed they would spend on their practice and decreased the hours they would spend on their families. Grant and her colleagues (1987) conclude that the entrance of women into the medical profession has not changed the profession. Medical school training appears to be turning women into men and both women and men into physicians who are more focused on their practice and away from their families.

One of the characteristics of the medical profession that illustrates its "maleness" is that the "organization of work in medicine, the sequence of a medical career, and key professional norms are predicated on a conventional male role in the family and on the male biological clock" (Bourne and Wikler 1982, p. 113). The time period in which the physician is expected to be most intensely involved in training and building a career is the same time as the favored childbearing years for women (Hochschild 1971).

Women who enter the medical profession know they will have to play the roles of doctor, wife, mother, and social worker (to their professional husbands). They fear the logistical and personal difficulties that playing all of these roles may create (Bourne and Wikler 1982). The women medical students interviewed by Patricia Bourne and Norma Wikler, however, defined these difficulties as personal ones and put the burden on themselves to work it out. One student told them:

> When I was thinking of going into medicine, I told myself, "Well you're not going to have any children because you're not going to have any time. If you want to be a good mother, you're going to have to have all your time for the formative years." But now I feel differently. However, that hasn't changed my ideas about children, but I do feel it can be done. I think it requires more energy and a lot of planning and a lot of help from the outside. (p. 116)

Women physicians are encouraged to enter specific kinds of settings in which to practice their profession as a way of juggling work and family. One medical school dean suggested, "Let me give you an example—physicians in student health services in colleges and universities. It's an ideal situation for women physicians" (Bourne and Wikler 1982, p. 120).

In another interview, a male physician suggested that women work in a health maintenance organization:

> Medicine is a taxing field, around the clock. It's harder to accept the kinds of responsibilities that are necessary, if she has in mind having a family, if we were operating on the entrepreneurial model. Now there's a change toward shared responsibility. It's easier for women to fit in. At Kaiser, for instance, I know of two women who are splitting a position. (Bourne and Wikler 1982, p. 120)

Women physicians appear to be taking this advice, especially if they are mothers. The presence of children is the key factor in the reduced number of hours that women physicians practice (Grant, Sampson, and Lai Rong 1990). Women physicians tend to specialize in different areas, work fewer hours per week, and see fewer patients than men (Sidel 1990). "Women are far more likely to choose specialties with regular hours, such as dermatology or pathology. They are far less likely to choose surgery, which is often thought of as the most rigid and hierarchical of the medical specialties and which is known for its years of infamously arduous training" (Sidel 1990, p. 171).

Placement of women into positions that facilitate their ability to maintain their work in families by working in settings that are less difficult but also less prestigious and less lucrative has been dubbed the "mommy track" (Schwartz 1989) (see Box 6.3).

BOX 6.3

Is a "Mommy Track" the Solution to Juggling Work and Family?

Felice Schwartz (1989) proposes that corporations distinguish between women who are "career primary" and those who are "career and family." Women who are "career primary" are those who will not interrupt their careers for children and can, therefore, remain on the fast track with the men. Management should identify these women and then invest more in them, for example, by providing them with training and experience and by expecting more from them.

The women who are "career and family" are those who want to have time to raise children. They should be put on the Mommy Track. Mommy Track employees could then be allowed to stay in middle management and not be under pressure to excel and compete for promotions.

The Mommy Track may help women by allowing them time to be wives and mothers, but it diminishes them as professionals, reducing their pay and their prestige. For example, in the profession of medicine we have observed that women physicians often have different career patterns, at least in part because of their desire to marry and raise children. Women physicians also earn less. In 2004, for example, women physicians earned 52 percent of what men physicians did on the average (U.S. Bureau of Labor Statistics 2005e).

Second, women may be pushed into the track, not because of their own desires but because of the expectations of others. In the quotes in the discussion of women physicians, we see this advice being given by a medical school dean and a colleague.

Third, the Mommy Track can legitimate discrimination against women. For example, if you were an employer and had to choose whether to hire a woman on the Mommy Track or a man, whom would you choose?

(continued)

B O X **6.3** (continued)

Fourth, Glass (1992) notes that higher-level jobs, compared with middle- and especially lower-level jobs, actually give workers more flexibility and authority to create solutions to problems that stem from job–family conflicts. For example, compared with an hourly employee, a higher-level salaried employee has more control over when she comes to or leaves work. Because the salaried higher-level employee is paid for accomplishing tasks rather than putting in a certain number of hours, she could, for example, drive her child to school in the morning even if it meant being a few minutes late. An hourly employee would not have this option or at least would be docked pay for her tardiness.

And finally, the premise of Schwartz's argument for the Mommy Track is based on the assumption that employing women in management is more costly than employing men. There are no published data on this question (Ehrenreich and English 1989).

Can Families Put Pressure for Change on Employers?

The difficulty of negotiating work and family for some women, like those in medicine described earlier, can cause women to develop coping mechanisms. These difficulties can also encourage employees to make demands for changes in institutions like workplaces and in government policy to allow them to both work and enjoy a family life (Gerson 1998; Hyde and Essex 1991; Zigler and Frank 1988).

Flextime

These demands fall into two categories: alter the organization of work and provide help with family demands, especially child care. One type of alteration in the organization of work that has recently gained attention is flextime (Glass and Estes, 1997). Flextime refers to flexible work schedules (Rothman and Marks 1989). An innovation that began in the 1970s, flextime allows workers to vary their arrival and departure times each day and the total number of hours worked per week. One variation, the compressed work week, allows employees to complete a full-time work schedule in three workdays. Another version of flextime allows workers to work from their homes through computer networks. Although flextime would seem to address some of the conflicts of work and family, it often is not an ideal solution (Negrey 1990; Raabe 1998; Wharton 1994). First, flextime is flexible for employers as well as employees. Workers may be asked to work a different schedule every week, which interferes with their ability to plan other activities.

Second, flextime can mean that the number of hours is flexible as well as the schedule (Glueck 1979; Swart 1979). If workers on flextime wish to work as many hours as possible, they must always be on call in case their employer needs someone to work extra hours. Even when they have time away from the workplace, they are really never off the job since they must constantly be awaiting schedule changes. Others with flexible hours may find themselves working many more hours than they like (Wharton 1994).

Carol Wharton (1994) interviewed women real estate agents about this issue. Many of the agents had chosen the field because of the flexible work schedule. They believed that

---

BOX **6.4**

Where Are the Family Friendly Companies?

In addition to finding out information about what kinds of family friendly options are available to employees, researchers have also looked at what kinds of companies offer these programs. The type of industry is the most important factor. Companies that offer finance, insurance, and real estate services are most generous. Company size is also important. Larger companies are more likely to provide flexible work hours, longer maternity leave, some wage replacement for new mothers, paternity leaves, leaves for adoptive parents, and elder-care programs.

The third most frequent predictor of whether a company will provide employee supports is the proportion of top executive positions held by women. Thirty percent of the companies had no women in the top positions, but 70 percent had some women and 20 percent had half or more of their top positions filled by women. The more women in these top positions, the more likely the company provided work-life assistance:

> 82% of companies with half or more women executives provide flextime.
> 56% of companies with no women in top positions provide flextime.
> 19% of companies with half or more women executives provide on- or near-site day care.
> 3% of companies with no women in top positions provide on- or near-site day care.
> 60% of companies with half or more women executives provide dependent-care assistance plans.
> 37% of companies with no women in top positions provide dependent-care assistance.
> 33% of companies with half or more women executives provide elder-care referral plans.
> 14% of companies with no women in top positions provide elder-care referral.

---

setting their own schedules and appointments would allow them to integrate their family work with their paid work. They found, however, that the job was flexible but also demanding and required many hours of work. One woman explained that she liked being able to take time if her child needed to go to the doctor or to participate in school events but "some of it was a little disappointing, because you end up actually working more than 40 hours a week. You work a lot more evenings and you work three weekends a month minimum, if not four" (p. 196).

Third, if the number of hours is flexible, then pay also varies. Workers with varying number of hours may earn less than they need, first because they are working fewer total hours, but also because they earn less per hour. About 24 percent of all employees in the United States were part time in 2004 (U.S. Department of Labor 2004a). The wages of women in part-time and temporary jobs were 20 percent less than the wages of women in regular full-time positions. The wages of men in part-time and temporary jobs are 24 percent less than the wages of men in regular full-time positions (Mishel, Bernstein, and Schmitt 2001). In addition, workers who are part time usually do not receive the same benefits as those who work full time (Hartmann 1991; Bureau of Labor Statistics 2004b).

In a speech presented to Congress, Heidi Hartmann (1991), the director of the Institute for Women's Policy Research, outlined problems with flextime from the point of view of the employee. She concluded that in order to benefit employees, flextime needs to be accompanied by reliable and sufficient wages and benefits, and the decision to reduce hours needs to be made voluntarily by the employee (Negrey 1990). A large proportion of part-time workers are not in these positions because they have chosen to be. For example, in 1999, 57 percent of the employees in temporary-help agencies said they would prefer a standard (full-time, permanent) job (Mishel, Bernstein, and Schmitt 2001).

Family Leave

A second approach to alleviating tensions between work and family is to provide more support for employees, such as parental and family leave (Goodstein 1994). The Family and Medical Leave Bill, enacted in 1993, gives employees the right to take up to twelve weeks of unpaid leave from their jobs in a twelve-month period if they become seriously ill or if they wish to take care of a child, spouse, or parent who is ill. (See Box 6.5 for a description of the policy.) The bill also allows new parents to take time to care for newborns or to adopt a child. The bill is important because it means that people will not lose their jobs if they take time off to care for themselves or their family members (Kamerman 1991).

A Department of Labor study of the effect of the bill found that 58 percent of the leave-takers were women, and the largest age group was people between thirty-five and forty-nine years old (*World Almanac* 1997). The most common reason given for taking a leave was to address the employee's own serious health problem (59%), and the second most common reason was to take care of a sick family member (19%). Almost half (40%) of the leave-takers said that they had difficulty obtaining the leave.

Not everyone is covered by the law, however. While all government employees are covered, only about half (46.5 percent) of people who work for private businesses are. Box 6.5 explains which companies are not covered. In addition, employees sometimes hesitate to take leave because they do not know the laws and fear offending those who will evaluate them later in their careers (Ward and Wolf-Wendel 2004). But the biggest problem with the law is that the leave is unpaid (Bookman 1991). Of 168 nations, 163 have some kind of pregnancy leave. United States along with countries like Papau New Guinea and Swaziland are not among them. In contrast, European nations provide fourteen to twenty-six weeks of maternity leave paid at 100 percent (Mishel, Bernstein, and Allegretto 2005) In 2005, California decided to move ahead of the nation and become the first state to offer paid family leave (Quinn 2005).

BOX 6.5

Family and Medical Leave Act, 1993

What leave am I entitled to?
    Twelve weeks in a twelve-month period for
        Birth, adoption, or foster placement of a child
        Care of spouse, parent, or child with serious medical condition
        Care of your own serious medical condition

What workplaces are covered?
    Public-sector employer (local, state, federal, and school)
    Private-sector employer with more than fifty employees

What employees are eligible?

Worked for total of twelve months or more

Worked at least 1,250 hours in past twelve months

Workplace has fifty employees or more within 75 miles

Excludes key employees: salaried employees who are among the highest paid 10 percent of employees within seventy-five mile of the worksite can be denied leave by their employers even if they are otherwise eligible

Can I take the time in intermittent chunks or all at once?

You can take the time intermittently if you are sick or in order to care for an ill family member

If you take time for birth or adoption, it must be taken all at once unless your employer agrees to some other arrangement

What health conditions are serious enough for a leave?

Any period connected with an overnight stay in a hospital, hospice, or residential medical care facility

Any period that requires absence of more than three calendar days from work or school or other regular daily activities

Continuing treatment for a chronic disease that if untreated would likely result in incapacity for three or more calendar days

Prenatal care

What happens to my health insurance?

Employers are required to continue providing your health insurance under the same terms; you may need to pay your share of the premiums if they were being taken out of your paycheck

If you fail to return to work after your leave, some employers may make you repay the health insurance premiums they paid for during your leave

Will my job be there when I return?

You must be restored to your original job or its equivalent in pay, benefits, and other terms and conditions

What kind of notice must I give my employer?

Thirty-day advance notice if the need is foreseeable and notice is practical

Medical certification

Second or third medical opinions (at employers' expense) and periodic recertification

Source: Adapted from Levine and Pettinsky 1997. For more information, check the *Federal Register,* January 6, 1995.

The Micro–Macro Connection

In Chapter 1, I described the task of sociology as drawing connections between the individual microexperience and the broader macrolevel of social context. In this chapter we have been more specific, focusing our attention on the particular features of the social context—work and family. Furthermore, this chapter has emphasized the dialectical relationship between these two.

Dialectics is a philosophical term that describes the way in which various social phenomena interact with one another. In this chapter we have observed the dialectical relationship between work and family—work influencing and shaping families and families pushing back to affect and change work. This chapter has shown how features of the macrolevel can contradict one another. The macrolevel is not only multifaceted, the parts do not necessarily fit easily together. The relationship between work and family, furthermore, is only one level of interaction. A second dialectical relationship exists between individuals and their social context. Both of these large macrolevel social structures—work and family—affect individuals. Individuals are called on to figure out ways to blend the two in their own lives. This balancing act confronts most of us and insists that we create ways to accomplish it.

In the opening scenario, we observed two methods individuals might use to accommodate work and family. Cindy has decided to put marriage and children on the back burner while she emphasizes work in her life. Jordan believes that he, in partnership with his wife, will be able to combine both activities. The women physicians in the discussion of the Mommy Track provide a third alternative. They deemphasize their work in order to allow themselves an opportunity to marry and raise children.

The last two sections of the chapter suggest another approach. People working for policy reform like flextime and parental leave are demanding that employers change workplace organization to make it easier for employees to manage the balancing act. The deliberations of Congress on flextime and family leave reflect the frustration at the microlevel of society, where individuals feel they need structural change. And we see individuals organizing at the microlevel to restructure the macrosocial context by influencing the government.

7 Housework

Children contribute to their families by doing housework. The amount they do depends on their gender, age, race ethnicity, and whether they live in one- or two-parent households. (© Carrie Boretz/The Image Works)

Cassandra is a retired schoolteacher. Her severe arthritis has made it difficult for her to take care of herself, so she lives with her daughter, Delena. Delena has been married to Cedric for eight years, and they have three school-age children. Cedric works at the auto plant. When their youngest started first grade, Delena went back to work as a nurse at the local hospital. Like most people in the United States, they cannot get by without two paychecks.

Cassandra noticed that, at first, Cedric and the children pitched in to do the housework while Delena was at work. But they weren't very skilled. Bologna sandwiches and canned spaghetti seemed to be the most frequent dinner menu, and clean laundry took on shades of pinks and greys. The arguments and complaints escalated.

Soon Delena found that she spent every weekend and evening freezing meals to be prepared later, cleaning the house, and doing the laundry and most of the other jobs she had done when she wasn't working full time.

Cedric works hard and feels he needs some time after work to relax so that he can face going into the plant every day. Especially with all of the cutbacks and downsizing, he doesn't want to risk losing his job because of poor performance. Cedric and the children feel neglected because Delena is so busy, and Delena feels tired, angry, and overwhelmed. Cassandra worries that she is a burden, and she feels guilty about not being able to help out more. She also feels sad that the household does not run more smoothly.

Is housework work?

Have you ever described a woman as not working when you meant that she was a housewife?

Are Delena and Cedric typical in the way in which they divide housework?

Why do people make the decisions they do about how to divide housework?

How is housework tied to gender and gender politics?

How can Cedric and Delena's dilemma be solved? Will sharing help? What about hiring a maid?

Housework, the Invisible Occupation

Many activities take place within families. Among the most important are economic activities, the production and distribution of the necessities of life. Families pool their efforts to provide themselves with food, shelter, and all the other goods and services they need to survive.

The production of many of these necessities in a postindustrial society like ours is done outside of families in manufacturing plants, offices, and service industry sites like restaurants. Most of us go to work and earn wages to purchase these goods and services for ourselves and our families.

A significant amount of the activity necessary to keep us fed and sheltered, however, takes place within households and is unpaid. It is called housework.

Chapter 1 outlined several themes in a recent study of families. One of these themes was the linking of families to other social structures. Housework is a good contemporary example of how economic activities take place within families, blurring the boundaries between the social institution of the economy and the social institution of family.

A paid worker puts tomato soup into cans in the Campbell's plant. An unpaid worker opens the can and prepares the soup for a family to eat. Both are involved in the economic activity of providing members of society with the necessities of life. At these moments, the lines between economics and family cease to exist.

If we allow ourselves to see housework as work, we will then notice that it is the largest single occupation for American adults. Nearly half (44%) of adult women in the United States are year-round full-time housewives, and most other women and many men are part-time houseworkers (Berheide, Berk, and Berk 1976; Berk and Berk 1988; Oakley 1974; Bureau of Labor Statistics 2005a).

Most people do not consider housework part of the economic system. In spite of the enormous amount of human energy used to do the work and the necessity of the work to our existence, housework is usually not thought of as work. For example, "working women" are women who are not full-time housewives.

Housework is not only neglected in our thinking about the economic system, but it is also often neglected in our thinking in general. Housework is an invisible activity. In the scenario at the beginning of the chapter, the unpaid domestic work that Delena did at home was invisible until she entered the paid labor force. Then, when she had less time to do the chores, everyone in the household started to see the amount of time housework takes and the amount of skill the tasks involve. Housework at Delena and Cedric's home became more visible only when it became a problem.

The invisibility of housework is reflected in the field of sociology, where housework was not considered a suitable subject of scholarly study a few decades ago (Oakley 1974). Ann Oakley, a British writer, was a groundbreaker in the movement to acknowledge that housework is work and that scholars in the field of the sociology of work should, therefore, study it as they would other occupations. In the late 1960s when Oakley was a student at the University of London, she tried to register her thesis, titled "Work Attitudes and Work Satisfaction of Housewives," and was met with "frank disbelief or patronizing jocularity" (Oakley 1981a). She was asked how she could seriously study such a boring subject. But Oakley persisted, and since her "discovery" of housework a number of other scholars have also investigated it.

This chapter is divided into three major sections. The first is a description of the division of housework in households. It includes information on the question of who does housework and how the division of labor in families has or has not changed in the past few decades. The second section looks at three different theories that attempt to explain what causes housework to be divided as it is. The third section of the chapter addresses the problem of developing ways in which to make the division of housework more equitable.

What Is It Like to Be a Housewife?

Oakley wanted to find out what the job of housewife was like. The women Oakley interviewed described their job as difficult and told her that there were three problem areas in their work. First, regarding the work itself, housewives said that the tasks they performed were monotonous, never-ending, and lonely. One woman explained to Oakley:

> I always say housework's harder work, but my husband doesn't say that at all. I think he's wrong because I'm going all the time—when his job is finished, it's finished. Sunday he can

lie in bed till twelve, get up, get dressed and go for a drink, but my job never changes. (1974, p. 45)

Second, the housewives complained that the long hours of housework severely limit what women are able to do and what they are able to become. Organizing unions, running for political office, obtaining an education, and being involved in the arts are all activities, for example, that might be hindered by having to spend time doing housework.

The third set of problems the housewives mentioned were related to the fact that housework is unpaid. We have a money-based economy, and therefore the value of work is measured by how much it pays. Since housework is unpaid, the work is devalued; furthermore, the workers who perform the unpaid housework are devalued and have low social status. In addition, since wages are essential to obtaining the necessities of life, the housewife is entirely dependent on others for her survival because she earns no pay. Her social value is further diminished because it appears that she is unproductive and living off others. The ideology that those who do not earn money, regardless of the work they perform, are unworthy shows up in opinions about welfare mothers. Welfare mothers may work full time as housewives, but because that work doesn't count as real work, proposals are constantly being made to "put welfare mothers to work."

B O X 7.1

On Methods

Oakley's research on housework and houseworkers is an example of feminist ethnographic research (Reinharz 1992). Ethnography is a multimethod approach to social research that involves interviewing and observing people, participating in their activities, and examining artifacts in their social context. Ethnography is a methodology that is not exclusive to feminist researchers. Many feminists including Oakley, however, have argued that ethnography has great potential for getting at the reality of women's lives (Reinharz 1992).

In Oakley's (1974) investigation, she uncovered an important facet of the process of ethnographic research. When sociologists conduct research, they often do not reflect on or report the relationship between the researcher and the researched. Oakley, however, noticed in the transcripts of her interviews that the "subjects" asked her questions during the interview and that long-term friendships sometimes developed between the interviewees and herself. She argues that this is at least in part a result of the fact that both she and the "subjects" were women.

Oakley (1981b) concluded that (1) researchers should pay attention to the ways in which social research is a social interaction, a two-way street; (2) relationships of camaraderie are especially likely when both interviewers and interviewees are women; and (3) these special relationships produce the most valid kind of data.

Judith Stacey (1988) has questioned this last assertion. Stacey says that while it is true that women interviewing women may elicit responses that are more open and self-disclosing, this may cause problems. The methodology provides good data for the researcher, but it may also be more exploitative of the "subjects" since the women being interviewed let down their guard in ways they may not really wish to do to further the ends of a sociological study.

Who Does the Housework?

The answer to this question is women (Bianchi et al. 2000; Coltrane 1996; Shelton and John 1996; South and Spitze 1994). But changes have occurred in the past few decades. Since the 1960s, researchers at the Institute for Social Research have been conducting a huge project to see how Americans spend their time (Aachen and Stafford 2005). Thousands of subjects have been asked to fill out twenty-four-hour time diaries describing exactly what they do. Each diary provides a one-day snapshot. When the researchers put all the snapshots together, they have a picture of large trends for the whole country. In the research, they are careful to try to get a random sample of people to keep the diaries. They also are careful to try to ensure that the days are random—spread out throughout the week and throughout the seasons and the year.

One of the activities people report is the time they spend on unpaid housework. Those reports have changed over time from 1965 to 2005. The data from the study show that time spent on housework varies by gender and whether the respondent is employed or not. The research found that:

1. Women in all categories do more housework than men.
2. Unemployed men do more housework than employed men, and unemployed women do more housework than employed women.
3. Employed women do more housework than unemployed men.
4. The amount of housework women do declined from 1965 to 1995 from 33.9 hours per week to 19.4 hours.
5. The amount of housework men do increased from 1965 to 1995 from 4.7 hours per week to 10.4 hours.

Table 7.1 shows the division of housework in households between women and men in 2004. This table shows a little different information. Instead of looking at whether people are employed it looks at whether they have children. The table tells us that in households

TABLE 7.1   Hours Spent Doing Housework per Day, 2004

Tasks	With Children under 6		With Children 6–17		With No Children	
	Men	*Women*	*Men*	*Women*	*Men*	*Women*
Total housework activity	1.24	2.54	1.36	2.41	1.45	2.27
Housework	.22	1.15	.22	1.03	.24	.90
Food preparation and cleanup	.29	.99	.27	.86	.26	.70
Household management	.09	.14	.10	.14	.13	.19
Lawn and garden care	.24	.09	.19	.12	.30	.18
Child care	1.11	2.46	.41	.81	—	—

Source: Bureau of Labor Statistics 2005a.

with young children, under age 6, women, on the average, do about 17.78 hours of house-work per week, and men do about half as much, 8.68 hours per week. In households with older children, ages 6 to 18, women do a little less work and and men a little more and households without children under 18, women do even less and men more. But women are still doing one and one-half times as much work as do men in this last group (Bureau of Labor Statistics 2005a).

The table also tells us that women and men spend their time doing different kinds of tasks. Child care, cleaning, and cooking, in that order, take up the greatest proportion of the housework time of both women and men, but women spend more time doing all of these tasks. Lawn and garden care is where men surpass women in the hours spent.

How Are the Tasks Divided?

In her interviews, Hochschild (1989) noticed that men's jobs and women's jobs could be identified by three characteristics. First, women do most of the daily jobs and most of the jobs that are time-bound. For example, women cook dinner, while men change the oil in the car. Dinner must be cooked every day at a particular time. Changing the oil must be done only a few times a year and may be done any day at any time that is convenient.

Second, women more often multitask. They make dinner and do the laundry, while men either do the grocery shopping or mow the lawn.

Third, women are the time and motion managers, hustling the children through their baths and homework, getting everyone out the door to school and work in the morning. This third characteristic of a woman's housework is especially costly to mothers' relationships with their children. Mothers become "villains" in the process of doing housework and child care because they are always rushing the children through such maintenance tasks as eating, bathing, getting ready for school, or doing homework, when the children may prefer, or even need, to have someone stop and pay attention to them (Hochschild 1989).

So far, in the discussion of the ways adults divide housework, the focus has been on husbands and wives. When other kinds of couples are studied, some differences have been found. Gay and lesbian couples often distribute housework unevenly, but they are more likely to share equally than heterosexual couples (Kurdek 1993; Patterson 1995; Solomon, Rothblum, and Balsam 2005). In cohabiting heterosexual couples, men do similar amounts of housework as married men, but cohabiting women do less than married women (Denmark, Shaw, and Ciali 1985; Shelton and John 1993; South and Spitze 1994). Married couples also seem to distribute tasks more stereotypically (Blair and Lichter 1991).

Social-Class Variation.   The scenario describing the unequal division of labor in Cedric and Delena's household captures the experience for most households. Even though it takes place today, they are a two-paycheck family, and both the husband and wife see the division as unequal and problematic. Delena is still doing much more housework than Cedric is.

Cedric and Delena are a working-class couple. Does their social class exacerbate the inequality in their household? Research by Ellen Rosen (1987, 1991) suggests that blue-collar families have some of the same kinds of tensions around housework that white-collar families have. But a number of the women factory workers Rosen interviewed said that their husbands took primary responsibility for the housework or at least shared it with the wives. The men were especially likely to take over child care when the women were at work.

Eric Olin Wright was interested in how social class might affect the division of labor in families and decided to do a comparison. He and his colleagues (Wright et al. 1992) compared the division of unpaid household labor in couples in the United States and Sweden. In their research they divided people into four social classes: small employers, petty bourgeoisie, middle class, and working class. They concluded that social class had little systematic effect on the division of labor in households:

> There is a common stereotype in the popular media that working-class men do proportionately less housework than middle-class men. The macho worker whose identity is threatened by housecleaning and infant child care is contrasted to the egalitarian and enlightened yuppie who cooks elegant meals and pushes a stroller in the park—our data lend no support for such images. (p. 281)

Social class, however, does have an important effect on how much housework families do themselves and how much they are able to purchase (Brines 1994; Hanson and Ooms 1991). Philip Cohen (1998) examined families in four income categories, as shown in Table 7.2. The table shows that 18.8 percent of the richest group hired domestic help, much more than the other groups. They also spent more money eating out. Cohen's research also shows that it is not just household income that determines whether a family will purchase services like cleaning and cooking. Women's economic role in their families also seems to influence this decision. In families where women have a higher income, they are more likely to spend money to hire a housekeeper or take the family to a restaurant for dinner. Cohen concludes that both the position of families in the social-class system and the

TABLE 7.2   Household Spending on Housekeeping and Eating Out

	Percent That Purchased Housekeeping Help	Amount Spent on Eating Out
Household Income Levels		
$0–24,999	2. 5%	$ 864
$25,000–49,999	3.9%	$1,445
$50,000–74,999	5.6%	$2,244
$75,000+	18.8%	$3,266
Earner Composition		
Wife only earner	5.1%	$1,385
Husband only earner	6.3%	$1,509
Both earners	6.4%	$1,935
Race Ethnicity		
White couple	7.4%	$1,901
Black couple	3.0%	$1,150
Hispanic couple	1.7%	$ 990
Asian couple	2.7%	$2,556

Source: Philip Cohen, *Gender and Society* (12)2. Copyright © 1998 by Sage Publications, Inc. Reprinted by permission of Sage Publications.

women's position within those families determine whether families can relieve some of the pressure to do housework by hiring outside help.

Children's Work in Families. Most children do chores around the house. In the 1970s, Hedges and Barnett (1972) and Thrall (1978) found that when women worked outside of the home, their children were more likely than their husbands to take up the chores previously done by the women. Lynn White and David Brinkerhoff (1987) discovered that children begin doing chores in most households at a very young age, and by the time children are ten years old, over 90 percent of them are responsible for at least some housework. At all ages, however, the number of hours most children put into housework is small.

Table 7.3 also shows gender differences by indicating in the two columns on the left-hand side which tasks are done by boys and which are done by girls. The columns give the percentage of boys and girls who say they have done the tasks listed. Like the data on the division of labor in families between adults, this table indicates that boys and girls often do different jobs. Both boys and girls are likely to clean their room and clean the house, and neither spend much time taking care of elderly relatives. Girls are much more likely to do the dishes and the laundry. Boys are much more likely to do yardwork and take out the trash (Aronson et al. 1996).

The two columns on the right-hand side provide some additional information. These columns report the average number of hours spent doing these tasks by those who say they

TABLE 7.3   Children and Household Work

Task	Percentage Who Report Doing Task		Average Hours Spent per Week by Those Who Perform Task	
	Girls	*Boys*	*Girls*	*Boys*
Cleaning my room	93.1%	84.5%	1.6 hours	1.2 hours
Cleaning the house	86.8	74.2	2.2	1.4
Laundry	78.7	56.7	2.9	2.0
Doing the dishes	75.1	53.4	2.0	1.4
Cooking	68.0	62.3	2.6	1.8
Taking care of pets	49.8	53.1	4.0	3.8
Shopping for food	42.3	31.8	1.8	1.3
Setting the table	39.1	35.0	.7	.5
Taking out the trash	37.4	69.7	.6	.6
Yardwork	22.3	63.9	1.2	1.8
Caring for younger children	37.5	23.1	13.8	6.0
Caring for elderly relative	4.7	6.3	4.6	3.1
Other tasks	40.5	44.2	3.8	5.5
n	506	446		

Source: P. Aronson, J. Mortimer, C. Zierman, and M. Hacker, in J. Mortimer and M. Finch (eds.), *Adolescents, work and family: An intergenerational developmental analysis* (pp. 25–62). Copyright © 1996 by Sage Publications. Reprinted by permission of Sage Publications.

perform them. For example, the table indicates that similar proportions of boys (62.3%) and girls (68%) cook. But when those who cook are asked how much time they spend per week cooking, the boys say 1.8 hours and the girls say 2.6 hours. These contrasts are most remarkable for caring for younger children. About 37.5 percent of the girls and 23.1 percent of the boys say they spend time taking care of younger children. But the girls spend 13.8 hours per week compared with only 6 hours per week for the boys who do child care. The information on what tasks are done by boys and girls and on how much time is spent doing them shows that gender plays an important role and that, overall, girls are doing more work.

These difference between boys and girls have an important implication in the division of housework in future families. If boys are not being encouraged to learn how to perform tasks and are not required to notice and take responsibility for housework, it is less likely that they will increase their involvement in housework as men. This aspect of gender socialization—learning to do housework—may play a critical role in determining whether future families will divide work more equally (Goldscheiter and Waite 1991). And it appears that in many homes the status quo is being perpetuated.

The data in Table 7.3 indicate differences only by gender, but families differ in other ways, such as by race and whether they have one or two parents. How do these variables affect the amount of housework children do? Goldscheiter and Waite (1991) found that in two-parent families African American children, compared with white children, were responsible for significantly more (21% more) housework. African American children were more likely than white children to perform more hours of both less-skilled work like washing dishes and more-skilled jobs like grocery shopping and babysitting.

In one-parent households the amount of work performed by children is similar for African American and white families. Children in one-parent families, regardless of race, were likely to perform a much larger share of the housework than children in two-parent households.

White and Brinkerhoff (1987) examined the reasons parents gave for why they asked their children to do housework. The most common reason (given by 72% of the parents) was that doing chores was an important part of helping children build character and learn responsibility. For example, one parent replied that asking the children to do work "gives them a sense of responsibility. Makes them appreciate what they have. I think it helps them grow into responsible adults" (p. 209). Twenty-five percent of the parents said they had their children do housework because it was the child's duty to help out; 23 percent said it was because the parents needed the help; and 12 percent said that children needed to learn the skills in order to be able to take care of themselves as adults.

In Chapter 2 we examined the historical change of the conceptualization of the value of children from useful to priceless. Zelizer (1985) traced this history from the turn of the nineteenth century to more recent times. She argues that, early in the twentieth century, children were valued for the contribution they made to the household as workers. Now children are valued for the love and affection they provide and are not thought of as valuable workers. The large number of parents in White and Brinkerhoff's (1987) study who explain that they ask their children to do chores because it helps the children develop character and responsibility is an example of contemporary ideologies about children. Housework is not done by children for the benefit of adults as it might have been early in the twentieth century. Many postmodern parents emphasize the value that the activity of doing housework has for the child.

This view of children's housework, however, may vary by social class. A study of low-income families shows that parents and children in these families believe that the work that children do is essential. It is not for the good of the children but rather for the survival of the household and may in fact harm children because the work they do pulls them away from other important childhood tasks like doing well in school (Dodson and Dickert 2005). Daughters across social classes are especially likely to be required to spend long hours caring for younger children and doing household chores. But in low-income and single-parent households those jobs may be especially time consuming because there is no one else to do it except older sisters when parents are working long hours and the family does not have enough money to hire others to help with the work. As fifteen-year-old Ella (High School Study cited in Dodson and Dickert 2005, p. 319) told researchers, "I have to take care of the house and take care of the kids and I don't go outside. I have to stay home. They have to work and so I take over."

In addition, children in low-income single-parent households often do a lot of emotional work helping their parents cope with the difficulties. Marline, fifteen years old (High School Study cited in Dodson and Dickert 2005, p. 320), spoke of trying to advise her mother on how to leave Marline's abusive father. She said, "I was like, ma, you can do it. I know you can." Marline collected information about battered women's shelters and helped her mother plan financial and physical escape. She said, "I felt like I was the only person who could do it [assist her mother] but sometimes I couldn't sleep."

Unlike the parents who say that doing housework benefits children by teaching them responsibility and how to take care of themselves, researchers in low-income neighborhoods found that the children, especially daughters since they do most of the work, do not benefit. Girls have little time for school and their role as "little mothers" may push them into early pregnancy perpetuating their low-income status.

Feeding the Family

Much of the discussion thus far has been based on the conceptualization of housework presented by Oakley (1974). Within this framework, housework is seen as an economic activity that is comparable in many ways to other occupations. Others (Devault 1991) maintain that conceptualizing housework as a job is only partially correct and that housework includes other social facets as well (Berheide, Berk, and Berk 1976).

Marjorie Devault interviewed thirty women and three men about the unpaid work they did to feed their families. She found that (1) the intimacy of the work created requirements that would not have been present if feeding were just a job and not an aspect of familial relationships; (2) the work done by people (most often women, as we have observed in the tables) who purchase, prepare, and serve food to their families is not only work from the point of view of the women but it is also an act of love; and (3) feeding families not only nourishes family members, but also it is a process that helps to socially construct families. Meals are social events that involve patterns of interaction and bring family members together to interact.

Devault argues that although feeding goes on day after day, it is not a mechanical task. Especially because of its connection to the personal relationships of family members, it involves coordination and interpersonal work. Before food is prepared, it must first be determined what family members wish to eat. Restaurant owners might advertise their food or do a marketing survey to determine customers' preferences, but housewives must interact with family members on an intimate level in order to decide what to have for dinner. Housewives must be aware of individual preferences, often with few direct responses from family members. Devault observed in her interviews: "Many women complained that they could not just ask their husbands what they wanted: 'I'll call the office and ask, "Is there anything special you'd like for dinner?" and his standard answer is "Yes, something good" ' " (Devault 1987, p. 183).

Housewives also must coordinate tastes, unlike restaurant owners who can let customers order from a menu. And housewives have a special concern for the health of their families they must consider in planning meals.

The activity of feeding families is also different for housewives compared with restaurant owners because wives and mothers are concerned with the social interaction that takes place at meals. Many families use mealtime as an opportunity to talk with each other, and they also use it as a place to monitor and control children's behavior and model adult behavior. Devault concludes that eating and the work involved in feeding families is "at the center of family life and sociability" (1987, p. 190).

The second observation made by Devault is that a link between feeding and love is often noted. One woman explained to her how important the connection between feeding and love is and how feeding involves both labor and love. She said, "In preparing food, you know, there's a lot of work that goes into preparing food. Therefore, for one to commit himself to the work, that's love, that's shared with those people that the food was being prepared for. I think love has a lot to do with it" (1987, p. 180).

The third major finding of Devault's work is that in addition to being acts of love, feeding activities also represent the social processes that create families. Devault discovered, for example, that working-class women preserved their family and ethnic heritage in the foods they prepared. They also used feeding as a means by which to bring together members of an extended family, for example, at holiday meals.

Socialization Goals while Feeding Children.   In a study comparing Puerto Rican and Anglo mothers, researchers found that basic values were reflected and transmitted in their feeding of their young children (Harwood et al. 2000). Five goals were identified in the feeding and the beliefs mothers expressed about their children:

- Self-maximization: wanting children to feel that the world is their oyster, to succeed in a career and to feel good about themselves
- Self-control: insisting that children be able to tolerate frustration of their wishes
- Lovingness: feeling that a children be friendly, warm, and able to form close ties with others
- Decency: wanting children to be able to meet basic social standards such as being a hard worker, honest, and drug free
- Proper demeanor *respeto:* insisting that children know courtesy and decorum required in relations with other people and that they learn to be acceptable to the larger community

Mothers were asked about their expectations for their children, and they were observed while they fed their young (approximately 1 year old) children. Practices were observed such as holding the child on their lap or sitting them in chair, spoon feeding or allowing the child to eat with hands, and making suggestions to the child about how and what to eat.

Puerto Rican mothers were more likely to hold the child in their lap and spoon feed them. The children were not often allowed to feed themselves, and Puerto Rican mothers emphasized proper demeanor in their expectations and in their feeding interactions. Anglo mothers were more likely to emphasize self-control and self-maximization in their views of their children, and they were more likely to place their child in a high chair with the food in front of them to feed themselves with their hands. They also asked the children "do you want more juice?" rather than saying "here's your juice." Feeding the family teaches many lessons about food and eating, as well as larger issues about interacting in the world.

The Difference between Full-Time Housewives and Part-Time Housewives

Research on the time spent on housework among women who work outside the home and women who are full-time housewives shows that full-time housewives do much more housework than women who are in the paid labor force. Why are there such large differences? There are two possible answers to this question. Either full-time housewives do a lot

---

BOX 7.2

Ethnomethodologists

Devault's work fits into the broad theoretical framework called ethnomethodology. Ethnomethodologists focus their attention on the methods people use to create a shared perception of social order (Chafetz 1988). "Ethnomethodologists assume that people work constantly and hard at recreating the social order in order to achieve a sense that the world is orderly and predictable. They seek to understand the everyday, taken-for-granted implicit rules people use in interacting with one another that allow them to create such a sense" (p. 20).

The observations Devault (1991) makes of the everyday interactions and activities that take place in feeding a family reveal the way in which women, along with men and children, work to create their vision of a family. Implied in their feeding work are many beliefs about families. For example, the descriptions in Devault's interviews reveal beliefs that families are connected by love, that parents should model the behaviors they wish their children to adopt, and that housewives should nurture their families physically and socially.

Ethnomethodologists have emphasized the importance of verbal interaction as a critical process in the social construction of everyday life. Devault's book differs somewhat in that it explores a less-researched activity, the importance of the work people do in that process. Devault's ethnomethodology examines not only what people say to each other but also what they do to and with each other in their everyday interactions.

of unnecessary work, or, the quality of life of people in families where women are employed outside the home is diminished because a lot of necessary work is not being done.

In Chapter 1, I referred to a book written in the 1960s by Betty Friedan, *The Feminine Mystique* (1963). This book played an important role in revealing the problematic character of the idealized family of the 1950s in which men were supposed to be the primary bread-winners and women were to stay home to care for their husbands and children. Friedan argued that these "ideal" families were more like prisons, and she disclosed her discovery of "the problem without a name." The problem she wrote about was the isolation, fatigue, and depression of middle-class housewives whose lives were filled with boring, thankless tasks that were easily undone and never seemed to be finished. Housework filled every moment available. Magazines and television commercials told women their dishes should sparkle, their floors should gleam, their laundry should smell like fresh air, and their dinners should be carefully prepared and served to entice every sense. Many women suspected that much of this work was unnecessary, but they were trapped with a set of goals and standards that required many hours to achieve.

The difference in the hours spent on housework by women employed outside the home and women who are full-time housewives may be a result of unnecessary housework being added to necessary housework to fill the time available. It is unnecessary, for example, to have floors so shiny "you can see yourself in them." But these kinds of expectations are incessantly promoted by the media. Housewives and others who evaluate their work may come to believe the ads, and even the most outlandish expectations can become requirements of the job.

The other explanation for the difference in the number of hours of housework done by full-time housewives compared with women in the paid labor force is that the work (at least most of it) done by the full-time housewife is necessary and that the families of women who cannot put in those hours do not have as high a standard of living. Employed women in some households may be able to purchase some products and services, allowing them to replace the labor of a full-time housewife (Berheide 1984; P. Cohen 1998). In many cases the services may be too expensive or inaccessible, and families without a full-time housewife go without. Families without a full-time housewife, for example, may have dirtier houses, less nutritious or diverse foods, less child supervision, or less entertainment, like birthday parties.

Although these kinds of deficits in the quality of life may be felt by all family members, living in a house without a full-time housewife may be especially bad for women in those families. Research shows that working mothers have higher self-esteem and less depression than housewives, but they also have more anxiety (Thoits 1985). For example, Hochschild (1989) found that many of the women she interviewed felt their quality of life was greatly diminished by their attempts to maintain the house and work outside the home. The women spoke of being tired, sick, and emotionally drained:

> Many women I could not tear away from the topic of sleep. They talked about how much they could "get by on" six and a half, seven, seven and a half, less, more. They talked about who they knew who needed more or less. Some apologized for how much sleep they need, "I'm afraid I need eight hours of sleep" as if eight was "too much." These women talked about sleep the way a hungry person talks about food. (p. 9)

The unstructured, overburdening expectations of the job cause significant problems for some of the women and men who try to fulfill the job description of housewife. Many researchers have found that when women spend a lot of time on housework and feel that they are doing an unfair share, they are likely to become depressed (Glass and Fujimoto 1994). Men may also report feelings of demoralization, sadness, helplessness, and hopelessness when they participate in housework (Rosenfield 1992). Both women and men sometimes even find that household labor negatively affects their physical health (Bird and Fremont 1991).

Hidden behind the numbers that show different amounts of housework being done by full-time housewives and employed women are two different possibilities: too much unnecessary housework is done in houses with full-time housewives, and too little necessary housework is done in houses with employed women. Behind the statistics, however, in both family types there are similar problems of women feeling overworked and overwhelmed. Women who are full-time housewives are troubled by the invisibility of their work, its lack of structure, and the enormity of the task. Women who are employed are troubled by their inability to do it all and by the lack of support they receive from other members of the household.

High Tech and Housework

The most striking feature of the data presented is the inequality between women and men in the division of housework. But equally impressive is the total number of hours that men and women engage in housework. In our world of fast food, microwaves, and wash-and-wear fabrics, one might think that housework would disappear or at least decrease. In some activities this has occurred. In 1997, for example, Americans, for the first time, spent more money eating out than eating at home (*Economist* 1998). Since the turn of the nineteenth century, however, overall the time spent doing housework has changed little, although the tasks that are done have changed dramatically (S. Jackson 1992; Schor 1991). Ruth Cowan (1983) compared the housework done in the early part of the twentieth century to housework done in the 1970s. She found that housework is really made up of several sets of tasks. Although some tasks have become more efficient and less time consuming, others have become more time consuming. She explains

> Twentieth-century household technology consists of not one, but of eight interlocking technological systems: the systems that supply us with food, clothing, health care, transportation, water, gas, electricity, and petroleum products. The household transportation system has developed in a pattern that is precisely the opposite of food, clothing and health-care systems: households have moved from the net consumption to the net production of transportation services and housewives were moved from being the receivers of goods to being the transporters of them. (p. 58)

Cowan (1983) argues that people are now more likely to purchase food, clothing, and health care than to produce these things in their homes. But in order to use these items, we have to bring them to us or us to them. Icemen, breadmen, and milkmen no longer deliver; physicians no longer make house calls. Transportation has become the most significant work of the American housewife.

There have also been changes in the systems of water, gas, electricity, and petroleum products. We no longer have to haul water and build fires, and we have indoor plumbing and electric vacuums to help clean. But we also have much higher standards of cleanliness, larger houses, and bigger wardrobes. Cowan explains, "Some of the work was made easier, but its volume increased: sheets and underwear were changed more frequently, so there was more laundry to be done; diets became more varied, so cooking was more complex; houses grew larger, so there were more surfaces to be cleaned" (1989, p. 66).

The end result is that people are doing only slightly fewer hours of total housework than they did fifty years ago. Despite significant changes in technology and the social organization of tasks associated with domestic work, the number of hours devoted to housework remains substantial.

A Recent Addition to the Tasks of the Housewife

Cowan (1983) did her research in the late 1970s and early 1980s. She found that between 1920 and 1980 one activity that diminished within households was the provision of health care. Earlier in the century, families took care of sick people in their homes. But as the years passed, these activities increasingly were done by paid professionals in hospitals and nursing homes.

Nona Glazer (1990, 1993), working in the late 1980s, however, discovered that this trend had been reversed by new federal laws. In 1983, Congress passed the Social Security Amendments, ruling that, whenever possible, Medicaid and Medicare patients should use outpatient clinics instead of hospitals and that reimbursement for inpatient care should be sharply restricted. As a result of these changes, patients are sent home sicker than when they were allowed to stay longer in the hospital to recuperate. Most of these still ill patients are discharged to homes where family members do for free the work once done by paid health service workers.

This shift is not an economically small one. "The insurance industry estimates a $10 billion savings in wages because of unpaid family work. Of course, the 'family and friends' doing the work are mostly women" (Glazer 1990, p. 488).

Many of the people receiving in-home care are older people. Several demographic and social changes are causing elder care to increasingly be part of the public discussion about families. Judy Singleton (1998) has outlined the following important changes:

- Kin networks are becoming increasingly top heavy, with more older family members than younger. For the first time in history, the average married couple has more parents than children.
- Longer life expectancy and lower birthrates are causing shifts to occur in time spent in various family roles. Middle-generation women in the future will spend more years with parents over sixty-five than with children under the age of eighteen.
- Declining birthrates also mean fewer siblings. More women will be the only children or the only daughters and will, therefore, have fewer people to share the care of their elderly parents.

- Childbearing at later ages means that women will more likely be simultaneously caring for young children and aging parents.
- High divorce rates may eliminate care for the elderly by their spouses, shifting the responsibility to children of those older people.

Despite the fact that elder care is a growing problem, employers are still unlikely to help much with it. A large survey of companies that provide various support for their employees who are taking care of older family members found that about one-quarter provide information on where to find help. But only a few provide insurance for long-term care (9%) or financial support for elder care (5%). This work is left to families (Bond and Galinsky 1998).

Currently 83 percent of long-term care for dependent elderly people is provided by relatives (Abel 1986; National Alliance for Caregiving and the AARP 2004). About 10 percent of older people would need to be in nursing homes if their families were not taking care of them in their homes. Only about one-third of those older people who do need care are living in nursing homes (Brody 1983).

Furthermore, nearly all of the work that is done for ill or dependent elderly people in households is done by women, and the women who are providing the care are likely to be older themselves. For example, 60 percent of those who care for older people are wives caring for older disabled husbands. Seventy-three percent of these wives are over sixty-five (Cantor 1994; National Alliance for Caregiving and AARP 2004).

In the United States women caregivers provide more hours and higher levels of care than do men (National Alliance for Caregiving and AARP 2004). Research by British scholars reveals that the ratio of work done by women compared with men in homes that include an elderly dependent person is nineteen to one (Abel 1986). Women take on this responsibility for a number of reasons. First, external sources push them into caring for their relatives. These include a dominant ideology that says that women are natural caregivers, and lower pay for women so that their economic contributions from paid work are more disposable. In addition, women caregivers themselves believe that the sacrifices they make in caring for their parents are necessary and honorable (Abel 1986; see also J. Aronson 1992).

The tasks themselves are not easy. In many sick people's homes, nonprofessional women use high-tech equipment to deliver treatments for acute and chronic conditions and to treat systemic infection and cancer. They supervise exercise, give mechanical relief to patients with breathing disorders, feed by tubes those unable to take food orally or digest normally, give intramuscular injections and more tricky intravenous injections, and monitor patients after antibiotic and chemotherapy treatments (Glazer 1980).

Why Is Housework Divided Unequally?

Thus far, this chapter has described the way in which housework is divided in households. We can conclude that, while there is historical change and variation from one household to another, housework appears to be a powerful example of gender inequality. In this section we ask why housework is divided unequally.

This section is divided into three subsections. The first describes how a socialization theorist might explain the unequal division of labor in families. The second presents the work of Gary Becker, who would contend that, for the most part, housework is divided in households on the basis of rational decisions by the members as a working team. The third section presents the work of Sarah Fenstermaker Berk and Heidi Hartmann, who argue that the division of housework is both a reflection and an expression of gender inequality. They would contend that the division of unpaid labor in households is a political question: He who has the power does not do the dishes.

Socializing Housewives

Socialization is the process by which children learn how to understand people in their society and what is expected of them. Many kinds of socialization take place, and gender socialization is a major type. Boys and girls learn how to be boys and girls as well as what will be expected of them when they become adult men and women. In Chapter 13, we look in depth at the process of gender socialization when we examine the experience of children in families. In this section we briefly review some socialization issues that might be related to the question of the division of unpaid work in families.

Spencer Cahill (1983) cites three sources of gender socialization: adult models; cultural artifacts like gender models in books, television, and toys; and peers. According to Cahill, childhood is a time of dress rehearsal in which children act out and refine their notions of gender and the skills necessary for playing the part of girl, boy, woman, or man.

Each of the three sources of gender socialization cited by Cahill (1983) is likely to play a role in preparing girls to be housewives while preparing boys to avoid housework. The first source is adult models. This chapter has shown overwhelming evidence that children are much more likely to see women performing housework. In addition, the section on children and housework indicated that parents differentially assign housework to their sons and daughters.

Second, Cahill suggests that cultural artifacts encourage boys and girls to learn or not learn the skills associated with housework. In a study of the bedrooms of middle-class children, Rheingold and Cook (1975) found significant differences in the kinds of toys girls and boys had. Girls' bedrooms had dolls and toy appliances. Boys' bedrooms had athletic equipment, military toys, and building and vehicular equipment. Advertisers and toy stores almost always divide their stock into girl toys and boy toys. In addition, girl toys are largely miniature tools of housework: toy stoves, dishes, doll houses and furniture, cooking sets, fake food, ironing boards, vacuum cleaners, and all of the equipment necessary for baby care (Schwartz and Markham 1985; L. Shapiro 1990). Not only do these toys teach girls the mechanical skills associated with housework; they also teach the value of nurturance, a major component in the ideology of housework (Miller 1987). When we reviewed the activity of feeding the family in this chapter, we noted the importance women gave to buying, preparing, and serving food as a way of showing their love (Devault 1987).

Finally, Cahill suggests that peer interaction forms an important component of gender socialization. Girls playing house and doctor help each other learn how to be good housewives. Boys playing football and war do not.

Making a Rational Choice

Gary Becker (1981) is an economist who has studied the way in which households divide all the work that is done. His analysis of the question of why men and women divide housework in a gendered way is less related to childhood socialization and more concerned with the task faced by adult men and women who are trying to survive and excel in a competitive economic system. Socialization theorists focus attention on what the individuals are like who are dividing the housework and how they came to be the people they are. Becker's work focuses on the decisions those individuals must make. He has examined the ways in which household members divide both housework and market work. Market work refers to employment in the paid labor force.

Becker argues that households work as a team seeking to divide these two types of work in the most rational and efficient manner. Households take into consideration factors like who can earn the highest wages in the paid labor force and who is most skilled at doing housework (Brines 1993).

In Chapter 1, we looked at the functionalist analysis of family organization. Functionalists assert that in order to maintain an advanced industrial society, the best (most functional) family is one in which men earn the living and women take care of the family.

Becker's analysis is similar to the functionalists' because he, too, is arguing that housework is distributed to men and women in families in unequal ways because that is the most efficient means of dividing the work. In Becker's assessment, there is no consideration of issues such as justice or conflict of interest. The fact that women do most of the housework in most families is explained as a result of rational cooperative decisions made by households.

Just as feminists were critical of Talcott Parsons and other functionalist sociologists, feminists have also been critical of Gary Becker's work. Sarah Fenstermaker Berk (1985) has criticized Becker for assuming that households, not individuals, maximize their interests. She maintains that Becker incorrectly assumes that rational decisions for the group affect all members of the group in the same way.

Take, for example, the case of Cedric and Delena in the scenario at the beginning of the chapter. Becker would argue that since Cedric makes more money and, therefore, his job in the labor market is more valuable to the household, it is a rational decision for the family as a unit to have him do less housework so that he can be rested and able to keep his job. Arranging housework so that Cedric is less responsible for domestic work is further supported within Becker's analytical framework by observing that Delena is more skilled at doing housework. When she does the laundry it does not turn pink, and her dinners are more nutritious and appealing. What Becker does not acknowledge about cases like Cedric's and Delena's is that although the division of labor appears to reflect this rational assessment by the household, Cedric and Delena may have very different points of view on the efficacy of the arrangement. The balance sheet that leads to this decision is rational only if the costs to Delena are ignored. Berk (1985) points out that Becker's assessment of decision making among married couples contrasts with his analysis of decision making by couples before marriage:

> Becker's theory of marriage asserts that marriage decisions are based on the self-interested assessments of individuals with respect to the best marriage "bargain" that they can achieve.

Yet once the bargain is struck and household production begins, a unitary utility function prevails. (Berk 1985, p. 26)

A second criticism made of Becker by Berk is that he assumes that it is rational and efficient for wives to do more housework because, in many households, women's time spent in the paid labor force is worth less than men's because they make less money. However, Becker never questions why women earn less. Gender inequality in the labor market is taken as a given and is then used to explain and rationalize gender inequality in households (Brayfield 1995).

Unequal Work and the Politics of Gender

Feminists have developed an alternative analysis to that of writers like Becker. Chapter 1 showed that one of the themes of the recent rethinking of the family is around the question of the undifferentiated experience. Feminists point out that it is not accurate to speak of the family as if it were one single unit because there are different experiences within each family. "Women and men, young and old officially participate in the same families but their experience of them may be quite different" (Rapp, Ross, and Bridenthal 1979, p. 177).

Furthermore, that differential experience is both separate and unequal. Differential experience in households is organized around relationships between political unequals. According to family scholars who take this point of view, housework is an excellent example of the politics of gender. Heidi Hartmann has assessed the way in which men and women divide housework and has concluded that "the family is a primary arena in which men exercise their patriarchal power over women's labor and that time spent on housework can be fruitfully used as a measure of power relations in the home" (1981, p. 377).

Natalie Sokoloff (1980) argues that the unequal division of housework both expresses and promotes the subordination of women. Women do more housework because they are unequal to men. But that is only half the story. Women are unequal to men because they do more housework. In order to remedy the unequal division of labor, we must devise ways to increase equality in the way housework is divided. We must, however, also address this underlying political relationship—the difference in power between women and men in all corners of our society—in order to make those changes possible.

Heidi Hartmann and Natalie Sokoloff are socialist feminists (Lengermann and Niebrugge-Brantley 1992). Socialist feminism is a theoretical framework that seeks to synthesize two major theoretical paradigms, Marxism and radical feminism. Socialist feminists draw from radical feminism a concern for gender inequality and the oppression of women. They draw from Marxist theory a concern for the economic factor in understanding the oppression of women. A major component of a Marxist outlook is the recognition of economics as an essential factor in the consideration of all human interaction. Hartmann agrees that understanding economics is key to unlocking the mystery of gender inequality and the oppression of women. Her work begins with the question of how men and women differ in their contribution to the economic life of the community. Hartmann's work, like that of other socialist feminists, differs from Marxism in its broad view of economic activity, which includes unpaid housework (Lengermann and Niebrugge-Brantley 1992).

BOX **7.3**

Can Housework Cause Gender Inequality?

Many people are aware that gender inequality causes imbalanced divisions of labor in families. Berk (1985) has examined the other side of this picture: What effect does an unequal division of housework have on gender stratification?

Berk uses Goffman's (1977, 1979) and West and Zimmerman's (1987) work to try to explain the way in which households are "gender factories." Goffman used the term *gender displays* to describe the sex-specific ways of appearing, acting, and feeling that people use to let others know what gender they are. For example, as signs to others we wear certain colors and styles of clothes and hair, we move our bodies in "gender-appropriate" ways, and, as Berk points out, we perform certain household tasks.

According to Goffman, these displays serve to establish or reaffirm what gender we are and to align ourselves to interact with others in gender-appropriate ways. The gendered division of housework provides a constant way in which people can reaffirm who they are and how they relate to others (Potuchek 1992; West and Zimmerman 1987).

Men can reaffirm their masculinity by not washing the dishes. Women can reaffirm their femininity by doing them. This division also reaffirms their relationship to each other—women work for men; men dominate; women are subordinate (Berk 1985).

Every day, several times a day, the division of housework allows us and/or forces us to practice gender. Then, when we display those behaviors and relationships, it serves to reinforce for ourselves and others the validity of that division of labor and those expressions of gender. Dividing housework unequally between women and men is more than just getting the job done, and it is more than just an illustration of the oppression of women. It is a way in which to strengthen, perpetuate, and create gender in our society.

But does this mean that we can never alter our gender arrangements? Scott Coltrane (1989) investigated the link between the ways in which husbands and wives distributed housework, specifically child care. He found that their activities did influence their ideas and behaviors about gender. But he found that dividing housework does not have to maintain or enhance men's dominance over women. Some of the couples he observed shared child care quite equitably, and this in turn seemed to influence them to behave in less gender-differentiated ways with their families.

Berk (1985) emphasizes the ways in which others reprimand those who do not display gender appropriately. Coltrane (1998a) says that people can and sometimes do break the rules of gender. He reports, furthermore, that fathers who participated fully in child care were often described as transformed—more sensitive to their children and their wives and more likely to understand the drudgery of housework and the need for making it easier by obtaining the proper tools, like a good vacuum or an effective bathroom cleaner.

In most Marxist writing, the economy of a capitalist system like that in the contemporary United States is viewed as those activities that directly contribute to the accumulation of capital. When employees go to work and build cars that are worth more than the wages the workers are paid, the surplus gained from the sale of the cars is returned to the owner of the car factory. This return is called profit, or the accumulation of capital. Although housework amounts to a lot of work, it does not directly create a profit for anyone because housewives are not employed, the products of their labor are not sold, and no one is able to directly accumulate capital because of their work.

Socialist feminists would argue that housework should nevertheless be considered part of the economic system because it *indirectly* enhances profitability. For example, a socialist feminist would maintain that when Cedric arrives at work rested and fed and therefore able to work harder, his boss is able to profit from the unpaid labor of Delena, who fed and cared for him. Socialist feminists, furthermore, would draw attention to the way in which both capitalist bosses and men workers benefit from the superexploitation of working-class housewives.

What Can Be Done about the Inequality in the Division of Housework?

The first two major sections in this chapter have looked at the way in which housework is divided and the contrasting analyses of the reasons for this division. In this section, the issue we turn to is what can be done about the inequality of the division of housework. The number of two-paycheck couples who will be faced with the problem of dividing housework is increasing. Sixty percent of wives and mothers now work outside the home. In a survey of 200,000 first-year college students in 1988, fewer than one percent said they planned to be full-time homemakers (Hochschild 1989; see also Johnston and Bachman 1995).

Table 7.4 shows the trends in labor-force participation rates for women and men. The table shows the rates for women increasing and the rates for men decreasing. The rates appear to be converging in paid work, making women and men more equal. How can we achieve more equality in unpaid work?

Negotiating New Ways to Divide Work

One way to solve the problem is to attempt to resolve it at the microlevel between husbands and wives. Negotiating housework is an important part of many marriages. The strategies that women and men use to try to resolve the problem of dividing housework become a constant source of tension (Hochschild 1989).

TABLE 7.4   Labor Force Participation Rates for Civilians Aged Sixteen and Over, by Sex, 1970 to 2008

	Participation Rate (Percent)				
	1970	*1980*	*1990*	*1999*	*2008 (Projected)*
Total Population	60.4	63.8	66.5	67.1	67.6
Women	43.3	51.5	57.5	60.0	61.9
Men	79.7	77.4	76.4	74.7	73.7

Source: U.S. Census Bureau 2000g. p. 403.

Within couples, men and women use different approaches to try to come to some agreement. The strategies women use to resolve the problems include (1) marrying men who share the work; (2) actively trying to change husbands who do not share the work; (3) passively trying to manipulate their husbands; (4) becoming "supermoms"; and (5) cutting back on work, marriage, self, and children (Hochschild 1989).

Men use other strategies in the struggle. They share the work equally, or they resist by (1) disaffiliating themselves; (2) reducing the need for the tasks; (3) substituting offerings; and (4) selectively encouraging their wives (Hochschild 1989). Hochschild uses the phrase "disaffiliating themselves" to describe the way in which men passively avoid taking responsibility for the work by forgetting things, doing tasks in an unskilled way, and waiting to be asked.

Some men take responsibility for the work, but they reduce the need for tasks to be done by redefining the situation. They might argue, for example, that there is no need for clothes to be ironed or sheets to be changed, and that McDonald's is good enough for dinner.

Other men do not do the work, but they try to alleviate the tension by offering substitute support to their wives. For example, this kind of husband might patiently listen to his wife and offer her advice while she struggles to balance her home and paid work. Such a man does not increase his material support for his wife by doing more of the housework, but he increases his emotional support of his wife to make the problem a little less difficult for her. Finally, husbands avoid sharing the work by praising their wives for the efficient, organized way in which the women get the work done (Hochschild 1989). Despite great pressure in the households Hochschild examined, as in many households, husbands and wives do not seem to be sharing housework equitably. These forms of resistance were more common than equitable distributions of the work.

In those cases where couples did share more equally, one variable that Hochschild (1989) found to be important was gender ideologies. Those couples who had more egalitarian ideas about what women and men should be like also tended to share housework more equitably. The work of Wright et al. (1992) also found small differences of increasing egalitarianism in the division of work in households where people, especially men, had more egalitarian beliefs. This suggests that one way to improve the division of labor in households is to encourage the adoption of more egalitarian gender ideologies, particularly among men.

Mothers as Gatekeepers

This discussion of housework poses the problem as a struggle between women and men in households over who should do the work. In-Sook Lim's (1997) research on Korean immigrants in the United States found that other voices can also enter this debate—mothers and mothers-in-law. Lim interviewed Korean couples where both the husband and wife worked outside the home. Husbands and wives found themselves trapped by Confucian patriarchal ideals that demand that women serve their families and do not challenge their husbands. "Confucian patriarchy [is] characterized by the Rule of Three Obedience, which emphasized women's subordination to men: A woman should obey her father before her marriage, her husband after marriage and her son(s) after her husband's death" (Lim 1997, p. 33).

In addition to these ideological restraints, economic factors also keep women dependent on men. Many immigrant Korean families employ all family members in family businesses. This necessitates much cooperation among family members for the business to succeed; conflict is discouraged and even dangerous to their livelihood. Regardless of an individual's contribution to the work, family members usually do not receive separate paychecks. As individuals, they are unpaid and therefore cannot accumulate or even acknowledge their own personal resources. Despite these constraints, immigrant Koreans living in the United States find themselves in a different culture that challenges their ideas and a different economy that places significant physical demands on women who are supposed to both work in the family business and try to maintain a household. This results in many women defying their role as solely responsible for household tasks, and marital conflict has increased.

One important additional factor, however, serves to keep wives resigned to their position in their families—their mothers and mothers-in-law. Grandmothers buffer the difficulties of raising children, keeping house and working for the family business by helping their daughters do everyday housework and especially care for children. Grandmothers also try to maintain traditional ways of doing family work in a manner that keeps husbands away from these domestic responsibilities. The grandmothers do not complain about doing family work, but they restrain daughters from pressuring their husbands to help out. One woman described her situation: "My mother shouts at me and scolds me for making my husband do the family work. Saying, 'why do you demand that your husband do family work even though there are two women in this house?'" (Lim 1997, p. 45).

Lim's observations show us that tension over housework occurs between husbands and wives, but other voices are also significant. Some of the voices are ancient religious ideas like Confucianism. Some of them are other people in our immediate environment who are important to us, like our mothers, but they could be other family members or even friends, coworkers, and neighbors.

Hiring a Maid

When sharing the housework does not work, another strategy is to hire someone to do the housework in the home, but this solution is not completely satisfactory. Some households are wealthier than others and are more likely to be able to accomplish this, as we noted in the discussion of Table 7.2. This solution is, therefore, available only for a limited number of people.

Hiring a maid is also a problem even for those households that can afford it because this solution may create another form of inequity, this one between employer and maid. Hiring a maid might help eliminate the inequality between a woman and man in a household, but it reveals race and class inequality between the employer and the maid, since the people hired to do domestic work have historically been working-class women, particularly working-class racial ethnic women. Domestic work has been an especially low-paid, devalued, oppressive, and difficult occupation.

Until the middle 1960s, the largest single occupation of African American women was domestic work. "By 1950, 60% of all black working women (compared to 16% of all white working women) were concentrated in institutional and private household service jobs" (J. Jones 1985, p. 235). In the late 1800s, Chinese men were likely to be domestic workers (Katzen 1978). And later, Japanese and Filipino men were often engaged in this kind of work (Chan 1991; Espiritu 1995, 1998). Today almost half (44%) of domestic workers are from Central American nations and Poland (Bernstein 2005).

Until World War II, domestic service was also the most common form of nonagricultural employment for Japanese American women, whether they were American born or Japanese born (Glenn 1990). In 1940, more than 50 percent of Japanese American women in San Francisco were employed in domestic work. In addition, West Indian and Chicana women have been likely to work as domestics. "The racial stratification of the occupation is so apparent that Judith Rollins (1985, p. 4) characterizes the situation as 'the darker domestic serving the lighter mistress'" (Romero 1988, p. 321). Today that is still mostly true. Forty-four percent of today's low-wage immigrant workforce tending to domestic needs are Mexican, Central American, and Polish women (Bernstein 2005).

For women who work as maids, domestic work has meant especially long hours away from their own families (Dill 1994). For most of its history, domestic work was a live-in occupation. This meant that domestic workers were able to see their own families only every other weekend. In addition, "work hours were open-ended with the domestic 'on call' most of her waking hours" (Glenn 1990, p. 450).

One of the most important battles won by domestic workers in the twentieth century was the right to day work instead of live-in work, which allowed domestic workers to go home to their own families at night (Dill 1983). This struggle and its importance in the first half of the century were discussed in Chapter 3.

The battle between mistress and maid continues even today. Mary Romero (1988, 1992) interviewed Chicana women who work as maids. She states that domestic work is characterized by four issues: (1) the work involves the extraction of emotional labor from the maid; (2) mistresses use various methods to maintain superiority and control while creating an informal and apparently companionable relationship; (3) domestic workers use various strategies to minimize the subjugation and unwelcome familiarity they face on the job; and (4) the work involves a constant struggle between employer and employee over the control of the work process.

The extraction of emotional labor refers to the way in which domestic workers are expected to fulfill not only technical roles, but also emotional and caring roles. Chicana domestics told Romero that they often felt called upon to be surrogate mothers for their younger employers.

Because the employer and the domestic worker live in different social worlds, the employer may feel free to tell the maid about her personal problems without fearing that the maid will look down on her or retaliate against her. This sharing of intimacy, however, is not reciprocal. The employer can choose to obtain consolement, but she does not have to return it, and the maid is not really free to offer her true feelings. The relationship, thus, only appears to be friendship, and it results in the employee doing additional work as she provides a source of emotional support.

Control over the relationship is maintained by the employer in ways such as allowing the domestic worker to sit only in the kitchen and to eat only after the employee's family has been served; to insist that a maid wear distinguishing clothes (a uniform), at least on special occasions like a dinner party; and generally to demand deferential treatment.

Another way in which the boundaries between maid and mistress are maintained by what appears to be friendly interaction is through the giving of gifts to a maid. Domestic workers frequently receive gifts of castoffs from the employer. Judith Rollins (1985, p. 193) argues that these gifts serve to "communicate to the parties involved and to the larger social group who the giver and the receiver are and what their relationship to each other and the community is." The message to the maid is that "you are only good enough to wear clothes that are no longer good enough for me" (p. 333). Even the giving of legitimate gifts and bonuses can serve to control employees, if they are given in lieu of benefits and raises.

Domestic workers have not easily given in to this second-class status. They have attempted to retain their control over the work by demanding proper equipment and to be allowed to define the methods of cleaning, standards, and the order and pace of the work. Employees also attempt to have greater control of their work by making agreements with employers based on specific tasks rather than the number of hours worked.

Maids have also tried to achieve more control over their work by eliminating the demands for emotional nurturance. Chicana workers in Romero's (1992) study said that one way to do this is to take positions where they work in homes when the employer is away.

Romero (1997) summarizes the kinds of strategies Chicana domestic workers use to maintain control over their work into six categories: (1) making the job more flexible; (2) increasing pay and benefits; (3) specifying tasks; (4) minimizing contact with employers; (5) defining themselves as expert housekeepers; and (6) creating a businesslike environment. The overriding goal is to move away from selling their labor and to move toward selling a service. Rather than purchasing a person whom they will supervise, customers now must negotiate a contract with a professional who will make decisions about the best way to conduct the work. This transition modernizes the relationship between the homeowner and the domestic worker. No longer are they mistress and maid. Their new relationship is between professional small business owner and customer, eliminating much of the exploitative and degrading potential of the mistress-maid relationship.

In their push to make this transition, many domestic workers use these strategies in their day-to-day interactions with employers. In addition, as we observed in Chapter 3, there is a long history of collective action and attempts to unionize by domestic workers throughout the United States. Among the goals of domestic workers who have sought to organize unions are "raising wages to minimum wage; providing common working benefits such as paid vacations, holidays, sick leave, and workers' unemployment compensation; changing attitudes toward the occupation; and creating awareness among workers about the value of their work" (Romero 1988, p. 340). United Domestic Workers of America continue to fight legal and political battles for their workers (www.udwa.org 2005).

We can see that from the point of view of working-class women, especially working-class racial ethnic women, purchasing housework by hiring people to do it is not necessarily a good solution to the problem of gender inequality in the division of labor between women and men. As long as the conditions of work remain as they are between maid and mistress, this "solution" helps perpetuate race and class inequality. Hiring a maid may eliminate the problem between a woman and man sharing a household; it can also create or exacerbate other inequalities in those households.

Solving the Problem of Housework through Policy Change

These two solutions to the problem of dividing housework more equitably by getting husbands to share and hiring a maid are based on decisions and actions within households. Neither has been satisfactory. Other solutions have been offered that look to larger institutions for change. These include changing laws to require that housewives be paid and socializing housework.

One public policy solution that has been suggested is to require that husbands pay housewives. In a 1985 survey, 42 percent of the women and 26 percent of the men said that men should have to pay for the housework their wives do (Hochschild 1989). Paying wages is a good way to recognize and reward the extra contribution that women make. The problem of the time constraints for women who also work outside of the home, however, is not addressed by this solution. Requiring that husbands pay their wives for domestic work is also problematic because it reinforces the subordinate relationship between husbands and wives. It also leaves unanswered questions like how the work would be evaluated and by whom. Also, the proposal that husbands pay wives is meaningless for the majority of couples who live paycheck to paycheck and whose combined earnings barely pay the bills for the entire household. In addition, this solution, like the solution of sharing housework, ignores the situation of single-parent households.

A second solution is for the government to pay housewives or at least to cover them by Social Security so they can retire with a pension. Putting housewives on a government payroll shares many of the weaknesses of the proposal to have husbands pay their wives. First, it does nothing to eliminate the idea that housework is primarily women's work. It also does not solve the problem of time constraints for wives, and it ignores single-parent households. Plus, once again, how would the work be evaluated? Who would determine whether the housewife had done her job adequately? And, finally,where would the money come from to pay this huge group of workers?

A third option is to socialize housework. Socializing housework means to making it the responsibility of the entire community rather than the responsibility of each individual household. This effort to spread out the work can be accomplished by radically restructuring the entire society, or it can be done in a less dramatic fashion by using the government to facilitate sharing the burden.

This solution has been considered by feminists for some time. Around the turn of the nineteenth century, Charlotte Perkins Gilman (1898/1966), a leader in the fight for women's suffrage in the United States, argued that the housework done privately in separate homes was an intolerable waste of human energy and a basis of gender inequality. Gilman proposed building houses without kitchens and establishing cooperative dining rooms, laundries, and nurseries.

A less utopian and perhaps more attainable model for socializing housework is represented by family policy in countries like Sweden (Moen 1989). In Sweden, socializing housework has meant that everyone pools economic resources in order to allow households, especially those with children, to divide work more equitably. This model includes reforms that provide for parental leave for either a father or mother after the birth of a child, that entitle either a father or mother to work six-hour days, and that explicitly encourage men and women to share child care and domestic work (Wright et al. 1992).

The Micro–Macro Connection

Housework, like many activities that take place within families, is experienced at the microlevel as a personal issue. Cassandra, Delena, and Cedric, whose story was told at the beginning of this chapter, feel bad as individuals because of their inability to divide housework in their household in a satisfying manner. Oakley has explained that housewives feel overworked and devalued. Hochschild found that women felt tired, overwhelmed, and frequently like villains in their attempts to keep house, raise children, and maintain outside jobs. The experience of housework for many individuals and families is not very pleasant.

In addition, the experience is different for women and men. Compared with women, men do less work, do different jobs, and have different strategies for avoiding housework. The experience of housework for men at the microlevel, however, is also problematic because, in dual-income families, housework may go undone and wives are not happy with the way in which the work is distributed.

One possible solution to the problem of housework is to hire people to do the work. But because of the system of class and race inequality in our society, this means that domestic work is done mostly by working-class racial ethnic people, and the work is difficult, low paid, and oppressive.

These microlevel personal experiences between husband and wife and between mistress and maid are embedded in larger macrolevel social structures that include our ideas about work and the way in which paid work is organized. Families are also affected by the macrolevel organization of the government, for example, in its attempt to shift costs from taxpayers to housewives through changes in health care funding. Housework is also affected by the system of gender relations, which includes ideologies about what women and men should do, as well as about the differential skills of women and men and the differential power of women and men to bargain for the division of tasks.

Macrolevel social structures—ideologies; race, gender, and class stratification; and the government—shape the experiences that individual people have with each other at the microlevel within their families. People like Cassandra's family are trapped in a web that cannot be altered by themselves alone.

Individual people at the microlevel can, however, work together to alter the web. Advocates of government-funded child care, paying housewives, and socializing housework have offered suggestions about what might be changed at the macrolevel to make sure that the housework gets done in a more satisfactory and equitable manner.

This chapter also shows another twist on the effect of microlevel activities in its discussion of Berk's notion of the gender factory (Box 7.3). The gender factory, which is comprised of the microlevel interactions of women and men around housework, helps create and sustain the macrolevel system of gender inequality. Although this book has emphasized the way in which microlevel activities can help transform the organization of our society, the gender factory reminds us that everyday microlevel activities also serve to reproduce the status quo.

CHAPTER

8 Love and Sex

Love and romance are closely linked in our culture. Specific activities like eating French food, watching a sunset, and dancing are part of the rituals of romance in our post-modern society. (Joe Jaszewski/Getty Images)

Lori instant messages her friends Kamika and Stacey. She writes, "Started my new job at the phone sex company. You would not believe the guys that call."

Kamika breaks in. "I can't believe you took that job. It's sick. Sex should be for lovers, not strangers on a telephone."

Lori responds, "I can't see the appeal myself, but if it makes these guys happy, what do I care? And besides, it's a job. Sex doesn't have to be only for people in love, you know."

"Well, I'd be afraid one of them might find out who I am or where I live," says Stacey.

Lori replies, "Nobody is going to find out where I live, and maybe I'm doing the community a service. Maybe they would be out doing something really terrible in the street if they couldn't have the telephone sex outlet."

"Yeah, maybe you're right. I sure don't want to be telling people what kind of sex they ought to have. Kristy and I get enough of that when we hear people talk bad about us just because we are lesbians. But I don't know, it seems like some of this stuff can get so far out it gets exploitative and doesn't seem like real sex anymore, more like rape or something. Don't you feel kind of used?"

"No, not really. I like sex. It seems kind of fun, you know, taking a risk, trying something new," Lori says.

Kamika shakes her head. "I like sex, too. But what's wrong with sex with love and marriage? Personally, I do not intend to jump into bed with anyone but my husband, and I do not intend to try any of that kinky stuff even with him."

"Well, I gotta go. I need to get up early for the prochoice rally."

"Yeah, us too. See ya."

In approximately what year is this scene taking place? How do you know?

How are the choices these young women face a reflection of the times in which they live? How have the choices changed since the 1990s? Since the 1970s? Over a long historical period?

Although each of these women has a different opinion about the relationship between sex and love, the fact that this relationship is one to consider is part of their thinking. What do you think is the proper relationship between sex and love? What about the relationship between sex and marriage?

How are gay men's and lesbians' sexual relationships different from those of heterosexuals? How are they similar?

How do each of these women emphasize different aspects of sex—its dangers or its pleasures?

The scenario ends with the young women planning to go to a prochoice rally. How is the issue of abortion tied to the expression of sexuality?

This chapter examines these issues as they are expressed in theory and in real experience. Like all social phenomena, love and sex are dynamic, changing over time. The history of that change is a central theme in the chapter as well. In addition, we pursue our exploration of the relationships among love, sex, and several other facets of our society, including politics, economics, technology, and especially families.

The chapter is divided into four sections. The first is a review of the issue of love, including the difficulty of defining the term and its historical development in Western society. The second section reviews the topic of sex and addresses issues like standards for evaluating legitimate sex, laws about sex, and quantitative and qualitative research on the experience of sex in the contemporary United States. In the third section, two theoretical debates are reviewed: theories about categorizing sexuality and theories about the basis of sexuality. The fourth section explores the way in which the microlevel has had an effect on the macrolevel in an examination of the abortion rights movement.

What Is Love?

Many scholars have sought to answer this question (Lee 1974; Verne 1995). In their attempts to develop a definition, they have concluded that love is multifaceted and that one definition will not suffice. Rollo May (1969) said that love in Western society can take four forms and that the real human experience of love is a blend of the four in a variety of proportions:

1. Lust, sex, or libido.
2. Eros, which identifies a feeling or relationship that moves us to a higher level, closer to our uniquely human potential.
3. Friendship, or the brotherhood and sisterhood of humans. May uses the word *philia* to identify this kind of love, as in Philadelphia, the city of brotherly love.
4. Caring and devotion to the welfare of the other, which is sometimes called agape.

Research on love shows that in addition to being complex and variable, love is also gendered. Women and men, on the average, seem to have different perceptions and experiences of love, although the love gap may be closing. In 1976 and again in 1984, researchers questioned college students about how important love was to them. The students were asked whether they would marry someone whom they did not love. Men were more likely than women to say no (Wood 1996). In 1991, similar research found that this gender difference had diminished. Women and men were about equally likely to say they would not marry someone they did not love. But women were still more likely to be concerned about the earnings potential of their love (Allgeier and Wiedener 1991). Women want to fall in love *and* find a good provider. Women still feel that they need to be more cautious in love, while men feel they have more freedom to choose (Coltrane 1998b).

Historical Development of Love

Like many issues in this book, love is a phenomenon that only appears to be natural, inevitable, and unchanging. When examined historically, love is revealed as highly variable from one time period to another. Our ideas about love and our experience of love have changed throughout history. One of the most significant changes concerns the connection between love and marriage. It is only relatively recently that this link has been idealized (Hendrick and Hendrick 1992).

Love existed in the ancient societies of Greece and Rome. In fact, much of the symbolism and language of contemporary love, such as Cupid, Venus, Eros (erotic), and Aphrodite (aphrodisiac) come from the names of gods and goddesses of those civilizations. In those ancient societies, love and marriage were kept separate. In classical Greece, for example, aristocratic men married women, but the lovers about whom they wrote were teenage boys with whom they had sexual relationships. In medieval Western society, the aristocracy carefully arranged their marriages as ways to annex land and wealth and to avoid or win wars. Among the peasants, marriages were also economic arrangements, not sentimental ones.

The concept of romantic love emerged during the thirteenth century. Unlike the ancient Greeks, for whom love meant primarily a sexual, not an emotional, relationship, romantic love in medieval society was frequently characterized by the lack of physical consummation. The rules of romantic love demanded that the lovers be emotionally devoted to one another, but they were not necessarily supposed to maintain a sexual relationship and they would never be married to each other.

During the colonial period in the United States, the economic and political reasons for marrying became less rigid, and couples began to have more of a choice in the matter. Both love and sex began to replace business interests as a basis for partnerships, and marriage was linked to love and sex.

In the late eighteenth and early nineteenth centuries, the agrarian-based economy began to change into an industrial-based one. Families of the industrial period were characterized, at least for middle-class whites, by a split between work and home. Love was idealized as the asexual love between mother and child (Cancian 1987). The split between work and family was paralleled by a split between women and men. As described in Chapter 2, the Puritan patriarchal household was replaced by the urban middle-class household. Husbands were dominant in both cases, but in the modern family of the industrializing nation, women and men led separate lives. Their emotional attachments were therefore segregated. In Puritan society, the key relationship was between husbands and wives. In the modern society of the nineteenth century, "the key relationship was an intense emotional tie between mothers and children and raising moral, respectable and healthy children was a woman's major task" (Cancian 1987, p. 31). During the twentieth century, the focus moved back to relationships between husbands and wives with an emphasis on developing intimacy and emotional connection.

Postmodern Romance

Human emotions may seem to be natural and biologically based. Sociologists, however, are increasingly learning that emotions are shaped by social forces. While the general responses of fear, anger, and attraction are connected with physiological states, the meaning, significance, and way in which we react to these feelings are determined by our social environment. Hochschild (1983) calls this emotion work. She notes that we have to learn and practice our emotional responses. Love is one of the emotions we have to work at. Our culture tells us how to translate our emotional experiences in four ways:

1. Our social environment provides us with meanings for our feelings of physical arousal. Our heartbeat may speed up and our pupils dilate when we are confronted with certain people or situations, but we need to learn what these biological reactions mean. People and other sources of information like the media tell us that this is what it feels like to love someone or to be angry at them.
2. Our social environment tells us how to manage and control our feelings in order to conform to cultural norms. Whether we should speak to people, what we should say, and how should we act are all prescribed by our culture.
3. Our social environment tells us how to measure the intensity. Do our feelings register as slight attraction or madly in love? We have to learn whether the feelings are significant and how much so.

4. Our social environment provides us with symbols to display our emotions. For example, flowers are often offered as an expression of love in U.S. culture.

Eva Illouz (1997) interviewed people about the images and experiences they associated with love. The responses were remarkably similar, and many clustered into three dominant categories: travel, nature, and eating. When she asked people to describe a romantic moment, they often described eating. Going out to a restaurant and eating special foods—French cuisine—were strongly linked to romance. The interviewees also talked about natural surroundings—watching a sunset or walking on the beach. Finally, they placed themselves in exotic places—a cruise in the islands, a weekend in Rome.

In her observations of what our culture tells us is romantic, Illouz (1997) notes that our images of romance are often associated with consumption—spending money and buying things. Nearly all the activities people spoke of in her research involve buying and consuming goods and services. Not surprisingly—because romance translates into needing money to buy the proper setting and artifacts—social-class differences emerged in her interviews. Middle-class people were more likely to identify consumption as part of their romantic images, while working-class people were more likely to describe romantic moments that involved less consumption.

One investment banker described an experience he had which he thought was very romantic:

> It has been a while, um, probably when I was traveling with someone through Italy and we were on the Spanish Steps in Rome. The moon was out, we bought some wine, and we sat on the steps. We were a little older, everybody around was students and I started to sing. I was an opera singer and a whole group came and surrounded me, was applauding me. And after they left it was just the two of us. It was a very special moment, a very special feeling. (Illouz 1997, pp. 264–65)

A working class housewife described a romantic moment she had experienced:

> I would drive to his house—this is back to the gasoline crisis and we would drive together to work. Naturally, he was always dressed with a shirt and tie. This particular day he had no tie and his shirt open and there he was, and I thought wow. It seemed like Robert Redford walking in the street. Like that feeling when you see somebody you like in a movie. (Illouz 1997, p. 265)

Human Sexuality

As you probably noticed, discussing love and sex as two separate issues is somewhat artificial. The tension between love and sex and the way in which the relationship between the two varies historically and from one individual to another make them almost inextricable. In this section, our focus moves to a consideration of sex as a phenomenon that is sometimes tightly bound to love and other social factors as well.

One characteristic that distinguishes humans from other animals is sexuality. Animal sexuality is "limited, constricted, and pre-defined in a narrow physical sphere" (Padgug

1979, p. 19). Human sexuality, in contrast, is marked by its richness, plasticity, and diversity. Human sexuality, like animal sexuality, is involved with biological sexuality, but biology is only a precondition, and human sexuality stretches far beyond it in an apparently infinite number of ways (Padgug 1979; Richardson 1996; Schneider and Gould 1987).

Issues like what we view as sex, what we view as sexual, who we perceive to be legitimately involved in sexual activities, and what conditions we believe must be part of valid sexuality vary from one culture to the next, from one historical period to the next, and from one individual to another (Jacobs, Tomas, and Long 1997). For example, among the Ik in East Africa, masturbation is the primary form of sexuality, and intercourse is accepted as an occasional extension of masturbation (Turnbull 1972). Among the Aranda in central Australia, boys are not eligible to marry until they have been initiated into sex through homosexual relationships with older men (Bullough 1976). These behaviors are quite different from what our society presents as sexual standards. On the other hand, activities we might see as normal would be viewed as exotic by others. For example, "Kissing, especially for anything longer than a brief peck, appears to be a feature of only a few, mostly Western cultures. Kissing is viewed unfavorably by many African and Asian cultures" (Reinisch 1990, p. 103).

Sexual Standards

As in all societies, in contemporary U.S. society certain standards tell us how we are supposed to feel and act sexually (Kelly 1992). This list of standards is not a formal set of rules by which we must abide, but it makes up a dominant sexual ideology in our society and is reflected in the media, in political rhetoric, and in some cases in the law. The standards also describe the actual sexual experience of many people. But many people, probably most people at some time, do not abide by the standards. Which ones are part of your beliefs about sex? Which describe your sexual experience? Do any of these standards hurt people? Is it necessary to have sexual standards? Is it inevitable?

1. Heterosexual standard: We are supposed to be sexually attractive to and attracted by the opposite sex and to desire to be sexually involved with them (Altman 1982). This is discussed later in the chapter. The proportion of people who say they believe that homosexual sex is "always wrong" declined between 1985 and 1994, but the majority of people, 53 percent still give this response in opinion polls (Pew Research Center 2003).

2. Coital standard: We are supposed to view sexual intercourse between a woman and a man, or coitus, as the ultimate sexual act. All other sexual activities, such as oral-genital contact or manual stimulation, are considered foreplay, implying that they are not really sex but can lead to the real thing. According to this standard, a person may have much sexual experience, heterosexual or homosexual, but can consider himself or herself to be a virgin because he or she has not participated in coitus. In 1998, the *Journal of the American Medical Association* reported that 60 percent of young people surveyed said that oral sex was not sex.

3. Orgasmic standard: We are supposed to experience orgasm as the climax of any sexual interaction. This standard has been prevalent for men for a long time in Western society, and more recently it has become the rule for women as well.

4. Two-person standard: We are supposed to view sex as an activity for two people. Masturbation has become more acceptable, but it is still seen as a substitute for real sex. Sexual activity involving more than two people is supposed to be perceived as exotic and unseemly.

5. Romantic standard: Sex and love are supposed to be tied together. Love without sex is seen as incomplete, and sex without love is perceived to be shallow and exploitative.

6. Marital standard: Marriage must include sex. Sex in marriage is the norm to which other sexual activity is compared. For example, we use the words *premarital sex* and *extramarital sex* to describe sex between people who are not married to each other. The use of these terms illustrates how sex in marriage is the "normal" reference point, although other kinds of sexual relationships are recognized and sometimes even accepted as legitimate (standards 2–4 from Kelly 1992).

Sex and the Law

Some characteristics of the sexual standards described earlier were formally sanctioned in law until very recently. During the twentieth century, legal interference in sexual relationships declined, but many restrictions still remain (Friedman 1993). For example, until 2003 over one-half of the states had laws that deemed some forms of nonmarital and extramarital sexual activity as crimes. These include adultery, fornication, sodomy, and oral sex (Stetson 1991).

The first standard mentioned, the heterosexual standard, is one that has been formalized by laws. In 1962, Illinois was the first state to decriminalize homosexual behavior practiced in private between consenting adults. About half of the rest of the states had followed suit by the 1990s (Kelly 1992).

In 2003 in a Supreme Court decision, *Lawrence et al.* v. *Texas,* the court ruled that the Texas statute making it a crime for two persons of the same sex to engage in certain intimate sexual conduct violates the Due Process Clause and is therefore unconstitutional. The ruling declared that sodomy laws can no longer be enforced when applied to noncommercial consenting adults in private. The remaining thirteen states with these laws are expected to see them overturned by the national ruling. But the process is slow and courts must sort through a wide range of cases. Of the thirteen states with sodomy laws, four—Texas, Kansas, Oklahoma, and Missouri—prohibit oral and anal sex between same-sex couples. The other nine ban consensual sodomy for everyone: Alabama, Florida, Idaho, Louisiana, Mississippi, North Carolina, South Carolina, Utah, and Virginia.

Private consensual sex between homosexuals and lesbians continues to be subject to legal action. The federal government, for example, discharges several hundred men and women (women are much more likely to be discharged) each year from the armed forces for violating a directive to refrain from homosexual activities (Kelly 1992). Military Courts of Appeal have so far not acknowledged the *Lawrence* v. *Texas* decision as reason to abolish laws against soldiers who are gay and lesbian. But the numbers of discharges has dropped dramatically in the past few years from a high of 1,227 in 2001 to 653 in 2004 (Nieves and Tyson 2005).

Other aspects of the standards listed in the previous section have also been formalized into law. For example, twenty states have laws that provide for misdemeanor charges for adultery, although they are rarely enforced (Katchadourian 1985). Regarding the last standard listed in the earlier section, the marital standard, the law views sexual intercourse as a required feature of marriage in a few states. If a marriage is not sexually consummated, it can be annulled. This means that if sexual intercourse does not take place between a wife and husband, the marriage can be said to never have existed.

Problems in Sex Research

Research on sex has been hampered by several problems. Some of the data are old; some are not representative; and some do not completely reveal the significance and meaning of sexuality (Schneider and Gould 1987). Until quite recently, sociologists often relied on the Kinsey Reports, which were done in the late 1940s and early 1950s, as the most comprehensive set of information we had on sexual attitudes and behaviors that reflected the whole nation. In the 1980s, researchers went to the federal government to obtain funding to conduct research on sex in the United States. In 1991, led by Senator Jesse Helms, the Senate passed an amendment to prohibit the government from funding such studies. Edward Laumann, Robert Michael, Stuart Michaels, and John Gagnon were forced to find lesser funding from other private sources, but forged ahead with their project—the National Health and Social Life Survey (Michael et al. 1994; Laumann et al. 1994). They hired 220 interviewers and collected data from 3,432 adults in the early 1990s. Their findings are reported in a number of figures and tables in this chapter. In 2002, a large study (12,571 men and women ages 15 to 44) was done by the Center for Disease Control (CDC) on sexual behavior and health in the United States (Mosher, Chandra, and Jones 2005). Their findings are also reported in this chapter.

There is still much work to do, however, because sexuality is difficult to understand by numbers alone. The significance and meaning of events can be critical. Qualitative data can sometimes help in this regard by offering some explanations and critiques of the numbers and their meaning in real lives.

You should recall from Box 2.1 in Chapter 2 that sociological research can be divided into two approaches: those that collect quantitative data that report numbers and those that collect qualitative data that describe and try to understand the meaning of those numbers. Both kinds of research are important. Quantitative data usually provide a stronger sense of the representativeness of the social phenomena because these projects are usually conducted on large representative samples. If we know what proportion of a large population, such as the nation, is affected by the issue, we have a better sense of how important it is to the society as a whole. For example, on the question of premarital sex, we find that over the past century increasing numbers of people are engaging in coitus at younger ages and that the gap between women and men is closing (Michael et al. 1994).

Qualitative research helps us see the complexity of the issues. Numbers can have many different meanings. Thompson's and Rubin's work shows, for example, that while the closing gap in quantitative measures of premarital coital experience between women and men indicates that one feature of sexual experience may be more equal, many other gender differences remain, and in some cases the gap between women and men may actually be increasing (Schneider and Gould 1987).

Ideas about Sex

Sex is a topic about which there are a wide range of ideas. Michael and his colleagues (1994), however, found that based on their responses to a questionnaire, people can be grouped into three categories: traditional, relational, and recreational. Table 8.1 shows nine key questions they asked.

The first group, traditionals, comprised about one-third of the total. They said that religion always guided their sexual activities, homosexuality was always wrong, abortion should be restricted, and premarital, extramarital, and teen sex were always wrong. The second group, relational, was the largest group, about half of all those interviewed. They believed that extramarital sex was wrong, premarital sex was okay, and they would not have sex with someone they did not love. The third category, recreational, made up almost one-quarter. They said that sex does not have to be connected with love, and they strongly oppose restrictions on pornography.

Michael et al. (1994) also found that various social factors seemed to be related to the category into which people fit. Table 8.2 shows how gender, age, marital status, education, religion, and race intersected with the traditional, relational, and recreational categories. Gender shows up throughout the table, and women in all categories are more likely to fit into the traditional and relational groups and less likely to fit into the recreational group than men. Younger people are more likely to fit into the recreational group than older people. Conservative Protestants are most likely to fit into the traditional group, while more of those with no religion show up in the recreational category. Better educated people are more likely to find themselves in the recreational category compared with those with less education, who are more traditional in their ideas about sex.

Race and gender combine in some interesting ways. Black men are more likely than men in the other two racial ethnic groups to fit into the recreational category, but black women are much less likely to fit into the recreational group compared with women and men in other racial ethnic categories.

Gail Wyatt and her colleagues (1998) have looked at African American women and sex and conclude that African American women's sexuality is a product of three important factors: socialization, economics, and beliefs. Wyatt et al. (1998) argue that the sexual

---

TABLE 8.1   Nine Key Questions about Sex

1. Premarital sex is always wrong.
2. Premarital sex among teenagers is always wrong.
3. Extramarital sex is always wrong.
4. Same-gender sex is always wrong.
5. There should be laws against the sale of pornography to adults.
6. I would not have sex with someone unless I was in love with them.
7. My religious beliefs have guided my sexual behavior.
8. A woman should be able to obtain a legal abortion if she was raped.
9. A woman should be able to obtain a legal abortion if she wants it for any reason.

Source: Michael et al. 1994, p. 147.

TABLE 8.2   Who Is Traditional, Relational, and Recreational?

	Traditional	Relational	Recreational
Gender			
Men	26.9%	40.1%	33.0%
Women	33.7	47.6	18.7
Age			
Men			
18–24	17.4	46.9	35.7
25–29	21.0	46.2	32.9
30–39	26.2	38.6	35.2
40–49	31.2	38.2	30.5
50–59	40.1	31.3	28.6
Women			
18–24	23.0	51.8	25.3
25–29	27.5	54.6	17.9
30–39	34.6	46.6	18.8
40–49	34.5	44.9	20.6
50–59	47.0	43.4	9.6
Marital Status			
Men			
Noncohabiting	18.4	39.7	42.0
Cohabiting	8.6	48.4	43.0
Married	36.4	39.0	24.5
Women			
Noncohabiting	31.9	46.8	21.3
Cohabiting	23.9	50.4	25.6
Married	36.2	48.1	15.8
Education			
Men			
Less than high school	31.6	39.5	28.8
High school or equivalent	28.3	40.9	30.8
Any college	25.0	39.8	35.2
Women			
Less than high school	36.6	47.6	15.9
High school or equivalent	38.3	46.0	15.7
Any college	30.4	48.7	20.9
Religion			
Men			
None	11.7	39.1	49.2
Mainline Protestant	24.2	43.8	32.0
Conservative Protestant	44.5	30.1	25.3
Catholic	17.8	49.6	32.6
Women			
None	10.4	44.4	45.2
Mainline Protestant	30.9	51.4	17.7
Conservative Protestant	50.5	38.4	11.2
Catholic	22.2	58.0	19.8

(*continued*)

TABLE 8.2 (*continued*)

	Traditional	Relational	Recreational
Race and Ethnicity			
Men			
White	26.1%	41.6%	32.2%
Black	32.4	25.4	42.3
Hispanic	25.3	45.1	29.7
Women			
White	30.5	48.3	21.1
Black	45.3	45.8	8.9
Hispanic	40.7	43.2	16.1

Source: Michael et al., 1994, pp. 148–49.

socialization of many African American women emphasizes no sexual knowledge, no sex before marriage, and a preference for vaginal-penile sex.

African American women's sexuality is also affected by the economic context of their lives. Because they often have access to fewer economic resources, they are more dependent on their male partners and therefore are more likely to defer to their partners' sexual decisions. Finally, Wyatt et al. (1998) maintain that, compared with white women, African American women's beliefs include more taboos against body touching and masturbation and less planning for sex because purchasing condoms or taking birth control pills represent a conscious decision to have sex and therefore violate the rules inherent in their beliefs.

Michael et al. (1994) conclude that social forces have strong influences on our attitudes about sex. Our position in racial ethnic and gender systems and our experience in social institutions like schools and churches shape our ideas about a wide range of sexual issues. Michael et al. do not have conclusions about why these forces affect us the ways in which they do or what implications our identification with any of these categories have. Perhaps we could argue that the effect of religion is obvious, since religions have explicit messages they deliver to their members about sexual topics. Wyatt et al. (1998) give us some ideas about the sources of attitudes for African American women, but what about the other differences by race ethnicity, gender, and education? Why do these patterns emerge?

The effects of these differences are also unknown, although they undoubtedly are important. In a general sense, the wide range of opinions suggests that sex will remain a controversial public debate. In more private settings, relationships among people who live with each other and especially who engage in sexual relationships with each other must be complicated by these patterns of difference.

Premarital Sex

The issue of premarital sex is one example of an area in which researchers had not maintained long-term, consistent data collection from a large, representative, cross-national population before the National Health and Social Life Survey (Laumann et al., 1994). Lau-

TABLE 8.3   Trends in Heterosexual Experience among Teens

Era When Subjects Were in High School	Proportion Ever Had Intercourse	
	Men	*Women*
1925–1930	50	8
1945–1950	74	22
1982	76	62
1991	78	67

Source: Laumann et al., 1994.

mann and his colleagues asked people to provide their age and their sexual history, allowing us to see what the long-term changes have been. Table 8.3 shows the proportion of women and men who said they had sexual intercourse by the time they were seniors in high school. The data are divided into four cohorts (age groups). The first were in high school in the late 1920s. Since the data were collected in the early 1990s, these people were in their seventies. The second group were in high school in the late 1940s and were in their late sixties and early seventies when the data were collected. The third group were in high school in 1982 and were close to forty. The fourth group were in high school in 1991 and were twenty-something at the time of the research.

The table shows that the proportion of young men having intercourse by the time they finished high school rose from about 50 percent in the oldest age group to 72 percent in the three younger groups. For women, the proportion rose from less than 10 percent in the oldest age group to 20 percent in the second age group to about 60 percent in the last two age groups. The gender gap is closing, and when we hear of greater sexual freedom among today's young people, we are referring mostly to changes in young women's experience (Schwartz and Rutter 1998).

At the same time changes in behavior were occurring, attitudes toward premarital sex were also becoming more tolerant. Table 8.3 shows how these attitudes changed between 1972 and 1994. In the NORC general survey, a large national survey of a representative sample in the United States carried out by the National Opinion Research Center at the University of Chicago, the subjects were asked, "There's been a lot of discussion about the way morals and attitudes about sex are changing in this country. If a man and woman have sex relations before marriage, do you think it is always wrong, almost always wrong, wrong only sometimes, or not wrong at all?" The majority of people still think premarital sex is wrong at least sometimes. But the percentage of people answering "not wrong at all" gradually increased from 27 percent in 1972 to 41 percent in 1994.

In 1991, Michael and his colleagues (1994) asked a second question of people who said they thought premarital sex was always wrong. The researchers asked them if they had themselves engaged in premarital sex. Fifty-eight percent said they had. Behavior and beliefs are not always consistent. Darling, Kallen, and VanDusen (1992) argue that changes in premarital sex moved through three stages in the twentieth century. They call the first stage, which lasted from 1900 to the early 1950s, the era of the double standard. During this period, men often experienced sex before marriage, but women rarely did.

The second era they label the era of permissiveness with affection. This was the transition period in the 1960s and 1970s during which the proportion of men experiencing premarital sex continued to increase and the proportion of women began to catch up with the men.

The 1980s they describe as a period in which premarital sex was expected of young men and women and in which sex in nonlove relationships was acceptable. This era might be called permissive. The picture of that decade that emerges is one of more sexual activity, fewer emotional restrictions on that activity, and a fair amount of gender equality (Reiss 1986).

Schwartz and Rutter (1998) speculate on what they believed to be occurring at the close of the twentieth century. As the 1980s proceeded, the "fun and games encouraged in the 1960s and 1970s [and early 80s] stopped with a rather dull thud" as the population aged and AIDS became an epidemic (p. 146). The opening decade of the twenty-first century is marked by concern over people who cannot control their sexual contacts—"sexual addicts"—and the option of celibacy. Nevertheless, sex persists as a popular activity (T. Lewin 1994). Ninety-seven percent of men ages twenty-five to forty-four have had sexual intercourse with a woman, 90 percent have had oral sex, and 40 percent have had anal sex. The numbers are nearly the same for women (Mosher, Chandra, and Jones 2005). Men now have a median of six to eight sex partners in their lifetime, and women have about four (Mosher, Chandra, and Jones 2005). Twenty-six percent of people report one partner, and the largest number of partners reported were 1,016 for one man and 1,009 for one woman. The top three attractions are vaginal intercourse, oral sex, and watching one's partner undress (Laumann et al. 1994).

Teen Romance

In the 1990s, about 65 percent of women age eighteen said they had had intercourse, and about 75 percent of men. The most recent study, based on data collected in 2002 found that young people are sexually active although they are not restricting themselves to intercourse and may be replacing intercourse with oral sex. In addition, young women are reporting having had intercourse more often than do young men. Fifty-five percent of fifteen- to nineteen-year-old men and 54 percent of women reported getting or giving oral sex, compared with 49 percent of men and 53 percent of women the same ages who reported having had intercourse (Mather, Chandra, and Jones 2005).

Table 8.4 shows that, although the gap has closed in the experience of women and men, the reasons for having first intercourse are still quite different. The table doesn't tell us the ages of the people who are responding, so differences in age might be significant, and perhaps younger women and men are more similar to one another than they are to older people. The table does tell us that if we take the population as whole, important differences exist in the reasons. Women are twice as likely to name affection as the reason for first intercourse, and men are twice as likely to name curiosity/readiness for sex.

Table 8.3 gave us some information about teens and sex, but not much about what the experience was like. Table 8.4 gives us some important hints about how the experience might be different for women and men. Sharon Thompson's (1984) qualitative research fur-

TABLE 8.4   Reasons for Having First Sexual Intercourse (First Intercourse Wanted)

Reason	Men	Women
Affection for partner	25%	48%
Peer pressure	4	3
Curiosity/readiness for sex	51	24
Wanted to have a baby	0	1
Physical pleasure	12	3
Under influence of drugs/alcohol	1	0
Wedding night	7	21

Source: Michael et al., 1994, p. 93.

ther expands our knowledge about the character of first sexual experiences among young women. She interviewed fifty working-class teenage girls between 1978 and 1983 to find out what their perceptions of their own sexual experiences were. Her work uncovered three factors: (1) the lower age of first coitus does not necessarily mean that young people are more sexually active; (2) although young women are engaging in coitus at an earlier age, they may not be enjoying their encounters; and (3) young women spend an enormous amount of energy infusing romance into their sexual experiences.

The statistics report that young women and men are having coitus at a younger age than in previous decades. But loss of virginity requires only one act of intercourse, and research shows that first coitus does not mark the beginning of high levels of sexual activity (Zelnick, Kanter, and Ford 1981). In her interviews, Thompson (1984) found that "having sex all the time is rarely the aftermath of first sexual intercourse for teenage girls" (p. 368). She argues that it is easier to say no after saying yes once because intercourse no longer carries symbolic weight. In another study by Lillian Rubin (1991), two-thirds of the teenage women said they had tried sex once and then decided to "put the issue on hold" (p. 62).

Thompson observes that at least for some women, first coitus was perceived more as meeting a challenge or moving through a rite of passage rather than as satisfying sexual desire. Rubin found this to be true among the adults—both men and women—she interviewed. When describing their first experience with coitus, Rubin's subjects used phrases like "crossing the great divide—the pressure was off—a burden was lifted—a hurdle was gotten over" (1991, p. 43).

Thompson (1984) observes, furthermore, that higher rates of coitus at earlier ages do not necessarily mean that more sexual activity is taking place. She argues that coitus has taken on such significance in recent decades that other forms of sexual activity may have lessened. In Kinsey's research in the 1930s and 1940s, for example, respondents spoke of extensive noncoital petting and orgasmic sexual play. Her subjects in the 1970s and 1980s, in contrast described their sexual activities as more limited: "fewer partners, a limited repertoire of sexual activities and relatively little pleasure, particularly orgasmic pleasure" (p. 363). Subjects in Rubin's research described the loss of pleasure in their own lives when they moved from "the kid stuff" to the "real thing." One woman who was nineteen when she first had intercourse described it this way:

I mean it was directed to his coming, no sensuality, nothing soft and pleasurable. The so-called kid's sexual experiences I had before, with whatever guy I was with, were much more in the nature of mutual pleasuring. I used to think about those experiences and miss them and wonder why I ever got into the so-called real thing. (1991, p. 57)

Schwartz and Rutter call this the "lost art of petting." They note that petting—or kissing, touching, feeling, rubbing, and groping—used to be the center of young romance. These days, people move quickly from first kiss to first intercourse, leaving little time for these intervening activities. And even people who have been engaging in sex with each other for some time may move rapidly in each encounter from touching and foreplay to genitally focused sex and intercourse. Schwartz and Rutter speculate that recent concern about HIV/AIDS may alter this trend as people increasingly try to find ways to enjoy safer sex. "Petting, sexy talk, and other old-fashioned methods of sexual intimacy have come back into vogue out of necessity" (Schwartz and Rutter 1998, pp. 94–95).

The second theme that emerges in Thompson's work is the frequent lack of enjoyment associated with coitus. Some young women spoke of physical discomfort; others just were disappointed that coitus hadn't lived up to their expectations. One teenager said, "I was expecting it to be much nicer than it felt. It didn't hurt or anything. It just didn't feel really good" (1984, p. 365).

The third theme in the interviews Thompson conducted was the elaborate romanticized context the women created around their sex lives. They spoke for long periods of time about the men, talking about details about his appearance, the first time they met, how they broke up, and their feelings for him. They spent hours with their girlfriends rehearsing and embellishing these stories. Romance was the focus of her subjects' discussion of sex.

A final issue is the question of the double standard—condoning sex for boys and condemning it for girls. Darling, Kallen, and VanDusen (1992) argue that the statistics indicate that the double standard has disappeared as young women and men become increasingly similar in their experience. Rubin's (1991) qualitative work suggests that the issue is more unsettled than the numbers might suggest. She describes the current period as one of tolerance and entitlement, where both teenage women and men feel entitled to engage in sex. Important gender differences, however, still emerge around the question of monogamy.

Rubin found that women who "sleep around" are consistently condemned, while men who are not monogamous are often not criticized. She observed that even the terms the people she interviewed used for this behavior—"stud" for men and "slut" for women—suggest admiration for the men and disparagement for the women. When Rubin asked college-aged men if they wished that women were less sexually available, they always said no, but they also frequently complained of women who were "too sexually active, too easy or who come on too strong" (1991, p. 118). And 40 percent of the women interviewed said they understated their sexual activity because "they fear people wouldn't understand or would think they were sluts or their boyfriends would be upset" (p. 119).

Table 8.5 shows the frequency of sex among different kinds of couples. The table compares single/never married people, married people, divorced/cohabiting people, and never married/cohabiting people. The table indicates that divorced people have the lowest frequency of sex, followed by single/never married people and married people. Cohabiting people have the most sex with divorced cohabitors having less sex than cohabitors who

TABLE 8.5   **Marriage Status and Average Sexual Frequency per Month**

	Men	Women
Single/never married	5.6	6.2
Divorced	5.5	5.1
Married	6.9	6.5
Divorced/cohabiting	7.9	7.4
Never married/cohabiting	8.3	8.5

Source: Data from Laumann et al., 1994.

have never been married. The table also shows that the numbers are almost identical for women and men, although women who are single/never married report a little more sex than men in this category. The range of all responses is fairly small, between five and nine sexual encounters per month.

The Marriage Bed

Laumann et al. (1994) provide us with numbers about the sexual experience of married people in the 1990s, but their data do not tell us what people think about their sexual experience in marriage. Rubin (1976) interviewed working-class couples to try to answer that question. She found that women and men experienced sex differently, especially in their expectations about sex. Although married couples may be engaging in more oral sex, husbands and wives frequently disagree about whether this is producing more sexual gratification for both of them. And the expectation that oral sex should be a part of their experience sometimes caused difficulties between the husbands and wives.

On the average, men and women in her study differed in their desire to experiment in sex. As an example, Rubin quotes a husband and wife who were interviewed separately. The husband says:

> I've always been of the opinion that what two people do in the bedroom is fine; whatever they want to do is okay. But Jane, she doesn't agree. I personally like a lot of foreplay, caressing each other and whatever. For her, no. I think oral sex is the ultimate in making love; but she says it's revolting. I wish I could make her understand. (Rubin 1976, p. 138)

His wife has a different opinion:

> I sure wish I could make him stop pushing me into that (ugh, I even hate to talk about it), into that oral stuff. I let him do it, but I hate it. He says I'm old-fashioned about sex and maybe I am. But I was brought up that there's just one way you're supposed to do it. I still believe that way, even though he keeps trying to convince me of his way. How can I change when I wasn't brought up that way? I wish I could make him understand. (Rubin 1976, p. 138)

Rubin discovered that part of the womens' reluctance was based on their belief that if they indulged in sexual behavior other than coitus, they might be judged as slutty or cheap by their husbands. Most of the husbands said they would not judge their wives' behavior that way.

The husbands, however, also expressed pride in their wives' sexual naivete. The husbands frequently made statements like "She was like an innocent babe, I taught her everything she knows" (Rubin 1976, p. 142). These comments were made even by husbands whose wives were in their second marriage. Rubin concludes that wives receive mixed messages. They are supposed to be interested in trying new sex techniques, but they are also supposed to appear to be innocent and naive.

Women are not the only ones who question the liberalization of sex. Men, too, sometimes express discomfort and apprehension. Their anxiety seems to center around the fear of losing control, since an important feature of the social construction of masculinity in our society is control. Sex can make men feel out of control and at the mercy of women. One man told Rubin (1981) in another set of interviews she conducted:

> I'm not always comfortable with my own sexuality because I can feel very vulnerable when I'm making love. It's a bit crazy, I suppose, because in sex is when I'm experiencing the essence of my manhood and also when I can feel the most frightened about it—like I'm not my own man, or I could lose myself or something like that. (p. 107)

In a similar vein another man said, "Sometimes I can get scared. I don't even know exactly why, but I feel very vulnerable, like I'm too wide open. Then it feels dangerous" (Rubin 1981, p. 109).

Nonmonogamous Activity

The percentage of people who say that extramarital sex is always wrong has fluctuated since the early 1970s, but the general trend is in the direction of a greater proportion agreeing with this statement. A very large percentage (68–80%) in all years say that extramarital sex is always wrong (Gallup Organization 2005).

In spite of the belief among many people that extramarital sex is always wrong, Table 8.6 shows that quite a few married people have engaged in nonmonogamous behavior. The table shows the proportion of married people who say they ever had a nonmonogamous experience. The data are divided into four age groups, and the numbers report information for women and men in each category. About 7 percent of the men in the youngest category

TABLE 8.6   **Lifetime Rates of Nonmonogamy among Married People**

Age	Men	Women
22–33	7	12
34–43	20	14
44–53	31	19
54–63	36	11

Source: Data from Laumann et al., 1994.

report they have been nonmonogamous, and the proportion rises with each age group to a high of about 37 percent among men aged fifty-four to sixty-three. For women the pattern is different. In the young age group, 12 percent of the women say they have been non-monogamous, and that proportion rises to the third age group, forty-four to fifty-three, where about 20 percent say they have been. The fourth age group of women, age fifty-four to sixty-three, has a smaller proportion (12 percent) reporting nonmonogamy.

Besides gender, other factors seem to influence the probability that a person has had an extramarital affair (Laumann et al. 1994). People who did not complete high school and those with graduate education are more likely to have been nonmonogamous than college graduates. Living in a city and being less religious also predicted greater nonmonogamy. Poor people were more likely to have had affairs compared with rich people, and those who had been married more than once were more likely than those in a first marriage.

HIV/AIDS

Concern about STDs (sexually transmitted diseases), and especially HIV/AIDS may alter our experience and ideas about sex. More than one million people (1,185,000) in the United States are living with HIV/AIDS. About one-quarter are unaware of their infection. AIDS is now among the top causes of death in the country. For African American women age 25–34 it is the number one cause of death (CDC 2003c; 2005c). Some people say that they are changing their behavior as a result of their fear of AIDS, as shown in Table 8.7.

Given the gravity of the issue, however, the number of people who have not changed their behavior is large, especially married people, women, and whites. It is difficult to interpret the meaning of the numbers, however. The small number stating they have changed their behavior could mean that most people, especially people in those categories, are foolishly unconcerned. The data could also be interpreted, however, as evidence that most people in the low-number categories were not engaged in behaviors associated with AIDS. For example, those who are celibate or who are involved in long-time monogamous relationships in which both partners are sexually exclusive and neither has been exposed to someone else's blood may feel that they do not have to change their behavior. (Knowing whether

TABLE 8.7   People Who Have Changed Their Sexual Behavior as a Result of Their Fear of AIDS

Married	12%
Never married	52
Whites	26
Blacks	46
Men	35
Women	25
Under 25	43
Age 25 to 29	36

Source: Laumann, Gagnon, Michael, and Michaels 1994, p. 434.

one's partner is monogamous, however, is impossible.) The numbers probably reflect a combination of valid and irrational reasoning

Research also reports that some people who may have changed their behavior in general to avoid HIV/AIDS are still engaging in risky behavior, such as not using a condom, in certain circumstances, like when they drink or when they are in love (Pilkington, Kern, and Indest 1994; Sigmon and Gainey 1995). Only 39 percent of men age fifteen to forty-four who had at least one sexual partner in the past year say they used a condom in their most recent contact. And only 14 percent of men who consider themselves heterosexual had gone for HIV testing (Mosher, Chandra, and Jones 2005).

Some Theoretical Debates on Sexuality

The description of sexual behaviors and ideologies shows them to be diverse and dynamic, changing over time. What exactly is sexuality? Can people be categorized by sexuality? Is sexuality repressed in our society? In this section we will discuss two of the theoretical debates over the answers to these questions, beginning with the question of sexual categories.

Heterosexuality, Homosexuality, and Lesbianism

In some of the tables discussed in the previous section, respondents were divided into three groups—heterosexual, homosexual, and lesbian. Most people in the United States identify themselves as heterosexual, homosexual, lesbian, or bisexual. These distinctions are politically and socially important. A large and important gay and lesbian movement is based on the recognition of the validity of sexuality that is not heterosexual.

Some theorists argue that distinctions between heterosexuals and homosexuals are biologically or socially determined early in a child's life. This point of view is an essentialist argument: Sexuality is perceived to be an orientation that is given, an essential, immutable part of an individual's character. Researchers from this point of view search for a gay gene or some other biological evidence of their assertion (DeCecco and Parker 1995).

Other theorists (D'Emlio 1998) argue, in contrast, that the categories are socially constructed. According to social constructionist, "Sexuality is situational and changeable, modified by day-to-day circumstances throughout the life course" (Blumstein and Schwartz 1990b, p. 173). They maintain that there are no scientific criteria by which to sort people into this limited number of categories (Simons 1996). Human sexuality is much too fluid and diverse to capture in the four slots commonly referred to in our society: heterosexual, homosexual, lesbian, and bisexual. Table 8.8 illustrates some of the complexity by showing how people identify themselves, what relationships they have engaged in, and whether they find the idea of same-sex relationships appealing.

Sexuality, however, is even more complex and includes self-identification, sexual histories, large ranges of sexual activities, physical arousal, opinions, ideologies, fantasy, and physical contact.

For example, many people have had sexual contact with someone of the same sex but identify themselves as heterosexual; others have had sexual contact with someone of the other sex and consider themselves homosexual. Many people's choices of partners vary by

TABLE 8.8   Homosexuality and Lesbianism

	Women	Men
Identify as gay or lesbian	2.3%	2.3%
Identify as bisexual	1.8	1.8
Identify as heterosexual	90	90
Had homosexual or lesbian experience	11.0%	6.0%
Had sex with same sex partner in last year	4.0	3.0
Had sex with same sex partner and opposite sex in last year	3.0	1.0
Sexually attracted to opposite sex only	86	92
*Find the fantasy of homosexual or lesbian experience appealing	5.5%	6.0%

Source: *Laumann, Gagnon, Michael, and Michaels, 1994; all other data from Mosher, Chandra, and Jones, 2005.

sex over time. Some people experience a dissonance between their ideas and their physical reactions and are physically aroused by sexual stimulation they believe to be disgusting. Some people are aroused by viewing the sexual activity of others but do not participate.

For example, heterosexual men may enjoy viewing erotic films of lesbians. People fantasize during sex about having sex with someone of a different sex. People engage in group sex, and so on. The social constructionists believe that attempting to create a sexual typology that could differentiate among all the possibilities would result in a large number of categories and would make the whole effort meaningless. Social constructionists point out that the task would be further complicated if one were to look at the issue historically. A review of the history would show that the practice of dividing people into categories based on their sexual activity has existed for only a little more than a hundred years. Karl Kertbeny coined the terms *heterosexual* and *homosexual* in 1868 in Germany. The first documented use of the term *homosexual* in the United States was in 1892 (Katz 1995).

Homosexual and heterosexual behavior existed prior to the invention of these terms. The important change the words indicate, however, is the identification of individuals as a function of their sexual activity. Before the nineteenth century, people were known to participate in sexual activities with those of their own sex. This activity, however, was not seen as indicative of a particular type of person. For example, sometimes men would engage in anal intercourse with other men; sometimes they might perform it on women. In either case, they were not seen as therefore being a homosexual or a heterosexual.

The social constructionists argue that the rational alternative is to accept the diversity and not try to fit people into sexual types. Kinsey wrote, "The world is not to be divided into sheep and goats. Only the human mind invents categories and tries to force facts into separate pigeonholes. The living world is a continuum" (Kinsey 1948, p. 689).

This rational alternative, however, ignores the importance of the oppression of people because of their sexuality and the social movements that have developed to try to end that oppression. Altman summarizes this dilemma:

> On one level to love someone of the same sex is remarkably inconsequential—after all, but for some anatomical differences, love for a man or a woman is hardly another order of things

> yet society has made of it something portentous, and we must expect homosexuals to accept this importance in stressing their identity. (1971, p. 219)

Sexuality remains a salient political arena for gay men and lesbians. And self-identification as homosexual, bisexual, or lesbian is an important aspect of the affirmative character of the gay and lesbian rights movement. The debate around questions like the essentialism or social construction of sexuality and our sexual identities are called queer theory (Beemyn and Elliason 1996; Duberman 1997a, 1997b; Warner 1993).

Explaining the Focus on Sex

The discussion of sex in this chapter reveals an assumption in the writings of many authors that sexuality is a powerful natural force controlled by society and that those restraints have recently been lessened. Researchers like Hunt (1974), Blumstein and Schwartz (1990b), and Gayle Rubin (1984) focus their attention on the positive features of unleashing sexuality from the tight grip of society. Others (Dworkin, 1981; MacKinnon 1982; Rich 1980) have been concerned with the problems that come with breaking down barriers to the expression of sexuality. All these scholars, however, share a conceptualization of sex as a human drive that is ever-present and restrained, repressed, or set free by the social systems in which humans live.

In the scenario at the beginning of the chapter, one of the comments Lori makes illustrates the popular notion of this idea. She says that she might be doing the community a favor by helping the telephone callers release their sexual tensions by talking on the phone rather than in some other, less acceptable behaviors. The underlying assumption is that sex is a powerful force that must be expressed in some form and that a community should be concerned with controlling and directing its expression. This point of view is rooted in the works of such scholars as Sigmund Freud (1963), Wilhelm Reich (1945), and Herbert Marcuse (1966). According to this framework, sexuality is a strong essential drive that has been repressed in order to establish and maintain civilization. As a matter of necessity, sexuality has become "subservient to labour discipline, to subdue hedonism in the interest of progress" (Brake 1982a).

Michael Foucault's (1978) work represents an important critique of this point of view. He posits that sex is not a biological urge repressed by society but a socially constructed urge with socially constructed means to satisfy that urge. He argues that our recent concern with sex is not because it has been set free but because our society emphasizes certain forms of sexuality. Jeffrey Weeks explains Foucault's point of view: "We give supreme importance to sex in our individual and social lives today because of a history that has assigned a central significance to the sexual. It has not always been so; it need not always be so" (1985, p. 3).

The important political implication of Foucault's and Weeks's position is that we can and must decide what place sexuality should have in our lives and in our society. The debate over sexuality cannot be one of repression versus freedom. Instead we need to do even more fundamental thinking and planning about what sex is and how it should be structured within our society.

According to theorists like Foucault and Weeks who emphasize the importance of social context in understanding sexuality, the key factor in how sex is socially constructed in our society is its commodification and therefore its growth along with the development of consumer capitalism (Altman 1982; D'Emilio and Freedman 1988). Sex is a lucrative business. Industries use sex to sell everything from cars to blue jeans. In addition, sex itself is for sale in a vast array of formats, including films, television, music, clothing, books, and Internet sites. The commercialization of sex has had an enormous impact on the promotion, repression, and all-around shaping of sex in contemporary U.S. society. Sixty-four percent of television shows include some sex talk or interaction and a scene depicting some sexual act occurs about every fifteen minutes. Sexual intercourse is portrayed about once an hour although it is often under the sheets (Kunkel et al. 2003). Foucault and Weeks would see these as examples of the commodification of sex.

This section has reviewed two important theoretical debates on sexuality. In the first subsection we looked at the question of diversity in sexuality. The dominant ideology about sex in our society posits that each individual can be identified as one of four types: heterosexual, homosexual, lesbian, or bisexual. Theorists assert that individual sexuality is much more variable and complex than any system of categorization could capture.

In the second subsection, our attention turned to the question of whether sex is an intrinsic human drive that is always repressed and controlled by society. This view comes especially from Freudian thought. Others, like Foucault and Weeks, maintain that sex is both created and shaped by social interaction at both the micro- and macrolevels.

In the next section we move to a more concrete issue that has taken center stage in political debates in the United States. The question of whether abortion should be accessible to women is an example of a practical but volatile issue within the debate over how sexuality should be organized and especially how its expression among women should be constructed and controlled.

Abortion

Thus far, this chapter has shown the way in which the macrolevel of our society has had an important effect on the microlevel of our most intimate social relationships, love and sex. An economic system commercializes sex and a political system passes laws to control it. We have also observed the way in which the macrolevel has been challenged and shaped by the microforces of individuals interacting with one another to form social movements to re-create sexuality. The abortion rights movement is a particularly important social movement that has organized to allow its view of sexuality, particularly women's sexuality, to exist. The abortion rights movement will be the focus of our attention in this section.

One issue that has become central in the debate over women's sexuality is the legality of abortion. When the Second-Wave feminist movement emerged in the late 1960s, abortion was not legal in the United States. The fight to make it legal was a top priority on the feminist agenda and has continued to be a rallying point (Ellis 1983). Feminists organized marches, educational programs, and rallies for abortion rights, and feminist-identified lawyers argued the *Roe* v. *Wade* case that made abortion legal in 1973 (Joffe 1986).

The legal restrictions prior to *Roe* v. *Wade,* however, did not stop abortions from being performed. Leo Kanowitz (1969) estimated in the late 1960s that more than a million illegal abortions were performed each year and that between five thousand and ten thousand women died every year from complications from these back-alley procedures.

In 1965, the Supreme Court ruled that it was legal to sell contraceptives to married people. The growing feminist movement of the 1960s joined this battle, claiming that legal access to abortion was intrinsic to the right to control one's own body and was necessary if women were to claim equality (D'Emilio and Freedman 1988). In 1973, *Roe* v. *Wade* was hailed as a major victory by the women's movement.

In the *Roe* v. *Wade* decision, the Supreme Court ruled that states could not pass laws that made abortion illegal during the first trimester of a pregnancy. The decision also declared that states could regulate abortions in the last six months of pregnancy, but those regulations must be based on restrictions related to maternal health. Finally, *Roe* v. *Wade* stated that only in the last ten weeks could states ban abortion entirely.

Table 8.9 shows the proportion of people who approve of abortion for various reasons. The table indicates that a large percentage of people think that abortion should be available, at least in some instances. A large proportion think it should be available in all cases, and the numbers are generally rising. Although abortion has been especially important to feminists, these statistics show that many others who would not necessarily consider themselves feminists think abortion should remain a legal right.

Today those who are opposed to legalizing abortion call their movement prolife. Those who advocate keeping abortion legal call their movement prochoice. Kristin Luker (1984) interviewed activists on both sides of the issue and found that people in each group shared a cluster of beliefs in addition to their opinions about whether abortion should be legal. The views of the prolife group included the beliefs that the purpose of sex is to have children; that sex is sacred but is currently being profaned; that making contraception available only encourages young people to be sexually active; and that the way to halt what they believed to be immoral behavior of unmarried teenagers is to eliminate sex education and the availability of birth control. Many prolife activists also believe that women and men should have equal status but that they cannot be equal in all regards because of their biological differences. Prochoice activists believe that the primary purpose of sex is communica-

TABLE 8.9   Percentage Approving of Legal Abortion for Various Reasons

Reason	1972	1985	1996
Pregnancy poses serious health endangerment for woman	87.4%	89.9%	91.5%
Strong chance of serious defect of fetus	78.6%	78.9%	81.1%
Pregnancy resulted from rape	79.1%	81.5%	83.7%
Parent(s) low income—cannot afford a child	48.9%	43.2%	45.7%
Unmarried woman who does not want to marry father	43.8%	41.2%	44.3%
Married woman who does not want more children	40.2%	40.7%	46.2%
Woman wants an abortion for any reason	NA	37.0%	44.6%

Source: Koch 1998, p. 237.

tion, not necessarily to have children. Their view of parenting is that it must be purposeful and designed to give children every possible advantage. Prochoice activists believe that women should be equal to men, and abortion is one part of a package that includes birth control and sex education and that it is designed to give women maximum control over their lives (Luker 1984).

Since the passage of *Roe* v. *Wade,* prolife activists have organized and lobbied at the state level for restrictions that have subsequently been brought to the U.S. District Court and overturned. For example, in 1984 the state of Rhode Island passed a law (which was eventually overturned) requiring that physicians notify a woman's husband before performing an abortion (Lott 1987).

At the federal level, prolife activists successfully lobbied Congress to pass the Hyde Amendment in 1977. The Hyde Amendment, named after Senator Henry Hyde, allows states to prohibit the use of public funds (Medicaid) to pay for abortions of poor women, unless it can be proven that an abortion is necessary to save the mother's life or that the pregnancy was a result of rape or incest. All but fourteen states (Alaska, California, Colorado, Georgia, Hawaii, Maryland, Michigan, New Jersey, New York, North Carolina, Oregon, Pennsylvania, Washington, and West Virginia) and the District of Columbia passed laws eliminating state funding. This means that if poor women wish to obtain an abortion in the other thirty-six states, they must find their own funds to pay for it (Petchesky, 1990).

The *Webster* decision in 1989 dealt another blow to *Roe* v. *Wade.* Although the Supreme Court did not overturn *Roe* v. *Wade* in deciding *Webster,* the justices upheld the constitutionality of four aspects of the Missouri law that were under consideration. The Missouri law (1) states that the life of each human being begins at conception; (2) prohibits using public facilities or employees to perform abortions; (3) prohibits public funding for abortion counseling; and (4) requires that physicians conduct viability tests on fetuses of twenty weeks or more before aborting those pregnancies (Stetson 1991).

The decision in 2003 to make so-called partial birth abortions illegal has added to the confusion surrounding abortion and has further restricted it. Partial birth abortion is not a medical term. Physicians use the term dilation and extraction of a late term (second or early third trimester) pregnancy, which also describes the procedures most commonly used in terminating pregnancies. Does this mean that all or most abortions after the first trimester have been banned because the procedure used is now illegal? Physicians and legal experts are having difficulty determining exactly what is and what is not illegal. In addition, the law has been judged unconstitutional in courts in at least four states, California, Nebraska, New York, and Missouri, because it does not protect the health of the mother, which is required by the *Roe* v. *Wade* decision.

In 2006, South Dakota approved the most far reaching ban on abortion. In South Dakota it is now a felony for a doctor to perform an abortion except to save the life of a pregnant woman. Even a woman whose health might be seriously damaged or who has become pregnant as a result of rape or incest cannot obtain an abortion in South Dakota. Other states, Ohio, Indiana, Georgia, Tennessee, and Kentucky have introduced similar measures. Since the law seems to directly contradict the Supreme Court decision of *Roe* v. *Wade,* which states that states cannot restrict abortion in the first twelve weeks of a pregnancy, the case will undoubtedly end up in the Supreme Court. Planned Parenthood will challenge the ban (Nieves 2006).

The issue of parental consent is another area of contention. A number of states have passed laws requiring that parents be notified if a minor obtains an abortion. In 1990, this restriction was widely publicized after the death of Becky Bell, an Indiana teenager who died from an illegal abortion. She felt forced to have an illegal abortion because, in order to obtain a legal abortion in Indiana, she would have had to inform her parents first, something she did not wish to do. Table 8.10 shows that young single white women like Becky Bell make up a significant proportion of the people seeking abortions.

Table 8.10 also indicates that the largest proportion of women obtaining abortions are over twenty, with almost half over twenty-five. Abortion is an issue for a broad range of women, although the issue of parental consent makes it especially problematic for women who are minors.

In addition to the changes in the legal issues surrounding abortion, the 1980s brought a technological change that further intensified the debate (Norsigian 1990). In 1988, the French government approved the use of a new drug, RU486. RU486 is a steroid that comes in pill form. If taken along with an injection of progesterone by a pregnant woman within forty-nine days of her last menstrual period, it causes her body to terminate the pregnancy and expel the embryo. RU486 is an effective replacement for the more complicated and more invasive surgical means of abortion that are currently in use in the United States (Lader 1991). RU486 was approved for use in the United States in 2000.

Another recently developed drug, called Plan B, cannot terminate a pregnancy but it can prevent a woman from becoming pregnant by preventing ovulation, preventing fertilization, or preventing implantation of the embryo in the uterus. Plan B is a concentrated dose of the medicines found in birth control pills and is effective if taken within a few hours or days of intercourse. It is especially good as a back up contraceptive—a Plan B—in the case of contraceptive failure or sexual assault. The Food and Drug Administration (FDA) voted to approve selling the drug over the counter, rather than by prescription only in the

TABLE 8.10   Who Obtains Abortions? 2001

	Percent
Age	
Under 20	16.1%
20–24	33.4
Over 25	48.5
Race	
White	55.4
Black	36.6
Other	8.0
Hispanic	17.1 (both white and black)
Marital status	
Married	18.4
Unmarried	81.6

Source: CDC 2004a.

United States in 2003, but the director of the agency's drug center, Steven Galson, decided to override the advisory committee and the staff members and reject the application because he feared that girls younger than sixteen might engage in riskier sex if they knew that the morning-after pill was easily available.

At this point, the conflict over abortion rights exists in a number of arenas: the courts, political campaigns, and the streets. Prolife advocates have staged civil disobedience actions, such as Operation Rescue, and have blocked entrances to clinics. In 1982 antiabortion activists began fire-bombing abortion clinics, and these incidents increased during the 1980s and 1990s. In 1993, Congress passed a law making abortion clinic violence a federal crime. In that year a new strategy emerged of targeting physicians who perform abortions, and the first such physician was killed. Since then seven clinic workers have been murdered.

In a postmodern political action, terrorists began creating Web sites that provide information on physicians who perform abortions, listing them as "baby butchers" and giving their names, photos, addresses, children's names, and automobile license plate numbers. The sites did not explicitly threaten the physicians, but when a physician was killed, his name was shown crossed through. In 1999, the Supreme Court ruled that such sites must be closed and that the organization that created them had to pay $200 million in damages to a group of doctors who had brought suit (Sanchez 1999).

Prochoice advocates have provided escorts through the blocked entrances, staged the largest protest marches in recent history in Washington, D.C., and launched their own program of nonviolent civil disobedience, Operation Fight Back. The latest political debate is over the Supreme Court itself. The political position of newly appointed justices on the question of legal abortion will determine which way the laws will be decided for a long time to come.

Debates about Abortion

Because of its historic link to the legalization of abortion, its contribution of a specific category of abortion personnel, and its ongoing engagement with the defense of abortion in the courts, the feminist movement can sustain a claim to ownership of the abortion issue (Joffe 1986, p. 37).

The battle over whether to keep abortion legal is a heated one. Proponents of both sides—prochoice and prolife—have widely disparate beliefs not only about whether abortion should be legal but also about what women and men should be like.

In the nineteenth century, feminists were in favor of restricting abortion, but in the late twentieth century, abortion rights have become a central component of the women's movement. Many proabortion rights activists are feminists, and most feminists are in favor of keeping abortion legal (Simon and Danziger 1991).

Ellen Willis (1983) argues that the reason abortion is so important to feminists is because it allows women to break the tie between sex and reproduction. The data presented in this chapter show that women are becoming increasingly engaged in marital and nonmarital coitus. Both unmarried and married women appear to be more sexually active but desire fewer children. Contraceptives are available, but some are dangerous and none are totally effective. Feminists view access to legal abortion as a way to guarantee that women can be heterosexually active and not be forced to continue an unwanted or unsafe pregnancy (Petchesky 1990).

Besides debates between prochoice activists and prolife activists, the question of abortion has also elicited debates between Second-Wave and Third-Wave feminists (Petchesky 1990). Recall from discussions in previous chapters that Second-Wave feminists emerged during the late 1960s. Their emphasis is on the issues they believe are shared by all women in the sisterhood of women. Third-Wave feminists have emphasized the differences among women, especially differences of race and class. In the recent history of the debate over abortion, both Second-Wave and Third-Wave feminists agree that abortion should be kept legal. Third-Wave feminists, however, have been critical of Second-Wave feminists for stopping there, and they have called for an expansion of the agenda (Davis 1991; Fried 1991, Walker 1990).

From the Third-Wave feminist point of view, legalizing abortion alone will do little to increase its accessibility to poor and working-class women. Third-Wave activists have demanded that abortion rights be promoted as part of a package that includes economic as well as legal access to abortion. Third-Wave feminists, furthermore, have insisted that women should not only have the right to choose abortion but also should have the right to bring a pregnancy to term within a health care system that provides them with prenatal, maternal, and pediatric care (Rodrique 1990).

Racial ethnic women have taken a particularly strong stand on this question because of the way in which their right to bear children has been restricted. For example, in 1976 it was revealed that three thousand Native American women had been sterilized after signing inadequate consent forms (Hartmann 1987). In 1970, a federal district court found that "an indefinite number of poor people had been coerced into accepting a sterilization operation under the threat that various federally supported welfare benefits would be withdrawn unless they submitted to irreversible sterilization" (Hartmann 1987, p. 241). Nearly all the cases heard on sterilization abuse have involved poor women who were African American, Chicana, Puerto Rican, or Native American (Lopez 1997; Petchesky 1990; Roberts 1998). As recently as 1987, a study of court-ordered cesarean sections shows that 81 percent were for black, Hispanic, and Asian women, and 24 percent of the women were not native English-speaking (Kolder, Gallagher, and Parsons 1987).

In the late 1970s, federal reforms were put in place to halt the abuse. They included "more rigorous informed consent procedures, a thirty-day waiting period, a prohibition on hysterectomies as opposed to tubal ligations for sterilization purposes, and a moratorium on federally funded sterilization of minors, the involuntarily institutionalized, and the legally incompetent" (Hartmann 1987, p. 241). But evidence remains that abuse continues, and recently proposals have been made to require that welfare recipients agree to using contraceptive implants in order to continue receiving their grants (Lewin 1991).

In 1990, the FDA approved Norplant, a contraceptive that works as long as five years after it is implanted in a woman's upper arm. By 1991, one hundred thousand women had received the implant, and it was fully covered by Medicaid—federally funded health benefits for poor people. While its easy use could make it highly beneficial to women, it also could be used in a coercive manner. Unlike other forms of contraception, the presence of Norplant could be easily monitored by welfare officials or parole officers (Lewin 1991). In Louisiana, State Representative David Duke, a Nazi Party and Ku Klux Klan member, proposed that welfare recipients be offered $100 a year to use Norplant. The ACLU (American Civil Liberties Union) is concerned that these proposals will escalate (Lewin 1991).

Third-Wave feminists share this concern and have called for a reconceptualization of reproductive rights that is broader in its view. Speaking from the Third-Wave feminist point of view, Fried (1991, p. ix) asserts:

> The public has been galvanized by the *Webster* decision to fight for legal abortion. But for what—freedom of choice circumscribed by race and class, removed from feminists' demands about women's autonomy, and shrouded in "privacy," or reproductive freedom for all women? We have an opportunity to move ahead with a positive reproductive rights agenda. Doing so requires that we build the kind of movement we have not had in the past, one that is broad based in its membership, its leadership, and its politics; a movement that goes beyond reaffirmation of *Roe* to demand access not just to abortion, but to the full range of reproductive rights; a movement that is based on a class- and race-conscious feminism.

BOX **8.1**

Was Abortion Illegal in the United States until the *Roe* v. *Wade* Decision?

Many people believe that *Roe* v. *Wade* marked a turning point in American history, making abortion legal for the first time. In fact, prior to about the middle of the nineteenth century, abortion was not a criminal issue in the United States, nor was it condemned by the Catholic or Protestant Churches if it occurred in the first few months of pregnancy, before quickening.

Quickening was the term used to refer to the moment at which the fetus was believed to gain life and therefore a soul. There were a variety of opinions throughout the centuries as to when this moment occurred, and it was believed that the sex of the fetus affected the moment of quickening. For example, Aristotle estimated that quickening occurred for a male fetus at forty days after conception and for a female fetus at ninety days after conception (Gordon 1977). Since technology did not exist that could precisely identify the time of conception, in practice quickening was identified as the point at which a pregnant woman felt the fetus move. Removing the contents of the uterus by chemical or surgical means before the woman felt movement was therefore not a crime or a sin. It was thought of as correcting the regularity of a woman's menstrual cycle (Petchesky 1990).

Abortion services and chemicals that could be used by women themselves to initiate an abortion were widely advertised. During the nineteenth century, advertisements referred to contraceptives as French; for example, condoms were called French letters. The term *Portuguese* referred to abortifacients. One ad in the *New York Times* in 1871 read, "A great and sure remedy for married ladies—the Portuguese female pills always give immediate relief—price $5" (Gordon 1977, p. 54).

In 1854, the Catholic Church began to alter its opinion, and by 1869, abortion had become grounds for excommunication. In 1895, the church tightened its opinion and declared that even when the woman's life was threatened, abortion could not be performed (Blanchard 1994).

But physicians, especially allopathic physicians, were probably most instrumental in the change in laws that resulted in abortions being illegal in all states by the end of the nineteenth century. Allopathic physicians are what are now called medical doctors. Although allopaths have become so dominant that we now reserve the title of physician for them, in the nineteenth century they were just one group of health care practitioners among many. During the 1800s, many different kinds of health care providers existed, including homeopaths, osteopaths, allopaths, midwives,

(continued)

B O X **8.1** *(continued)*

and abortionists. During the last half of the nineteenth century, U.S. allopaths began a campaign to make abortion at any time in the pregnancy illegal. Part of the reason they took on this political crusade was to enhance their position in the competitive field. To wage their battle against abortion, allopaths formed the American Medical Association (AMA), passed a formal resolution against abortion, and then convinced Congress that abortion should be made illegal and that allopaths should be the only legitimate decision makers about whether a therapeutic abortion was justified. The AMA argued that abortion and contraceptives were part of a dangerous female folk culture that was destined to destroy The Family and domestic order in general.

A surprise in the history of abortion in the United States is that nineteenth-century feminists advocated making abortion illegal (Gordon 1982). Nineteenth-century feminists supported criminalizing abortion because they felt that legal abortion encouraged promiscuity among men, who did not have to take responsibility for the pregnancies they caused (Ginsberg 1990). The AMA and feminists were joined by the New York Society for the Suppression of Vice, headed by Anthony Comstock. In 1873, Congress passed the Comstock laws. Among other things, the Comstock laws made it illegal to give information about abortions and contraception and to perform abortions.

The Micro–Macro Connection

We often use the word *choice* when we discuss sex. Abortion rights are called prochoice. Whether a person identifies himself or herself as gay or heterosexual is referred to as sexual choice. Our ideas and experience of sex are supposedly personal ones, largely carried in our own minds and only occasionally shared with a few close friends or relations. This chapter, however, has revealed that although sexuality is experienced by people at the microlevel, sexuality is pressured, shaped, and molded by macrolevel social forces.

Factors at the macrolevel that affect sexuality include economic institutions, laws, stratification, and ideologies. Economic institutions that sell sex or use sex to sell other goods affect our ideas and experience of sex. Laws determined by political bodies rule on the legitimacy of various forms of sex and even whether studies about sex should be conducted using public money. Social stratification, especially by gender, has a critical effect on sex. Ideologies rooted in competing theories about sexuality also influence us at the microlevel. When we enter into a sexual relationship with another person, we bring with us to this microencounter an array of forces emanating from the macrolevel of social organization.

As I have emphasized throughout the book, the microlevel has also had an effect on the macrolevel on the issue of sex. These ideologies, economic arrangements, and laws were developed through the interaction of individuals with one another at the microlevel. Allopathic physicians, feminists, prolife and prochoice activists, and gay rights activists are just a few of the microlevel groups that have worked and continue to work to influence the organization of sexuality in the contemporary United States.

CHAPTER

9

Marriage

Until the 1960s, marriage between people of different racial ethnic groups was illegal in the United States. The numbers have increased since that time, but it is still relatively unusual for people to marry across racial ethnic lines. (Patric Molnar/Taxi/ Getty Images)

Sharon Kowalski and Karen Thompson lived together as committed partners in Minnesota. Because the state of Minnesota does not allow people of the same sex to marry, they were not legally married to each other. The two women, however, had fallen in love, vowed their commitment to each other, exchanged rings, and bought a house together (Griscom 1992).

After they had been living together for four years, Sharon was nearly killed in a head-on car collision. The crash left her almost completely paralyzed and unable to speak. She eventually was able to use a typewriter and even to speak a few words, but she remained almost immobile. Immediately following the accident, Karen stayed by Sharon's side for hours at a time, reading and talking to her and massaging her muscles so that they would not be damaged by the inactivity. At first Sharon's parents accepted Karen's presence, but after a short time Sharon's father told Karen that only family could love his daughter and that Karen should not spend so much time with her. Sharon's father also disagreed with Karen about the care Sharon was receiving. He preferred to place her in a nursing home that offered little rehabilitation service. Karen believed that Sharon was making progress and would improve with sufficient care. But since Karen was not legally married to Sharon, she had no legal right to be involved in decisions about her partner's care or even to visit her.

Karen decided to file for guardianship of Sharon. She and Sharon's father went to court to decide who would have control over Sharon's life. After a long series of decisions and counterdecisions, the court awarded Sharon's father full guardianship. Karen was not permitted to visit Sharon for three years. While the court was deliberating, Sharon submitted testimony that she could communicate with a typewriter and that she was gay and wished to live with her lover, Karen Thompson. In her last visit with Karen before her father barred Karen from seeing her, Sharon typed to Karen: "Karen, help me. Get me out of here. Take me home with you" (NC NOW 1992). However, the court ruled that Sharon was incompetent to testify in her own behalf.

Sharon's father transferred her to a small nursing home with few rehabilitation services. Before the move, Sharon had begun to stand and feed herself. In the new home, Sharon was locked away for three years with a feeding tube and was given insufficient stretching and exercise. She was unable to leave the home and prohibited from seeing her friends and her lover. Her physical condition deteriorated, but both she and Karen continued their efforts to live together again. Eight years after the accident, overwhelming medical testimony that it would be in Sharon's best interest to live with Karen was presented and the court finally decided to allow Sharon to go home.

> How would this story have been different if Karen and Sharon were a legally married couple?
>
> What is a marriage? Is it only a legal institution, or does it consist of other factors like commitment, economics, power, love, or sex?
>
> Is the partnership between Karen and Sharon a marriage?
>
> In answering this question, what criteria are you using for defining marriage? What do those criteria imply for both gay and lesbian couples and heterosexual couples?
>
> What kinds of problems have been caused by the institution of marriage for those who are currently legally allowed to marry?
>
> Although many gay and lesbian couples have fought for the right to marry, others have argued that the institution of marriage is so fraught with problems that it is not a worthwhile goal. What is your opinion of this debate? Should everyone be allowed to marry? Should no one be allowed to marry? Or is there a middle ground?

Characteristics of Marriage

To answer the questions, you are asked to define marriage: who qualifies as married and what rights and obligations does that entail? Coming up with a definition is difficult because marriage is a many-faceted social institution. It is defined by law, but it also includes economic arrangements and sexual, political, and emotional factors like love and commitment. This chapter investigates the various facets of marriage and their often problematic character.

The chapter is divided into four major sections. The first looks at the different factors that go into defining marriage. The second section presents data on the incidence of marriage and a description of the changes in our experience of marriage in the past two centuries. In the third section, a theoretical model that links class inequality, gender inequality, and marriage is reviewed. The fourth section examines the political debate over whether marriage is a valuable and humane institution or one that should be radically restructured.

Marriage Is a Legal Contract

Marriage is a social institution that has several components. These include legal, economic, emotional, sexual, and political factors. In this section we explore each of these factors as an aspect of marriage, beginning with the link between marriage and the law.

Marriage is a legal contract in the United States. The macrolevel legal organization of marriage has a powerful effect on the microlevel experience of people who enter into marriage with each other. Even though we think of marriage as a private affair, a marriage contract actually gives more control to the government and less to the contracting partners than do other kinds of legal contracts. The duties and rewards are specified by the government, not by the parties who enter into the contract, the husband and wife. This means that the particular arrangements a couple makes are legally invalid if they conflict with the duties and privileges specified by public policy (Stetson 1997). Marriage is a legal contract that is tightly controlled by the government. Only certain people can legally marry, and those who do marry enter into a contract that is largely determined by law rather than by the parties who are marrying.

For example, if you wished to sell a car, you could set up nearly any contract to which you and the buyer agreed. The state would interfere with the contract by requiring that certain taxes be paid and that certain assurances of the mileage and ownership of the car were valid. But issues like who can buy and who can sell, when and where the exchange would take place, and the price and payment schedule would be up to you. The details of a marriage contract, in contrast, are specified, and when the contract is ended through divorce, the state makes the final decision over nearly all arrangements.

One important specification of the marriage contract in the contemporary United States is that the couple must be heterosexual. Gay men and lesbians do not have the legal right to marry except in the state of Massachusetts. And amendments are currently being considered that may curtail or abolish that right even in Massachusetts (Johnson 2005). This restriction has been criticized because it prevents gay and lesbian couples from making choices about their lives and because it implies that homosexuality and lesbianism are bad or unnatural.

The restriction prohibiting marriage for gay people also creates practical problems. For example, a gay couple may live together for years, pooling their resources. They often are not be allowed, however, to carry each other on health insurance policies or life insurance policies when that benefit is provided by their employer for workers' spouses. As we read in the account of Sharon Kowalski and Karen Thompson, their lack of rights to behave as a couple—to choose to live together, to take care of each other, and to make decisions with each other about health care—led to a long and painful court battle.

In a few places in the United States, some concessions have been won. In New York, a gay person may inherit an apartment lease if a partner dies. A number of employers provide partner benefits for unmarried partners of their employees, including gay and lesbian partners. Civil unions are legal in Vermont and Connecticut, reciprocal beneficiaries are the law in Hawaii, and domestic partnerships are recognized in Maine, New Jersey, and California. All of these arrangements address some of the legal and economic difficulties faced by couples like Sharon and Karen in the opening scenario. But marriage advocates believe they fall short of full legal equality of gay and lesbian partnerships with heterosexual marriage.

Civil unions are certified by a Justice of the Peace, a judge, or member of the clergy, and grant the couple rights and responsibilities similar to those of marriage for heterosexuals. For example, civil partners can claim each other for tax and insurance benefits, and they have the right to make decisions for one another in crisis like that faced by Sharon and Karen in the opening scenario. Finally, couples who become civil union partners and decide to separate must go through the Family Court and obtain a formal dissolution, similar to a divorce for married couples (Ferdinand 2000).

At the national level, gay rights to marriage have suffered setbacks in the past decade. Forty-two states now have specific legislation forbidding same-sex marriages. Federal laws prohibit gay couples to receive federal marriage benefits such as time off under the Family and Medical Leave Act, veteran's benefits, and Social Security. In addition, the Defense of Marriage Act signed into law in 1997 defines marriage as only legal between one man and one woman and allows states to ignore marriages that have occurred between same-sex partners in other states.

The United States is behind many countries in the world on this issue. In 2005, South Africa joined Canada, Denmark, and Holland as the fourth nation to allow same sex marriage, and several nations in Europe recognize same-sex partners (Krauss 2005). Ten nations in Europe, New Zealand, and Israel extend immigration rights to include same sex partners. And many nations are considering extending marriage rights to gay and lesbian couples.

Three Periods of Marriage and Family Law.   Dorothy Stetson (1997) observes that there have been three major periods of marriage and family law in U.S. history. The first was the doctrine of couverture, which defined marriage as a unity in which husband and wife became one, and that one was the husband. Stetson quotes an early nineteenth-century document to explain what couverture meant. "By marriage, the husband and wife are one person in law: that is, the very being or existence of the woman is suspended during marriage, or at least is incorporated and consolidated into that of the husband" (Blackstone 1803, p. 442).

Under the doctrine of couverture, married women could not own property. They had to turn over their wages to their husbands. If someone wanted to sue a married woman, she or he had to sue the woman's husband.

The second period was marked by the passage of the Married Women's Property Laws, which were first passed in Mississippi in 1839 and eventually were passed in all the states by the end of the nineteenth century. These laws allowed women the right to own property and to control their own earnings. Marriage during this period was perceived as a union between two separate and different but equal individuals (Stetson 1997). Women and men had different responsibilities and rights in marriage, but neither was supposed to overshadow the other. The wife was expected to provide services for her husband. One court case, for example, specified that a wife was "to be his helpmate, to love and care for him in such a role, to afford him her society and her person, to protect and care for him in sickness, and to labor faithfully to advance his interests" (Weitzman 1981, p. 60). The husband in turn was obligated to provide for the economic needs of his family.

You can see how a separate but equal notion of marriage is closely tied to the ideology of separate spheres that dominated during the nineteenth century. In Chapters 2, 3, and 6, we observed the problems associated with this ideology and the way in which the system was not one of equality. Although some women gained certain rights during the nineteenth century, they were still very much under the control of men.

In addition, in Chapter 2 we noted the way in which the ideology of separate spheres was class based. The only people who could live up to the ideal were wealthy and middle-class whites. The case that opened the door for married women to own property in Mississippi was a dramatic example of this kind of class and racial ethnic difference. The property about which the woman brought suit and was granted the right to own was a slave.

The separate but equal notion of marriage persisted until the 1960s, when the third period of marriage law began to emerge. The third doctrine identified marriage as a shared partnership in which spouses would have equal and overlapping responsibilities for economic, household, and child care tasks. This development of greater equality in the legal definition of marriage has been welcomed by many. We have seen, however, that this legal equality has not necessarily meant social equality. The way in which housework, market work, and child care are divided are all influenced by gender.

In addition, the third doctrine has created problems in some cases in which equality between women and men is upheld. For example, changes in laws that make women more equal to men in divorce proceedings are based on assumptions that women are equal to men in their responsibility for children and in their ability to earn an income. The laws assume equality between women and men, which is a valuable reform. But since women and men remain unequal in reality, problems have developed for divorcing women, especially when they are awarded the custody of children. We examine these issues further in the discussion of no-fault divorce in Chapter 10.

Marriage Is an Economic Arrangement

In the history of marriage as a legal contract, one of the factors that was important, especially in earlier days, was the economic responsibilities that come with entering into a marriage. During the colonial period, marriages were more likely to be arranged by a patriarch. A critical issue in his decision was the economic deal that could be struck with the parents of the prospective spouse of his son or daughter. Although the opinion of the potential bride and groom increasingly gained control over the decision throughout the nineteenth century, economics continued to play a role. The legal contract of marriage is filled with references to issues like whether a married person can be sued and by whom, and to whom the property of a married person belongs.

Today, economics remains an essential feature of marriage. The organization of our economic system at the macrolevel has great importance for decisions about marrying and the experience of marriage at the microlevel. As we observed in Chapter 4, the economic facet of marriage may be especially salient for those in the owning class. Owning-class mothers work hard to ensure that their children interact socially with others of their class, for example, by arranging debutante balls, in order to find a suitable person—a class peer—for a mate.

But even for those not in the owning class, economics plays a major role in marriage around the issue of mate selection. Nearly all people in the United States marry within their own social class, and even when people marry outside of their class, they marry someone who is close to their position in the class system (Carter and Glick 1976; Gardyn 2002; Lee 2005). There are interesting gender differences among those who do marry outside of their class. Women tend to marry up, and men tend to marry down. The tendency of women to marry up is called hypergamy. Hypergamy results in decreased marriage opportunities for women at the top of the stratification system and men at the bottom of the stratification system compared with those in the middle. The greater ability of women to marry up, however, is countered by men's greater ability to move up in the class system through occupation. Furthermore, not all women can use the marriage option. The ability to marry up among white women seems to be tightly tied to appearance. The bigger the step up, the more attractive she must be (Elder 1969). In contrast, men's ability to move up through their occupation is related to their IQ. And black women's tendency to marry up is related to their education (Udry 1977).

The relationship between economics and marriage was investigated in Chapters 6 and 7 in the discussion of the division of paid and unpaid work as a central aspect of intimate relationships. In Chapter 10 we look at the organization of divorce in our society and see how marriage is most clearly revealed as an economic institution when a couple divorces. Later in this chapter, we look at the importance of economic factors in shaping the marriage opportunities of African Americans.

In your assessment of the scenario at the beginning of the chapter, did the fact that Sharon and Karen had bought a house together influence your thinking about the validity of their relationship? Suppose you were in a heterosexual relationship and planning to marry, and your prospective husband or wife told you she or he would not proceed with the marriage plans unless you agreed to sign a contract allowing his or her finances to be kept entirely separate and unknown to you. Would you be surprised or unhappy?

Marriage Is a Sexual Relationship

Randall Collins and Scott Coltrane state that "the core of the marital relationship is a claim to permanent and exclusive sexual possession of one's partner" (1991, p. 638). Marriage law requires that in order to consummate a marriage—to bring the wedding ritual to completion—a couple not only must have sex with one another, but also they must have a particular form of sex, intercourse. On the other hand, social norms and laws in many areas in the United States prohibit sex between people who are not married to one another. Of course the real experience of sexuality is much broader than this.

In Chapter 8 we explored the relationship between sex and marriage. The important point to be considered in this chapter is that sex is tightly bound to marriage, legally, ideologically, and for many people experientially. Marriage is at least partly defined by its link to sex (Reiss 1986).

In addition, sex is at least partly defined by its link to marriage; sex outside of marriage is invalid. In Sharon and Karen's case at the beginning of the chapter, their sexual relationship was not perceived by Sharon's father and the courts as a valid basis for arguing that their relationship should be supported and that Karen should have the right to participate in decision making about Sharon's treatment. Their sexual relationship, in fact, was perceived to be a reason to keep them apart. In the court proceedings, Sharon's father argued that he did not want Karen to see Sharon because he believed that Karen would sexually molest her. The court initially granted him guardianship even after Karen stated that she was gay and that Sharon was her lover (Griscom 1992).

Marriage Means Commitment

Jessie Bernard is recognized as a founding mother of family sociology. Much of her work has focused on relationships between women and men in marriage. She writes, "One fundamental fact underlies the conception of marriage itself. Some kind of commitment must be involved. Without such a commitment a marriage may hardly be said to exist at all, even in the most avante garde patterns" (Bernard 1972, p. 79).

Part of the meaning of this commitment is often the promise of mutual sexual exclusivity. But the concept of commitment includes other aspects as well. Bernard (1982) reviewed marriage vows to determine the content of commitment. She writes that in the most traditional wedding ceremonies in the contemporary United States, the commitment is to love, honor, and obey. In more modern examples, couples vow to commit themselves to a variable array of values and behaviors, including truth, honesty, personal growth, allowing one's mate to grow, and respecting differences.

Bernard (1989) maintains, however, that permanence has historically been the essential component of commitment in marriage in cultures heavily influenced by Christian belief, like the United States. The line in a traditional wedding ceremony, "till death do us part," is a reflection of this definition of commitment.

According to Bernard, a definition of commitment centered on permanence has recently given way to another essential component, love. In some contemporary marriages, couples vow to stay together "as long as ye both shall love." In Chapters 2 and 8, we observed the way in which this ideal of the companionate marriage emphasizing love and affection developed relatively recently in the United States. An examination of contemporary Japanese American marriages indicates that the transition to marital commitment based on love is still occurring among some groups of people in the United States.

First-generation Japanese Americans are called Issei, and second generation are called Nisei. Sylvia Yanagisako (1985) interviewed couples from both generations to find out their perceptions of ideal marital relationships. She found that both generations viewed Japanese marriage as based on and maintained by *giri* (duty) and believed that American marriage was based on and maintained by romantic love. Issei couples sought to model their marriages after the Japanese type. They recognized that husbands and wives may develop strong emotional feelings for each other, but those feelings were secondary in their marriage. The more basic and essential component was duty and ethical commitment. Nisei couples believed that this view of marriage was often emotionally ungratifying. Nisei couples, however, were also wary of what they perceived to be the whimsical and dangerously unstable character of American marriage. They attempted to create an alternative to these two views by combining ideas of duty and romantic love in order to redefine commitment as an expression of both.

Commitment can be added to our list of components defining marriage. Bernard even goes so far as to assert that without it, a marriage does not exist. In trying to capture the meaning of marriage, we have looked at the law, economics, sex, and now the emotional feature of commitment. Commitment itself, however, is not easy to define. The term is slippery, variable, difficult to measure, and changing. How important is commitment to defining marriage? When the story of Sharon and Karen is presented in the press and in this chapter, they are described as having pledged their commitment to one another. How important should this act have been to the courts deciding their case?

Marriage Is a Political Arena

The last feature of marriage is the question of power. Claire Renzetti and Daniel Curran write, "In short, marital relations are fundamentally power relations—usually the power of husbands over wives" (1992, p. 136). Power in marriage is a question that has been investigated for some time by family sociologists.

What exactly is power? Recall that in Chapter 1 politics was defined as the "process whereby individuals or groups gain or maintain the capacity to impose their will upon others, to have their way recurrently, despite implicit opposition through invoking or threatening punishment, as well as offering or withholding rewards" (Lipman-Blumen 1984, p. 6). This definition comes from a Weberian perspective. Max Weber was a nineteenth-century sociologist. He proposed that power was the chance that one actor in a social relationship is able to impose his or her will on another (Fishman 1978).

Since Weber made his proposal, Berger and Luckmann (1966) have suggested another feature of power. They assert that power is more than being able to force someone to do something. It includes the ability to force one's definition of reality on others. In Berger and Luckmann's framework, "Power is the ability to impose one's definition of what is possible, what is right, what is rational, what is real" (Fishman 1978, p. 397).

Both kinds of power are a feature of married life. A husband may enforce his will on his wife by insisting that he decide whether they will move from one community to another. He may also successfully convince his wife that his control over the decision is the only rational and legitimate way in which to make family decisions. Keep these two forms of power in mind as we examine some of the research on power relations in marriage.

In 1960 Robert Blood and Donald Wolfe surveyed married couples in Detroit about the division of power in their marriage. This survey has become a classic in family studies, and variations of the study have been replicated several times since then (Peplau and Campbell 1989). Blood and Wolfe used decision making as their measure of marital power. They questioned more than nine hundred married women about who made various decisions in their families. They asked, for example, who had the final say in deciding to buy a car, to move, which physician a family member should see, and whether a wife should seek employment. The researchers found that husbands usually had more power in their marriages because they had the final say in more decisions.

Blood and Wolfe also found that when wives brought more social resources to the marriage, like a higher education or income, they had greater control over decisions (Gillespie 1971). Letitia Peplau and Susan Campbell (1989) conducted a similar study of dating couples and found that 49 percent of the women and 42 percent of the men reported equal power in their current dating relationships. Peplau and Campbell, like Blood and Wolfe, found that when women had more resources they had more power in their relationships with men. Peplau and Campbell identified gender ideologies, career goals, and involvement in the relationship as important resources for dating couples. Women who had more liberal gender ideologies, stronger career goals, and less involvement in the relationship had greater power than women who did not. Gender ideology and involvement in the relationship also affected men, although the correlation between liberal ideas about men and women and power in the relationship was inverse for the men. Career goals did not appear to affect men. For example, the higher the academic degree to which women aspired—BA, MA, or PhD—the greater their power in the relationship. This correlation between academic aspiration and power in the relationship was not evident for men.

I cited the Blood and Wolfe study in Chapter 6 as an example of an exchange theory perspective, and I noted some of the theoretical criticisms of exchange theory. Blood and Wolfe's study has also been criticized for four methodological problems.

First, this study and others like it have been criticized because they do not distinguish among different decisions. They give the same weight to choosing a physician and choosing whether a wife should seek employment (Safilios-Rothschild 1970).

Second, Blumstein and Schwartz (1983) have criticized Blood and Wolfe, arguing that women sometimes make decisions because they have been assigned that task by their husbands. The "power" they have, for example, to purchase furniture, comes from the more fundamental decision by the husband that the wife should do so.

Third, Blood and Wolfe have been criticized because, rather than observing the behavior of the subjects, they only asked them what they do. Surveys like theirs may be a better measure of what wives believe their marriages should be like or what they believe they should say their marriages are like than an accurate assessment of power and/or decision making in their households (Renzetti and Curran 1992).

The failure to distinguish between ideals and behavior has been especially evident in studies of Chicano families (Baca Zinn 1982). Quantitative research studies that rely on questionnaire data fail to tap the experience of Chicano husbands and wives. Although the popular image of Chicano families is one in which husbands have absolute authority, the reality may be one in which women have some power and/or at least the question of power is contested terrain (N. Williams 1990).

Baca Zinn (1982) set out to examine this question using more qualitative methods: focused interviews and participant observation of a small sample of wives. Baca Zinn found important differences *entre dicho y hecho* (between what is said and what is done). The women she interviewed and observed all supported patriarchy as an ideology. For example, one woman said, "You know I'm slowly becoming equal with Nabor even though he will always be the head of the family. No matter how much money I make, even if I get a master's degree he will always be the head" (p. 73).

In the women's behavior, however, Baca Zinn (1982) found that the patriarchal model was not always followed. Especially when women were employed outside the home, they were likely to abandon the patriarchal ideal by challenging their husbands, making independent decisions, and taking actions with which their husbands did not agree (see also N. Williams 1990).

Baca Zinn's research shows the way in which the two definitions of power, Weber's and Berger and Luckmann's, do not necessarily mesh in real people's lives. According to Weber's definition, power is the ability to impose one's will on another. The husbands in Baca Zinn's sample were not always able to induce their wives to follow their directions. The husbands did not have power over their wives in the Weberian sense. From the Berger and Luckmann perspective, however, husbands did have power. The husbands were able to impose their definition of what was rational and good on their wives' thinking.

Fourth, Blood and Wolfe have been criticized because of the measure they used to indicate power. Decision making may not be the best measurement or even an accurate measure at all of power in marriages. For example, in Chapter 7, Heidi Hartmann was quoted as defining power in intimate relationships as being best indicated by who did or did not do the housework. Others (Gordon 1988) have suggested that violence is the most critical indicator of power (see Chapters 11 and 13). Patterns of communication have also been cited as an important indicator of power in relationships between women and men, including marriage (Fishman 1978).

An important component of marriage is the relationship of power. Such relationships can be expressed in a variety of ways, including communication. Women and men communicate differently. For example, men talk more and are more likely to choose the topics of conversation. These differences can mean that men use verbal interaction to wield power in their relationships with their wives.

Power in Communication. One of the ways in which researchers have observed the distribution and negotiation of power in marriage is in nonverbal and verbal communication between husbands and wives. In 1964, Berger and Kellner proposed their view of the social process of marriage. They argued that newly married husbands and wives come to a marriage with different biographies and work together to create a mutually shared view of the world (Glenn 1987). This work is accomplished through conversation, which includes verbal communication as well as other forms of social interaction. This interpretation of communication in marriage focuses on cooperation and the creation of a consensual view of the relationship and the world. It is an example of interactionism, a theoretical framework closely identified with George Herbert Mead (Glenn 1987).

Glenn (1987) argues that this kind of interactionist theory focuses too narrowly on consensus—what do people share and how do they negotiate a shared vision? This kind of analysis ignores equally salient factors such as conflict, inequality, and power. Feminist researchers have been interested in incorporating conflict, inequality, and power into their assessments of the process of communication between intimate partners.

Fishman (1978) investigated communication between men and women to see whether there were differences in or evidence of conflict and power. In her research, she asked couples who identified themselves as egalitarian to record spontaneous conversations in their homes. The couples were requested to turn on an audio recorder and allow their conversations to be taped for her to listen to and analyze. The conversations were about mundane everyday topics like what happened at work or what to have for dinner. Fishman looked for differences in the ways in which men and women talked to one another. Like other researchers in this field she found that men talked more and interrupted more, while women asked more questions and used more qualifiers and more passive ways of entering into conversations. For example, men would begin a conversation with a direct statement; women would begin with a tag like "Isn't this interesting," or "Let me ask you this."

In her research, Fishman also found that while men controlled conversations, women did most of the work. By this she means that women offered an array of possible conversation topics. Men chose which topics, if any, they wanted to discuss. Conversations frequently followed the pattern of a woman offering a topic through a question and a man either stopping the conversation by a short response—yes, no, uh-huh—or accepting the topic and then expounding on it as the woman interjected supportive words to keep the conversation going. If the man declined the topic by cutting it short, the woman would continue her work, offering other possible topics from which he could select.

According to Fishman, these language differences are signs of power differences. Men do not need to ask to be heard. They are the center of attention. Their communication dominance, in terms of controlling topics and of the time spent speaking, are indications of their social dominance, even in these self-described egalitarian couples.

Religion, Politics, and Marriage.   One social arena in which the proper character of marriages and relationships between husbands and wives has gained attention in recent years is religion, especially within fundamentalist religious groups. Fundamentalism can be a segment of any religion, and we hear about the activities of Muslim fundamentalists in Afghanistan and Iran and Jewish fundamentalists in Israel. But in the United States, most people are Christians, and therefore Christian fundamentalism is particularly important.

You should recall from Chapter 1 that families can be political in two ways: when issues related to families are addressed in public political debates in the media and in the government and within families in the power struggles among family members. The debate between fundamentalist Christians and others about how best to organize families and the debate within fundamentalist Christian households between husbands and wives illustrate both of these political sides of families.

Fundamentalist Christians are the most conservative wing of Evangelicals. Evangelicals maintain that the Bible is literally true and that it can and should serve as a practical guide to everyday living. They also believe that it is important for them to commit themselves to spreading the word by sharing their faith with others. Most important, they claim to have a deep personal relationship with Jesus Christ, whom they believe intervenes regularly in their individual lives (Stacey and Gerard 1998). Not surprisingly, their family lives and their ideas about families are entertwined with their religious beliefs and religious experience.

In 1990, one fundamentalist Christian, Bill McCartney, decided to share his ideas and his commitment on a broad scale by creating an organization to articulate and promote a Christian fundamentalist view of marriage and family. McCartney, a football coach at the

BOX **9.1**

American Poll on Marriage

The Gallup Poll (Newport 1996) is a respected polling agency that has conducted surveys on many issues in American life for many years. The pollsters select a random group and ask them a series of questions. Since the people answering the questions are randomly selected, the pollsters argue that their responses are representative of the total population. We see how important these polls are during elections, when they are used to predict winners, but many other issues are investigated as well.

When a sample of Americans were asked in 1996 how they would grade their marriages, 80 percent said they would give them an A (Newport 1996). Most of the rest said they would give their marriages a B. Only 10 percent graded their marriages C, D, or F, and most of them were Cs. Husbands and wives are very similar in their grades, and older couples give their marriages higher grades than younger couples.

Most people—80 percent—knew their spouses pretty well, having dated at least a year before marriage. But the amount of time they dated before marriage didn't seem to be related to what grade they gave their marriages. Some people who gave low grades said they had dated for a long time—two years or more—and some had dated only a short time.

One factor that did show up as related to marital happiness was satisfaction with their spouse's weight. About 20 percent of the respondents said "if they had their way," they would like their spouse to lose weight. Wives were slightly more critical of husbands than the reverse. Married people who were least happy with their marriage were most likely to think their husband or wife should lose weight. Forty percent of those who graded their marriage C, D, or F wanted their spouse to lose weight. Those who were very happy with their marriage, in contrast, were much less likely to think their spouse should lose weight. Only about 14 percent of those who gave themselves an A wanted their spouses to take off some pounds.

Does this mean that fat causes marital discord and if we would slim down marriages would be happier and divorces would decline? Or does it mean that "beauty is in the eye of the beholder" and that people who are unhappy in their marriages are more likely to note flaws, including excess weight in their partners (Newport 1996)?

University of Colorado, pulled together seventy men to found an organization called the Promise Keepers. Two years later, the Promise Keepers began to arrange massive conferences of thousands of people across the country to call attention to their activities (Ruth 1998). The Promise Keepers have had organizational and financial difficulties in more recent years, but their ideology provides a good example of fundamentalist Christian views of marriage and family and the political character of marriage.

The centerpiece of the Promise Keepers' message is that men need to reclaim leadership of their families. They explain this message in their public speeches and written documents like the book, *Seven Promises of a Promise Keeper:*

> I can hear you saying, "I want to be a spiritually pure man. Where do I start?"
>
> The first thing you do is sit down with your wife and say something like this: "Honey, I've made a terrible mistake. I've given you my role. I gave up leading this family, and forced you to take my place. Now I must reclaim that role."

Don't misunderstand what I'm saying here. I'm not suggesting that you ask for your role back. I'm urging you to take it back.

There can be no compromise here. If you're going to lead, you must lead. Be sensitive. Listen. Treat the lady gently and lovingly. But lead! (Phillips 1994, pp. 79–80).

Darlene Wilkinson, another fundamentalist Christian with similar ideas, has written about what women need to do to live by "God's ideal plan for man and woman" (Wilkinson 1998, p. 137). She argues that God does not think that women are lesser than men, but rather that women and men are called to different tasks. The task of leader should fall to men, and the task of helper should be taken by women:

Seven Affirmations of a Perfect Helper

- I am the perfect helper for my husband, for God chose me out of all the women in the world especially for him.
- I am the perfect helper for my husband, for I share his hopes and dreams and bear his hurts and frustrations along with him.
- I am the perfect helper for my husband, for I bring him before God's throne in prayer every day.
- I am the perfect helper for my husband, for I encourage and comfort him at strategic moments.
- I am the perfect helper for my husband, for I put his sexual and emotional needs ahead of my own.
- I am the perfect helper for my husband, for I love him unconditionally.
- I am the perfect helper for my husband, for I enable him to become all God wants him to be and I assist him in accomplishing God's purposes. (p. 139)

Promoting this ideal meets with difficulty among people who do not consider themselves fundamentalist Christians and do not share this view of marriage and gender. But the ideal also has problems within the conservative Christian community and even within the conservative Christian household. First, the gender arrangement advocated by the Promise Keepers and Wilkinson assume that both the husband and wife in a household share a common view of religion. In fact, more women than men are fundamentalists, and women are often at least the most enthusiastic or first in their households to convert. This creates the perplexing situation in which the woman is in fact the spiritual leader in her family—the first or only person to agree with the ideas. But the correct role for women is not leader but helper (Ammerman 1987).

A second problem has to do with the range of ideas about what the Bible says about the proper relationship between husbands and wives. Some fundamentalist Christians believe it should be as the Promise Keepers describe, but another voice in the Evangelical community is that of Evangelical feminists, who also call themselves Biblical feminists or Christian feminists. They share many beliefs with fundamentalists about the importance of living directly by the word of the Bible, cultivating a close personal relationship with Jesus Christ, and bringing the "good news" to others. But Evangelical feminists have some important differences, too. First, they claim the right of women to be leaders within the Christian community. They also assert that the Bible uses inclusive language, for example, by speaking of God as a being without sex rather than as a male. Third, they challenge the scriptural basis for the subordination of women, noting that passages cited for this purpose are often taken out of context or misrepresented. When it comes to marriage, Evangelical feminists argue that the Bible teaches that husbands and wives must be mutually submissive to each other and that an unequal marriage is an un-Christian one (Stacey and Gerard 1998).

Power appears to be an aspect of marriage that takes a variety of forms. Marriages are an arena of struggle over power and the mechanisms by which power can be maintained or changed. Differences in power between women and men have become less overt at the macrolevel in marriage law but remain salient in other social institutions, like religion. And, at the microlevel, they are pervasive in every aspect of even the smallest social encounter between husbands and wives. Jessie Bernard (1972) coined the term *his and her marriage* to describe gender differences in the experience of marriage, even within the same marriage. Later in this chapter we return to the theoretical question of gender politics as a critical aspect of relationships within marriage. But before moving to that issue, let us take a look at data on the incidence of marriage in the contemporary United States.

Statistics on Marriage

In this section, we examine the demographic data on marriage. How prevalent is marriage? How do race, gender, and religion affect marriage rates and the age at which people marry?

Nearly all Americans marry at some time in their lives (U.S. Census Bureau 2002b). Figure 2.1 in Chapter 2 shows the rate of marriage as it has changed in this century. The rate is calculated as the number of first marriages per thousand single women between the ages of fourteen and forty-four. The figure shows that the rate of first marriage has fluctuated greatly over the past sixty years, although in the past twenty years the rate has begun to level off.

Table 9.1 shows the marital status of people over the age of eighteen in the United States in 2000. The table indicates variation by race ethnicity. It shows that whites are most likely to be married, followed by Hispanics and blacks. It also shows that whites are least likely to never have been married, followed by Hispanics and blacks.

TABLE 9.1   Marital Status by Race, 2000 (Percent of Population 18 Years and Older)

	White	Black	Hispanic
Never married	21.4	39.4	28.0
Married	60.2	40.7	56.2
Widowed	6.9	7.0	4.2
Divorced	9.8	11.5	7.7

Source: U.S. Census Bureau 2000e, 2000b, p. 238.

TABLE 9.2   Median Age at First Marriage
by Sex, 1890–2003

Year	Men	Women
1890	26.1	22.0
1900	25.9	21.9
1910	25.1	21.6
1920	24.6	21.2
1930	24.3	21.3
1940	24.3	21.5
1950	22.8	20.3
1960	22.8	20.3
1970	23.2	20.8
1980	24.7	22.0
1990	26.1	23.9
2000	26.8	25.1
2003	27.1	25.3

Source: U.S. Census Bureau 2003b.

Age at First Marriage

Table 9.2 shows changes in the last century in the median age at first marriage for women and men. (Recall that half the population falls below and half the population falls above the median point.) The table indicates that the median age at first marriage has risen for both women and men since the 1950s. Changes since the beginning of the twentieth century in age at first marriage have differed for men compared with women. Men's age at first marriage dipped in the middle of the twentieth century and recently has risen to the highest recorded, but it is this older age is similar to that of men marrying in the early 1900s.

Women now are also marrying later than women did earlier in the century. But for women, this later age of first marriage is higher than at any previously recorded time in the United States and is not a return to a previous level as it is for men.

Racial Ethnic Differences in Age at First Marriage.   Until the 1950s, African Americans tended to marry at an earlier age than white Americans. Since the 1950s, African Americans have married at increasingly later ages. They now marry later than any other group of Americans. The percentage of African Americans who have not married by the time they are twenty-nine years old is higher than for any other racial ethnic group in the United States. This proportion, furthermore, has increased in the past two decades.

Table 9.3 provides information similar to that in Table 9.1, except that it shows how these proportions have changed over time. Table 9.3 divides the population into black, white, and Hispanic and shows the percentage of people who had never married in 1970, 1980, 1994, 1999, and 2003.

The table indicates that for all three racial ethnic groups, the percentage of those who are over eighteen years old and have never married has risen over the past two decades.

TABLE 9.3   Percentage of People 18 and Older Who Have Never Been Married, 1970–2003

	1970	1980	1994	1999	2003
White	15.6	18.9	20.9	21.4	21.4
Black	20.6	30.5	38.9	39.2	39.4
Hispanic	18.6	24.1	29.8	29.0	28.0

Source: U.S. Census Bureau 1994c, p. vi; 2000, p. 51; 2005e.

There are differences, however, by race ethnicity. Whites are least likely to have never married, and blacks are most likely to have done so in all three periods. The increase for whites has also been less dramatic, especially in comparison to blacks.

Table 9.4 shows the changes over time on the question of whether people are in intact marriages. The category "in intact marriages" excludes both those who have never married and those who might have married but are now divorced or widowed. The data on those in intact marriages also show differences by race ethnicity. Blacks are less likely to be in intact marriages than whites or Hispanics.

Three explanations have been offered for this difference between African Americans and others (Glick and Norton 1979; Taylor et al. 1992). One explanation is that African Americans, especially African American men, do not desire to marry; the gap is a result of

---

BOX **9.2**

The Native American Marriage Gap and the Sociological Research Gap

The marriage gap between whites and African Americans has begun to receive attention. Researchers have gathered data and tested hypothesis to determine what the reasons for the different rates are. There is also a large marriage gap between Native Americans and whites. The statistics for Native Americans are similar to those for African Americans. The 2000 census reported that 48 percent of Native American women were currently married, 32 percent had never married, and 21 percent were divorced or widowed (U.S. Census Bureau 2000). Take a look at Table 9.1 to see the contrast with African Americans, whites, and Hispanics. The marriage gap for Native Americans is striking (Johnson 1995). Little (or no) research has been done on why this gap exists and what its consequences might be for Native Americans and their community.

Perhaps some of the same explanations that have been revealed in the research on African Americans will also be valid for Native Americans. But as we have seen in other comparisons among racial ethnic people, we need to be careful not to make assumptions about similarities across racial ethnic lines without finding out what the evidence supports. One of the important changes occurring in sociology today is the recognition of the multicultural character of American society. Today the census includes a range of different racial ethnic categories. Black people have become increasingly visible in sociological research, and now we are beginning to look at "others" as well. We have many interesting questions to explore (Strauss 1995).

TABLE 9.4   Percentage of People 18 and Older Who Are in Intact Marriages, 1970–2002

	1970	1980	1994	1999	2002
White	72.6	67.2	63.0	62.0	61
Black	64.1	51.4	42.9	41.4	38
Hispanic	71.8	65.6	58.3	59.4	58

Source: U.S. Census Bureau 1994c, p. vi; U.S. Census Bureau 2000, p. 51; CDC 2004b.

choices made by African Americans. This explanation has received little support in the scientific literature (Tucker and Mitchell-Kernan 1995).

The second explanation is that higher rates of unemployment and underemployment among African Americans cause them to delay marriage longer as they wait to become more financially secure (Edin and Kefalas 2005; Lichter et al. 1992; Shock, Manning, and Porter 2005; Testa and Krogh 1995). Most of the research findings support this theory. For example, a study in inner-city Chicago found that employed fathers were twice as likely as unemployed fathers to marry the mother of their first child (Testa et al. 1989). In another study of men and marriage, researchers (Tucker and Taylor 1989) determined that the higher a man's personal income, the more likely he was to marry. For these men, income was unrelated to whether they were involved in a nonmarital romantic relationship. This means that men continue to become involved in romantic relationships with women regardless of their income. Deciding to marry, however, seems to be a step that is inhibited by insufficient income.

A third explanation for why African Americans marry later than whites or not at all is called the "marriage squeeze." This theory has also been supported by research. In the United States, women tend to marry men who are two or three years older than themselves. If the population is increasing, there are more younger people than there are older people. This means that men (who seek younger partners) have a larger pool from which to choose than women (who seek older partners) (Rodgers and Thornton 1985; Schoen 1983; Taylor et al. 1992). Birthrates in the United States increased from 1933 to 1960 and from 1973 to 1990. Assuming that people will marry sometime in their twenties, those women who sought a husband between 1954 and 1982, or beginning in 1997 had a harder time finding one who is older than themselves.

This problem of pool size exists for all women born during years of larger total births, but it may be especially evident for black women because of the higher mortality rates for black men. Not only are there fewer black men born a year or two before the women who will be seeking them as husbands, black men are likely to die young. An African American woman seeking to marry an African American man who is a few years older than herself may find the number of eligible people to be insufficient (Guttentag and Secord 1983). Furthermore, it is relatively unusual for an African American woman to marry a man who is not African American.

In sum, an African American woman who wishes to marry a man who is a few years older than she faces an insufficient pool of potential mates because of (1) the marriage squeeze if she was born in a year of a larger numbers of births; (2) a higher mortality rate among black men; and (3) unlikely prospects of crossing racial ethnic lines to marry.

Marrying across Racial Ethnic Lines

The marriage squeeze is at least partly due to the fact that Americans do not often marry across racial ethnic lines. Americans tend to marry people like themselves (Skolnick 2005). Seventy-two percent of us marry people of our religion; 78 percent of us marry within five years of our age group; 82 percent of us marry people of similar educational backgrounds; and 93 percent of us marry people of the same racial ethnic group (Laumann et al. 1994). Until 1967, it was actually illegal in many states for a black person and a white person or an Asian person and a white person to marry (Harrison and Bennett 1995).

Table 9.5 shows the number of interracial ethnic marriages. The table shows that the total number of couples who marry across racial ethnic lines has risen steadily since 1980 and was much larger in 2000 than in previous years. The proportion of people who marry across racial ethnic lines, however, remains small. In 2000, interracial couples accounted for just over 5 percent of all married couples (Lee and Edmonston 2005).

Marriages of whites and African Americans are still especially rare throughout the country while intermarriages between Native Americans, Hawaiians, and multiple race people are most common (Lee and Edmonston 2005; Staples 1998). Black–white married couples made up 2.9 percent of all married couples (U.S. Census Bureau 2003b). About two-thirds of black-white couples are those with a black husband and a white wife. Black women have the highest odds overall of marrying a person of the same racial ethnic group (Taylor, Jackson, and Chatters 1996). In addition, 30 percent of white Americans and 20 percent of black Americans say they they do not approve of marriages between black and white people (Goodhart 2004).

Paul Rosenblatt and his colleagues (1995) interviewed twenty-one black-white couples to find out what their experience was like. The people with whom he spoke characterized themselves as "feeling ordinary in a relationship others see as unusual" (Rosenblatt, Karis, and Powell 1995, p. 24). One man explained, "We're no different than anybody else. We have the same concerns for a family, the kids—if you have any—my house, my dog, my job, my daily life concerns" (Rosenblatt, Karis, and Powell 1995, p. 24).

TABLE 9.5   Interracial and Interethnic Marriages Increasing

	Number of Couples in Thousands		
	1980	*1990*	*2000*
Black/white	167	211	307
White/other (not black)	450	720	983
Black/other (not white)	34	33	27
Hispanic/non-Hispanic	891	1193	1647

Source: U.S. Census Bureau 2000, p. 51.

Another said that, despite the fact that he felt ordinary, he often felt he was being treated as an oddity:

> Because of our relationship, [I] sometimes feel called upon by people to make a speech. They are making presumptions about my political beliefs, and that our relationship is somehow a philosophical decision that had been made and that I should be able to make an eloquent speech I've always felt I'm not up to the task. I didn't choose to marry her to make speeches (Rosenblatt, Karis, and Powell 1995, p. 32).

The couples had felt opposition from their families on both sides, although black parents were more accepting of their relationship than white parents. Some also experienced intolerance and even attacks from friends, the police, church, and real estate agents and had received hate mail. Others, however, noted the "special blessings," the positive results of their relationship. One woman reviewed what she had gained because of her interracial marriage:

> I'm glad you asked that question, because my pet peeve for years and years is that there have been studies that focused on problems and I think because of that give an extremely distorted view of what's going on. I would say that not only the interracial marriage but children has probably broadened and enriched my life in ways that no other single experience could do. And I think that for the kids too, that they would say and see themselves as being wealthier culturally rather than having any problems. And that's absolutely across the board, and it far exceeds any minor inconveniences and hassles (Rosenblatt, Karis, and Powell 1995, p. 251).

Long-Term Marriage

As we will see in the next chapter, many marriages end in divorce. Perhaps surprisingly, researchers also report that a growing number of people live in long-term marriages (Field and Weishaus 1992). For example, at the end of the nineteenth century, on average people had been married twenty-eight years when their spouse died. Today, those couples who stay together until the death of a spouse have been married an average of forty-three years (Hooyman and Kiyak 1996).

Robert Lauer and his colleagues (1995) interviewed a hundred couples living in a retirement community who had been married a long time to find out what those relationships were like. These couples had a median 54.5 years of marriage, with a range from 45 to 64 years. Ninety-two percent of them said that they were happy or extremely happy in their marriage. Seventy-eight percent said they always or almost always agreed on a range of activities and ideas, including recreation, religion, affection, friends, sex, proper behavior, philosophy of life, life goals, time together decisions, housework, and career decisions. They also found that 85 percent of the couples confide in their mates all or most of the time; 98 percent kiss each other every day; and 74 percent laugh together every day. The researchers cited all of these experiences as evidence of the happiness of these long-term ties.

Another similar study (Mackey and O'Brien 1995) reported that five issues seemed to have a positive effect on stable and high-quality long-term marriages. Mackey and O'Brien identified, first, containment of conflict. The couples they interviewed who had

BOX **9.3**

Mail-Order Brides

One questionnable kind of interracial marriage involves mail-order brides. Finding hard data on the numbers of men who find their wives through catalogs is difficult. Correspondence services like those commonly listed in newspapers advertise "Asian women desire romance" and "Attractive Oriental ladies seeking friendship, correspondence." Men who respond to these ads receive pictures and descriptions of women, along with addresses, for a small fee (Agbayani-Siewert and Reeilla 1995).

The Philippines is the major source of mail-order brides from Asia. The Philippines report that nineteen thousand mail order brides leave the Philippines every year to marry men in other countries (Tolentina 1996). Many of these women come to the United States, although we don't know the exact number. Many women also come from other areas of the world as mail-order brides for American husbands.

Some of these arrangements result in happy marriages, but there are some important problems that can occur. The first problem with this practice is the possibility that the women involved are not making their own choices to enter themselves into the service. Researchers have found that many of the mail-order women who seek counseling in Seattle do not speak English and come from isolated rural areas (Mochizuki 1987). One might suspect, therefore, that they did not make a free and/or informed choice to be listed in the magazines or to marry someone in the United States. Perhaps the choices they had were so limited that they cannot really be considered a humane range of options.

Other researchers have found that the level of marital satisfaction among mail-order brides is similar to that of other intermarried Asian women who found their husbands through other means. Mail-order brides, however, reported more physical and psychological abuse (Lin 1991).

---

been married a long time and said their marriages were happy ones faced a variety of problems from outside their household as well as interpersonal problems. Those couples who figured out ways to contain the conflict—to come to a mutually satisfying resolution through negotiation—were more likely to stay together and to stay happy.

The second factor was mutuality in decision making—relying on each other and sharing decisions throughout their marriage about such issues as children, careers, and problems. Third was quality of communication. Fourth was values. People who remained in long-term marriages valued trust, respect, empathetic understanding, and equity. Finally, sexual and psychological intimacy played an important role in these marriages. Mackey and O'Brien looked at the evolution of long-term marriages over a lifetime. In addition to finding that these issues were important across time, they also discovered that the skills necessary to the five factors developed over time. People learned or adapted to the model of these five ingredients.

All couples who stay together in marriage for a long time are not necessarily happy. Finnegan Alford-Cooper (1998) interviewed couples who had been married a long time. Many of them were happy, and most said their love for each other had grown over time. In this study, 90.8 percent of the women described themselves as very happy or happy, as did 94.8 percent of the men. Those who were happy said they stayed married to each other because they loved each other and enjoyed their spouse's company. "They have created a life together, which they cherish. Usually they share similar backgrounds and values. They have compatible interests; they love and respect each other; they are committed to each other and to the marriage; and they communicate and compromise, and are willing to sacrifice for each other" (Alford-Cooper 1998, p. 192).

A small proportion of couples had stayed together even though they were not happy, often because of religious beliefs or a sense of commitment, or because they felt they didn't have any alternatives. Women were especially likely to mention lack of educational or work opportunities that would have allowed them to be financially independent. "After fifty years of marriage, those who were less happy had accommodated themselves to the situation, most often by pursuing other interests and investing themselves in activities outside of their marriage or in their children. The unhappily married couples had developed an interdependence of sorts and had a lifetime of memories and experiences together. They knew each other well, whether they liked what they knew or not" (Alford-Cooper 1998, p. 134).

Widowhood

One of the interesting differences in long-term marriages is that men are more likely to live out their lives in a marriage, while women are likely to be widowed. Because women live longer than men, marry men who are older than they, and are less likely to remarry after the death of a spouse, women are much more likely to be widows than men are to be widowers. About one-third of women over sixty-five are widows, and on the average widows live about fifteen years after their husband's death (O'Bryant and Hansson 1995; Federal Interagency Forum on Aging Related Statistics 2005). At every age, men are much more likely to be married and much less likely to be widowed.

On average, 70 percent of men over sixty-five live with a wife, while 35 percent of women over sixty-five live with a husband (Federal Interagency Forum on Aging Related Statistics 2005). Sixteen percent of women who are widowed or otherwise single live with other relatives, compared with 7 percent of men who live with other relatives. Nearly the majority of women over sixty-five—49 percent—live alone compared with only 21 percent of men who are over sixty-five (U.S. Census Bureau 2000b).

Table 9.6 shows the proportion of all women and men who are widowed. The table shows that race ethnicity creates some differences. Gender differences are striking for all people. These data tell us what proportion of people in 2004 were widowed. You should recall from Chapter 1 that an important demographic change is the aging of the population. We can expect that the percentage of people who are widowed and the proportion living alone will rise as our population includes larger proportions of older people. In 2000, 9.8 million people over sixty-five lived alone. Demographers project this number to increase to 15.2 million by 2020 (Fields and Casper 2001).

The death of a spouse is a difficult event, initially causing emotional distress and even decline in physical health. Seventy percent of widows say it is the most stressful event in their lives. But by two years after their spouses' death, most people recover from their grief

TABLE 9.6   Proportion of Widows and Widowers in the United States, 2004

Race Ethnicity	Women	Men
White	9.8%	2.5%
Black	9.2	2.6
Hispanic	5.5	1.3

Source: U.S. Census Bureau 2004k.

and even feel good about themselves as they have learned new skills necessary to their survival (Lopata 1973, 1996; O'Bryan and Hansson 1995; Pellman 1995). Widows are often helped by their children, especially by their daughters (Horowitz 1985). Racial ethnic comparisons show that Hispanic widows receive the most help from their children and whites the least, with blacks between.

Transition to Marriage

Although the word sounds quaint, sociologists refer to the period between singlehood and marriage as courtship. The preceding discussion of racial ethnic groups and marriage has identified several important factors affecting the transition from singlehood to marriage. The microlevel interaction of courtship is affected by the macrolevel issues of economics, population changes, and racial ideologies and laws restricting marriage between members of different racial ethnic groups.

The two most significant characteristics of courtship today are the delay of first marriage and the increase in cohabitation. These factors have become increasingly important, and we examine them in the next section. But before moving on, let us look at a brief history of courtship in order to get a sense of where our present practices emerged from.

Cate (1992) traced the historical evolution of courtship in the United States and noted the transition in the early twentieth century from men calling on women to the incorporation of dating into courtship. Calling involved only visiting; dating brought something new to the activity—going out and doing things in public. Since the 1970s dating has changed, becoming more informal, less focused on the goal of marriage, and more likely to be substituted with mixed group activities that do not involve pairing up. Two trends in courtship developed throughout the nineteenth and twentieth centuries: (1) the lessening of parental involvement in the process, especially in selecting partners for their children, and (2) a growth in the demand for emotional intimacy as the criterion for continuing a relationship and particularly for deciding to marry (Cate 1992; Coontz 1988).

While courtship continues to change, some factors remain strikingly consistent (Basow 1992). In 1989, college students were asked to list the content and sequence of events that would occur on a first date. The students were very much in agreement in their responses, and the image they conveyed was highly gender-stereotyped. The focus of first dates for women was concern about their appearance, making conversation, and limiting sexual activity. The focus of first dates for men was planning activities, paying for the date, and initiating sex (Rose and Frieze 1989). Other research supports these observations. For example, reviews of personal ads show that men are looking for women with particular physical characteristics, while women emphasize a potential male date's status characteristics (Davis 1990). Women who initiate dates are viewed more negatively than men who initiate dates (Green and Sandos 1983). Men have higher sexual expectation on a first date than do women (Morr and Mongeau 2004).

One group of people we might not immediately think of in our images of dating are older couples. In Chapter 1, we saw statistics on the growing proportion of older people in our population. As their numbers grow, researchers have begun to look at a wide range of activities, including courtship. Most of the research shows few surprises. People over sixty-five who date are seeking romance, sex, and companionship, and they meet through friends as well as formal organizations (Lopata 1979). Two surprises in the literature are related to gender differences. First, older men are much more likely to date than older women. When asked if they had dated in the last month, one-third of the men said they had, but only 6.7 percent of the women said they had. Men and women also had different reasons for dating. Men said they dated as an "outlet for self disclosure," meaning they looked forward to going out with a woman in order to talk with her about their feelings. Women said they dated because it increased their prestige among their friends (Bulcroft and Bulcroft 1985). In addition, it might be surprising to find that older daters may be more creative than younger ones finding dates at church and outdoor clubs but also speed dating events, the Internet, personal ads, and matchmaker services (Mahoney 2003).

Cohabitation and Domestic Partnerships

Table 9.7 shows the growth in the numbers of couples who are cohabiting from 1960 to 2004. The table shows a steady increase, with a steep jump beginning in 1970. The numbers went from fewer than 500,000 couples in 1960 to more than 5 million in 2004. During this

TABLE 9.7   Number of Unmarried Couples Cohabiting

Year	Number (in Millions)
1960	.439
1970	.523
1980	1.589
1990	2.856
2000	4.736
2004	5.080

Source: Fields and Casper 2001; U.S. Census Bureau 1995, 2000, 2004h.

same time period, the proportion of cohabitors among all heterosexuals living together as married or unmarried partners went from 1.1 percent in 1960 to 6.3 percent in 2000 (Abma et al. 1997; Fields and Casper 2001; Simmons and O'Connell 2003).

These percentages are small but growing. In addition, if we look at the proportion of people who have ever cohabited, the experience of cohabitation appears to be becoming the norm. In 1970, 11 percent of the population had cohabited before a first marriage. In 1989, 50 percent had (Bumpass, Sweet, and Cherlin 1998). Choosing to delay marriage and to remain single, sometimes indefinitely, has become a sign of our times. But many people who remain single choose to cohabit, and an equally important sign of the times is the growing number of heterosexual couples who live together without being legally married. A number of researchers assert that cohabitation is becoming institutionalized as a new phase of mate selection in the United States (Gwartney-Gibbs 1986).

In fact, when the growing numbers of couples who cohabit are considered, the decline in marriage rates is offset to a large extent (Bumpass, Sweet, and Cherlin 1991). The movement away from legal marriage has been accompanied by a movement toward nonmarital unions (Surra 1991). Cherlin (1992a) notes that despite the rising age of marriage, young adults are almost as likely now as they were in 1970 to be sharing a household with a partner.

Older people are part of the growing trend in cohabiting. In 1970, 115,000 couples over the age of sixty-five said they were unmarried and cohabiting. In 2000, 9.7 million people over age sixty-five were unmarried and cohabiting (Greider 2004). And demographers expect the proportion of senior couples to grow dramatically in the next few decades (Fields 2001).

The length of time people cohabit with one partner is usually fairly brief. About half of all domestic partnerships dissolve within sixteen months. About 60 percent of the time, cohabitation ends with the marriage of the partners; 40 percent break up. Black cohabiting women have the lowest odds of moving to marriage from cohabiting (CDC 2002). For white women marriages that are preceded by cohabitation are more likely to end in divorce than marriages that do not. Black and Mexican American women who cohabit before marriage are not more likely to divorce (Phillips and Sweeney 2005).

Cohabitation is less stable than marriage for whites, but researchers are not sure why. Perhaps the most straightforward reason is that people who cohabit are less traditional in their family values. When couples of similar age and duration of partnership are compared, 55 percent of cohabitors agree that "marriage is a lifetime relationship and should never be ended except under extreme circumstances," while 71 percent of married people agree (Bumpass, Sweet, and Cherlin 1998, p. 155).

Who are heterosexual domestic partners? Fifty-five percent are younger than thirty-five. Over half (59%) had never been married before they cohabited, and about one-third (28%) are divorced. Forty percent of cohabitors live with children in the home, although usually they are children of a previous marriage (Bedard 1992; Bumpass and Sweet 1991; U.S. Census Bureau 2005c).

Education has an inverse relationship to cohabitation. This means that the more education a person has the less likely he or she is to have cohabited (Whitehead and Popenoe 2005). This runs counter to the image of college students as the primary cohabitors. College students did increase their likelihood of cohabiting in the 1970s and 1980s, but so did most other groups, and people with less education were cohabiting at higher rates prior to the 1970s. College students were imitators, not innovators, of cohabitation (Cherlin 1992a).

Singles

Most people in the United States eventually marry, and a number of those who are not married cohabit within heterosexual and gay and lesbian domestic partnerships. Many people also remain single, at least for some part of their lives. In 2000, 26 percent of all households were those in which an individual lived alone (U.S. Census Bureau 2000b). As we have already noted, some of those who claim to live alone may in fact be involved in domestic partnerships while they maintain separate residences (Nock 1987). On the other hand, other singles may not be revealed in census data because they live with relatives or friends with whom they are not domestic partners.

Many of the 61 million people who are single are single by choice and enjoy the single life. Peter Stein (1981) interviewed single people and found that they named freedom, career opportunities, friendship, self-sufficiency, and sexual relationships as being enhanced by their single status. Other researchers have found that single people spend more time having fun (Cargan and Melko 1982). Compared with married people, they go out more often, visit places of entertainment more often, and have more sex partners.

Some single people may remain single although they would prefer to marry. Marriage rates have historically declined when the economy declines. And since, as we have noted in Chapter 4, the current period is marked by economic difficulty, singlehood may be at least partly a result of inability to marry rather than a matter of choice (Bedard 1992). Our examination of the marriage gap between whites and African Americans illustrates how financial problems can create barriers to marriage (Phillips and Sweeney 2005).

Theoretical Debate on Marriage

This chapter has revealed a number of problems in the institution of marriage. Some theorists believe that marriage may be the key to the creation and maintenance of gender inequality and the oppression of women and that therefore the institution of marriage must be dismantled in order to restructure intimate relationships, especially those between women and men, more humanely and more equally.

Frederick Engels was the first scholar to assert women's status relative to men's as sociologically based rather than biologically determined (O'Toole and Sullivan 1997). He believed that marriage was a central factor in the oppression of women. He wrote that the invention of the social institution of monogamous marriage was the moment of the "world historic defeat of the female sex" (Engels 1884/1970, p. 87).

To those of us living in the twenty-first century, the idea that marriage was a social invention may at first sound strange, but as we have observed throughout this book, history shows us that the way we organize our social lives is created by humans. Marriage is an institution that exists in some societies but not in others and varies greatly from one society to the next. Therefore, the idea and practice of monogamous marriage must have been created for the first time at some specific moment in history. According to Engels, it was created for a particular purpose—to control women and children.

Engels, who was a collaborator of Karl Marx, developed an elaborate theory explaining why women were oppressed and the link of the invention of marriage to this oppression. He argued that, early in human history, people lived in small groups in which there was no class inequality and in which women were not oppressed. Although women and men had some different responsibilities in these societies, these differences did not include a power differential. In fact, he argued, if anything women may have been more powerful as a group than men because of their importance in reproduction. Women's power in these small societies was indicated by the matrilineal organization of kin relationships in which women and their children formed the core. Men were connected to the system through their mothers and sisters. Men's biological children were considered part of the mother's family, and men had stronger social relationships with their sisters' children than with their own offspring.

After describing these ancient matrilineal egalitarian societies, Engels pointed out the striking inequality between women and men in modern capitalist states and asked, "How did society change to produce the oppression of women?" He answered by asserting that as the egalitarian hunter-gatherer groups became more efficient at producing their own food and shelter rather than finding it in the wild, they were able to produce a surplus. For example, after animals were domesticated, herders could begin to raise more animals than they needed to provide enough food for the clan. When they were not forced to use up the animals every year for food, they could accumulate larger and larger herds. Those people who owned the herds gradually gathered more and more of this surplus, and class inequalities began to emerge. Those who owned herds had something to offer or to withhold from others in order to gain control over decisions made by the clan. Furthermore, Engels argued, men, not women, were more likely to be herders, and it was men and not women who came to make up this emerging dominant owning class.

The dominance of men in terms of ownership of wealth did not fit well with the egalitarian matrilineal kinship system. Men who were able to accumulate property through the ownership of their herds and through trading were unable to pass their inheritance to their own children because of the matrilineal kinship system, in which inheritance would pass from a man to his sister's children. In order to create a system of inheritance that allowed the passage of property from a father to his children, a mechanism had to be created to ensure that (1) a man's children were in fact his own, and (2) kinship and inheritance would be traced through the father's line. The mechanism that provided for these two needs was patriarchal monogamous marriage. This kind of marriage required women to be sexually exclusive in order to guarantee that any children were the husband's. Marriage allowed property-owning men to consolidate their wealth and to pass it on to their biological and legal heirs.

According to Engels, marriage was a critical initial social underpinning of both class inequality and the oppression of women. Marriage aided the consolidation of wealth, locking in class inequality. Marriage guaranteed that men would control women and thereby control the products of their reproduction—children—locking in male dominance of women.

Engels tried to support his theory by citing empirical evidence gathered by nineteenth-century anthropologists. The data he amassed did back up his ideas, but other anthropologists have since found conflicting evidence as well. Most scholars now argue either that there is insufficient empirical evidence to support or refute Engels's theory or that the empirical evidence refutes his theory. Anthropologists do not agree about whether Engels was correct in his depiction of the process by which social classes developed or men came to control women. Nevertheless, the framework remains a powerful theoretical argument for analyzing the historical roots of the oppression of women because it suggests a way of understanding the oppression of women in contemporary society (Leacock 1973; Lengermann and Niebrugge-Brantley 1992; Lerner 1986).

The importance of Engels's theory to this chapter is that it points out the centrality of the organization of marriage to the existence of gender inequality and the oppression of women. Throughout this chapter, we have noted contemporary authors who argue that the current organization of marriage, despite a history of reform, still aids men in their dominance over women. Engels's theory gives us some clues to understanding why women are oppressed by men and how they are kept under men's control (Rapp 1982).

Why are women oppressed? Engels proposed, as we have seen, that the reason women are oppressed by men is that in order to maintain the class system, wealthy men need a mechanism for keeping their wealth together from one generation to the next rather than dispersing it. Upper-class men need a family system that allows them to pass their inheritance to their own biological heirs. Therefore, they need a means to guarantee their wives' sexual exclusivity and dependence on them. How do upper-class men accomplish this? By maintaining a family system that is patrilineal and that demands that women be monogamous by maintaining the institution of marriage. Engels argued that marriage was an institution that served the interest of ruling-class men. He asserted that relationships between working-class women and men were not bound by the same needs and that another kind of marriage, a nonoppressive form, existed or potentially existed between working-class women and men. He argued that as working-class women became economically independent by entering the paid labor force, they were freed to enter into egalitarian relationships with working-class men. This is where Engels has been criticized by marxist and socialist feminists.

During the emergence of Second-Wave feminism, Engels's theories were widely discussed. Socialist feminists agreed that the oppression of women was tied into the maintenance of class systems like the capitalist system in the United States and believed Engels's theory provided a convincing argument for how marriage acted as a mechanism to connect these two systems of oppression, capitalism and patriarchy (Eisenstein 1979). Socialist feminists, however, disagreed with the assertion that working-class men did not benefit from an organization of marriage that placed women in a dependent, subordinate position. They also argued that entering the labor force did not eliminate the oppression of women. The oppression of women served ruling-class men in two ways—by helping maintain the system of class inequality and by helping maintain the system of gender inequality. But according to socialist feminists, the oppression of women also served working-class men by granting them a position of dominance in their relationships with women of their class. Male dominance exists in many working-class marriages even when the woman is earning wages outside of the home (Hansen and Philipson 1990; Kain 1993).

The debate over whether class inequality is more salient than gender inequality or vice versa and whether ending class inequality will lead to gender equality continues (Shelton and Agger 1993). The problematic character of marriage and its importance in the maintenance of class and gender oppression, however, is agreed on by theorists from Marxist, socialist feminist, and radical feminist frameworks.

This chapter began with a story in which a couple faced a dilemma that might be solved or alleviated if they had the right to marry. Much of the rest of the chapter has described the difficulties in the instituion of marriage for those who are allowed to marry in our society. Is marriage the problem or the solution? The debate over this question has been an important one, not only among theorists but also among political activists, especially those involved in the gay rights movement. This debate is the topic of the next section.

Families We Choose

Throughout this book, I have argued that people consistently challenge their society in an attempt to adjust the macrolevel of social organization. The case of marriage is no different. Individuals interacting with one another have expressed unhappiness with the way in which marriage is organized, especially in the law, and have sought to challenge that organization. One important issue that has been subject to public debate is homosexuality and gay and lesbian rights. Polls show that public opinion about homosexuality has become more accepting in recent years.

One of the specific family issues around which there has been public debate is the question of whether gay people should be allowed to legally marry. Surveys in 2005 that asked whether gay men and lesbians should be allowed to marry found that more than half (53%) of Americans said they should not be granted this right (Pew Research Center 2005). Gender makes a difference in the responses. More than three-quarters of men said gay marriage should not be legal, while 61 percent of women said they should not. Age also was important. Eighty-six percent of men over sixty-five said it should not be legal while only 40 percent of young women under thirty though gay marriage should not be legal.

Whether to identify the right to marry as a political goal has been an issue of controversy within the gay community. Gay men and lesbians are divided on the issue. Should the political battle be to allow marriage for gay people, or should gay rights activists lead the challenge to reconstruct intimate relationships in ways other than the marriage model?

Andrew Sullivan (1992) argues that gay couples should be allowed to marry. He writes that marriage allows couples to make a deeper commitment to one another and to society, and that in return society allows them certain benefits. Those benefits include legal rights. Sullivan also maintains that marriage provides emotional benefits: "Marriage provides an anchor, if an arbitrary and weak one, in the chaos of sex and relationships to which we are all prone" (Sullivan 1992, p. 77). Furthermore, he asserts that legalizing and encouraging marriage among gay couples would provide role models for young gay people and would help bridge the gulf between gay people and their parents.

Paula Ettlebrick (1992) strongly disagrees. She asks, "Since when is marriage a path to liberation?" Her concern is that gay couples would be caught in the oppressive trap of the institution of marriage as it is currently organized. In addition, she worries that the more gay people choose to fashion their relationships after conventional heterosexual relationships, the more that diversity will be discredited as a valuable feature of our society. Both heterosexual and gay people who chose not to pattern their relationships on a conservative marriage model would be subjected to social and legal sanction even more than they are now.

Kath Weston (1991) refers to this debate as the dilemma of assimilation or transformation. Sullivan is promoting assimilation, and Ettlebrick is criticizing it. According to Weston, the alternative is to identify factors that could and in many cases are transforming intimate relationships among gay people. Weston asked gay men and lesbians about their families and their intimate relations in order to find clues about how a transformed family might look. She found that gay people often live in social arrangements that include intimate relationships between couples and close familial relationships among other adults and among adults and children. She refers to these arrangements as "families we choose." Sociologists often refer to two types of families: family of orientation and family of procreation. A family of orientation is the one into which a person is born. A person's ties to a family of orientation is a blood relationship; if the person was adopted, the relationship is a legal one that is modeled after a blood relationship. A family of procreation is a person and his or her spouse and children. The relationships in a family of procreation are based on the legal tie between a husband and wife and the blood tie between parents and their children and the legal tie between parents and children who are adopted.

Families we choose may include blood relationships and legal relationships, but they also include equally and often more important relationships that are not legally or biologically based but are chosen and consciously built. Weston found that lesbians and gay men were actively building families they chose. Their families of orientation were sometimes part of this effort. The act of coming out frequently puts relationships with families of orientation to the test. Not all gay people are willing to test their family of orientation, but many are willing to break these ties if necessary to attempt to create stronger, more honest ties. One man told Weston, "If you can't be honest with somebody, then what kind of relationship are you really salvaging? What are you giving up if they react badly and they're gone? What have you really lost?" (Weston 1991, p. 52).

Gay men and women also created families they chose as alternatives to families of procreation. These families often did include procreation, sometimes by bringing children from previous heterosexual relationships, sometimes by adopting children as a gay couple or single, and sometimes by organizing reproduction through alternative insemination.

When Weston (1991) asked the gay men and lesbians she interviewed whom they considered to be members of their families, they consistently counted lovers as family, usually at the top of the list. They also included children and other relatives of their lovers as family and people who were not their lovers but with whom they shared a household. In addition, they often named former lovers as more distant, but still connected, parts of the family they chose.

Families we choose expand beyond a couple and their children to include fictive kin who become an extended family. One woman described her family:

> When I go to have a kid, I'm not gonna have my biological sisters as godparents. I'm gonna have people that are around me, that are gay. No, I call on my inner family—my community, or whatever—to help me with my life. So there's definitely a family. And you're building it; it keeps getting bigger and bigger. (Weston 1991, p. 108)

One of the problems gay couples and the families they chose faced was that without rituals declaring the validity of their relationship, it was sometimes difficult to know how shared the relationship was. For example, one person may consider another as part of his or her family but may not know for sure if that person feels likewise. Gay weddings and rituals are one way to try to affirm the connections.

Weston (1991) concludes that gay men and lesbians, in their efforts to create families they choose, present a challenge to an organization of marriage and family fashioned after the conservative model. The first feature of this challenge is the support of diversity. Families we choose are not monolithic; they are individually tailored. Second, families we choose prioritize social relationships over legal or biological relationships. Familial relationships in families we choose are not assumed. Instead they are created, tested, and revised through the social interaction of their members.

The Micro–Macro Connection

This chapter has once again shown us the way in which the seemingly personal character of microlevel family relationships is influenced and sometimes determined by large macrolevel social structures and forces. A marriage is a microlevel relationship between two individuals, but that relationship is affected by the macrolevel organization of society, including such factors as legal issues, economic opportunities, and ideologies. Who can marry, when they marry, and what a marriage entails are defined by factors beyond the individuals who are marrying.

Both the social structural macrolevel factors and the microlevel features of marriage are dynamic and change over time. In recent years, marriage laws, the experience of marriage, and ideas about marriage have all changed rather dramatically. And at the same time that changes in the macrolevel have affected the microlevel experience of marriage, people interacting at the microlevel have also had an effect on the macrolevel. Many are attempting to transform the organization of marriage through conscious political work and through the day-to-day acting out of alternative family forms. Increasing numbers of people who are choosing to live together without marriage are challenging and altering the institution, often in an unconscious way. In addition, some people, like those involved in the gay rights movement, are debating among themselves and with the wider society about the best way to organize our personal lives and whether marriage should be transformed or left as it is.

CHAPTER

10 Divorce and Remarriage

Divorce is a legal issue and has been subject to laws and courtroom proceedings in the United States since Colonial days. The 1970s marked an important transition in divorce laws and changes to what is known as no-fault divorce during that decade have had significant effects on divorcing couples and their children. (© Frank Siteman/PhotoEdit)

Teresa and Manny were recently divorced after eight years of marriage. For most of their marriage, they were both happy, and when their daughter Maria was born, they excitedly looked forward to watching her grow up together.

Teresa speaks, "Divorce teaches you a lot about marriage. I had some very romantic ideas about what marriage is, and when we couldn't seem to match those dreams I felt so unhappy I couldn't stay married anymore. It has been almost two years since we got our divorce. For me it was a major turning point. Mostly it's the money. We had to sell the house in the divorce settlement, and my check is pretty good but not enough to buy a house or even rent in our old neighborhood. Maria has to go without sometimes, and it makes me feel bad. Manny is supposed to send child support, but sometimes he doesn't. He says his job is not going that well, but sometimes I think he doesn't send the check because he likes to keep me on edge. Divorce isn't all bad, though. I've had to take care of Maria and myself, and I've done it. That feels pretty good."

Manny speaks, "I liked being married, but Teresa and I didn't see eye to eye on what a good marriage is. She was always wanting me to try harder and make more money to get ahead, and I wanted to enjoy life a little. At the end I was going out with other women because I needed some sympathy. Divorce has been hard on me. Most of our friends were Teresa's, and they stopped seeing me when we split up. Teresa gets mad when I don't send the child support check, but work is off in construction and we don't get that much. Plus I feel like I hardly know Maria any more. We get together on weekends and holidays, but it's not natural picking her up and making arrangements. Her friends are in her new neighborhood, and sometimes it seems like I'm imposing on her new life. I hope I can get back to normal when I remarry next spring. My girlfriend Carol has helped me a lot."

Maria speaks, "I hate it that my parents got a divorce. They don't argue as much, but I don't see why they couldn't have worked it out. It's embarrassing not to have a father at home. People think he left us or that there was something wrong with my mother or him. And besides, I miss him. When they decided to split up, I thought it was my fault because I wasn't doing so well in school. Now I know it was their problems, but I keep thinking maybe I could have done something. Divorce is between two adults, but it affects us too. Kids have nothing to say about it. When I get married, I will be different."

> How do our ideas about what marriage should be like affect the possibility that we will divorce?
>
> Besides ideas, what other social factors put pressure on marriages?
>
> How is divorce experienced differently by women and men and by parents and children?
>
> Divorce is usually a crisis because it creates difficult changes in people's lives. Can those changes be positive as well as negative? Can divorce be both a trauma and an opportunity?
>
> Manny looks forward to his second marriage as an opportunity to correct some of the mistakes he made and to start over. While remarriage does provide a second chance, what kinds of problems do couples who are marrying for a second time have?
>
> Since divorce is such a common experience, why do people feel as if they are facing an unexplored and difficult mystery when they decide to divorce?
>
> Divorce is a social problem because it is experienced by so many people. How can our society create ways to ease that experience? Should we make divorce more difficult to obtain? Should we create supports that make it easier to endure?

Divorce is common in the contemporary United States. Everyone knows someone who has divorced, and many of us have lived through a divorce of our own or of our parents. Despite its commonness, however, divorce is difficult to understand. In this chapter, we examine the nature of divorce and offer some suggestions for how to use the Sociological Imagination to try to understand why the process is so painful and how it might be made more humane. The chapter is divided into four sections. The first describes the incidence of divorce in the United States and reviews the history of change in divorce since the colonial period, with an emphasis on the way in which the macro-organization of law has had an important effect on the microlevel experience of divorce. The next section deals with what happens after a divorce and is divided into five subsections: social stigma, economic difficulties, divorce as an opportunity, remarriage, the experience of children with divorce. In the third section, the effect of the microlevel on the macrolevel is reviewed in a discussion of the development of divorce law.

How to Measure Divorce

In the introduction to this chapter, I asserted that divorce is a common experience and asked that you recall your personal experience as evidence of its pervasiveness. Scholarship, however, demands that additional evidence be provided. How often does divorce occur? This is a question that demographers have grappled with, and the answer is surprisingly difficult to obtain (Heuveline 2005).

Demography is the study of the size, composition, and distribution of human populations. Demographers record and analyze statistics about issues such as birth, death, marriage, and divorce. It may seem that the demographers' task of measuring divorce is an easy one. Since divorce is a legal transaction, there is a record in the courts of every divorce. Reporting the absolute number of divorces, however, is not very useful unless it is compared with some other number like population size, number of marriages, or number of potentially divorcing people. When demographers wish to report the number of divorces, therefore, they confront difficult choices.

There are five possible ways to report the number of divorces. Each of these methods has drawbacks (Crosby 1980).

1. Reporting the number of divorces per year is one method for arriving at the rate of divorce. This measure is unsatisfactory because it does not take into account the changing numbers of people in the population. For example, if we found that the absolute number of divorces was larger in 1970 than it was in 1870, we would not know how much of this increase was a result of the increase in the total population and how much was a true measure of the increase in divorce.

2. The crude divorce rate is the number of divorces per 1,000 population. This technique corrects for the size of the population mentioned in the discussion of the first method. But many people in the general population—those who are single adults and those who are children—are not able to divorce. If the proportion of single adults or children in the total population changes, it will appear that the divorce rate has changed, even though it has remained the same. For example, suppose the total population remains the same, but the birthrate rises and children make up a larger proportion of the total population in 1990 compared with 1970. Then we might find that the crude divorce rate falls during that period. This decline might mean that divorces have really diminished, or it might mean that fewer people were married and divorce was actually more common.

3. Measuring the ratio of current marriages to current divorces is a third way of finding the divorce rate. The problem with this method is that the ratio between marriages and divorces can fluctuate because of changes in the rate of marriage, as well as changes in the rate of divorce, and the ratio does not tell us which number is fluctuating. For example, suppose we compared the ratio between the number of marriages and the number of divorces in 1960 with the ratio in 2000 and found that the ratio was higher in 1960. This could mean that there were more marriages in 1960 than there were in 2000, or that there were fewer divorces in 1960, or both. But we do not know which of these possibilities is being reflected in the ratio.

4. The refined divorce rate is the number of divorces per 1,000 married women over age fifteen. This is the measure that is most commonly used and is considered the best available. It accounts for changes in the population and eliminates the problem of a fluctuating number of children (too young to marry) and a fluctuating number of singles (not able to divorce). This method of measurement, however, is not completely satisfactory because it does not give any indication of what the possibility is of divorcing at any time in one's life or at any particular age. It does not include information on the relationship of years of marriage to divorce. We do not know from the refined divorce rate how long people have been married. The refined divorce rate tells how many people in a given year are divorced, but it does not tell us how many of those who are currently married will divorce at some time in their lives.

5. Data from longitudinal studies would correct this problem by following married couples over their lifetimes to look at patterns of marriage and divorce over time. A longitudinal study would be the best way to report divorces (Crosby 1980). This technique, however, is expensive and time consuming and, therefore, has been used only in small surveys.

Rates of Divorce

The National Marriage Project (Whitehead and Popenoe 2005) reports that one in two marriages end in divorce. Divorce is so common that it will touch nearly all of us as spouses, children, or at least friends or relatives of divorcing couples.

The experience of divorce by such large numbers of people is a relatively recent phenomenon. As we saw in Chapter 2, the divorce rate in the United States increased after the turn of the century. Until the mid-1960s, the increase was gradual, except for a brief but intense increase immediately following World War, II. From 1965 to 1975, however, the rates rose dramatically, nearly doubling. The refined divorce rate went from 9.2 divorces per 1,000 married women over age 15 in 1960 to 10.6 in 1970. The rate peaked at 22.6 in 1980, and then began to decline to 20.9 in 1990, 18.8 in 2000, and 18.4 in 2002 (Whitehead and Popenoe 2005).

Table 10.1 shows the percentage of divorced adults in four censuses. This is not the divorce rate, but rather the proportion of divorced people. The table shows that the proportion has increased. It also shows that the proportion of divorced people is highest for blacks and lowest for Hispanics, with whites falling in between.

TABLE 10.1   **Percentage of People Who Are Divorced, 1970–2001**

	1970	1980	1994	2001
White	3.1%	6.4%	8.6%	10.3%
Black	4.4	8.4	10.0	10.6
Hispanic	3.9	5.8	6.9	7.5

Source: Kreider 2005; U.S. Census Bureau 1994c, p. 1; U.S. Census Bureau 2000f, p. 51.

What Are the Correlates of Divorce?

Divorce is such a common experience in contemporary America that it crosses many social lines such as race, age, class, education, and age. Sociologists, however, have found patterns indicating that particular factors make a couple more or less likely to seek a divorce. Several factors seem to lessen the risk of divorce. Researchers (Whitehead and Popenoe 2005, p. 19) have found that the following factors reduce the probability of divorce in the first ten years of marriage by particular percentage points:

Factors in Risk of Divorce	Percent Decrease
Annual income over $50,000 (vs. under $25,000)	−30
Having a baby seven months or more after Marriage (vs. before marriage)	−24
Marrying over 25 years of age (vs. under 18)	−24
Own family of origin intact (vs. divorced parents)	−14
Religious affiliation (vs. none)	−14
Some college (vs. high-school dropout)	−13

This means that although the married people in the United States as a whole have about a fifty/fifty chance of divorcing, if they are are reasonably well educated with a decent income, come from an intact family and are religious, and marry after age twenty-five without having a baby first, their chances of divorce are quite low (Whitehead and Popenoe 2005).

Divorce rates also vary by race ethnicity. Once again, however, the variation is complex. African Americans are more likely than Euro-Americans to divorce (Thornton and Freedman 1983). The greater likelihood of divorce among African Americans has been linked to other issues, such as pressures from discrimination and lower incomes. However, Latinos who share some of these problems with African Americans have divorce rates that are only slightly higher than Euro-Americans. Furthermore, there is great variability in divorce rates as well as other family issues among different groups of Latinos—for example, Cubans, Mexicans, Puerto Ricans, and Central Americans (Baca, Zinn, and Eitzen 1990).

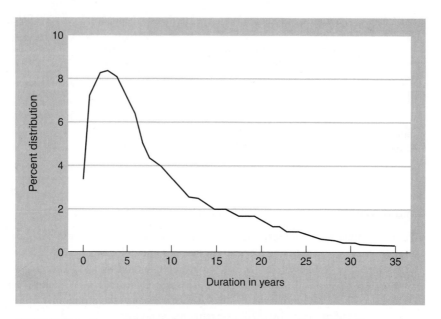

FIGURE 10.1   Percent Distribution of Divorces by Duration of Marriage

Source: National Center for Health Statistics, 1995, p. 4.

Chinese Americans, on the other hand, have very low rates of divorce. This may be because among Chinese Americans, husbands and wives are not just marriage partners, but are often also business partners. Their livelihood is tied to their marriage because they work for a family business, making divorce especially difficult to consider (Glenn 1991). Although there do seem to be relationships between race ethnicity and divorce, the underlying reasons for these relationships and what the differences mean are only partially understood.

Divorces are also more likely to occur for couples who have been married between about two and four years. Figure 10.1 shows the distribution of divorces by the amount time couples have been married. The figure indicates that the rate rises rapidly during the first year, and that it peaks in about the second year, when it drops sharply. Couples who have been married twenty years or more are much less likely to divorce (Kreider 2005).

Divorces also vary by occupation and historical circumstances. Divorces rose 78 percent among Army officers between 2003 and 2004 and are now three and half times the rates they were in 2000 before the beginning of the Afghanistan and Iraq wars (Zoroya 2005).

Historical Changes in Divorce

Although the rates of divorce in the last decade are near record highs, divorce is not new to this country. The first husband and wife to obtain a legal divorce in North America were granted their decree in 1639 (Riley 1991). The divorce was filed by the wife on the grounds of bigamy when she found that her husband was already married to another woman. For nearly four hundred years, divorce has been part of the American tradition.

As we observed in Chapter 2, the Godly family was established by Puritans fleeing a society in England of which they did not approve. Divorce was part of their new society. Divorce was not available at all in England until the late 1600s, and until 1853, it could be obtained only by a decree from Parliament. In contrast, in the colonies in North America, Plymouth officials in 1620 declared that marriage was a civil rather than an ecclesiastical matter, making divorce possible. This declaration directly "defied English colonial policy that stipulated English laws—in this case anti-divorce laws—be established in parts of the empire that lacked pre-existing legal codes" (Riley 1991, p. 12).

Divorce, however, has not been a settled issue in the United States (Riley 1991). Throughout the almost four hundred years of divorce in America, the issue has been debated by two opposing sides, the antidivorce-rights faction and the prodivorce-rights faction. The opponents of divorce rights have usually believed there is only one legitimate reason for allowing divorce, and that is adultery. Sometimes they have also accepted insanity or consanguinity—marriage between blood relatives—as legitimate reasons for granting a divorce.

Prodivorce-rights advocates believe that divorce is a citizen's right in a democratic society. They also believe that divorce is a symptom, not a cause, of underlying problems in marriage and society. Historically, supporters of divorce rights have argued that divorce is sometimes a solution to certain kinds of problems. For example, they hoped that making divorce easier to obtain might lead to greater equality in marriage.

In the 1970s, major changes consistent with the prodivorce perspective took place in the legal structure of divorce. Before 1970, divorce laws were based on the concept of fault. Someone who wanted a divorce had to prove that his or her spouse had committed adultery, cruelty, or desertion (Stetson 1997). Divorcing couples were "already engaged in a furious pitched battle, [and] forced by the fault issue to raise the stakes even higher" (Ahrons 1994, p. 1). Private detectives were hired, and even people who wanted to part amicably had to make a case that proved that their partner was bad enough to divorce.

In 1970, California instituted the first no-fault divorce law in the Western world. By 1985, all states had adopted some version of no-fault laws, although there are variations from one state to another, for example, in waiting periods between separation and divorce. The no-fault legislation had six major innovations:

1. No grounds are needed to obtain a divorce.
2. Neither spouse has to prove fault to obtain a divorce.
3. One spouse can decide unilaterally to obtain a divorce.
4. Financial awards are not linked to fault.
5. New standards for alimony and property awards seek to treat women and men equally.
6. New procedures aim at undermining the adversarial process and creating a social-psychological climate that fosters amicable divorce (Weitzman 1985, pp. 15–16).

In the 1990s, antidivorce-rights activists won some legal ground in their promotion of the covenant marriage to replace no-fault divorce. Louisiana, Arizona, and Arkansas have enacted covenant marriage legislation. Fifteen states have considered the laws and rejected them, and they are now being considered in about twenty other states (National Conference of State Legislatures 2005). Couples who choose a covenant marriage must receive premarital counseling and sign an affidavit that confirms their lifetime commitment to one another, as well as their understanding of the limited grounds under which they may receive a divorce. They cannot divorce except in extreme cases specified by the law. Regardless of the circumstances, covenant couples must also agree to go through counseling to work through problems before a divorce can be obtained.

The law states that those who marry under the covenant option can divorce only for the following reasons: adultery by the other spouse; commission of a felony that results in imprisonment or the death penalty; abandonment by the other spouse for one year or more; physical or sexual abuse of the spouse or child of either partner; living separately from the spouse for two or more years; habitual alcohol or drug abuse; and cruel treatment or severe ill treatment. Irreconcilable differences is not an acceptable reason for divorce in a covenant marriage (Laconte 1998).

Only a few hundred newlyweds have chosen covenant marriage so far, but several thousand couples who are already married signed covenant agreements. A number of churches have also declared their congregations to be "no-fault-free zones" and are refusing to marry people who do not choose the covenant option.

Another American History of Divorce.   Until about 1900, the Inuit in North Alaska, who are commonly called Eskimos, maintained a system of marriage and divorce that was quite different from that of the Euro-Americans who dominated North America. Burch (1970) noted that divorce among the Inuit consisted of the couple's ceasing to live with one another and to have sexual relations. A divorce, like a marriage among the Inuit, was accomplished without ceremony. The decision was made by the person who wanted the divorce regardless of whether the spouse agreed with that decision. All that was involved was for one or the other spouse to leave or to make the other one go. A husband or wife who wished to divorce needed only to walk out the door. A husband or wife who wanted his or her spouse to leave would scatter the spouse's belongings outside the door.

Unlike the legal systems of divorce in Euro-American society, Inuit divorce was not constrained by the problem of giving a reason for the separation or obtaining permission from the community and its institutions. While Euro-Americans argued about who should decide and what the grounds for those decisions should be, the Inuit agreed that individuals should be able to make the decision to separate and that any reason for their decision was a legitimate one.

Another characteristic that distinguished Inuit divorce from the legal system of divorce in the United States was the relationship between husband and wife after a divorce. Under the legal system created by Euro-Americans, divorce terminates the marital relationship between husbands and wives, so that, for example, if they decide to get back together again they must remarry. For the Inuit, the relationship between husband and wife is never terminated, but rather is deactivated. Burch describes this as similar to the phenomenon among Euro-Americans of inactive relationships with relatives outside of the immediate family. For example, we may have second cousins about whom we have heard, and we may even know where they live, but we have no direct contact with them. In one sense, we do not have a relationship with these cousins because we have no contact with them. On the

B O X **10.1**

Do Higher Divorce Rates Mean Fewer Intact Families?

Sometimes people who see the statistics indicating increasing numbers of divorces jump to the conclusions that contemporary Americans, compared with those of previous historical periods, are much less likely to live in intact families, children are less likely to be raised to adulthood by both of their natural parents, and more families include stepparents and step- and half-brothers and sisters. These conclusions are not entirely valid.

Peter Uhlenberg (1998) points out that while divorce was increasing, another demographic statistic, the mortality rate, was decreasing. For example, in 1900, 24 percent of children had lost one parent to death by the time they were fifteen, and one in sixty-two had lost both parents. In 1976, in contrast, only 5 percent had lost one parent, and one in 1800 had lost both.

Until the 1970s, mortality rates in the twentieth century dropped more rapidly than divorce rates rose. A husband or wife who married in his or her early twenties was much more likely to be widowed or divorced before reaching a fortieth wedding anniversary in 1900 than in 1976. Even though divorce rates rose during this time period, the net effect of marriages ending by *either* divorce or death actually declined. Writing in 1976, Uhlenberg states, "Decline in early widowhood more than offsets the rise in divorce so that the stability of marriage during the childrearing years has actually increased over this century" (1998, p. 92).

Since the late 1970s, this situation has changed somewhat. Divorces have come to represent a larger proportion of marriages that have ended. Divorce now has caused marital dissolution to rise to higher levels than in earlier years. But the change in the total is still relatively small. The proportion of people today who experience the early termination of a marriage is not dramatically different from what it was at the end of the nineteenth century (Weeks 1993). The reason for the end of a marriage, however, is different. At the beginning of the twentieth century, couples were separated by death, and now they are separated by divorce.

---

other hand, the potential relationship exists and can often be activated or reactivated if one of the cousins wishes to do so.

In traditional Inuit society, couples deactivated their relationship by ceasing to live with one another. If they decided to get back together, they reestablished their relationship by living with each other again. Solid data are not available on the divorce rate among the Inuit under this system, but Burch (1970) argues that the divorce rate approached 100 percent. Nearly all couples were separated at some time during their married lives, and many were separated a number of times. Divorce was a pervasive and fluid phenomenon in Inuit society.

Burch also looked at the reasons for divorce among the Inuit. He observed that three reasons seemed most common: infidelity, failure of either a husband or wife to meet economic obligations, and disagreements over child rearing. Burch also observed that the level of interpersonal difficulty caused by these activities was often quite low, but resulted in divorce nevertheless: "Indeed, some of the things we would scarcely regard as justification for an argument were sufficient grounds for an Eskimo divorce" (1970, p. 168). The relatively quick transition from problem to divorce in Inuit society was a result of the belief that relationships between husbands and wives were not supposed to contain any strains.

The ease and prevalence of divorce was coupled with a high rate of remarriage among the Inuit. Ex-spouses were obligated to treat each other in a friendly and supportive manner. The jealousy and mutual antagonisms often encountered in our society between new spouses and ex-spouses were not tolerated. New spouses and ex-spouses were required to avoid each other altogether or to get along on good terms (Burch 1970).

Following a divorce, the children of the divorced couple frequently stayed with their mother, although they could choose to live with the parent they preferred. A very young child was frequently adopted by another couple, usually a relative of the natural parents. In these adoptions, the child was not seen as having lost his or her natural parents, but rather as having gained another set of parents with whom to live.

Property settlements were also easy. Most property was individually owned, with little overlap between the sexes. Men owned the property associated with the economic tasks they fulfilled, such as hunting, manufacturing tools, and educating their sons. Women owned the property associated with the womanly work of butchering, making clothing, caring for small children, and educating their daughters. When couples divorced, they took with them the tools of their trades.

The difference between Inuit divorce and legal divorce in the United States in the nineteenth and twentieth centuries is striking. For the Inuit, the decision to divorce could be made by an individual and involved minimal action. The decision to remarry one's ex-spouse was equally simple. The two difficulties in legal divorce that we face—property settlement and child custody—were also handled in a humane and efficient manner.

Throughout this book, I have stressed the importance of observing the link between social context and family organization. The Inuit living in northern Alaska before 1900 existed in a social context that is much different from that of most people living in the contemporary United States. The Inuit system for organizing divorce, therefore, could not be directly incorporated into contemporary U.S. divorce law. However, the Inuit do provide us with some insight into the variety of ways in which divorce might be handled more effectively. This discussion also reminds us that the historical pool from which Americans might draw ideas should include ideas from small, relatively invisible, and disappearing—but equally American—cultures.

Why Do Women Choose Divorce?

Women are likely to be the initiators of divorce. Various studies show between two-thirds and three-quarters of divorces are initiated by wives. Demie Kurz (1995) interviewed women to find out about their experiences and why their marriages ended. Nineteen percent say they divorced because of personal dissatisfaction. Women in this category gave such reasons as they didn't love their husbands any more, they fought too often, or they didn't like the way their husbands treated them. One woman explained her personal dissatisfaction:

> I left him—he wasn't physically abusive, but he was emotionally abusive. I didn't like how he made all the decisions. He always argued very logically with what I said. So it always seemed like what I said didn't make any sense and what he said was right. I just didn't have the respect for him any more. I thought long and hard about leaving for over a year. I tried to

get him into counseling. He went but he didn't really participate. And when we got home it was just the same thing. (p. 21)

Violence was also an important reason. Seventy percent of the women in her sample said they had experienced violence at least once in their marriage. Nineteen percent said they sought a divorce because their husbands were violent.

Seventeen percent said they ended their marriages because of "hard living." Kurz uses this term to describe behaviors like heavy drinking, drug use, and frequent absences from home. Another 19 percent said their husbands had been involved with another woman, and either their husbands had left them or they had chosen to leave. The final category, "other reasons," accounted for 26 percent of divorces and included mostly women whose husbands left them.

Divorce Transitions

Constance Ahrons (1994, 2004a, 2004b) conducted a long-term investigation of 196 parents who divorced. Interviewing people periodically from the late 1970s to the mid-1980s, she was particularly interested in the process by which people divorce. Although it takes only a few minutes to issue a decree, divorce in real people's lives unfolds over a much more extended period of time. Ahrons (2004a) found that five transitions comprised the divorce experience: decision, announcement, separation, formal, and aftermath. The first three occurred before the formal divorce. First, people made the decision for themselves that they must divorce and shared this insight with their spouses, who may or may not have seen it coming. They also had to announce it to their friends and family. And they had to separate physically and emotionally. The formal divorce can occur quickly, but it too varies and can drag out for extended periods of time. The final transition occurred after the formal legal divorce and involved resolving emotions, reconstructing new relationships with the former spouse and new forms of coparenting, and creating new lives. Eventually, if remarriage occurred, it also involved reconstructing binuclear households (two separate households, one for each spouse) that might include subsequent spouses, cohabitors, and their children and families.

This section addresses this last transition by investigating four important issues that face people after they formalize their divorces: the stigmatization of divorced people; economic difficulties, especially for women; the unfolding of opportunities for personal growth after a divorce; and remarriage.

Social Stigmatization

Social stigmatization occurs when people are perceived to be different and less worthy than other people because of their appearance or behavior. When people are stigmatized, others see them as having something wrong with them. Erving Goffman described stigmatized people as those who are seen and come to see themselves as "of a less desired kind—

reduced in our mind from a whole and usual person to a tainted, discounted one" (Goffman 1963, p. 3).

Naomi Gerstel (1987) decided to try to find out if divorced people are stigmatized. Changes in the laws, especially the passage of no-fault laws, indicate that people are becoming more accepting of divorce and are less likely to blame divorced people for the divorce. In addition to changes in the laws, public opinion polls of divorce also show greater tolerance of divorce and divorced people than existed earlier in the twentieth century (Veroff, Douvan, and Kukla 1981). Polls in 1962 found that 51 percent of people believed that parents who were considering a divorce should not stay together for the sake of the children. In 1985, 82 percent said they should not (Kosmin and Lachman 1993). But is this greater level of acceptance of divorce reflected in the personal experience of individuals who are divorced?

Gerstel's (1987) interviews with 104 divorced and separated people showed that divorced people continue to be stigmatized in two ways. First, although disapproval of divorce as a general category has declined, divorced people experience disapproval related to the specific conditions of the divorce. The divorce is accepted only if it took place under certain conditions. Furthermore, these conditions vary by gender. Men who had begun affairs before their divorce experienced disapproval and were stigmatized as "cavalier home-wreckers" (p. 176). Women were more likely to be criticized if they divorced when they had young children. Gerstel explains that these women were "bad divorcees" when they did not or could not sacrifice for their children.

Second, divorced people still suffer informal relational sanctions. For example, divorced people feel they are punished for divorce by being forced to split friends and being excluded from social interactions. One man explained, "The couples we shared our life with, I'm an outsider now. They stay away. Not being invited to a lot of parties that we was always invited to. It's with males and females. It sucks" (Gerstel 1987, p. 173). And a woman stated, "Well, I now have no married friends. It's as if I all of a sudden became single and I'm going to chase after their husbands" (Gerstel 1987, p. 172).

As a result of their exclusion from married couple circles, divorced people, Gerstel found, tended to develop a social life among other divorced people. This is similar to the experience of other stigmatized people. Goffman (1963, p. 21), who studied many different kinds of stigmatized people, found that, in general, stigmatized people often come together to share their stories, offer comfort, and make one another feel at home like "a person who is really like any normal person."

Gerstel concludes that the divorced are no longer thought to be sinful or criminal, and many of the friends and families of divorced people do not disapprove of their divorce. "However, a decrease in statistical deviance, a relaxation of institutional controls by church or state, or a decline in categorical disapproval is not the same as the absence of stigmatization" (1987, p. 183). Divorce continues to set people apart and often to represent a mark against them.

Young Song (1991) has examined the negative results of divorce for Asian American women. She reports that Asian American women experience the stigmatization and self-blame described by Gerstel, but in an exaggerated form. Song argues that the divorced women she interviewed retained stronger ideas than other Americans did about the shamefulness of divorce and its identification with failure, particularly for women. As a result,

Asian American women are likely to suffer serious emotional hardships after a divorce. These problems are further exacerbated by the cultural value placed on controlling and hiding negative feelings.

Economic Difficulties for Women

In 2005, women who divorced, on average, experienced a 50 percent decline in their family income and at least a 20 percent decline in the per capita income of their household (Family Research Council 2005). Despite the economic decline, many women say they still feel more satisfied with their financial situations after the divorce because they feel more in charge, able to make their own decisions, and relieved they don't have to account to their husbands for their choices (Ahrons 1994). Nevertheless, the reduction in income that occurs for most women after divorce has created problems (Mulroy 1995). Thirty-seven percent of single women with children live below poverty (U.S. Census Bureau 2005a).

When Kurz (1995) interviewed women who had divorced, she found that economics was a key issue for them. Kurz divided her sample into three categories: middle class, working class, and poverty level. Middle-class women worried about maintaining their lifestyles with car payments and tuition for their children, and especially mortgages. Working-class women struggled to meet basic expenses. They, too, were particularly worried about housing. Poverty-level mothers were unable to keep up with even basic necessities.

In order to make ends meet, the women took second jobs and moved in with their parents. Forty-eight percent of the poverty-level women, 30 percent of the working-class women, and 20 percent of the middle-class women relied on their parents for substantial support and said they would not be able to make it without their parents' help (Kurz 1995). Poverty-level women also sought help from social-welfare programs.

Terry Arendell (1986) interviewed sixty middle-class divorced women. She found that nearly all of them faced serious economic hardship after their divorces: "90% of them found divorce immediately pushed them below the poverty line, or close to it" (p. 231). Their economic decline was not temporary. One woman described her experience:

> I've been living hand to mouth all these years, ever since the divorce. I have no savings account. The notion of having one is as foreign to me as insurance—there's no way I can afford insurance. I have an old pickup that I don't drive very often. In the summertime I don't wear nylons to work because I can cut costs there. Together the kids and I have had to struggle and struggle. There have been times when we've scoured the shag rug to see if we could find a coin to come up with enough to buy milk so we could have cold cereal for dinner. (p. 231)

Because women nearly always have custody of their children, divorce also causes poverty among children. Another woman told Arendell:

> I had $950 a month. My son qualified for free school lunches. We'd been living on over $4,000 a month before the divorce and there we were. That's so humiliating. What that does to the self-esteem of a child is absolutely unbelievable. And it isn't hidden: everybody knows the situation. They knew at school that he was the kid with the free lunch coupons. My son is real tall and growing. I really didn't have any money to buy him clothes. So he

was wearing these sweatshirts that were too small for him. Then one day he didn't want to go to school because the kids had been calling him Frankenstein because his arms and legs were hanging out of his clothes they were too short. (1986, p. 240)

The poverty of women and children is further exaggerated by its contrast to the lives of the ex-husbands. The same woman who was concerned about finding sufficient food and clothes for her son explained how the situation was different in the father's new household:

His father seldom buys him anything. But his stepmother does. She can give him all these nice things. She's given him nice books, a stereo headset—it's a very funny feeling to know that I can't go and buy my son something he would love to have, but this perfect stranger can. But it's kind of ironic—I helped establish that standard of living but I end up with none of it, and she has full access to it. (Arendell 1986, p. 234)

Why does divorce have such negative economic consequences for women? In the 1970s, the reforms initiating no-fault divorce were put into effect at least in part to eliminate the hostile, undignified, and sometimes fabricated evidence common in divorce proceedings under the previous laws. No-fault divorce laws have undoubtedly alleviated at least some of the adversarial and rancorous character of divorce, but they have also created some unintended economic consequences.

No-fault divorce laws are based on the premise of equality between women and men. The laws themselves are gender-blind. Women and men in our society, however, are not equal in marriage or outside of it. Since the premise of equality is invalid, no-fault laws do not work as they were intended and, in fact, actually exacerbate gender inequality. The change in divorce laws to no-fault altered one important facet of the macrolevel of social organization, but it left other facets intact. In the following discussion, we examine gender inequality in three areas that have interfered with the ability of no-fault divorce laws to work in an equitable manner: marriage, the labor market, and divorce proceedings. In many households, marriage has a different effect on women's and men's earning capacity. One of the most important investments people make is the investment in their careers and in their ability to earn money. Married couples tend to make these decisions in a way that diminishes wives' earning capacity while enhancing husbands' earning capacity (Waldfogel 1998).

For example, a couple may decide that one spouse will work while the other obtains an education, a license, or a membership in a professional organization. They may decide to move in order for one of them to accept a better job, or they may decide to stay in an area so that one person can build seniority, a professional practice, or a pension. If these kinds of decisions are made to improve the earning ability of the husband, they enhance the economic standing of the couple as long as they remain married. But after a divorce, this investment may not be part of the property to be divided equally, but rather is the "property" of the husband to take with him from the marriage.

If wives invest less in their earning capacity, they may leave a marriage with less ability to support themselves. Some wives, of course, do not allow marriage to stand in the way of earning an education and building a career. But even these wives leave marriage at a disadvantage compared with their husbands because education and labor market participation do not necessarily result in equal pay for women.

TABLE 10.2   Median Weekly Earnings for Full-Time Wage and Salary Workers by Gender and Race Ethnicity, 2004

Racial Ethnicity	Men	Women
White	$782	$584
Black	569	505
Hispanic	480	419
Asian	802	613

Source: Bureau of Labor Statistics 2004c.

Table 10.2 compares women's and men's wages. The table shows that women in every racial ethnic group still earn substantially less than do men in the same group. No-fault divorce laws make the incorrect assumption that wives are equal to their husbands in the labor market.

Alimony is money the court requires one spouse to pay to support another after a divorce. Historically, alimony was a payment a husband was required to make when separating from or divorcing his wife. Theoretically, alimony was a way in which to overcome the inequity between women and men in the labor market. Divorced women were assumed to be unable to earn as much money as their husbands, and alimony was a method of closing the gap between their incomes. In reality, however, alimony was always rare, and the payments were small.

Alimony is now called spousal support. Many people believe that most women receive spousal support when they divorce. The real number, however, is only 14 percent, and that proportion has remained steady since the late 1960s (Stetson 1997).

The third disadvantage women have when they divorce is in the division of property in the divorce proceedings. In most divorces, the largest asset recognized by the court that couples own is a family house. Prior to no-fault divorce, judges were likely to award the house to the parent who was raising the children, usually the mother, in order to allow them a stable, continuous residence. Since the passage of no-fault, judges are more likely to divide all property down the middle and to insist that the house be sold and the husband and wife divide the equity between them. A woman, of course, is legally allowed to purchase the house from her husband, which would enable her to remain there with her children. But usually women are financially unable to do this.

In the opening scenario, Teresa says that the house that she and Manny shared was sold as part of the divorce settlement. Not only was she unable to afford to buy her old home, she was unable to rent or buy in the same neighborhood. In addition to leaving the house in which they had lived, she and Maria also were forced to leave the community.

A second problem with the division of property in divorce is that it assumes that the property is to be equally divided between the divorcing adults. Since mothers are usually awarded custody of the children, in households where there are children the property may be divided down the middle, but it is awarded to two different-sized groups. One-half goes to the husband and one-half goes to the wife and children.

Third, what is defined as property may not include some of the most important assets a couple owns. For example, pensions and education are not treated as marital property (Weitzman 1985). As I described earlier, couples are more likely to have made investments in the education and pension plan of the husband in the belief that as long as the man and woman remain married, these decisions would benefit the entire household. In a divorce, state law varies, but in most cases the state does not recognize these investments as property to be divided between the spouses equally, and the husband is likely to leave the marriage with more of the assets.

For a brief period in the mid-1980s, it appeared as if the problem of dividing family assets more equitably in divorce courts was beginning to be addressed by public officials. In 1983, the Congressional Caucus on Women's Issues pushed a bill through Congress that allowed military pensions to be considered as marital property to be divided in a divorce. Since then, however, the courts have allowed people to convert their military pensions into disability benefits, which can be excluded from property settlements (Stetson 1997).

In 1998, Lorna Wendt won a $20 million divorce settlement that did take into consideration the enhanced earnings with which her husband was leaving the marriage. Wendt was married to the CEO (chief executive officer) of GE Capital. During the divorce, she contended that over the course of their thirty-two-year marriage, she had been a business partner entertaining extensively, traveling, maintaining the household, serving in the community, and taking care of her husband. Based on this work, she maintained that she was entitled to his earnings potential in the form of future stock options and pensions. The judge ruled in her favor. The ruling is significant for wives of this elite strata (Morris 1998). In more typical households, the average assets amount to a few thousand dollars and are divided fifty-fifty with no regard for future earnings (Kurz 1995).

This section has described the importance of gender inequality in the issue of divorce. Gender inequality is both a cause and an effect in relationship to divorce. Gender inequality in marriage, the labor market, and divorce proceedings shapes divorce.

Divorce in turn reinforces and helps create gender inequality. A woman and a man who are leaving a marriage find themselves even more unequal in some ways than when they were in the marriage. This gender inequity is especially remarkable in its expression in financial status. Divorce appears to be an important factor in the growing impoverishment of women and their dependent children.

Divorce as an Opportunity

As we have seen in the previous discussion, divorce is often accompanied by enormous pain. The difficulties of divorce, especially in regard to children and child custody, are discussed later in this chapter. Divorce can, however, have a positive effect on people's lives by allowing them to end difficult and sometimes destructive relationships (Lund 1990). In the scenario at the beginning of the chapter, Teresa says that in spite of the difficulties, divorce has allowed her to test herself and to successfully accomplish tasks she did not know she would be able to do.

Divorce creates such a powerful break that it can be used as an opportunity to make dramatic, positive personal changes. Lund explains:

Divorce can be seen as a traumatic life crisis for any adult. It means the dissolution of dreams, hopes and the security of a socially acceptable and often secure family form. It can also be viewed as an opportunity for tremendous personal growth for women and men as they gain a new sense of competence, autonomy and individuation. (1990, p. 65)

In Ahrons's (1994) interviews, she found that most people said they were happier several years after their divorce than they were when they were married. Many also added that the one regret they had was not divorcing sooner.

Kurz's (1995) research similarly found that, despite hardships, 61 percent of the women had positive feelings about their divorce five years later. Some focused on the positive experience of getting away from the difficulties of the marriage, and others talked about their feelings of independence and personal growth.

Catherine Reissman (1991) interviewed women and men who had recently divorced and found that their experience of personal growth after divorce fell into three categories: management of daily life, social relationships, and identity. Women spoke of their delight in finding themselves competent to do things they had not done before. They talked of learning to fix things, managing their own money, and making choices about entering jobs or school. One woman spoke of her financial abilities:

> I've managed to get almost everything I've wanted. Everything you see here I bought, this is all mine, I have done it in less than two years. I did this, while with him I never got anything. It was either "We can't afford it" or "We need the money for something else." (p. 272)

Another spoke of her newfound skills as a labor organizer:

> When I first was asked to speak at the strike I had no voice, I lost my voice, but I was the spokesman—they said, "You're the one that's got to go to the meeting, they're ready to endorse this." And I can't even talk. Well, nobody else could do it, so off we rushed, and I spoke to all those people and TV and radio. (p. 273)

Women also talked about positive changes the divorce brought to their social relationships. They felt they could be themselves and that they learned to spend time alone. They also noted how they were forced to develop ties with others in order to survive. Their relationships with friends became closer as they reached out for comfort and advice. One woman explained:

> Marriage assumes that you are, that the couple is self-sufficient. It's harder to reach out. It's funny, I hadn't thought about this but it is true. You're not supposed to be needy when you're married. It's like a betrayal of this myth that marriage provides everything. (p. 269)

Third, women spoke of newfound identity revealed because of the freedom granted with the divorce. Our society highly values individuality and individual freedom. For many people, especially women, this individuality is submerged in marriage (Bellah et al.

1985). Divorce for some becomes an opportunity to "take back" their lives (Reissman 1991, p. 270).

Remarriage

Remarriage is a fourth example of what happens after a divorce: for many, divorce is followed by remarriage. In 2001, the Census Bureau reported that in more than 37 percent of all the marriages that year, the bride or groom or both partners had been married previously. This number has risen in past decades. In 1970, for example, the percentage was 31 percent (Census Bureau 1989d; Kreider 2005).

The Census Bureau also reports that 75 percent of those who divorce will eventually remarry. There are a number of factors, however, that influence the rate of remarriage. Age is one important variable. Usually, young people who divorce quickly remarry; older people are much less likely to do so. For example, 81 percent of those who divorce before they are twenty-five years of age remarry, while 61 percent of those divorcing after they are twenty-five remarry (CDC 2002).

Race ethnicity is also important. Fifty-four percent of all women will remarry within five years after they divorce. But the numbers are quite different for each racial ethnic group: 58 percent of white women, 44 percent of Hispanic women, and 32 percent of black women (CDC 2002).

Gender and the custody of children are additional factors. Eighty-one percent of women without children remarry, compared with 73 percent of women with one or two children and 57 percent of women with three or more children (Spanier and Glick 1981). Men are more likely to remarry than women, and they tend to remarry more quickly (Glick and Lin 1986). Finally, remarriage rates have changed over time. The rates of remarriage have fluctuated dramatically throughout the twentieth century and are now much lower than they were earlier (Brofenbrenner et al. 1996, p. 95).

The transition from singlehood to first marriage is not entirely unlike the transition from first marriage to remarriage, but there are differences. The couple in a first marriage must work out ways to integrate themselves into their two families of origin—the families into which they were born. Remarried people also have this task. Couples who are remarrying additionally have to integrate their ex-spouses, their children, and perhaps the families of their previous marriage (Ahrons and Rodgers 1987; Levin and Sussman 1997; Stacey 1990).

Constance Ahrons and Roy Rodgers (1987) use the term *complex binuclear family* to express the situation. They described this type of family as it existed for two children in a divorced family they encountered in their research:

> Their family looks like this: They have two biological parents, two stepparents, three stepsisters, a half-brother and a half-sister. Their extended family has expanded as well: They have two sets of step grandparents, two sets of biological grandparents, and a large network of aunts, uncles and cousins. In addition to this complex network of kin, they have two households of "family." (p. 279)

Among U.S. children, 28 percent live with one parent—23 percent with their mothers and 4.6 percent with their fathers. Another 4.2 percent live with someone else (U.S Census

BOX **10.2**

Lessons from African American Men on Easing the Divorce Transition

How do black men cope with divorce? And how does their experience differ from that of white men? Erma Jean Lawson (1999) investigated these questions by interviewing black men about what helped them adjust to their divorces. In their descriptions of what helped, the men named a number of supports including church, work relations, friends, and new heterosexual relations (Lawson and Thompson 1999). The literature on white men shows them to be more socially isolated than their wives after a divorce. The black men Lawson talked to, in contrast, were reaching out for social support to help them through the divorce (Reissmann 1991).

In addition to this general difference, three factors showed up in Lawson's interviews that indicate the unique character of black men's coping with divorce. The first of these was the importance of their mothers, who provided them with emotional and tangible support. One man described the significance of his mother as follows:

> My mother gave me so much emotional support that helped me to cope with the divorce. She understood that I was losing a wife and that it would be painful. That helped a lot. One day mom asked, "Have you tried praying?" From then on, mom and I often read the Bible together and prayed. Mom provided so much positive support and it was a relief to know that she was there for me. (1999, p. 116).

The second unique feature of black men's coping techniques was their optimism. Other scholars have noted the optimism of black Americans despite adversity (Billingsley 1992; Hill 1993). One man articulated this connection:

> My ancestors suffered and believed that they would overcome oppression one day. My forefathers and foremothers kept on going, even though they were slaves. Knowledge of their strength has given me determination and inspiration to keep on going, despite obstacles I face in trying to re-establish my life. (Lawson 1999, p. 119)

A third unique feature was the maintenance of attachment to their wives after divorce. The men reported that they remained emotionally and physically attached to their wives, although that attachment decreased over time. They also reported that maintaining the connection helped them adapt to the divorce. One man explained:

> Initially I called about everything—to see if the car insurance had been paid, to see if the grass had been cut, or if the garbage had been taken out. After a year, I stopped calling and waited for Thelma to get in touch with me, in other words, the relationship just faded. But our initial relationship helped me to adjust to living alone. (Lawson 1999, p. 121)

Bureau 2004c). Table 10.3 shows that 71 percent of children live with two parents, and 64 percent are in homes with both of their own biological or adoptive parents. About 7 percent live with one biological parent and one stepparent. These numbers show only a snapshot and do not provide information on the experience of children over time. Although a large

TABLE 10.3   Children Living with Two, One, or Neither Parent, 1996

Parents	Total Percent	Whites Percent	Blacks Percent	Hispanic Percent
Two parents	71%	77%	38%	68%
Both biological/adoptive	64	70	33	63
One biological/adoptive and one stepparent	7	7	5	5
One parent	25	20	54	27
Biological/adoptive mother	22	17	52	26
Biological adoptive father	2.5	2.7	1.9	0.2
Stepparent	0.2	0.3	0.3	0.1
Neither parent	4	3	8	5

Source: Fields 2001.

proportion of children live with their biological parents at the moment the snapshot is taken, many will at some time live in other arrangements.

Judith Stacey conducted extensive ethnographic research on two women and their families in a working-class community in Silicon Valley in California. One of her findings was that a new version of extended family had emerged. She describes it as follows: "Your basic extended family today includes your ex-husband or -wife, your ex's new mate, your new mate, possibly your new mate's ex, and any new mate that your new mate's ex has acquired. It consists entirely of people who are not related by blood, many of whom can't stand each other" (Stacey 1990, p. 23).

Although these kinds of blended families are quite common and are experienced as complete in real people lives, socially they are incomplete institutions (Cherlin 1978). First, our language gives us no words to describe the relationships or the people Stacey describes. In a sense they are invisible. Some African American families have addressed this naming problem in the case of biological fathers and stepfathers by using the name *father* for a natural father and *daddy* for a man who takes care of the children. Frank Furstenberg and his colleagues' study of blended African American families found these two terms used, while the word *stepfather* was never used (Furstenberg, Sherwood, and Sullivan 1992).

Second, there are few legal regulations or protections. For example, a mother and a stepfather might raise a child together for many years, but if the biological parent dies and the stepfather has not legally adopted the stepchild, he may have difficulty retaining custody. Third, there is little support from other social institutions besides the legal system. Hospitals and schools, for example, do not have forms that recognize complex binuclear families and sometimes have restrictions that prevent people with close ties from participating fully in each other's lives.

Besides these external difficulties, people in remarriages also face internal difficulties negotiating all the relationships. One remarried stepmother explained the special difficulties remarried people face:

When Jim and I decided to get married, I was real excited to get married again and give Jamie more of a dad. But it's not working out that way. Jamie is angry a lot about not having time alone with me, which ends up with Jim and me fighting a lot. Jim feels badly about not spending enough time with his kids and when the kids are together it just seems to be everyone fighting over Jim. And I feel resentful not having enough time alone with Jim. Between every other weekend with his kids and the long hours we both work we never seem to have time alone together. Last Friday we were finally spending an evening all alone and just as I was putting dinner on the table, Nancy Jim's ex-wife called. Jim and I spent the next two hours talking about Nancy. It ended up spoiling our evening. (Ahrons and Rodgers 1987, p. 282)

Despite the challenges of creating blended families, first remarriages have about the same probability of divorce as first marriages. Statistics on all remarriages (not just first ones), however, show that remarriages are more likely to end in divorce than first marriages. The jump in the probability of divorce occurs after the second remarriage, when rates of divorce begin to increase progressively with every remarriage (Cherlin 1992a; Cherlin and Furstenberg 1998).

Children and Divorce

In the opening scenario, Maria complains that divorce is discussed as an issue for husbands and wives, but that children are involved, too. In this next section, we look at some of the issues that relate to children's experience with divorce. Some scholars believe that divorce causes great difficulty for children (Marquardt 2005). For example, 34 percent of parents who are separated or divorced say that their children have behavioral problems in school, compared with 20 percent of parents in intact families. It is not easy to tell, however, whether the problems of children of divorced parents are caused by their parents divorcing, by the troubles in the family leading to the divorce, or by the economic decline experienced by divorced single-parent families (Coontz 1999).

Amato and Booth (1997) assert that low parental marital quality lowers children's well-being and that parental divorce lowers it even further. About 30 percent of marriages are highly conflictual, and in these cases divorce is beneficial for children. About 70 percent of marriages that end in divorce, however, are low conflict, and divorce for children in these families may cause more problems than it resolves. Parents and children, therefore, may experience marriage as well as divorce differently. Furstenburg and Cherlin (1991) conclude that "the best predictor of children's adjustment is a good relationship with the mother, and a low level of conflict between the mother and father" (Kurz 1995, p. 206).

Abigail Stewart and her colleagues (1997) asked children whose parents had recently divorced how they felt about their parents' separation. Table 10.4 shows their responses. The table indicates that sadness was the most common emotion: 82 percent of the children said they felt at least a little sad. Confusion and fear were also quite common. About one-third, however, said they felt at least a little glad. These same children were interviewed a year later, and some of their negative feelings had diminished. Twenty-eight percent said they didn't feel sad at all, and 80 percent said they didn't feel guilty at all. When asked what

BOX 10.3

Researching Divorce

Many people believe that divorce is inevitably a bad experience. Constance Ahrons has written a book called *The Good Divorce* (1994). She maintains that as a general event divorce is not necessarily good or bad. Rather, it can be good or bad depending on how it is handled. For example, in her discussion on children and divorce, she presents two principles to help create a good divorce from the point of view of children. She says that a good divorce, one that does not injure children, should allow them to continue relationships with family members who were important to them before the divorce. A good divorce is also one where parents cooperate with one another and are supportive of their children after the divorce.

Trying to explore divorce in such a nonjudgmental way is difficult. Many people in our culture identify divorce as synonymous with bad. We call families where a divorce has occurred broken, with the implication that all divorced families have something wrong with them and are damaged and incomplete.

According to Ahrons, researchers looking at divorce sometimes fall into this assumption as well. They ask divorced parents questions like "What problems have you faced with finances since your divorce?" or "What made your divorce emotionally difficult?" or "What negative effects has divorce had on your children?"

Ahrons tells a story about a researcher who asked her assistant to have children draw a picture of a person as part of the data they were collecting. When she began to examine the pictures, she picked up the first one, noticed it was a tiny little figure, and wondered what this meant in terms of the child's state of mind or view of the world. As she began to look at other pictures, she realized that they were all tiny, so she asked her assistant what the exact instructions given to the children were. The assistant said the children were told "draw a picture of a small person on the paper." The children had followed the directions explicitly and drawn a *small* person.

This story tells us that when we do research, we need to be careful about the questions we ask in order to allow people to provide us with information from their point of view, even if that point of view is not our own or is not the dominant point of view. In the case of divorce, Ahrons tried to find out what the experience was like—good, bad, and neutral. She tried to ask questions that did not lead interviewees to respond with only negative examples but instead led them to provide their point of view, which included benefits, reliefs, gains, and steps forward as well as difficulties.

---

was worse about their lives since the divorce, one-third said not having their father in the house, and one-third said that nothing was worse.

In Kurz's (1995) interviews with divorced mothers, she asked what they felt the effect of the divorce had been on their children. A small percentage (8%) of mothers felt that the divorce had a positive effect. They explained that the violence in the marriage had stopped with the divorce, and this had been a benefit. About half (46%) felt that the children had not experienced any particular problems with the divorce, although they also didn't describe it as beneficial. These mothers thought that the children had handled it well and so far did not seem to be adversely affected. More than one-third (38%) of the mothers reported concerns about their children, describing them as angry, hurt, or worried.

TABLE 10.4   Children's Feelings about Their Parents' Divorce (Asked Six Months After)

Feelings	A Lot	A Little
Sad	50%	32%
Confused	22	34
Scared	22	36
Surprised	15	27
Like it's partly my fault	4	31
Angry	13	33
Glad	11	20

Source: A. Stewart, A. Copeland, N. Chester, J. Malley, and N. Barenbau. 1997. *Separating together: How divorce transforms families.* New York: Guilford Press. Reprinted with permission.

Two key factors seemed to distinguish between children who had been damaged by divorce and those who had not. The first condition that contributed to the well-being of children was that their parents remained cooperative with one another and mutually supportive of the children. Second, children who were allowed to maintain relationships with family members who were important to them before the divorce were less likely to be negatively affected by divorce. This of course includes fathers who were important positive parts of their lives, but it also includes grandparents, stepsiblings, and others who are sometimes cut off from children after a divorce (Ahrons 2004a, 2004b). Children do seem to be remaining in better contact with their noncustodial fathers than in the past. In 1978, a national sample found that 50 percent of children had seen their fathers in the past year, and 17 percent reported visiting with their fathers every week. A 1988 survey found that 25 percent of divorced fathers saw their children at least once a week, and 82 percent had seen their children in the past year (Coontz 1999). By 1999, 84 percent of children of divorced mothers had seen their fathers in the previous year, and 28 percent had visited with him at least once a week (Koball and Principe 2002).

Child Custody

Child custody has changed over the past few centuries. These changes illustrate the way in which alterations in macrolevel factors in society (e.g., laws) have a critical effect on whether the custody of children will be awarded to their mothers or their fathers in a divorce and what the basis of that decision will be. Whether a child lives with one parent or the other seems like a choice that should be made at the microlevel among those directly concerned with the question. A historical review of the issue, however, shows that what the choices are and whether children are likely to live with a mother or father after a divorce are largely determined by laws that have changed over time.

In the opening scenario, Maria is living with her mother. You may have thought that this was a result of choices she or her parents made. The fact that her mother had custody of her, however, was determined by the social context in which the divorce took place. If Manny and Teresa had divorced in the nineteenth century, the decision probably would have been different.

Until the middle of the 1800s, fathers retained the right to custody of children after a divorce. Unless a court found "clear and strong case of unfitness" of the father, he was granted custody (Polikoff 1983, p. 186). In 1848, at the Seneca Falls Convention (mentioned in Chapter 2), one of the demands made by early feminists was that mothers be awarded custody of their children if they divorced.

Throughout the nineteenth century and into the first half of the twentieth, the laws gradually changed, and more and more mothers were awarded custody of their children. These changes were partly based on an increased emphasis on motherhood and a new idea called "the principle of tender years." According to this principle "special, even mysterious, bonds existed between mother and young child which, all other things being equal, made her the preferred parental custodian" (Sheppard 1982, p. 230). In addition, as we saw in Chapter 2, this historical period was one in which reliance on children for labor was diminishing. Therefore, fathers were perhaps less likely to appeal for custody or to be granted custody because they needed a child to work in the business.

More recently, ideas about marriage have changed to emphasize shared partnership and equality in child custody decisions. These changes have resulted in an erosion of the "tender years principle." Laws in nearly all states now have replaced it with the new principle of "best interest of the child." But 85 percent of children are still awarded to the custody of their mothers (U.S. Census Bureau 2003c).

The women in Kurz's (1995) research expressed a great deal of concern about child custody, relating stories about fathers threatening to take the children. Others described incidents of violence, kidnapping, and other conflict that was part of their custody negotiations. When she asked mothers, however, why they felt that so many mothers (90% in her sample) had custody of their children, the women most often said that they and their husbands felt that it was more natural for mothers to keep the children with them. But these ideological reasons were also mixed in with other factors, like the beliefs that the fathers didn't know how to care for the children, were not interested in having custody, or had problems like drug and alcohol abuse that made them less fit parents. A second explanation comes from organizations like Fathers' Rights of America and the National Congress of Men who believe that women are more often awarded custody because fathers are discriminated against.

A third answer to the question of why do women so often end up with custody of their children after a divorce is that women are more likely to be granted custody because they are more likely to file for custody (Polikoff 1983). About 80 percent of child custody decisions in a divorce case are uncontested (CANOW.org 2005). Although women are currently more likely to be granted custody of their children, control of this decision is in the hands of fathers. "The power to decide child custody often lies with the father, not the mother. If he wishes to exercise that power, he is likely to win" (Polikoff 1983, p. 185). In the 20 percent of the child custody cases today where there is a contest, fathers are likely to be granted either joint custody or sole custody in a majority of the cases (Goodman 2004).

Fathers' success in the courts is based on two factors: economic advantage and ideologies about parenting. Fathers have an economic advantage in seeking custody because they are more likely to have the money to hire attorneys to seek custody. Fathers are also advantaged because the courts are increasingly choosing to select the parent who they believe can best provide for the material needs of the child.

One ominous aspect of fathers seeking custody is that men who have battered their wives are two times more like to seek sole custody of children in divorce cases (CANOW.org 2005). This is not to say that fathers who wish to have custody of their children are abusive. It does suggest that abusive men use child custody contests as ways to punish their wives who choose to divorce.

In addition to economics, the courts are also influenced by what is considered "normal" parenting. For example, fathers who hire housekeepers to be primary caregivers to their children are seen as normal, while mothers who work outside the home and can spend only a few hours with their children are perceived as neglectful.

Mothers are also sometimes judged as inappropriate parents because of their sexual behavior. A custody-seeking mother's sexual activity is especially likely to be at issue if she is a lesbian (Causey and Duran-Aydingtug 1997). Gay fathers are also discriminated against on these grounds (Causey and Duran-Aydingtug 1997; Connolly 2002; Polikoff 1990).

Child Support

Child support is money to be paid by the noncustodial parent to the parent with whom the child lives. Since most children live with their mothers after a divorce, child support is usually supposed to be paid by men to their ex-wives. Although women are much less likely to be the noncustodial parents, they are just as likely as men to be in arrears on child support. Attention has been focused on noncustodial fathers because they are a larger group.

Children's family income declines by 37 percent when their father moves out of the household (Family Research Council 2005). Child support could be a way of eliminating this fall in income, but child support has two problems: the awards are not sufficient, and the support is not paid.

Almost 63 percent of divorced single mothers who live with minor children were awarded child support in 2001. The proportion of women who were awarded child support and actually received the full amount (45.4%) has risen since 1978 (Koball and Principe 2002). These numbers are worse if we look at poor women. Table 10.5 shows the percentage

TABLE 10.5   Child Support-Award and Recipiency Status of Custodial Parent: 2001

	Percent Granted Award	Percent Receiving Full Award	Percent Receiving None of Award	Mean Amount of Award Received Per Year Per Child
Poor Fathers	43.8%	22.2%	39.3%	$2,622
All Fathers	38.6	39.0	32.6	$4,273
Poor Mothers	53.6	27.0	28.9	$3,078
All Mothers	63.0	45.4	25.3	$4,274

Source: U.S. Census Bureau 2003c.

of women who were awarded and received child support divided into two groups: all women and poor women. Only 55.7 percent of poor women were awarded child support in 2001, and only about 29 percent of those awarded support received the full payment (Census Bureau 2003c).

Table 10.6 shows that the average amount of child support awarded to white women is higher than that granted to Hispanics and blacks. A bill passed in 1988 required states to set formulas for awarding benefits so that awards are fair and consistent and do not vary from judge to judge; the bill also required states to allow immediate wage withholding for the amount of child support awarded (Kurz 1995; Renzetti and Curran 1992). In addition, the awards are also supposed to conform more closely to real costs of raising children, and delays in processing must be decreased. Individual states have implemented even stronger laws that place liens on real estate, seize lottery winnings, and refuse to issue professional licenses, driver's licenses, fishing and hunting licenses, and car registration when a parent is behind in child care payments (Kurz 1995).

One problem that remains is interstate cases. About 30 percent of child support cases involve parents who live in different states than their children. Only about 10 percent of child support is paid in these cases. Another problem is the inequity in the treatment of parents in arrears. Low-income fathers are more likely to be incarcerated, and they pay higher rates than do fathers in higher income brackets (Kurz 1995). Despite the important changes, a report in 1995 estimated that only about 63 percent of the $28.3 billion owed to custodial parents was paid (Cohen 1999).

In sum, in spite of changes in the laws that have helped increase the proportion of child support awards to be paid, many custodial parents still receive no payments or only partial payments. Furthermore, even if the total is paid, child support awards pay less than half the costs of child care alone. Children, of course, incur many other expenses besides child care, such as food, clothing, health care, education, and recreational expenses (Kurz 1995). Kurz also notes that child support doesn't take into account the additional costs that a single parent might have, since the awards are based on costs for raising children in a two-parent household. For example, single parents must pay for child care or after-school care that might be handled by a second parent in a two-parent household. In addition, child support usually ends at eighteen, although in many families, children are far from independent at that age.

TABLE 10.6   Mean Child Support Payments by Race

	Mean Payment, 2002
White women	$4,704/year
Black women	$3,043/year
Hispanic women	$4,014/year

Source: U.S Census Bureau 2003c, p. 16.

Why Don't Men Pay?   One common explanation for why men don't pay is that they do not have sufficient funds to make the payments. Noncompliance, however, occurs across several income brackets, including relatively high ones (Meyer and Bartfeld 1996).

Another explanation that has been suggested is that men are retaliating for visitation problems. Researchers (Wallerstein and Blakeslee 1989) have found little evidence of mothers sabotaging visitation, and in fact found that most mothers felt that mothers and children benefited when divorced fathers participated in raising their children.

When researchers interview noncustodial fathers about this question, the men report that they do not make child support payments because they feel their relationships with their children are no longer close (Chambers 1979). In the scenario at the beginning of the chapter, Teresa claims that Manny misses child support payments as a way to get at her. But Manny expresses the feeling suggested by Chambers's research; he no longer feels a part of Maria's life. Others have found that fathers say they do not pay because they believe that the mother does not spend the money on the child (Haskins 1988) or that the judges are biased and set unreasonably high awards (Greif 1985).

When parents divorce, one or the other may be granted custody of the children, or they may obtain joint custody. Joint custody can be either joint legal custody or joint physical custody. Joint legal custody means that parents have equal rights and responsibilities in regard to their children, although the child lives primarily with only one parent. In joint physical custody, the child lives intermittently with both parents, trading residence by the day, week, or year (Arditti 1992). Joint legal custody is the more common form (Emery 1988).

Joint custody has been shown to have a beneficial effect on fathers. They report a higher frequency of contact with their children and greater satisfaction with custody arrangements (Arditti 1992). Noncustodial fathers suffer more emotional problems, such as guilt, anxiety, depression, and low self-esteem (D'Andrea 1983; Greif 1979; Hetherington, Cox, and Cox 1976).

For mothers, the benefits of joint custody include sharing responsibility and physical care for children. Some scholars have suggested that joint custody could improve the record of child support payments; if fathers are granted joint custody, they may be more likely to contribute financially. However, this connection is not clear in the research. Custody is only weakly linked to child support compliance (Arditti 1992).

The disadvantages for both parents are the logistical problems of moving between houses and being tied to a geographic area because of the ex-spouse's residence (Luepnitz 1982). Another problem that is especially likely to affect mothers (because they usually obtain custody) is that joint custody can be used as a means by which noncustodial fathers can negotiate lower child support payments (Weitzman 1985).

Joint custody compared with sole custody has been shown to be advantageous for children because it facilitates positive interactions between children and both parents (Bauserman 2002). In a qualitative study, children in joint custody arrangements said they preferred it because it made their lives "more fun, more interesting or more comfortable" (Luepnitz 1982, p. 47). Despite problems negotiating two households and two sets of rules, one girl explained that she preferred joint custody because "I love them both and would miss them too much" (Luepnitz 1982, p. 46). Other children, however, said that joint custody meant they missed one favored parent when they were in the custody of the other.

Divorced Fathers

Since children are so frequently placed in the physical custody of their mothers, fathers face special challenges in determining how or if they will maintain relationships with their children. Terry Arendell (1995) interviewed divorced men about their lives after divorce. She found that men faced a number of problems in divorce and found a range of ways of coping. Some of the men had resorted to such extreme measures as stalking their wives, using violence against them, and child abduction, as well as less severe responses such as refusing to pay child support or continuing to challenge child custody decisions. For many, divorce had elicited or exacerbated anger. One man provides an example in his description of his feelings about divorce:

> I was so depressed at first, it almost killed me. I couldn't even drag myself out of bed. But then I got to realizing that she had shafted me, shafted me. We made a deal, a vow, that's what marriage is. And she didn't honor it. She thought she could just up and break it off. Break a contract, a contractual arrangement. I became very angry; it was true I would yell at her from time to time. I can't imagine anybody being more angry than I was. I think I had good reason to be angry. (p. 136)

The men Arendell interviewed developed a range of ways to cope with these experiences and feelings. She grouped men into three categories depending on their response style: traditionalist, neotraditionalists, and innovators.

Traditionalists had limited contact with their wives and continued to define them as the enemy. They were especially distressed about the loss of control over their wives and children that resulted from the divorce. Their main way of responding was to disengage, avoiding contact or responsibility for their ex-wives or children. One traditionalist father explained how he had come to this response:

> I finally decided that I was putting too much into this divorce war with my ex-wife. We've played this game for over four years. So I pulled out. She didn't know when to quit. Someday, if my son wants to get to know me, he can find me. My daughter, she could care less. She's been totally brainwashed by her [the former wife]. (Arendell 1995, p. 145)

Neotraditionalists had some of the same animosity toward their wives but wanted to maintain contact with their children and felt that collaboration with their ex was possible. They wanted to stay close to their children while avoiding their wives. They were especially concerned about being the male role model for their children and about sustaining a meaningful relationship with their children, rather than being just a weekend visitor:

> She [the former wife] complains about my teaching them to shoot and hunt; she says its dangerous and unnecessary. "Too macho," she says. But what's really bugging her is that she can't stand it that I have something to offer them that she can't. They're boys. I understand that. She doesn't. They need this sort of input from me. She can't give it to them. (Arendell 1995, p. 173)

Innovators focused on their own parental responsibility for their children rather than their rights as fathers. They did not find it easy to develop cooperation with their wives, but they were willing to be very flexible, rearranging schedules, and finding options in order to create parenting partnerships with their ex-wives. They were more able to set aside their anger at their wives and to dismiss conventional views of masculinity than the other two types of divorced fathers. An innovative father said:

> Our relationship is amicable, if that's the proper word. I would describe it that way, an amicable relationship. I don't particularly go out of my way to talk to her. I have my moments and sometimes I really want to talk to her. Other times I don't want to talk to her at all and I just leave, I don't want to be there. We're both concerned about the children. We went together to see the principal. We also went to see the school counselor. Or if my son has a soccer game, we'll be together. (Arendell, 1995, p. 190)

Finding Solutions: Where Were the Feminists?

A number of macrolevel factors affect the organization of divorce in our society. In particular, law has played a central role, but economics and gender stratification have also influenced divorce. In turn, the organization of divorce has affected the microlevel—the relationships of women, men, and children in families that divorce. Like all macrolevel social phenomena, the legal organization of divorce has been shaped by microlevel forces of people working together to try to reform the system. As we have observed in this chapter, changes in the organization of divorce in recent years have been a significant result of the passage of no-fault divorce laws. Furthermore, these changes have created especially difficult economic problems for women and their children.

How did this come about? Why did recent changes in the laws result in the creation of such problems for women? Herbert Jacob (1989) argues that although divorce reform occurred during a period in which the women's movement was extraordinarily active. "There were few connections between feminist activity and divorce reform" (p. 482). When legislation was being passed to change divorce laws in the 1970s, feminists were missing in action. Divorce is a critical issue to many women, and it has been an aspect of the feminist agenda since the nineteenth century when Elizabeth Cady Stanton spoke out for the liberalization of divorce laws. But during a critical moment in divorce history, feminists failed to mobilize around the issue.

In this section we examine the way in which the microlevel successfully changed the macrolevel—divorce reformers passed no-fault divorce laws. A central question of our inquiry will be why a feminist perspective was not part of that divorce reform movement.

In 1969, California was the first state to pass no-fault, and in 1985, South Dakota was the last state. Jacob (1989) argues that this activity constituted a long-term reform movement in which feminists were only faintly visible. He suggests that there are three possible reasons why feminists were not part of the movement:

1. Women, who Jacob believes may have been more likely than men to hold feminist views, had not effectively penetrated decision-making agencies and, therefore, had no avenue for representing feminist views.
2. Feminist organizations were inadequate to the task, both because they organized too late and because they focused on national rather than state issues.

3. Feminist organizations concentrated on other issues that they believed at the time to have higher priority.

The first possibility is that few women were insiders in the judicial and legislative arenas in which divorce reform was being proposed and debated. In 1977, only 110 state judges out of 5,940 were women. Although women increasingly gained seats on state legislatures during the 1970s, their relative numbers remained small. In addition, Jacob (1989) traced the history of committees that sought divorce reform, especially the National Conference of Commissioners on Uniform State Laws (NCCUSL), and found that not only were women scarce, but also frequently there were no women present. For example, the original NCCUSL was an entirely male initiative. Jacob found, furthermore, that women who eventually joined the conference did not identify themselves as feminists and showed little concern with the way in which various reforms would differentially affect women and men. In addition, after reviewing the hearings of a number of study panels that eventually led to no-fault divorce reform, Jacob found that there was no testimony by feminist groups. Jacob did find there had been feminist input in a few cases in New York and Wisconsin, but he concludes that even when a feminist viewpoint was articulated it did not prevail.

The second factor in the absence of a feminist voice in divorce reform is the possible inadequacy of feminist organization. Jacob maintains that the women's movement in the late 1960s and early 1970s, when divorce reform was taking place, was not organized well enough to demand (as outsiders to the legislative bodies) that their voice be heard. In addition, those women's organizations that were strong enough to make themselves heard focused their attention on federal rather than state laws, and divorce reforms occurred at the state level.

The third factor cited by Jacob was the low priority given by feminists to divorce law revision. "Divorce law revision did not attract the feminist movement because it neither threatened basic values nor promised widespread benefits" (p. 483, 1989). Leaders in the women's liberation movement focused their attention on issues like pay equity, the equal rights amendment, and abortion rights, which they believed to be most important. The general membership may not have agreed with these priorities. Freeman (1975) observed that the most well-attended workshops at the 1973 NOW (National Organization for Women) meetings were those on family, marriage, and divorce. Divorce reformers may have contributed to the neglect of the issue by feminists because the reformers presented the issues as if they were technical, legalistic, procedural issues of little interest to political organizations (Jacob 1989). Most feminists did not see divorce reform as a threat to women until after the no-fault legislation was enacted.

Since feminists were not central to the movement for divorce reform, who were the divorce reformers? Two groups played a major role in the enactment of no-fault (Jacob 1989). Lawyers were one group that worked both to initiate the legislation and to testify on its behalf before legislative bodies. Some lawyers saw no-fault as a way to keep divorces in their own states, thereby improving their case load. For example, California lawyers explicitly mentioned that no-fault in California would keep divorcing couples from taking their cases to Nevada.

A second group of divorce reformers were men's rights groups. They were especially active around child custody reforms that increased the likelihood of fathers' being granted custody or joint custody. Jacob (1989) argues that they were more likely to have the ear of legislators, who were nearly all men and many of whom were divorced fathers.

The Micro–Macro Connection

Divorce is a critical turning point in family life. The voices of the people we hear in the interview data tell us exactly what the experience of divorce and remarriage feels like at the microlevel. Their stories help us see the human faces behind the statistics and the complex, unforeseen consequences of these events.

An underlying theme in the stories is the mysterious and unknown quality of divorce and remarriage. We hear of people who did not expect to become poor, to be stigmatized, to have their new marriages overshadowed by the old ones, or, on the other hand, to discover unknown strengths and opportunities for personal growth.

All these microlevel experiences are framed by macrolevel structures and events. Ideologies, economic opportunities, mortality rates (that are themselves altered by health care, technology, nutrition, violence, and discrimination), and especially the legal structure, have a profound effect on what divorces are like and sometimes whether they can even occur.

History plays a role, too, as these macrolevel institutions change, sometimes dramatically, over time. Teresa's and Manny's stories would be quite different had they been told in 1850 or in 1650.

Two important components of the macrolevel—the organization of gender and the organization of divorce—have a mutual effect on each other. Gender inequality in marriage, the labor market, and divorce proceedings shapes the experience of divorce. Divorce plays a critical role in maintaining and exacerbating the economic inequality between women and men.

Macrolevel institutions have been changed at least in part as a result of microlevel organizing. The two opposing factions on the question of divorce, prodivorce-rights activists and antidivorce-rights activists, have affected our options and our experience of those options. Feminists have played a surprisingly small role in these debates. Increasingly, feminists, especially feminist scholars rather than activists, have recognized the importance of divorce reform and the necessity of having a voice in its creation. Their work, however, follows the enactment of sweeping changes and the passage of no-fault in all fifty states, which means that feminist activists must work to further alter the laws so that they more effectively benefit all parties, including women. Today their work is even more difficult as new laws press to return to conservative divorce legislation, like covenant marriage.

CHAPTER

11 Battering and Marital Rape

The police have been a focal point in the attempts to address the problem of battering of women. Before the recognition of battering as a social problem, police were likely to try to calm the couple down. They did not treat domestic violence like other assault cases. Laws have changed, however, and police departments are increasingly required to arrest batterers. (© Rhoda Sidney/PhotoEdit)

Linda married Ron when she was twenty-three. She was a teacher, and he was an engineer. Before they married, Linda noticed that Ron became jealous if she spoke to any other men. But he was also attentive and charming when they were together. She wasn't bothered too much by his bursts of anger; they were not directed toward her, and they seemed to be part of his aggressive, self-confident style, which she admired. And, anyway, she figured, he would mellow after they were married and he was assured that she was all his.

After they were married for two years, Linda became pregnant, and Ron's outbursts became physically abusive. At first it was a shove or a slap, but by the time the baby arrived,

Linda found herself making excuses to her friends and her obstetrician about the bruises. Linda did not know what to do. She hoped she could change Ron, and she blamed herself— maybe if she had been a better wife, a better lover, a better mother. Linda also thought she was unique. This kind of thing doesn't happen in good families like hers.

> How unusual is Linda's marriage?
>
> Is it reasonable for Linda to blame herself for the violence inflicted on her?
>
> Is it useful to try to solve the problem by changing Ron only?
>
> Linda says she is not sure what to do. What might happen to convince her to take action?
>
> What social structural factors might be related to Linda's plight?
>
> Why do we admire men who are physically aggressive, self-confident, and domineering?
>
> What social-structural barriers might Linda find if she tries to leave Ron?
>
> What help might Linda find from a battered women's shelter? Were such shelters available for her mother's generation? Where did they come from?
>
> If violence against women in families has been present in society for hundreds or thousands of years, why is it only recently being recognized as a social problem?

An event as personal as a husband beating his wife is difficult to conceptualize as a social problem rooted in the organization of our society, not in the individuals who experience the difficulty. When we hear about battering or experience it in our own family, we tend to think about it as an individual problem. We ask why Linda doesn't leave, and what is wrong with Ron.

As we have observed in this text, in order to answer these questions, we must look at the interplay between social organization and individual people's lives, between history and biography. We must ask questions that examine social structure and its role in creating or allowing violence in families. In order to understand the abuse of Linda, we need to understand the way in which the macrolevel of social organization creates opportunities to abuse women and barriers to stopping the violence. We also need to discover the way in which the microlevel, individuals interacting with one another, can alter the macrolevel to allow us to address the problem of battering and to end it.

The chapter is organized into three main sections. The first presents information on the prevalence of battering and marital rape. The second section discusses two theoretical issues that emerge in the analysis of violence in families. One is the debate among three competing theories on why violence occurs in families. These three theories differ in their assessment of the way the macrolevel of social organization—economic decline, the isolation of families, ideologies, and gender stratification—affects the microlevel of individual heterosexual couples interacting in abusive ways. The other theoretical issue explored in this section is the question of why battering has recently become identified as a social problem.

The third section investigates the effect of the microlevel of social organization on the macrolevel. How have people worked to create solutions to violence in families by reshaping social institutions like the police and shelters?

Prevalence of Violence in Families

Although research shows that the rate of violent crime has plummeted in recent years, we still live in a violent society. Almost 1.5 million violent crimes were reported in 2002 (U.S. Census Bureau 2005g). We only have to turn on the television, read the newspaper, or look at our history to see that violence is very much part of the American experience. Families are affected by the social system in which they are embedded. The rates of violence in families are also declining but they remain high. More than 2 million violent crimes against familiy (and close friends) were reported to the police between 1998 and 2002, and these probably represent only about 60 percent of those committed (Durose et al. 2005).

More men than women are victims of reported violence in our society, but the gap between women and men is closing as fewer women and many fewer men are victims of violence. In 2004, about 17 women in every 1,000 were victims of violent crimes—murders, rapes, robberies, and assaults. About 25 men in every 1,000 were victims. Since 1973, the rates for men declined from about 70 per 1,000. The rates for women during this period also decreased from about 31 per 1,000 in 1973 (U.S. Department of Justice 2005).

When we look at the relationship of the victims of violence and the perpetrators, women's and men's experience continues to be very different. Men are victims of violence half the time by strangers (50%) and about half the time by people they know but not intimately (46%). Only 4 percent of violent crimes against men are committed by women who are their intimates. For women who are victims of violent crimes, about one-quarter (21%) are by intimates, one-third (34%) are by strangers, and the rest (45%) are by people they know but who are not their boyfriends, husbands, or other family members (U.S. Department of Justice 2003).

In addition, women differ from men in their experience of violence in families. Women are much more likely than men to be victims of abuse in families, and men are much more likely to be the ones inflicting the abuse. Seventy-three percent of all victims of family violence are women and girls; 84 percent of victims of spouse abuse are women; and 75 percent of the perpetrators of violence in families are men (Durose et al. 2005).

Women also differ from men in terms of the injuries they sustain in assaults. When women are victims of violence, they are most likely to sustain injuries when the assailant is an intimate. In sum, if women are violently assaulted, it is most likely by a husband or boyfriend. And when they are assaulted, they are more likely to be injured if they had a close relationship with the perpetrator (Tjaden and Thoennes 2000).

Violence permeates the macrolevel of our society and is played out in the microcosm of intimate relationships like those in families. But we are surprised when we hear about violence in families because we think about families as a place where people love each other and treat each other well. Our media and our culture are filled with images of loving, gentle families. The data reporting violence between people in families seem surprising, but if we stop to think about it, if we have ever been hurt by another person, that person was likely to have been someone in our family. Probably all of us have been hit by a parent or sibling. Probably few of us have been hit by a stranger, a boss, a teacher, or a coworker.

Because we think of families as private places and because, in fact, families are frequently isolated and secluded, it is difficult to find real numbers when it comes to child abuse, incest, woman battering, husband abuse, and marital rape. Researchers have used a variety of methods to try to find out what the numbers are. They have gone to police records, but all violent attacks are not reported to the police. Researchers have therefore also gone to hospital emergency rooms, family court records, divorce records, and random surveys (Anderson 1988). In this chapter we explore the problem of violence in families among adults. In Chapter 13 we investigate family violence against children.

Woman Battering

Michele Bograd (1988, p. 12) defines woman battering or wife abuse as "the use of physical force by a man against his intimate cohabiting partner. This force can range from pushes and slaps to coerced sex to assaults with deadly weapons." Batterers use a broad range of methods against their wives, including:

> Economic abuse (taking her money or not allowing her to earn money; giving her an allowance; making her account for every penny she spends); emotional abuse (humiliating and verbally abusing her); threats and coercion (threatening suicide; making her engage in illegal activities; sexual coercion); social isolation (controlling whom she sees and talks to; where she goes; limiting her contact with her family); intimidation (destroying her property; hitting walls instead of her; looks that threaten violence); and using male privilege (defining roles; making major decisions; treating her like a servant). (O'Sullivan 1998, p. 86)

All these are important, and sometimes it is difficult to distinguish among them (Dobash and Dobash 1998). In this chapter, however, we focus our attention on physical abuse.

Murray Straus, Richard Gelles, and Suzanne Steinmetz were the first sociologists to systematically study physical violence in families, and they have published more than any other social scientists on the physical abuse of wives by their husbands (Kurz 1989). Their research shows that more than 2 million Americans have been abused by a spouse. If that number is divided by the number of seconds in a year, it reveals that a woman is beaten every eighteen seconds in the United States—a statistic commonly used in public education about abuse.

In one of the large surveys Straus, Gelles, and Steinmetz (1980) conducted, they interviewed 2,143 married people and found woman battering in every class and at every income level. Sixteen percent of their sample, or one in every six couples, had experienced some form of violence in their marriage during the previous year, and 28 percent of the couples reported at least one incident of violence at some time during their marriage.

Straus, Gelles, and Steinmetz's (1980) surveys used a random sample. A random sample is one in which researchers choose subjects without regard to any of their individual characteristics. Researchers then argue that it is statistically probable that the sample is not unique and that it can be said to represent the larger population from which it was drawn. Based on the assumption that the sample is representative, sociologists who conduct large surveys on random samples argue that the percentages of people who were involved in various kinds of activities in the sample can be extrapolated to the entire population. For example, if 7 percent of their sample of 2,143 people had experienced one spouse throwing something at the other, then it is safe to assume that 7 percent of the total 300 million or so people in the United States also experienced this form of violence.

Therefore, although the percentages appear relatively small, if they accurately represent the entire population in the United States, the actual numbers are very large. For example, the percentages indicate that "over 1.7 million Americans had at some time faced a husband or wife wielding a knife or gun, and well over two million had been beaten up by a spouse" (Straus, Gelles, and Steinmetz 1988). Straus, Gelles, and Steinmetz (1980) also suggest that these percentages are probably underestimates. They maintain that "it seems likely that the true rate is closer to 50 or 60 percent of all couples than it is to the 28 percent who were willing to describe violent acts to our interviewers" (p. 36).

Straus, Gelles, and Steinmetz describe three important sources of underestimation in their research. First, for many people, these kinds of violent events are so much a part of normal family life that they might not even be remembered. Second, people who do not believe violence in families is normal might feel too guilty or ashamed to admit they had been either perpetrators or victims. Finally, in the particular study done by Straus, Gelles, and Steinmetz, only couples who were currently living together were interviewed. Couples who had been divorced—perhaps because of violence—were excluded. The sample, therefore, eliminated many potentially high-violence cases. You should remember from Chapter 10 that almost one-fifth of women who divorce said that they had sought a divorce because of abuse. Seventy percent of divorced women said that violence had occurred in their relationship, although it was not necessarily the most important reason for their seeking a divorce (Kurz 1995).

Throughout this book, we have been paying attention to diversity among families. Race ethnicity is one of the important ways families vary in the United States. Looking at the ways in which families in different racial ethnic groups experience violence is therefore important. Government statistics on violence by intimates reports that on average between 1992 and 1996, 12 per 1,000 black women experienced violence by an intimate compared with 8 per 1,000 white women and 7 per 1,000 Hispanic women. For men the differences were much smaller (Greenfield et al. 1998).

One problem with these data is that African Americans may be more likely to come to the attention of the police and therefore to show up in the crime statistics. About two-thirds of black women compared with about one-half of white women who have been victims have reported the crime to the police. In addition, economic status may also affect whether police are called and therefore whether incidents show up in crime statistics. Wealthier women may have resources other than the police to call upon to protect themselves from abusive husbands. For example, they may have money to leave the house more easily. In addition, wealthier families may have bigger houses and yards—and therefore more privacy, preventing neighbors from calling the police. Since African Americans are more likely to be poor, their numbers may be exaggerated compared with people in more affluent neighborhoods who are more likely to be white. Figure 11.1 shows the incidence of intimate violence by income categories. The figure reveals that for women, household income is an important predictor of reported violence, with those in the poorest category much more likely to be victimized than those in richer households. The effect of income on men's victimization rates is not as clear.

Age of victims has a dramatic influence on victimization. Figure 11.2 shows the distribution of victims of intimate violence by age among women. The figure indicates that women between the ages of 20 and 24 are most vulnerable and that nearly all victims of intimate violence are between the ages of 16 and 34 (Greenfield et al. 1998).

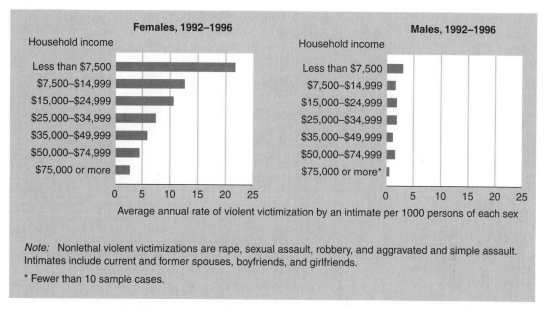

FIGURE 11.1   Intimate Violence against Women and Men by Household Income, Averages for 1992–1996
Source: Greenfield et al., 1998, p. 14.

What provokes an incident of violence in a family? A large study of violent men revealed four themes in the disagreements leading to abusive conflicts: men's possessiveness and jealousy, disagreements about money and housework, men's belief in their right to punish "their" women, and the importance men give to maintaining and exercising their authority (Dobash and Dobash 1998).

The men do not mention alcohol and drugs. But these have gained much attention from researchers and the public. Research reports a high incidence of alcohol and drug use in battering cases (Busch and Rosenberg 2004; Thompson and Kingree 2004). But we don't know how they are linked or why. We do not know, for example, if alcohol lowers inhibitions or clouds judgment in ways that cause some people to become violent. We also do not know if alcohol and drugs cause abuse or if they are used to excuse abuse that would have occurred regardless of intoxication (Gelles 1993). Furthermore, the Department of Justice reports that in 75 percent of the incidents of intimate violence, the offender had not been drinking (Greenfield et al. 1998). Most batterers are not alcoholics or drug addicts (Gelles 1993).

Most of the studies of intimate abuse focus on heterosexual couples. Gay and lesbian couples also sometimes experience violence in their relationships, but we do not have good estimates of the prevalence (McClennan 2005; Renzetti and Curran 1999). Gay and lesbian partners face some of the same constraints on their ability to leave abusive situations, such as emotional attachment and economic dependence. In addition, most services are designed for heterosexual women, and gay men and lesbians may not feel welcome (Renzetti 1992).

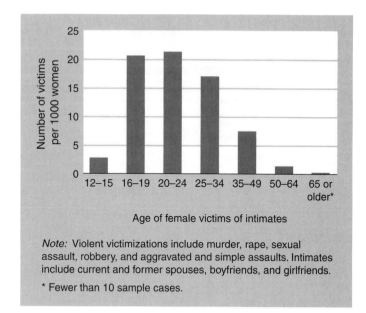

FIGURE 11.2   Victims of Intimate Violence by Age, Average per 1000 Women, 1992–1996

Source: Greenfield et al., 1998, p. 13.

Note: Violent victimizations include murder, rape, sexual assault, robbery, and aggravated and simple assaults. Intimates include current and former spouses, boyfriends, and girlfriends.

* Fewer than 10 sample cases.

Another intimate relationship between adults that sometimes becomes abusive is that between adult children and their parents. Elder abuse affects an estimated 300,000 to 1 million each year (Griffin, Williams, and Reed 1998). Some older people are abused by people outside of their families, like nurses or health aides. Some are abused by spouses. But many are abused by the adult children who are taking care of them. Thirty-seven states now have laws making it mandatory to report elder abuse (Renzetti and Curran 1999).

Murder by Intimates

Since 1976, the overall murder rate by intimates has been falling, but the numbers are still substantial. In 2001, about 16,000 murders were committed in the United States. Men, especially black men, are likely to be victims of homicide. The murder rate per 100,000 people in 2001 was 2.6 for white women, 7.2 for white men, 7.4 for black women, and an astounding 38.3 for black men (U.S. Census Bureau 2005g).

The situation changes somewhat when we look at homicides of intimates. Almost one-quarter (22%) of all homicides are committed against family members and close friends, such as boyfriends and girlfriends of the murderer. Eighty percent of murders of intimates are committed by men, and 76 percent of the victims are women (Durose et al. 2005; Fox and Zawitz 2004). When statistics on murder victims are looked at by race ethnicity and gender, black women are most likely to be killed by a husband, ex-husband, or boyfriend, and white men are least likely to be killed by intimates. Fortunately these numbers are also declining as violent crime has been going down rapidly in recent years. Change over the past two decades has been most dramatic for black men, who used to be much more likely than people in the other three categories to have been killed by a wife, ex-wife, or girlfriend (U.S. Department of Justice 2004). For both white men and white women, the numbers have also declined although the change has been much less than for black men and black women.

Another breakdown of these data, distinguishing not only by race ethnicity and gender but also the relationship between the murderer and victim, shows one group did not see a drop in their victimization—white girlfriends. The proportion of white women who were killed by their boyfriends was the only category to rise during the last two decades of the twentieth century (Greenfield et al. 1998, p. 8).

BOX 11.1

How Different Are Battered Women Who Kill Their Husbands from Battered Women Who Do Not?

The proportion of murders that occur among family members is much higher in the United States than in other nations. About one-quarter of murders are by a relative; about one-eighth are by a spouse. Wives are the victims in two-thirds of these cases. Men are more likely to murder their wives than vice versa. The number of wives who kill their husbands is significant, however, because women are so much less likely to commit murder in general. Only about 15 percent of all homicides are committed by women. Women are seven times more likely than men to have committed murder in self-defense. In addition, women charged in deaths of their husbands have the least extensive criminal records of any female offenders (Browne 1987).

Angela Browne (1987) interviewed forty-two battered women who killed or attempted to kill their husbands to examine the circumstances of their cases and to compare their situations to those of 205 battered women who had not used lethal means to end the violence. Their stories were typical of abusive relationships. The battering usually started after marriage. What first appeared to be concern and care by the men escalated to extreme possessiveness and jealousy. The women sought help from ministers and were told to be better wives. They sought advice from lawyers and were told to see marriage counselors (Browne 1987).

Browne (1987) found few differences in the two groups of women—those who murdered their husbands and those who did not. The biggest differences were between the husbands who were murdered and those who were not. The men who had been killed (or nearly killed) were significantly more likely to have threatened to kill their wives, battered their wives more than once a week, caused more severe injuries (multiple and to the head and body rather than to extremities), abused children also used drugs and/or alcohol daily, and raped their wives.

Earlier research shows that murder weapons differed by gender; women used weapons to kill their husbands, and men beat their wives to death. In Browne's (1987) sample, 81 percent of the women used guns, 7 percent used knives, 7 percent used a car, and 5 percent used something else.

Previous reviews of the cases of wives who murdered their husbands show that they are more likely to be charged with first- or second-degree murder, rather than lesser charges, and to receive longer sentences (Browne 1987). In Browne's sample of the thirty-six whose husbands died, twenty-seven were charged with first-degree murder, and nine were charged with second-degree murder. Twenty received jail terms; twelve received suspended sentences or probation; nine were acquitted; and one case was ruled self-defense and charges were dropped.

Marital Rape

Marital rape is another form of family violence. Until the 1970s, husbands could not rape their wives because a wife was legally obligated to have sex with her husband whenever he desired it. What was defined as a felony when it occurs between a man and a woman who are not married to each other was defined as just another sexual technique when the man and woman were married. Since then important changes have taken place in the laws, and marital rape is now a crime in all fifty states (Bintliff 1996). But some states still retain remnants of the old laws, for example, the punishments are lighter and the standard of evidence required to convict a husband rapist is higher (McElroy 2005).

Researchers estimate that about 10 percent of all married women have been raped by their husbands. In a random survey conducted by Diana Russell (1986) of 930 women over the age of eighteen, 14 percent were victims of at least one attempted or completed rape by their husbands or ex-husbands. Among battered women, the numbers of women raped by their husbands are even higher. "Studies of battered women regularly show that anywhere from a third to a half of them are victims of marital sexual assault" (Finkelhor and Yllo 1989, p. 387).

Russell argues that in spite of the care taken in the research, these numbers are probably underestimates for two reasons. First, the numbers may be underestimates because the sample did not include women in mental hospitals, prisons, nursing homes, and shelters, who may represent a category of women especially vulnerable to all types of violence, including marital rape.

Second, sex can be coerced through social factors, which sometimes makes it difficult for women to identify sex as being forced and therefore as rape by their husbands. For example, wives may participate in sex although they do not wish to because they believe it is their wifely duty or because they fear their husband will leave, cut off money, hurt her or publicly embarrass her if she will not have sex (Finkelhor and Yllo 1983).

Marital rape appears to be a chronic constant threat, not a single event. In Russell's research (which included both battered and nonbattered women), one-third of the wife rapes were isolated cases, one-third of the women had been raped between two and twenty times, and one-third had been raped more than twenty times by their husbands. Fifty percent of the battered women Finkelhor and Yllo (1989) interviewed had been raped twenty times or more by their husbands.

Women who are raped by their husbands use several strategies to manage their experience (Mills 1985). Some women attempt to minimize the risk of the violence by actively resisting. Others avoid damage by giving in, especially if their husbands raped them with objects and they feared internal damage. Some women avoid their husbands as much as possible or placate them by being "good wives," avoiding friends their husband don't approve of and making sure the children are quiet at all times (Bergen 1996).

Women who cannot avoid the physical confrontations develop ways to cope emotionally. Most commonly, they describe psychologically removing themselves from the scene. Debbie explained, "He would be all over me, and then I just went out in my mind—I just wasn't there anymore. I took myself somewhere else, and I found out later that I had done that a lot. Even growing up, and all, if anything hurts me, I orb out—I get totally numb" (Bergen 1996, pp. 30–31).

In order to leave their husbands, battered women who have been raped must redefine the behavior as rape and as unacceptable. Three factors seemed to trigger this event: (1) the violence approached the level of severity they associated with stranger rape; (2) the violence became abnormal; and (3) the women received help from an outsider (Bergen 1996).

Victims of prolonged trauma of battering and marital rape can recover by moving through three stages, which must take place in the context of supportive social relationships (Herman 1992):

> First survivors must establish a feeling of safety. Second they must remember and mourn the traumas they have undergone; through mourning, grief slowly diminishes. Finally they must make new connections with ordinary life. (M. Lewin 1992, p. 16)

Measuring the Social Costs of Domestic Violence

In addition to the personal costs to individual women, domestic violence also has costs for society. There are two types of costs—direct costs and indirect costs (Zuckerman and Friedman 1998). Direct costs are the value of the goods and services used to treat or prevent domestic violence, such as health care, emergency shelter, police time, social services, counseling, and property damage.

Indirect costs include lost productivity for employed women, such as job loss or absenteeism, death of a battered woman, and social and psychological costs. Social and psychological costs include relocating, severing social ties with friends and family, and staying in remote locations in order to avoid the batterer and embarrassment.

The Centers for Disease Control (2003b) estimate that these add up to about $8.3 billion a year. This is equal to 8 million days of paid work. They estimate 32 million people a year are affected by spouse abuse, resulting in about 2 million injuries. Each incident costs about $948 in health care costs for women and $387 in health care costs for men. In addition, the dollar amount placed on production lost from each injury incident is $257 for a woman and $224 for a man.

This section has described the incidence and effect of battering and rape. In addition to providing descriptive information about violence in families, scholars have also developed theories to explain the phenomenon. In the next section, we explore some of the explanations for the data we have reviewed.

Theories about Violence in Families

People who are concerned about the problems of battering and rape wish to see changes that will stop the violence. To aid them in this work, they have developed ways of understanding the problem—analyses of the problem—that allow them to determine ways in which to best address it.

A number of scholars have attempted to develop theories about how to understand violence in families in our society. One set of theoretical issues centers around the quesiton of why violence occurs. Three important frameworks have been developed to address this question. The first argues that the characteristics of the battered woman and the battering man are the crucial factors. The second focuses on the importance of social structure. The third also views social structure as crucial but emphasizes that gender inequality is a determining factor. Another set of theoretical issues centers around the question of how a social issue comes to be identified as a social problem. Woman battering and marital rape appear in ancient documents and seem to have been part of many human societies for a long time. Why has it been only recently that they have been identified as social problems? This is the question some theorists have addressed. We will investigate both of these in the second part of this section on theory.

Why Does Violence Occur?

Explaining Woman Battering as a Result of Individual Characteristics.   What causes violence in families? In trying to answer this question, one set of theorists has developed an analysis that focuses on the individuals who are battered and on those who are batterers. This kind of individualistic understanding is sometimes called a therapeutic model (Dobash and Dobash 1998). Within this framework, battering is defined as a phenomenon rooted in the genetic makeup or learned characteristics of individuals who experience the problem. Sometimes the man is blamed; sometimes the woman is blamed; sometimes both may be seen to be at fault. Within this framework, battering is caused by men who are either inherently violent or have been socialized to be violent, cruel people. Women within this framework are perceived to be either inherently weak or socialized to be weak, ineffective, passive victims.

Lenore Walker (1979) is one of the best-known advocates of this point of view. She argues that men and women have learned to play the roles of batterer and battered. Based on her interviews with battered women and their husbands, she claims that as a result of their social experience many women have become unresourceful, downtrodden victims. Walker named the concept "learned helplessness" or "the battered woman syndrome."

Walker maintains that some girls are socialized to behave in a passive, helpless manner. These behaviors make them likely to become victims of violence. They do not know how to tell their husbands what they want and how they believe a husband should behave, and they are unable to make decisions and take actions that would remove them from violent relationships.

While girls are learning to be passive and helpless, some boys have learned to take advantage of them. Boys who become batterers have been socialized to expect a woman to make their lives less stressful, to expect violence in homes, to expect women to behave in gender-stereotyped ways, and to intermittently use charm and anger to manipulate others' behavior (Walker 1983).

The socialization of men into the role of batterer takes place during their childhood. The socialization of women into the role of battered woman takes place during two time periods in their lives. First, young girls are socialized by their parents. Second, adult women who may not have learned these behaviors as children may be socialized by their husbands. Some wives who do not enter a marriage helpless and passive may become so as a result of the pressure placed on them by their abusive husbands.

Women within this framework are said to exhibit the battered women's syndrome of low self-esteem, depression, and difficulty making decisions, especially the decision to leave. Men who batter exhibit the following cluster of common characteristics:

1. "Excessive" jealousy, which makes them suspicious of their wives and any possible interactions with other men.
2. Victim-blaming and denial of their violence; they believe that they're the real victims and have no sense of agency about the violence they inflict.
3. A belief that sexual infidelity in men is acceptable, even necessary, but must be punished in women, and that their wives must be sexually available to them at all times.
4. A belief that women, especially their wives, are incompetent and infantile as well as manipulative and deceitful.
5. A belief that they are entitled to respect as men, and that disrespect for their "manhood" must be punished.
6. The belief that they are entitled to "discipline" or retaliate physically against wives who violate their "rules" or disappoint their expectations.
7. A belief that they might have an anger problem and sometimes "lose control." (O'Sullivan 1998).

Walker's theory has gained enormous attention among professional and community organizations in the United States. The prevalence of a therapeutic model perhaps should not be surprising in a country that employs one-half of the world's clinical psychologists (Dobash and Dobash 1992). Her theory, however, is controversial. She has been criticized for emphasizing psychology too much. Although psychological characteristics may play a role, the large number of women who are battered by their husbands and the way in which battering permeates every sector of our society indicate that the problem is a systemic one, embedded in our society. According to Walker's critics, the focus must be shifted from an individualistic framework to one that acknowledges the social context in which violence in families occurs.

Dobash and Dobash (1988), two of Walker's critics, write, "The analysis of Walker's own data demonstrates that the explanation of why women remain in a violent relationship lies much more in social and economic circumstances (employment, housing, number of dependent children, and so on) than in individuals' supposed helplessness" (p. 64).

Walker's critics have been especially concerned with the way her theory falls into blaming the victim. They argue that the theory of learned helplessness has become part of the ideology that maintains that women are inferior and the source of their own problems. If the problem of battering is essentially a problem of learned helplessness, then the solution must be for women to change, which blames women for their victimization (Dobash and Dobash 1988).

Violence-Prone Family Structure in Our Society. A second group of theorists has shifted their examination of battering to focus on social-structural factors that may create social contexts in which even strong women may find themselves being battered. Theorists who take a structural point of view blame the organization of our society for the violence in families and therefore call for changes at a societal level as a way to address the problem. Straus, Gelles, and Steinmetz (1988) are examples of those who take a structural view of violence in families. They describe three structural factors as key causes of violence in contemporary American families: stress, privacy/isolation, and the cultural acceptance of violence (Kurz 1989). This framework is sometimes called the family violence model.

Stress includes unemployment, poverty, and health problems. Chapter 4 on families and the economy showed that unemployment and poverty are common experiences of contemporary American families. Furthermore, in our society, families are the social institution that are frequently called on to provide a lifeboat in an economic crisis. The simultaneous demand placed on families to provide for economic survival and the inability of large numbers of families to do so adequately creates a stressful situation that may cause violence to erupt. Conger and his colleagues (1990) describe the ways in which Iowa farm families suffered economic losses in the 1990s that caused people to leave bills unpaid, postpone necessary purchases or medical care, and seek loans from family. In many of these families, men reacted violently to their problems.

Stress may also result from critical events more internal to families, such as the birth of a child, the death of a family member, illness, divorce, and remarriage. These events are considered most appropriately handled by individual families, rather than other institutions in the community. When people run into any difficulty in handling them, it is expected that families will be the major source of support. If a family cannot cope with the crisis, a situation is created that can push family members toward violence (Straus, Gelles, and Steinmetz 1988).

In the scenario at the beginning of the chapter, Ron becomes more abusive of Linda when she is pregnant. Having a baby puts a lot of pressure on parents. There may be excitement and anticipation, but parents-to-be may also worry about how successful they will be as parents, whether they will be able to afford the child, and whether their spouse will still have time for them. In Chapter 12 you will learn that one of the characteristics of parenting in contemporary American culture is the lack of training for the job. Without an opportunity for learning what exactly is expected of them, parents-to-be may feel stressed.

Isolation, the second causal factor, is both an ideological and a structural characteristic of U.S. families. That is, many of us hold strong beliefs that families should be private and separate from the rest of the world. And we frequently experience isolation of our families.

Isolation may be especially characteristic of families where violence occurs. "All forms of abuse have been associated with families that are isolated and that have few community ties, friendships, or organizational affiliations" (Finkelhor and Yllo 1989, p. 407). Isolation causes violence by diminishing the possibility of outside interference that could stop conflicts from developing into physical violence. Dobash and Dobash (1979) interviewed 109 Scottish women who were in relationships that involved battering. One of the common patterns they found among the women was that as the couple became more committed to each other and the relationship became more serious, the women spent less time with their own friends.

Table 11.1 shows the correlation between actions husbands took to isolate their wives and whether serious, nonserious, or no violence occurred in their relationships. The table lists questions that were asked of women in three categories and shows the percentage of women who answered yes to each question. The table shows that much higher pro-

TABLE 11.1   Percentage of Women Agreeing to Five Statements about Their Husbands According to Type of Violence Perpetrated by Their Husbands, 1993

Statements	None (n = 7060)	Nonserious (n = 1039)	Serious (n = 286)
He is jealous and doesn't want you to talk to other men.	3.5%	13.0%	39.3%
He tries to limit your contact with family or friends.	2.0%	11.1%	35.0%
He insists on knowing who you are with and where you are at all times.	7.4%	23.5%	40.4%
He calls you names to put you down and make you feel bad.	2.9%	22.3%	48.0%
He prevents you from knowing about or having access to the family income, even if you ask.	1.2%	4.6%	15.3%

Source: Wilson, Johnson, and Daly 1995. Reproduced by permission of the *Canadian Journal of Criminology.* Copyright by the Canadian Criminal Justice Association.

portions of the women who had experienced violence said that their husbands had tried to limit their behavior. In particular, women who had experienced serious violence requiring medical attention were likely to say that their husbands had tried to psychologically and socially isolate them.

Sometimes the ideology that families should remain private can inhibit victims of abuse from seeking help. Some battered women may go so far as to try to keep the abuse hidden. For example, in the scenario at the beginning of the chapter, Linda expresses the belief that her abuse is a personal problem that she should be able to resolve. Although she is unable to develop a solution on her own, she has not sought help from people outside of her family.

In addition, even if the victim does wish to seek help, if she is kept secluded and isolated from others, she may be unable to make contact with someone who could help her. Linda says she does not know what to do about Ron's abuse. This implies that perhaps, if she had more social contacts or more knowledge about the community, she might discover a range of options about which she is currently unaware.

The isolation of a family also means that it is unlikely that someone who could offer unsolicited help will even know about the abuse. The people who are in contact with Linda—her physician and her friends—have seen only the bruises, and so far Linda has been able to convince them the marks are the result of something other than purposeful abuse. The violent interactions between Ron and Linda are apparently taking place in private, and others may not know about them.

Finally, even if the violence is not private and others know about it, if those others believe that it is essential to maintain family privacy, outside interference is unlikely to occur. In some cases, real physical isolation of families may not exist, but if people believe that "outside interference" is inappropriate, they may not act to intervene. When asked why they did not report violence in families to the police, the most common response (34%) is "it is a private personal matter" (Durose et al. 2005). Perhaps Linda's friends do suspect that she is abused, but they believe, as she does, that husbands and wives should settle their own problems and that friends should not pry into their family affairs.

The third social-structural factor frequently cited as a cause of family violence is the acceptance of violence as a means of solving conflicts. Straus, Gelles, and Steinmetz (1980) found in their research that 25 percent of the wives and 33 percent of the husbands thought that "a couple slapping one another was at least somewhat necessary, normal and good."

We learn that violence is legitimate from movies, cartoon shows, other television programs, music, and even nursery rhymes. We also learn it from parents who practice violence. Many researchers have discussed the way in which the exposure of children to family violence may play an important role in causing them to behave violently as adults (Bernard and Bernard 1983; Fagan, Stewart, and Valentine 1983; Spinetta and Rigler 1972; Walker 1979).

The Gallup Poll (Moore 1994) conducted research in four time periods—1968, 1985, 1992, and 1994—to determine whether our ideas about using violence in families have changed. People were asked whether they could imagine any situations in which they would approve of a wife slapping her husband's face or a husband slapping his wife's face. The proportion of people approving of this behavior was about the same for husbands and wives in 1968. About 21 percent said they could imagine a situation in which the behavior would be appropriate. When they were asked what the situation might be, about three-quarters said they would approve if the spouse had been sexually unfaithful. After 1968, the proportion approving of a wife slapping her husband stayed about the same. The proportion approving of a husband slapping a wife, however, steadily declined to less than 10 percent in 1994. Young women between eighteen and thirty were especially likely to approve of a wife slapping her husband but not the reverse.

A Feminist Social-Structural View on Battering and Marital Rape.   Chapter 1 introduced six themes. One of these themes was paying attention to the different way in which different family members experience events that occur within their families. The most dramatic example of this differentiation is violence in families. The experience of violence in families may be radically different for different family members. One person may be a batterer, another a victim, and another unaware of the abuse. The differences in terms of who is a batterer and who is a victim are not random, but tend to lie along lines of gender and generation. Batterers are usually men; victims are usually women. Abusers are usually parents; the abused are usually children, although elder abuse can reverse the relationship. The description above of three structural sources of violence in families shows us that men, women, and children who call themselves a family can treat each other in cruel ways without being pathological individuals or even unusual or deviant people. The source of the violence is found both in the way we organize families—for example, as isolated units that allow and sometimes even encourage people to treat each other badly—and in the social context of families, such as during an economic crisis. Demie Kurz (1989) has named the theory that takes a social structural approach, which does not emphasize gender, as the family violence approach. The family violence approach does not entirely ignore the importance of women's subordinate position in family violence situations; adherents believe it is only one of several contributing factors.

TABLE 11.2   What Should Be Done When a Man Hurts a Woman?

	Percent of Respondents Who Believe:			
	He Should Be Arrested		*She Should Leave Him*	
Action of Abusive Man	Women	Men	Women	Men
When he screams abusive things				
White	1%	2%	8%	5%
African American	9	6	12	9
Latinos	3	3	6	3
Asian American	32	23	16	24
When he threatens her				
White	22	17	39	28
African American	33	29	31	21
Latinos	24	22	21	16
Asian American	47	39	33	57
When he grabs and shoves her				
White	35	29	44	38
African American	33	25	36	28
Latinos	35	26	28	20
Asian American	49	56	34	58
When he slaps her hard				
White	52	51	61	54
African American	47	39	46	39
Latinos	56	49	46	43
Asian American	58	69	51	55
When he punches her				
White	83	77	81	73
African American	64	57	53	62
Latinos	85	78	69	62
Asian American	82	84	66	86

Source: E. Klein, J. Campbell, E. Soler, and M. Ghez, *Ending domestic violence: Changing public perceptions/ halting the epidemic.* Copyright © 1997 by Sage Publications. Reprinted by permission of Sage Publications.

Some scholars have argued that the family violence approach does not pay sufficient attention to differentiation within families (Klein et al. 1997). Kurz (1989), for example, asserts that the family violence approach is correct in some ways but is insufficient. She maintains that gender inequality and the oppression of women is the central feature of violence in families and must always be considered in our analysis.

Kurz (1989) names Murray Straus, Richard Gelles, and Suzanne Steinmetz as the scholars who are best identified with the family violence approach, and she compares their point of view with other social structuralists who have made gender more central in their assessment of violence in families. Kurz cites Russell (1986), Dobash and Dobash (1979), Bowker (1986), Yllo (1988), Pagelow (1981), and Stark and Flitcraft (1979) as examples of scholars who take a feminist approach.

Kurz notes that the family violence approach uses language to describe the problem that does not emphasize the gendered quality of the violence. For example, people writing from the family violence perspective use terms like *family violence* or *domestic violence* instead of *battering* or *wife rape,* and they use the term *spouse abuse* instead of *wife abuse.* These words "indicate that it is the family, not the relationship between women and men, which is the central unit of their analysis" (1989, p. 492).

Kurz (1989) argues that a feminist approach is different from and better than the approach proposed by the family violence theorists. The feminist approach makes the politically unequal relationship of men and women the center of the analysis and views gender inequality as the most critical factor in violence. According to the feminist approach, in attempts to understand violence in families and to develop solutions to the problem, special attention must be paid to the unequal political relationship between women and men both in and outside of families (Stark and Flitcraft 1996).

Family violence researchers note the importance of cultural norms that condone violence in general. Feminists point out that, additionally, there are norms (and historically, even laws) that condone violence against women. For example, in the nineteenth century many states had laws specifically approving wife beating (see Dobash and Dobash 1979 for a history of battering).

Feminists also note the way that gender interacts with social-structural factors like economic distress to exacerbate violence. For example, imagine a family in which the husband has been the main breadwinner and is downsized. His frustration and economic difficulties might cause him to feel angry and erupt into violence. It would seem that if his wife could work and their bills were paid, he could relax and his violent behavior might stop. Researchers have found, however, that if a wife is earning more than her husband, tension and violence increase. A disparity in economic success with the wife on top, in fact, is more predictive of violence than overall family resources (McCloskey 1996). When women's economic resources approach or exceed their partners', the women are more likely to be victims of violence. If we pay attention only to economic stress and ignore gender, we will have only a partial and distorted understanding of the issue.

Feminist researchers, furthermore, argue that battering is not just a reflection of the inequality between women and men, but is also a conscious strategy used by men to control women and maintain the system of gender inequality (Kurz 1989). In interviews with violent men, Dobash and Dobash (1998) found that for these men the violence itself was not the key issue when they were violent with women. The men often minimized or denied the violence. When the men described violent encounters with women, the key issue was the outcome—influencing the woman's behavior—which they viewed as just (Anderson and Umberson 2001).

Theorists who take a feminist approach also argue that gender inequality enters into the problem of violence in families by creating barriers to stopping the violence. Economic inequality between women and men, for example, keeps women tied to men who are batterers. Wives with the most resources were the first to leave physically abusive husbands (Pagelow 1981).

Family violence theorists and feminist theorists share some ideas. They both maintain that social structure, not individual psychology, best explains the problems of woman battering and marital rape. But they are quite different in another respect. "For family violence researchers, violence is the primary problem to be explained, while for feminists an equally important question is why women are overwhelmingly the targets of the violence" (Kurz 1989, p. 498).

The Controversy over the Battered Husband Syndrome.   In 1980, the debate between the family violence model and the feminist model made the news for the first time. It continues to be a controversy today. Straus, Gelles, and Steinmetz, spokespersons for the family violence perspective, reported that husband abuse is equally as common as wife abuse, and their findings were picked up by the popular press. When random samples were asked about violence used against a partner, similar percentages of women and men answer yes. For example, 2.8 percent of husbands and 5.2 percent of wives say they have thrown something at their spouse; 10.7 percent of husbands and 8.3 percent of wives say they have pushed, grabbed, or shoved their partners; 2.4 percent of husbands and 3.1 percent of wives have kicked, bit, or hit their spouses with a fist; and 2.2 percent of husbands and 3.0 percent of wives hit or tried to hit their spouses.

Straus (1986, p. 472) argues that "violence by wives has not been an object of public concern. There has been no publicity, and no funds have been invested in ameliorating this problem because it has not been defined as a problem."

Feminists strongly criticized Straus, Gelles, and Steinmetz's conclusion that similar reports by husbands and wives meant that husband abuse is a problem equal or nearly equal to wife abuse (Dobash and Dobash 1988; Pleck et al. 1977–78). The first criticism centered on how the researchers categorized the answers to their survey questions:

> Included in the "high risk" category is "trying to hit with something" and excluded from it is "slapping." Yet, our own research, which does examine injuries sustained from particular attacks, demonstrates that a slap can result in anything from a temporary red mark to a broken nose, tooth, or jaw and that trying to hit with something never results in anything unless the blow is landed. (Dobash and Dobash 1988, p. 59)

Self-defense was another issue of concern to the feminist critics. They claimed that issues like who initiated the attack and who acted in self-defense were not taken into consideration in the data that were used to make the argument that husbands are victims of spouse abuse as often as wives. Dobash and Dobash wrote:

> Indeed our research and virtually everyone else's who has actually studied violent events and/or their patterning in a concrete and detailed fashion reveal that when women do use violence against their spouses or cohabitants, it is primarily in self-defense or retaliation, often during an attack by their husbands. On occasions, women may initiate an incident after years of being attacked but it is extraordinarily rare for women to persistently initiate severe attacks. (1988, p. 60)

Finally, feminist critics point out that Straus, Gelles, and Steinmetz's work is based on self-reporting. Data obtained from sources that report the effects of violence, like police and hospital records, show that nearly all violence between spouses is directed at women by men. In the latest reports, 84 percent of the victims of spouse abuse were women (Durose et al. 2005).

Berk and his colleagues (1983) investigated 262 cases of domestic disturbance to determine whether these incidents were primarily mutual combat or woman battering. They coded the severity of injuries on an eight-point scale from no injury to high injuries (combinations of concussions, internal injuries, broken bones, and damaged sense organs). Their sample showed that 43 percent of the women and 7 percent of the men were injured. When only injury-producing incidents were examined, women comprised 94 percent of the victims. This percentage is similar to the 95 percent figure reported in the National Crime Survey. Furthermore, in 39 percent of the cases only the woman was injured, while in 3 percent of the cases only the man was injured. Berk et al. (1983, pp. 204–7) conclude, "This implies that if there is anything to the battered husband syndrome, it either has nothing to do with injury or is relevant to very few couples. When injuries are used as the outcome of interest, a marriage license is a hitting license, but for men only."

Family violence scholars respond to this kind of information by arguing that the reports of battered husbands are exceedingly low because men hesitate to come forward, fearing stigma (Dobash and Dobash 1992). Feminists reply that women are also unlikely to report being battered. Dobash and Dobash (1992) estimate that of 35,000 cases of woman battering they examined, about 2 percent were reported. Others (Rouse, Breen, and Howell 1988) have compared women's and men's response to being assaulted by a spouse and found that men were more likely than women to call the police. Kincaid's (1982, p. 91) review of 3,125 cases found that men were also more likely to press charges: "While there were 17 times as many female as male victims, only 22% of women laid charges, while almost 40% of the men did so." In addition, men were four to five times more likely to pursue a complaint and less likely to drop charges (Kincaid 1982).

Three Points of View, Three Strategies for Policy.   This review of the literature on violence in families shows three distinct points of view: an individualistic framework, a family violence framework, and a feminist framework.

These three different points of view have important implications in terms of policy. The individualistic framework implies social policy that seeks to change the individuals who live in violent families. For example, in the scenario at the beginning of the chapter, the individualistic framework would call for resocializing Linda to be more assertive and to gain a stronger sense of self-worth. At the same time, Ron would be advised to learn to hold less dominating beliefs about relationships and more appropriate ways in which to express his anger.

The family violence approach seeks policies that call for changes in the social-structural system. For example, family violence approach theorists would call for reforms that alleviate problems like unemployment. They might also work to eliminate ideologies that promote violence, for example, by protesting media images that glorify and romanticize assaults and other violent behavior.

The feminist approach calls for similar changes in the social structure but insists that each of these changes be made in light of the gendered character of violence. For example, they would call not just for eliminating violence in the media but also for eliminating the glorification of woman battering and rape in particular.

Feminists also observe the need for an elimination of the oppression of women in all areas of society as essential for ending violence in families. For example, from the feminist point of view, policies that could help reduce battering and rape would include equal pay for women to allow them to afford to leave violent relationships. Feminists would point out that even though Linda is a professional, as we observed in Chapter 10, if she chooses to leave Ron she will probably see a drop in her standard of living. Abuse would be more likely to end if Linda were better able to live independently from Ron, and she would be able to live independently from him more easily if she were financially self-sufficient.

The Discovery of Violence in Families

The second set of theoretical issues that have emerged around the study of violence in families revolves around the question of why now. Woman battering and marital rape have been around for a long time. Why have they just recently been discovered as important social problems? How did this apparently old problem become visible? This is a question of interest to sociologists with a social constructionist perspective (Loseke 1992).

Social constructionism is a theoretical framework that posits that what we perceive to be real is a product of social interaction among many people. In the case of the issues of wife abuse and battered women, the social constructionist would argue that these issues were not only invisible before the 1970s, but that they actually did not exist. "Most certainly some husbands always have victimized their wives—the historical record is clear on that—but assault could not be an instance of 'wife abuse' until the label was available" (Loseke 1992, p. 38).

The label that allows us to begin to recognize and understand the phenomenon of wife abuse is created by many people and groups of people interacting with one another. The ongoing activity of the social construction of wife abuse and battered women has been an important development because it allows us to begin to think of ways to address the problem now that it is recognized. But much work had to be done to create the images and make the claims that battering did exist and that it was a serious social problem.

In the review of the history, we have seen that feminists played an important role in constructing wife abuse as a social problem. But many others were involved as well, including battered women, social service agencies, police departments, and scholars. Because wife abuse and battering are socially constructed by many different people, the meanings of the concepts and the issues behind those concepts are contradictory and dynamic. The character of wife abuse and its causes and solutions had to be hammered out by these various interests, and many debates remain about what wife abuse or a battered woman is.

For example, is it wife abuse to "just" slap a woman? If a woman gets drunk, slaps her husband, and then is beaten up by him, is she a battered woman? What about a woman who has not yet been physically assaulted by her husband but has been threatened and believes the problem could easily escalate to physical violence?

These questions demand that we continue, as a society, to revise and reconstruct our ideas about battering. Loseke (1992) observed the operation of a shelter in California and found that this effort of socially constructing battered women is a continuing one among those in the front lines, the workers in the shelters. Every day the employees and volunteers at shelters for battered women must make decisions based on their understanding of what wife abuse is and who a "real" battered woman is. They make these decisions in social contexts, interacting with other workers and residents in the shelters, with funding agencies, and with the public. Their task of socially constructing wife abuse, battered women, and shelters for battered women is difficult. It requires a lot of thought and creates frustration, anger, and sometimes shame if shelter workers are unable to come to an acceptable understanding. The decisions they make, based on their construction of the problem, can have profound consequences for the women seeking shelter.

The issues of battering and marital rape are so unsettling and so pervasive that it is sometimes difficult to figure out how to understand them, not to mention how to stop them. Social constructionist theory helps us think more clearly about battering and see the most important factors. Social constructionist theory suggests that we need to be sure to consider the dynamic and complex process by which battering and rape and their causes and consequences are socially constructed. Who is involved in socially constructing the problem? What are their relationships to the problem? What are their relationships to each other?

Finding Solutions

Thus far this chapter has reviewed the incidence of violence in families and has discussed a number of theories about violence. The emphasis has been on the way in which the macrolevel of society shapes and determines the microlevel relationships between women and men in marriage and especially how those relationships are often marked by violence. People have also resisted violence in their microlevel relationships. Sometimes their resistance has taken the form of microlevel changes, such as removing themselves from the relationship or altering the relationship. In addition, people have organized themselves at the microlevel to put pressure on the macrolevel of society. They have worked for alterations in social institutions like the police force and have invented a new social institution—the battered women's shelter—to help stop the violence. In this section, we turn our attention to these efforts, beginning with an examination of efforts made by individuals to alter their social context at the microlevel and then moving to two examples of how the microlevel affects the macrolevel.

As we have seen in the discussion of the prevalence of battering and marital rape, determining the number of women, men, and children who are victims of violence in families is a difficult task. Even more difficult is determining the number who solve the problem for themselves. Our image of the battered woman is a person who is under attack, in crisis, and undecided about what to do about it. Linda in the opening scenario projected such an image. At the particular moment we meet her, she is confused about what has happened to her and ambivalent about what to do.

One step women can take is to call the police. Miller and Krull (1997) report, however, that fewer than half of the calls to the police about domestic violence were made by the victims. The remaining calls were made by children or other family members living in the household or by neighbors. Hesitating to contact the police might be an indication of confusion and ambivalence. When asked why they did not call the police, however, some women said that it was not because they were confused or ambivalent but because they chose not to for rational reasons. The three most common reasons given for not calling the police were that the women feared injury by the suspect as punishment for calling, believed that the police would make things worse, and had no access to a telephone. Almost half of the women interviewed said they believed that police intervention in the past had caused a variety of problems, including violent retaliation by the suspect, and other financial, family, and legal problems. Research on mandatory arrest shows that police intervention can be a powerful mechanism for constraining abusers and protecting victims. Police intervention, however, does not have uniform results, and women must make decisions about what is best in each particular situation.

Many women take the next step by determining that they must leave the abuser and establish an independent and unbattered life. What are the catalysts for women making this move?

Kathleen Ferraro and John Johnson (1990) interviewed 120 women who passed through a shelter and asked them how they had decided to leave. They found six factors that served as catalysts. The first was a change in the level of violence. The kind of change that was especially important was a sudden one in the direction of increased abuse that the women perceived as a direct threat not just to their physical well-being but to their lives. For example, one woman explained that the deciding factor in her decision to leave her abusive husband was when he held a gun to her head.

The second catalyst was a change in resources. Women began to reinterpret the violence as unacceptable when other forms of support became available to them, such as jobs and shelters for battered women.

A third catalyst was a change in the relationship. Several researchers describe the pattern of abuse as one that includes intermittent periods of violence and then remorse on the part of the batterer (Walker 1979). The women who spoke to Ferraro and Johnson said that their decision to leave was triggered when the periods of remorse shortened or disappeared.

The fourth catalyst Ferraro and Johnson discovered was despair. For some women, the hope that things would get better prevented them from leaving. When this last hope seemed to disappear, their despair forced them to make a change.

The fifth catalyst was a change in the visibility of the violence. "Battering in private was degrading, but battering in public was humiliating" (Ferraro and Johnson 1990, p. 113). One woman explained:

> He never hit me in public before—it was always at home. But the Saturday I got back [returning to her husband from the shelter], we went Christmas shopping and he slapped me in the store because of some stupid joke I made. People saw it, I know, I felt so stupid, like, they must think what a jerk I am, what a sick couple, and I thought, "God, I must be crazy to let him do this."

The sixth catalyst was external definitions of the relationship. When a woman was offered responses from others that encouraged her to see the abusive man as intolerable, she was more likely to leave. Ferraro and Johnson (1990) argue that this is an indication of the importance of shelters because they provide just such an outside opinion.

The women Ferraro and Johnson interviewed took it upon themselves to resist the violence against them by leaving their abusive husbands. These women have taken action at the microlevel to make changes in their own lives.

Violence in families has also caused activity at the microlevel with the intention of changing macrolevel social institutions. For example, resistance against violence in families has taken a place at the community level in the form of social movements that have demanded two important changes in the availability of community resources for battered women: the get-tough campaigns in police departments and the provision of shelters for battered women.

Table 11.2 shows the distribution of various groups in terms of their opinions about these two solutions to the problem of battering. The table shows the percentage of people who believe that a batterer should be arrested for certain behaviors and the percentage of people who believe the woman should leave (and possibly go to a shelter) if she is treated in a particular way. The table shows that gender and race ethnicity affect people's opinions on these questions, but in all cases a large proportion of people believe that arrest and encouraging women to leave are essential tools to stop battering.

The Get-Tough-with-Abusers Campaign

Since the recognition in the early 1970s that violence in families is a crucial social issue, significant changes have taken place in the laws, making it easier and sometimes mandatory for the police to arrest men who batter women in family fights.

In 1984, Lawrence Sherman and Richard Berk studied the effect of police arrest in Minneapolis as a deterrent in domestic violence. They concluded:

> Arrest was the most effective of three standard methods police use to reduce domestic violence. The other police methods—attempting to counsel both the parties or sending assailants away—were found to be considerably less effective in deterring future violence in the cases examined. (p. 262)

Why does arrest reduce the incidence of repeated wife assault? First, the arrest acts as a deterrent—something the men do not wish to have happen again. Second, an arrest alters the power dynamic between the men and their wives. Batterers perceive a power shift emanating both from the wife's willingness to call the police and from the criminal justice system's willingness to defend her (Dutton et al. 1992).

Furthermore, an arrest prevents batterers from minimizing and rationalizing the abuse because it makes the incidents public and subject to others' perceptions and evaluation, which might be quite different from the abuser's (Anderson and Umberson 2001). Some batterers minimize and deny the effects claiming they were not violent; their wives just bruised easily. Others rationalize the violence as, for example, a result of some unique personal flaw such as an inability to use self-control. One batterer explains, "When I got violent, it was not because I really wanted to get violent. It was just because it was like an outburst of rage" (Ptacek 1988, p. 143).

Other batterers explain the behavior as unusual and out of character, caused by peculiar circumstances such as being drunk. One man said, "I've been involved with AA, and that's why I'm much better. And a lot of my problems—not all of them, but most of my problems at the time were due to that. And it's just amazing to know there was a reason for the way I acted" (Ptacek 1988, p. 142). Some men rationalize the violence by claiming that it had been provoked. One man blamed his wife this way: "She was trying to tell me, you know, I'm no fucking good and this and that, and she just kept at me, you know. And I couldn't believe it. And finally I got real pissed and I said wow, you know, you're going to treat me like this? Whack. Take that" (Ptacek 1988, p. 144).

Police departments were made aware of Sherman and Berk's (1984) findings in a publicizing effort unprecedented for a scholarly work in criminal justice (Binder and Meeker 1992). Few departments, however, implemented mandatory arrest in domestic violence cases. A court case brought against the police in 1983, however, turned the tide (Halsted 1992).

In 1982 and 1983, Tracy Thurman called the police or came to police headquarters at least seven times, begging for protection from her husband, Buck. Although she signed several sworn statements, the police hesitated to act. On the last call, the officer took twenty minutes to arrive because he stopped to go to the bathroom. When he arrived he witnessed Buck stabbing and kicking Tracy. He convinced Buck to give him the knife but did not handcuff him. Buck then ran into the house to get their son and began kicking Tracy in the head in front of the officer. Six more officers arrived but still did not arrest Buck. They restrained him only after he again assaulted Tracy as she lay on a stretcher being carried to the ambulance.

Tracy Thurman sued the police department and won $2.3 million in compensatory damages. The judge ruled in 1985 that Tracy Thurman had been denied equal protection under the law simply because she was married to the assailant (Halsted 1992).

The 1980s and 1990s saw a wave of new laws designed to remove discretion from police and require them to arrest batterers. Twenty states now have mandatory arrest statutes (Coyle 2005). Mandatory arrest means that police officers are required to arrest batterers. Warrantless arrest statutes allow police to arrest batterers if there is due cause. This means that if, for example, an officer sees an injured woman who has called for help, the officer can arrest the batterer without having actually witnessed the assault.

These changes in the law are important successes in the struggle to protect people, especially women, from battering, and we have seen from the decrease in the numbers of people assaulted and murdered by intimates, they are saving lives. Two problems, however, remain. First, requiring the police to arrest the batterer regardless of the woman's wishes removes any choice she may have. Furthermore, it ignores the validity of her fears that the abuser may retaliate even more harshly against her if he is arrested. Second, even if the laws have been altered, the actual policy being implemented by the police in these cases may have changed little (Ferraro 1989).

Kathleen Ferraro (1989) has investigated this second issue. She was interested in whether change in policy did create a change in the behavior of the Phoenix police. She and her assistants rode in police cars and witnessed police handling of domestic disputes.

In Phoenix in 1984, both the law and the stated policy of the police chief was to arrest batterers. The researchers found, however, that the laws and departmental policy are only one set of factors influencing police decisions to make arrests in family fights. The police were also influenced by legal, ideological, practical, and political considerations.

An example of a legal consideration was the question of property damage. In several incidents, the women had not been physically injured but their house doors had been kicked in, their tires slashed, and their windshields smashed. The officers did not arrest the men, explaining to the women that Arizona is a community property state. In a community property state, all property acquired during a marriage belongs to both the husband and wife. When married men destroy property that they or their wives have acquired, the men are destroying their own property, and the act is therefore not illegal (Stetson 1997).

Racist, classist, and homophobic ideology was also a critical issue. Officers believed that arrests were a waste of time if the people lived in housing projects or were Mexicans, Indians, or gay. The police referred to them as "low life" and "scum" and insisted that "arrest was meaningless because violence is a way of life for them" (Ferraro 1989, p. 67).

Practical considerations were the third factor interfering with making arrests. If an arrest involved finding shelter or information (e.g., about legal rights) for the women and children, the police would often choose to avoid making it. Transporting women and children and processing them through the bureaucracies of shelters, foster care, and legal and social services is time consuming and often requires long-term involvement. The police preferred to take the most expedient course that required the least additional involvement. Another practical consideration is the presence of the abuser. The batterer often leaves before the police arrives, and in some cities policies require that arrests be made on the scene. In all cities, finding him would create much additional police work.

Finally, the police were influenced by their perception of political matters. Since there were no explicit rewards for compliance with the new policies nor punishment for noncompliance, they interpreted the policies as just talk and relatively unimportant. They decided, therefore, that making arrests was not politically important to them and was unnecessary to maintaining their good standing in the department.

Ferraro (1989) concluded that changing laws is not enough. Her review of the factors that entered into the decision to arrest indicates that creating a mandatory policy might be a good idea, but its implementation is likely to be disrupted by the four factors.

Many other reports show that Ferraro's findings are not unique (Dobash and Dobash 1992). In a recent study in D.C. although departmental policy called for arrests, police frequently did not abide by the policies (Cassidy, Nicholl, and Rose 2001).

The Battered Women's Movement

Police departments are not the only social institutions that have been called on to address the problem of battering. Another institution—the battered women's shelter—was invented for that purpose in the early 1970s. As Table 11.2 indicated, many people believe that women should leave if their husbands treat them in abusive ways. Until the 1970s, women who wished to leave often had no place to go. During the 1970s, many states began to use marriage license fees to fund shelters (E. Pleck 1991). The development of the battered women's shelter is a second example of the way in which microlevel activity of people working together has had an effect on the macrolevel of social organization.

BOX **11.2**

Do Restraining Orders Help?

One legal procedure now often used by battered women is a restraining order. These are orders given by the court to make abusive men change their behavior. For example:

1. An offender is ordered to move out of a domicile or not to use certain property, like a car, even if the title to the property is in the name of the offender.
2. An offender is ordered to refrain from further physical or psychological abuse.
3. An offender is ordered to refrain from any contact with the victim.
4. An offender is ordered to enter counseling and to finish the program.
5. An offender is directed to pay support, restitution, or attorney fees.
6. Provisional custody of minors is granted to the victim and drafted onto the protective order (Halsted 1992, p. 153).

In twenty states, the police are required to make an arrest when the defendant violates an order of protection (Coyle 2005). These orders can have important positive effects. Chaduril and Daly (1992) found that they increased police responsiveness, increased arrest rates of repeaters, reduced the chance that the man battered again, and empowered women to end abusive relationships. The researchers caution, however, that one in ten men retaliated by beating or threatening his wife for obtaining a restraining order, and one-third of the men ignored the order. In addition, a new ruling by the Supreme Court seems to weaken the protection given to people who take out a protective order (Greenhouse 2005).

In 2005, an important decision was made by the Supreme Court that seems to reverse the legal trend of increasing protection for battered women and their children (Greenhouse 2005). The justices ruled against Jessica Gonzalez in her case against the police department of Castle Rock, Colorado. Gonzalez had obtained a protective order against her estranged husband. One evening her husband picked up their three daughters, ages 7, 9, and 10, outside her house and took them to a local amusement park. She called the police repeatedly that evening and told them that her husband was unstable and that he was not legally allowed to come to her house or to take the children. She pleaded with them to find her husband and bring the girls back home. The police ignored the protective order violation saying that he was their father and that going to an amusement park didn't seem like something they should be worried about. The father showed up at the police department later in the evening with three dead children in the back of his truck. He had shot them all and then turned the gun on himself.

The Supreme Court ruled that she did not have the right to expect the police to enforce the protective order because there is a well established tradition of police using their own discretion in spite of mandatory arrest statutes. Not all of the justices agree with the majority ruling. Justices Stevens and Ginsburg, in their dissenting opinion, said that the elimination of police discretion was an important legal development in the 1990s designed to address domestic violence cases and that the police should not have used their discretion but have abided by the protective orders (Greenhouse 2005).

Shelters are residential refuges that offer a free place for women and their children who are fleeing an abusive home to stay. Most shelters in the United States limit the stay to four or six weeks. Shelters usually provide services for residents like personal counseling, job counseling, legal assistance, assistance in obtaining welfare and food stamps, and information on education. In the 1990s on average about 160,800 women got help from victim service agencies including shelters every year (Greenfield et al. 1998). There are more than two thousand shelters in the United States now but the available beds still fall far short of the need (NPR 2002).

Violence against Women Act

In 1994, the federal government passed a series of laws collectively known as the Violence against Women Act (VAWA) as a result of many years of work by feminists, politicians, other activists, police, and social service providers. VAWA is a landmark piece of legislation that has provided crucial aid to women, men, and children experiencing violence. VAWA programs and services, with the support of federal, state and private funding, have changed and improved our nation's responses to violence at the federal, state, local, campus, institutional and tribal level.

The act provides for a wide range of activities, granting money for research to determine the extent of the problem and to develop and implement education programs for police and prosecutors. Reforms in the legislation create new offenses and tougher penalties. For example, the act makes it a federal crime punishable by up to five years in prison to cross state lines to do bodily harm to spouses or intimate partners. It also allows a state to prosecute stalkers and those subject to protective orders as felons if they travel to another state to harass spouses or intimate partners. In addition, it makes it a federal crime for anyone convicted of an offense involving domestic violence to continue to own or acquire a firearm (Landner 1999). One of the most controversial sections is the "civil rights for women" provision. "Under the statute, a person who commits a crime of gender motivated violence is liable to the injured party and is subject to compensatory and punitive damages" (Shagall 1999).

The act also provides money to fund services for victims, especially shelters, and for a national 1-800-799-SAFE hotline for domestic violence information and help (Biden 1997). The hotline has now answered well over one million (1,240,000) calls (www.ndvh .org 2006).

Besides funding the national domestic hotline, VAWA 2000 provided $925 million for services to train police officers and prosecutors; $875 million for shelters; $200 million for legal services for victims; and $140 million to address violence against women on college campuses. The act also grants funding for programs that address stalking and domestic violence, teen dating violence, domestic violence in the workplace, and disability and sexual assault. In addition, it authorizes money for transitional housing and training programs for child protective service workers and judges. Immigrant women have especially welcomed the renewal of the act because it allows them to seek legal residency in the United States and avoid deportation to protect themselves from batterers.

When former President Clinton signed VAWA in 1994, $1.62 billion were authorized for the law's first six years. The act was renewed in 2000 and again in 2005.

The Micro–Macro Connection

We began this chapter with a story about Linda and Ron. Linda thought that the troubles she was having were hers alone and that the violence she was experiencing existed apart from the rest of society. If we use the sociological imagination, we see many connections between Linda's personal troubles and social structures.

The social context shapes the behavior of Linda and Ron and limits their ability to eliminate the battering in their lives. Social-structural issues such as poverty and unemployment cause stress. The demands placed on families in our society to resolve or cope with these stresses may make families violence prone.

Another factor in the social context, ideologies that condone violence against family members, and especially ideologies that condone violence against women and children, "justify" battering and child abuse. Furthermore, isolation of families and the lack of economically feasible alternatives to violent marriages for battered women limit the possibility for individual women and children to escape the violence. Macrolevel social organization both causes the problem and limits its solution.

Gender inequality, a feature of several social institutions at the macrolevel, such as the labor market and the legal system, plays a central role in the creation and perpetuation of battering and marital rape. Furthermore, violence against women at the microlevel of social interaction is an important way in which gender inequality is maintained at both the micro- and macrolevels.

Individuals also affect their social environment. Over the last two decades, we have seen changes in thinking, policy, and social organization in attempts to stop the violence. Individual women at the microlevel have sought to change their immediate surroundings by leaving abusive situations. People organized at the microlevel have also created changes in the macrolevel of the law and in the way in which the police are supposed to handle battering.

Other changes include the invention of shelters for battered women and the creation of VAWA. All these activities appear to be working to slow down the violence in families, but there is still a lot more work to do.

The sociological imagination allows us to see both the personal suffering from violence and the social forces causing and perpetuating that violence. Most important, it also shows us a way out. It will not be easy to make the necessary changes to stop the violence, but understanding problems is a crucial first step to solving them.

CHAPTER

12 Parents

Many people believe that children today do not spend as much time with their parents as children in the past. Research shows that when the number of children each parent is responsible for plus the time spent with children is considered, parents spend more time per child than they did 30 years ago. (© Bob Daemmrich/The Image Works)

Kimberly and Michael (from Chapter 1) have been married for six years, and they have three-year-old twins, Anna and Elizabeth. While the girls play in a makeshift play area, Kimberly busily stuffs envelopes at the campaign headquarters of Lynn Wilson for Congress. The centerpiece of the Wilson campaign is her support of a child care bill that would create more high-quality day care centers, raise the pay for workers at the centers, and federally subsidize children from middle- and low-income families.

Another volunteer asks Kimberly how she got involved. Kimberly says, "When I first got married, I planned on having children and staying home with them until they went to kindergarten, but I've been forced to change my thinking since then." She explains that when the twins were born, she was totally unprepared for the amount of work required to care for them. She also did not anticipate how children change a household—the sleep interruptions and eating schedules, the mess and lack of privacy, and the shifting of activities from those for adults to those that include children. After the initial shock wore off and she and Michael established a schedule, she began to feel lonely and isolated, and she realized that the bills were piling up. She decided to go back to work. But finding someone to take care of the twins was more of a challenge than she had counted on.

"I never gave child care much thought. I noticed the day care centers around town and figured it was no problem finding a place. But when I went out to look around for myself, I discovered that some were dreary establishments with no learning program, and since the girls weren't toilet trained, they weren't eligible for many centers. Plus the expense for two children meant that nearly all my take-home pay would be eaten up in child care."

The other volunteer asks, "What about Michael? Can't he help?" Kimberly explains that Michael does consulting work and is out of town a lot. He spends time with the kids on the weekends to give her a break, and he is getting better with them but he really had no experience taking care of babies.

"That's why I'm here. Lynn Wilson is a mother herself, and that will help her bring a fresh outlook to Washington. I know she will work to make the government pay attention to parents and children," Kimberly concludes, as she excuses herself to track down Anna and Elizabeth.

> When we last heard from Kimberly in Chapter 1, she had different ideas. How is the real experience of parenting different from the anticipated one?
>
> What is it about parenting that makes it different from other activities, and how does the experience differ for women and men?
>
> How does the experience of parenting influence our thinking about other activities?
>
> Kimberly is married and middle class. How would her experience be altered if she were single, a teenager, a lesbian, or poor?
>
> Some people argue that the division of child care between Kimberly and Michael is inevitable because it is rooted in biological differences. What are the weaknesses of that argument?

Parents and Parenting

In this chapter and the next, we examine parents and children. Parents and children create a relationship within families. Separating the two, therefore, is somewhat artificial. On the other hand, parents and children are separate categories, and they do have different responsibilities and interests in their relationship with each other. Nevertheless, when you read about parents and parenting, keep in mind how they affect children and childhood, as well as how they are shaped by children.

This chapter is divided into three sections: parenting, the question of biological destiny, and the political debate around child care. The discussion begins with a summary of the characteristics of parenting and then moves to examining the way in which gender affects parenting—motherhood and fatherhood. Since parenting can be so readily divided into two categories by gender, the question that emerges is whether this distinction is biologically determined. Are mothering and fathering different because of physical differences between women and men? The theoretical debate over the answer to this question is reviewed. The final section of the chapter concerns an important political debate on the question of child care.

Parenting Role

Being a parent is unlike any other activity in which we participate. But what exactly is unique about the role of parent compared with other roles in our society? Alice Rossi (1992) suggests that there are four salient features of parenting: (1) cultural pressure to assume the role, (2) onset of the role, (3) irrevocability of the role, and (4) preparation for parenthood.

Much pressure is placed on people to assume the role of parents. This is especially true for women. In order for men to secure their status as adults they must be employed. For women, adulthood is marked by maternity, whether they are employed or not. But both women and men in the United States are usually expected to become parents (Rossi 1992).

By onset of the role, Rossi means the way in which parenthood begins. Unlike many activities in which we participate that have an equal effect on our lives, becoming a parent almost always includes an element of surprise. Most pregnancies are unplanned. About one-half of pregnancies are unintended (Alan Guttmacher Institute 1999). Among those that are planned, few are timed exactly, and even when children are adopted, there is a broad range of time in which the child arrives in the new parents' home. Parenthood, therefore, may be intentional or unintentional, but the moment at which one becomes a parent is unpredictable. Furthermore, the transition to pregnancy and from pregnancy to parenthood is an abrupt one.

The third feature of parenting noted by Rossi is its irrevocability. Once a child is born or adopted, there is little opportunity for terminating one's status as a parent. Parents can and do place their children for adoption, but this is relatively unusual and does not necessarily end the relationship for the parent or the child.

The last factor intrinsic to parenthood is the lack of preparation parents are given for their new role. There are few informal and even fewer formal opportunities for learning how to be a parent.

Scholars who have studied Asian American families would add a fifth feature to Rossi's list—primacy of the parent-child relationship. Sylvia Yanagisako (1985) says that a difference between traditional Japanese families and contemporary white middle-class American families is the importance given to parent-child relationships in contrast to husband-wife relationships. When she interviewed Nisei (second-generation Japanese Americans), she found that they felt they were in the middle of these two cultural groups. Nisei believed their parents' generation overemphasized the parent-child relationship and ignored the relationship between husbands and wives. They described their mothers and fathers as having "lived for their children and in turn of having expected too much of them" (Yanagisako 1985, p. 110).

Nisei, in contrast, believe that the conjugal relationship between husband and wife should be the closest. One woman explained, "You have to have more than kids, because the kids are going to leave; you have to think not only of now, but later. You need marriage not only for now but later for the companionship" (Yanagisako 1985, p. 110).

Nisei, however, were also critical of "American" marriage because it goes too far in the other direction. Nisei believed that "American-style parents are too eager to leave their children at home while they seek entertainment and pleasure for themselves. Their egoistic selfish concern for their own interests and recreational pursuits may lead to the neglect of children—a neglect they pay for in problem children, juvenile delinquency, rebellion and ultimately rejection" (Yanagisako 1985, p. 111).

Transition to Parenting

What is the transition to parenthood like for couples expecting their first child? Changes take place in five domains of family life. First, men's and women's identity and inner lives alter after the baby. They feel responsibility they may have never experienced before, and they may feel concerned about problems in the world about which they previously did not worry.

Second, their roles and relationships with each other change as work increases to care for the baby and nurturance for each other may be in shorter supply. Third, they may see shifts in the relationships between themselves and their parents. Grandparents need time to develop a relationship with the new baby and with their children who are now in the new roles of parents. Fourth, roles and relationships outside the family are modified. Friends, coworkers, and bosses may not recognize the energy it takes to be a parent and may expect new parents to continue in their old ways. The fifth domain is new parenting roles and relationships. Even couples who believe that they know how their partner feels about parenting and that they share parenting values may be surprised by the real thing—what the baby should eat or wear, what risks he or she should be exposed to, and how a good parent should respond to the baby's demands. New parents may feel ambivalent about their own feelings as well as critical of those of their spouse (Cowan and Cowan 1999).

This discussion of what parenting and the transition to parenting consists of gives us some good ideas, but it lacks one ingredient—gender. Men and women are similar in some ways in their experience of parenting, but whether one is a mother or a father creates significant differences.

Interviews with new mothers and fathers show, for example, that both men and women are stressed about the amount of time spent with the baby (Walzer 1998). Their experience, however, is quite different. Women worry they do not have enough time to spend with the baby. Men worry that the time they spend with the baby is causing them to be unable to get other tasks done. Mothers and fathers also experience taking care of the baby differently. Mothers describe motherhood as a job. Fathers talk about time with the baby as a pleasurable alternative or escape from the job.

Parenting in the twenty-first century remains a strongly gendered experience. In the following sections, we look at parenting as a gendered experience, examining the experience of mothering and fathering and the differences and tensions between them.

BOX **12.1**

Neglected Children?

Many people believe that children today do not spend as much time with their parents as children did in the past. Parents worry that work and other activities are causing families to neglect children by not being with them as much as mothers and fathers were in previous generations. However, data on the amount of hours available for each child in families today show that the amount of time per child is actually growing.

When we think about time spent with children, we need to think about not only hours spent with our families but also the number of children in families among which a parent's time must be shared. Because the number of children in households has shrunk, parents today are spending more time per child than they were twenty or thirty years ago. Table 12.1 shows this trend. The table indicates that it is true that number of hours of family time declined between 1970 and 1992, but the number of hours per child increased over that same period.

TABLE 12.1   Hours Available for Children per Week

Year	Hours Available per Child's Family	Hours Available per Child
1970	162.8	68.1
1980	154.0	77.5
1990	146.7	76.4
1992	145.6	76.0

Source: Mayer, Susan, 1997. "Indicators of economic well being and parental employment," pp. 237–57, in R. Hauser, B. Brown, and W. Prosser (eds.). *Indicators of children's well being.* New York: Russell Sage.

Mothering

Raising children can be a delightful and gratifying experience. Because of these attractive features of parenting, most women in our society would like to have children, and the favorite number is two (Abma et al. 1997). Genevie and Margolies (1987) asked one thousand one hundred women in a nationally representative sample about their experience of being mothers. About 25 percent of the women said the experience had been mostly positive, and 20 percent said the experience had been mostly negative. The majority of women (55%), however, said they felt ambivalent. Although there were wonderful aspects to being a mother, they also had experienced disillusionment when real mothering did not match the ideal. They were especially disappointed when mothering was boring and burdensome and their husbands were not as involved as they wished.

Although there are real, positive aspects to mothering, in our culture motherhood is idealized. Our ideas about motherhood ignore the problems and sometimes overemphasize the benefits and pleasures. As a result, when women become mothers they may be unprepared for the real experience, and they may feel guilty and inadequate when their own experience does not match the ideal (Lazarre 1986).

This idealized version of motherhood is called the motherhood mystique. The word mystique means that the description has little to do with reality, although people may believe it is the truth or at least something to which they should aspire (Hoffnung 1989). The motherhood mystique tells us that:

1. Women achieve their ultimate fulfillment by becoming mothers. In contrast, fathers are supposed to be delighted by their children, but their other interests are also supposed to continue.
2. The body of work assigned to mothers—caring for child, home, and husband—fits together in a noncontradictory manner. But real mothers often experience difficulties finding time and energy to do all the jobs.
3. In order to be a good mother, a woman must like being a mother and all the work that goes with it.
4. Mothers cannot be independent from men. They must be heterosexual; lesbians cannot be good mothers. The children of single women are "illegitimate."
5. A woman's ardent, exclusive devotion to mothering is good for her children.

Choosing Single Motherhood

Single parent-headed households are a rapidly growing category of family. Nearly one-quarter of never-married women age fifteen to forty-four were mothers in 2000 (Maher 2002). Today 12 percent of white children, 43.1 percent of black children, and 21.3 percent of Hispanic children live with a single mother (Dupree and Primus 2001).

One reason for the sharp increase in births outside of marriage is a decreasing tendency for single women to marry if they become pregnant. In the early 1960s, 52.2 percent of unmarried women between fifteen and thirty-four who became pregnant married before the baby was born. In 1994, this proportion was only 23 percent (Gerstein 2000).

Single mothers are more likely than other parents to be poor. Families least likely to live in poverty are those with one child and two parents (9%). Table 12.2 shows the percentage of households within different racial ethnic categories who live below the poverty line. The table shows that single women householders in all the racial ethnic groups, but

TABLE 12.2   Households Living Below Poverty by Race Ethnicity and Household Type, 2002

Household type	White	Black	Asian	Hispanic
Married couple	5.0%	7.9%	5.9%	15.0%
Single woman headed	22.6	35.8	14.2	35.3
Single man headed	9.9	20.9	12.4	17.0

Source: U.S. Census Bureau 2002c.

especially African American and Hispanic women, are very likely to be poor (Roosa et al 2002; Schaffer 1996).

Single mothers also face greater stress than other parents. McLanahan (1983) examined the Michigan Panel Study of Income Dynamics and found three types of stress in families: the presence of chronic life strains, the occurrence of major life events, and the absence of social and psychological supports. She compared two-parent families to single-parent families and found a higher incidence of major life events among the single-parent families. These included voluntary and involuntary job changes, decrease in income, moves, and illness.

One important source of stress for single mothers is much lower levels of psychological support. Others (Belle 1982) have suggested, however, that support can sometimes involve strain as well. For example, if single mothers seek support among others who themselves are in need of material and social support, they must be willing to reciprocate with the few resources they do have.

As a result of these stresses, poor and single mothers suffer psychological effects (Mednick 1992). These include depression, lower self-esteem, lower feelings of efficacy, and greater pessimism.

Why do women choose single motherhood? Some women do not make a real choice. They choose from limited options when they find themselves with unplanned pregnancies and reluctant grooms or abusive husbands. Others find themselves single parents when their spouse dies.

Some women, however, actively choose to be single parents. Jean Renvoize (1985) interviewed women who had chosen to be single mothers. Many of the women were active in an organization called Single Mothers by Choice a twenty-five-year-old organization that worked to support single mothers, to educate the public about the validity of single-parent families, and to help women thinking about becoming single mothers make their choices (Harmon 2005a). One woman explained why she had made the choice: "I felt that I could go through life without being married, I could be fulfilled without having a man in my life, but I knew I couldn't be fulfilled without at least having experienced a pregnancy and raising a child" (Renvoize 1985, p. 91). About one-third of single women over forty with high-status jobs and no children say they regret not having a child much more than never having married (Harmon 2005a).

Regardless of the way in which people became single parents, those who move from being parents in two-parent households to being single heads of households face a difficult transition. Polly Fassinger (1989) investigated the experience of women and men who became single parents when their marriages ended in divorce. She was interested in finding out how the type of marriage individuals had affected their experiences as single parents.

Fassinger divided marriages into four types: segregated, modified segregated, integrated, and primarily wife-shaped. Segregated marriages were ones in which husbands and wives controlled different sets of tasks—men were breadwinners and decision makers, women were homemakers and mothers. When these couples were divorced and women found themselves single parents, they responded to their new and drastically different situation with feelings of doubt and being overwhelmed, but also with some satisfaction as they became more experienced in making decisions in the areas that had been dominated by their husbands. One woman in this category explained:

I was a dependent wife. My first thought was how am I going to survive? Not financially, but who is gonna make my decisions? But when he was gone, I wondered, "Now, how is this gonna work? Where is my decision-maker?" I wasn't prepared for it. (1989, p. 170)

Men from segregated marriages who became single parents after a divorce felt confident and claimed they saw little difference in their roles.

Modified segregated households are similar to segregated ones, except the wife played the role of a junior partner. The experience of the single parents from these households was similar to that of the parents from segregated marriages. The wives had feelings of self-doubt and uncertainty, but much less so than wives from segregated marriages. Husbands in this group said they did not think there had been much change, although they were slightly more likely to acknowledge the loss of aid from their partners.

Integrated marriages were those in which husbands and wives shared relatively equally in tasks and decision making. Fassinger's sample did not include any wives who had come from this kind of marriage. The single men said that the transition from an integrated marriage to single head of household was significant. They were not sure at first if they would be able to handle it and regretted not having someone with whom to check their decisions. They were the most hesitant and doubtful group of single fathers. One man in this group said:

I think the worst part of that is being wholly responsible for the decisions and nobody really to try out those decisions on. To test them out and talk about them. That's really one of the tougher things. That really wears you down after a while. It's always on you. (1989, p. 176)

The fourth category is the primarily wife-shaped marriage. Although husbands in these marriages retained significant influence and veto power, the wives were active decision makers and handled finances. There were no men in Fassinger's sample who came from this type of marriage. The women who had come from primarily wife-shaped marriages felt little disruption in their transition to single parenthood and expressed satisfaction and enjoyment in their new role. A woman in this category described her experience as a single parent: "I think I felt real stifled living with this person. So many times when I would suggest something it was laughed at or, 'We can't do that.' Now all that's not there, I don't have to worry about it. And if I want to do something, I do it" (1989, p. 172).

Fassinger concludes that gender combines with marriage type to create patterns of reactions to single parenthood. Gender is a key factor in the organization of marriage and together with the variation of marriage types has a critical effect on the experience of the divorced women and men who move from those marriages into single-headed households. Women from segregated marriages and men from integrated marriages have remarkably similar reactions to that transition. And women and men from segregated marriages have dramatically different reactions.

Lesbigay Parents

About 3 million gay men and lesbians are parents and are raising between 5 and 10 million children in their households (Allen 1998). In 2000, one in five gay couples had children under the age of eighteen and one in three lesbian couples did. Approximately one in twelve children in the United States has at least one parent who is lesbian, gay or bisexual (Stacey and Biblarz 2003). Children have been raised by lesbigay parents for as long as they have been by heterosexual parents, but the idea that gay men and lesbians have families is only a decade or so old (Joos 2003). The ideas and the numbers are now growing so rapidly, however, it has been dubbed the "gayby boom" (Salholz 1990; Lotozo 2003).

These families come in three varieties: blended, single parent, and couples having children together. The most common type is blended families to which lesbian mothers bring children from previous heterosexual marriages into their new households, where they share parenting with a partner. A fairly recent development, which is quickly expanding, is the third option—individual lesbians and gay men and couples choosing to become parents (M. Sullivan 1996; Connolly 2002).

Many major cities have support groups for prospective lesbian mothers. Gay fathers are less likely to have support from the gay community (Basow 1992). Books and manuals are being written for all lesbigay parents, and nearly half of Fortune 500 companies now offer domestic partner benefits and many cover a partner's children and provide assistance for adoption by domestic partners (Amour 2005).

Some lesbians choose to become pregnant through sexual intercourse, although this sometimes creates additional social problems because it involves biological fathers rather than unknown sperm donors. New reproductive techniques (NRTs) ranging from low-tech artificial insemination to in vitro fertilization also allow lesbians to bear children.

Surrogate mothers provide opportunities for gay men to become biological fathers. This option, however, has difficulties because the relationship of the biological mother to the child is socially more complicated. In addition, the arrangements usually involve men with substantial financial resources and women in need of money (Benkov 1999).

Adoption is still difficult because the right of lesbians and gay men to adopt is a highly contested political issue. Some political figures have been critical of gay and lesbian parents. Social scientists have played an important role in making the case that LGBT (lesbian, gay, bisexual, and transgendered) families are valid and their children are not adversely affected (Joos 2003). The research provides overwhelming evidence that children who are raised by gay and lesbian parents do not suffer harm as a result of the sexuality of their mothers and fathers (Ferraro, Freker, and Foster 2005).

By the early 1990s, much scientific investigation had been done on this question. The studies show no significant differences between children raised in heterosexual households and those raised by lesbigay parents (Joos 2003). Lesbigay parents are comparable on measures of mental health, self-esteem, parenting skills, and commitment to parenting. Children who are raised by lesbigay parents are no different from those raised by heterosexual parents on measures of psychological well-being and social adjustment such as self esteem, anxiety, depression, behavioral problems, school performance, extracurricular activities, IQ, and ability to make friends. LGBT parents provide their children with as wide an array of role models as from both genders (Allen and Burrell 1996; Joos 2003; Patterson 1992; Patterson and Redding 1996).

A second area of research has shown, in fact, that children who are raised in LGBT households are advantaged in some ways. Lesbigay parents are somewhat more nurturant and tolerant than heterosexual parents. Their children are more open minded and express a greater sense of social responsibility. Daughters have higher self-esteem and higher aspirations to enter careers that are male dominated such as astronauts, engineers, and physicians. Sons are less physically aggressive, more caring, have higher self-esteem, and aspire to a wider range of careers (Joos 2003).

In the 1990s, tens of thousands of mental health professionals from every major organization that works with children and families, including the American Psychological Association, the American Academy of Child and Adolescent Psychiatrists, and the National Association of Social Workers, have declared that in their professional opinion "presumption that a parent who is in an openly gay or lesbian relationship is an unfit custodian has no basis in fact" (Patterson and Redding 1996, p. 45).

The American Psychological Association (APA 1995) issued the following summary of their findings on children in gay and lesbian households.

> The results of existing research comparing gay and lesbian parents to heterosexual parents and children of gay or lesbian parents to children of heterosexual parents are quite uniform: common stereotypes are not supported by the data. . . . In summary, there is no evidence to suggest that lesbians and gay men are unfit to be parents or that psychosocial development among children of gay men and lesbians is compromised in any respect relevant to that among offspring of heterosexual parents. Not a single study has found children of gay or lesbian parents to be disadvantaged in any significant respect relative to children of heterosexual parents. Indeed, the evidence to date suggests that home environments provided by gay and lesbian parents are as likely as those provided by heterosexual parents to support and enable children's psycho-social growth.

Despite the political debate, the legal system is beginning to catch up with the professional community and increasingly supports the rights of gay men and lesbians to adopt children. Nine states (CA, MA, NJ, NM, NY, OH, VT, WA, WI, RI, and Washington, D.C.) currently allow openly gay and lesbian parents to adopt children as a couple. All but six other states allow single gay men and lesbians to adopt and foster children. Five states have restrictions (UT, MS, AR, ND, OK) and only one, Florida, has banned it (National Adoption Clearing House 2005; National Gay and Lesbian Task Force 2005). Lesbians and gay men who wish to be adoptive parents have been most successful making private arrangements with biological parents. The placement must still be approved by a state or private agency that may have policies restricting lesbian and gay access to adoption. Since the evaluation of the adoption takes place after the child is with the new parents, however, it is more likely to be positive.

In 2005, an important legal decision was made by the California Supreme Court, declaring that "We perceive no reason why both parents of a child cannot be women." The decision broke new legal ground for same-sex parents by ruling that lesbian and gay partners who plan a family and raise a child together should be considered legal parents after a breakup, with the same rights and responsibilities as heterosexual parents.

This was the first time a court granted full parental status to same-sex partners regardless of their marital status or biological connection with their children. The judges were ruling on three cases in which lesbian partners had cooperated in conceiving and rearing children in a family setting but then parted. The court decided that they were both legal parents—entitling them to visitation over an ex-partner's objections and requiring them to pay child support. The ruling will also apply to gay men who agree to raise a child together (Egelko 2005).

The growing number of gay parents is not just a result of changes in technology and legal policy. Changes have also occurred in the gay community. You should recall from Chapter 9 that there is a debate within the community over the question of marriage. Some gay people believe that assimilation into the dominant society is personally and politically useful, and they support obtaining rights to marriage. Others in the gay community prefer to create new forms of intimacy and family that are not modeled after heterosexual marriage and that are not tied to the current laws—families we choose. Choosing children also reflects this debate as lesbian mothers try to be good mothers without accepting too many of the oppressive features of motherhood and without falling into gender-stereotyped roles with their partners (Sullivan 1996).

One special problem nearly all lesbigay parents face, however, is homophobia. Homophobia is the hatred and fear of homosexuals and lesbians. Homophobia is often expressed in the courts. In divorce and custody decisions, lesbian mothers must face accusations that they are not adequate mothers even though research indicates that they are similar to other mothers and that they appear, in fact, to be more child-centered. Lesbian mothers are likely to lose custody in divorce cases and gay men also face this kind of discrimination (Falk 1989; Kendell 2003; Perrin 2002; Robson 1992).

Children of gay parents also face challenges. Children from gay and lesbian households face more stigma from peers about their own sexuality (Joos 2003). In addition, their interactions within families with their parents must negotiate stigmas from the outside world. Bozett (1984, 1988) interviewed children of gay fathers to examine their experience. He found that while the children accepted their fathers' homosexuality, they worried others would think they were gay because their fathers were. The children used a number of strategies to address this dilemma. Some attempted to control their father's behavior, for example, by not allowing him to appear with a lover in their presence. Others would not allow certain friends to meet their father. Bozett also found that gay fathers frequently tried to protect their children by avoiding disclosure of their homosexuality or advising their children to refer to the father's lover as uncle or housemate. Some fathers who had custody of their children placed them in schools outside the neighborhood in order to give the children more privacy. The fathers Bozett interviewed, however, were also concerned that their children understand that, although the wider society disapproves of homosexuality, it is not a negative attribute, and the gay fathers are as moral and virtuous as other men.

Lesbian mothers and their children also face overt hostile remarks and ostracism by homophobes in other settings, such as schools and the community. Such adversity is not necessarily all bad, however, because it allows opportunities for the children of lesbian mothers to learn about standing up for their convictions (Drexler 2005; Garner 2004; Rohrbaugh 1979).

Teenage Mothers

Between 1955 and 2003, the adolescent fertility rate dropped sharply. That's right, the proportion of teenagers who bore children has declined in the past five decades and now is at a record low of 22 births per every 1,000 women aged 15 to 17 (National Institutes of Health

2005). Table 12.3 shows the decline in birthrate from 1955 to 2000 (Alan Guttmacher Institute 2004). The birthrate is the number of live births per 1,000 women. The table shows the birthrate for all women nineteen years old and younger by race. The rate is higher for black women and Hispanic women. The rates declined in all racial ethnic categories. Data for Hispanic, Native American, and Asian American women are not available in many years. The rates for Asians are lowest, and the rates for Native Americans are between whites and blacks.

At the same time that the birthrate has been declining, concern over adolescent pregnancy and childbearing has grown. In 1995, President Clinton declared teen motherhood as America's most serious problem (Glassner 1999). Googling teen mothers problem brings up millions of sites dedicated to this issue. In the political scene, President Bush is now recommending spending $270 milllion to persuade young people to practice premarital abstinence (Reuters 2005).

Why is concern growing while the incidence of teen pregnancy is declining? There are several different points of view on why teen mothers are seen as so problematic. Some scholars maintain that health problems are more common in pregnancy and childbirth for young women. "Compared to mothers who have babies later in life, teen mothers are in poorer health, have medically more treacherous pregnancies, more stillbirths and newborn deaths, and more low-birthweight and medically compromised babies" (Luker 1992, p. 164). But this view has been questioned by others. First, they argue that solid evidence of a link between health problems and youth is lacking because few studies have been done, and those that have tend to overstate the negative aspects of early motherhood (Furstenberg, Brooks-Gunn, and Morgan, 1987; Lamb and Elster 1986).

Second, critics maintain that the health problems that have been associated with young women having babies are more likely a result of socioeconomic factors than age. According to this perspective, poverty, not youth, should be blamed for most health problems of teen mothers and their babies. Research indicates that when young mothers are provided with good nutrition, prenatal care, and pediatric care, the outcomes for them and their children are good (Carlson et al., 1986; Furstenberg, Brooks-Gunn, and Morgan 1987). When socioeconomic variables are considered in research that compares younger and older mothers, the differences in health outcomes are greatly reduced or disappear (Phoenix 1991).

TABLE 12.3   Birthrates for Teenage Mothers, 1955–2000, by Race

	1955	1960	1965	1970	1975	1980	1990	2000	**Percent Decline**
White	79.1	79.4	60.6	57.4	46.5	44.7	48	43.2	45.4 (since 1955)
Black	167.2	156.1	144.6	140.7	111.8	100.0	110	77.2	70.7 (since 1955)
Hispanic	—	—	—	—	—	—	101.6	87.1	14.3 (since 1980)
Native American	—	—	—	—	—	—	82	72.0 (1998)	21.0
Asian	—	—	—	—	—	—	29	28.0 (1998)	3.0

Source: Alan Guttmacher Institute 2004; Lewin 1998, p. A21; U.S. Census Bureau 2000g; U.S. Department of Health and Human Services 1990, p. 78.

A third critique of the argument that teen childbirth is medically problematic is that positive outcomes for younger mothers have been ignored. Arline Geronimus, for example, reported to the American Association for the Advancement of Science that at least some health problems may actually be greater for women beyond their teens. Her research shows that poor women who delay childbirth risk greater health problems and possible sterility. Furthermore, Geronimus notes that social support from the pregnant teens' mothers on whom they rely for help in raising their babies may not be as accessible if those grandmothers are older (*Charlotte Observer* 1990).

Finally, even if health problems are a result of youth, we are still left with the question of why teen pregnancies were perceived to be so much more prevalent and problematic in the past few decades than they were in previous decades. E. Jones et al. (1986) has examined that question.

Jones argues that there are five reasons why concern emerged and escalated. First, because of the baby boom, in the 1960s and 1970s teenagers made up a large proportion of the total population, and anything they did became a matter of controversy and concern.

Second, while the proportion of teens who bear children has declined, it has not declined as rapidly as the fertility rate for nonteens. This means that of all the babies born in the United States, the proportion of babies born to teenage mothers has increased. Furthermore, compared with other industrialized Western countries, the rate of teenage pregnancy in the United States is much higher.

Third, pregnant teenagers are more visible because until 1972 they could be legally expelled from school. Since 1972, however, it has been illegal to expel pregnant students, and therefore they remain more active and visible in the community.

Fourth, unmarried teenage mothers are now more likely to keep their babies rather than to have them adopted. This also makes their fertility rate more visible.

Fifth, while the birthrate among teens has declined in the past forty years, the rate of pregnancy has not declined as rapidly. Among women under age 19, the birthrate dropped by 26 percent between 1991 and 2001. But the pregnancy rate only declined by 19 percent during that same time period (U.S. Department of Health and Human Services 2002). Many young women who become pregnant but do not give birth have obtained abortions. About one-fifth of all abortions performed on women in the United States are for those under the age of nineteen (U.S. Census Bureau 2005a). And as we saw in Chapter 8, abortion is a controversial practice.

Finally, fewer teen mothers are getting married. In the 1950s, many teenagers became pregnant but were quickly married, which "hid" them. Unmarried teen mothers are no longer hidden. In 1970 one-third of teen mothers who gave birth were single. In 2003, 81 percent were single (CDC 2005a).

Ann Phoenix (1991) argues that it is this factor that is most responsible for making teen childbirth a problem. She asserts that the difference between teen pregnancy in the 1950s and in the 1980s is that contemporary teen pregnancy makes more visible the sexual activity of young unmarried women. This creates a moral dilemma, especially for growing conservative forces who believe only married people should be sexually active.

In addition, because young single women are less likely to have access to jobs that will allow them to earn enough to financially support their children, they make visible another politically difficult question: Who should be responsible for poor children? In

Chapter 4 we observed that poverty is a growing problem and that young people are especially likely to be poor because they are attempting to enter the labor market during a time when jobs are diminishing. Young mothers are trapped in the position of being poor and responsible for children, a combination that is condemned (Bonell 2004).

The debate continues between those who advocate eliminating young mothers' poverty and those who advocate eliminating their childbearing. The governmental office on adolescent pregnancy, the numerous state task forces, proposed programs on abstinence, and media articles are examples of the latter. They maintain that young women's childbearing must stop. They suggest policies that punish young women who bear children by placing their children in foster homes and preventing the mothers from obtaining welfare (Luker 1992).

On the other side of the debate are welfare rights organizations and the young women themselves, who argue that the elimination of poverty should be the target. Young women who have few other options because of poverty, poor job prospects, and school difficulties are more likely to get pregnant (Luker 1996; Musich 1993; Sonfield and Gold 2005). Teenage parents, contrary to popular images, are not middle-class people who became poor simply because they had babies. Rather, they became teenage parents because they were poor to begin with. When young women see little hope for their futures, they may drift into sexual relations, pregnancy, and parenthood (Corsaro 1997). Creating better life opportunities will lower the birthrate among young women (Luker 1999b).

Others argue that that lack of access to sex education and contraceptives are part of the problem, and these issues need to be addressed. They note that federal funding for family planning dropped drastically in the 1980s and 1990s and although it has inched up since then it still has not recovered from those cuts (Sonfield and Gold 2005). If we want to help young women avoid pregnancy, we need to ensure access to birth control information and materials.

Finally, some women prefer to have children while they are young and single, and the health care and sustenance for those babies and mothers should be guaranteed. Furthermore, the structural factors such as low-wage jobs and unemployment that make young women unable to support themselves should be addressed (Williams and Kornblum 1991).

The discussion so far suggests that young women exercise some choice in their sexual behavior and in their pregnancies. Sometimes they make an informed decision that runs contrary to the dominant ideas. They choose to be sexually active, become pregnant, and raise their children despite their youth and usually despite their singlehood. Sometimes they make these choices from a limited set of alternatives. But there is a third category that has recently gained attention and that is much more problematic. These are young women who may have had little choice in their sexual encounters because they were involved with men much older than they.

A national survey of ten thousand teen mothers found that half of the fathers of the babies born to fifteen- to seventeen-year-old women were over twenty. Twenty percent of the fathers were more than six years older than the young women. The younger the mother, the larger the age gap. Fathers of the high school girls' babies were 4.2 years older. Fathers of the junior high school girls were 6.7 years older. A similar study in Washington State found that the average age of men who had impregnated twelve- to seventeen-year-old mothers was twenty-four (Corsaro 1997). Can a thirteen-year-old girl make real choices about sexuality and pregnancy with an eighteen-year-old man? Can a fifteen-year-old girl with a twenty-six-year-old man?

What Do Teen Mothers Have to Say about Motherhood?   Being a young mother is not the same experience for all women. One study of teenage Chicana mothers found that they fell into three very different categories in describing their experience (Valdez 2004). Some felt that being a mother was burdensome especially because of the work that was involved and the difficulties interacting with the father and other family members. One young woman said, "It's hard. I like to sleep late but my son doesn't. He wakes up every two hours and wants milk so I have to get up. I can't do my chores around the house because he cries. When he was born I used to work, go to school and go to night school. I stay home more because I was afraid he would think granma was mom" (Valdez 2004, p. 110).

Others had a more mixed perception seeing motherhood as a huge responsibility but one that also had rewards. A third group felt that being a young mother had important benefits. One explained, "I was excited when I was pregnant with her, knowing she was going to be born and I could finally hold her in my arms, I really enjoyed being a mom, feeding her and caring for her." Another described how being a mother had changed her positive ways. She said, "I am more patient now, which I wasn't before he came along" (Valdez 2004, p. 105).

Delaying Childbirth

At the other end of the spectrum are the increasing numbers of women who are delaying childbearing. Table 12.4 shows the number of births to women over thirty. The table indicates that a growing number of babies are born to women in this older age group.

Compared with other mothers, women who delay childbirth have more education, more prestigious jobs, higher incomes, and fewer children; are more likely to have planned the pregnancy; and spend more money on their children (Baldwin and Nord 1984).

When the larger proportion of older women bearing children and young women bearing children are taken together, a trend becomes evident. Mothering has changed in its link to a particular age. Women as a group appear to be extending their childbearing over a

TABLE 12.4   Birthrates for Mothers over 30, 1980–2002 (Live Births per 1,000 Women over 30)

Age	1980	1985	1990	1996	2002
30–34	61.9	69.1	80.8	82.1	91.5
35–39	19.8	24.0	31.7	34.9	41.4
40–44	3.9	4.0	5.5	6.8	8.3

Source: CDC 2003a.

longer time. This change in itself is unsettling to those whose ideas about motherhood limit it to a specific age range—early twenties to early thirties. When these mothers are poor or unmarried, it is viewed with even greater skepticism.

High Technology and Mothering

A central theme of this book is the recognition of the importance of social context to the organization of families. The effect of advanced technology on mothering is a dramatic example of this relationship. For many centuries people have used contraceptives and performed abortions, which are examples of the application of technology to mothering. In recent years, the use of these applications, which are now called new reproductive technologies (NRTs), has been stepped up.

NRTs can be divided into three categories: (1) those that inhibit the development of new life; (2) those that monitor it; and (3) those that create it (Achilles 1990). The inhibition of new life includes contraception, abortion, and sterilization. The general character of technology used for this purpose has not changed dramatically, although recent applications are often more effective and efficient. Some are also more dangerous, like the birth-control pill and some IUDs.

NRTs that monitor new life include ultrasound, amniocentesis (sampling fetal cells by extracting some of the amniotic fluid), chorionic villi sampling (sampling fetal cells from the pregnant woman's cervix to determine abnormalities and the sex of the fetus), fetal monitoring (monitoring fetal heartbeat, especially during labor), and fetal surgery (Achilles 1990).

The third type of NRT, concerned with the creation of life, is the newest and has produced the most difficult ethical and political questions. These techniques include alternative insemination (sperm is inserted into a woman's vaginal canal by some means other than sexual intercourse), sperm banks, surrogate mothers, in vitro fertilization (an egg is fertilized outside of a woman's body and then implanted in her uterus), frozen embryos, and surrogate embryo transfer (Achilles 1990). Sperm banks pay men about $50 to $100 (men with PhDs can charge more for their sperm) a vial and then sell it to customers for $150 to $600, which includes shipping and handling. They estimate that about thirty-thousand children are born every year with sperm donor fathers (Harmon 2005b).

Advances to overcome infertility can be seen as a wonderful opportunity, but they can also create problems for the infertile individual or couple. About 10 percent of Americans of reproductive age experience some kind of infertility, and it appears to be a growing phenomenon (National Center for Health Statistics 1997). In one-third of the cases, the infertility is attributed to the man, in one-third to the woman, and in one-third to either unknown causes or those shared by the couple (Achilles 1990).

The procedures sound straightforward, technical, and unproblematic. The social meanings of the activities and their product, however, are much messier (Stanworth 1990). For example, the Catholic Church considers alternative insemination adulterous. Others may not take this position but are troubled by the way in which sperm donors are chosen. Currently sperm donors are actually sperm vendors who may sell their sperm for about $25 per ejaculate. One vendor in Achilles' (1990) research had donated 240 times. Recently the

FDA has established strict tissue donation regulations that may address some of these technical problems (Kaiser Family Foundation Report 2004).

A second set of issues arises from the way in which these NRTs redefine infertility. A woman who in previous years would have been told she could not have children is now told she might be able to if she is willing to go through sometimes enormous physical procedures. Some women may welcome any opportunity to conceive. Others may feel pressured to try to overcome infertility (E. May 1995). Some of the procedures used include hysterosalpingograms (dye is injected into the fallopian tubes and uterus), endometrial biopsies (surgical removal of samples of tissue from inside the uterus), and drugs to regulate ovulation or sustain pregnancy (Achilles 1990). In vitro fertilization involves taking drugs to stimulate egg production, daily blood tests, pelvic examinations, ultrasound, and when the technique is successful, an increased number of multiple births.

Third, NRTs create problems for children. The product of the procedures is a child. Since the relationships among surrogates, gamete donors, and recipient donors is a financial one, the child is a commodity. If the commodity is "imperfect," "damaged," or "defective," the consumers may find it unacceptable, and the child may be abandoned by all parties. Such a case was documented when a handicapped child was born to a surrogate mother (Rosenblatt 1983). Older children may also feel concern about "missing" relationships with biological fathers and especially siblings.

They may be able to find some of the relatives through Donor Sibling Registry, a Web site that allows parents and offspring to enter their contact information and search for others by sperm bank and donor number. Most of the matches are between half-siblings. One teenage daughter of a sperm donor described her encounter with another offspring of the same donor, #150, "The first time we were on the phone, it was awkward," Danielle said. "I was like, 'We'll get over it,' and she said, 'Yeah, we're sisters.' It was so weird to hear her say that. It was cool." In an e-mail, she explained the irony of having children with anonymous sperm donors. "I hate when people that use D.I. [donor insemination] say that biology doesn't matter (cough, my mom, cough). Because if it really didn't matter to them, then why would they use D.I. at all? They could just adopt or something and help out kids in need" (Harmon 2005b).

BOX **12.2**

Childbirth

One area of parenting on which medical technology has had a strong effect throughout most of the twentieth century is childbirth. For many women in the United States, birth was a medical event in which they played what seemed to be a minor part. And the part they did play, especially before the 1970s, was primarily to stay out of the way of the real actors, the physicians (Rothman 1982, 1989b). In the early 1970s, Nancy Stoller Shaw (1974) observed a typical American birth:

> The woman was placed on a delivery table similar to an operating table. The majority were numbed from the waist down, while they lay in the lithotomy position (legs spread apart and up in stirrups), with their hands at their sides, often strapped there, to prevent their contaminating the "sterile field."

The women were unable to move their bodies below the chest. Mothers were clearly not the active participants. That role was reserved for the doctor. (Rothman 1989b, p. 156)

Rothman (1989b) defines *ideology* as the way in which a group looks at the world and organizes its thinking about the world. The ideology that underlies the scene above of the woman in labor is a medicalized one. The birth is a medical event. The woman is a patient under the supervision of physicians. She is in a position—on her back with her feet lifted and spread apart—that is to the advantage of the physician. She is in a hospital where, if the birth does not go in the manner described in the medical texts, medical equipment is available. She is in a sterile environment, hooked up to an IV and monitors to assess her condition.

This medical view of birthing has been widely criticized, and other birth formats have been allowed to creep back in. These alternative birthing experiences are informed by alternative ideologies. Alternative birth settings are homes and birthing rooms. The women are not lying flat; they may not even be lying down. Birth may occur with the woman in a squatting position, using gravity to help her push. She is surrounded by people she knows, not hospital workers. She becomes the centerpiece of the event rather than just a birth canal.

Rothman claims that the changes in birthing that have occurred as a result of the demand for midwives, home births, and birthing rooms have had a radicalizing effect on the health care workers who attend births and have called into question so-called facts about giving birth (1989b).

For example, many physicians had believed that vomiting and nausea were a natural and common part of labor. Midwives who do not work in a medical setting and who do not forbid women in labor to eat and drink, as the hospitals do, have found that nausea is uncommon.

Another example of this contrast is in the medical setting when full dilation of the cervix occurs. If the mother does not immediately begin pushing the baby out, the situation is called second-stage arrest and is considered pathological. The physician uses drugs or mechanical techniques to end the interruption and continue the birth. In the nonhospital setting, midwives have observed women who were exhausted after reaching full dilation take a nap before resuming labor, and deliver healthy babies (Rothman 1989b).

These examples, and there are many more, show that the medicalization of birth has created medical problems, which have then been reformulated to be the normal, natural experience of birth. Demedicalizing the experience and working with a mother as a unique individual and the central figure will improve not only the emotional and social experience of birthing but also the physiological one as well.

Demedicalizing birth, however, continues to be a political question. Midwives provide an alternative to medicalized birth. Midwives treat pregnant and birthing women as people who must be seen as part of the whole social context, not as draped bodies that arrive at the delivery table. "Midwives do not 'deliver' babies. They teach women how to give birth" (Rothman 1989b).

Heavily medicalized births in the traditional sense, however, continue. For example, between 1970 and 1989 the rate of cesarean sections increased from 5.5 percent to 23.8 percent. Since then it has remained stable and was about 22 percent in 2000 (Martin, Hamilton, and Venture 2001).

What about Fathers?

"Like mothering, fathering should be thought of as a social relationship" (Rothman 1989a, p. 536). In the discussion on Baby M later in the chapter, Rothman explains her assertion that the link between children and parents should not be regarded as primarily a genetic one. She argues that it is our social relationship with children that creates parenthood. For biological mothers this relationship begins with the physical contribution women make to their children's lives in pregnancy and birth. For fathers it begins with the care a father provides for his child through his care for the pregnant mother and for the child after he or she is born. Fathering, according to Rothman, cannot be defined as impregnating a woman who will then raise the child. Fathering must involve "doing the work of attentive love" (Rothman 1989a, p. 537).

Bringing Fathers into Parenting

Many people share the opinion expressed by Rothman that men should be more involved in child raising (Pleck 1987; Rotundo 1985). Pleck (1987) notes that ideas about fathers have changed over time and that recent images include a stronger role for fathers in the care of their children. According to Pleck, in the late nineteenth and early twentieth centuries the dominant image of the father was as distant breadwinner. Then from 1945 until the mid-1960s, fathers were the sex-role model. Since then a new model of father has emerged—father as nurturer (Coltrane 1996; Pleck 1987).

Ralph LaRossa (1992) suggests that this change has been more a change in the culture of fatherhood than in the conduct of fatherhood. By this he means that, on the average, ideas and rhetoric about fathering have outstripped real behavior changes. In Chapter 7, for example, we discovered that women are still responsible for the majority of unpaid domestic work, including child care. And many fathers still think of themselves and are thought by others as their wives' helpers in child care (Walzer 1998).

Lamb's (1987) work measures changes in the last two decades in the amount of time mothers and fathers spent with their children. Lamb defines engagement as "time spent in one-on-one interaction with a child (whether feeding, helping with homework, or playing catch in the back yard)" (LaRossa 1992, p. 524). The amount of engagement time increased among fathers by 26 percent between 1976 and 1981, while it increased for mothers by only 7 percent (Lamb 1987). It is necessary to look at the actual number of hours for mothers and fathers in order to get a complete picture, however. The number of hours of engagement time for fathers went from 2.29 to 2.88 hours per week. For mothers, engagement time went from 7.96 to 8.54 hours per week. For both mothers and fathers, this amounts to an increase of about 5 minutes per day, and mothers still spend much more engagement time with their children than do fathers.

Others (LaRossa and LaRossa 1981) have found that in addition to spending different amounts of time, fathers also do different things with their children than do mothers. Fathers spend a larger proportion of their engagement time playing with their children, while mothers spend more time in caregiving activities. The kinds of play that fathers engage in often were those that could be carried out in a semi-involved manner, such as watching television together. In addition, others sometimes view their involvement with their children as a job, an activity in which they had to participate, and they prided themselves on discovering ways to make child care as noninterfering as possible with their other activities. For example, in one study, a father explained that the hours for which he was responsible for his infant son were hours that the baby slept, and he could get two hours of his own work done while watching the baby sleep.

Our expectations about fathers are increasingly calling for greater involvement of men in all kinds of care for their children. The behavior of fathers, however, sometimes falls short of those expectations. What happens when ideas about fatherhood and the experience of fatherhood are disparate? LaRossa and LaRossa (1981) refer to this as asynchronous social change. They argue that the result is mixed messages for children who are spending more time with their fathers but who may become aware of the burdensome job-like character with which their fathers view that time. It may also create marital conflict and guilt-ridden fathers.

New Fathers in Word and Deed

Nevertheless, in some households men have attempted to bring their conduct as fathers in line with their beliefs and have begun to play an important part in the raising of children (Hertz 1998). One recent study shows that African American men and Hispanic men may be taking the lead in this regard. Black children's fathers were less warm but monitor their children more than do white and Hispanic fathers. Both Hispanic and black fathers take more responsibility for child rearing than do white fathers (Hofferth 2003).

Diane Ehrensaft (1987) looked at what happens in families where men took an active role with their children. She defines mothering as an activity having two components in which both men and women can participate. First, it involves the day-to-day primary care of a child. Second, it includes a consciousness of being directly in charge of the child's upbringing. Ehrensaft chose a group of heterosexual couples with children who shared mothering and asked them about their experience. She found that shared mothering is difficult to implement. Both men and women find that there are barriers to shared mothering within themselves and from the outside.

Men are rewarded for mothering by their increased access to children. The trade-offs are difficult, however. Men who mother must give up the privilege of being the distant father, and they must do work like changing diapers that is regarded as debasing in our society. Fathers who mother are also likely to be responded to negatively by others, who feel they are behaving in an unmanly manner or shirking their real duties when they are caring for their children (Ehrensaft 1987).

In order to be involved, men often must be willing to resist the claims that paid employment makes on their time. These fathers must challenge three powerful cultural values. First, they must set aside the importance of materialism in order to reduce living expenses. Second, they must alter their belief that to be successful, a man must be successful at work. Third, they must relinquish privileges their gender often holds to have priority relative to their wife when decisions are made about how to allot household time outside of family (Daly and Dienhart 1998).

Women benefit from relinquishing some of their responsibilities for mothering because it allows them more time to participate in other activities. Women may also find, however, that sharing mothering is difficult for them as well. First, although they are able to share the physical tasks of mothering, they may still feel guilty for not doing them. Second, they may discover that mothering is an important part of their identity, and if they are unable to establish themselves as successfully as they would like in extra-mother activities like paid work, they may feel caught between identities, without an arena of success.

Ehrensaft claims that despite these difficulties, shared mothering is a worthy goal because it can have important positive effects on parents, children, and our society. She lists seven specific results of having both women and men mother:

1. Liberates women from full-time mothering.
2. Affords opportunities for more equal relationships between women and men.
3. Allows men more access to children.
4. Allows children to be parented by two nurturing figures and frees them from the confines of an "overinvolved" adult who has no other outside identity.
5. Provides new socialization experiences and possibly increases the likelihood of less gender-stereotyped behaviors and ideologies in children.
6. Challenges the myth that women are better equipped biologically for parenting.
7. Puts pressure on political, economic, and social structures for changes such as paternity and maternity leaves, job sharing, and freely available child care facilities. (Ehrensaft 1987, p. 45)

Single Fathers

Much of the literature on fathers compares fathers to mothers in two-parent families. One in every six single-parent households is headed by a father. Although the percentage is small—2.4 percent of all households—the numbers are substantial—2 million households (U.S. Census Bureau 2004h). And almost three and a half million children live with their single fathers. In addition, the single-father-headed household is a rapidly growing family type up from 393,000 in 1970 (U.S. Census Bureau 2004h).

What happens when fathers are left to parent on their own in single-parent households? Barbara Risman (1987) investigated this question using a questionnaire survey examining parenting in four family types: single mothers, single fathers, two-parent households where the father was in the paid labor force and the mother was not, and two-paycheck households.

Risman (1987) measured variation in parenting by looking at three factors: time spent in housework, parent-child intimacy, and overt affection. She found that single fathers, single mothers, and housewives spent more time than married fathers or married employed mothers on housework. Single fathers did not hire others to do the work for them and were forced to take responsibility for these household tasks.

The second factor, parent-child intimacy, was measured by how often children shared their emotions—sadness, loneliness, anger, happiness, pride—with their parents. Here she found that femininity was the most important predictor of parent-child intimacy. Parents who considered themselves more feminine on a range of issues were more likely to report higher rates of parent-child intimacy. This was true regardless of the sex of the parent. Fathers who were more feminine (according to personality scales) were more likely to report parent-child intimacy than mothers or fathers who were less feminine. Single fathers reported levels of femininity similar to those of employed mothers, suggesting that the activity of parenting may create different expressions of personality, which in turn helps fathers build parent-child intimacy.

The third factor was overt affection, which was measured by the amount of physical contact—hugging, cuddling, wrestling—children had with their parents and the kinds of interactions that took place when the parent and child were alone with each other. This factor was affected by the sex of the parent and the parental role. Mothers, regardless of household type, reported displaying more overt affection. But parents in two-paycheck families were more likely to report overt affection than single mothers or fathers and married fathers in one-paycheck families. In this case, both single fathers and single mothers report less overt affection than married mothers in two-paycheck families.

Risman (1987) concludes that the activities of parenting have an important effect on the behavior and personalities of people who do that parenting. Fathers who become primary parents learn to be capable of caring for their children, and they begin to behave similar to women parents. The change cannot begin with ideas but with action that engages men in the activities of primary caregivers.

Other Fathers

In Chapter 5 we looked at the concept of other mothers, which refers to women who cooperate with legal and biological mothers to help raise children in extended community-based families (Collins 1990). Other mothers is an idea that emerged in research on African American families; other fathers also appear to be an important part of African American families (Lempert 1999). Other fathers are men who "assume financial responsibility in part or in whole for the children of other men; or who model honesty, respectability, social wisdom and race pride; or who consistently maintain a positive, interactive presence in the lives of children in their extended families or the community" (Lempert 1999, p. 190). Lempert has named three kinds of other fathers: one-step-removed fathers, stand-up fathers, and stand-in fathers.

One-step-removed fathers are grandfathers who step in to raise grandchildren when the children's parents are unable. They assume responsibility as financial providers, major decision makers, disciplinarians, and role models.

The second type is stand-up fathers. In poor and minority neighborhoods, almost one in three African American men aged twenty to twenty-nine is either in prison, on probation, or on parole (Lempert 1999). Incarceration pulls these men away from their families. Even though the fathers are out of the household, however, some remain active in their children's lives. In Lempert's interviews, one such man called his daughter every day to express his concern for her and to continue to be involved in her everyday activities.

The third type of other fathers are stand-in fathers. Some of these men are extended family members like uncles and cousins, or fictive kin relations. Others are members of the community or church, and some are members of organizations like Boys Club. They provide role models of successful and nurturant men, opportunities to participate in community resources on field trips, and academic support and encouragement.

Coparenting

So far this chapter has been divided by gender looking at the experience of being mothers or fathers. What about the experience of being a parent, coparenting with another parent? Researchers who have looked at coparenting in Mexican American families find that six dimensions play an important role in that experience: joint decision making, support, coordination, compensation, cooperation, and conflict. These dimensions are important when both mothers and fathers live with their children as well as when coparents are divorced but continue to raise their children together.

Coparents speak of joint decision making, negotiating behind the scenes in order to present a united front to their children. One mother explained, "But I'll never say anything in front of the girls. We always make that it's where we can talk about it, because then they're always going to be either coming to mom or going to dad trying to take sides" (Cardera et al. 2000, p. 116).

A second dimension is supporting one another by one parent playing a leading role while the other backed him or her up. The united front was often not just two equal parents, but one parent taking the lead. Parents described ways they backed one another up or took over when the other parent had either already tried or was being challenged by the children.

Third, coparents talked about coordination. This included logistical negotiations like who would pick someone up from school or who would bathe the baby while the other made dinner. Parents worked a "split shift" coordinating their activities so that they both shared the work and the pleasures.

Compensation was the fourth dimension. Mothers and fathers talked about the ways in which they compensated for each other's strengths and weaknesses. One father explained, "Well, when you tell your daughter to do something 'Hey do it and don't question my authority.' Where with her mother, you know, she can try her to the end" (Cardera, Fitzpatrick, and Wampler 2000, p. 121).

The fifth dimension was conflict. Mothers and fathers recognized that they did not always agree. Some of them went along with the other to maintain the united front despite their misgivings. Others debated the issues and tried to change the other parent's behavior. The most difficult issues they described had to do with punishment where one parent felt the other was too harsh.

The sixth dimension was cooperating. Parents viewed each other as equally capable and equally responsible, but they might not necessarily agree about what a child should be doing. In those cases they had to cooperate by negotiating a compromise.

This study reminds us that coparenting may be different than being a mother or a father and that it requires many complex skills and practice to raise children, especially in cooperation with other adults.

Childless by Choice

Women today are the first generation to have nearly equal opportunities in education and careers which increases the cost of having children. Legal access to abortion and contraceptives also means they have grown up assuming they have control over when and if they will have children, and many are making the choice not to have children (Fisher 2003). But American society continues to be one where we are surrounded by messages that say we must bear children in order to be normal adults. We are also surrounded by people having children. In the late nineteenth century, research showed that 30 percent of wives were childless, often by choice, using abstinence, abortion, diaphragms, and condoms to limit their fertility (Degler 1980). We now have more effective contraception, but in 2002, 82 percent of all women in the United States between the ages of forty and forty-four had borne at least one child (U.S. Census Bureau 2003f). A substantial number of women are childless by choice. In 1995, 5.4 million women had no children and expected none in the future; 6.6 percent (4.1 million) of all women were voluntarily childless; and 2 percent (1.2 million) were involuntarily childless. The proportion of childless women ages 40 to 44 has steadily increased since 1976 (U.S. Census Bureau 2003f).

What is the experience of people who are childless in such a pronatalist environment? Couples who have chosen to remain childless are often met with negative reactions because of their choice. The negative reactions can be divided into three categories: the diagnostic model, the deprivation model, and the labeling model (Veevers 1980). The diagnostic model refers to people who believe that a person who chooses to remain childless is maladjusted by virtue of that fact alone.

The deprivation model describes people who believe that people without children are not maladjusted because they have chosen childlessness. They believe they become maladjusted, however, because they are not allowed the experience of having children. People with this point of view argue that having children is a critical factor in developing full emotional and sexual maturity.

The third model, labeling, refers to people who claim that people who choose to remain childless are not necessarily maladjusted and that the experience of having children is not necessary to fully maturing. They believe that remaining childless, however, does put a person at a serious social disadvantage because of the way in which others perceive childless people.

Veevers (1980) interviewed 156 married women and men who had deliberately avoided having children to see what their experience had been. He looked at the factors involved in their decisions, the pressures they felt, the way in which they coped with pronatalism, and the character of their child-free marriages.

The couples Veevers studied followed two paths in their decision not to have children. In one-third of the couples, at least one person had decided before marriage that he or she did not want to have children, and an agreement was made between the man and woman as part of the marriage "contract." In two-thirds of the couples, the decision was made after marriage in a series of postponements.

Those who postponed having children moved through stages. First they postponed pregnancy for a specific period. Then they postponed it indefinitely. Next they deliberated the pros and cons of parenthood, and finally they accepted permanent childlessness.

As the wife became older and the couple feared they would need to make a decision, the possibility of adoption emerged as a way of further delaying childbearing. Veevers (1980) found that most couples did not seem to have much knowledge about adoption as a real option. Symbolically, however, the possibility of adoption allowed them to decide not to have children when they could claim they had not really made that decision yet.

Couples faced many outside forces attempting to compel them to have children. Pressure to have children was especially intense in the first six or seven years of the marriage. Their sexual ability was questioned, especially the husband's. They were required to explain themselves to friends, physicians, acquaintances, and would-be grandparents.

Childless couples found some ideological support in maintaining their lifestyle from organizations that were concerned with population problems, such as Zero Population Growth.

What are relationships like between husbands and wives in childless couples? Veevers (1980) found that the most salient feature of these marriages was the intensity of the relationship. Although Veevers had no way of determining whether these marriages were happier than those with children, the people perceived them to be happier. Veevers also noted that the childless couples he interviewed had more egalitarian relationships.

Some people do not choose to be childless and would like to have their own biological children but cannot because one or both members of the couple are infertile. Couples who find themselves in this situation are stigmatized. You should remember from Chapter 10 that stigmatized people are seen as different and inferior to others. The stigmatization of infertile couples is often associated with one of three beliefs: that the infertility is psychologically based, that the infertility is related to sexual incompetence, and that the infertility is the woman's problem (Greil 1998).

Arthur Griel (1998) interviewed couples who were infertile. They told him that fertile people often invade their privacy, asking them why they do not have children or why they have not tried some particular "cure" for infertility. They also spoke of the way in which people trivialized infertility as something easily solved. One woman described the way people always asked her if she was pregnant yet: "Finally I got to the point where I just said, 'Well, when I am, I'll let you know.' Because it was like, after surgery, that was all I ever heard, 'well are you pregnant yet?' I felt like saying 'Well don't you think if I was I would have told you?'" (p. 246).

Some people also mentioned that they felt they had to admit infertility in order to avoid what they believed would be even greater stigmatization for choosing to remain childless. One woman described a scene in which a friend berated her for not having children:

> We had been married about four years. We walked into a bar one night and acquaintances of ours sat down and suddenly decided to have this long talk with us. Who were we getting off being married four years and not having any children? Didn't we know that money wasn't everything? Why were we so money hungry, and why was I being such a bitch to my husband not giving him the children that he rightly deserved? (Griel 1998, p. 247).

Grandparents

We often associate grandparents with old-fashioned families. Grandparenthood, however, became a nearly universal experience only after World War II (Cherlin and Furstenberg 1999). At the turn of the nineteenth century, few people lived long enough to be grandparents. By 1970, however, 75 percent of people experienced grandparenthood, and 50 percent experienced great-grandparenthood (Robertson 1995). Not only have the statistics changed, lifestyles have also changed. Between 1880 and 1970, the images of grandmothers in *Good Housekeeping Magazine* changed from kindly, aged, passive women knitting and rocking to active midlife jugglers (Bengston 1985). Real grandmothers today are also likely to be in the labor force and helping to take care of their grandchildren.

Grandparents' connections with their grandchildren have also been enhanced by more modern technological developments. Ninety-seven percent of our homes have telephones, and one-third of grandparents reported that they had spoken to their grandchild once a week or more during the past year (Cherlin and Furstenberg 1999). Studies have not yet been done on grandparenting on the Internet, but some of you probably communicate with grandparents through e-mail as 67 percent of people aged 55 to 64 and 26 percent of people over 65 use the Internet (Pew Internet and American Life Project 2005).

Improvements in transportation also help people visit grandparents more easily. At the end of World War II, only about half of American households had cars. Nearly everyone owns a car today, and billions of miles of highway have been built since then (Cherlin and Furstenburg 1999).

Today, about 5.8 million grandparents have their grandchildren living with them, and about 42 percent of them were the primary caretakers of those children (U.S. Census Bureau 2003d). This is a growing trend. About two-thirds of these households also include one or both parents of the children. About half (51%) include both a grandmother and a grandfather, and almost half (43%) include only a grandmother. Six percent are headed by a single grandfather (Casper and Bryson 1998).

Table 12.5 shows the percentage of children live with grandparents. The table shows that the likelihood of a child living with a grandparent varies by race ethnicity. African American children are more likely to live with a grandparent than white children or Hispanic children.

Grandparent-headed households cover a wide range of economic situations, although on the average they tend to be poorer than households headed by parents. Incomes range from a mean of $19,750 for households headed by single grandmothers to $61,632 for households with both grandparents and one or both parents living in them. Children in grandparent-headed homes are also less likely than other children to have health insurance. This problem is worse in families with both grandparents and no parents, where 56 percent of the children are not insured (Casper and Bryson 1998).

Grandchildren often have more contact with their mothers' parents compared with their paternal grandparents. They are also more likely to be in contact with grandmothers compared with grandfathers. Part of this difference may be because grandmothers live longer (Roberts and Stroes 1995; Uhlenberg 1998).

Grandparents who maintain close contact with their children report both problems and rewards. One difficulty they experience is long-term, open-ended responsibility for grandchildren. One grandfather described his difficulties: "I've had all three of my grandchildren since they were born. The oldest one is now 13 and the youngest 7. I had no idea I would be raising these children this long but their parents are in no shape to raise them

TABLE 12.5   What Percent of Children in Different Racial Ethnic Groups Live with Their Grandparents? (2000)

White (49% of total child population)	39.0%	Black (15% of total child population)	32.3%	Hispanic (17% of total child population)	21.1%

Source: U.S. Census Bureau 2004d.

right. I am going to be raising kids all my life, I just know it. I just know it" (Burton and de Vries 1993, p. 105).

Another problem grandparents report is keeping up with their grandchildren's needs. One seventy-five-year-old grandmother said, "Can you just see me out there trying to get on a roller coaster at my age? I'm going to have to hire someone younger than me to take him there so he can have some fun" (Burton and de Vries 1993, p. 105).

Grandparents also describe rewards from their close relationships with their grandchildren. These include getting a second chance at parenthood and enjoying the feeling that they are nurturing a legacy. One grandfather put it this way: "I feel blessed that I can see our family line being carried down through my grandchildren. I'm going to invest all I can in them because our name needs to go on and our belief in God has to be carried forth" (Burton and de Vries 1993, p. 107).

In spite of the worry and work that sometimes accompany child raising, companionship and love are also treasured rewards. An eighty-year-old great-grandmother explained her feelings: "I don't know what I would do without my granddaughter. She is my best friend. With her here with me, even though she did have a baby, I feel like I will never be alone" (Burton and de Vries 1993, p. 107).

Grandparents are more involved in their grandchildren's lives not only because they are living longer and because of the personal enrichment they feel from maintaining close relationships with grandchildren. Certain social problems may also be growing, and grandparents are stepping forward to try to address those problems by providing care for grandchildren. Four problems have been identified as pushing grandparents into caretaking roles. The most common is parents abusing drugs and alcohol. The other three are incarceration of parents, parents abusing or neglecting their children, and parents who have died from AIDS or other illnesses or accidents. These triggers to grandparent caretaking are not only serious problems, but they also create problems in grandchildren that may make the caretaking more arduous. For example, children whose parents have these difficulties may have physical problems themselves, like fetal alcohol syndrome or HIV/AIDS, or they may have psychological, emotional, or academic problems because of their experience (Pinson-Melburn et al. 1999).

Is Biology Destiny?

Thus far we have examined a number of issues related to parenting. Gender appears to be an important factor in determining what that experience is like. The question of why gender is so salient is an important theoretical issue. Are differences in mothering and fathering biologically rooted? In this section we review the theoretical debate around this question.

This book has presented much evidence that families vary by race, class, and historical period. The idea, however, that some features of families are natural, unchanging, invariable, and essential is a powerful one in our culture. Beliefs about parents and children seem especially vulnerable to assumptions that some aspects of families are not socially determined. Perhaps lingering in your mind is the belief that there is something intrinsic to the relationship between parents and children that cannot be altered by time, place, or the society in which that relationship exists. This belief is called essentialism and is tied to a belief in biological determinism.

Recall from Chapter 8 that essentialism is a philosophical viewpoint that posits that there are certain phenomena that are essential; they cannot be omitted or altered but must be accepted as a given. In the case of parenting, essentialism is the belief that biological parents have a biologically determined (or at least partly biologically determined) social relationship to their children.

Essentialists argue that it is in our genes for biological parents to care for their young; if they do not, our species is threatened. Because males and females are biologically different, within this framework they have different biologically determined roles they must play in raising the next generation. In sum, this point of view asserts that biological mothers must raise children because they are physically best equipped to do so, and that if women do not take this responsibility the survival of our species is at risk.

In sociology, this argument is put forward by sociobiologists (Wilson 1975). After World War II, biological determinism fell into disrepute because of its association with nazism. In the past twenty years, a resurgence of interest in the approach has occurred (Segal and Kilty 1998).

Alice Rossi has been an important figure in the sociobiological view of parenting. Rossi (1964) was one of the early writers in the second-wave feminist movement in the late 1960s. In 1977, she published an article that was met with strong criticism from other feminist scholars (Breines, Cerullo, and Stacey 1978).

Rossi (1977) argued that the responsibility of women for child care and cooking are "the products of an innate physiological disposition supported by natural selection and a long evolutionary heritage" (Breines, Cerullo, and Stacey 1978, p. 46). In other words, women have been genetically programmed to be effective parents and cooks.

A second factor in Rossi's argument is that men have not been biologically programmed to be as proficient in these activities. Regardless of social factors, therefore, men cannot be as good at parenting as women: "Unisex socialization has proven insufficient to remove whatever sex differences currently exist" (Rossi 1977, p. 45).

Third, Rossi asserts that because human babies have such a prolonged dependency on their parents, they require the formation of strong bonds between themselves and their parents in order to survive and flourish psychologically and physically. Therefore, it is necessary for mothers, because they can best provide the relationship infants need, to take responsibility for this essential activity. Child raising cannot be left to the inferior parents, fathers.

Rossi's work, for the most part, ignores men (Breines, Cerullo, and Stacey 1978). Other than being inferior parents, they are not a problem; in fact, they are quite invisible.

Other sociobiologists (Barash 1977; Wilson 1975) have proposed a theory about men as well as women. They argue that because they are biologically different, men and women have a different way of contributing to the perpetuation of the species. Women are genetically programmed to be careful when selecting a mate, and they need to have sex only every couple of years in order to best preserve their genes.

Men, on the other hand, are genetically programmed to invest little in the raising of children because they are not as skilled. Instead, men must go for quantity. According to sociobiologists, the best mating strategy for men is to impregnate as many women as possible. The maximum advantage goes to men with fewer inhibitions. A genetically influenced tendency to "play fast and loose" and "love 'em and leave 'em" may well reflect more bio-logical reality than most of us care to admit (Barash 1977, p. 48).

What Is Wrong with the Sociobiological Model?

Ruth Bleier (1984) is a biologist who has carefully analyzed the sociobiological model and discovered three problems with its premises. First, sociobiology presumes that certain human behaviors and certain differences between males and females are universal, when in fact they do not exist in all times, in all societies, or even among all people in a particular time and place. The behaviors that sociobiologists define as masculine, like competitive-ness, aggression, and selfishness, may be an important part of men's character in white upper-class American and British society, but they are not important in many other cultures (Bleier 1984; Lorber 1996; Sydie 1987; van den Wijngaard 1997). A critical issue for the argument Rossi makes about mothering is the variation of the separation of childbearing from child care. Although it is always women who bear children, there is enormous varia-tion in the role that fathers, mothers, and others play in child rearing.

Second, sociobiologists often call on research on other animals as evidence for their arguments. For example, Rossi (1977) cites evidence from primate studies of maternal dep-rivation. This practice is questionable for several reasons. It is impossible to show how translatable one set of behaviors is from one species to another. How significant is it to explaining human behavior if we show that gorilla females are more likely to take care of their young than gorilla males are? Even though primates are our closest contemporary rel-atives, the first hominids split off from apes between 5 and 15 million years ago, and both branches continued to evolve. The species from which *Homo sapiens* evolved is extinct. Making comparisons even with our nearest relative involves a huge evolutionary leap (Sperling 1991). Sociobiologists, however, are often quite unconcerned with even larger leaps, like comparing humans to birds. For example, among mallards, a female is chased by several males who then appear to roughly jump on her and "force" her to allow them to copulate. This behavior has been cited by some sociobiologists as evidence of rape among animals and therefore as evidence of the naturalness of rape by male animals, including humans (Judd 1978).

Another problem with extrapolating from the behavior of one species to another is the arbitrariness with which examples are chosen (Bleier 1984). For example, a silver-backed gorilla male may dominate the movement of the troop. In other species, however, like the Japanese macaques, females form the core of the hierarchy. And in many primate species, dominance hierarchies do not exist at all. Sociobiologists are especially prone to omitting species that do not fit their model.

Using data from other species is also questionable because it assumes that animals do not socialize their members. Perhaps part of a gorilla's behavior is a result of what it has learned (Bleier 1984).

In addition, animals vary within groups. The behaviors that are identified in some members of a species may not be universal within that species (Bleier 1984; Sperling 1991). For example, animals may have different ways of handling child care or territory disputes in different communities. This is particularly important because a number of studies cited by sociobiologists are based on research on animals held in zoos that subsequently have been determined to behave quite differently in the wild (Lewontin, Rose, and Kamin 1984).

The third area Bleier (1984) identifies is the problem of separating biology from other factors. She says it is not possible to tease genetic and other factors from learning and environment in human behavior. From conception, humans are affected by their environment. For example, pregnant mothers can respond to social factors with different hormonal output, which can then affect the fetus. Or mothers may have more or less access to food or health care depending on their social situation, which can affect their children even before birth. After birth, Bleier (1984) declares that biology and social and physical environment are not polar opposites to be unwound. They are fused in the lives of humans. Both biology and social experience influence our lives, and they both influence each other.

If Biology Is Not Destiny, Are Men and Women Identical as Parents?

Liberal feminism is a theoretical position that takes the opposite position of sociobiologists. Liberal feminists posit that inequality between women and men "results from the organization of society, not from any significant biological or personality differences between women and men" (Lengermann and Niebrugge-Brantley 1992, p. 462). The goal of liberal feminism is to make the world see how similar women and men are and to organize ways in which to treat them equally. For the liberal feminist, "a woman lawyer is exactly the same as a man lawyer. A woman cop is just the same as a man cop. A pregnant woman is just the same as." (Rothman 1989a, p. 248).

This quotation illustrates a problem in liberal feminism. In nearly every human activity, women and men are the same, or the differences between one woman and another woman are as great as or greater than they are between a woman and a man. But pregnancy and childbirth make some women different from all men, and pregnancy and childbirth have an especially important effect on parenting.

Both women and men contribute equal amounts of genetic material to a fetus, but it is only the female's body that contributes nine months of gestation and the labor of giving birth. Rothman (1989a) argues that this difference is important and should play a role in legal battles, like that in the case of Baby M.

Bill Stern wanted a child who came from his sperm, but his wife Betsy had multiple sclerosis and had been told that bearing a child might worsen her condition. The Sterns decided to hire Mary Beth Whitehead as a surrogate mother to carry Bill's child. For a fee Whitehead allowed herself to be alternatively inseminated with Stern's sperm and agreed to give the baby to the Sterns. Whitehead, however, changed her mind after the child was born and hid herself and the baby for four months while the courts deliberated the case.

The court said that the contract between the Sterns and Whitehead was not binding. However, because the child was genetically related to Bill Stern, he had the right to sue for custody. According to the court, he and Whitehead were equally parents. The case was then decided on the basis of who would be a better parent: Stern, a wealthy professional, or Whitehead, a working-class wife and mother. In the proceedings, evidence was presented that Whitehead had been a go-go dancer, had dyed her hair, and had trouble with her husband (Rothman 1989a, p. 24). The court decided in Stern's favor.

According to Rothman (1989a), the mother's link to the child was incorrectly reduced to that of the father's, thereby making them equal parents. Bill Stern and Mary Beth Whitehead had equal genetic links to Baby M. The baby was a product of equal parts of Stern's and Whitehead's genes. But Rothman argues that the fact that Whitehead had the additional connection to the child of being a pregnant and birthing mother should not have been dismissed as irrelevant. The court's decision was based on the liberal feminist assumption that men and women are equal. Even though men and women are not equal in their contribution to reproduction, the factors that make them unequal were ignored, and the one way in which they are equal—their genetic contribution—was the only criterion acknowledged.

Rothman (1989a) demands that a new framework be developed that can capture the need for women to be treated equally to men while not dismissing the unique character of the relationship between biological mothers and their children. She proposes a policy in which the contribution biological mothers make in pregnancy and childbirth and the contribution fathers, mothers, and others make in caring for children after they are born is factored into equations leading to decisions about questions like custody. Specifically, Rothman suggests that policy should be based on the following rules:

1. Infants belong to their mothers at birth because of the unique nurturant relationship that has existed between them up to that moment; genetic ties will not give parental rights.
2. Adoption can only occur after birth, and the birth mother has six weeks in which to change her mind.
3. All custody cases after six months will be determined by the amount of care provided by the adult with joint custody if this role is fully shared.
4. There is no such thing as surrogacy under this system. Every woman who bears a child is the mother of the child she bears, with full parental rights regardless of the source of the egg or the sperm (pp. 254–60).

Child Care

Our focus thus far has been on the microlevel of parenting and how the microlevel is affected by the macrolevel. Our attention has been on the diverse experience of parenting and how social factors, especially the social construction of gender, shape that experience. The microlevel has also affected the macrolevel. People have tried to influence the organization of parenting and the social context that affects it. One of the most direct examples is the political battle for increasing public responsibility for child care.

In more than half (61%) of all married couple households with children under eighteen today, both parents are employed (Bureau of Labor Statistics 2005c). In 1940, 10 percent of children under the age of six had mothers in the paid labor force. In 2004, 62 percent did. Sixty-three percent of the 18.5 million children under five years of age are in some type of regular child care arrangement (Johnson 2005).

Table 12.6 shows the types of child care parents use while they are at work. The table reveals that about 25 percent of children are in the care of the father, 28 percent in the care of the grandparent, and 11 percent are being cared for by a sibling. Twenty-one percent are

TABLE 12.6   Regular Child Care Arrangements for Children under 5 Years Old, 2002

Characteristics	Type of Nonparental Arrangements			
	No Regular Care	*In Relative Care*	*In Nonrelative Care*	*In Center*
Total	37%	32%	14%	24%
Race-Ethnicity				
White	7	35	25	35
Black	7	45	17	40
Hispanic	6	56	19	31
Asian and Pacific Islander	NA	47	10	32
Mother's Employment Status				
Full time	6	39	24	39
Part time	9	44	20	27
Poverty status				
Below poverty	12	47	20	29
At or above poverty	6	39	23	36

Source: Johnson 2005.

in a day care center, and 22 percent have multiple child care arrangements. Race ethnicity affects the kind of child care arrangements parents have made. For example, a larger proportion of Hispanic children are cared for by siblings or other relatives other than grandparents (19%) compared with white children (8%) (Johnson 2005).

A little over half (54%) of employed women with children under the age of fifteen report making cash payments for child care (U.S. House of Representatives 2004). Often this is because parents work different shifts so that one parent can care for the children while the other is at work (Casper 1997). In addition, many parents who cannot afford to place their children in licensed day care facilities rely on unlicensed babysitters, who are paid less than a minimum wage and who do not claim these earnings on their federal income tax forms. Since several aspects of these arrangements are illegal, they probably are not reported, and therefore the number of people reporting cash payments is less than the number who actually make cash payments.

The number of slots available for parents seeking day care is insufficient in some areas, especially for infants and very young children. But availability of child care is a less significant issue than the quality of care available and the cost (Eyer 1996, Hofferth and Phillips, 1987).

One of the problems with the quality of child care is the rapid turnover of personnel in day care centers. Day care workers have a turnover rate about twice as high as the national average. This is undoubtedly related to the demanding work coupled with the low pay (Bureau of Labor Statistics 2005b; Wrigley 1995; Zigler and Long 1991). In spite of great responsibility and expertise, child care workers receive no respect and have little authority in their workplaces and in the lives of the children in their care (Rutman 1996).

They are also underpaid. On the average, day care workers have nearly two more years of education than other workers in the United States, but they only earn about $9.50 an hour (Bureau of Labor Statistics 2005b). In addition, the workload for day care workers has increased as child-to-staff ratios have increased (Taylor 1991).

Another problem families face is the difficulty of finding child care for sick children. This is particularly a issue for mothers. In dual income families, 83 percent of mothers say they are more likely to take time off, compared with 22 percent of fathers who say they are more likely to take time off when a child is ill (Bond and Galinsky 1998).

Parents are also concerned about the lack of an educational component at child care centers that provide full day care. One large study found that only one in seven American child care centers provides high-quality child-development and learning programs (Helbern et al., 1999).

In addition to these quality issues, parents are also faced with financial problems in child care. In 1985, on the average, families spent about $67 per child per week. In 2002, that cost had risen to $95 (Johnson 2005). On the average, families spend 11 percent of their income on child care. For poor and moderate-income families, however, this proportion can rise much higher, especially if there is more than one child in the family. Families below poverty pay an average of 30 percent of their income for child care (U.S. House of Representatives 2004). Parents who seek child care face the dilemma of "incompatible desires" (Wrigley 1995). Julia Wrigley interviewed parents and child care providers. She found that mothers and fathers want a child care provider who is independent, caring, and creative in taking care of their children. But they also want an employee who is "inexpensive, reliable and controllable"—not a likely combination. Providers in this relationships are left feeling exploited and faced with overwhelming tasks. Parents worry that their children are not being well cared for or at least not cared for in a manner consistent with their own values. Wrigley concludes that individual families cannot solve the dilemma by themselves. She advocates developing public day care with protections for employees.

Currently the federal government supports child care in two ways. First, the government provides direct subsidies through social service block grants to states, but those subsidies are drying up as programs are cut at the state and federal level. Second, the government allows tax credit to parents who spend money on child care and to employers of parents. Many middle- and high-income parents tax advantage of the tax credits. The credits, however, do not help low-income families whose income is not high enough to pay income tax, and few employers take advantage of the tax incentives (Burman, Maag, and Rohaly 2005; Friedman 1988).

Only 5 percent of businesses provide financial assistance for child care for their employees, and only 9 percent provide child care near or onsite (Bond and Galinsky 1998). When parents have child care problems, however, they can cause businesses problems. Bond and Galinsky estimate that employers lose $3 billion a year when employees miss work to care for children. Some companies are beginning to look at child care as an issue they may need to address.

In addition to difficulties convincing government and business to create and support child care for working parents, ideas about good parents and especially good mothers interfere with providing child care (Hays 1995; Ribbens 1994). Lynet Uttal (1999) has looked at the way in which mothers think about child care and has found three dominant views. The first group of mothers think about child care as custodial care. They believe mothers are the primary socializers and child rearers. Child care providers meet the immediate emotional and physical needs of the children when the mothers are not there, but they are not substitute mothers. Mothers with this point of view think that child care should provide safe physical surroundings and occupy children's time, but they are less concerned that caregivers have similar values and they do not believe they influence children's social and moral development. One woman who fit into this category thought about child care as intellectually enriching and the child care provider as a teacher rather than a parental figure:

> They are not there as a parent or trying to take the place of a parent. They are there to do a job. A teacher is more structured, a teacher has certain things to do at a certain time, a time for talking, cuddling; or whatever, the time for art. When you're hurt, when something happens to you as a child, who do you want? You want your parents. (Uttal 1999, p. 567)

The second category were those who viewed child care as surrogate care. These mothers thought about the child care provider as a substitute mother, and they also felt distressed that another person was taking this role. One mother said she was "sometimes sad because he knows that I'm his mother, he loves me, but for everything he looks for her. Everything. When he's hungry, when he's bored, just for everything, he prefers her" (Uttal 1999, p. 569).

The third category were mothers who viewed their relationship with the child care provider as coordinated care. They shared mothering and used words like *comother* and *my baby's other parent* to describe the child care provider. They felt it was important for the provider to share their values and often mentioned that they wanted the provider to also be able to teach their culture, for example, by speaking Spanish. One mother in this category said, "It would be what I'd do if I were taking care of him If I'm not going to be in the position for one reason or another to interpret the world for him in that way, to reframe situations in order for him to see that there's a better way of doing things, then I want someone else to do that" (Uttal 1999, p. 572).

Children whose parents are employed spend many hours in the care of child care workers. Coordinated care is the most realistic view of child care. This view, however, challenges the dominant view of mothering because it suggests that children can have more than one mother and that the other person does not have to be biologically or legally related (Uttal 1999). Shared mothering is good for children, and it is well suited to the time that children spend in the care of people other than their parents. But shared mothering or coordinated care is a controversial idea for many people to accept or even consider because it demands that we rethink some of our most fundamental ideas about parenting, especially motherhood (Chira 1998).

Our contradictory ideas about child care and good parenting has been called the "mommy wars" (Hays 1995). In the beginning of this chapter, we looked at the motherhood mystique. The mystique tells us today that parents, and especially mothers, are supposed to be intensely involved in mothering. They are supposed to be engaged in every aspect of their children's lives, creatively developing ways to ensure that their children have all of the emotional, social, and intellectual skills they need in order to succeed. Good mothers should also provide a buffer from the worst of the outside world. The ideology of intense mothering additionally promotes the idea that only mothers can provide the highest quality of care for their children. Paradoxically, this ideology about mothering exists in a society where child rearing is generally devalued, while profit, efficiency, and getting ahead are given highest recognition.

> What this creates is a no-win situation for a women of childbearing years. If a woman voluntarily remains childless, some will say that she is cold, heartless and unfulfilled as a woman. If she is a mother who works too hard at her job or career, some will accuse her of neglecting the kids. If she does not work hard enough some will surely place her on the mommy track and her career advancement will be permanently slowed by the claim that her commitment to her children interferes with her workplace efficiency (Schwartz 1989). And if she stays home with her children, some will call her unproductive and useless. A woman, in other words, can never fully do it right. (Hays 1999, p. 434)

In order to resolve this contradiction, we need to re-examine both the ideology of intensive mothering and the value we place on profit, efficiency, and getting ahead. Because women appear to be permanently in both the child raising and the paid labor force, their lives show us that we cannot settle the problem by separating the two activities and asking people to choose one or the other. Nor can we expect people to add one task to the other and still do a good job and feel good about themselves (Hays 1995).

Lessons from History

During World War II, child care centers were established in forty-seven states, Alaska, Hawaii, and Washington, D.C. Millions of dollars were spent by the government to house thousands of children whose mothers were needed in war industry. You should remember the story of Rosie the Riveter from Chapter 2. These centers were not sufficient for the needs of all children, but they helped a large number of parents. After the war, most of the centers were shut down as women were laid off. In California, however, legislation was passed that kept the centers open.

Why were child care advocates successful in California? Ellen Reese (1996) argues that there were many child care workers and clients who wanted to keep the centers open, and they were able to create an effective strategy. Most important, they used the rhetoric of maternalism to make their case. In arguing to retain the child care centers, they focused on how they met children's needs. In the 1940s, there was little support for backing parents in their efforts to find child care. But legislators and the public did respond to keeping the centers because of the service they provided for children. In addition to a winning strategy, child care advocates also built a useful network of alliances among unions and veterans' organizations. The women and men in these working-class organizations recognized the need for their wives or themselves to earn wages and the need for care for their children when parents are in the paid labor force. Finally, Reese notes that the economic and political contexts were ideal, too. The opposition was quiet; public officials were supportive; and a budget surplus helped California retain the child care system that vanished in other places after the war.

The Micro–Macro Connection

Despite the popular notion of the essential character of parenting, we can see that the social context and the interplay between the micro- and macrolevels of the social context have a defining influence on parents. An exploration of parenting shows that the microlevel experience of parenting is affected by macrolevel social structural factors of the legal system that define parents as those who are genetically linked to children. The microlevel is also affected by the macrofeatures of gender stratification, technology, essentialist ideology, and the organization of health care.

In the opening scenario in Chapter 1, Kimberly and Michael look forward to marriage and parenting with little knowledge about the limitations that will be placed on them as they begin these activities. The technology of reproduction and birth, the ideologies that promote the idea that women should be the primary parents, and limited support from the community around such needs as child care all influence their experience of parenting, the problems they face, and the possible solutions available to them.

Microlevel forces have also affected the organization of parenting by contesting the medicalization of birthing and developing alternative birthing methods. The political battle of people at the microlevel who are attempting to alter the macrolevel of government is most clear in the effort to promote legislation to bring more public support of child care.

CHAPTER

13 **Children**

Socialization is the process by which people learn what to expect from their society and how they in turn are expected to behave. Gender socialization teaches children how to be masculine or feminine. (© Will Hart)

Mrs. Gonzalez teaches sixth grade at an elementary school in Chicago. The school year is just beginning, and as a way to help the students get to know one another, she asks them to talk about their summer vacation. The school is located in a neighborhood that includes a broad range of classes and cultures.

Rodriguez quickly raises his hand. "We had a lot of excitement this summer. Our house burned down. Lucky for us we weren't in it. My brother and mother and me had to move in with my grandma. My mother says we're sure poor now."

Mrs. Gonzalez calls on Amy next. She says, "My brother and I both got to go to camp this summer. My father said that just because he and my mother were at work every day we weren't going to spend the summer in front of the TV. My brother picked basketball camp, and I chose to go to ballet camp. We had to practice every day and at the end there was a beautiful recital."

Neu is next. "My parents got separated this summer. I had to help. Everyday when my mother went to work, I stayed home and took care of the two babies. I also had to make the dinners and do the dishes. Every few days I took the clothes to wash them at the laundromat. That was pretty fun."

"My aunt made me and my cousin go to summer school," says Jamal. "Last year I did real well in math, and they made me take enrichment classes at the Afro-American Center this summer so that I could get into the advanced classes."

Mrs. Gonzalez notices that Jennifer is sitting quietly at her desk. Two years ago, Jennifer's older sister Melissa was in her class. Melissa had confided that she was being sexually abused at home, and Mrs. Gonzalez had helped their mother work with protective services to have the father removed from the home. She wonders if Jennifer has been molested as well. Mrs. Gonzalez notes to herself that she will need to make a special effort to get to know the quiet girl.

Which of these children have better lives, in your opinion?

How do you define "better," and from where do your ideas come about what children should be like and how they spend their time? Would those ideas be different if you lived in 1900? In 1400?

What different relationships do children have in families?

What are all of the roles children may play in families? Are they students to be taught? Workers? Burdens? Victims?

Why are families an important arena for gender socialization? What about other kinds of socialization? Are families the only place children are socialized?

How do class, race, and family organization affect children's lives?

Children's lives are diverse, frequently difficult, and always shaped by the social context in which they live. Most children grow up in families. But the kind of families in which they live can vary by race and class and by household arrangements—who they live with and what their relationships are to those people. Some children face great difficulty, for example, if they are abused or poor. Children's lives are influenced by factors at the microlevel, the relationships and interactions in which they are involved with family members and others they see day to day. Children's lives are also affected by large macrolevel social structures like the media, the organization of education, the government, the economy, and the social system of stratification.

This chapter examines the experiences of children in families in the United States. The chapter is organized into three main sections. The first is a review of the three dominant images of children in our society: social learners, threats to adults, and victims. The second section examines two theoretical issues: the way in which children and childhood are socially constructed and the insufficient character of our current images of children.

The third section introduces political activities that attempt to improve the quality of life for children.

Postmodern American Children

Barrie Thorne (1987) has examined the place of children in our society, especially their relationship to adults. She asserts that contemporary American images of the relationship between children and adults fall into three categories: (1) children as learners of adult culture, (2) children as threats to adult society, and (3) children as victims of adults. Each of these are important aspects of family life for children.

Thorne argues, however, that these three images fall short of capturing reality because they ignore many other aspects of children's lives, including their experience in families. In the second section of this chapter, we look at the question of whether we need to broaden our conceptualization of children and what theoretical tools might be most useful in that effort. But first we focus our attention on the three dominant images of children, beginning with the image of children as learners.

Children as Learners of Adult Culture

The first image of children is that of learners of adult culture. Families are an important site of this learning activity, which is called socialization. Socialization is the process by which people learn to behave in an acceptable manner in their society; they learn what behaviors are considered appropriate or inappropriate and what they might expect in response to those activities. Through socialization we learn how to express our feelings, how to respond to events and people, and how to understand other people's behavior.

One type of socialization to which social scientists have paid special attention is gender socialization. Gender socialization is the process by which people learn what it is to be masculine and feminine. Chapter 5 described how gender is socially constructed. One of the ways in which people work to construct gender is by teaching each new generation how to behave in "masculine" and "feminine" ways. Learning how to be masculine or feminine requires a lot of effort because there are so many rules and nearly every facet of our lives is gendered. Gender socialization includes a wide variety of lessons, like learning how to walk, talk, play, and express our feelings.

Masculinity and femininity also differ from one culture to the next and across classes. Some rules that exist in one society may be exactly the opposite in another. For example, in the United States we learn to display gender through our clothing. One rule is that skirts and dresses are feminine and for women only. But in Scotland male soldiers wear kilts, and in Saudi Arabia men are expected to wear long gowns. Since the rules about how to be masculine and feminine are complex and arbitrary, intense socialization is required for us to learn the lessons.

When we learn about gender through socialization, we learn not only what to do but also how to do it. We are not outside observers. The lessons are absorbed and become part of us. *Sex typing* is the term that psychologists use to refer to the acquisition of gender-appropriate preferences, skills, personality attributes, behaviors, and self-concepts.

Although gender socialization takes place in families, many other people and institutions socialize children (Coltrane and Adams 1997). For example, in the scenario at the beginning of the chapter Amy tells about how she and her brother attended separate camps, where he learned about a masculine activity—football—and she learned about a feminine one—ballet. Camps, schools, and the media all play important roles in socializing children. In this section we look at the way in which families socialize children and then move to other socializing institutions, like television.

Gender Socialization in Families.   Sandra Bem (1983) has been interested in sex typing, the acquisition of gender through socialization, in families. Her goal is not only to understand the process better but also to develop ways for parents to short-circuit sex typing in order to eliminate gender restrictions in their children's lives.

Because she is a psychologist, Bem emphasizes the internal psychological processes and the social interaction between individuals at the microlevel that create gendered people. Four theories dominate this social-psychological view of gender socialization: psychoanalytic theory, social learning theory, cognitive-developmental theory, and gender schema theory.

Psychoanalytic theory was initially developed by Sigmund Freud in the 1920s and 1930s. Large pieces of Freud's work have been rejected. Some of his insights, however, had a tremendous effect on twentieth-century psychology and continue to play a role in the field. Scholars who use Freudian theory argue that children learn to be gendered individuals by interacting with their mothers. Females notice that they are physiologically like their mothers and develop an attachment and identity with them as women. Males learn to be masculine by noticing that they are dissimilar to their mothers and developing a sense of themselves as different from women (Chodorow 1978b).

Freudian theory has been criticized on several counts. First, some critics argue that little empirical evidence exists to support the argument that the psychological development that Freud proposed actually takes place. Second, the model does not account for the large number of children who grow up in single-parent families and who become "properly" gendered (Maccoby and Jacklin 1974).

Third, Freud asserted that females are in a subordinate position in our society because of inferior genital structure rather than because of sexism. He maintained that girls are disappointed when they discover they do not have penises and and that they develop penis envy and a disdain for women. Researchers question whether this is a valid conclusion. Girls' preference for boys' activities could be a result of the greater social value placed on boys, men, and masculinity rather than the superiority of male genitals. Or girls might prefer "masculine" toys and games because the "masculine" activities are intrinsically more entertaining. Boys' toys are more varied, encourage activity outside of the house, and are more challenging (Basow 1992).

Social learning theory is a second model that has been proposed to explain gender socialization. This model grew out of stimulus-response theory, or behaviorism (Stockard and Johnson 1992). Social learning theorists argue that children learn gender through reward and punishment. They display those behaviors for which they are rewarded and avoid displaying those behaviors for which they are punished.

Social learning theorists believe that sometimes children are directly taught that some behaviors are good and others are bad. For example, girls may be told by their parents that their behavior is not ladylike, or boys may be told not to play with dolls or wear lipstick because those things are for girls. Sometimes children are taught these rules more indirectly, through modeling. Modeling is the process of learning by seeing others behave in appropriate ways and being rewarded or seeing them punished for aberrant behavior. For example, boys would frequently see their mothers wear lipstick but not their fathers. A boy might hear others comment on how pretty his mother looks with lipstick or how lipstick is taboo for men. Television is an important source of models, and TV programs include gender and racial ethnic stereotypes.

Critics of social learning theory note that people stick with gender-appropriate behavior even if it is not rewarding. For example, even though men are paid more than women and are more likely to hold political office, few women are willing or able to behave like men to obtain these rewards. Social learning theory, however, implies that any behavior, including behavior associated with gender, is readily learnable and unlearnable. Social learning theory has also been criticized because it assumes that children are entirely passive in the process.

The third theory of gender socialization, cognitive-developmental theory, improves on social learning theory by recognizing the child as an active participant in the process. This theory also differs from social learning theory because it proposes that age is a critical factor; exposure to rules is experienced differently by different age groups. According to cognitive-developmental theorists, children must be at the appropriate age to be able to receive the message being sent to them.

Cognitive-developmental theorists argue that children move through stages of psychological maturity. A child who has reached the appropriate stage identifies unalterably as either a boy or a girl. This judgment of a child's own sex then determines whether she or he will accept or reject punishments and rewards. For example, once a boy determines that he is a boy, those activities and behaviors that he perceives to be masculine become intrinsically positive regardless of their real effect on him. He may feel uncomfortable wrestling on the playground and prefer to play with dolls, but he may perceive wrestling as consistent with his sex and therefore good, and playing with dolls as inconsistent and therefore bad.

Bem (1981) criticizes cognitive developmental theory. Most important, she says that the theory ignores the significance of society in the "choice" children make to use sex as a central organizer of their lives. Children could, for example, choose size, color, or age as the way to organize their world and the basis for selecting certain behaviors as consistent or not. Cognitive-developmental theory does not ask why children decide that sex is going to be the central organizer. Bem, however, does ask this question and answers it by pointing out that our society's emphasis on sex causes our children to use sex as the most important way to determine their place in the world and their decisions about how they should think, feel, and act.

Bem (1981) proposes gender schema theory as the fourth and best theory to explain gender socialization. Like cognitive-developmental theory, gender schema theory argues that children are active participants in their socialization. Children are exposed to rewards, punishments, and models of various behaviors, and they interpret and select based on their belief that gender is an important organizer of people's lives.

Gender schema theory is different from cognitive-developmental theory, however, because it assumes that the "choice" to make gender the central factor is itself determined by the culture in which the child is living. It is, therefore, not inevitable. One could imagine a society in which gender is not a critical factor and that is what Bem emphasizes in her conclusions.

In a culture like ours, however, gender is enormously important, so children use gender as the main criterion for determining whether a behavior is good or bad for them. Children look around and see that virtually everyone can be distinguished as either masculine or feminine, and that many factors in their environment fit one category or the other—names, colors, games, jobs, clothes, language, interests, and so on.

This implies that if we wish to eliminate gender inequality, we must introduce children to the idea that gender could be a much less important factor. Children could learn that it is good for both males and females to behave in a variety of ways. More important, children could learn that there are only a few instances in which sex should play a role at all in assessments of how they should think, feel, act, or relate to one another.

For example, if a man wished to find a person with whom to conceive a child, it would be important to pay attention to the sex of the other person. She would need to be a female. (She would also have to possess a number of other characteristics: fertility, interest in having a child, and interest in having intercourse with him or being alternatively inseminated by his sperm.) Very few other activities would necessitate acknowledging sex.

Gender schema theory goes beyond suggesting that we teach children that it is all right for boys to like nail polish and girls to like football. Gender schema theory suggests that we need to teach children that gender is an irrelevant issue in determining what is good, acceptable, or fun.

Bem emphasizes the role parents play in gender socialization and concludes her review by asking what parents can do to try to eliminate gender restrictions in their children's lives. Bem suggests that we need to take an active part in presenting alternatives to our children. If we just ignore gender, children will learn the dominant gender ideology in our society, which insists that gender is a central way to organize people and that the two types, girls and boys, must learn many rules to differentiate themselves.

Bem has two specific recommendations for counteracting this message and raising gender-aschematic children. First, parents should emphasize the biological distinction between males and females. If children are aware of real physical distinctions between males and females and the limited significance those differences have in nearly all situations, they will be better able to distinguish biological differences from socially determined ones.

Second, parents must propose an alternative set of criteria for assessing how people should think, feel, and act. Bem suggests that parents create new materials like stories, games, and toys that do not teach gender stereotypes and instead stress commonalities among people and individual nongender-related variation. Parents must also censor cultural messages in television programs and books.

Finally, Bem argues that teaching alternatives is not enough. Children must be shown how to actively resist gender socialization and gender inequality. She asserts that parents must teach the child to be "morally outraged by and opposed to whatever sex discrimination she or he meets in daily life" (Bem 1983, p. 615).

One of the central themes of this book is the importance of the resistance movements of people working together at the microlevel to change their immediate social circumstances and especially to change the macro-organization of their society. Bem's suggestions for how to raise gender-aschematic children provide a specific plan for challenging gender inequality, especially at the microlevel. Parents in microlevel, face-to-face interactions with children are encouraged to behave differently in a way that diminishes the role of gender.

Social Interactionist Theory.   Bem's advice acknowledges and encourages the resistance behavior of parents, but it still leaves children in a largely passive, recipient role. Social interaction theory, a fifth model, forces us to notice the reciprocal relationship between children and others and the active role that we all play in creating gender (Cahill 1983; Thorne 1987). Social interactionists West and Zimmerman (1987) call this doing gender. They argue that gender socialization theory conveys the idea that gender is achieved at an early age by people doing things to us and by our responses. A social interactionist approach, in contrast, notes the way gender is an active, ongoing, ever-present process. We are almost constantly practicing gender, and we practice it not just as children and not just in relationships that entail socialization. In Chapter 7, for example, we discussed Sarah Fenstermaker Berk's (1985) work examining housework from a social interactionist perspective. She argued that in doing housework, women and men were doing gender. They were practicing and displaying the supposedly appropriate activities of masculine and feminine people. Thorne's (1993) work on children shows the importance of schools, classrooms, and playgrounds as arenas for the construction of gender for young people.

One of the most important places where boys do gender is in sports (Messner 1998). Boys' masculinity is often evaluated according to their athletic abilities, and when boys and men participate in sports they are doing gender. Michael Messner interviewed men who had been athletes. Many of them talked about how their fathers, in particular, had encouraged or even pushed them into athletic activities. One man described his introduction to baseball:

> I still remember it like it was yesterday—Dad and I driving up in his truck, and I had my glove and my hat and all that—and I said, "Dad, I don't want to do it." He says, "What?" I says "I don't want to do it." I was nervous that I might fail. And he says "Don't be silly. Lookit: there's Joey and Petey and all your friends out there." And so Dad says, "You're gonna do it, come on." And in my memory he's never said that about anything else; he just knew I needed a little kick in the pants and I'd do it. And once you're out there and you see all the other kids making errors and stuff, and you know you're better than those guys, you know: Maybe I do belong here. As it turned out, Little League was a good experience. (p. 113)

The participation of boys in athletic events allows them to do gender. In particular, they are doing masculinity, practicing to be competitive, aggressive, physical, and successful.

Socialization theory implies that gender is an aspect of who we are—I am a woman, therefore I behave in certain ways. Social interactionist theory conceptualizes gender as what a person does recurrently in interaction with others. Socialization theory suggests that we can alter patterns of gender by changing socialization practices. Social interactionist theory demands that we alter all of our social interactions that include doing gender.

The theory also reminds us that these interactions make up a large proportion of our encounters and that they are as common to adults as they are to children.

Racial Socialization.   Gender inequality and the oppression of women are important social problems. Bem tells us that socialization of children in families can operate as a mechanism of social control or can generate new ideas, new behavior, and challenges to the organization of gender in our society.

As we have seen throughout this book, inequality by race ethnicity is also an important social problem. Racism is a salient factor that black parents are very much aware of: "An inescapable aspect of the socialization of Black children is that it prepares them for survival in an environment that is hostile, racist and discriminatory against Blacks" (Peters 1988, p. 237). Socialization in families can help counter the effects of racism. Through racial socialization, children can learn what racism is and how best to confront it. Like gender socialization, racial socialization can often take place in families.

In response to the hostile environment, African American families have devised ways to buffer some of the demeaning messages African American children receive outside of the community (Carrothers 1998; Ogbu 1978; Peters 1985, 1988; Richardson 1981; Scanzoni 1971; Willie 1988). Marie Peters (1985) refers to the special attention African American families give to preparing their children for being an African American in the United States as "racial socialization."

Peters (1985) followed the child rearing practices of the parents of thirty African American children for two years to examine racial socialization. All the mothers in the study were conscious of racism, and they offered examples of their experience of discrimination in the course of their daily activities. They described incidences of being ignored or treated badly or unfairly by employers, store clerks, waitresses, and bank officials (see also Sigelman and Welch 1991).

Because of the parents' own experiences, they felt responsible to teach their children to understand that they might be discriminated against and how to survive in a hostile environment. One mother explained, "It's most important for me to teach my sons how to deal with a society as it is—to let them know they're protected as long as they're at home, but when they get out there in the world, they're not protected anymore" (Peters 1985, p. 164).

Parents also attempt to counteract racism by presenting an alternative. They actively try to instill pride, self-respect, and assurance of love as protection against negative images the children might encounter. A mother explained to Peters: "I'd like them to have enough pride, because if you have enough pride or self-confidence in yourself, you'll let a lot of things roll off your back" (1985, p. 165).

Racial socialization strategies fall into three categories: the mainstream experience, the minority experience, and the black cultural experience (M. Thornton 1997). In the mainstream experience, parents emphasize the fundamental equality among people and try to develop positive self-images in their children. They might be likely to tell their children, "You are as good as anyone else."

The second strategy, the minority experience, underscores the social restrictions placed on people as a result of racism. Parents in this category warn their children about barriers they will face and try to show them ways to cope with mistreatment.

The third category, the black cultural experience, teaches children about racial pride and the tradition and history of African American people. Parents who use this strategy sometimes go beyond relying solely on informal socialization within families. They also create formal rituals to socialize children into their community. The Passage, described in

BOX **13.1**

The Passage

The Passage is an initiation rite created by Nathan and Julia Hare (1985) for African Americans. The rite consists of a year of activities beginning with the eleventh birthday and culminating with a celebration on the twelfth birthday. The rite is primarily guided by family members, but the wider community is also involved. The purpose of the Passage is to socialize African American boys into the black community.

During the year, the boy is expected to accomplish a number of tasks, including:

1. Keeping a log.
2. Reading about African American culture and history.
3. Developing a list of his relatives and their residences.
4. Providing service to the community.
5. Adopting a senior citizen.
6. Preparing for future education.
7. Practicing courtesy and making contact with public officials to begin taking leadership in his community.
8. Preparing for the Passage Celebration, which includes fasting, presenting a speech, and responding to questions from a panel of adults.

Box 13.1, is one way parents approach racial socialization from this third point of view (Hare and Hare 1985).

The racial socialization strategies of the African American parents in these studies in some ways sound like the proposals made by Bem (1983) in her discussion of gender schema theory. African American parents teach their children to be aware of race discrimination and to develop alternative ways of seeing themselves and of confronting inequality. Bem calls for teaching children to become morally outraged at sex discrimination and to oppose it in their lives. Peters and Thornton find that African American parents also teach their children to cope with and resist racism.

Euro-American children also learn about racism and how to behave in racist or non-racist ways. Robyn Holmes (1995) interviewed kindergarteners about their perceptions of race, racism, and people of different racial ethnic groups. She concludes that five-year-olds have unclear ideas about race and racism. She argues that this is an ideal time to teach tolerance and respect for diversity. She recommends exposing children to many different people from a range of racial ethnic groups so that they do not form ideas about a group based on only a few people or a narrow sample of people. She also suggests being careful not to reinforce stereotypes and negative associations even through abstract factors such as associating the color black with evil or badness. In addition, Holmes recommends that teachers and parents create cooperative groups of children that are multicultural and provide opportunities for children to learn to appreciate people who are different in some ways from themselves.

This discussion of race and gender socialization shows the ways in which adults can socialize children into values and behaviors that contradict and counteract dominant ideologies. In this case, the dominant ideologies are racist or sexist, and the parents and other adults in the community are offering alternative ideas and behaviors to resist those ideas.

In some communities in the United States, parents and children find themselves at odds about whether to accept or reject the dominant value system. Immigrant children sometimes must negotiate two different social worlds—the world from which their parents came and the one in which they are currently living (Igoa 1995). Vietnamese immigrant children attempt to figure out what exactly is American while they argue with their parents about abandoning Vietnamese ways in order to become American. In one study, children commonly complained that their parents were too old-fashioned or too Vietnamese. One young woman said, "They don't understand about life here. They want us to do everything the way they did things when they were in Vietnam. And it isn't the same" (Zhou and Bankston 1998, p. 182).

A central contrast between the two cultures is the individualism of American society and the collectivism of Vietnamese culture. A young Vietnamese woman explained this difference:

> This may sound very silly, but a youngster who is becoming too American is the one who is having too much fun, too much fun in doing nontypical Vietnamese things such as enjoying yourself, unwilling to do hard work, and not obligating yourself to your family's best interests. To be an American you may be able to do whatever you want. But to be a Vietnamese, you must think of your family first. (Zhou and Bankston 1998, p. 166)

Obligation to family is a quality that is especially valued in daughters. One Vietnamese father said: "It is important that all children obey their parents. But it is more important for daughters to obey. The daughters will be mothers one day and they must be good mothers. So, they must obey their parents today" (Zhou and Bankston 1998, p. 175).

Television Socializes Children.   This discussion has emphasized the importance of families as a key place where children are learners of adult culture. Barbara Risman (1998) examined "fair families" that were trying to re-create alternative ideas and behaviors in regard to family and gender. These families practiced much of what Bem recommended, and their promotion of fairer, less gender-stratified families had an effect on their children's ideas. But the children also were influenced by the media, school, and especially their peers. Risman concludes that changing families is crucial to creating gender vertigo, which occurs when we go beyond gender whenever we can, ignore gender rules, and "push the envelope until we get dizzy." She argues that the destabilized moments when gender vertigo appears and our deeply held but incorrect beliefs about the "natural" differences between women and men are shaken allow an essential step in building a post–gender society in which gender is irrelevant. Gender vertigo can be created in our microlevel encounters in families, but change in individual identities and families alone is insufficient. Alterations must occur on many levels across wide areas of the social landscape.

One of the most important forces outside of families that can create gender vertigo or gender maintenance for children is the media, especially television. Children spend many hours watching television and learning about our culture. Ninety-eight percent of homes in the United States have television sets, more than have indoor toilets and telephones (U.S. Census Bureau 2001). The average American household has at least one television running over eight hours a day (Nielsen Media Research 2005). Two-thirds of all eight-to-eighteen-year-olds have a TV in their room (Kaiser Family Foundation 2005) Children as young as two or three have favorite programs. In addition, children and teens are spending increasing amounts of time on new media like the Internet and video games without cutting back on the time they spend watching TV. Eighty-six percent of children live in a house with a computer (Day, Janus, and Davis 2005)

Boys and girls watch TV about the same amount of time, and households of different social classes do not vary much in terms of television watching. Race ethnicity does seem to have an influence on how many hours are watched. On average white children age eight to eighteen spend 2.45 hours watching television every day; Hispanic children spend 3.23 and black children spend 4.05. In addition white children spend another 1.03 hours playing video games and watching movies. Hispanic children spend 1.22 and black children 1.52 on these latest electronic media (Rideout, Roberts, and Foehr 2005).

When children watch television they are being sold images, and those images are frequently gender stereotyped (Witt 2000). Sarah Sobieraj (1998) sampled toy ads to see what gender images were being promoted. She found that toy companies were selling boys the image of aggressive dominator and girls the image of pretty vanity. Sixty-nine percent of ads directed toward boys contained incidents of physical and verbal aggression. None of the ads directed toward girls showed any acts of violence. In addition, nearly all of the acts of violence were depicted as having positive consequences—victory, smiles, "high fives," and laughter on the part of the aggressors. Domination was another difference in the ads. The researchers looked for words like *control, boss, power,* and *in command* to measure dominance. In the ads for girls there was little competition, and in only 2 percent of the advertisements was there any mention of domination. For boys, competition was a constant theme, and the toys' ability to place the boys in command was frequent, with overt statements describing toys such as action figures as "an eternal hero with power and friends by his side" (Sobieraj 1998, p. 25).

The toy advertisements with only girls in them had messages focused on physical attractiveness. Fifty-six percent of the ads directed toward girls had references to physical attractiveness. None of those for boys did. The ads frequently used words like *gorgeous, pretty,* and *beautiful.* They also showed girls posing in front of mirrors, combing hair, applying cosmetics, sighing and gasping over clothes, and receiving admiring glances from others (Sobieraj 1998).

In regular programming as well as ads, gender stereotyping occurs (Witt 2000). For example, men are more visible on TV. During prime time, women continue to be outnumbered by men, with little change since the 1950s. Female characters are younger, less mature, and less authoritative than males. Female characters are also less diverse in appearance than male characters. Although both men and women on TV tend to be young, thin, and attractive, men are more likely to vary from this model than women.

Men and women also behave differently on television. TV women are more emotionally expressive and seven times more likely than men to use sex or romantic charm to get what they want.

The settings for women's activities are also different from those of men. Women characters are more often shown at home. Even when women characters are employed outside of the home, they usually are not shown on the job, and the plots revolve around family matters and interpersonal relationships. The most important message the media gives us about girls and women is that looking good is their most important achievement (Warlamount 1993).

The activities in which men and women participate are different on TV. Women do the housework, while men rarely are seen working in kitchens and laundry rooms. In Chapter 7 we noted that women do about two times as much housework as men do in real life. On television women are shown doing housework five times as often as men (Keller 1999). Men are much more likely than women to appear in action/drama programs and to be problem solvers. Men are also more likely than women to be violent or criminal.

Television also plays a role in socializing us about race ethnicity, and the messages are distorted and biased. All racial ethnic people are less likely to appear on television than European Americans, and the nonwhites who are shown are almost always African Americans. And even African Americans do not often appear as experts on television. In 2004, 8 percent of guests on news shows were black, and almost all these appearances were of three individuals: Colin Powell, Condoleezza Rice, and Juan Williams (National Urban League 2005).

Latino Americans are especially invisible relative to their real numbers in the population. Although Latinos are the largest minority group in the United States (about 13% of the population), they make up only 4 percent of the regular characters on television (LaPrensa 2004). And when they do appear, they are portrayed in narrow ways. Latinos are twice as likely to appear as criminals than whites and four times as likely as African Americans (Condry 1989). In addition to the role of lawbreaker, Latino Americans are most frequently shown as needy victims—patients in medical programs. Asian Americans are given the role of "exotic" and are rarely shown in familiar, commonplace roles of spouse or parent (National Asian Pacific American Legal Consortium 2005). Native Americans are so invisible that it is difficult to do research on their images on television. In the past two decades, Native Americans have appeared in only five series and two advertisements on television. In addition to the invisibility and stereotyping of racial ethnic groups, people of diverse race and ethnicity are rarely shown interacting with each other, particularly as friends (Graves 1996).

Race stereotypes are combined with gender stereotypes, resulting in the portrayal of African American women in a negative manner. Non–Euro-American women are even more invisible than men, and only one-third to one-half as likely as racial ethnic men to appear. When African American women are shown, they are depicted as unskilled, unpolished, and lacking decorum; rarely in control of situations; financially dependent on a parent or even a white family; never giving information unless it is about child care or housekeeping; and, if single, desperately preoccupied with finding a husband (Renzetti and Curran 1992, p. 116). In the most recent reality television, African American women appear as perpetually perturbed, tooth-sucking, finger-wagging harpies, the "sista with an attitude" (Wiltz 2004).

Age stereotypes are also combined with gender. Women, especially older women, portray victims of crimes. Condry (1989) found that older women are victims of violent attacks on television thirty times more than they are in real life.

When we think of the socialization of children, we tend to emphasize the importance of families. We can see from the enormous amount of time that children are exposed to television and the powerful messages being delivered by the media that forces outside of families also play a critical role in socializing children and that the lessons children learn from the media can influence their behavior and experience in families.

Television is a feature of the macrolevel of social organization. The huge television industry is itself shaped by governmental regulation and business pressures. This review of TV in children's lives shows the way in which the macrolevel of society has an important effect on children, if only in terms of the amount of their time it consumes. In addition, the images undoubtedly have an effect on the thinking and behavior of children. A child's individual family is an aspect of the microlevel of social organization. The microlevel interaction that takes place in families is a critical factor in socialization. But the macrolevel, in this case TV, plays an important role as well.

Children as Threats

The second dominant image of children is that they are threats to the community and to their families. There is some evidence that children can have a negative effect on their families. For example, children may have a detrimental effect on parents' mental health. In an extensive review of the literature, Sara McLanahan and Julia Adams (1987) conclude that parents with children at home are worse off than nonparents on a number of indicators of psychological well-being. Compared with nonparents, parents are less happy and satisfied, and they are more worried, depressed, and anxious. One man in a study of people who had been married for many years summed it up for the researcher: "When the kids come along, they have a way of bursting the bubble and making things less than perfect" (Mackey and O'Brien 1995, p. 62).

Mothers who are primarily or solely responsible for children are further negatively affected by them because of the additional work they create. Mirowsky and Ross (1989) examined the depression levels of husbands and wives. They found that unemployed wives without children and employed mothers whose husbands shared responsibility for child care had lower than average levels of depression. But wives with small children, paid jobs, difficulty finding child care, and sole responsibility for child care had much higher than average levels of depression. When we looked at the division of child care and housework in families in Chapter 7, we saw that this last type of situation is the most typical one.

Children may also have a negative effect on their parents' marriages. "Satisfaction with marriage decreases with the birth of the first child, and does not return to prechildren levels until all the children have left home. As the number of children, especially young children, increases, marital satisfaction decreases" (Mirowsky and Ross 1989, p. 103).

The negative effect children have on parents' psychological well-being may be related to the decreased amount of time husbands and wives have to spend together (Belsky and Kelly 1998). In addition, even when parents do get time alone without the children, they must spend much of it considering issues that relate to the children (Mirowsky and Ross 1989; White, Booth, and Edwards 1986).

Children may also cause distress for their parents by increasing the economic strains on families (Mirowsky and Ross 1989). Women's earnings fall about 7 percent for each child they raise (Budig and England 2001). Furthermore, with every addition to a household, each dollar must be stretched further to cover food, clothes, and all the other necessi-

TABLE 13.1   What's It Going to Cost to Raise a Child from Birth to Age 18?

Total	Housing	Food	Transport	Clothing	Health	Education/ Child Care	Miscellaneous
Couples with income less than before taxes $41,700							
$134,370	$44,580	$26,490	$18,660	$8,490	$10,680	$12,090	$13,380
Couples with income before taxes between $41,700 and $70,200							
$184,320	$61,650	$31,770	$25,980	$9,930	$13,830	$21,180	$19,980
Couples with income before taxes more than $70,200							
$269,520	$100,080	$39,570	$34,860	$12,810	$15,870	$33,870	$32,460

Source: U.S. Department of Agriculture 2004

ties. More people in a household also increases the pressure for a larger, more expensive place to live.

Table 13.1 shows the cost of raising one child for families from different income brackets in 2004. The total ranges from $134,370 to $269,520. The biggest expense is for housing. These estimates take children only up to age eighteen. A four year degree on average will cost an additional $45,416 at a state school and $110,064 at a private institution (Wang 2005).

Given the inadequacies of child care in our society, which are discussed in Chapter 12, having children frequently makes it more difficult for all of the adults in a household to be in the paid labor force, which further increases the financial strain. Hofferth and Phillips (1987) found that the birth of a first child had a greater negative effect on family finances than the birth of subsequent children and that reductions in income with each birth are related to reductions in the labor force participation of their mothers. These foregone wages can cost between $466,613 and $1,885,454 (Longman 1999).

The economic strain of children in families may be prolonged as young adults delay moving out of their parents' homes (L. White 1994). In 2002, about 55 percent of men between 18 and 24 and 46 percent of women between 18 and 24 were living in their parents' homes. This is compared with 52 percent of men and 35 percent of women of these ages who were residing with their parents in 1960 (U.S. Census Bureau 2003). These statistics also may be deceptively low because they can include college students who are counted as living away when really they are dependent on the parents, at least financially (Ambert 1997). Several factors influence young people to stay in their parents' homes, including delay in age of first marriage, reluctance to set up a separate household because their incomes are low and/or their expenses are high, and tendency to return home after a divorce.

About half of children return home for a least a brief period of time after first leaving. The proportion of those who remain in their parents' homes declines with age. Seventy-four percent of 18- to 19-year-olds lived with their parents, while 40 percent of those aged

20 to 24 and 16 percent of those aged 25 to 29 did. Gender also creates differences. Women leave their parents' homes earlier then men, and they are less likely to return. Young men also differ from women because the men are more likely to believe that it is their right to receive financial assistance from their parents (Ambert 1997). Race ethnicity shows variation as well. Vietnamese, Korean, Filipino, and Chinese young people over eighteen are more likely to live with their families than whites. But Japanese are less likely. African Americans and Hispanics are much more likely than non-Hispanic whites to live in extended families (L. White 1994).

When Thorne (1987) proposed that children are frequently thought of as threats in our culture, she noted such examples as images of gangs and youthful criminals that are common in the media. Her emphasis was on the way in which we perceive children to be a threat rather than the way in which children might pose real threats to adults.

Research by other scholars on the mental health, marriages, and financial situation of parents, however, shows that the image of children as threats is not entirely without an empirical basis. Research indicates that when children are in families, psychological distress, marital unhappiness, and financial strain increase. People raising children seem to have problems in these areas that are more intense than those for nonparents.

The Positive Effects of Children on Parents

The prior section has focused attention on the problems children can sometimes cause their parents. Children can have a positive effect on their parents as well. Elise Boulding (1980) has investigated empathy among children and the way they nurture their parents. Boulding defines *empathy* as the ability to understand how another person is feeling without actually experiencing what the other person is experiencing. She argues that children develop the capacity to empathize at a remarkably early age.

Boulding asked adolescents and college students to give an example in writing of when they had been supportive of their father or mother before they were fifteen and another example from after they were fifteen. Nearly all the respondents were able to provide examples. They described incidents from when they were as young as five years old. Incidents included everyday situations like making a Father's Day card to providing support during such family crises as illness, job problems, death, and divorce. The respondents remembered performing chores, providing companionship, listening, and counseling. One woman remembered at age nine taking care of two infant brothers so that her mother could have some time to herself. Another remembered running with her father while he was training for the Boston Marathon. A man remembered dropping out of school for a year to help his father rehabilitate after surgery. Boulding concludes that her findings reinforce the need for sociologists to pay more attention to the positive character of children's contribution to their parents' lives and, perhaps even more important, to reconceptualize children as active, autonomous social beings.

Beverly Purrington (1980) is another scholar who investigated the positive effects of children on their parents. She interviewed seventy parents, asking them how they perceived that their children had affected their lives. The responses to this question fell into two broad categories. Parents said that having children necessitated commitment and decision making that made them feel good about themselves, like responsible adults. In addition, parents

BOX 13.2
Birth Parents, Children, and Adoption

Should birth parents be able to keep their records sealed from the children they have given up for adoption? Should the courts refuse to provide information on such children to their birth parents? These controversial questions pose the interests of a child against his or her birth parents. Many birth parents wish to protect their anonymity when they choose to place their children for adoption. Many children who have been adopted do not want to be contacted by their birth parents. But what if there is disagreement on this question between birth parent and child? What if one wishes to make contact and the other does not?

Adoptions in United States are marked by two factors: legality and confidentiality. The relationship established between the child, birth parents, and adoptive parents is legally binding, and the entire procedure is focused on protecting the privacy of all parties.

Three ways of handling adoption have been practiced in the United States: confidential, mediated, and fully disclosed. In confidential adoptions minimal information is exchanged between the adoptive family and the birth family; information is never exchanged directly; and sharing of information ends with the adoption. In these cases the records are sometimes sealed, and adoptive parents may not reveal to anyone, including the child, that the child was adopted. Mediated adoptions may include some exchange of personal mementos like letters, pictures, or even personal meetings. But no fully identifying information is revealed. In fully disclosed adoptions, exchanges and meetings may be frequent and direct and sometimes include contact with extended family, as well the birth parent and the immediate adoptive family.

Recently the trend has been in the direction of opening up adoption. Advocates for more open adoption argue that it helps humanize the process. It is better for birth parents because it makes them feel less guilty. It is better for adoptive parents because it can help them answer questions about their child, and it may increase their ability to find a child since birth parents feel more comfortable with the process and may therefore be more likely to consider adoption as an option. It is better for adoptive children because knowledge of one's past is a basic human need (Grotevant and McRoy 1997).

Critics, however, maintain that in spite of these advantages there are also risks. Birth mothers may find it more difficult to overcome their guilt and move on with their lives. Adoptive parents may feel they never quite become "real" parents. Adoptive children may have identity problems.

---

said that having children allowed them to be more childlike by legitimizing more open reactions to experiences and more heightened emotional responses to their surroundings.

One man explained how being a parent made demands on him that he felt good about being able to meet: "It's fun to just have the ability to be a protecting force in somebody's environment—it gives you a sense of accomplishment and importance—it's easy to get that with a kid. It's much easier to get that with a kid than an adult" (Purrington 1980, p. 124).

Several parents told stories of how having a child allowed them to be more open to participation in activities they otherwise might have felt were unseemly for adults, such as watching cartoons and playing on swings. One father said:

> Suddenly 'cause you have a kid you have a license to do all of these things again. And that's fun, that's really terrific—one of the good things, the greatest joys of having kids is that you

can be a kid again, you're suddenly allowed to do things that when you're grown up you're no longer supposed to do, you know—suddenly Christmas is Christmas again. You know, you remember Christmas as a kid was great joy, and then it got sort of dull, 'cause the miracle had gone out of it and then suddenly you have kids and oh boy, it's just a miracle to them and then you can enjoy it that way. (Purrington 1980, p. 64)

In addition to giving access to certain activities, children also provided access to memories. Parents spoke of remembering their own childhoods only after seeing their children involved in activities and situations that had been part of their childhoods.

Parents also believed that having children allowed them to experience an intensity of emotion they would not otherwise have felt. A mother described the way being a parent had helped her to express love: "There's real warmth there that I never felt with any other person, but I guess that's been a positive influence in learning how to love" (Purrington 1980, p. 107). A father described the intensity of emotion he experienced at the birth of his children:

I was there in the delivery room right there when they were both born and that is just the most fantastic emotion you have ever experienced. It's just such an amazing feeling of relief and joy and happiness—it's like nothing else you've ever experienced—you both just start crying. (Purrington 1980, p. 100)

Boulding's and Purrington's work shows us how children can make a positive contribution to their parents' lives. Research on Salvadoran and Guatemalan families who immigrated to the United States shows another example of how children can become important members of the family, in this case because of their ability to learn the language more quickly than adults. One refugee explained:

I see a lot of situations where [the parents] will take a young child to get their gas installed, to ask why their services were shut off, to pay the bill. So it's the children here who learn to read and write for their parents who brought them. In that sense the children play a different role from other children because they are secretaries or assistants to their parents in order to function. (Dorrington 1995, p. 121)

Boulding's, Purrington's, and Dorrington's work is unusual because of its focus on the autonomy of children and their beneficial effect on their parents. The perception of children as threatening to their parents' well-being is much more prevalent in the literature.

Why are children perceived to be threats in our society? And why are they blamed for problems like financial difficulties in families that could just as easily be blamed on inadequate social institutions? Letty Pogrebin (1983) argues that the perception of children as threats is rooted in an ideology that prevails in our society. She contends that "America is a nation fundamentally ambivalent about its children, often afraid of its children, and frequently punitive toward its children" (p. 42). Pogrebin has named this ideology *pedophobia,* from *ped* meaning child and *phobia* meaning fear, dread, aversion, or hatred. Pogrebin argues that pedophobia is expressed not only in an ideology that perceives children as threats, but also in the victimization of children, the third image that Thorne (1987) observed was dominant in our culture.

According to Pogrebin (1983), the victimization of children can be categorized into two types: individualized pedophobia and institutionalized pedophobia. Individualized pedophobia is the cruelty of parents who physically and sexually abuse their own children. Institutionalized pedophobia is made up of the public policies, practices, and institutions that keep children impoverished, malnourished, unhealthy, and frequently unable to survive.

Children as Victims: Child Abuse

Children are often victims of a number of types of abuse in families. They are at high risk for abuse for three reasons. First, they are dependent on adults and have little freedom to make independent choices. Second, they are smaller and weaker. Third, they have little legal protection (Finkelhor 1994; Finkelhor and Dziuba-Leatherman 1995).

The numbers of children who were reportedly abused dropped by half between 1993 and 2001, but the numbers are still high. In 2003, about 1.9 million investigations concerning the welfare of children were made by Child Protective Services: 60 percent were for neglect, 19 percent were for physical abuse, 10 percent were for sexual abuse, and 5 percent were for emotional maltreatment. Children from birth to age three had the highest rates of victimization (U.S. Department of Health and Human Services 2005). Girls (51.7%) were a little more likely to be victims than boys (47.9%) (U. S. Department of Health and Human Services 2002).

The U.S. Department of Health and Human Services asserts that these numbers are serious underestimates. Their research with child-serving professionals estimates that the true numbers are probably triple the number officially reported by public agencies (Walker, Brooks, and Wrightsman 1999).

In the Child Abuse Prevention and Treatment Act (CAPTA) of 1974, Congress defined *child abuse* as overt acts of aggression such as excessive verbal derogation, beating or inflicting physical injury, and sexual abuse. *Child neglect* means repeatedly failing to provide adequate physical and emotional care. In some states, it is further defined as leaving a child under six unattended in a car. *Medical neglect* is failure to provide or cooperate with essential medical care. *Emotional abuse* or *neglect* means intentionally being overly harsh and critical, failing to provide guidance, or being uninterested in the child's needs. Professionals who deliver health services are required by law to report these abuses in all fifty states. The federal law also requires states to grant immunity to persons who report abuse and neglect of children (Walker, Brooks, and Wrightsman 1999).

Although all of these harm children, the public's attention has been almost exclusively focused on physical abuse, and there is little discussion of or political activity around the other, "lesser" forms of abuse. In this section, we examine the problem of physical abuse of children and then move to a discussion of the sexual abuse of children in families.

Even though every state now has compulsory child abuse reporting laws, it is difficult to obtain accurate statistics because much abuse still goes unreported. One in seven Americans reports having been physically disciplined in ways that would be defined as abuse by CAPTA: punched, kicked, choked, or even more severely punished (Moore 1995). These reports come from adults describing their childhood experiences. The numbers reported by adults recalling childhood are seven times higher than the numbers elicited from parents who are asked about their own behavior with their children.

Murder, which is the most extreme example of child abuse, is the fifth highest cause of death among children (Gelles and Cornell 1985). In 2000, about 1,400 children died from

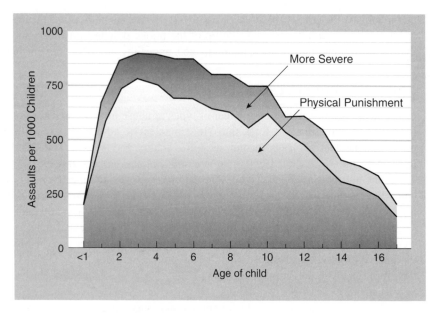

FIGURE 13.1   Physical Punishment and Severe Assaults of Children by Age

Source: R. Gelles and M. Straus, 1995, *Physical Violence in American Families.* Copyright © 1995 by Transaction Publishers, Inc. Reprinted by permission.

abuse or neglect. As many as 60 percent of deaths of children resulting from abuse or neglect may not be reported as murder. Children under age four are the most frequent victims of child fatalities accounting for 86 percent of the victims (U.S. Department of Health and Human Services 2004).

Figure 13.1 shows the distribution of abuse by age. Among every 1,000 infants below the age of one, 209 experienced physical violence at least once during the year. The rate peaks at 905 per 1,000 among three- to four-year-olds and declines with age to 180 per 1,000 among seventeen-year-olds (Gelles and Straus 1995).

Parents are not the only ones involved in violence against children in families. Sibling violence is also common, although it is rarely reported. Gelles (1977) found that 80 percent of children who had sisters and brothers reported that they had tried to hurt a sibling during the previous year. Fifty percent said they had kicked, punched, or bitten a sibling. Forty percent had hit a sister or brother with an object, and 15 percent had beaten one up. Parents reported that their children used on average twenty-one acts of violence a year on their siblings (Straus, Gelles and Steingmetz 1980). If these percentages are extrapolated to the entire population, 36 million attacks occurred between siblings that legally could have been considered assault (Steinmetz, Clavan, and Stein 1990). When (simple) assault is reported to the police, in about 70 percent of the cases the victim is the offender's brother or sister (Durose et al. 2005).

Mothers, Fathers, and Child Abuse.   In Chapter 11, we concluded that men are usually the perpetrators of violence and wives the victims in violent encounters between adults in

BOX 13.3

Spanking Controversy

Child abuse is defined as extreme acts such as kicking, biting, punching, beating, burning, scalding, threatening with a knife or gun, and using a knife or gun. In the United States, spanking or hitting a child with an object such as a stick or belt is not considered abuse according to the law and informal norms (Straus and Mathur 1996). This definition is currently being debated. Some argue that "mild physical punishment" is necessary and useful. Others contend that trivializing terms like *spank, smack,* and *slap* hide seriously degrading and damaging treatment of children. Phillip Davis (1999) has analyzed the way in which spanking has been covered by the popular press to trace the contrasting views and changes in opinions over the past five decades. He found five key groups among those who advocate using spanking.

First, there are those who maintain that spanking is a sign of nonpermissiveness. Children who are raised permissively are believed by this group to be in danger of becoming vandals, thieves, and too selfish for enduring marriages. A second group asserts that spanking prepares children for the real world, making them tough enough to endure tribulations they will face in adult life. A third group claims that spanking is biblically sanctioned. The phrase they often quote—"spare the rod and spoil the child"—is not from the Bible, however, but from a poem by Samuel Butler published in 1664. The fourth group defines spanking as a morally neutral technique for child rearing. According to these advocates, spanking is quick, effective, and rational. The fifth group emphasizes the psychic release of spanking. They claim that spanking allows parents to relatively harmlessly release their anger while it simultaneously allows children to relieve themselves of guilt.

Arguments from the critics of spanking fall into three categories. The first group maintains that spanking is compulsive. Parents mindlessly spank their children because the behavior has become habitual. Their child behaves in some way they disapprove of, and they reach out with little thought and slap him or her. A second group asserts that spanking is a demeaning and violent act. Spanking is degrading for both the parent and child, and it perpetuates a cycle of solving problems with aggression and violence. The third group claims that spanking is abusive. Physical attacks are legally permitted on no other social category except children (Straus 1991). Even prisoners have more rights than children to avoid physical punishment (Walker, Brooks, and Wrightsmen 1999).

A majority of people still approve of spanking. Straus and Mathur (1996) warn, however, that people have many ways of defining *spanking* and use the word to describe any form of corporal punishment that falls short of physical abuse. Women are less likely to approve of spanking. Age also influences this opinion. Older men over fifty (81%) are more likely than younger men under thirty (60%) to agree with the statement that "a good hard spanking is sometimes necessary."

There has been a change over time in the percentage of people who say they approve of spanking. Acceptance of corporal punishment may be declining, or at least approval of spanking is going down (Straus 1994; Straus and Maher 1996). In 1968, 94 percent of the population approved of spanking a child who misbehaves. Straus and Mathur (1996, p. 94) define *spanking* as hitting a child on the buttocks. Straus and Maher applaud the decline shown, but caution that a backlash may occur as those who favor corporal punishment organize to prohibit public policy from punishing parents who use corporal punishment. They note, for example, a bill that was passed by the Florida legislature that prohibited child protective services from ruling that a child had been abused if the only evidence was that the parents had used corporal punishment and the child showed welts or bruises (Finkelhor 1994).

families. Along with gender, generation is important in violence against children. Exactly which of these is more important depends on which statistics you look at. In FBI reports men are more likely to commit violent acts against their children. Biological fathers account for about 41 percent of violent offenses reported to the police against juveniles, while mothers account for 20 percent (Finkelhor and Ormrod 2001).

In studies of abuse reported to protective services, women acting alone (40% of cases) are more likely than fathers acting alone (19%) to abuse their children. Eighteen percent of children were abused by both parents (U.S. Department of Health and Human Services 2002). The large proportion of child abuse for which women are responsible can be explained partly by the greater amount of time women spend with children. If children spend most of their time with their mothers, and fathers are still responsible for half of the child abuse, women must be significantly less likely to abuse children than are men. Judith Martin's (1983) work supports this contention. She found that mothers are as likely as fathers to abuse young children, but three out of four abused adolescents had been abused by their fathers. Adolescents are also likely to spend more time than infants with their fathers.

The large share of abuse for which women are reported may also be a result of the way in which research has been conducted (J. Martin 1983). For example, nearly all of the research on single-parent families and the incidence of abuse is on mother-only families, and in general researchers who study child abuse have tended to focus on mothers. Nevertheless, women must take responsibility for a significant proportion of the physical abuse of children.

Incest.   Incest is another form of child abuse. Incest refers to sexual contact between close kin. The word *incest* can refer to sexual relationships that are not abusive. For example, a sister and brother might choose as adults to have sexual contact in a mutually consenting relationship. In most of the literature in contemporary sociology, however, the word *incest* is used to mean sexual abuse by a relative.

The prohibition against incest is so widespread in human societies that the incest taboo is called a cultural universal (Murdock 1949). In the United States (and probably most other societies) the taboo, however, is much stronger in ideology than it is in actual behavior. Relatively large proportions of people report incestuous experiences. For example, Diana Russell (1986) found that 16 percent of a random sample of 930 adult women had been sexually victimized as children by a relative. Self-report studies of adults indicate that 20 percent of women and 5 to 10 percent of men recall a child sexual assault or sexual abuse incident (Fineklhor 1994). Furthermore, the actual incidence of incest is probably substantially higher than the reported rate.

Gender is an important factor in incest. For example, in Finkelhor's survey 93 percent of the people who said they had experienced incest said it had involved an older man and a girl (Finkelhor 1979). Russell (1986) found that uncles were the largest category of perpetrators, accounting for 25 percent of the incidents. Uncles were followed closely by fathers and stepfathers, who accounted for 24 percent of the incidents (National Council for the Prevention of Child Abuse 1991).

The incidence of reported child abuse including sexual abuse as well as physical injury, emotional abuse, and neglect, increased from about 700,000 in 1976 to almost 2 million in 1985. During this same time period, incest comprised an increasingly larger pro-

BOX **13.4**

Has the U.S. Government Always Sought to Protect
Children from Abuse?

Although child abuse has occurred throughout U.S. history, until about twenty-five years ago most physicians, even pediatricians, denied that abuse occurred. The legal system also failed to protect children by either providing no laws restricting child abuse or insufficiently supporting laws that did exist (Johnson 1991).

Early American common law stated: "If one beats a child until it bleeds, then it will remember the words of its master. But if one beats it to death, then the law applies" (Radhill 1968, p. 4). While murder was illegal, anything short of murder in the treatment of a child seemed to be acceptable. John Johnson (1991) describes a famous case that illustrated this assumption and created the impetus for establishing the Society for the Prevention of Cruelty to Children:

> In 1875 the American Society for the Prevention of Cruelty to Animals (ASPCA) in New York City was asked to intervene for the purpose of protecting Mary Ellen, a nine-year-old girl who had been neglected, beaten and even slashed with scissors by her foster parents. Earlier efforts to intervene had failed, because the parental right to discipline had been heretofore considered absolute by law. So the ASPCA was asked to intervene to protect Mary Ellen on the argument that she was a member of the animal kingdom and thus the legitimate recipient of laws already on the books to protect animals. (Johnson, 1991 p. 673)

As recently as the 1960s, child abuse and neglect were still invisible. Among a few professionals, their existence had been suggested but dismissed as invalid accusations. In 1962, the first study of child abuse was done by the American Humane Association, and in 1963 the government finally began to take the initiative to both study and address the problem. By 1967, forty-nine states had new laws mandating reporting child abuse (Johnson 1991).

---

portion of this growing total. In 1976, about 3.2 percent of the reported cases of child abuse and neglect were for sexual abuse. By 1985, sexual abuse accounted for 11.7 percent of the total (American Association for Protecting Children 1985).

Although incest is illegal in every state, the legal system is organized in a way that hinders the ability of victims to protect themselves. During a trial, a child may be cross examined by an attorney or even the father or other accused molester. In some states, victims must provide other witnesses, which is of course difficult to do.

In a study of 256 known cases of sexual abuse of children involving 250 offenders conducted by the Brooklyn Society for the Prevention of Cruelty to Children, parents and family found the police process so trying and frightening to the children that 76 cases were dropped, leaving 174 cases eligible for prosecution. Once charges were officially made, the number of interrogations and court appearances resulted in such trauma to the children and their families that another 77 families were so discouraged that they, too, dropped the charges. This left 97 cases. Of this number, 39 offenders either absconded, were acquitted, or were convicted on a lesser charge, such as assault, rather than rape or incest; and 5 were committed to mental institutions. Of the 53 found guilty of sexual abuse (excluding the 5 sent to mental institutions), 30 escaped jail sentence by suspension or fine, 18 were sentenced to jail for from six months to a year, and 5 received indeterminate sentences (Begus and Armstrong 1982, p. 243).

How harmful is incest? Researchers have made careful studies of adult women who describe the great pain and feelings of powerlessness, degradation, and wrongdoing they carry into adulthood (Russell 1986).

Russell (1986, p. 139) interviewed a sample of 151 women who had been incest victims as children. Twenty-five percent reported many long-term effects from the abuse; 26 percent reported some effects; 27 percent reported few effects; and 22 percent reported no long-term effects. The most frequently mentioned long-term effects were negative feelings about men in general and about the perpetrator; negative feelings about themselves, such as shame and guilt; and negative feelings in general, such as fear, anxiety, depression, and mistrust.

Radical Feminist Theory on Incest.   Radical feminism sees society as permeated by oppression of many types—race, class, age, and sexuality. But gender oppression is the most salient and the focus of their attention. From the radical feminist point of view, the most basic power resource that men hold in their oppression of women is physical force, with violence as the last line of defense in the maintenance of the system (Lengermann and Wallace 1985).

Radical feminists use the term *patriarchy* to describe the system of oppression of women that they believe underlies all other systems of oppression (Firestone 1970). The term *patriarchy* can be used in a variety of ways. One use of the term refers to a historically specific form of male dominance. For example, patriarchal families in Puritan communities were ones in which fathers dominated entire households, including younger men, women, and children who were both kin and nonkin. In a second, more general, sense, *patriarchy* means the dominance and control of women by men in nuclear families and extended households, as well as in nonfamily social institutions such as government and work. Herman and Hirschmann (1977) have used the second concept of patriarchy to explain the particular problem of incest.

Herman and Hirschmann (1977) examined the relationship between incest and the structure of patriarchy and conclude that (1) the social sanctions against father-daughter incest are relatively weak in a patriarchal family system like that of the contemporary United States; and (2) within individual families, incest occurs most frequently in families characterized by extremely dominant fathers or stepfathers. Incest, they conclude, is a result of patriarchal families within a patriarchal society (Herman and Hirschmann 1977, p. 741).

In further research, Herman (1981) began to specify the characteristics of patriarchal incestuous families. She compared families where fathers and daughters had seductive but not sexual relationships to families where incest had occurred. She found that incest was more likely to occur in families that (1) rigidly conformed to traditional gender roles, (2) had fathers who dominated through the use of force and expressed no contrition for their behavior, and (3) had mothers who were physically or psychologically disabled (Devlin 2005; Gordon and O'Keefe 1984).

BOX **13.5**

Ten Myths That Perpetuate Corporal Punishment

Murray Straus (1994) has been an active researcher in the area of corporal punishment and violence in families. He defines corporal punishment as "the use of physical force with the intention of causing a child to experience pain, but not injury, for the purpose of correction or control of the child's behavior" (p. 4). This definition includes spanking. Straus assessed the social science research on corporal punishment, spanking, discipline, and parenting. Based on his review, he concluded that corporal punishment of children in the United States is extremely common and fraught with myths. He has proposed that ten important myths serve to obscure our understanding of violence against children in families.

Myth 1: Spanking works better.
Research shows that corporal punishment is no more effective than noncorporal punishment like reasoning and "time out" and that sometimes it is less effective. Even if hitting a child stops the immediate behavior, in the long run it makes the job of parenting more difficult because children are more likely to do what their parents want them to when they feel a strong bond of affection. Spanking can reduce those feelings.

Myth 2: Spanking is needed as a last resort.
Using spanking as a last resort is probably the worst time because by the time parents believe they are at the last option, they are very angry. Most episodes of physical abuse started as physical punishment that got out of hand.

Myth 3: Spanking is harmless.
Research shows that harmful long-term side effects include increased risk of delinquency and criminal behavior, wife beating, depression, masochistic sex, and lowered earnings.

Myth 4: One or two times won't cause any damage.
Greater risks of negative side effects are associated with a higher incidence of corporal punishment, but even a smaller incidence is associated with some negative effects, like later abusing children, depression, and violence and crime.

Myth 5: Parents can't stop without help.
All of us could use help learning to be better parents, but all of us can stop using corporal punishment by asserting that we will not under any circumstances hit a child.

Myth 6: If you don't spank, your children will be spoiled or run wild.
Children who behave most aggressively are those whose parents ignore their aggression and use high levels of corporal punishment. Children who behave least aggressively have parents who condemn aggression and use low degrees of corporal punishment.

Myth 7: Parents spank rarely or only for serious problems.
Parents who spank tend to use this method of discipline almost any time their child misbehaves. Often parents use it as a first resort, without trying anything else and without offering any explanation to the child who is being hit.

(continued)

B O X **13.5** (continued)

Myth 8: By the time a child is a teenager, parents have stopped.
About half of parents of thirteen- and fourteen-year-olds report slapping their children. Even when children are as old as seventeen, 20 percent of parents are still hitting them, although by the teens it is usually a slap in the face rather than on the bottom.

Myth 9: If parents don't spank, they will verbally abuse their children.
Research shows that those parents who do the least hitting also use the least verbal aggression.

Myth 10: It is unrealistic to expect parents to never spank.
It is always difficult to stop everyone from behaving in a particular manner, especially if their behavior is widely accepted, as spanking is. Nevertheless, changing ideas and even laws can help alter actions. Norway, Finland, Denmark, Austria, and Sweden have passed laws forbidding corporal punishment of children by their parents. Public opinion has increasingly supported these laws. Seventy-one percent of people in Sweden favor managing children without the use of corporal punishment.

Children as Victims: Poverty

A second type of victimization of children is through poverty. The poverty rate for children fell from about 27 percent to about 14 percent between 1959 and 1970, and in the early 1970s rose again until it peaked in 1993 and then fell. About 22 percent of children now live below the poverty line.

You should recall from Chapter 5 that poverty varies by race ethnicity among children. Although the majority of poor children are white, the proportion of children who are poor is higher in all racial ethnic groups compared with whites (Roosa et al 2002): 34 percent of black children are poor, 30 percent of Latino children are poor, 12.5 percent of Asian children are poor, and 10 percent of white childen are poor (Children's Defense Fund 2004).

Family structure also has an important effect on poverty and children. Of the 23.1 million children under the age of six, 71 percent lived in two-parent households, and relatively few of them (10.5%) were poor. The next largest group are children who lived with their single mothers. They made up about one-quarter of all children, and more than half of them were poor. Almost a third of those in father-only families (4% of the total population of children) or living with someone else (2% of the total population of children) were poor.

The United States does not rank well in comparisons to other industrialized nations (Children's Defense Fund 2004). Table 13.2 shows the proportion of children who are poor in eighteen countries. The lowest proportion is in Denmark, where 2.4 percent of the children are poor. The highest percentage is 27.2 percent in Mexico. The United States has the second-highest proportion of poor children at 21.9 percent.

Every day in America twenty-seven children die from poverty-induced causes. Although this number is shocking, it is not surprising when we look at the U.S. infant mortality rate, especially as it compares with other nations.

TABLE 13.2   Child Poverty in Rich Countries, 2005

Country	Percentage of Children Below National Poverty Lines	Country	Percentage of Children Below National Poverty Lines
Denmark	2.4	Greece	12.4
Finland	3.4	Poland	12.7
Norway	3.4	Spain	13.3
Sweden	4.2	Japan	14.3
Switzerland	6.8	Australia	14.7
Czech Republic	6.8	Canada	14.9
France	7.5	United Kingdom	15.4
Belgium	7.7	Portugal	15.6
Hungary	8.8	Ireland	15.7
Luxembourg	9.1	New Zealand	16.3
Netherlands	9.8	Italy	16.6
Germany	10.2	United States	21.9
Austria	10.2	Mexico	27.2

Source: UNICEF 2005. Child poverty in rich countries

The infant mortality rate is the number of children who die before their first birthday among every 1,000 babies born. Infant mortality is related to such factors as nutrition, housing, and access to health care. All these factors are related to poverty. Because the United States is such a wealthy nation, it is surprising to find that the infant mortality rate is so high.

Despite the wealth of the nation as a whole, 6.8 babies died for every 1,000 live births in the United States in 2001 (U.S. Census Bureau 2001). This rate is higher than in nations that are much poorer than the United States, such as Singapore, Hong Kong, Spain, and Ireland.

Black American children are at especially high risk. "A black child born in the inner-city of Boston has less chance of surviving the first year of life than a child born in Panama, North or South Korea or Uruguay" (Children's Defense Fund 1990, p. 6). The poverty and inadequate shelter and access to health care that result from racism take a heavy toll on black children.

Children do not have to die to be devastated by poverty. In 1991, the Stanford Center for the Study of Children, Family and Youth interviewed homeless children to find out how homelessness affects them. The research team asked the children what they would wish for if they had three wishes. One child said, "I wish we could be less poor. Not rich. But have enough to eat" (Stanford 1991, p. 22). Another wished for a car, a bed, and a kitchen for his family. One boy's list included enough money so that his father could buy food, money to rent an apartment, and, if there was money left over, a bike. The children were also asked what they liked most about themselves. One ten-year-old girl answered, "That I haven't gone crazy yet" (Stanford Center for the Studies of Families, Children, and Youth 1991, p. 25). The comments of these children show that poverty has deprived them of the most fundamental human needs and that their hopes and even their ideas about themselves have been dashed by homelessness.

The Children's Defense Fund (CDF) argues that the well-being of children cannot be left to their parents alone, but that the public and its representatives must act to raise children out of poverty. To encourage officials to take action to invest in our children, the CDF asserts that we must write or call the president and our state and national legislators. The CDF recommends that we educate our representatives by bringing them to visit children in day care centers, public housing, schools, and homeless shelters to see the problem for themselves. If our representatives do not respond to this type of education, the CDF suggests that we might run for office ourselves and that we must at least monitor public officials and use the ballot box to make our views known.

This point of view implies a focus on sources outside of families to take responsibility for children. In the scenario at the beginning of the chapter, Rodriguez told the class how his mother had found a way to survive the fire that destroyed their family's house and belongings. The solution she found was an individual one, and it was only partially successful. Rodriguez says they are poor now. Should his mother be left to solve these economic problems on her own? Who is responsible for children? Should their fate be left in the hands of parents alone, or should we, as the CDF suggests, call on the community and the government to provide for their well-being? These questions are further examined in the next chapter.

Sisters and Brothers

This discussion has focused on relationships between adults and children in families, but another set of relationships is also very important in our lives, that between siblings. The median number of siblings fell dramatically from 1865 to 1994. You should remember that the median refers to the midpoint. Half the people had more siblings than the number indicated and half had less. In 1856, the median was about seven sisters and brothers. In 1994, the median was about two brothers and sisters. As we grow older, we lose siblings. Twenty percent of Americans over sixty-five have no siblings. But most of us have had a sister or brother at some time. Only about 5 percent of the population have never had a sibling (Crispell 1999).

Our relationships with our siblings vary depending on how much we interact with them. Table 13.3 shows how often adults visit with their sisters and brothers. Older people are more likely to not see their siblings at all than younger adults. Probably this is because of physical distance between older adults and their siblings. Seventy percent of adults over seventy-five have a sister or brother living more than three hundred miles away (Crispell 1996). Adults between the ages of twenty and thirty-four are most likely to see their siblings very often, two or three times a week. Notice that the table does not give specific information about adults between eighteen and twenty-five because the sample size of this group in the study wasn't large enough to be reliable.

One particular kind of interaction sisters and brothers engage in is exchanging cards and gifts. Once again, older people are less likely than younger to send cards and gifts to siblings, but large proportions in all age categories exchange gifts and cards. Between 60

TABLE 13.3   Keeping in Touch

Age	No Visits	Once to Several Visits a Year	Two or More Times a Week
25–34	3.8%	31.8%	30.5%
35–44	7.4	44.2	16.9
45–54	11.4	51.3	11.6
55–64	10.8	45.5	11.5
65–74	17.7	47.4	11.2
75 and older	19.2	46.6	10.1
All adults over 18	9.4	42.7	18.1

Source: Crispell 1996, p. 201. This chart first appeared in the August 1996 edition of *American Demographics Magazine.* It is reprinted with permission.

and 85 percent of people say they exchange birthday and holiday gifts, and about four out of five say they send each other cards for holidays and special days.

When people need help they first look to their partners, children, and friends. But siblings are also an important resource. About one-fifth of people say they would turn to a sister or brother as a first or second choice when having difficulty with a spouse (23%), feeling depressed (20%), wanting to borrow money (19%), needing help during an illness (18%), to get advice (17%), or for help with household chores (16%). Specifically, they said they looked to brothers for physical help and sisters for emotional support (Crispell 1996).

Sibling relationships are important in families especially when we are children. As we grow older we are less likely to visit with our sisters and brothers but we still keep in touch by sending cards and gifts. (Ruth Root, Kalamazoo, Michigan)

Theoretical Problems in the Study of Children

Thus far, this chapter has described three dominant images of children in our society. In this section we turn our attention to two theoretical issues that emerge in our attempts to understand who children are and where they fit in families and in their community. The first issue addresses the question of how we conceptualize children and childhood and how that has changed historically. The second issue addresses the problem of the limiting character of the three dominant images and how feminist theory might help us uncover a fuller and more realistic picture of children and childhood in our society.

How Do We Think of Children and Childhood?

Most of us think of childhood as a natural process that is similar in all societies and historical periods. Human beings go through a fairly long period of being generally smaller and weaker, frequently less knowledgeable about their society and the world, and certainly less powerful than adults. In our society, we take it for granted that the people who fit into this category should be set off from the rest of us and given a special name—children. We also assume that these child-humans should be treated differently—in dress, responsibility, activities, and authority.

Historical evidence suggests that it is not valid to assume that there is a natural category of children. Furthermore, it is not valid to assume that there is an unchanging way to experience being a child in all societies. Childhood varies from one society to another and from one historical period to the next.

Sociologists speak of childhood as being socially constructed. This means that, although it is a physical fact that human children are younger, smaller, weaker, and generally less experienced, they do not necessarily constitute a separate category that must be treated differently. They must wear clothes, for example, that are smaller, but they do not need to wear clothes that are different from adults' in any other way. They cannot do all of the tasks that adults can do because they are not as strong, but they need not necessarily be restricted from working in factories, mines, fields, and offices.

When we treat children differently from adults (as we do in our society), we have constructed a social category called children. Along with the category, we have also constructed a set of characteristics appropriate for the people in the category and a set of relationships others should have with those people.

One of the strongest pieces of evidence to support the argument that the concepts of children and childhood are socially constructed and not inevitable is the way in which children and childhood vary historically. Phillip Aries (1962), a French historian, was one of the first modern scholars to investigate the concept of childhood. In his research on Europe, he discovered that both the perception and the experience of childhood changed over time.

Children's status has moved through three distinct stages (Mandell 1988). The first stage characterized European society before 1500 and might be called the period of indifference toward childhood. The second stage ran from the 1600s until the mid-1800s and could be called the emergence of childhood. The third period is the ascendency of childhood, which dates from the mid-1800s and continues to develop.

John Demos (1986) examined childhood in U.S. history during the period of the emergence of childhood. He discovered that childhood was quite different during the colonial period from what it is today. Children were more similar to adults, and the period that we would recognize as childhood was much shorter: "If childhood is defined as a protected state, a carefree period of freedom from adulthood responsibilities, then a Puritan childhood was quite brief. Childhood abruptly came to an end around the age of seven" (Mintz and Kellogg 1988).

Puritan children worked alongside adults doing the same kinds of work as their elders—caring for domesticated animals, gardening, spinning, making candles, and preparing food. Sons were miniature versions of their farmer fathers, and daughters were models of their mothers (Demos 1986).

In addition to doing the same work as adults, children in this period also looked more like their parents. Before age six, both boys and girls wore frocks or petticoats. At around age six, they began to wear the same clothes as their parents. Boys wore breeches, shirts, and doublets; girls wore caps, chemises, bodices, petticoats, and skirts (Mintz and Kellogg 1988).

Children were not seen as equal to their parents, but as morally and physically inferior. The difference between children and adults, however, was not in what they did but rather in how well and how much they performed (Demos 1970). On the other hand, children were not seen as a special group with their own needs and interests, as they are in our society (Demos 1970).

Throughout the last three centuries, children have increasingly been differentiated from adults. Labor laws prohibit them from taking most jobs. Huge industries in children's clothes, toys, and media—like children's books and cartoons—have been created. Organizations such as the Boy Scouts, Girl Scouts, and Little League have been developed to allow children to participate in children's activities.

Public education separates the lives of children from adults and further segregates children by age in class levels and in schools—elementary, middle, junior high, and high school. Childhood in our time is perceived as a period that is very different from adulthood, and childhood itself can be differentiated into many stages.

In the scenario at the beginning of the chapter, one girl, Neu, tells how her parents' separation has meant that she must spend a lot of time working in her family, caring for her brothers and sisters, and doing the housework. Because we think of childhood as a period in which children should participate in children's activities and not those of adults, we might respond to her story with pity for her and criticism of her mother. How are our responses shaped by the dominant ideas about childhood in our society? Are other conceptualizations of childhood, like that of Puritan society, wrong or inhumane?

The review of this literature suggests that ideas about childhood and children are shaped and even determined by the social era in which they exist. In this chapter we have observed that contemporary ideas about children in the United States are dominated by three images. A theoretical point of view that acknowledges the way concepts of childhood and children are affected by historical context suggests that these images are a product of our times. The images are an aspect of the macrolevel of society that influence our thinking and our experience, but the images in turn are created by other macrolevel factors that predominate in this particular historical period.

How Accurate Is Our Image of Children?

The second theoretical issue that has emerged in our examination of children is the question of the accuracy of the images of children in our society. Thorne (1987) argued that the three images of children as learners, threats, and victims do not capture the range of experiences and influence that children have.

Children's lives are more varied than the three dominant images suggest (Medrich et al. 1982). In addition to the time they spend in school, children spend time in five other kinds of activities: activities with their parents, working both at home and outside the home, participating in organized activities like sports and cultural programs, watching TV, and spending time on their own in unstructured activities. On an average weekday, children spent about seven hours a day in school; three to four hours watching television; two to three hours on their own (this category included activities with friends or alone and excluded watching TV) playing, reading, doing homework, and relaxing; one to one-half hours with their parents; less than an hour on chores; and a little less than an hour on organized activities like lessons and athletic teams. Medrich and his colleagues' findings, as well as those of Purrington (1980) and Boulding (1980), suggest that children are involved in many activities about which we know little and that do not fit easily into the categories of learner, threat, or victim.

Medrich and his colleagues' (1982) work, however, is unusual. Part of the limited nature of the three dominant images may be a result of the lack of research directed toward understanding children and childhood. Family scholars have focused much more attention on the experience of adults than on that of children.

Table 13.4 shows that the proportion of the population that is under nineteen is declining but that children remain a significant percentage of our population. In 1970, children comprised 37.8 percent of the population, while in 2002, they comprised 28 percent. These numbers vary by race ethnicity. For example, 43.2 percent of Mexican Americans are under the age of 21, as are 21.6 percent of Cubans (Solis 1995); 32.5 percent of African Americans and 27 percent of Asians are under 18 (U.S. Census Bureau 2000e). The study of children would seem to be an obviously important area. But the study of children and childhood has been much less attended to than other issues by many scholars, even those who study families.

Thorne (1987) argues that feminist family scholars, in particular, need to pay more careful attention to the experience of children because the fates and definitions of women

TABLE 13.4   Percent of Total Population under 19, 1970–2002

	1970	1980	1991	2002
Under 5	8.4%	7.2%	7.5%	7.0%
5–9	9.8	7.4	7.3	7.1
10–14	10.2	8.1	6.9	7.5
15–19	9.4	9.3	7.2	6.7
Total Children	37.8	32.0	28.9	28.3

Source: U.S. Census Bureau 1992c, and 2000e, p. 13; U.S. Census Bureau 2002a.

have been so closely tied to those of children. Children are intertwined in many women's lives and in the images, expectations, and controlling mechanisms that exist for women in our society. Scholars who are interested in women's lives must look at the relationships between children and adults, especially women, in order to unravel the question of gender inequality.

Children must also be studied in their own right, and the insights that feminists have brought to the sociological study of women can be useful in helping us examine the experience of children. Thorne (1987) says that feminists have revisioned women, acknowledging that (1) women are not just passive victims but are active agents in society; (2) women are diverse; and (3) gender exists in all corners of our society, in all social institutions. These principles need to be applied to our study of children, recognizing their agency, diversity, and activity throughout society.

In this chapter we have focused on the three images of children in the United States—as learners, threats, and victims. Most research on children fits into these three categories. If we take Thorne's advice, however, we will need to broaden our vision of children to examine more fully their position in society as sexual beings, workers, athletes, teachers, artists, leaders, and in any number of other roles, including as political activists.

Resistance against Child Abuse and Incest

This chapter has reviewed much research on children in the United States and has offered some suggestions about the kinds of theoretical questions that have been uncovered and need to be studied further. In this section we look at a few examples of the political activities that have developed in the effort to improve children's lives. The discussion of child abuse and incest reveals some of the most devastating information about the condition of children in our society. Not surprisingly, this is where political activists have focused their efforts.

Resistance against child abuse and incest has a long history. Like Jennifer's sister in the vignette at the beginning of the chapter, victims of incest have a long history of fighting back. In Gordon's (1988) investigation of records of incest, she found that girls who were victims of incest were likely to resist by running away, fighting back, or informing the police or others. In addition to these individual acts of rebellion, organizations have also been active in seeking recognition of the problem and in proposing specific policy changes to increase the power of children in our society so that they might be better able to protect themselves from assault and so that they might be better able to see that their assailants are punished.

Gordon (1988) studied the records of child abuse, incest, and neglect cases from 1880 to 1960. Her data came from the case records of "child saving" agencies in Boston. In earlier years, the clients of the agencies were mainly poor Catholic immigrants from countries like Italy, Ireland, and Canada. In later years, clients were likely to be African Americans and West Indians.

The cases revealed at least three sets of political relationships: (1) between husbands and wives, (2) between parents and children, and (3) between white Anglo-Saxon Protestant (WASP) social workers, who represented the dominant culture and its agencies of control, and working-class racial ethnic people who were their clients.

Each of these three political relationships included oppression of the subordinate group. Men battered women and sexually abused children. Women abused and neglected children. Throughout the period studied, mothers and fathers were approximately equally likely to be the assailants in reported incidents of child abuse. Social workers degraded, disrespected, punished, and attempted to control their clients.

At the same time, the victims in each of these relationships were also likely to resist actively. As a way to draw attention to the importance of the resistance, Gordon (1988) titled her book *Heroes of Their Own Lives.* Incest victims resisted their fathers' assaults. Battered women and abused children fought back against their husbands and parents. And communities, families, and individuals struggled against the authorities for the right to create their own definitions of family, morality, and child care.

A key feature of Gordon's analysis is the political quality of the relationships that make up the issue of violence. Like the radical feminists discussed in the section on incest, Gordon centers her discussion around the concepts of oppression and control.

The picture Gordon presents of the history of family violence differs from the one presented by radical feminists, however, in its complexity. Gender inequality is at the heart of the violence she examines, but equally important are generation and class inequality. The complexity of the situation is further illustrated by the the active resistance to oppression by women and others that her work uncovers.

PFLAG Does Real Family Values

GLBT (gay, lesbian, bisexual, and transgendered) young people face many difficulties in school. The average high school student hears twenty-five antigay slurs daily, and 97 percent of students say they hear homophobic comments regularly (GLSEN 1999; www.pflag.org 2005; VanWormer and McKinney 2003). Boys who are gender nonconformist are more likely to be harrassed by actions ranging from a slap in the hall to rape. This kind of harassment takes a toll. Gay and lesbian youth are more likely to skip classes, drop out, and commit suicide. Four of ten students who have been bullied about their sexuality have attempted suicide or harmed themselves in some way (Charles 2000).

PFLAG (parents, friends, and family of GLBT) is an organization that addresses these issues through its "From our house to the schoolhouse" program. In the discussion in this chapter on violence against children, we have seen how families sometimes harm their children. PFLAG is an example of families rallying behind children to support them and to help create a more hospitable and nurturant community for them.

In 1972, the idea for PFLAG was created when the mother of a gay young man marched by his side in a gay pride march. The mother was concerned because her son had been beaten in a gay rights rally the previous week and the police had stood by and watched. Within a year she and her allies had formed PFLAG which now has about 500 chapters and 200,000 members.

PFLAG has been successful in its establishment of safe schools for gay, bisexual, and lesbian youth. Their mission is to promote the health and well-being of GLBT and their family and friends and works on a wide range of projects of support for individuals and families, public education, and political advocacy (www.PFLAG.org 2005).

In a recent study of schools they found that (PFLAG 2005):

59 percent did not include GLBT in their student harassment/non-discrimination policies.

75 percent did not include gender identity/expression in their student policies.

61 percent had no support groups for GLBT students.

83 percent had little or no GLBT information in library for students.

81 percent rarely or never addressed GLBT issues in the curriculum (48% never).

41 percent had a diversity coordinator.

80 percent never responded/responded sporadically to complaints.

95 percent of counseling services had little or no GLBT resources.

99 percent of counseling services had little or no transresources.

70 percent had no training for staff on how to stop GLBT bullying/harassment.

92 percent had no training for students on how to stop GLBT bullying/harassment.

91 percent provided little or no multicultural training of any kind.

62 percent of staff rarely or never used GLBT inclusive language.

75 percent reported that they felt that GLBT students were unsafe in their school.

In short, schools are not addressing the needs of GLBT youth and are leaving their students in an unsafe situation. PFLAG's goal now is to make these gaps known and to help schools create policies and practices that support all the young people who attend them.

PFLAG's work is an example of subverting hegemonic meaning by reframing issues from alternative point of view that makes diversity and human rights central (Broad, Crawley, and Foley 2004). This means that PFLAG members take the discourse (what is being said) about family values and use those words and their meanings to create an alternative "real family values" to the conservative rhetoric often referred to as "family values." PFLAG is concerned about families and children, but they assert through their work that many kinds of families need to be recognized and respected. And the children in those families need to be protected and nurtured by the whole community.

The Micro–Macro Connection

This discussion of children in families and children's families in society helps us see the multiple layers of macrolevel forces. Our society makes children primarily the responsibility of their families, but as we have noted, neither families nor children exist in a vacuum. Families play an important role in many children's lives, but they are not the only factor.

Other macrolevel institutions that affect children's lives directly and through families include an economic system that does not provide sufficient access to food, shelter, and health care for many families. This makes children who are economically dependent on those families especially vulnerable and frequently unable to survive. Children's lives are also affected by a legal system that does not adequately protect them from sexual and physical abuse and schools that do not adequately support them. The media, in addition, play a role in limiting children's opportunities, particularly in terms of their ability to see gender-less and racial ethnic stereotyped images.

Ideologies are a part of the macroforces in society. They help us see or ignore what exists, and they provide a way of understanding what is happening, why it is happening, and what its significance is. Children are a large segment of our population and an important factor in many families, but they are strangely invisible in much of the work done on families. When our ideas about children assume that children and childhood are something natural, they need little explanation. But the historical evidence suggests that children and childhood are socially constructed and therefore need intense examination. Furthermore, that examination should pay attention to children not as just victims, learners, and threats but also as social actors in all arenas of human life.

Macrolevel forces in society are numerous, and they are also contradictory. Ideologies that have paid attention to issues related to children, for example, are not in agreement. In this chapter we have examined competing sets of ideas about how gender is learned and maintained. We have also looked at two competing models of how to understand and address the problem of incest and child abuse.

Political action by feminists and organizations like the Children's Defense Fund and PFLAG show us the ways in which the microlevel can affect the macro level. These groups claim that in order to provide humane environments for children, our ideas about children and their relationships with families must be assessed and changed by activities ranging from scholarly work to running for office. CDF challenges fundamental ideas about who should be responsible for children—individual families or the broader community. Radical feminists, who have worked on issues such as incest, insist that we reexamine and change our assessment of relationships within families.

Gordon's (1988) uncovering of the resistance of children to child abuse and incest also provides an example of the way in which the microlevel can put pressure on the macrolevel for social change. Bem's (1983) review of gender socialization in child rearing techniques and Peters's (1988) review of race socialization in child rearing also provide examples of resistance and the ongoing active struggle of people to reconstruct their families and their societies in more just ways.

14 Families, Family Policy, and the State

Welfare policy has affected family life in the United States, especially low-income families. Welfare policy has changed throughout the twentieth century and into the twenty first century. In the mid-1990s it took an important turn with the establishment of Temporary Assistance for Needy Families (TANF). (© Lara Jo Regan/SABA Press/Corbis)

We want jobs, low-income housing, and our rights as true American citizens. We want to reinvent the social system of America from the bottom up, not from the top down. Remember "We the people"? We are following American tradition. It was the poor people that fled all those countries and came to America to make it wealthy and great and what it is today. The best story in my history book was the one about the Boston Tea Party where they weren't being represented and so they dumped all of the tea into the ocean. And I feel the same way. Like we're not being represented by the king and queen of America and we've gotten so far away from democracy. (Mary Uebelgunne, a homeless woman from North Carolina who organized a homeless organization called Home Street Home, speaking at a rally, quoted in Aulette and Fishman 1991, p. 247)

Women are more aggressive when they see something harming their kids. When the strikebreaker or the scab, he's taking her husband's job away, taking the food away from your kids, taking the shoes off their feet, I think women are the first to respond to that. They're seeing the destruction of the family, and they are going to come out with tooth and nail. (Anna O'Leary, president of the Morenci Miners' Women's Auxiliary, an organization of wives of copper miners who struck against Phelps Dodge, quoted in Aulette and Mills 1988)

Native women struggle against government and corporations, as well as against all individuals or interest groups who will stop at nothing in their dedication to obliterating the American Indian people. We must work to maintain tribal status; we must make certain that the tribes continue to be legally recognized entities, sovereign nations within the larger U.S., and we must wage this battle in a multitude of ways—political, educational, literary, artistic, individual, and communal. We are doing all we can—we daily demonstrate that we have no intention of disappearing, of being silent or of going along quietly with our extinction. (Paula Gunn Allen, a Native American woman, writing in 1986, p. 410)

So what we did was we organized to fight back and to take what's ours because we are the sons and daughters, sisters and the brothers and the aunts and the uncles of the people who built this country and this is ours. And we challenge you, America, to take back and distribute the wealth among the people that need it. We're talking about the welfare movement. We're talking about the mothers with the babies. We're talking about childcare. We're talking about education. And that's why I'm here today and I'm pretty sure that's why you're here because we're tired. But we're not that tired and we're going to keep on struggling and the fight has just begun. (Leona Smith, a welfare mother, speaking out at Survival Summit in Philadelphia, quoted in Aulette and Fishman 1991, p. 247)

There's one good thing about welfare. It kills your illusions about yourself, and about where this society is really at. It's laid out for you straight. You have to learn to fight, to be aggressive, or you just don't make it. If you can survive long enough on welfare, you can survive anything. It gives you a kind of freedom, a sense of your own power and togetherness with other women. (Johnnie Tilmon, founding president of National Welfare Rights Organization, quoted in Abramowitz 2000, p. 134)

These are voices of people who want to see change in America and have called on the government as a place to begin making those changes.

What do these people want for their families and what do they think the government can do for them?

What do these people think is wrong with the government?

What values do the voices express about democracy, freedom, rights, and support?

What is a government, and what is its relationship to the nation-state and social policy?

The United States is one of a few wealthy industrialized countries that does not have an explicit, official family policy. Based on the statements made by these people, what kinds of issues do you think would need to be part of a family policy in the United States?

In answering these questions, you have had to think about what a government is and how government operates in the United States. This chapter discusses various points of view about the character and activities of our government, especially in regard to problems that families face.

Throughout this book, we have observed the ways in which people have looked to the government to address the problems their families experience. For example, in Chapters 2 and 3 we saw how people successfully changed public policy, laws, and even the government itself when the women's movement fought for the right to vote and own property, when the labor movement demanded that the government pass family wage laws, and when slaves and other antislavery forces toppled the slave system. In Chapters 4 through 7, we examined the more contemporary demands of housing for the homeless, living wages, family leave legislation, civil rights for racial ethnic people, and wages for housework. In Chapters 8 through 10, we added to this list the right to marriage for gay couples and divorce reform. Chapters 11 and 13 explored the need for changes in policy and law to protect children and adults from violence in families, and Chapter 12 reviewed the movement around government support of child care.

The discussions of these issues in the previous chapters described the different groups and their points of view about what needs to be changed and how. The way in which the government is organized and the structural and ideological roots of that organization have not been emphasized. In this last chapter, we take a closer look at the organization of the government and its potential for supporting families making needed changes. The discussion of the government centers around one particular set of laws and policies that has been especially important for families—the welfare system.

The chapter is divided into five major sections. The first is a brief discussion of terms that are used to talk about public policy. The second section describes the current organization of the welfare system. The third section reviews the historical roots of the welfare system and recent trends. The fourth section addresses the question of why the welfare system and family policy in general seem so inadequate in the United States by discussing three theoretical conceptualizations of the nation-state. In the final section, the activities of people resisting current policies and seeking to reformulate welfare and the government are explored.

The Welfare State and Family Policy

Since World War II, most of the industrial capitalist nations, including the United States, have come to identify themselves as welfare states. Welfare states can be divided into two types: programmatic welfare states and redistributive welfare states. Programmatic welfare states are ones in which a "capitalist state devotes a portion of its gross national product, through taxation, to the solution of certain social problems without changing the basic nature of the economy" (Atherton 1989, p. 169). Redistributive welfare states are those whose primary aim is to restructure the economy by redistributing wealth and resources.

For example, suppose a U.S. company decides to close a plant because it wishes to move its operation to Mexico, where labor is cheaper and profits higher. A programmatic welfare state would provide help to workers and their families in the region where the plant closed. Benefits like unemployment, TANF (Temporary Aid for Needy Families), and food stamps would be provided to the families whose breadwinners had been laid off. A redistributive welfare state might take more radical action, for example, by making it illegal to close the plant. In this case, the resource that would be redistributed is the power to decide whether a business should move. The goal of the programmatic welfare state is to help people get by when the normal functioning of the economy causes them problems. The goal of the redistributive welfare state is to alter the normal functioning of the system. The United States is a programmatic welfare state (Atherton 1989).

Within these two broad categories is a range of support for the welfare state. While most Western industrial nations would be considered programmatic welfare states, most of them spend a larger proportion of their gross national product (GNP) on welfare than does the United States, and they have older and more extensive programs (Chelf 1992; OECD 2004).

Governments develop and implement these kinds of programs through policies. Policies are lines of action that allow countries to extract resources from and control people residing in them (Skocpol and Amenta 1986). Policies include nearly everything the government does, from collecting taxes to imprisoning criminals.

Social policies are government "activities affecting the social status and life chances of groups, families and individuals" (Skocpol and Amenta 1986, p. 132). Such policies would include, for example, the provision of public education, regulations affecting working conditions and the environment, and protection of vulnerable populations like children, the elderly, and the disabled. As a programmatic welfare state, the United States has an enormous array of social policies that are designed to help provide people with food, shelter, health care, and education. All these programs have a powerful influence on families (Zimmerman 1992). The United States, however, remains unusual among developed industrialized nations because it does not have an official family policy (Bane 1980; Kamerman and Kahn 1978).

The lack of an explicit family policy is a problem. First, without an overarching organized family policy, the policies that do touch families lack continuity, vision, and coherence. For example, one agency or program may provide work training for parents, while another provides day care support and still another provides health care benefits. These programs may or may not be coordinated with one another.

Second, problems can occur when services emerge for families by accident or as outgrowths of policies intended primarily for attaining a national objective other than serving those families. Because they were not intended to address the needs of families, they may be distorted by the interests they were designed to serve and, therefore, may be less useful to families (Schorr 1962). For example, the Housing Act of 1949 was a policy that directly affected families. The intention of the act, however, was not to serve families but rather to guarantee housing starts in order to avoid postwar deflation (Moen and Schorr 1987). Choices about where and for whom the housing would be built were based on the goal of providing economic support for communities and industries, not necessarily to provide shelter for individual families.

Social Policy and Families:
The Case of the Welfare System

In this section, we look at one set of social policies that has been particularly important to families—welfare policy. One of the first observations we can make about social policy when we look at the welfare system is that it is sometimes as important to notice what is missing as what is included. In the United States, most of the care of families is not provided by the government. An official social policy is missing in the provision of welfare even in cases where it is sorely needed.

One could say that the largest welfare system in the nation is the one provided by individual families (Moen and Schorr 1987). Although he was writing in 1949, Reuben Hill's thoughts about this are still valid:

> For too long the family has been called upon to take up the slack in a poorly integrated social order. If fiscal policies are bungled producing inflation, the family purse strings are tightened; if depressions bring sudden impoverishment, family savings and families' capacity to restrict consumption to subsistence levels are drawn upon; if real estate and building interest fail to provide housing, families must adapt themselves to filtered down, obsolete dwellings or double up into shoehorned quarters with other families. (p. ix)

The second largest welfare system in the United States is the one provided by the government (Moen and Schorr 1987). While the United States does not have an explicit, official family policy, the welfare system is a good example of a set of programs that would be an important part of family policy if we had such a thing. The welfare system provides an example of a large and influential social policy that has great importance for many families. In 2000, 17 percent of households received public assistance or noncash benefits from the government, and another 26 percent had received social security benefits (U.S. Census Bureau 2000; 2000). The Census Bureau further reports that about one-half of the households in the United States have used the welfare system at some time (Chisman and Pifer 1987). This section describes the system before we move to a discussion of its historical roots and current direction.

One distinction that can be made among social welfare services in the United States today is that only some are means-tested. Means-tested programs are ones in which recipients must prove that they need the service and that they cannot provide it for themselves. For example, unemployment is an entitlement program that is not means-tested. Any person who qualifies by such criteria as length of employment and being laid off can collect unemployment. Unemployed people do not have to prove they are impoverished. They are not asked about how much money they have in savings accounts or whether they own property. They are entitled to the benefit because they worked for an employer who paid into the system and now they are unemployed. TANF (Temporary Assistance to Needy Families) recipients, in contrast, are means-tested. In order to receive a grant, they must prove that they are impoverished and that they have no other way to support themselves.

A second distinction among services is that they provide either cash assistance or in-kind support. Cash assistance refers to programs that provide money to eligible persons who can then decide how best to use it. In-kind programs provide specific services, such as medical care and housing, and vouchers that can be used only to purchase specific items. For example, food stamps are an in-kind benefit since they can be used only to purchase food.

The services provided by these programs varies greatly from one state to another. Some programs are funded by federal funds and supplemented by state and local agencies. In addition, since 1996 some federal funding, in particular funding for TANF, comes in block grants. In a block grant, a state is given a sum of money by the federal government, and within certain guidelines the state can determine how the money will be spent. In addition, each state can create waivers within federal guidelines for qualifying for support. This means that states vary in the programs they provide, the funding available for each program, and the criteria used to determine who will receive assistance.

Some policy makers believe that this flexibility is useful because it allows states to be innovative with their welfare systems and it allows them to tailor programs to the particular needs of the locales in which they are being implemented. Others, however, assert that the variation can create unfair inequities for people who live in states that design particularly punitive or inadequate systems (Blank 1995).

Regardless of variation from state to state, the amount of money available to families is low everywhere. In 2001, the average monthly grant for a TANF family was $351 (U.S. Department of Health and Human Services 2001). Another key characteristic of the welfare system is the differential manner in which needy people are treated by various programs within the system (Abramowitz 1996). When the programs were initiated in the 1930s, two kinds of cash benefits were created—social insurance and public assistance. Social insurance included a pension for retired workers (called Social Security) and unemployment insurance. People who received these benefits were treated as deserving recipients. Public assistance included Old Age Assistance (OAA), Aid to the Blind (AB), Aid to the Permanently and Totally Disabled (APTD), and Aid to Dependent Children (ADC). Recipients in these programs were more stigmatized, especially the women and children in the ADC program, and were seen as less deserving. Widows, who were regarded as women who had become single mothers through no fault of their own, remained in the Social Security system and were not part of ADC. Women who were in single female-headed households because of divorce or having never married were put into a separate program called ADC (which later became AFDC). Widows in the Social Security program were regarded as the deserving poor, while AFDC was for women who were seen as having failed in their family responsibilities. This distinction still exists. Women who receive public money as a result of their relationship to a deceased husband remain better off, and the gap between the two programs continues to grow (Folbre 1987).

Welfare policy always reflected a perception that AFDC mothers are bad women and need to have their personal lives monitored and controlled. Until the 1960s, states cut aid to women who had relationships with men. For example, Arkansas did not allow aid to be given to mothers who were engaged in a "nonstable illegal union." Texas barred women from aid if they were in "pseudocommon law marriages." Michigan excluded women in households with "male boarders" (Folbre 1987; Patterson 1981). TANF mothers are no longer monitored this way, but the perception of them as immoral and irresponsible remains. This perception is part of a set of myths about welfare mothers.

Persistent Myths about Welfare Mothers

Myth 1. Welfare mothers form single-parent households in order to obtain welfare. If single-mother families were forming in order to become eligible for welfare, we would expect to see a larger proportion participating in AFDC/TANF over time because the number of single-mother families is increasing. Research on families headed by single women shows they are much less likely now to be receiving welfare than they were in the past. In 1972, 62 percent of single-mother families received AFDC. In 1992, that proportion had declined to 49 percent (Mishel, Bernstein, and Schmitt 1997). Since the passage of welfare reform legislation in the mid-1990s, the proportion has continued to decline. The numbers of single-mother-headed households is growing, however, the proportion receiving welfare has continued to drop dramatically (U.S. Census Bureau 2005).

Myth 2. Welfare mothers purposely bear children in order to increase their grants. In 2002, welfare families had an average of 1.9 children, which is smaller than the national average, and the longer a woman remains on welfare the less likely she is to have a baby (Rank 1989; U.S. Department of Health and Human Services 2004).

The economics of welfare grants make additional children highly unprofitable. Grants increase an average of $60 a month with the birth of a new child, not enough to provide for a child and certainly not likely to allow a mother to use childbirth as a money-making scheme. Although the empirical evidence refutes the myth that welfare mothers have babies as a way of enriching themselves, policy makers continue to create programs that are based on this false premise. A major change in welfare laws in 1996 that replaced AFDC with TANF allows states to place a cap on welfare payments, eliminating increases with the birth of a baby. Before 1996, families receiving welfare would receive a small increase to cover the cost of another mouth to feed. Now states can refuse to increase benefits to a family that increases its size, leaving parents to stretch their budgets even further.

Myth 3. Welfare accounts for a huge proportion of the national budget. Many people believe that welfare payments make up a large part of the federal budget. This belief is not well founded. Welfare accounts for only a small proportion, while other expenses, such as defense and Social Security, are much larger public expenses. Table 14.1 shows the way the federal government spends money. Only about 3 percent of the federal budget is allocated to welfare and social services and 1 percent to food stamps, much smaller numbers than for Social Security (21%) or defense (18%) (Pitzer and Tsehaye 2003).

Myth 4. Most families on welfare stay on it for many years even for generations. Studies have shown that women who received welfare as children are more likely to seek welfare as adults. But the connection between these two factors is not clear. First, most women who received welfare as children do not turn to welfare when they are adults. Growing up in a family that relied on welfare does not inevitably or even usually cause children in those families to enter the welfare program when they become adults.

Second, children of welfare mothers may seek welfare as adults because they never escaped poverty, not because of their experience growing up (Abramowitz 1996). Children of poor parents are almost four times as likely to be poor as adults than children of

TABLE 14.1   Federal Outlays by Function, 2004

Social Security	21.3%	Pensions and unemployment	1.8%
Defense	18.4%	Supplementary Security income	1.5%
Net interest	9.8%	Food stamps	1.0%
International affairs	0.6%	Welfare and social services	2.8%
Medicare	12.5%		
Medicaid	8.1%		

Source: Pitzer and Tsehaye 2003.

middle-class people. The poorer their parents are, the more likely they are to be poor. Gender also makes a difference. Adult sons are more likely to escape poverty than adult daughters.

Myth 5. Welfare recipients refuse to work. Most poor people are in the paid labor force. Nearly two-thirds (63%) of poor families have at least one worker. Welfare mothers averaged 950 hours a year, about the same as all mothers, in the labor force (Abramowtiz 1996). Forty-four percent of welfare mothers held two or more jobs. Welfare mothers who were employed averaged thirty-four hours per week. But they also averaged four months a year laid off or looking for work. This means that they tend to have jobs that are sporadically full time, rather than steady part-time jobs. Their average pay was $4.40 an hour, and the most common job was in fast food. Other typical jobs included working as cashiers, nurses' aides, janitors, and machine operators (Handler 1999).

Welfare and Gender and Race

The welfare system continues to have an influence on the organization of gender. Women are the major consumers of welfare, and they are also overrepresented among workers in the welfare system. Several authors have also examined the way the welfare system enforces a particular organization of gender, especially a subordinate and oppressed role for women (Abramowitz 1989; Cohen and Katzenstein 1992; Miller 1990; Pearce 1989). The welfare system pushes women into marriage as the only alternative for survival. Marriage in turn operates as a way to keep women dependent on and controlled by men. Those women who insist on remaining single usually cannot maintain themselves financially because of inequality in the labor market and are therefore punished and controlled by the state through its welfare system (Miller 1990). In Chapter 10 we explored the impoverishment of women associated with divorce and single parenting. One place divorced women might look for financial assistance is the welfare system. Our review of the system, however, reveals that it is inadequate to the needs of poor families.

In the 1970s, Johnny Tillmon, a welfare mother and president of the National Welfare Rights Organization, observed the relationship between AFDC mothers and the welfare system and the way in which that relationship represented and enforced gender inequality and the oppression of women. She summed it up this way:

> AFDC is a supersexist marriage. You trade in "a" man for "the" man. But you can't divorce him if he treats you bad. He can divorce you of course, cut you off anytime he wants. But in that case "he" keeps the kids, not you. "The" man runs everything. In the ordinary marriage, sex is supposed to be for your husband. On AFDC, you're not supposed to have any sex at all. You give up control over your body. It's a condition of aid. "The" man, the welfare system, controls your money. He tells you what to buy, and what not to buy, where to buy it, and how much things cost. If things—rent, for instance—really costs more than he says they do, it's too bad for you. (1976, p. 356)

Race ethnicity also plays a role in the welfare system (Mink 1990; Quadagno 1994). African American families and Hispanic families are more likely to participate in the system. Thirty-eight percent of TANF families are black, 32 percent are white, and 25 percent are Hispanic (U.S. Department of Health and Human Services 2004). African American women are even more disadvantaged by the system than are white women. One reason

African American women receive fewer benefits than white women is that African American women who receive TANF are more likely to live in the states with the lowest payments. Discrimination has also played a role in diminishing African American women's access to welfare benefits. For example, although the provision of economic assistance for single mothers and their children was developed as a national system in the 1930s, it was not until the 1960s and the civil rights movement that African American women in the South were allowed to participate. Caseworkers in the Southern states assumed that "black mothers had always worked in the past, that they had more job opportunities than did white mothers, and that they had their children's grandmothers to provide childcare" and so they were systematically denied ADC (Sarvasy 1988, p. 255).

In summary, the welfare system is a huge, complex system of programs that vary widely from one state to another and from one program to another. The programs are inadequate for the needs of poor people, and they are decreasing in their ability to meet those needs. The welfare system plays a particularly important role in women's lives because women are the majority of the system's workers as well as of the clients. In addition, the welfare system creates a mythical image of poor women as undeserving people who should be held responsible for their poverty and who are a serious drain on the nation's resources. Finally, the degrading treatment women receive in the welfare system may influence their lives by forcing them to stay in marriages or to enter marriages because they have no other means of survival.

History and Trends for the Future in Welfare

This chapter has described the current organization of the welfare system. Next we move to a brief history of its emergence and evolution and discuss how it is developing in the twenty-first century. We will see that the welfare system is continuing to deteriorate and that the insufficient funds that are provided seem to be headed toward further decline.

The Social Security system was set up during the Great Depression in the 1930s as a way to address the potentially volatile impoverishment of large sections of the American population (Abramowitz 1989). Before the Depression, most relief for the poor came from private sources. In 1928, for example, only 12 percent of the money for relief in the fifteen largest U.S. cities came from public funds (Chelf 1992). As the Depression deepened, these private agencies were increasingly unable to obtain funds or provide services for the growing number of people who needed them. Local public agencies and eventually the federal government were called on to play a larger role. The 1935 Social Security Act established a federally funded and publicly administered welfare system. This act, regarded as the cornerstone of the federal welfare state, was composed of two components, social insurance and social assistance, and was funded by taxes from individuals and employers (Chelf 1992).

World War II pulled the U.S. economy out of the Depression, and concern for poverty waned. In the 1950s and 1960s, writers like Michael Harrington (1962) and John Kenneth Galbraith (1958) called political leaders' attention to the poverty that still existed in the prosperous United States (Gilbert and Kahl 1993). These books, along with the civil rights and poor people's movements and the rebellions in the impoverished inner cities of large urban areas such as Los Angeles, Detroit, and Newark, sparked a rediscovery of poverty and inequality. A new wave of policies appeared in the Kennedy and Johnson administrations, which came to be known as the War on Poverty. The War on Poverty introduced food stamps, Medicare, Medicaid, Head Start, the Job Corps, Legal Services, and many other welfare programs. This period is regarded as one of tremendous welfare expansion. The number of people covered and served by government assistance grew during these years.

Programs were initiated and expanded. Equally significant, people who were eligible were applying for and receiving help. The ability to access programs was an important step forward for poor people. A Field Foundation team that had previously visited poverty-stricken areas in the Bronx, Appalachia, Mississippi, and Texas revisited those areas in 1977 after the start of the War on Poverty. One physician who made both trips reported that nutrition and food stamp programs had nearly eliminated hunger (Katz 1996).

> There can be little doubt that significant change has occurred since 1967. Nowhere did I see the gross evidence of malnutrition among young children we saw in 1967. It is not possible any more to find very easily the bloated bellies, the shriveled infants, the gross evidence of vitamin and protein deficiency in children that we identified in the late 1960s. (Quoted in Schwartz 1983, p. 45)

Most of the dollars (75%) spent on social welfare during the period of expansion in the 1960s and 1970s, however, were spent on people who were not poor. AFDC, which was for poor people only, grew during this period. Social Security, which is available to nonpoor as well as poor people, however, exploded. Social Security is designed to keep pace with the cost of living; AFDC was not.

Today, Social Security benefits many poor people, but it continues to benefit many people who are not poor. In 2004, 50 percent of single-recipient households and 40 percent of married couple recipients remained poor even after receiving the benefit, but many people who receive Social Security would not be poor if they did not receive Social Security checks (Koenig and Rupp 2003/2004).

The 1980s and 1990s were marked by additional changes in the provision of welfare with the introduction of the Family Support Act and the trend toward privatization. Unlike the changes in the 1930s and 1960s that expanded welfare programs, especially those that served low-income people, the 1980s were a time of cutbacks in programs. From the War on Poverty, we moved to a war on welfare (Trattner 1999).

One of the ways in which these cuts in federal support for low-income people took place was through the creation of policies that transferred the responsibility for the provision of welfare services from the government to individuals and private institutions like churches and community organizations (M. Brown 1988; Eisenstein 1984; M. Katz 1996; Starr 1989). This process is called privatization (Kamerman and Kahn 1989; Smith and Stone 1988).

In 1987, the Reagan administration created a commission to investigate and propose changes in the division of responsibility between the federal government and the private sector in nine areas (President's Commission on Privatization 1988). The report that was issued the following spring recommended that the federal government divest itself as much as possible from its welfare responsibilities by substituting the private sector as the provider. Housing topped the list of areas in which it was recommended that the government pull out and let private business and humanitarian community organizations take over (Stoesz 1987).

One proposal that illustrates privatization in housing in the 1980s is a program called Stepping Stone Housing. Stepping Stone Housing also provides good examples of the kinds of problems low-income families face when welfare programs are privatized (Aulette 1991).

Stepping Stone Housing identified people living in public housing whose income, according to the government, was adequate enough—over $12,500—to allow them to move into unsubsidized housing. These people were asked to participate in a seven-year transition program to make that move. The households—with incomes that averaged $16,000—that entered the Stepping Stone program were allowed to stay in public housing, paying monthly rents of $250 for a one-bedroom and $300 for a two-bedroom apartment, for two years. For the third through seventh years, their rent was raised to 30 percent of their monthly income. The Housing Authority, however, continued to keep only $250 to $300 of those payments. The rest of the money was placed in a savings account for the renter. At the end of the seven years, the participants had to leave their subsidized apartments, and, according to the Housing Authority, the households would have about $2,700 in their savings, which they could then use as a down payment on a house or as a security deposit on a privately owned apartment (E. Martin 1988).

The advantages to the participant are cheaper rent for two years, regardless of income, and the savings account created for them during the third through seventh years. The program, however, entails some risk because once a person decides to enter Stepping Stone, he or she cannot quit and is required to leave public housing at the end of seven years, regardless of any other changes that might have occurred in the seven-year period. Getting back into public housing is next to impossible. In most cities, the waiting lists in the mid-1980s were enormous and had been closed for years (Reyes and Waxman 1986).

I interviewed people who had been identified as targets of this program to see what they thought about the idea of moving from government-subsidized apartments to private houses and apartments (Aulette 1991). All the respondents said that they had thought about moving, and all had criticisms of the housing provided in the project. They did not, however, agree with the government about their ability to handle the finances of a transition to private housing. Some people noted that even though their income appeared to be above the poverty line, their ability to provide for their families was barely adequate, even while living in subsidized housing. For example, one woman said, "My children were pressuring me to move, but I set them down and showed them what my check was, all the little charges and things I had to buy to make them look halfway decent when they go to school. I couldn't afford it" (Aulette 1991, p. 155).

Others pointed out that even if they could afford it now, they might run into unforeseen difficulties such as losing their job or becoming ill. One person explained:

> I was looking for a house and I found one I could afford but then I looked at my paycheck and said: "Oh! What if my little girls get sick?" like my mama had to go to the emergency room and I could do it but I can't afford a house too. Being in the projects, it helps you a lot. (Aulette 1991, p. 155)

For the people in the study, public housing operated like insurance, allowing them to feel more secure, knowing that if they ran into economic difficulties their rent would fall on the sliding scale and they would be less likely to become homeless. In addition, the income identified by Stepping Stone as adequate to finding housing in the local private market was unrealistic. The average price of a house in the city in which they lived was $104,633. The Stepping Stone participants who would be seeking housing would have an average annual income of about $16,000 and savings of about $3,000. Even finding a rental unit would be difficult. The average monthly rent on a two-bedroom apartment was $415. This is a little less than 30 percent of their average income, but there were no provisions for a decline in income due to illness or job loss (Aulette 1991).

Privatization plans like Stepping Stone Housing frequently fail to provide for people's needs. In Chapter 4, we observed how the Great U-turn was characterized by a decline in the incomes of working-class and middle-class people. The policy makers who designed Stepping Stone Housing are assuming that people will see their incomes rise or at least remain the same. The people in the study were more cognizant of the Great U-turn and fear that the risk of losing their place in public housing would cost them everything.

Family Support Act

A second example of changes in welfare policies in the 1980s and 1990s was the introduction of the Family Support Act. Privatization indicates a change in thinking on the part of policy makers on the question of who should provide welfare for needy people. The Family Support Act indicates a change in thinking about what that support should look like.

The Family Support Act made a number of changes, including increasing the ability of the government to more aggressively obtain child support from noncustodial parents who fail to make payments. The centerpiece of the legislation, however, is its emphasis on making recipients of welfare work for their grants. The word used to describe this policy is *workfare* (Katz 1989).

Workfare is the requirement that welfare recipients must work in exchange for receiving their grants (Block and Noakes 1988). Workfare exists under several names, like Community Work Experience Program (CWEP), Job Opportunity and Basic Skills (JOBS), Work Incentive Program (WIN), and Jobs Training Partnership Act (JTPA). The concept began to be introduced to welfare policy at the federal level in the late 1960s and was increasingly promoted throughout the 1980s and early 1990s. In 1996, workfare became a central feature of TANF.

Included in workfare programs are a variety of supportive programs that are supposed to assist people with education, job searches, transportation, and child care. Although the idea of helping welfare recipients find good jobs is one that many support, the reality of workfare programs has not lived up to expectations. Most of the workfare jobs provide either no wages—recipients receive their grants for working at unpaid jobs—or the minimum wage, with no benefits, and are insufficient to raise families above the poverty line (Harlan 1989; Katz 1989). Seventy-five percent of the programs reporting in 1987 averaged wages of less than $4.47 per hour (Abramowitz 1989). A study of workfare workers in Massachusetts found that 45 percent had no health coverage at their jobs (Amott 1990). Support for workfare employees like education, transportation, and child support was nearly nonexistent, and most of the assistance provided was in small programs that taught participants how to search for jobs. The issue of child care is especially important because the families targeted by workfare are frequently composed of single parents and children.

Because many workfare programs are mandatory, people who refuse to participate can be sanctioned. For example, a mother may refuse to participate because she cannot find adequate child care, or she may not have money to purchase special clothing necessary for the job (Sarvasy 1988). In Michigan, for example, people were placed in outside construction crews in the winter, which meant that they needed expensive insulated jackets and boots. When an adult is sanctioned, his or her entire family loses its grant. This means that if an adult does not participate adequately, children who have no control over the situation must suffer.

Furthermore, it appears that a large proportion of those who are sanctioned have been treated unfairly. One study in New York, for example, found that eight thousand people had received sanctions in a six-month period, but 98 percent subsequently won reversal of the sanctions because of administrative incompetence or outright harassment (Abramowitz 1989). Legislation has attempted to provide minimal employment standards for workfare employees, but despite changes in policy, many workfare participants continue to suffer working conditions that are vastly inferior to employees in "regular" jobs (Dietrich, Emsellem, and Paradise 2000).

Workfare is also problematic from the point of view of workers who are not receiving welfare. When the welfare system mandates that welfare recipients take jobs, they have no control over wages and no right to belong to or organize unions. This means they are forced to become low-wage, nonunion competitors for jobs, which eliminates job openings and union strength among "regular" workers. In spite of these problems, by 1987 forty-two states operated optional work programs, and twenty-six states required able-bodied AFDC parents to work off their grants at unpaid jobs. Workfare became universal in 1996 when massive welfare reform was instituted.

Personal Responsibility and Work Opportunity Reconciliation Act

In 1996, the federal government created a welfare reform package that pulled together all the pieces of workfare and privitization and other changes that had been emerging in state and local welfare offices in the 1970s, 1980s, and early 1990s. The Personal Responsibility and Work Opportunity Reconciliation Act replaced the sixty-year-old AFDC program with a new program called TANF, Temporary Aid to Needy Families (Trattner 1999).

TANF included major alterations in existing welfare programs:

1. Welfare is no longer an entitlement. Before TANF, AFDC was guaranteed to eligible Americans. The federal laws demanded that the state governments provide grants for needy families that qualified. The new law is a block grant, which means that the federal government provides a set amount of funds to each state. The states in turn must create their own systems of dispersing the funds. The federal money is now capped at $16.5 billion annually. When the funds run out, states are not legally obligated to provide services, even for families that would otherwise be eligible.

2. Time limits were placed on the number of years people are eligible for grants. Households are eligible for support for only two years at a time and for five years in the lifetime of any adult in the household, regardless of need.

3. Legal immigrants are barred from receiving TANF and food stamps. Undocumented immigrants were already barred from receiving any assistance except for emergency medical care or education for their children.

4. Criteria for receiving disability payments are more stringent. About 135,000 disabled children lost welfare assistance with the new laws.

5. The food stamp program was cut by $27 billion. No legal immigrants are allowed to receive food stamps, and able-bodied adults under the age of fifty are restricted from receiving food stamps for more than three months in a three-year period.

6. States are allowed to place caps on the number of people within a household who are considered eligible for support. States can, for example, refuse to pay larger sums to larger households or to parents who have children while they are on welfare. This restriction is based on the assumption that limiting welfare will reduce fertility among recipients. Ironically, lower birthrates are associated with more generous welfare programs in countries in Western Europe, Scandinavia, and Canada.

7. Poor families can own larger amounts of assets and still be eligible for assistance. Previously, a family could have only a vehicle worth up to $1,500, a burial plot, and $1,000 in other assets. Now families are allowed to save some money for education or buying a home.

8. States are required to assign all individuals in a welfare household to job-training and job-finding activities. People may be exempt because they are ill, incapacitated, aged, under sixteen or in school full time, already working at least thirty hours per week, more than six months pregnant, caring for an ill or incapacitated family member in their home, or caring for a young child. States have much flexibility defining these exemptions. For example, Massachusetts allows parents of children under six years old to be exempt to take care of their children. Michigan exempts only parents of babies younger than three months (Greenberg 1999).

9. Medicaid coverage continues for persons who leave welfare to go to work for one year after they leave welfare (Walker, Brooks, and Wrightsman 1999).

10. States are not required to provide child care for children of TANF recipients who participate in job support programs (Walker, Brooks, and Wrightsman 1999).

In the first eighteen months of implementation, welfare caseloads dropped 27 percent (Greenberg 1999). Wisconsin, which has been called the epicenter of the TANF reforms, reported 9,000 families relying on public aid in 1999 compared with 100,000 a decade earlier (DeParle 1999). Some of this decline may have been because welfare recipients were more strongly motivated to aggressively seek work and stop depending on welfare. Some may have been because, coincidentally, the economy generated more low-skill jobs during this time, providing greater opportunities for welfare recipients to obtain employment and leave the welfare rolls. Some of the decline represents people without other economic resources who were forced from the system because of more restrictive rules, creating larger numbers of poor people uncovered by public support.

What happens to poor people who cannot find adequate work and no longer have access to public support? One resource that is called on are grandparents. In Chapter 13 we looked at "skip generation" households, where grandparents were raising grandchildren without parents present. This kind of household has increased 52 percent since 1990. Many of these households are headed by single grandmothers with average annual incomes of $13,400. They are helping people hang on, but their resources are too meager to provide a widespread permanent solution (DeParle, 1999).

BOX 14.1

Earned Income Tax Credit

AFDC was being cut during the 1970s and 1980s and was eventually eliminated in 1996. During this same time, another program was being expanded, the Earned Income Tax Credit (EITC). EITC is a tax credit on federal income tax. The credit works on a sliding scale and varies by household size. For example, imagine a single mother who is earning wages and who has two or more children. She can apply for a credit of 40 percent of her income under $8,890. If she earned $5,000, she can get a credit for $2,000. If she earned the maximum, $8,890, she could receive a credit of $3,356. If she earned anything between $8,890 and $11,610, her credit remains the same, $3,356. If she earns over $11,610, she loses the credit at a rate of 21 cents for every dollar over that amount. If she earned $15,610, she would lose $840 from the $3,356 maximum credit. At $27,000 she would no longer be eligible for the credit.

The strength of this program is that it provides assistance to the working poor (Handler and Hasenfeld 1997). It also removes some of the stigma of receiving help because it is a tax credit, not welfare. The downside of the policy is that it provides the least assistance to the very poorest working poor, and it provides no assistance to those who are unemployed and most needy. The program also provides income in one lump annual sum, but poor families living so close to the edge need stable, consistent support to pay the rent and buy groceries. We would not expect a single parent with two children who earns about $200 a week to save 40 percent of his or her income. But because the benefit is paid as a tax credit, the system forces households to juggle their finances all year waiting for the annual check.

In addition to the practical pros and cons of EITC, the abolishment of AFDC and the simultaneous growth in EITC also marks a change in American ethics. Mimi Abramowitz (1996) writes that two important values in the United States are the work ethic and the family ethic. The work ethic says that it is essential that everyone contribute to society and that contribution must come in the form of paid labor. As we explored in Chapter 7, many activities that take place in families, like child care and housework, are not considered work because they do not generate wages. The family ethic says that families are the building block of the nation and that families should have an adult (woman) who nurtures its members. In particular, children should be cared for by their mother, and mothering requires much time and attention. In Chapter 12 we examined this ideology and the problems encountered when parents, especially mothers, cannot devote all of their attention to their children.

A tension between these two ethics has always existed in the welfare system. ADC was originally premised on the idea that children need to have full-time mothers and that the government, therefore, should provide financial assistance to single poor mothers. This premise has been shaky, particularly in the case of African American women who were frequently barred from ADC. The

(continued)

BOX **14.1** (continued)

abolishment of AFDC in 1996 marks a turning point. The government has abandoned the family ethic. And yet, as noted in Chapter 1, some of the political leaders who have strongly supported the 1996 act are also most vocal about maintaining the family ethic.

The tension between the work ethic and the family ethic and the personal impact of the government's demanding that welfare mothers abandon the family ethic is illustrated by a welfare mother in Wisconsin who quit going to a job-search program because she was going to school and also trying to find time to spend with her children. Her caseworker insisted that she must find time to do all of these things. The mother explained her dilemma. "I know I can [go to the job search program and go to school], but who would my kids be eating dinner with? Who would put them to bed if I were to work nights and go to school during the day? Even AFDC kids need their moms" (Abramowitz 1996, p. 41).

Johnnie Tillmon, an African American woman from Los Angeles who was president of the National Welfare Rights Organization (NWRO), had an idea about how to reconcile these two ethics. She suggested that we start counting family care as work:

> If I were President, I would solve this so-called welfare crisis in a minute, and go a long way toward liberating every woman. I'd just issue a proclamation that women's work is real work. In other words, I'd start paying women a living wage for doing the work we are already doing—child raising and housekeeping. And the welfare crisis would be over. Just like that. (Quoted in West 1981, p. 91)

Why Is There No Explicit Family Policy in the United States?

The United States is unusual among Western industrialized countries because it does not have a formal family policy. What has prevented this country from developing such a policy? Phyllis Moen and Alvin Schorr (1987) argue that the lack of a family policy in the United States is a result of three factors: an individualist ideology, an economy based on free enterprise, and a heterogeneous population.

A major tradition in the United States is the belief in individualism. The individual is perceived to be the fundamental element in society, and policy has tended to be directed toward individuals rather than families (Bellah et al. 1985):

> Individualism is at the very core of American culture. We believe in the dignity, indeed the sacredness, of the individual. Anything that would violate our right to think for ourselves, judge for ourselves, make our own decisions, live our lives as we see fit, is not only morally wrong, it is sacrilegious. (p. 142)

This belief in the value of individualism has had an effect on public policy. First, it has made social policy itself difficult to develop because calling on the community and the government to provide for others through public tax systems goes against the ideal of individual responsibility. Second, even when this hurdle has been overcome and the public and the government agree to provide for some members of the society, the focus is on providing for them as individuals, not as members of families. Moen and Schorr (1987) note, for example, that the Social Security Act of 1935 was implemented to provide economic security for elderly individuals and to encourage retirement to create job openings for the unemployed. The notion that Social Security might serve families of individuals developed later.

An economic system based on free enterprise is a second factor that has inhibited the development of a family policy. The commitment to free enterprise has made any governmental action that interferes with the free market subject to scrutiny and criticism. All of us do not agree about whether the free market should be interfered with, but this question always emerges in national discussions about social policy. Bellah et al. (1985) write that our ambivalence as a nation is expressed in the debate between those who are welfare liberalists and those who are neocapitalists. Both of these groups are concerned about how much the government should "interfere" with business. The neocapitalists argue that interference should be minimal. Welfare liberalists argue that capitalism cannot be maintained unless it is compassionate and therefore provides for the less fortunate in the system (Hewlett 1991).

The third inhibition to developing a family policy is the heterogeneity of our large and diverse nation. Variability by region, state, family organization, and race ethnicity has made it difficult to agree on what a family is, as well as what the government should be doing for families. Throughout this book, we have seen both the diversity of families and the problems scholars and policy makers have in trying to agree what a "real" family is. For example, we reviewed recent cuts in welfare grants to young, single, poor women who have babies. These policies imply a belief that these women and their children are not real families or good families, or at least not families the government wishes to help support.

In addition to the lack of an explicit family policy, the United States is characterized by a lack of understanding about the effect of the policies that do touch families. Schorr (1962) notes that much of the effect is accidental. *Family impact analysis* is the term used to describe assessments of how a policy might affect families. Family impact analysis would take into consideration issues like the intensity of consequences of policies on families and whether those consequences would be short or long term. It would also assess the range of families that would be affected and the perception of those effects by the families themselves. Moen and Schorr (1987) assert that although much discussion has promoted the idea that family impact analysis is essential, little has actually been accomplished.

Moen and Schorr (1987) conclude their discussion of families and social policy with four orientations they believe must be adopted by policy makers if we are to see any improvement in family policy. First, policy makers must acknowledge families as active agents, not just reactors, and therefore participants in finding and implementing solutions. Those who make policy related to families are usually not those whose lives are most affected by it. For example, Congress and the president's cabinet do not include middle- or low-income people, single parents, or welfare recipients.

Second, policy makers must be informed about the diverse and changing nature of families. For example, single-parent families are a growing form. Rather than ignoring single-parent families or trying to make them go away, policy makers should come to grips with the problems single-parent families face and the support the government might provide them.

Third, policy makers should emphasize families as their unit of analysis rather than focusing on individuals in families as their targets. For example, poverty among children cannot be solved by programs for children alone.

Fourth, family impact orientation is necessary to foresee potential inadvertent results of policies. For example, cutting programs that provide food and medical care for pregnant women and infants may result in the worse problems of very ill mothers and children.

What Is a State?

This chapter has provided a description of social policies that are critical for families through the example of welfare policy. We have seen some of the problems and shortcomings of the policies, their historical evolution, and future trends. We have observed the way in which the macrolevel of social organization, in the form of social policy, has important effects on the microlevel experience of people who seek support from that system. The macrolevel of government and policy making, however, exists within an even broader social system, the state. In this section we review the organization of the state and the theoretical debates that have developed around questions concerning its organization.

Throughout the chapter, I have used the term *government* to describe the public institutions that make laws, provide for welfare, and use force. A government is part of the state, which is the broad political organization that organizes and wields power in our society.

In the United States, the word *state* is commonly used to describe the fifty political and geographic units that make up the country. For example, we talk about the states of California, Iowa, and Georgia. When social scientists use the term *state* they mean something different. Sociologists refer to the state to indicate a social institution that can operate at several levels within a country. For example, in the United States the state would include the Supreme Court, the president, the armed forces, the IRS, the Census Bureau, and Congress at the federal level, as well as governors, legislatures, and more local bodies like city councils, school systems, welfare offices, and local police departments. Theda Skocpol and Edwin Amenta offer the following definition: "States are organizations that extract resources through taxation and attempt to extend coercive control and political authority over particular territories and the people residing in them" (1986, p. 131).

This definition makes certain assumptions about the kind of society in which a state may exist. First, it assumes that people are living in some kind of settled community associated with a particular geographic site. Nomadic hunter-gatherers, for example, were not subjects of a state. The emergence of states in human history is associated with the development of permanent settlements of people, first into cities and then into larger areas or nations.

A second factor that is associated with the emergence of the state in human history is the development of economic productivity through the invention of agriculture, manufacturing, and trade, and population growth to a level that allowed for establishing a state. Skocpol and Amenta's (1986) definition assumes that economic productivity is at a level that can both maintain the survival of at least a substantial portion of the population and allow for some surplus that can be extracted through taxes. A society that is small and able to provide only subsistence for its members would not have enough that could be given to state officials without jeopardizing the existence of the group. States demand material support in order to run their affairs. States also need to be able to maintain people in authority positions to run the state, and these people would not have time to produce their own food and shelter.

For most of human history, people lived in stateless societies. There may have been rulers, but there was no organized system of political and military support to maintain those rulers and to give them authority. About ten thousand years ago, when the agricultural revolution became firmly established in the Middle East, city-states like Mesopotamia, which is in the region now known as Iraq, were created.

Modern states, which are called nation-states, came about with the emergence of nations and developed with the growth of industrialization. Modern nation-states are marked by sovereignty (authority over a given area), citizenship (consciousness of people that they have certain rights and obligations by virtue of living in a state), and nationalism (identification of individuals with the state as a unified political community). In earlier states, most of the people had little conscious connection to their state. In a modern nation-state like the United States, people are aware of the authority of the state and understand themselves to be citizens of it (Giddens 1991). For example, in the quotes at the beginning of the chapter Leona Smith says this is our country. She is identifying herself as a member of the nation-state. Paula Gunn Allen, the Native American speaker, on the other hand, reminds us that the absorption of Native American nations by the nation-state known as the United States occurred by force, was not accepted by many Native Americans, and continues to be an unsettled issue.

States, then, are a relatively new phenomenon in human society. Their emergence is tied to changes that took place a few thousand years ago. Since then, states have extended their reach into our lives and, through the use of policy, play an important role in nearly all social interactions, including those related to families.

The State and Inequality

As you read the section on welfare policy, you may have begun to wonder why the welfare system is organized as it is. Why is it so inadequate? Why is it so complex? Why does it treat poor people inhumanely? Why is there a push toward workfare and privatization? The answers to these questions depend on the point of view you use to examine them. In this section, we explore some of the theoretical frameworks that currently propose explanations for the organization of the welfare system, and in particular we try to uncover whose interests are served by its current organization.

In the previous discussion, I described two features of the historical development of human society that allowed and/or necessitated the emergence of the state. I noted that in order for a state to exist, a society must include permanent settlements of people in specific geographic sites. In addition, a society must be capable of producing, on the average at least, a surplus that can be taken in the form of taxes to maintain the state. In this section we examine a third feature of the emergence of the state—inequality. The state became necessary because of a diversity of interests in society that necessitated some institution either negotiate a compromise among the adversarial parties or act on behalf of one party to control the others.

There are many perspectives on the question of whether, in a capitalist nation-state like the United States, the state acts as a negotiator on behalf of everyone or on behalf of

TABLE 14.2   Theories of the State

Liberal Democrats:	The state operates as a neutral arbiter among all interest groups in the country. Different values and ideas create critical delineations among interest groups, but other factors like gender, race ethnicity, and region are also important.
Marxist	
Instrumentalists:	The state serves the interest of the capitalist class.
Structuralists:	The state negotiates among different interests in the capitalist class.
Feminists	
Class Focus:	The state controls/oppresses women to better serve the interests of the capitalist class.
Gender Focus:	The state controls/oppresses women as a way to maintain male dominance.
Combination:	The state controls/oppresses women to maintain male dominance and the capitalist class.

certain strata. Two of the most popular points of view are the liberal democratic and the marxist positions (Abramowitz 1989; Pupo 1988). These viewpoints are summarized in Table 14.2.

According to liberal democrats, the state is a neutral arbitrator among the numerous interest groups in a pluralist democracy like the United States. This model sees the United States as a nation of many different people, classes, and organizations. Each group works to influence the state through activities like lobbying, gaining media coverage, and running candidates. The state acts as a vehicle by which these opposing interests can come together to create a fair and humane compromise. The state operates with the vague mission of providing for the social good (Pupo 1988). Liberal democrats would argue that the welfare system is a product of much negotiation among many different parties. They would assert that the character of the system is a result of the ability of different interests to implement their will. Those who are better able to make their wishes known and build political support for their proposals will have a larger say in how the system operates. Liberal democrats would contend that the complexity of the welfare system is due to the complex sets of competing interests. For example, there are debates among federal, state, and local authorities about how best to spend money. There are different sets of interests among taxpayers and those who receive welfare grants. There are also differences in ideology among various groups. The dilemma posed earlier in Box 14.1, for example, illustrates one debate between those who advocate a work ethic and those who wish to advocate a family ethic.

The second major framework that seeks to understand the organization of the state is the marxist position. Marxists maintain that the state is not a neutral arbiter but works to serve the interest of the ruling class, those who own the wealth. Wealth refers to cash, property, stocks, buildings, factories, and mines. Wealth can take the form of personal property, which means it is consumed by those who own it. This would include mansions, yachts, cars, jewels, and spending money. Wealth can also take the form of private property, which means that it is used to generate more wealth. This would include stocks, money invested in loans, factories, rental buildings, and mines. The people who own the majority of the wealth in a capitalist system like the United States are called capitalists. Remember from Chapter 5 that this includes a small number of people, but they own a large proportion of all the wealth in the United States. Furthermore, because they own the places of business where other classes of people work, they have a class relationship with working-class and middle-class people. In contrast to the liberal democrats who emphasize ideology, Marxists emphasize class position as a source of motivation and power for the contending forces vying for power in the state.

The marxist position on the state can be divided into two points of view, the instrumentalist perspective and the structuralist perspective. Instrumentalists contend that the state accomplishes its mission of serving the capitalist class by operating directly under its instruction. Instrumentalists, for example, would point out that the majority of members of Congress come from wealthy families and that some individuals float back and forth between leadership positions in business and leadership positions in the government. Structuralists, on the other hand, believe that there is so much conflict in the capitalist class that the state must act somewhat independently of any particular capitalist and instead behaves as an arbiter among various factions. For example, the structuralist would point out that capitalists who produce goods in the United States to sell here would advocate high tariffs on goods produced elsewhere. Capitalists with branches in other nations who wish to sell to the U.S. market would advocate lower tariffs for those same imported goods. The state must negotiate this difference of opinion by coming to some agreement about what is best for the maintenance of the political economy as a whole.

Both instrumentalist and structuralist marxists assert that within a capitalist society, the state has two main tasks: to facilitate accumulation of capital by the capitalists and to maintain the system by either legitimating it in the eyes of the populace or by providing for some other form of social control, like the police (O'Connor 1973). To facilitate the accumulation of capital by the capitalists, the state, for example, provides for a properly educated workforce (Bowles and Gintis 1976). It also designs tax laws to keep money in the hands of the wealthy, and it builds and maintains an infrastructure of roads, airports, and mail, water, and sewage systems to allow the capitalists to produce and distribute commodities.

The maintenance of the system is accomplished by a number of state agencies. Information dissemination, education, and the welfare system help inhibit those who are not in the ruling class from understanding that they are oppressed and taking action to change the system. If that does not work, however, the state can also use the courts, the police, and the army to keep the peace.

Marxists argue that the welfare system is organized to support the two major tasks of the state, accumulation and legitimation. Accumulation is facilitated by paying as few benefits as possible in order to keep more money available to the capitalists. Accumulation is also facilitated if the welfare system keeps more people seeking work in order to increase competition among workers and thereby lower wages. Legitimation is facilitated by stigmatizing welfare recipients and promoting a victim-blaming image of poverty that deflects criticism away from the economic system and the political organization, which are actually the root of the problem.

A third school of thought on the state—feminist theory—is a recently emerging one that incorporates the notion of gender inequality in its assessment of state activity (Connell

1987; Marshall 1996; Zaretsky 1982). This framework can be divided into three types. The first group of theorists contend that the state seeks to control and shape gender and sexuality to accomplish its primary mission of maintaining the capitalist system. For example, this approach would argue that the state does not demand equal or comparable pay for women primarily because keeping women as a cheap source of labor lowers production costs for business interests, thereby improving profitability and strengthening the capitalists.

The second group argues that the state operates to protect the patriarchy (MacKinnon 1982). Theorists in this school of thought emphasize the way an insufficient welfare system—one that is means-tested, inadequate, constricting, and stigmatizing—coupled with unequal wages for women help preserve male dominance by providing men with more money and by keeping women more dependent on men. For example, consider a woman with children who wishes to leave an unhappy marriage. In Chapter 10, we saw that she is likely to retain custody of the children but unlikely to receive child support from her husband. If she finds employment, she is likely to be paid less than her husband and certainly less than they made as a two-income household. If she cannot find employment and child care, she can apply for TANF, but will find that her financial status falls below the poverty level. In short, she can choose to be poor or she can choose to stay with her husband. If the welfare system provided sufficient support, it would create an avenue of independence for women. Advocates of this framework insist that our analysis of the state must fully appreciate the gender politics of the state and the coercive manner in which the state controls women and benefits men.

The third group of theorists argues that the state is used to promote both the dominance of capitalists over the working class and the dominance of men over women. Furthermore, the state serves as an arbiter between these two competing ruling strata: those who dominate by gender—men—and those who dominate by class—capitalists (Eisenstein 1984b; Petchesky 1990).

Resistance to the Welfare System

This chapter has explored the way in which the macrolevel of social policy and the government create problems for people and the way in which policy makers and the government exist within an even broader system called the state. In this section we turn our attention to the way people at the microlevel respond to and resist the problems that are created for them by these macrolevel institutions.

The welfare system appears to be fraught with problems. It is discriminating, inadequate, cumbersome, and deteriorating. How do recipients respond? Some people have created ways to try to transform the system. Others have attempted to cope with the system by devising ways to combine welfare with other resources in order to patch together a survival package. These two methods of resistance are the subject of this section, beginning with those who cope with the system.

Kathryn Edin (1991) examined this issue by interviewing fifty Chicago-area mothers who received welfare. Edin found that all the women in her study supplemented their grants from AFDC and food stamps by using at least one source of unreported income: income from work or assistance from family, friends, boyfriends, or the fathers of their children (Edin and Lein 1997).

Because their budgets were so tight, the women were able to give extremely accurate accounts of how much money they spent and how much money they took in. The average woman spent a total of $864, with $501 going for housing and food. The remaining $363 was spent on items like a telephone, clothing, school supplies, transportation, toiletries, health care, diapers, burial insurance, and furniture. The average AFDC grant amounted to $324, and the average food stamps were $197. The mothers also received income from other sources totaling $376—an average of $166 from work and $210 from family and friends. This left a shortfall of about $343 per month.

The women explained to Edin (1991) how this constant shortfall affected them. One woman said, "I don't ever pay off all my bills, so there isn't ever anything left over. As soon as I get my check, it's gone, and I don't have anything left" (p. 465).

If they had not received money from sources other than welfare, the women would have been even deeper in debt. Some of the money they obtained was from family and friends, and some was from jobs. Receiving these funds and not reporting them to the welfare office, which would result in a cut in the grant received, is illegal. One woman explained that although she felt bad about having to lie, she saw no other way to survive:

> Public Aid is an agency that I believe can teach a person how to lie. If you tell them the truth, you won't get any help. But if you go down there and tell them a lie, you get help. And I can't understand it, and every woman on Public Aid will tell you the same thing. It teaches you to lie. It won't accept the truth. So when you deal with Public Aid, you have to tell them a tale. (Edin 1991, p. 469)

According to the respondents in Edin's work, many people who receive welfare resist the system by not complying with the regulations. A second form of resistance is through organizations like the National Welfare Rights Organization (NWRO), which works to transform the system itself in order to make it more effective for the people who seek assistance (Piven 1990).

The NWRO flourished in the 1960s and 1970s (G. West 1981). During that time, the organization mobilized thousands of welfare recipients and their advocates and millions of dollars and other resources. The movement gained national recognition after a ten-day march on Columbus, Ohio, in 1966, which was coordinated with protests across the country. NWRO activities included lobbying, courtroom contests, public protests, education, and advocacy with individual welfare cases. NWRO's strategy was to flood the welfare system with eligible applicants in order to expose the inadequacy of the system and force change. The goal was to obtain a guaranteed income system in the United States.

Although NWRO did not obtain a guaranteed income, it was successful in some of its efforts (Amott 1990). NWRO educated potential applicants about available services and helped guide people through the complex system. The number of AFDC families tripled between 1965 and 1976, the period in which NWRO was largest and most visible (Miller 1990). In addition, some of the most punitive features of welfare, such as midnight raids on AFDC mothers, were contested in court by NWRO and eventually ruled illegal. NWRO declined in the late 1970s as a national organization, although a few local Welfare Rights Organization groups remained strong throughout the 1980s and into the 1990s (*Welfare Mother's Voice* 1992).

During the late 1970s and into the 1980s, welfare rights advocates took another tactic and sought positions within the welfare system, where they continued to work for change, an issue that Nancy Naples has investigated. Naples (1991) interviewed forty-two women who had been unpaid community activists and had become paid workers in the state system, working in community action programs (CAPs). CAPs are publicly funded programs that provide information, education, and other services to residents of low-income neighborhoods. The women successfully challenged the organization of CAPs in four ways. First, they broadened the range of activities that were seen as part of their job. For example, traditional social service professionals worked from 9 A.M. to 5 P.M. and then went home. The community activists were in paid jobs from 9 A.M. to 5 P.M., but their work continued after hours because of their membership and participation in the community.

Second, they contested the reliance on credentials as the most important or only criterion for being able to provide quality service. Third, they demanded that those who worked for the state should also be involved in challenging the state, instead of playing the role of neutral observer. The supervisors attempted to stop paid workers from participating in political actions, but workers ignored or resisted these regulations. Fourth, they insisted that their work with the people in their communities emerges from their relationship with their neighbors and that the services they provided and the way in which they were provided be appropriate to the particular community. For example, program administrators who attempted to manage centers from a central office were met with resistance by workers at various branches. Naples (1991) concludes, however, that despite the importance of their work in the community and the influence of their resistance on the bureaucracy of the CAPs, the cuts in welfare spending have eliminated many of the positions the women held.

In 1988, on the twenty-fifth anniversary of the founding of NWRO, the National Welfare Rights Union (NWRU) emerged and held its first annual convention in Detroit. Its leadership had come out of NWRO. In 1989, NWRU formed a coalition with the National Union of the Homeless and the National Anti-Hunger Coalition and organized a conference titled "Up and Out of Poverty, Now!" (Abramowitz 1996). The NWRU has taken a more militant stand than the women in the Naples study. NWRU members maintain that poor people must openly confront the government for failing to provide a society in which all people can attain social justice and a decent standard of living. In the 1980s and 1990s, they "turned up the street heat" by staging sit-ins in welfare offices and takeovers of empty housing owned by government housing authorities, by appropriating abandoned buildings to create community centers, and by agitating in local and state government offices. In 1995, NWRU worked hard to try to convince President Clinton not to sign the 1996 welfare reform legislation. They were joined in their efforts by the National Organization for Women (NOW) and ninety other organizations (Abramowitz 2000).

NWRU believes that the victims of poverty, not their advocates, must take the leadership in the welfare-rights movement. They also believe that they must build coalitions with homeless unions, labor unions, students, women's organizations, and churches in order to wage their fight to "educate, organize and empower" (Kramer 1988).

In its statement of purpose, NWRU wrote:

The current welfare system destroys families by keeping the husband/father out of the household, penalizes the parents who are trying to work themselves out of welfare, and punishes people, especially the children, for being poor. All people should have adequate income, regardless of their work, a guaranteed annual income so that no one in this nation should live in poverty. All people should be able to live a life of dignity with full freedom and respect for human rights. All low-income people and public assistance recipients should enjoy a fair and open system which guarantees the full protection of the U.S. Constitution. All low-income people and public assistance recipients should participate directly in the formation of decisions affecting their lives. (National Welfare Rights Union 1988, p. 11)

Since 1988, NWRU has continued its effort through national and local Survival Summits, marching for justice protesting at the Democratic and Republican conventions, testifying at United Nations hearings on poverty and human rights, and joining with international organizations in protest of the G8 summits (www.kwru.org 2005; www.nationalwru.org 2005). NWRU declares:

The NWRU will take our movement into the streets of this nation from the farms of rural America to the tenements of the inner city, from the homeless ghettos to the college campuses, from the Halls of Congress to the hearing rooms of our state houses. We are building a movement to insure a better world for our children and ourselves. We are building a movement that cannot be stopped. (National Welfare Rights Union 1988, p. 12)

BOX 14.2

Sociologists Making a Difference

The NWRU asserts that the movement to solve the problems welfare recipients face should be led by the welfare recipients themselves. This is a good principle, but does it mean that sociologists have no role to play? Arloc Sherman and Jodi Sandfort (1998) write that researchers can be an important asset in these endeavors. The passage of TANF and its renewals and further cuts were major setbacks in welfare rights, but sometimes changes can open the door to further change, and we may be able to create positive policies in the wake of the dismantling of the old system. The cracks are small and they may close quickly, but there may still be some opportunities to create beneficial changes for low-income families.

Part of the political organizing will entail gathering information and disseminating it to the press, the public, and policy makers. Professors and students can become scholar-activists and play an important role in this effort. We may need to learn to work within or at least alongside activist organizations. We will need to gear our research to the questions that matter to political actors. We will also need to be sure we are communicating effectively and clearly. Sometimes the language and style of writing for the scientific community is not suitable to providing information to a broader audience. Scholar-activists also need to find outlets for distributing their work to an audience far beyond our usual academic circles. Sherman and Sandfort (1998) suggest the following topics as most critical to the current debate around welfare and families: the consequences of child poverty, the effects of state programs and policies, and action research and assistance to "community monitoring" efforts.

The Micro–Macro Connection

In this chapter our focus has been on the way in which the government uses social policy, especially welfare policy, to influence families. The welfare system directly affects poor families, but it also affects other families as well, by defining what a family is and what a proper relationship should be between women and men and adults and children.

The book has discussed a number of other ways in which the state influences families. For example, one prominent aspect of the state is legislation. We have explored the way in which the laws shape and define The Family and issues related to families such as sexuality, reproduction, marriage, divorce, relationships between parents and children, and violence in families. We have also noted how the financial activities of the state, such as collecting taxes and setting a minimum wage, have affected families. The state also includes the institutions of coercive control, and here we have seen how the police have played a role in families on questions such as sexuality and violence.

We have also observed the way in which various factors at the macro level may influence each other. For example, the welfare system is influenced by the government, which is influenced by the organization of the state; and the state is influenced by cultural values as well as by the stratification systems of class, gender, and race. A variety of macrolevel forces play on each other.

In addition, the microlevel of society affects the macrolevel. Families and individuals at the microlevel have sought to resist and transform the macrolevel of social organization. For example, welfare mothers have responded to the welfare system by attempting to cope with the inadequacies of the services. In addition, the microlevel has also worked to alter the organization of the welfare system. Community activists attempt to try to influence the provision of services to low-income communities by working within the system. The National Welfare Rights Organization was able to win concessions in the 1960s and 1970s, and its members, now in the National Welfare Rights Union, continue their efforts to transform the system into a more effective and humane one. Scholar-activists are being called on to join this effort.

REFERENCES

Abel, Emily. 1986. Adult daughters and care for the elderly. *Feminist Studies* 12 (3):479–493.

Abma, J., A. Chandra, W. Hosher, L. Peterson, and L. Piccinino. 1997. Fertility, family planning and women's health: New data from the 1995 national survey of family growth. *Vital Health Statistics* 23 (19).

Abramowitz, Mimi. 1989. *Regulating the lives of women: Social welfare policy from colonial times to the present.* Boston: South End Press.

Abramowitz, Mimi. 1996. *Under attack and fighting back: Women and welfare in the U.S.* New York: Monthly Review Press.

Abramowitz, Mimi. 2000. *Under attack and fighting Back: Women and welfare in the U.S.* 2d ed. New York: Monthly Review Press.

Achen, Alexandra, and Frank Stafford. 2005. *Data quality of housework hours in the panel study of income dynamics: Who really does the dishes?* Ann Arbor: Institute for Social Research (September).

Achilles, Rona. 1990. Desperately seeking babies: New technologies of hope and despair. In K. Arnup, A. Levesque, and R. Pierson (eds.), *Delivering motherhood: Maternal ideologies and practices in the 19th and 20th centuries* (pp. 284–312). New York: Routledge.

ACORN Living Wage Resource Center. 2005. www.acorn .org Brooklyn, New York (accessed May 29, 2006).

Acuna, Rodolfo. 2003. *Occupied America,* 5th ed. Boston: Longman.

AFL-CIO. 2005. *Facts and statistics.* www.aflcio.org (accessed July 19, 2006).

Agbayani-Siewert, Pauline, and Linda Revilla. 1995. Filipino Americans. In P. Min (ed.), *Asian Americans: Contemporary trends and issues* (pp. 95–133). Thousand Oaks, CA: Sage.

Aguilar-San Juan, Karin, ed. 1994. *The state of Asian America: Activism and resistance in the 1990s.* Boston: South End Press.

Ahrons, Constance, and Roy Rodgers. 1987. *Divorced families: A multidisciplinary view.* New York: Norton and Norton.

Ahrons, Constance. 1994. *The good divorce.* New York: Harper-Collins.

Ahrons, Constance. 2004a. *The good divorce* (Updated). New York: Harper-Collins.

Ahrons, Constance. 2004b. *We're still family.* New York: Harper-Collins.

Alan Guttmacher Institute. 1994. *Sex and America's teenagers.* New York: Guttmacher.

Alan Guttmacher Institute. 1999. *Sharing responsibility: Women, society, and abortion worldwide.* New York.

Alan Guttmacher Institute. 2004. *U.S. teenage pregnancy statistics* (February).

Albers, Cheryl. 1999. *Sociology of families readings.* Thousand Oaks, CA: Pine Forge.

Alford-Cooper, Finnegan. 1998. *For keeps: Marriages that last a lifetime.* Armonk, NY: M. E. Sharpe.

Allan, Graham. 1985. *Family life: Domestic roles and social organization.* New York: Basil Blackwell.

Allen, Katherine. 1998. Lesbian and gay families. In T. Arendell (ed.), *Contemporary parenting* (pp. 196–218). Thousand Oaks, CA: Sage.

Allen, Mike, and Nancy Burrell. 1996. Comparing the impact of homosexual and heterosexual parents on children. *Journal of Homosexuality* 32 (2):19–35.

Allen, Paula Gunn. 1986. *The sacred hoop.* Boston: Beacon Press.

Allgeier, E., and M. Wiederman. 1991. Love and mate selection in the 1990s. *Free Inquiry* 11:25–27.

Alliance Housing Council. 1988. *Housing and homelessness.* Washington, DC: Alliance to End Homelessness.

Altman, Dennis. 1971. *Homosexual: Oppression and liberation.* New York: Outerbridge and Dientsfrey.

Altman, Dennis. 1982. *The homosexualization of America.* Boston: Beacon Press.

Amato, Paul, and Alan Booth. 1997. *A generation at risk.* Cambridge, MA: Harvard University Press.

Ambert, Anne-Marie. 1997. *Parents, children, and adolescents: Interactive relationships and development in context.* New York: Haworth Press.

American Association for Protecting Children. 1979. *National study on neglect and abuse reporting.* Denver, CO: American Humane Association.

American Association for Protecting Children. 1985. *National study on neglect and abuse reporting.* Denver, CO: American Humane Association.

Ammerman, Nancy Tatom. 1987. *Bible believers: Fundamentalists in the modern world.* Rutgers: Rutgers University Press.

Amott, Teresa. 1990. Black women and AFDC: Making entitlement out of necessity. In L. Gordon (ed.), *Women, the state and welfare* (pp. 280–300). Madison: University of Wisconsin Press.

Amott, Teresa, and Julie Matthaei. 1991. *Race, gender and work: A multicultural economic history of women in the United States.* Boston: South End Press.

Amour, Stephanie. 2005. Gay parents cheer a benefit revolution. *USA Today,* 9 January.

An act for the better ordering and governing of Negroes and slaves, South Carolina, 1712. 1992. In P. Rothenberg (ed.),

Race, class and gender in the U.S.: An integrated study. 2d ed. (pp. 258–264). New York: St. Martin's Press.

Anderson, Dilworth. 1993. Extended kin networks in black families. In L. Burton (ed.), *Families and aging* (pp. 57–63). Amityville, NY: Baywood.

Anderson, E. 1990. *Streetwise: Race, class and change in an urban community.* Chicago: University of Chicago Press.

Anderson, Elaine A. and Sally A. Koblinsky. 1999. "Homeless policy: The need to speak to families." In L. Stone (ed.), *Selected readings in marriage and family.* San Diego, CA: Greenhaven Press.

Anderson, Kristin, and Debra Umberson. 2001. Gendering violence. *Gender and Society,* 15 (3):358–380.

Anderson, Margaret. 1988. *Thinking about women: Sociological perspectives on sex and gender.* 2d ed. New York: Macmillan.

Anderson, Sarah and John Cavanaugh. 2000. *Field guide to the global economy.* New York: The New Free Press.

Andler, Judy, and Gail Sullivan. 1980. The price of government funding. *Journal of Alternative Human Services* 6 (2):15–18.

APA. 1995. Lesbian and gay parenting: A resource for psychologists. *American Psychological Association.* www.apa.org/pi/parent/html (accessed May 29, 2006).

Appelbaum, Richard. 1989. The affordability gap. *Society* 26 (May/June):6–8.

Appelbaum, Richard, and Peter Dreier. 1992. Census count no help to the homeless. In P. Baker, L. Anderson, and D. Dom (eds.), *Social problems: A critical thinking approach* (pp. 336–337). Belmont, CA: Wadsworth.

Applebaum, Richard, and William Chambliss. 1997. *Sociology.* New York: HarperCollins.

Aptheker, Herbert. 1943. *American Negro slave revolts.* New York: International Publishers.

Arditti, Joyce. 1992. Differences between fathers with joint custody and noncustodial fathers. *American Journal of Orthopsychiatry* 62 (2):186–195.

Arendell, Terry. 1986. *Mothers and divorce: Legal, economic and social dilemmas.* Berkeley: University of California Press.

Arendell, Terry. 1995. *Fathers and divorce.* Thousand Oaks, CA: Sage.

Arendell, Terry. 1997. Divorce and remarriage In T. Arendell (ed.), *Contemporary parenting* (pp. 154–195). Thousand Oaks, CA: Sage.

Aries, Philippe. 1962. *Centuries of childhood: A social history of family life.* New York: Knopf.

Aronowitz, Stanley and Wiliam DiFazio. 1994. *Jobless future.* Minneapolis: University of Minnesota Press.

Aronson, Jane. 1992. Women's sense of responsibility for the care of old people: "But who else is going to do it?" *Gender and Society* 6 (1):8–29.

Aronson, Pamela, Jeylan Mortimer, Carol Zierman, and Michael Hacker. 1996. Generational differences in early work experiences and evaluations. In J. Mortimer and M. Finch (eds.), *Adolescents, work and family: An intergener-ational developmental analysis* (pp. 25–62). Thousand Oaks, CA: Sage.

Associated Press. 2004. Gap between haves and have nots expands. www.truthout.org (accessed May 29, 2006).

Atchley, Robert. 1992. Retirement and marital satisfaction. In M. Szinovacz, D. Ekerdt, and B. Vinick (eds.), *Families and retirement* (pp. 145–158). Newbury Park, CA: Sage.

Atherton, Charles. 1989. The welfare state: Still on solid ground. *Social Service Review* 63 (June): 169–178.

Aulette, Judy. 1991. The privatization of housing in a declining economy: The case of Stepping Stone Housing. *Sociology and Social Welfare* 18 (1):149–164.

Aulette, Judy, and Trudy Mills. 1988. Something old, something new: Auxiliary work in the 1983–1986 copper strike. *Feminist Studies* 14 (2):251–268.

Aulette, Judy, and Walda Katz Fishman. 1991. Working class women and the women's movement. In B. Berberoglu (ed.), *Critical perspectives in sociology* (pp. 241–252). Dubuque, IA: Kendall Hunt.

Baca Zinn, Maxine, and D. Stanley Eitzen. 1999. *Diversity in families.* 5th ed. New York: Longman.

Baca Zinn, Maxine, and Stanley Eitzen. 1990. *Diversity in American families.* 2d ed. New York: Harper and Row.

Baca Zinn, Maxine. 1980. Employment and education of Mexican American women: The interplay of modernity and ethnicity in eight families. *Harvard Educational Review* 50 (1):47–62.

Baca Zinn, Maxine. 1982. Qualitative methods in family research: A look inside Chicano families. *California Sociologist* (Summer):58–79.

Baca Zinn, Maxine. 1987. *Minority families in crisis: The public discussion.* Memphis, TN: Memphis State University, Center for Research on Women.

Baca Zinn, Maxine. 1989a. Chicano men and masculinity. In M. Kimmel and M. Messner (eds.), *Men's lives.* 2d ed. (pp. 67–76). New York: Macmillan.

Baca Zinn, Maxine. 1989b. Family race and poverty in the eighties. *Signs* 14 (4):856–874.

Baca Zinn, Maxine. 1995. Social science theorizing for Latino families in the age of diversity. In R. Zambrano (ed.), *Understanding Latino families: Scholarship, policy and practice* (pp. 177–189). Thousand Oaks, CA: Sage.

Baca Zinn, Maxine. 1998a. Race and the family values debate. In D. Vannoy and P. Diebeck (eds.), *Challenges for work and family in the twenty first century* (pp. 49–64). New York: Aldine deGruyter.

Baca Zinn, Maxine. 1998b. Feminist rethinking from racial-ethnic families. In S. Ferguson (ed.), *Shifting the center: Understanding contemporary families* (pp. 12–21). Mountain View, CA: Mayfield.

Baca Zinn, Maxine, and D. Stanley Eitzen. 1998. "Economic restructuring and systems of inequality." In E. Chow, D. Wilkinson, and M. Baca Zinn (eds.), *Race, class and gender* (pp. 233–238). Thousand Oaks, CA: Sage.

Bachman, J., and J. Schulenberg. 1993. How part time work intensity relates to drug use, problem behavior, time use, and satisfaction among high school seniors: Are these consequences or merely correlates? *Developmental Psychology* 29:220–235.

Back, Gloria, 1985. *Are you still my mother?* New York: Warner Books.

Bahr, Stephen. 1974. Effects of power and division of labor in the family. In L. Hoffman and F. Nye (eds.), *Working mothers* (pp. 167–185). San Francisco: Jossey-Bass.

Baker, Laurence. 1996. Comparing women and men physicians. *New England Journal of Medicine,* 11 April.

Baldwin, Wendy, and Christine Nord. 1984. Delaying childbirth in the U.S.: Facts and fictions. *Population Bulletin* 39:1–37.

Balswick, Jack. 1979. How to get your husband to say "I love you." *Family Circle.*

Balswick, Jack, and Charles Peek. 1971. The inexpressive male: A tragedy of American society. *The Family Coordinator* 20:363–368.

Bane, Mary Jo. 1980. Toward a description and evaluation of U.S. family policy. In J. Aldous and W. Dumon (eds.), *The politics and programs of family policy* (pp. 155–191). Notre Dame: UND and Leuven University Press.

Bane, Mary Jo. 1986. Household composition and poverty. In S. Danziger and D. Weinberg (eds.), *Fighting poverty: What works and what doesn't* (pp. 209–231). Cambridge, MA: Harvard University Press.

Barak, Gregg. 1992. *Gimme shelter: A social history of homelessness in contemporary America.* New York: Praeger.

Barash, David. 1977. *Sociobiology and behavior.* New York: Elsevier.

Barerra, Mario. 1979. *Race and class in the Southwest.* Notre Dame: University of Notre Dame Press.

Barret, Robert, and Bryan Robinson. 1992. *Gay fathers.* Lexington, MA: Lexington.

Barry, Kathleen. 1981. *Female sexual slavery.* Englewood Cliffs, NJ: Prentice-Hall.

Bart, Pauline. 1983. Review of Chodorow's "The reproduction of mothering." In J. Trebilcot (ed.), *Mothering: Essays in feminist theory* (pp. 147–152). Totowa, NJ: Rowman and Allanheld.

Basow, Susan. 1992. *Gender stereotypes and roles.* 3d ed. Pacific Grove, CA: Brooks/Cole.

Bassuk, E., L. Rubin, and A. Lauriat. 1986. Characteristics of sheltered homeless families. *American Journal of Public Health* 76 (September):1097–1101.

Bauserman, Robert. 2002. Child adjustment in joint-custody versus sole-custody arrangements: A meta-analytic review. *Journal of Family Psychology* 16 (1):91–102.

Beals, Ralph, Harry Hoijer, and Alan Beals. 1977. *An introduction to anthropology.* New York: Macmillan.

Bean, Frank, and Marta Tienda. 1987. *The Hispanic population of the U.S.* New York: Russell Sage.

Beck, Barbara. 2004. "Wealth gap widens" Grantee press release. *Pew Charitable Trust,* DC October 18, 2004. www .civilrights.org/issues/labor (accessed May 29, 2006).

Becker, Gary. 1965. A theory of the allocation of time. *Economic Journal* 75 (299):493–517.

Becker, Gary. 1981. *A treatise on the family.* Cambridge, MA: Harvard University Press.

Becker, Howard. 1979. What's happening to sociology? *Society* 15 (5):19–24.

Bedard, Marcia. 1992. *Breaking with tradition: Diversity, conflict and change in contemporary American families.* Dix Hills, NY: General Hall.

Beemyn, Brett, and Mickey Elliason (eds.). 1996. *Queer studies: A lesbian, gay, bisexual and transgender anthology.* New York: NYU Press.

Begus, Sarah, and Pamela Armstrong. 1982. Daddy's right: Incestuous assault. In Diamond (ed.), *Family politics and public policy: A feminist dialogue on women and the state* (pp. 236–249). New York: Longman.

Bellah, Robert, Richard Madsen, William Sullivan, Ann Swidler, and Steven Tipton. 1985. *Habits of the heart: Individualism and commitment in American life.* New York: Harper and Row.

Belle, Deborah. 1982. *Lives in stress: Women and depression.* Beverly Hills, CA: Sage.

Belsky, Jay and John Kelly. 1994. *The transition to parenthood.* New York: Delacorte Press.

Bem, Sandra Lipsitz. 1981. Gender schema theory: A cognitive account of sex typing. *Psychological Review* 88 (4):354–364.

Bem, Sandra Lipsitz. 1982. Gender schema theory and self-schema theory compared: A comment on Markus, Crane, Bernstein, and Siladi's "self schemas and gender." *Journal of Personality and Social Psychology* 43 (6):1192–1194.

Bem, Sandra Lipsitz. 1983. Gender schema theory and its implications for child development: Raising gender-aschematic children in a genderschematic society. *Signs* 8 (4):598–616.

Benenson, Harold. 1985. The community and family bases of U.S. working class protest, 1880–1920. In L. Kriesberg (ed.), *Research in social movements, conflicts and change* (pp. 112–126). Greenwich, CT: JAI Press.

Bengston, V. 1985. Diversity and symbolism in grandparent roles. In V. Bengston and J. Robertson (ed.) *Grandparenthood* (pp. 11–26). Beverly Hills, CA: Sage.

Benkov, Laura. 1999. Reinventing the family. In A. Skolnick and J. Skolnick (eds.), *Family in transition.* 10th ed. (pp. 322–344). New York: Addison Wesley.

Bennett, Neil, David Bloom, and Patricia Craig. 1989. The divergence of black and white marriage patterns. *American Journal of Sociology* 95:692–722.

Bennett, Neil, Jiali Li, Young Hwan Song, and Keming Yang. 1999. *Young children in poverty: A statistical update.* New York: National Center for Children in Poverty.

Bennett, Nichole. 2001. "Action Alert" *SWS Network News* 18 (2):9–11.

Benson, Susan. 1978. The clerking sisterhood: Rationalization and the work culture of saleswomen in American department stores, 1890–1960. *Radical America* 12 (2):41–55.

Benston, Margaret. 1969. The political economy of women's liberation. *Monthly Review* 21:13–27.

Berberoglu, Berch. 1988. Labor, capital and the state: Economic crisis and class struggle in the U.S. in the 1970s and 1980s. *Humanity and Society* 12 (1):1–20.

Berberoglu, Berch. 1992. *The legacy of empire: Economic decline and class polarization in the United States.* New York: Praeger.

Berberoglu, Berch. 2002. The political economy of labor process. In M. Lanham (ed.), *Labor and capital in the age of globalization.* New York: Rowman & Littlefield.

Berberoglu, Berch. 2005. *Globalization and change.* Lexington, MA: Lexington Books.

Bergen, Raquel. 1996. *Wife rape: Understanding the response of survivors and service providers.* Thousand Oaks, CA: Sage.

Berger, Brigette, and Peter Berger. 1974. *The war over the family.* New York: Anchor.

Berger, Peter, and Hansfried Kellner. 1964. Marriage and the construction of reality. *Diogenes* 46:1–32.

Berger, Peter, and Thomas Luckmann. 1966. *The social construction of reality.* New York: Random House.

Berheide, Catherine, Sarah Fenstermaker Berk, and Richard Berk. 1976. Household work in the suburbs: The job and its participants. *Pacific Sociological Review* 19 (4):491–518.

Berheide, Catherine. 1984. Women's work in the home: Seems like old times. *Marriage and Family Review* 7 (Fall/Winter):37–50.

Berk, Richard, and Sarah Fenstermaker Berk. 1979. *Labor and leisure at home: Content and organization of the household day.* Beverly Hills, CA: Sage.

Berk, Richard, and Sarah Fenstermaker Berk. 1983. Supply side sociology of the family: The challenge of the new home economics. *Annual Review of Sociology* 9:375–395.

Berk, Richard, and Sarah Fenstermaker Berk. 1988. Women's unpaid labor: Home and community. In A. Stromberg and S. Harkess (eds.), *Women working.* 2d ed. (pp. 287–302). Mountain View, CA: Mayfield.

Berk, Richard, Sarah Berk, Donileen Loseke, and David Rauma. 1983. Mutual combat and other family violence myths. In D. Finkelhor et al. (eds.), *The dark side of families* (pp. 197–212). Beverly Hills, CA: Sage.

Berk, Sarah Fenstermaker. 1985. *The gender factory: The apportionment of work in American households.* New York: Plenum.

Bernard, Jessie. 1972. *The future of marriage.* New Haven: Yale University Press.

Bernard, Jessie. 1989. The dissemination of feminist thought: 1960–1988. In R. Wallace (ed.), *Feminism and sociological theory* (pp. 23–33). Newbury Park, CA: Sage.

Bernard, M., and V. Bernard. 1983. Violent intimacy: The family as a model for love relationships. *Family Relations* 32 (April):283–286.

Bernstein, Jared, and Lawrence Mishel. 2004. Weak recovery claims new victim: Workers' wages. *Economic Policy*

Institute. Issue Brief #196. (February 5). www.epi.org (accessed May 29, 2006).

Bernstein, Jared. 1999. The living wage movement: Pointing the way toward the high road. *Community Action Digest.*

Bernstein, Nina. 2002. Once again trying housing as a cure for homelessness. *New York Times,* (23 June).

Bernstein, Nina. 2005. Invisible to most, immigrant women line up for day labor. *New York Times,* 15, August. www.nytimes.com/2005 (accessed May 29, 2006).

Berube, Alan. 2005. "Mobility and place." *Social Mobility and Life Chance Forum.* Washington, DC: Brookings Institution.

Bhatia, Juhie, and Teresa Braine. 2005. "Mothering from afar exacts heavy price" May 7, 2005 www.womensnews.org.

Bianchi, Suzanne M., Melissa A. Milkie, Liana C. Sayer, and John P. Robinson. 2000. Is anyone doing the housework? U.S. trends and gender differentials in domestic labor. *Social Forces,* 79 (1):191–228.

Biden, Joseph. 1999. The VAWA is just. In J. Torr and K. Swisher (eds.), *Violence against women* (pp. 122–126). San Diego: Greenhaven.

Billingsley, Andrew. 1968. *Black families in white America.* Englewood Cliffs, NJ: Prentice-Hall.

Billingsley, Andrew. 1992. *Climbing Jacob's ladder: The enduring legacy of African American families.* New York: Simon and Schuster.

Billington, Ray. 1949. *Westward expansion: A history of the American frontier.* New York: Macmillan.

Binder, Arnold, and James Meeker. 1992. Arrest as a method to control spouse abuse. In E. Buzawa and C. Buzawa (eds.), *Domestic violence: The changing criminal justice response* (pp. 129–140). Westport, CT: Auburn House.

Bintliff, S. 1996. Domestic violence: Myths and barriers. *Hawaii Medical Journal,* 55 (9):159–161.

Bird, C., and A. Fremont. 1991. Gender, time use and health. *Journal of Health and Social Behavior* 32:114–129.

Blackstone, William. 1803. *Commentaries on the laws of England.* Book 1. 14th ed. London: Strahan.

Blackwood, Evelyn. 1984. Sexuality and gender in certain Native American tribes: The case of cross-gender females. *Signs* 10 (1):27–42.

Blair, S. 1992a. Children's participation in household labor: Socialization versus the need for household labor. *Journal of Youth and Adolescents* 21 (2):241–258.

Blair, S. 1992b. The sex typing of children's household labor: Parental influence on daughters' and sons' housework. *Youth and Society* 24:178–203.

Blair, S., and D. Lichter. 1991. Measuring the division of household labor: Gender segregation of housework among American couples. *Journal of Family Issues* 12:91–113.

Blanchard, Dallas. 1994. *The antiabortion movement and the rise of the religious right.* New York: Twayne Publisher.

Blank, Rebecca. 1995. "Poverty and public policy in the 1990s" pp. 60–75 in G. Demko et al (eds.) *Populations at risk in America.* Boulder, CO: Westview.

Blassingame, John. 1977. *Slave testimony: Two centuries of letters, speeches, interviews and autobiographies.* Baton Rouge: Louisiana State University Press.

Blau, Francine and Ronald Ehrenberg. 1997. *Gender and family issues in the workplace.* New York: Russell Sage.

Blau, Peter, and Otis Dudley Duncan, with Andrea Tyree. 1967. *The American occupational structure.* New York: Wiley.

Blauner, Robert. 1964. *Alienation and freedom.* Chicago: University of Chicago Press.

Bleier, Ruth. 1984. *Science and gender: A critique of biology and its theories on women.* Elmsworth, NY: Pergamon Press.

Block, Fred. 1984. Technological change and employment: New perspectives on an old controversy. *Economia and Lavora* 18:3–21.

Block, Fred. 1988. Rethinking responses to economic distress: A critique of full employment. In P. Voydanoff and L. Majka (eds.), *Families and economic distress: Coping strategies and social policy* (pp. 190–206). Beverly Hills, CA: Sage.

Block, Fred, and J. Noakes. 1988. The politics of new style workfare. *Socialist Review* 18 (3):31–58.

Block, Fred, Richard Cloward, Barbara Ehrenreich, and Frances Fox Piven. 1987. *The mean season: The attack on the welfare state.* New York: Pantheon.

Blood, Robert, and Donald Wolf. 1960. *Husbands and wives: The dynamics of married living.* New York: Free Press.

Blumstein, Phillip, and Pepper Schwartz. 1983. *American couples: Money, work and sex.* New York: William Morrow.

Blumstein, Phillip, and Pepper Schwartz. 1990a. Getting and spending money among American couples. In J. Heeren and M. Mason (eds.), *Windows on society* (pp. 124–129). Los Angeles: Roxbury Publishing.

Blumstein, Phillip, and Pepper Schwartz. 1990b. Intimate relationships and the creation of sexuality. In D. McWhirter, S. Sanders, and J. Reinisch (eds.), *Homosexuality/heterosexuality: Concepts of sexual orientation* (pp. 96–109). New York: Oxford University Press.

Bograd, Michele. 1988. Feminist perspectives on wife abuse: An introduction. In K. Yllo and M. Bograd (eds.), *Feminist perspectives on wife abuse* (pp. 11–27). Beverly Hills, CA: Sage.

Bond, James, and Ellen Galinsky. 1998. 1997 National study of the changing workforce. New York: Families and Work Institute.

Bonell, Chris. 2004. Why is teenage pregnancy conceptualized as a social problem? A review of quantitative research from the USA and UK. *Culture, Health, and Sexuality,* 6 (3) (May–June).

Bonomo, Thomas. 1987. Working class movements in the Reagan era: The potential for progressive change. *Humanity and Society* 11 (1):12–39.

Bonomo, Thomas. 1993. Personal communication.

Bookman, Ann. 1991. Parenting without poverty: The case for funded parental leave. In J. Hyde and M. Essex (eds.), *Parental leave and children: Setting a research and policy agenda* (pp. 66–89). Philadelphia: Temple University Press.

Boris, Eileen, and Peter Bordaglio. 1983. The transformation of patriarchy: The historic role of the state. In I. Diamond (ed.), *Families, politics and public policy: A feminist dialogue on women and the state* (pp. 70–93). New York: Longman.

Bose, Christine. 1987. Dual spheres. In B. Hess and M. Ferree (eds.), *Analyzing gender* (pp. 267–285). Newbury Park, CA: Sage.

Boulding, Elise. 1980. The nurturance of adults by children in family settings. In H. Lopata (ed.), *Research in the interweave of social roles.* Vol. 1 (pp. 167–189). Greenwich, CT: JAI Press.

Bourne, Patricia, and Norma Wikler. 1982. Commitment and the cultural mandate: Women in medicine. In R. Kahn-Hut et al. (eds.), *Women and work: Problems and perspectives* (pp. 111–112). New York: Oxford University Press.

Bovee, Tim. 1993. Interracial marriage on rise: "It's a very normal thing." *Charlotte Observer,* 12 February, 1A, 5A.

Bowker, Lee. 1986. *Ending the violence: A guidebook based on the experience of 1000 wives.* Holmes Beach, FL: Learning Publications.

Bowles, Samuel, and Herbert Gintis. 1976. *Schooling in capitalist America.* New York: Basic Books.

Bowman, Madonna, and Constance Ahrons. 1985. Impact of legal custody status on fathers' parenting post divorce. *Journal of Marriage and the Family* 47:481–488.

Boyett, Joseph, and Henry Conn. 1992. *The revolution shaping American business.* New York: Plume.

Boyle, James. 1913. *The minimum wage and syndicalism.* Cincinnati: Stewart and Kidd.

Bozett, Frederick. 1984. Parenting concerns of gay fathers. *Topics in Clinical Nursing* 6:60–71.

Bozett, Frederick. 1988. Gay fatherhood. In P. Bronstein and C. Cowan (eds.), *Fatherhood today: Men's changing role in the family* (pp. 60–71). New York: Wiley.

Bozett, Frederick. 1993. Children of gay fathers. In C. Brettell and C. Sargent (eds.), *Gender in crosscultural perspective* (pp. 191–200). Englewood Cliffs, NJ: Prentice-Hall.

Brake, Mike. 1982a. Sexuality as praxis—A consideration of the contribution of sexual theory to the process of sexual being. In M. Brake (ed.), *Human sexual relations: Towards a redefinition of sexual politics* (pp. 13–34). New York: Pantheon.

Brake, Mike, ed. 1982b. *Human sexual relations: Towards a redefinition of sexual politics.* New York: Pantheon.

Braun, Denny. 1991. *The rich get richer: The rise of income in inequality in the U.S. and the world.* Chicago: Nelson Hall.

Braverman, Harry. 1974. *Labor and monopoly capital: The degradation of work in the twentieth century.* New York: Monthly Review Press.

Brayfield, April. 1995. Juggling jobs and kids: The impact of employment schedules on fathers' caring for children. *Journal of Marriage and the Family* 57:321–332.

Breines, Wini, Margaret Cerullo, and Judith Stacey. 1978. Socio biology, family studies and antifeminist backlash. *Feminist Studies* 4 (1):43–67.

Brewer, Rose. 1988. Black women in poverty: Some comments on female-headed families. *Signs* 13 (2):331–339.

Bridenthal, Renate, and C. Koonz, eds. 1977. *Becoming visible: Women in European history.* Boston: Houghton Mifflin.

Brines, J. 1993. The exchange value of housework. *Rational Sociology* 5:302–340.

Brines, J. 1994. Economic dependency, gender and the division of labor at home. *American Journal of Sociology* 100:652–688.

Bringing America Home Campaign. 2005. Bring America Home Act. bringinghomeamerica.org (accessed May 29, 2006).

Brinkerhoff, David. 1981. The sexual division of labor. *Social Forces,* 60 (1):170–181.

Broad, K. L., Sara Crawley, and Lara Foley. 2004. Doing real family values: Social movement framing, discourse, and interpretive practice. *Sociological Quarterly,* 45(3):509–527.

Broder, David. 1983. Phil Gramms' free enterprise. *Washington Post,* 16 February, A1.

Brodie, Mollyann. 2002. 2002 *National survey of latinos.* Washington, DC: Pew Hispanic center.

Brody, E. 1983. Parent care as normative family stress. *The Gerontologist* 25:19–30.

Brody, Jane. 1989. Who's having sex? Data are obsolete, experts say. *New York Times,* 18 February, A1.

Bronfenbrenner, Urie, Peter McClelland, Elaine Wethington, Phyllis Moen, and Stephen Ceci. 1996. *The state of Americans.* New York: Free Press.

Brown, Judith. 1977. Economic organization and the position of women among the Iroquois. *Ethnohistory* 17:151–167.

Brown, Michael, ed. 1988. *Remaking the welfare state: Retrenchment and social policy in America and Europe.* Philadelphia: Temple University Press.

Brown, Prince. 1997. Biology and the social construction of the "race" concept. In J. Ferrante and P. Brown (eds.), *The social construction of race and ethnicity in the U.S.* (pp. 131–138). New York: Longman.

Brown, Rita Mae. 1976. *Plain Brown Rapper.* Baltimore: Diana Press.

Browne, Angela. 1987. *When battered women kill.* New York: Free Press.

Bryson, Ken, and Lynne Casper. 1997. Household and family characteristics: March 1997. *Current Population Reports.*

Bryson, Ken, and Lynne Casper. 1999. *Coresident grandparents and grandchildren.* Current Population Reports PD23-198. Washington, DC: Bureau of Census.

Budig, Michele, and Paula England. 2001. The wage penalty for motherhood. *American Sociological Review,* 66: 204–225.

Bulcroft, K., and R. Bulcroft. 1985. Dating and courtship in later life: An exploratory study. In W. Person and J. Quadagno (eds.), *Social bond in later life.* Thousand Oaks, CA: Sage.

Bulcroft, K., and R. Bulcroft. 1991. The nature and functions of dating in later life. *Research on Aging* 13 (2):244–260.

Bullough, Vern. 1976. *Sexual variance in society and history.* New York: John Wiley.

Bumpass, Larry. 1990. What's happening to the family? Interactions between demographic and institutional change. *Demography* 27:483–490.

Bumpass, Larry, and James Sweet. 1985. *The national survey of families and households.* Madison: University of Wisconsin-Madison, Center for Demography and Ecology.

Bumpass, Larry, and James Sweet. 1989. National estimates of cohabitation. *Demography* 26:615–625.

Bumpass, Larry, James Sweet, and Andrew Cherlin. 1991. The role of cohabitation in declining rates of marriage. *Journal of Marriage and the Family* 53 (November):913–927.

Bumpass, Larry, James Sweet, and Andrew Cherlin. 1998. "The role of cohabitation on declining rates of marriage" pp. 146–160 in S. Ferguson (ed.) *Shifting the Center.* Mountain View, CA: Mayfield.

Burch, E. S. 1970. Marriage and divorce among North American Eskimos. In P. Bohannon (ed.), *Divorce and after* (pp. 152–181). New York: Doubleday.

Bureau of Justice Statistics. 1995. *Violence against women: Estimates from the redesigned survey.* Special Report, August, NCJ 154348.

Bureau of Labor Statistics. 2003a. *Historical data for the "B" tables of the employment situation release* (June 6 U.S. Dept. of Labor). Washington, DC: USGPO.

Bureau of Labor Statistics. 2003b. *Labor force statistics from the current population survey.* U.S. Dept. of Labor. (February) Washington, DC: USGPO.

Bureau of Labor Statistics. 2004b. *Division of labor force statistics.* U.S. Dept. of Labor. (March 5) Washington, DC: USGPO.

Bureau of Labor Statistics. 2004b. *Unemployment,* p. 149. Washington, DC: Department of Labor.

Bureau of Labor Statistics. 2004c. *Household data. Annual averages.* Table #37. U.S. Dept. of Labor. Washington, DC: USGPO.

Bureau of Labor Statistics. 2004d. *Occupational outlook handbook. Tomorrow's jobs* U.S. Dept. of Labor. June 2. Washington, DC: USGPO.

Bureau of Labor Statistics. 2004e. *Women's bureau. Women in the labor force in 2004.* U.S. Dept. of Labor. Washington, DC: USGPO.

Bureau of Labor Statistics. 2005a. *American time use survey,* U.S. Dept. of Labor. September. Washington, DC: USGPO.

Bureau of Labor Statistics. 2005b. *Career guide to industries,* 2004–05 ed. Child Day Care Services. www.bls.gov (October).

Bureau of Labor Statistics. 2005c. *Current population survey. Employment characteristics of families in 2004* U.S. Dept. of Labor. June Washington, DC: USGPO.

Bureau of Labor Statistics. 2005d. *The employment situation,* U.S. Dept. of Labor. July. Washington, DC: USGPO.

Bureau of Labor Statistics. 2005e. *Women in the labor force: A data book* U.S. Dept. of Labor. May. Washington, DC: USGPO.

Burgess, Ernest, and L. Cottrell. 1939. *Predicting success or failure in marriage.* New York: Prentice-Hall.

Burgess, Ernest, and Harvey Locke. 1945. *The family: From institution to companionship.* New York: American Book.

Burman, Leonard E., Elaine Maag, and Jeffrey Rohaly. 2005. *Tax credits to help low income families pay for child care.* Urban-Brookings Tax Policy Center, No. 14 (July).

Burris, Beverly. 1991. Employed mothers. *Social Science Quarterly* 72 (March):50–66.

Burstein, Andrew, Nancy Isenberg, and Annette Gordon-Reed. 1999. Three perspectives on America's Jefferson fixation. *The Nation,* 16 January.

Burton, Linda, and Cynthia de Vries. 1993. Challenges and rewards: African American grandparents as surrogate parents. In L. Burton (ed.), *Families and aging* (pp. 101–108). Amityville, NY: Baywood Publishing.

Burton, Linda, Donald Hernandez, and Sondra Hofferth. 1998. *Families, youth and children's well being.* Washington, DC: American Sociological Association.

Busch, Amy and Mindy Rosenberg. 2004. Comparing women and men arrested for domestic violence. *Journal of Family Violence,* 19 (1):49–57.

Bushnell, Don, and Robert Burgess. 1969. Some basic principles of behavior. In R. Burgess and D. Bushnell (eds.), *Behavioral sociology* (pp. 27–48). New York: Columbia University Press.

Business. 2004. rediff.com (March 17).

Buss, D. M. 1985. Human mate selection. *American Scientist* 73:48.

Butler, Sandra. 1979. *Conspiracy of silence: The trauma of incest.* San Francisco: New Glide.

Cahan, Sucherg. 1991. *Asian Americans: An interpretive history.* Boston: Twayne.

Cahill, Spencer. 1983. Reexamining the acquisition of sex roles: A symbolic interactionist approach. *Sex Roles* 9 (1):1–15.

Calvert, Karin. 1992. *Children in the house: The material culture of early childhood, 1600–1900.* Boston: Northeastern University Press.

Camarillo, Albert. 1979. *Chicanos in a changing society: From Mexican pueblos to American barrios in Santa Barbara and Southern California, 1848–1930.* Cambridge, MA: Harvard University Press.

Cancian, Francesca. 1987. *Love in America: Gender and self development.* New York: Cambridge University Press.

Cancian, Francesca. 1993. Feminist science: Methodologies that challenge inequality. *Gender and Society* 6 (4):623–642.

CANOW.org. 2005. California National Organization for Women. Preparing Mothers for Custody Suites.

Cantor, Muriel. 1994. Family care-giving: Social care. In M. Cantor (ed.), *Family care-giving: Agenda for the future* (pp. 1–9). San Francisco: American Society on Aging.

Capps, Randy, Michael Fix, Jason Ost, Jane Reardon-Anderson, and Jeffrey Passel 2005. "The Health and Well-Being of Young Children of Immigrants," by Foundation for Child Development and Annie E. Casey Foundation. Available at http://www.urban.org/url.cfm?ID=311139.

Cardera, Yvonne, Jacki Fitzpatrick, and Karen Wampler. 2000. "Coparenting in intact Mexican American families." In Contreras, Kerns, and Neal Bennett (eds.), *Latino children and families in the United States,* (pp. 107–131) Westport, CT: Praeger.

Cargan, Leonard, and Matthew Melko. 1982. *Singles: Myths and realities.* Beverly Hills, CA: Sage.

Carlson, D., R. Labarba, J. Sclafani, and C. Bowers. 1986. Cognitive and motor development in infants of adolescent mothers: A longitudinal analysis. *International Journal of Behavior Development* 9 (1):1–14.

Carnegie-Mellon University, School of Urban and Public Affairs. 1983. *Milltowns in the Pittsburgh region: Conditions and prospects.* Pittsburgh: Carnegie-Mellon University.

Carothers, Suzanne. 1998. Catching sense: Learning from our mothers to be black and female. In K. Hansen and A. Garey (eds.), *Families in the U.S.: Kinship and domestic policies* (pp. 315–328). Philadelphia: Temple University Press.

Carter, Hugh, and Paul Glick. 1976. *Marriage and divorce: A social and economic study.* Cambridge, MA: Harvard University Press.

Casper, Lynne. 1997. My daddy takes care of me! Fathers as care providers. *Current Population Reports* P70–59 (September).

Casper, Lynne, and Kenneth Bryson. 1998. *Co-resident grandparents and their grandchildren: Grandparent maintained families.* Washington, DC: U.S. Bureau of the Census (March).

Cassidy, Michael, Caroline G. Nicholl, and Carmen R. Rose. 2001. *Results of a survey conducted by the metropolitan police department of victims who reported violence against women.* Washington DC: DC Metro Police Department.

Cate, Rodney. 1992. *Courtship.* Beverly Hills, CA: Sage.

Caulfield, Mina. 1974. Imperialism, the family and cultures of resistance. *Socialist Revolution* 20:67–85.

Causey, Kelly, and Candan Duran-Aydingtug. 1997. Tendency to stigmatize lesbian mothers in custody case. *Journal of Divorce and Remarriage.* 28 (1–2):171–182.

Cavan, Ruth, and Katherine Ranck. 1938. *The family and the Depression: A study of one hundred Chicago families.* Chicago: University of Chicago Press.

Center for Housing Policy. 2005. *Housing landscape for America's working families* 2005, May.

Centers for Disease Control (CDC). 1990. *National survey of family growth.* Atlanta: CDC and Prevention National Center for Health Statistics, Division of Vital Statistics.

Centers for Disease Control (CDC). 2002. Cohabitation, marriage, divorce, and remarriage in the United States. *National survey of family growth.* Atlanta, GA: CDC.

Centers for Disease Control (CDC). 2003a. *Births: Final data for 2002.* National Vital Statistics Report, Vol 52(10). (17 December). Atlanta, GA: CDC.

Centers for Disease Control (CDC). 2003b. *Cost of intimate partner violence against women in the United States.* www.cdc.gov.

Centers for Disease Control (CDC). 2003c. *HIV/AIDS surveillance report: HIV infection and AIDS in the United States.* www.cdc.gov.

Centers for Disease Control (CDC). 2004a. *Abortion surveillance—United States, 2001.* Surveillance Summaries, (26 November). Atlanta, GA: CDC.

Centers for Disease Control (CDC). 2004b. *Marital status and health: United States, 1999–2002.* Advance Data, No. 351, December. Atlanta, GA: CDC.

Centers for Disease Control (CDC). 2005a. *Births: Final data for 2003.* National Vital Statistics Report. Vol 54(2), (8 September). Atlanta, CA: CDC.

Centers for Disease Control (CDC). 2005b. *CDC Study Documents High Cost and Impact of Intimate Partner Violence.* Press Release. www.cdc.gov. (October 25).

Centers for Disease Control (CDC). 2005c. *Fact Sheet: HIV/AIDS Among African Americans.* Atlanta, GA: CDC.

Chaduril, Molly, and Kathleen Daly. 1992. Do restraining orders help? Battered women's experience with male violence and legal process. In E. Buzawa and C. Buzawa (eds.), *Domestic violence: The changing criminal justice response* (pp. 227–252). Westport, CT: Auburn House.

Chafetz, Janet. 1988. *Feminist sociology: An overview of contemporary theories.* Itasca, IL: Peacock.

Chambers, David. 1979. *Making fathers pay.* Chicago: University of Chicago Press.

Chan, Suchang. 1991. *Asian Americans.* Boston: Twayne.

Charles, D. 2000. Victims of gay bullying drop out of school. *London Times,* (18 July).

Charlotte Observer. 1990. Teenage mothers studied: Babies healthier, moms better off. 17 February, 16A.

Chelf, Carl. 1992. *Controversial issues in social welfare policy: The government and the pursuit of happiness.* Newbury Park, CA: Sage.

Cherlin, Andrew. 1982. The trends: Marriage, divorce, remarriage. In A. Skolnick and J. Skolnick (eds.), *Family in transition* (pp. 128–137), 4th ed. Boston: Little Brown.

Cherlin, Andrew. 1992a. *Marriage, divorce and remarriage.* Cambridge, MA: Harvard University Press.

Cherlin, Andrew. 1992b. The strange career of the "Harvard-Yale Study." In A. Skolnick and J. Skolnick (eds.), *Family in transition* (pp. 553–559). New York: Harper Collins.

Cherlin, Andrew, and Frank Furstenberg. 1998. Stepfamilies in the U.S: A reconsideration. In S. Ferguson (ed.), *Shifting the center: Understanding contemporary families* (pp. 448–467). Mountainview, CA: Mayfield.

Cherlin, Andrew, and Frank Furstenberg. 1999. The modernization of grandparenthood. In A. Skolnick and J. Skolnick (eds.), *Family in transition.* 10th ed. (pp. 385–391). New York: Addison Wesley.

Cherlin, Andrew. 1978. Remarriage as an incomplete institution. *American Journal of Sociology* 84: 634–650.

Chesler, Phyllis. 1986. *Mothers on trial: The battle for children and custody.* New York: McGraw-Hill.

Childe, J. Gordon. 1948. *The dawn of European civilization.* London: Kegan Paul.

Children's Defense Fund. 1988a. *A children's defense budget: An analysis of our nation's investment in children.* Washington, DC: Children's Defense Fund.

Children's Defense Fund. 1988b. *Vanishing dream: The growing economic plight of America's young families.* Washington, DC: Children's Defense Fund

Children's Defense Fund. 1990. *Children 1990: A report card briefing book and action primer.* Washington, DC: Children's Defense Fund.

Children's Defense Fund. 2004. *2003 Facts in Child Poverty in America,* (October) Washington, DC: Children's Defense Fund.

Children's Defense Fund. 2004. *Fiscal Year 2005 Budget Analysis,* Washington, DC: Children's Defense Fund, www.chn.org/pdf/fy05budgetanalysis.pdf accessed (May 29, 2006).

Children's Defense Fund. 2004. *State of America's Children 2004.* Washington, DC: Children's Defense Fund.

Chinen, Joyce, Kathleen Kane, and Ida Yoshinga. 1997. *Women in Hawai'i.* Honolulu: University of Hawai'i Press.

Chira, Susan. 1998. *A mother's place: Taking the debate about working mothers beyond guilt and blame.* New York: HarperCollins.

Chisman, F., and A. Pifer. 1987. *Government for the people: The federal social role, what it is, what it should be.* New York: Norton.

Chodorow, Nancy. 1976. Oedipal asymetries and heterosexual knots. *Social Problems* 23 (4):454–468.

Chodorow, Nancy. 1978a. Considerations on a biosocial perspective on parenting. *Berkeley Journal of Sociology* 22:179–197.

Chodorow, Nancy. 1978b. *The reproduction of mothering: Psychoanalysis and the sociology of gender.* Berkeley: University of California Press.

Chow, Esther. 1987. The development of feminist consciousness among Asian American women. *Gender and Society* 1 (September):284–299.

Chow, Esther Ngan-ling. 1998. Family, economy and the state: A legacy of struggle for Chinese American women. In S. Ferguson (ed.), *Shifting the center* (pp. 99–114). Mountain View, CA: Mayfield.

Chow, Esther, and Catherine Berheide. 1994. Studying women, families and policies globally. In E. Chow and C. Berheid (eds.), *Women, the family and policy: A global perspective* (pp. 1–32). Albany, NY: SUNY.

Chow, Esther, and Katherine Berheide. 1988. The interdependence of family and work. *Family Relations* 37 (January):23–28.

Clay, Phil. 1987. At risk of loss: The endangered future of low-income rental housing resources. *Safety Network* (May):1–7.

Close, Stacey. 1997. *Elderly slaves of the plantation south.* New York: Garland.

Cobb, S., and S. Kasl. 1977. *Termination: The consequences of job loss.* Cincinnati: NIOSH.

Cogan, Frances. 1989. *All American girl: The ideal of real womanhood in mid nineteenth century America.* Athens, GA: University of Georgia Press.

Cohen, David. 1999. *Map and track: State initiatives to encourage responsible fatherhood.* Baltimore: Annie E. Casey Foundation.

Cohen, Philip. 1998. Replacing housework in the service economy: Gender, class and race ethnicity in service spending. *Gender and Society* 12 (2):219–231.

Cohen, Susan, and Mary Katzenstein. 1992. The war over the family is not over the family. In M. Hutter (ed.), *The family experience: A reader in cultural diversity* (pp. 101–120). New York: Macmillan.

Cole, Jonathan. 1979. *Fair science: Women in the scientific community.* New York: Free Press.

Collier, Jane, Michelle Rosaldo, and Sylvia Yanagisako. 1992. Is there a family? New anthropological views. In B. Thorne with M. Yalom (eds.), *Rethinking the family: Some feminist questions* (pp. 31–48). New York: Longman.

Collins, Patricia Hill. 1989. A comparison of two works on black family life. *Signs* 14 (4):875–884.

Collins, Patricia Hill. 1990. *Black feminist thought: Knowledge, consciousness and the politics of empowerment.* New York: Harper Collins.

Collins, Patricia Hill. 1991. The meaning of motherhood in black culture and black mother-daughter relationships. In R. Scott et al. (eds.), *Double stitch: Black women write about mothers and daughters* (pp. 42–60). Boston: Beacon Press.

Collins, Patricia. 1998. *Fighting words: Black women and the search for justice.* Minneapolis: University of Minnesota Press.

Collins, Randall, and Scott Coltrane. 1991. *Sociology of marriage and the family: Gender, love and property.* 3d ed. New York: Nelson Hall.

Coltrane, Scott. 1996. *Family man: Fatherhood, housework, and gender equity.* New York: Oxford University Press.

Coltrane, Scott. 1998a. Household labor and the routine production of gender. In K. Hansen and A. Garey (eds.), *Families in the U.S.: Kinship and domestic politics* (pp. 791–808). Philadelphia: Temple University Press.

Coltrane, Scott. 1998b. *Gender and families.* Thousand Oaks, CA: Pine Forge.

Coltrane, Scott, and Michele Adams. 1997. Children and gender. In T. Arendell (ed.), *Contemporary parenting: Challenges and issues* (pp. 219–253). Thousand Oaks, CA: Sage.

Committee on Health Care for Homeless People (CHCHP). 1988. *Homelessness, health and human needs.* Washington, DC: National Academy Press.

Condry, J. 1989. *The psychology of television.* Hillsdale, NJ: Lawrence Erlbaum Associates.

Conger, R., G. Elder, F. Lorenz, K. Conger, L. Sions, S. Whitbeck, S. Huck, and J. Melby. 1990. Linking economic hardship to marital quality and stability. *Journal of Marriage and the Family* 53:643–656.

Connell, Robert. 1987. *Gender and power: Society, the person and sexual politics.* Stanford, CA: Stanford University Press.

Connolly, Catherine. 2002. Lesbian and gay parenting. *Studies in Law, Politics, and Society* 26 (1):189–208.

Connor, J., and L. Serbin. 1978. Children's responses to stories with male and female characters. *Sex Roles* 4:637–645.

Contreras, Josefina, Kathryn Kerns, and Angela Neal-Bennett (eds.) 2000. *Latino children and families in the United States.* Westport, CT: Praeger.

Conway, Elizabeth. 1990. Women and contingent work. In S. Rix (ed.), *The American woman, 1990–1991: A status report* (pp. 203–211). New York: W. W. Norton.

Coontz, Stephanie. 1988. *The social origins of private life: A history of American families, 1600–1900.* London: Verso.

Coontz, Stephanie. 1992. *The way we never were: American families and the nostalgia trap.* New York: Basic Books.

Coontz, Stephanie. 1997. *The way we really are: Coming to terms with America's changing families.* New York: Basic Books.

Coontz, Stephanie. 1999. Divorcing reality. In L. Stone (ed.), *Selected readings in marriage and family* (pp. 226–229). San Diego: Greenhaven Press.

Cornell, Stephen, and Doug Hartmann. 1997. *Ethnicity and race: Making identities in a changing world.* Thousand Oaks, CA: Pine Forge.

Corsaro, William. 1997. *Sociology of childhood.* Thousand Oaks, CA: Pine Forge.

Costello, C. 1985. "We're worth it." Work culture and conflict at the Wisconsin Education Association Insurance Trust. *Feminist Studies* 11 (Fall):497–518.

Coverman, Shelley. 1989. Women's work is never done. The division of domestic labor. In Jo Freeman (ed.), *Women: A feminist perspective* (pp. 356–370). Mountain View, CA: Mayfield.

Cowan, Carolyn, and Phillip Cowan. 1999. Becoming a parent. In A. Skolnick and J. Skolnick (eds.), *Family in transition* 10th ed. (pp. 189–201). New York: Addison Wesley.

Cowan, Ruth Schwartz. 1983. *More work for mothers: The ironies of household technology from the open hearth to the microwave.* New York: Basic Books.

Cowan, Ruth Schwartz. 1989. More work for mothers. In A. Skolnick and J. Skolnick (eds.), *Family in transition* (pp. 57–67). 6th ed. New York: Scott, Foresman.

Coyle, Laurie, Gail Hershatter, and Emily Honig. 1980. Women at Farah: An unfinished story. In M. Mora and A. del Castillo (eds.), *Mexican women and Chicano families* (pp. 117–144). Los Angeles: University of California, Chicano Research Center Publications.

Coyle, Marcia. 2005. Supreme Court to weigh in on due process and domestic violence—justices to decide if police are liable. *The National Law Journal* (March 9).

Craven, Diane. 1996. Female victims of violent crime. *Bureau of Justice Statistics.* December. NCJ-162602.

Crispell, Diane. 1996. "The sibling syndrome" *American Demographics* 15 (October):24–30.

Cronan, Sheila. 1971. Marriage. In *Notes from the third year: Women's liberation* (pp. 62–66). New York: Notes from the Second Year, Inc.

Cronin, A. 1996. Abortion: The rate vs. the debate. *New York Times,* 25 February, 4E.

Crosby, John. 1980. A critique of divorce statistics and their interpretation. *Family Relations* 29:51–68.

Crutsinger, Martin. 2000. Personal income dropped in October. AP.

Cullen, Countee. 1947. *On these I stand.* New York: Harper and Row.

Curie-Cohen, Martin, Lesleigh Luttrell, and Sander Shapiro. 1979. Current practice of artificial insemination by donor in the U.S. *New England Journal of Medicine* 300 (11):589.

D'Andrea, Ann. 1983. Joint custody as related to paternal involvement and paternal self-esteem. *Conciliation Courts Review* 21:81–87.

D'Emilio, John. 1998. *Sexual politics, sexual communities: The making of a homosexual minority in the United States, 1940–1970.* Chicago: University of Chicago Press.

D'Emilio, John, and Estelle Freedman. 1988. *Intimate matters: A history of sexuality in America.* New York: Harper.

D'Iorio, Judith. 1982. Feminist fieldwork in a masculinist setting: Personal problems and methodological issues. Paper presented at annual meeting of the North Central Sociological Association, Detroit.

Daly, Kerry, and Anna Dienhart. 1998. Negotiating parental involvement: Finding time for the children. In D. Vannoy and P. Dubeck (eds.), *Challenges for work and family in the 21st century* (pp. 111–122). New York: Aldine de Gruyter.

Damon, William. 1977. *The social world of the child.* San Francisco: Jossey-Bass.

Daniels, Arlene Kaplan. 1988. *Invisible careers: Women civic leaders from the volunteer world.* Chicago: University of Chicago Press.

Daniels, Cynthia. 1997. *The politics of domestic violence.* New York: University Press of America.

Daniels, Roger, ed. 1978. *Anti-Chinese violence in America.* New York: Arno Press.

Danziger, Sheldon, and Peter Gottschalk. 1985. The poverty of losing ground. *Challenge* 28 (May/June):32–38.

Darity, William, and Samuel Meyers. 1984. Does welfare dependency cause female headship? The case of the black family. *Journal of Marriage and the Family* 46 (4):765–779.

Darling, Carol, David Kallen, and Joyce VanDusen. 1992. Sex in transition, 1900–1980. In A. Skolnick and J. Skolnick (eds.), *Family in transition* (pp. 151–160). 7th ed. New York: Harper Collins.

Dassbach, Carl. 1986. Industrial robots in the American automobile industry. *Insurgent Sociologist* 13 (Summer):53–61.

Davis, Angela. 1981. *Women, race and class.* New York: Random House.

Davis, Angela. 1991. Racism, birth control and reproductive rights. In M. Fried (ed.), *From abortion to reproductive freedom: Transforming a movement* (pp. 15–26). Boston: Southend Press.

Davis, Jim, Thomas Hirschl, and Michael Stack. 1997. *Cutting edge: Technology, information, capitalism and social revolution.* New York: Verso.

Davis, Margaret R. 1982. *Families in a working world: The impact of organizations on domestic life.* New York: Praeger.

Davis, Phillip. 1999. Changing meanings of spanking. In L. Stone (ed.), *Selected readings in marriage and family* (pp. 176–187). San Diego: Greenhaven Press.

Davis, S. 1990. Men as success objects and women as sex objects: A study of personal advertisements. *Sex Roles* 23:43–50.

Day, Jennifer Cheeseman, Alex Janus, and Jessica Davis. 2005. Computer and internet use in the United States: 2003. *U.S. Census Bureau.* Current Population Reports (October).

De Anda, Roberto (ed). 2004. *Chicanos and Chicanas in contempoary society,* 2d ed. New York: Rowman and Littlefield.

DeCecco, John and David Parker. 1995. "The biology of homosexuality: Sexual orientation or sexual preference?" *Journal of Homosexuality* 21 (1–2):1–27

Degler, Carl. 1980. *At odds: Women and the family in America: From the Revolution to the present.* Oxford: Oxford University Press.

Deitch, Cynthia. 1984. Collective action and unemployment: Responses to job loss by workers and community groups. *International Journal of Mental Health* 13 (1–2):139–153.

Demos, John. 1970. *A little commonwealth: Family life in the Plymouth Colony.* New York: Oxford University Press.

Demos, John. 1986. *Past, present and personal: The family and life course in American history.* New York: Oxford University Press.

Denmark, F., J. Shaw, and S. Ciali. 1985. The relationships among sex roles, living arrangements, and the division of household responsibilities. *Sex Roles* 12:617–625.

DeParle, Jason. 1999. As welfare rolls shrink load on relatives grows. *New York Times,* 21 February, 1, 20.

Devault, Marjorie. 1987. Doing housework: Feeding and family life. In N. Gerstel and H. Gross (eds), *Families and work* (pp. 178–191). Philadelphia: Temple University Press.

Devault, Marjorie. 1991. *Feeding the family: The social organization of caring as gendered work.* Chicago: University of Chicago Press.

DeVault, Marjorie. 1996. Talking back to sociology: Distinctive contributions of feminist methodology. *Annual Review of Sociology* 22:29–50.

Devlin, Rachel. 2005. Acting out the oedipal wish. *Journal of Social History,* 38 (3):609–633.

Diamond, Irene. 1983. *Families, politics and public policy.* New York: Longman.

Diamond, Sara. 1998. *Not by politics alone.* New York: Guilford.

Dibble, Ursula, and Murray Straus. 1980. Some social structure determinants of inconsistency between attitudes and behavior: The case of family violence. *Journal of Marriage and the Family* 42 (February):71–80.

Dickerson, R., and L. Bean. 1915. *The single woman.* Baltimore: Williams and Wilkins.

Dietrich, Sharon, Maurice Emsellem, and Jennifer Paradise. 2000. Employment rights of workfare participants and displaced workers. *National Employment Law Project.* (March).

Dill, Bonnie Thornton. 1983. Race, class and gender: Prospects for an all-inclusive sisterhood. *Feminist Studies* 9 (1):131–150.

Dill, Bonnie Thornton. 1986. *Our mother's grief: Racial ethnic women and the maintenance of families.* Memphis, TN: MSU Center for Research on Women.

Dill, Bonnie Thornton. 1988. Making your job good yourself: Domestic service and the construction of personal dignity. In A. Bookman and S. Morgen (eds.), *Women and the politics of empowerment* (pp. 33–52). Philadelphia: Temple University Press.

Dill, Bonnie. 1994. *Across the boundaries of race and class: An exploration of work and family among black female domestic servants.* New York: Garland Publishing.

Dinnerstein, Dorothy. 1977. *The mermaid and the minotaur.* New York: Harper and Row.

Dobash, R. Emerson, and Russell Dobash. 1979. *Violence against wives: A case against the patriarchy.* New York: Free Press.

Dobash, R. Emerson, and Russell Dobash. 1988. Research as social action: The struggle for battered women. In K. Yllo and M. Bogard (eds.), *Feminist perspectives on wife abuse* (pp. 28–50). Beverly Hills, CA: Sage.

Dobash, R. Emerson, and Russell Dobash. 1992. *Women, violence and social change.* New York: Routledge.

Dobash, Rebecca Emerson, and Russell Dobash (eds.). 1998. *Rethinking Violence Against Women.* Thousand Oaks, CA: Sage.

Dobash, Rebecca, and Russell Dobash. 1998. Violent men and violent contexts. In Dobash R. and R. Dobash (eds.), *Rethinking violence against women* (pp. 141–168). Thousand Oaks, CA: Sage.

Dodson, Lisa, and Jillian Dickert. 2005. Girls' family labor in low income households: A decade of qualitative research. *Journal of Marriage and the Family,* 66 (2):306–332.

Dolbeare, Cushing, Irene Basloe Salaf, and Sheila Crowley. 2005. *Changing Priorities.* Washington, DC: National low income housing coalition.

Dolbeare, Cushing. 1983. The low income housing crisis. In C. Hartman (ed.), *America's housing crisis: What is to be done?* (pp. 32–47). Boston: Routledge and Kegan.

Domhoff, William. 1970. *The higher circles: The governing class in America.* New York: Random House.

Donnelly, Nancy. 1994. *Changing lives of refugee Hmong women.* Seattle: University of Washington Press.

Dorr, A., and B. Rabin. 1995. Parents, children and television. In M. Bornstein (ed.), *Handbook of parenting.* Vol 4; *Applied and practical parenting* (pp. 323–352). Englewood Cliffs, NJ: Lawrence Erlbaum.

Dorrington, Claudia. 1995. Central American refugees in Los Angeles: Adjustment of children and families. In R. Zambrano (ed.), *Understanding Latino families: Scholarship, policy and practice* (pp. 107–129). Thousand Oaks, CA: Sage.

Douvan, Elizabeth, and Joseph Adelson. 1966. *The adolescent experience.* New York: Wiley.

Drexler, Peggy. 2005. *Raising Boys Without Men.* Allentown, PA: Rodale.

Duberman, Martin. 1997a. *Queer representations: Reading lives, reading cultures.* New York: NYU Press.

Duberman, Martin. 1997b. *A queer world: Center for lesbian and gay studies reader.* New York: NYU Press.

DuBois, W. E. B. (1969/1908). *The Negro American family.* New York: New American Library.

Duncan, Otis Dudley, B. Featherman, and Beverly Duncan. 1972. *Social change in a metropolitan community.* New York: Russell Sage.

Dunkerly, Michael. 1996. *The jobless economy? Computer technology in the world of work.* Cambridge, UK: Polity.

Dupree, Allen, and Wendell Primus. 2001. Declining share of children lived with single mothers in the late 1990s. *Center on Budget and Policy Priorities.* Washington, DC (June 15).

Durose, Matthew, Caroline Wolf Harlow, Patrick A. Langan, Mark Motivans, Ramona R. Rantala, and Erica L. Schmidt. 2005. Family violence statistics. *U.S. Department of Justice.* Office of Justice Programs.

Dutton, Donald, Stephen Hart, Les Kennedy, and Kirk Williams. 1992. Arrest and the reduction of repeat wife assault. In E. Buzawa and C. Buzawa (eds.), *Domestic violence: The changing criminal justice response* (pp. 111–127). Westport, CT: Auburn House.

Dutton, Donald. 1986. Wife assaulters' explanations for assault: The neutralization of self-punishment. *Canadian Journal of Behavioral Science* 18 (4):381–390.

Dworkin, Andrea. 1981. *Pornography: Men possessing women.* New York: Putnam.

Dworkin, Andrea. 1987. *Intercourse.* New York: Free Press.

Eckenrode, John, and Susan Gore, eds. 1990. *Stress between work and family.* New York: Plenum.

Economic Policy Institute. 2005. State of Working America 2004/2005. Inequality. *Facts & Figures.* Washington, DC.

Economist. 1987. Homework, 26 September, 68–70.

Edin, Kathryn, and Laura Lein. 1997. *Making ends meet: How single mothers survive welfare and low-wage work.* New York: Russell Sage Foundation.

Edin, Kathryn, and Maria Kefalas. 2005. *Promises I Can Keep.* Los Angeles: University of California Press.

Edin, Kathryn. 1991. Surviving the welfare system: How AFDC recipients make ends meet in Chicago. *Social Problems* 38 (4):462–474.

Edwards, Richard. 1993. *Rights at work: Employment relations in a post-union era.* Washington, DC: Brookings Institution.

Egelko, Bob. 2005. Court grants equal rights to same sex parents. *San Francisco Chronicle,* (23 August).

Ehrenreich, Barbara. 1983. *Hearts of men: American dreams and the flight from commitment.* Garden City, NY: Anchor.

Ehrenreich, Barbara, and Dierdre English. 1989. Blowing the whistle on the mommy track. *Ms* 18:56–58.

Ehrenreich, Barbara, Beth Hess, and G. Jacobs. 1986. *Remaking love: The feminization of sex.* Garden City, NY: Anchor.

Ehrensaft, Diane. 1980. When women and men mother. *Socialist Review* 49:37–73.

Ehrensaft, Diane. 1987. *Parenting together: Men and women sharing the care of children.* New York: Free Press.

Ehrensaft, Diane. 1990. Feminists fight (for) fathers. *Socialist Review* 59:57–80.

Eisenstein, Zillah, ed. 1979. *Capitalist patriarchy and the case of socialist feminism.* New York: Monthly Review Press.

Eisenstein, Zillah. 1984a. *Feminism and sexual equality: Crisis in liberal America.* New York: Monthly Review Press.

Eisenstein, Zillah. 1984b. The patriarchal relations of the Reagan state. *Signs* 10 (2):329–337.

Eitzen, D. Stanley. 1985. *In conflict and order: Understanding society.* 3d ed. Boston: Allyn and Bacon.

Eitzen, Stanley, and Maxine Baca Zinn, eds. 1989. *The reshaping of America.* Englewood Cliffs, NJ: Prentice-Hall.

Eitzen, Stanley, and Maxine Baca Zinn, eds. 1992. *Social problems.* 5th ed. Boston: Allyn and Bacon.

Elder, Glen. 1969. Appearance and education in marriage mobility. *American Sociological Review* 34:519–533.

Elder, Glen. 1974. *Children of the Great Depression.* Chicago: University of Chicago Press.

Elder, Glen. 1986. Military times and turning points in men's lives. *Developmental Psychology* 22:233–245.

Ellis, Ellen. 1983. Abortion: Is a woman a person? In A. Snitow, C. Stansell, and S. Thompson (eds.), *Powers of desire: The politics of sexuality* (pp. 471–476). New York: Monthly Review Press.

Ellis, Joseph. 1998. *American Sphinx: The character of Thomas Jefferson.* New York: Vintage.

Ellison, Christopher, and W. Martin, eds. 1998. *Race and ethnic relations in the U.S.* Los Angeles: Roxbury.

Ellwood, David, and Lawrence Summers. 1986. Poverty in America: Is welfare the answer or the problem? In. S. Danziger and D. Weinberg (eds.), *Fighting poverty: What works and what doesn't* (pp. 78–105). Cambridge, MA: Harvard University Press.

Elsa Valdez. 2004. Chicana mothers: Acculturation, social support and perceptions of motherhood. In Roberto De Anda (ed.). *Chicanos and Chicanas in contempoary society* 2nd ed. (pp 99-111) New York: Rowman and Littlefield.

Emery, R. 1988. *Marriage, divorce and children's adjustment.* Newbury Park, CA: Sage.

Engels, Frederick. 1884/1970. *Origins of the family, private property and the state.* New York: International Publishers.

England, Paula. 1989. A feminist critique of rational choice theories: Implications for sociology. *The American Sociologist* 19 (Spring):14–28.

England, Paula, and B. S. Kilbourne. 1990. Feminist critiques of the separative model of self: Implications for rational choice theory" *Rational Sociology* 2:156–171.

Epstein, Cynthia Fuchs, and Anne Kallenberg. 2004. *Fighting for Time.* New York: Russell Sage.

Epstein, Cynthia. 1983. *Women in law.* New York: Anchor Press.

Erlichman, Karen. 1989. Lesbian mothers: Ethical issues in social work practice. In E. Rothblum and E. Cole (eds), *Lesbianism: Affirming nontraditional roles* (pp. 207–244). New York: Haworth Press.

Espiritu, Yen Le. 1995. *Filipino American lives.* Philadelphia: Temple University Press.

Espiritu, Yen Le. 1997. *Asian American women and men: Labor, laws and love.* Thousand Oaks, CA: Sage.

Espiritu, Yen Le. 1998. All men are not created equal: Asian men in U.S. history. In M. Kimmel and M. Messner (eds.), *Men's Lives.* 4th ed. (pp. 35–44). Boston: Allyn and Bacon.

Etaugh, C. 1980. The effects of non-maternal care on children: Research evidence and popular views. *American Psychologist* 35:309–319.

Ettlebrick, Paula. 1992. Since when is marriage the path to liberation? In G. Bird and M. Sporakowski (eds.), *Taking sides: Clashing views on controversial issues in family and personal relationships* (pp. 80–84). Guilford, CT: Dushkin Publishing.

Evans, Sara. 1979. *Personal politics: The roots of women's liberation in the civil rights movement and the new left.* New York: Knopf.

Evans, Sara. 1989. *Born for liberty: A history of women in America.* New York: Free Press.

Evans, Sara. 1991. The first American women. In L. Kerber and J. De Hart (eds.), *Woman's America: Refocusing the past.* 3d ed. (pp. 31–40). New York: Oxford University Press.

Exner, M. 1915. *Problems and principles of sex education: A study of 948 college men.* New York: Association Press.

Eyer, Diane. 1992. *Mother-infant bonding: A scientific fiction.* New Haven, CT: Yale University Press.

Eyer, Diane. 1996. *Motherguilt: How our culture blames mothers for what's wrong with society.* New York: Random House.

Fagan, J. 1993. Interactions among drugs, alcohol, and violence. *Health Affairs* 12 (4):65–79.

Fagan, Jeffrey, Douglas Stewart, and Karen Valentine. 1983. Violent men or violent husband? Background factors and situational correlates. In D. Finkelhor et al. (eds), *The dark side of families: Current family violence research* (pp. 49–68). Beverly Hills, CA: Sage.

Falk, P. 1989. Lesbian mothers: Psychological assumptions in family law. *American Psychologist* 44:941–947.

Faludi, Susan. 1991. *Backlash: The undeclared war against American women.* New York: Crown.

Falwell, Jerry. 1980. *Listen America.* New York: Doubleday.

Family Research Council. 2005. *Deterring Divorce* Washington, DC. (October 17).

Farel, A. 1980. Effects of preferred maternal roles, maternal employment and sociographic status on school adjustment and competence. *Child Development* 50:1179–1186.

Farley, Reynolds. 1996. *The new American reality: Who we are, how we got here, where we are going.* New York: Russell Sage Foundation.

Farrar, Eliza. 1837. *The young lady's friend.* Boston: Ticknor and Fields.

Fass, Paula. 1977. *The damned and the beautiful: American youth in the 1920s.* New York: Oxford University Press.

Fassinger, Polly. 1989. The impact of gender and past marital experience on heading a household alone. In B. Risman and R. Schwartz (eds.), *Gender in intimate relationships* (pp. 165–180). Belmont, CA: Wadsworth.

Feagin, Joe, and Clarice Feagin. 1990. *Building American cities.* 2d ed. Englewood Cliffs, NJ: Prentice-Hall.

Federal Interagency Forum on Aging-Related Statistics. 2005. *Older Americans 2004: Key Indicators of Well Being* (July). Washington, D.C.

Feldberg, Roslyn, and Evelyn Nakano Glenn. 1979. Male and female: Job versus gender models in the sociology of work. *Social Problems* 26:524–538.

Fengler, A. 1975. Attitudinal orientation of wives toward their husbands' retirement. *International Journal of Aging and Human Development* 6:139–152.

Ferber, M. A., and J. Nelson, eds. 1993. *Beyond economic man: Feminist theory and economics.* Chicago: University of Chicago Press.

Ferber, Marianne, and Brigid O'Farrell, eds. 1991. *Work and family.* Washington, DC: National Academy.

Ferdinand, Pamela. 2000. "Gays achieve breakthrough in Vermont" *Washington Post* (3/17):A1.

Ferman, Lewis, and Mary Blehar. 1983. Family adjustment to unemployment. In A. Skolnick and J. Skolnick (eds.), *Family in transition.* 4th ed. (pp. 587–600). Boston: Little, Brown.

Fernandez, Elizabeth. 1997. Life at the office. *People* 47 (20):71.

Ferraro, Eric, Joshua Freker, and Travis Foster. 2005. *Too High a Price: The Case Against Restricting Gay Parenting.* New York: ACLU.

Ferraro, Kathleen. 1981. *Battered women and the shelter movement.* Ph.D. dissertation, Arizona State University.

Ferraro, Kathleen. 1989. Policing woman battering. *Social Problems* 36 (1):61–74.

Ferraro, Kathleen, and John Johnson. 1990. How women experience battering: The process of victimization. In J. Heeren and M. Mason (eds.), *Sociology: Windows on society* (pp. 109–115). Los Angeles: Roxbury.

Ferree, Myra Marx. 1990. Beyond separate spheres: Feminism and family research. *Journal of Marriage and the Family* 52 (November):866–884.

Ferree, Myra Marx, and Beth Hess. 1985. *Controversy and coalition: The new feminist movement.* Boston: Twayne.

Field, D., and S. Weishaus. 1992. Marriages over half a century: A longitudinal study. In M. Bloom (ed.), *Changing lives* (pp. 269–273). Columbia: University of South Carolina Press.

Fields, Jason and Lynne Casper. 2001. America's family and living arrangements: March 2000, Current Population Reports, P20-537. Washington, DC: U.S. Census Bureau.

Fields, Robin. 2001. Seniors pick cohabitation rather than marriage. *Los Angeles Times,* (4 September).

Finkelhor, David. 1979. *Sexually victimized children.* New York: Basic Books.

Finkelhor, David. 1994. Current information on the scope and nature of child sexual abuse. *The Future of Children* 4 (2):31–53.

Finkelhor, David. 1994. The "blacklash" and the future of child protection advocacy: Insights from the study of social issues. In J. Myers (ed.), *The backlash: Child protection under fire* (pp. 1–16). Thousand Oaks, CA: Sage.

Finkelhor, David and Jennifer Dziuba-Leatherman. 1995. "Victimization prevention programs: A national survey of children's exposures and reactions." *Child Abuse and Neglect* 19(2):128–139

Finkelhor, David, and Kersti Yllo. 1983. Rape in marriage: A sociological view. In D. Finkelhor et al. (eds.), *The dark side of families* (pp. 119–130). Beverly Hills, CA: Sage.

Finkelhor, David, and Kersti Yllo. 1985. *License to rape: Sexual abuse of wives.* New York: Free Press.

Finkelhor, David, and Kersti Yllo. 1989. Marital rape: The myth versus the reality. In J. Henslin (ed.), *Marriage and the family in a changing society* (pp. 382–291). New York: Free Press.

Finkelhor, David, and Richard Ormrod. 2001. Child abuse reported to the police. *Juvenile Justice Bulletin* (May).

Firestone, Shulamith. 1970. *The dialectic of sex: The case for feminist revolution.* New York: William Morrow.

Fisher, Luchina. 2003. Working women delay, forgo, rethink motherhood. *Women's Enews Correspondent* (November 7).

Fishman, Pamela. 1978. Interaction: The work women do. *Social Problems* 25:308–406.

Flaks, P., I. Ficher, I. Masterpqua, and G. Joseph. 1995. Lesbians choosing motherhood: A comparative study of lesbians, heterosexual parents and their children. *Developmental Psychology* 31:105–114.

Flax, Jane. 1982. The family in contemporary feminist thought: A critical review. In J. Elshtain (ed.), *The family in political thought* (pp. 223–253). Amherst, MA: University of Massachusetts.

Flax, Jane. 1993. Women do theory. In M. Pearsall (ed.), *Women and values: Readings in recent feminist philosophy* (pp. 3–7). Belmont, CA: Wadsworth.

Fleming, Jeanne. 1988. Public opinion on changes in women's rights and roles. In S. Dornbusch and M. Strober (eds.), *Feminism, children and the new families* (pp. 47–66). New York: Guilford.

Folbre, Nancy. 1987. The pauperization of motherhood: Patriarchy and public policy in the U.S. In N. Gerstel and H. Gross (eds.), *Families and work* (pp. 491–511). Philadelphia: Temple University Press.

Forbes. 1992. Billionaires, July, 16–18.

Fortune. 1993. When will the layoffs end? 20 September, 40.

Foucault, Michael. 1978. *The history of sexuality.* New York: Pantheon.

Fowles, Deborah. 2006. New bankruptcy laws make it harder for some people to erase their debts NY: About.inc (*New York Times*). http://financialplan.about.com/od/creditand debt/a/bankruptcylaw.htm

Fowlkes, Martha. 1987. The myth of merit and mate professional careers: The roles of wives. In N. Gerstel and H. Gross (eds.), *Families and work* (pp. 347–361). Philadelphia: Temple University Press.

Fox, J., and M. Zawitz. 2004. Homicide Trends in the United States. U.S. Department of Justice Washington, DC: USGPO.

Francis, David. 2001. Bush tax cuts widen income gap. *Christian Science Monitor* 23 May.

Franklin, John Hope. 1988. A historical note on black families. In H. McAdoo (ed.), *Black families.* 2d ed. (pp. 23–26). Beverly Hills, CA: Sage.

Freedman, Estelle, and Barrie Thorne. 1984. Introduction to feminist sexuality debates. *Signs* 10 (Autumn): 102–105.

Freeman, Jo. 1975. *The politics of women's liberation.* New York: Longman.

Freeman, Jo. 1989. Feminist organization and activities from suffrage to women's liberation. In J. Freeman (ed.), *Women: A feminist perspective.* 4th ed. (pp. 541–555). Mountain View, CA: Mayfield.

Freising, David. 1998. Its the best of times. Or is it? *Business Week,* 11 January, 36–38.

Freud, Sigmund. 1954. *The origins of psychoanalysis: Letters to Wilhelm Fliess, drafts and notes, 1887–1902.* New York: Basic Books.

Freud, Sigmund. 1963. *Introductory lectures on psychoanalysis.* New York: W. W. Norton.

Fried, Marlene, ed. 1991. *From abortion to reproductive freedom: Transforming a movement.* Boston: Southend Press.

Friedan, Betty. 1963. *The feminine mystique.* New York: Dell.

Friedman, Dana. 1988. Estimates from the Conference Board and other national monitors of employer-supported child care. Unpublished memo. New York: The Conference Board.

Friedman, Lawrence. 1994. *Crime and punishment in American history.* New York: Basic Books.

Frisch, Michael, and Dorothy Watts. 1980. Oral history and the presentation of class consciousness: The *New York Times* vs. the Buffalo unemployed. *International Journal of Oral History* 1:89–110.

Frye, Marilyn. 1983. *The politics of reality.* Trumansburg, NY: Crossing Press.

Furstenberg, Frank. 1988. Childcare after divorce and remarriage. In E. Hetherington and J. Arosteh (eds.), *Impact of divorce, single-parenting, and step parenting on children* (pp. 245–261). Hillsdale, NJ: Lawrence Erlbaum.

Furstenburg, Frank. 1990. Divorce and the American family. *Annual Review of Sociology* 16:379–403.

Furstenberg, Frank, and Andrew Cherlin. 1991. *Divided families: What happens to children when parents part.* Cambridge, MA: Harvard University Press.

Furstenberg, Frank, K. Sherwood, and M. Sullivan. 1992. *Caring and paying: What fathers and mothers say about child support.* New York: Manpower Demonstration Resources.

Furstenburg, F., J. Brooks-Gunn, and S. Morgan. 1987. *Adolescent mothers in later life.* Cambridge: Cambridge University Press.

Furstenburg, Frank, S. Phillip Morgan, and Paul Allison. 1987. Paternal participation and children's well-being after marital dissolution. *American Sociological Review* 52:695–701.

Galbraith, John. 1958. *The affluent society.* Boston: Houghton, Mifflin.

Gallagher, E. 1986. *No place like home: The tragedy of homeless children and their families in Massachusetts.* Boston: Massachusetts Committee for Children and Youth.

Gallup Organization. 2003. *Current Views on premarital, extramarital sex.* Princeton, NJ: The Gallup Organization.

Gallup, George, and F. Newport. 1991. Babyboomers seek more family time. *Gallup Poll Monthly,* April, 31–38.

Garcia, Mario. 1980. La familia: The Mexican immigrant family 1900–1930. In M. Barrera, A. Camarillo, and F. Hernandez (eds.), *Work, family, sex roles, language* (pp. 117–140). Berkeley: Tonatius-Quinto Sol International.

Gardyn, Rebecca. 2002. The mating game—brief article. *American Demographics* (July 1).

Garey, Anita. 1998. Fertility on the frontier: Women, contraception and community. In K. Hansen and A. Garey (eds.), *Families in the U.S.: Kinship and domestic politics* (pp. 79–90). Philadelphia: Temple University Press.

Garner, Abigail. 2004. *Families Like Mine: Children of Gay Parents Tell It Like It Is.* New York: Harper.

Gaylord, Maxine. 1984. Relocation and the corporate family. In R. Voydanoff (ed.), *Work and family: Changing roles of women and men* (pp. 144–152). Palo Alto, CA: Mayfield.

Geerken, Michael, and Walter Gove. 1983. *At home and at work: The family's allocation of labor.* Beverly Hills, CA: Sage.

Gelles, Richard. 1977. Violence in the American family. In J. Martin (ed.), *Violence and the family* (pp. 169–182). New York: Wiley.

Gelles, Richard. 1993. Alcohol and drugs are associated with violence—They are its cause. In R. Gelles and D. Loseke (eds.), *Current controversies in domestic violence* (pp. 182–196). Newbury Park, CA: Sage.

Gelles, Richard, and Claire Cornell. 1985. *Intimate violence in families.* Beverly Hills, CA: Sage.

Gelles, Richard, and Murray Straus. 1976. Abused wives: Why do they stay? *Journal of Marriage and the Family* 38:659–668.

Gelles, Richard, and Murray Straus. 1987. Is violence toward children increasing? A comparison of 1975–1985 national survey rates. *Journal of Interpersonal Violence* 2:212–222.

Gelles, Richard, and Murray Straus. 1995. *Physical violence in American families: Risk factors and adaptations to violence in 8,145 families.* New Brunswick, NJ: Transaction.

Genevie, L., and E. Margolies. 1987. *The motherhood report: How women feel about being mothers.* New York: Macmillan.

Genovese, Eugene. 1972. *Roll, Jordan, roll: The world the slaves made.* New York: Pantheon.

Gerson, Kathleen. 1987. How women choose between employment and family: A developmental perspective. In N. Gerstel and H. Gross (eds.), *Families and work* (pp. 270–288). Philadelphia: Temple University Press.

Gerson, Kathleen. 1993. *No man's land: Men's changing commitment to family and work.* New York: Basic Books.

Gerson, Kathleen. 1998. Gender and the future of the family: Implications for the postindustrial workplace. In D. Vannoy and P. Dubeck (eds.), *Challenges for work and family in the twenty first century* (pp. 11–22). New York: Aldine de Gruyter.

Gerstein, L. 2000. Women aged 15 to 29 are increasingly having first children before marriage. *Family Planning Perspectives* (March/April).

Gerstel, Naomi, and Hannah Gross, eds. 1987. *Families and work.* Philadelphia: Temple University Press.

Gerstel, Naomi. 1987. Divorce and stigma. *Social Problems* 34 (2):172–186.

Giddens, Anthony. 1977. *Studies in social and political theory.* New York: Basic Books.

Giddens, Anthony. 1984. *The constitution of society: Outline of the theory of structuration.* Berkeley: University of California Press.

Giddens, Anthony. 1991. *Introduction to sociology.* New York: W. W. Norton.

Giddings, Paula. 1984. *When and where I enter: The impact of black women on race and sex in America.* New York: Bantam Books.

Giele, Janet. 1999. Decline of the family: Conservative, liberal and feminist views. In A. Skolnick and J. Skolnick (eds.), *Family in transition,* 10th ed. (pp. 449–472). New York: Longman.

Gilbert, Dennis, and Joseph Kahl. 1993. *The American class structure: A new synthesis.* Belmont, CA: Wadsworth.

Gilderbloom, John, and Richard Appelbaum. 1988. *Rethinking rental housing.* Philadelphia: Temple University Press.

Gillespie, Dair. 1971. Who has the power? The marital struggle. *Journal of Marriage and the Family* 31:445–558.

Gilligan, Carol. 1982. *In a different voice: Psychological theory and women's development.* Cambridge, MA: Harvard University Press.

Gillis, John. 1997. *A world of their own making: Myth, ritual and the quest for family values.* Cambridge, MA: Harvard University Press.

Gilman, Carolina. 1834. *Recollections of a housekeeper.* New York.

Gilman, Charlotte Perkins. 1898/1966. *Women and economics.* New York: Harper and Row.

Ginsberg, Faye, and Anna Lowenhaupt Tsing. 1990. *Uncertain terms: Negotiating gender in American culture.* Boston: Beacon Press.

Ginsberg, Faye. 1990. *Contested lives: The abortion debate in an American community.* Berkeley: University of California Press.

Gittens, Diane. 1998. The family in question: Is it universal? In S. Ferguson (ed.), *Shifting the center: Understanding contemporary families* (pp. 1–12). Mountain View, CA: Mayfield.

Glass, Jennifer. 1992. Gender, family and job family compatibility. *American Journal of Sociology* 98 (1): 131–151.

Glass, J., and T. Fujimoto. 1994. Housework, paid work and depression among husbands and wives. *Journal of Health and Social Behavior* 35:179–191.

Glass, Jennifer, and Sarah Estes. 1997. The family responsive workplace. In J. Hagan and K. Cook (eds.), *Annual review of sociology.* Vol. 23. (pp. 289–313). Palo Alto, CA: Annual Reviews, Inc.

Glassner, Barry. 1999. *The culture of fear.* New York: Basic Books.

Glazer, Nona. 1987. Servants to capital: Unpaid domestic labor and paid work. In N. Gerstel and H. Gross (eds.), *Families and work* (pp. 236–255). Philadelphia: Temple University Press.

Glazer, Nona. 1990. The home as workshop: Women as amateur nurses and medical care providers. *Gender and Society* 4 (4):479–499.

Glazer, Nona. 1993. *Women's paid and unpaid labor: The work transfer in health care and retailing.* Philadelphia: Temple University Press.

Glenn, Evelyn Nakano. 1987. Gender and the family. In P. Hess and M. M. Ferree (eds.), *Analyzing gender: A handbook of social science research* (pp. 348–380). Newbury Park, CA: Sage.

Glenn, Evelyn Nakano. 1990. The dialectics of wage work: Japanese-American women and domestic service, 1905–1940. In E. Dubois and V. Ruiz (eds.), *Unequal sisters: A multi-cultural reader in U.S. women's history* (pp. 345–372). New York: Routledge.

Glenn, Evelyn Nakano. 1991. Racial ethnic women's labor: The intersection of race, gender and class oppression. In R. Blumberg (ed.), *Gender, family and economy: The triple overlap* (pp. 173–201). Newbury Park, CA: Sage.

Glick, Paul. 1977. Updating the life cycle of the family. *Journal of Marriage and the Family* 39:5–13.

Glick, Paul. 1988. A demographic picture of black families. In H. McAdoo (ed.), *Black families.* 2d ed. (pp. 111–133). Beverly Hills, CA: Sage.

Glick, Paul, and Arthur Norton. 1979. Marrying, divorcing and living together in the U.S. today. *Population Bulletin* 32 (February):1–41.

Glick, Paul, and Sung-Ling Lin. 1986. Recent changes in divorce and remarriage. *Journal of Marriage and the Family* 48 (4):737–747.

GLSEN. 1999. *Gay, Lesbian, and Straight Network Report on Anti-Gay Violence.* www.Glsenla.org (accessed May 29, 2006).

Gluck, Sherna. 1987. *Rosie the Riveter revisited: Women, the war and social change.* New York: Twayne.

Glueck, W. 1979. Changing hours of work: A review and analysis of the research. *Personnel Administrator* 3:44–47.

Goffman, Erving. 1963. *Stigma: Notes on the management of spoiled identity.* Englewood Cliffs, NJ: Prentice-Hall.

Goffman, Erving. 1977. The arrangement between the sexes. *Theory and Society* 40:301–331.

Goffman, Erving. 1979. *Gender advertisements.* New York: Harper and Row.

Goldin, Cynthia. 1981. Family strategies and the family economy in the late nineteenth century: The role of secondary works. In T. Hershberg (ed.), *Philadelphia* (pp. 183–201). New York: Oxford University Press.

Goldman, Emma. 1910. *Anarchism and other essays.* Port Washington, NY: Kennikat Press.

Goldscheiter, Frances, and Linda Waite. 1991. *New families, no families: The transformation of the American home.* Berkeley: University of California Press.

Gonzalez, David. 2005. From margins of society to center of tragedy. *New York Times* 2 September.

Goode, William. 1964. *The family.* Englewood Cliffs, NJ: Prentice-Hall.

Goodhart, Adam. 2004. Change of heart. *AARP Magazine* (May).

Goodman, Ellen. 1992. The White House and your house. *Charlotte Observer,* 10 October, 2c.

Goodman, Jacqueline. 2004. Mothers and children caught in war zone. *Studies in Law, Politics, and Society* 32: 163–196.

Goodstein, J. 1994. Institutional pressures and strategic responsiveness: Employer involvement in work-family issues. *Academic Management Journal* 37:350–382.

Googins, Bradley. 1991. *Work/family conflicts: Private lives, public responses.* New York: Auburn House.

Gordon, David. 1996. *Fat and mean: The corporate squeeze of working Americans and the myth of managerial "downsizing."* New York: Free Press.

Gordon, Linda, and Paul O'Keefe. 1984. Incest as a form of family violence: Evidence from historical case records. *Journal of Marriage and the Family* 49:27–34.

Gordon, Linda. 1977. *Woman's body, woman's right: A social history of birth control in America.* New York: Penguin.

Gordon, Linda. 1982. Why nineteenth century feminists did not support birth control and twentieth century feminists do. In B. Thorne (ed.), *Rethinking the family: Some feminist questions* (pp. 40–53). New York: Longman.

Gordon, Linda. 1988. *Heroes of their own lives: The politics and history of family violence, Boston 1880–1960.* New York: Viking.

Gordon, Michael, ed. 1978. *The American family in social-historical perspective.* 2d ed. New York: St. Martin's Press.

Gordon-Reed, Annette. 1998. *Thomas Jefferson and Sally Hemings: An American controversy.* Charlottesville: University Press of Virginia.

Gorelick, Sherry. 1991. Contradictions of feminist methodology. *Gender and Society* 5 (4):459–478.

Gould, Meredith. 1984. Lesbians and the law: Where sexism and heterosexism meet. In T. Darty and S. Potter (eds.), *Women identified women* (pp. 149–162). Palo Alto, CA: Mayfield.

Gouldner, Alvin. 1970. *The coming crisis of Western sociology.* New York: Basic Books.

Gove, Walter. 1972. The relation between sex roles, marital status and mental illness. *Social Forces* 51:34–44.

Gramsci, Antonio. 1971. *Selections from the prison notebooks.* New York: International Publishers.

Granrose, Cheryl, and Eileen Kaplan. 1996. *Work-Family Role Choice for Women in Their 20's and 30's.* New York: Praeger.

Grant, Linda, Kathryn Ward, Donald Broom, and William Moore. 1987. Gender, parenthood and work hours of physicians. *Journal of Marriage and the Family* 52 (February):39–49.

Grant, Linda, Layne Sampson, and Xue Lai Rong. 1990. Development of work and family commitments: A study of medical students. *Journal of Family Issues* 8:176–198.

Graves, Sherryl. 1996. Diversity on television. In T. MacBeth (ed.), *Tuning in to young viewers: Social science perspectives in television* (pp. 61–86). Thousand Oaks, CA: Sage.

Greeley, Andrew, ed. 1995. *Sociology and religion.* New York: HarperCollins.

Greeley, Andrew, Robert Michael, and Tom Smith. 1990. *A most monogamous people: Americans and their sexual partners.* Chicago: NORC.

Green, Charles. 1992. Bush says test welfare limits plan. *Charlotte Observer,* 10 April, 1A.

Green, S., and P. Sandos. 1983. Perceptions of male and female initiators of relationships. *Sex Roles* 9:849–852.

Greenberg, Mark. 1999. Welfare restructuring and working poor family policy: The new context. In J. Handler and L. White (eds.), *Hard Labor* (pp. 24–47). New York: M. E. Sharpe.

Greenberger, Ellen. 1987. Children's employment and families. In N. Gerstel and H. Gross (eds.), *Families and work* (pp. 396–406). Philadelphia: Temple University Press.

Greenfield, Lawrence, Michael Rand, Diane Craven, Patsy Klaus, Craig Perkins, Cheryl Ringel, Greg Warchol, Cathy Maston, and James Fox. 1998. *Violence by intimates: Analysis of data on crimes by current or former spouses, boyfriends and girlfriends.* Washington, DC: U.S. Department of Justice. NCJ167237.

Greenhouse, Linda. 2005. Justices rule police do not have constitutional duty to protect someone. *New York Times* (28 June).

Greer, Germaine. 1970. *The female eunuch.* London: MacGibbon and Kee.

Greider, Linda. 2004. Unmarried together—more older couples skip the wedding but still find bliss. *AARP Bulletin Online* (October).

Greif, Geoffrey. 1979. Fathers, children and joint custody. *American Journal of Orthopsychiatry* 49:311–319.

Greif, Geoffrey. 1985. *Single fathers.* Lexington, MA: Lexington Books.

Greil, Arthur. 1998. A secret stigma: Interaction with the fertile world. In S. Ferguson (ed.), *Shifting the center: Understanding the contemporary families* (pp. 243–254). Mountain View, CA: Mayfield.

Gresham, Jewell. 1989. White patriarchal supremacy: The politics of family in America. *Nation* 249 (4):116–121.

Greven, Philip. 1978. Family structure in the 17th century. *William and Mary Quarterly* 23:234–256.

Griffin, L., O. Williams, and J. Reed. 1998. Abuse of African American elders. In R. Bergen (ed.), *Issues in intimate violence* (pp. 267–284). Thousand Oaks, CA: Sage.

Griscom, Joan. 1992. The case of Sharon Kowalski and Karen Thompson: Ableism, heterosexism and sexism. In P. Rothenberg (ed.), *Race, class and gender in the U.S.: An integrated study.* 2d ed. (pp. 215–224). New York: St. Martin's Press.

Grotevant, Harold and Ruth McRoy. 1997. "The Minnesota/Texas adoption research project: Implications of openness in adoption for development and relationships" *Applied Developmental Science* 1 (4):168–186.

Gutman, Herbert. 1976. *The black family in slavery and freedom, 1750–1925.* New York: Pantheon.

Gutman, Herbert. 1992. Americans and their sexual partners. In G. Bird and M. Sporakowski (eds.), *Taking sides: Clashing views on controversial issues and family and personal relationships* (pp. 254–262). Guilford, CT: Dushkin.

Guttentag, Marcia, and Paul Secord. 1983. *Too many women: The sex ratio problem.* Beverly Hills, CA: Sage.

Gwartney-Gibbs, Patricia. 1986. The institutionalization of premarital cohabitation: Estimates from marriage license applications, 1970–1980. *Journal of Marriage and the Family* 48:423–434.

Hacker, Andrew. 1992. *Two nations: Black and white, separate, hostile and unequal.* New York: Charles Scribner's Sons.

Hadden, Jeffrey. 1995. Conservative Christians, televangelism and politics: Taking stock a decade after the founding of the moral majority. In A. Greeley (ed.), *Sociology and religion* (pp. 420–433). New York: HarperCollins.

Haines, Michael R, and Richard H. Steckel (eds.). 2001. *A Population History of North America.* New York: Cambridge University Press.

Hall, E. T. 1983. *The dance of life: The other dimension of time.* New York: Anchor.

Halle, David. 1984. *America's Working Man.* Chicago: University of Chicago Press.

Halle, Robert. 1984. *America's working man: Work, home and politics among blue collar property owners.* Chicago: University of Chicago Press.

Halsted, James. 1992. Domestic violence: Its legal definitions. In S. Buzawa and C. Buzawa (eds.), *Domestic violence: The changing criminal justice response* (pp. 143–160). Westport, CT: Auburn House.

Hamilton, Brandy E., Paul D. Sutton, and Stephanie J. Ventura. 2003. *CDC. National Vital Statistics Report,* Vol. 51. No. 12. Revised Birth and Fertility Rates for the 1990s and New Rates for Hispanic Populations, 2000 and 2001: United States. Atlanta, GA: CDC.

Hamilton, Brandy E., Stephanie J. Ventura, Joyce A. Martin, and Paul D. Sutton. 2005. CDC. National Center for Health Statistics. *Preliminary Births for 2004.* Hayattsville, MD.

Handler, Joel, and Yeheskel Hasenfeld. 1997. We the poor people: Work, poverty and welfare. New Haven, CT: Yale University Press.

Handler, Joel. 1999. Low wage work as we know it: What's wrong/what can be done? In J. Handler and L. White, eds., *Hard labor* (pp. 3–23). New York: M. E. Sharpe.

Hansen, D., and V. Johnson. 1979. Rethinking family stress theory. In W. Burr et al. (eds.), *Contemporary theories about the family.* Vol. 1 (pp. 582–603). New York: Free Press.

Hansen, Karen, and Ilene Philipson, eds. 1990. *Women, class and the feminist imagination: A socialist-feminist reader.* Philadelphia: Temple University Press.

Hanson, S., and T. Ooms. 1991. The economic costs and rewards of two-earner, two parent families. *Journal of Marriage and the Family* 53:622–634.

Hardacre, Helen. 1994. Fundamentalism and society: The impact of fundamentalism on women, the family and interpersonal relationships. In M. Marty and R. Appleby (eds.), *Fundamentalism in Society* (pp. 129–150). Chicago: University of Chicago Press.

Harding, Susan. 1981. Family reform movements: Recent feminism and its opposition. *Feminist Studies* 7 (1):58–75.

Harding, Susan. 1987. *Feminism and methodology.* Bloomington: University of Indiana Press.

Hare, Nathan, and Julia Hare. 1985. *Bringing the black boy to manhood: The passage.* San Francisco: Black Think Tank.

Harlan, S. 1989. Introduction to welfare, workfare and training. In S. Harlan and R. Steinberg (eds.), *Job training for women* (pp. 359–364). Philadelphia: Temple University Press.

Harmon, Amy. 2005a. First comes the baby carriage. *New York Times,* (13 October).

Harmon, Amy. 2005b. Hello i'm your sister. *New York Times,* (20 November).

Harrington, Michael. 1962. *The other America: Poverty in the U.S.* New York: Penguin.

Harris, Diana. 1992. You're pregnant? You're out. *Working Woman,* November, 48–51.

Harrison, Althea. 1987. Images of black women. In *The American woman, 1987–1988: A report in depth.* New York: Norton.

Harrison, Bennett, and Barry Bluestone. 1988. *The Great U-Turn: The corporate restructuring and the polarizing of America.* New York: Basic Books.

Harrison, Lee. 1991. California report. *Personnel Journal* 70 (October):26.

Harrison, Roderick, and Claudette Bennett. 1995. Racial and ethnic diversity. In R. Farley (ed.), *State of the Union* (pp. 141–210). New York: Russell Sage.

Harry, Joseph. 1983. Gay male and lesbian relationships. In E. Macklin and R. Rubin (ed.), *Contemporary families and alternative lifestyles: Handbook of research and theory* (pp. 216–234). Beverly Hills, CA: Sage.

Hartmann, Betsy. 1987. *Reproductive rights and wrongs: The global politics of population control and contraceptive choice.* New York: Harper & Row.

Hartmann, Heidi. 1981. The family as the locus of gender, class and political struggle: The example of housework. *Signs* 6 (3):366–394.

Hartmann, Heidi. 1991. Women's work and diversity and employment stability: Public policy responses to new realities. Testimony before U.S. Senate Committee of Labor and Human Resources. Washington, DC: Institute for Women's Policy Research.

Hartmann, Heidi, and Diana Pearce. 1989. *High skill and low pay: The economics of child care work.* Executive summary. Washington, DC: IWPR.

Hartsock, Nancy. 1983. *Money, sex and power: Toward a feminist historical materialism.* New York: Longman.

Hartsock, Nancy. 1993. Feminist theory and the development of revolutionary strategy. In M. Pearsall (ed.), *Women and values: Readings in recent feminist philosophy* (pp. 8–17). Belmont, CA: Wadsworth.

Hartsock, Nancy. 1998. *The feminist standpoint revisited and other essays.* Boulder, CO: Westview.

Harvey, Elizabeth. 1999. Short and long term effects of early parental employment on children. *Developmental Psychology* 35 (2).

Harvey, Elizabeth. 1999. Short term and long term effects of early parental employment on children. *Development Psychology* 35 (2):445–459.

Harwood, Robin, Amy Miller, Vivan Carlson, and Birgit Leyendecker. 2000. Child-rearing beliefs and practices during feeding among middle-class Puerto Rican and Anglo mother infant pairs. In Kerns, Contreras, and Neal Bennett (eds.), *Latino children and families in the United States* (pp. 133–152). Westport, CT: Praeger.

Haskins, R. 1988. Child support: A father's view. In S. Kamerman and A. Kahn (eds.), *Child support: From debt collection to public policy* (pp. 306–327). Beverly Hills, CA: Sage.

Hayden, Dolores. 1981. *The grand domestic revolution: History of feminist designs for American homes, neighborhoods, and cities.* Cambridge, MA: MIT Press.

Hayghe, Howard. 1993. "Working wives contribution to family income" *Month Labor Review* 116 (8):39–43.

Hays, Sharon. 1995. *Cultural contradictions of motherhood.* New Haven, CT: Yale University Press.

Hays, Sharon. 1999. The mommy wars. In A. Skolnick and J. Skolnick (eds.), *Family in transition.* 10th ed. (pp. 432–448). New York: Addison Wesley.

Hedges, J., and J. Barnett. 1972. Working women and the division of household tasks. *Monthly Labor Review* 95 (1):9–14.

Hein, Jeremy. 1993. *States and international migrants: The incorporation of Indochinese refugees in the U.S. and France.* San Francisco: Westview.

Heintz, James, and Nancy Folbre. 2000. *The ultimate field guide to the US economy.* New York: The New Press.

Helbern, Suzanne, et al. 1999. *The Silent Crisis in U.S. Childcare.* Philadelphia: American Academy of Political and Social Sciences.

Heller, Celia. 1966. *Mexican American youth: Forgotten youth at the crossroads.* New York: Random House.

Hendershott, Anne. 1995. *Moving for work: The sociology of relocating in the 1990s.* New York: University Press of America.

Hendrick, Susan, and Clyde Hendrick. 1992. *Liking, loving and relating.* 2d ed. Belmont, CA: Wadsworth.

Henley, Nancy. 1977. *Body politics: Power, sex and nonverbal communication.* Englewood Cliffs, NJ: Prentice-Hall.

Henshaw, S., and J. Van Vort, eds. 1992. *Abortion services in the U.S.: Each state and metropolitan area, 1967–1988.* New York: Alan Guttmacher Institute.

Herman, Judith. 1981. *Father-daughter incest.* Cambridge, MA: Harvard University Press.

Herman, Judith. 1992. *Trauma and recovery.* New York: Basic Books.

Herman, Judith, and Lisa Hirschman. 1977. Father-daughter incest. *Signs* 2 (4):735–756.

Hernandez, Donald. 1993. *America's children: Resources from family, government, and the economy.* New York: Russell Sage Foundation.

Hernandez, Donald. 1995. *America's children: Lessons from family, government and the economy.* New York: Russell Sage.

Hertz, Rosanna. 1998. The parenting approach to the work-family dilemma. In K. Hansen and A. Garey (eds.), *Families in the U.S.: Kinship and domestic politics* (pp. 767–775). Philadelphia: Temple University Press.

Hess, Beth, and Myra Marx Ferree. 1987. *Analyzing gender: A handbook of social science research.* Beverly Hills, CA: Sage.

Hetherington, E. 1979. Divorce: A child's perspective. *American Psychologist* 34:851–858.

Hetherington, E., Martha Cox, and Roger Cox. 1976. Divorced fathers. *The Family Coordinator* 25:417–428.

Heuveline, Patrick. 2005. Estimating the proportion of marriages that end in divorce. *Council on Contemporary Families* (November 15).

Hewitt, John. 1984. *Self and society: A symbolic interactionist social psychology.* 3d ed. Boston: Allyn and Bacon.

Hewlett, Sylvia. 1991. *When the bough breaks: The cost of neglecting our children.* New York: Basic Books.

Heyman, D., and F. Jeffers. 1968. Wives and retirement: A pilot study. *The Gerontologist* 10:54–56.

Higgenbotham, Elizabeth. 1981. Is marriage a priority? Class differences in marital options of educated black women. In P. Stein (ed.), *Single life: Unmarried adults in social context* (pp. 259–267). New York: St. Martin's Press.

Hill, Martha S. 1985. Patterns of time use. In F. Thomas Juster and Frank P. Stafford (eds.), *Time, goods, and well-being* (pp. 133–176). Ann Arbor, MI: Institute for Social Research.

Hill, Martha, and Michael Ponza. 1983. Poverty and welfare dependence across generations. *Economic Outlook, USA,* Summer, 61–64.

Hill, Reuben. 1949. *Families under stress.* New York: Harper and Row.

Hill, Richard, and Cynthia Negrey. 1989. Deindustrialization and racial minorities in the Great Lakes region, USA. In D. Stanley Eitzen and M. Baca Zinn (eds.), *The reshaping of America: Social consequences of a changing economy.* Englewood Cliffs, NJ: Prentice Hall.

Hill, Robert, et al., eds. 1989. *Research on the African American family: A holistic perspective and assessment of the status of African Americans.* Vol. 11. Boston: Robert Trotter Institute, University of Massachusetts.

Hill, Robert. 1972. *The strengths of black families.* New York: Emerson Hall.

Hill, Robert. 1977. *Informal adoption among black families.* Washington, DC: National Urban League Research Department.

Hill, Robert. 1993. *Research on the African American family.* Westport, CT: Auburn House.

Hirschel, J. David, and Ira Hutchison. 1989. The theory and practice of spouse abuse arrest policies. Paper presented at the annual meetings of the ASC, Reno, NV.

Hochschild, Arlie. 1971. Inside the clockwork of male careers. In F. Howe (ed.), *Women and the power to change* (pp. 47–80). New York: McGraw-Hill.

Hochschild, Arlie. 1983. *The managed heart: Commercialization of human feeling.* Berkeley: University of California Press.

Hochschild, Arlie. 1989. *The second shift: Working parents and the revolution at home.* New York: Viking.

Hochschild, Arlie. 1991. The economy of gratitude. In M. Hutter (ed.), *The family experience: A reader in cultural diversity* (pp. 499–512). New York: Macmillan.

Hochschild, Arlie. 1997. *The time bind: When work becomes home and home becomes work.* New York: Metropolitan Books.

Hochschild, Arlie. 1998. The emotional geography of work and family life. In S. Levine, James and Todd Pettinsky (eds.), *Working fathers: New strategies for balancing work and family* (pp. 518–532). New York: Addison Wesley Publishing.

Hofferth, Sandra L. 2003. Race/ethnic differences in father involvement in two parent families: Culture, context or economy? *Journal of Family Issues* 24 (2):185–216.

Hofferth, Sandra, and Deborah Phillips. 1987. Childcare in the United States, 1970–1995. *Journal of Marriage and the Family* 49:559–571.

Hoffman, Lois. 1961. Effects of maternal employment on the child. *Child Development* 32:187–97.

Hoffman, Lois. 1984. Maternal employment and the young child. In M. Perlmutter (ed.), *Minnesota symposium in child psychology.* Hillsdale, NJ: Erlbaum.

Hoffman, Lois, and J. Manis. 1979. The value of children in the U.S.: A new approach to the study of fertility. *Journal of Marriage and the Family* 41:583–596.

Hoffman, Saul, and Greg Duncan. 1988. What are the economic consequences of divorce? *Demography* 25 (4):641–645.

Hoffnung, Michele. 1989. Motherhood: Contemporary conflict for women. In J. Freeman (ed.), *Women: A feminist perspective* (pp. 147–175). Mountain View, CA: Mayfield.

Hole, Judith, and Ellen Levine. 1971. *Rebirth of feminism.* New York: Random House.

Holmes, Robyn. 1995. *How young children perceive race.* Thousand Oaks, CA: Sage.

Homans, George. 1958. Social behavior as exchange. *American Journal of Sociology* 63:597–606.

Hondagneu-Sotelo, Pierrette. 1997. Overcoming patriarchal constraints: The reconstruction of gender relations among Mexican immigrant women and men. In M. Baca Zinn, P. Hondagney-Sotelo, and M. Messner (eds.), *Through the prism of difference: Readings on sex and gender* (pp. 477–485). Boston: Allyn and Bacon.

Hooks, Bell. 1984. *Feminist theory: From margin to center.* Boston: Southend Press.

Hooyman, Nancy, and H. Kiyak. 1996. *Social gerontology.* Boston: Allyn and Bacon.

Hope, Marjorie, and James Young. 1986. *The faces of homelessness.* Lexington, MA: Lexington Books.

Hope, Tina, and Cardell Jacobson. 1995. Japanese American families: Assimilation over time. In C. Johnson (ed.), *American families: Issues in ethnicity* (pp. 145–156). New York: Garland.

Horowitz, Allen. 1985. Sons and daughters as caregivers to older parents. *Gerontologist* 25:612–617.

Horowitz, Gad, and Michael Kaufman. 1987. Male sexuality: Toward a theory of liberation. In M. Kaufman (ed.), *Beyond patriarchy: Essays by men on pleasure, power and change* (pp. 81–119). New York: Oxford University Press.

Houseknecht, Sharon. 1987. Voluntary childlessness. In M. Sussman and S. Steinmetz (eds.), *Handbook of marriage and the family* (pp. 369–396). New York: Plenum.

Houseknecht, Sharon, Suzanne Vaughn, and Anne Macke. 1984. Marital disruption among professional women: The timing of career and family events. *Social Problems* 31 (1):273–284.

Huaco, George. 1986. Ideology and general theory: The case of sociological functionalism. *Comparative Studies in Society and History* 28:34–54.

HUD. 1998. *The state of the cities.* Washington, DC: GPO.

Hughes, Everett. 1945. Dilemmas and contradictions of status. *American Journal of Sociology* 50:353–359.

Hughes, Everett. 1958. *Men and their work.* Chicago: University of Chicago Press.

Hunt, D. 1985. Parents and children in history. In P. Worsley (ed.), *Modern sociology* (pp. 195–199). New York: Penguin.

Hunt, Morton. 1974. *Sexual behavior in the seventies.* Chicago: Playboy Press.

Hunt, Morton. 1983. Marital sex. In A. Skolnick and J. Skolnick (eds.), *Family in transition.* 4th ed. (pp. 219–234). Boston: Little, Brown.

Hunter, Andrea, and Sherrill Sellers. 1998. Feminist attitudes among African American women and men. *Gender and Society* 12 (1):81–99.

Hyde, Janet, and M. Essex. 1991. *Parental leave and child care.* Philadelphia: Temple University Press.

Hymowitz, Carol, and Michaele Weissman. 1978. *A history of women in America.* New York: Bantam Books.

Igoa, Cristina. 1995. *The inner world of the immigrant child.* New York: St. Martin's Press.

Illouz, Eva. 1997. *Consuming the romantic utopia: Love and the cultural contradictions of capitalism.* Berkeley: University of California Press.

Jackson, Margaret. 1994. *The real facts of life: Feminism and the politics of sexuality, 1850–1940.* London: Taylor and Francis.

Jackson, S. 1992. Towards a historical sociology of housework: A materialist feminist analysis. *Women's Studies International Forum,* 15:153–72

Jacob, Herbert. 1989. Women and divorce reform. In L. Tilly and P. Gurin (eds.), *Women, politics and change* (pp. 482–502). New York: Russell Sage.

Jacobs, Janet. 1990. Reassessing mother blame in incest. *Signs* 15 (3):500–514.

Jacobs, Sue Ellen, Wesley Tomas, and Sabine Long. 1997. *Two-spirit people: Native American gender identity, sexuality and spirituality.* Urbana, IL: University of Illinois Press.

Jagger, Alison. 1983. *Feminist politics and human nature.* Totowa, NJ: Rowman and Allanheld.

Janiewski, Doris. 1983. Sisters under the skin: Southern working women 1880–1950. In J. Hauks and S. Skemp (eds.), *Sex, race and the role of women in the South.* Jackson: University of Mississippi Press.

Janofsky, Michael. 2000. Home prices are out of reach for many, survey finds. *New York Times,* 12 June.

Jarrett, Robin. 1994. Living poor: Family life among single parent African American women. *Social Problems* 41 (1):30–49.

Jenkins, R., and N. Westues. 1981. The nurse role in parent infant bonding. *JOGN Nursing,* March/April.

Jensen, Joan. 1991. Native American women and agriculture: A Seneca case study. In E. Dubois and V. Ruiz (eds.), *Unequal sisters* (pp. 51–65). New York: Routledge.

Jessor, S., and R. Jessor. 1975. Transition from virginity to non-virginity among youth: A social-psychological study over time. *Developmental Psychology* 11 (4):473–484.

Jesu, Carolyn. 1995. Family resemblance: How new Asian immigrants compare with the "model minority." In C. Jacobson (ed.), *American families: Issues in race and ethnicity* (pp. 157–175). New York: Garland.

Joffe, Carol. 1986. *The regulation of sexuality: Experiences of family planning workers.* Philadelphia: Temple University Press.

Johnson, Cardell. 1995. *American families: Issues in race and ethnicity.* New York: Garland.

Johnson, Glen. 2005. Mass. sets gay marriage convention date. FindLaw. *Legal News and Commentary* (August 25).

Johnson, John. 1981. Program enterprise and official cooptation in the battered women's shelter movement. *American Behavioral Scientist* 24 (6):827–842.

Johnson, John. 1991. The changing concept of child abuse and its impact on the integrity of family life. In M. Hutter (ed.), *The family experience: A reader in cultural diversity* (pp. 671–685). New York: Macmillan.

Johnson, Julia Overturf. 2005. Who's minding the kids? Child care arrangements: Winter 2002. *Current Population Reports* (October).

Johnston, David. 2005. Richest leaving even rich far behind. *New York Times,* 5 June.

Johnston, L., and J. Bachman. 1995. Monitoring the future: Questionnaire responses from the nation's high school seniors, 1975. 1995. Ann Arbor: Institute for Social Research.

Jones, Barry. 1985. *Sleepers, wake! Technology and the future of work.* New York: Oxford University Press.

Jones, Elise, et al., eds. 1986. *Teenage pregnancy in industrialized countries.* New Haven, CT: Yale University Press.

Jones, Jacqueline. 1985. *Labor of love, labor of sorrow: Black women, work, and family from slavery to the present.* New York: Basic Books.

Jones, Jacqueline. 1989. The public dimensions of the "private" life: Southern women and their families, 1865–1965. In P. Cortelyou Little and R. Vaughn (eds.), *A new perspective: Southern women's cultural history from the Civil War to civil rights* (pp. 29–40). Charlottesville, VA: Virginia Foundation for the Humanities.

Joos, Kristin E. 2003. LGBT Parents and their children. *Sociologists for Women in Society.* SWS Fact Sheets (November).

Joseph, Janice. 1997. Woman battering: A comparative analysis of black and white women. In G. Kantor and J. Jasinski (eds.), *Out of the Darkness* (pp. 161–169). Thousand Oaks, CA: Sage.

Journal of the American Medical Association (JAMA). 1989. Abortion frequency before and after Roe v. Wade. *JAMA* 262:2076.

Judd, Ted. 1978. Naturizing what we do: A review of the film "Sociobiology: Doing what comes naturally." *Science for the People* 10 (1):16–19.

Kain, Edward. 1990. *The myth of family decline: Understanding families in a world of rapid social change.* Lexington, MA: Lexington.

Kain, P. 1993. Marx, housework and alienation. *Hypatia* 8 (1):121–144.

Kaiser Family Foundation. 2004. *Daily HIV/AIDS Report.* (May 21). Menlo Park, CA.

Kaiser Family Foundation. 2005. *Media multi-tasking. Changing the Amount and Nature of Young People's Media Use* (March). Menlo Park, CA.

Kamerman, Sheila. 1991. Parental leave and infant care: U.S. and international trends and issues, 1978–1988. In J. Hyde and M. Essex (eds.), *Parental leave and children: Setting a research and policy agenda* (pp. 11–23). Philadelphia: Temple University Press.

Kamerman, Sheila, and Arthur Kahn, eds. 1989. *Privatization and the welfare state.* Princeton: Princeton University Press.

Kamerman, Sheila, and Arthur Kahn, eds. 1991. *Child care, parental leave and the under three's: Policy innovation in Europe.* New York: Auburn.

Kamerman, Sheila, and Arthur Kahn. 1978. *Family policy, government and families in 14 countries.* New York: Columbia University Press.

Kamerman, Sheila, and Arthur Kahn. 1988. *Mothers alone: Strategies for a time of change.* Dover, MA: Auburn House.

Kandel, Denise, and Gerald Lesser. 1972. *Youth in two worlds.* San Francisco: Jossey-Bass.

Kandiyoti, D. 1988. Bargaining with patriarchy. *Gender and Society* 2:274–291.

Kanowitz, Leo. 1969. *Women and the law.* Albuquerque: University of New Mexico Press.

Kanter, Rosabeth Moss. 1977a. *Men and women of the corporation.* New York: Basic Books.

Kanter, Rosabeth Moss. 1977b. *Work and family in the United States: A critical review and agenda for research and policy.* New York: Russell Sage Foundation.

Kanter, Rosabeth Moss. 1986. Wives. In J. Cole (ed.), *All American women: Lines that divide, ties that bind* (pp. 155–171). New York: Free Press.

Kasarda, John. 1985. Urban change and minority opportunities. In P. Peterson (ed.), *The new urban reality* (pp. 33–67). Washington, DC: Brookings Institution.

Kasinitz, Phillip. 1984. Gentrification and homelessness: The single room occupant and inner city revival. *The Urban and Social Change Review* 17:9–14.

Kassoff, Elizabeth. 1989. Nonmonogamy in the lesbian community. In E. Rosenblum and E. Cole (eds.), *Lesbianism: Affirming nontraditional roles* (pp. 167–182). New York: Haworth Press.

Kastenbaum, Robert. 1998. *Death, society and the human experience.* Boston: Allyn & Bacon.

Katchadourian, Herant. 1985. *Fundamentals of human sexuality.* New York: Holt Rinehart and Winston.

Katz, Jonathan. 1995. *The invention of heterosexuality.* New York: Penguin.

Katz, Michael. 1989. *The undeserving poor: From the war on poverty to the war on welfare.* New York: Pantheon.

Katz, Michael. 1990. The invention of heterosexuality. *Socialist Review* 59:7–34.

Katz, Michael. 1996. *In the shadow of the poorhouse: A social history of welfare in America.* 10th ed. New York: Basic Books.

Katzen, David. 1978. Domestic service: Women's work. In A. Stromberg and S. Harkess (eds.), *Women working: Theories and facts in perspective* (pp. 377–391). Palo Alto, CA: Mayfield.

Keller, John. 1983. *Power in America.* Chicago: Vanguard.

Keller, Teresa. 1999. Lessons in inequality: What television teaches us about women. In C. Forden, A. Hunter, and B. Burns (eds.), *Readings in the psychology of women: Dimensions of the female experience* (pp. 27–35). Boston: Allyn and Bacon.

Kellman, Jeff. 1989. Decoding MTV: Values, views and videos. *Media and Values* 46:15–16.

Kelly, Gary. 1992. *Sexuality today: The human perspective.* Guilford, CT: Dushkin.

Kelly, Joan. 1979. The doubled vision of feminist theory: A postscript to the Women of Power Conference. *Feminist Studies* 5 (1):221–240.

Kelly, Liz. 1988. How women define their experience of violence. In K. Yllo and M. Bograd (eds.), *Feminist perspectives on wife abuse* (pp. 114–132). Newbury Park, CA: Sage.

Kendell, Kate. 2003. Lesbian and gay parents in child custody and visitation disputes. *Human Rights Magazine.* American Bar Association. Vol. 30 (3).

Kennel, John, and Marshall Klaus. 1972. Maternal attachment: Importance of the first postpartum days. *New England Journal of Medicine.*

Kennel, John, and Marshall Klaus. 1976. Mother infant bonding: The impact of early separation or loss on child development.

Kephart, William. 1967. Some correlates of romantic love. *Journal of Marriage and the Family* 29:470–474.

Kessler-Harris, Alice. 1982. *Out to work: A history of wage-earning women in the United States.* New York: Oxford University Press.

Kibria, Nazlia. 1993. *Family tightrope: The changing lives of Vietnamese Americans.* Princeton, NJ: Princeton University Press.

Kibria, Nazlia. 1996. Power, patriarchy and gender conflict in the Vietnamese immigrant community. In E. Chow, D. Wilkinson, and M. Baca Zinn (eds.), *Race, class and gender: Common bonds, different voices* (pp. 206–222). Thousand Oaks, CA: Sage.

Kieran, Scott, and Michael Warren. 1993. *Perspectives on marriage: A reader.* New York: Oxford University Press.

Kimmel, Michael, and Michael Messner. 1989. *Men's lives.* New York: Macmillan.

Kimmel, Michael, and Michael Messner. 1990. Men as "gendered beings." In S. Ruth (ed.), *Issues in feminism: An introduction to women's studies* (pp. 56–58). Mountain View, CA: Mayfield.

Kincaid, P. 1982. *The omitted reality: Husband-wife violence in Ontario and policy implications for education.* Maple, Ontario: Learner's Press.

King, Wilma. 1995. *Stolen childhood: Slave youth in nineteenth century America.* Bloomington, IN: Indiana University Press.

Kinsey, Alfred. 1948. *Sexual behavior in the human male.* Philadelphia: Saunders.

Kinsey, Alfred. 1953. *Sexual behavior in the human female.* Philadelphia: Saunders.

Kitano, Harry. 1976. *Japanese Americans: The evolution of a subculture.* 2d ed. Englewood Cliffs, NJ: Prentice-Hall.

Kitano, Harry, and Roger Daniels. 1988. *Asian Americans: Emerging minorities.* Englewood Cliffs, NJ: Prentice Hall.

Klein, Ethel, Jacquelyn Campbell, Esta Soler, and Marissa Ghez. 1997. *Ending domestic violence: Changing public perceptions/halting the epidemic.* Thousand Oaks, CA: Sage.

Klein, Laura, and Lillian Ackerman, eds. 1998. *Women and power in Native North America.* Norman, OK: Oklahoma University Press.

Kloby, Jerry. 1991. Increasing class polarization in the United States: The growth of wealth and income inequality. In B. Berberoglu (ed.), *Critical perspectives in sociology: A reader* (pp. 39–54). Dubuque, IA: Kendall/Hunt.

Koball, Heather L., and Desiree Principe. 2002. *Do nonresident fathers who pay child support visit their children more?* Washington, DC: Urban Institute.

Koball, Heather, and Ayana Douglas-Hall. 2005. *Marriage is not enough to guarantee economic security.* New York: National Center for Children in Poverty.

Koch, Patricia. 1998. Contraception, abortion and population planning. In P. Koch and D. Weis (eds.), *Sexuality in America: Understanding our sexual values and behavior* (pp. 216–239). New York: Continuum.

Kochiyama, Yuri. 1998. Then came the war. In J. Ferrante and P. Brown (eds.), *The social construction of race and ethnicity in the U.S.* (pp. 99–107). New York: Longman.

Koenig, Melissa, and Kalman Rupp. 2003/2004. SSI Recipients in Households and Families with Multiple Recipients: Prevalence and Poverty Outcomes. Social Security Bulletin, Government Printing Office, Vol 65(2).

Kohlberg, Lawrence. 1966. A cognitive developmental analysis of children's sex role concepts and attitudes. In E. Maccoby (ed.), *The development of sex differences* (pp. 82–173). Stanford, CA: Stanford University Press.

Kolder, V., J. Gallagher, and M. Parsons. 1987. Court-ordered obstetrical interventions. *New England Journal of Medicine* 316 (19):1192–1196.

Kolder, Veronica, Janet Gallagher, and Michael Parsons. 1987. Court ordered obstetrical interventions. *New England Journal of Medicine* 316:1192–1196.

Komarovsky, Mirra. 1940. *The unemployed man and his family: The effect of unemployment upon the status of the man in fifty-nine families.* New York: Dryden Press.

Komarovsky, Mirra. 1953. *Women in the modern world.* Boston: Little Brown.

Kong, D. 1998. Mergers with Catholic hospitals cut access to abortion, study finds. *Boston Globe,* 7 April, A10.

Koonin, Lisa, Lilo Strauss, Camaryn Chrisman and Wilda Parker. 2000. *Abortion Surveillance—United States, 1997.* Atlanta: Center for Disease Control.

Kosmin, Barry, and Seymour Lachman. 1993. *One nation under God: Religion in contemporary American society.* New York: Crown.

Kozol, Jonathan. 1988. *Rachel and her children: Homeless families in America.* New York: Crown.

Kramer, Marian. 1988. Report on National Welfare Rights Union to members and friends. *Convention Proceedings.* Detroit, MI: September 3–5.

Krauss, Clifford. 2005. Gay marriage is extended nationwide in canada. *New York Times,* (29 June).

Kreider, Rose M. 2005. Number, Timing, and Duration of Marriages and Divorces: 2001. Survey of Income and Program Participation. (February). Washington, DC: USGPO. U.S. Census Bureau.

Kunen, James. 1996 Hawaiian courtship: Hawaiian court ruling in favor of same-sex marriage. *Time,* 16 December, 44.

Kunkel, Dale, Erica Bielly, Kirstie Farer, Edward Donnerstein, and Rena Fandrich. 2003. *Sex on TV 2003.* Santa Barbara, CA: UCSB.

Kurdek, L. 1993. The allocation of household labor in gay, lesbian and heterosexual married couples. *Journal of Social Issues* 49:127–134.

Kurz, Demie. 1989. Social science perspectives on wife abuse: Current debates and future directions. *Gender and Society* 3 (4):489–505.

Kurz, Demie. 1995. *For richer or poorer.* New York: Routledge.

Kuznets, Simon. 1971. *The economic growth of nations.* Cambridge, MA: Harvard University Press.

Laconte, Joe. 1998. I'll stand bayou: Lousiana couples choose a more muscular marriage contract. *Policy Review* 89:30–35.

Lader, Lawrence. 1991. *RU486: The pill that could end the abortion wars and why American women don't have it.* New York: Addison-Wesley.

Ladner, Joyce. 1971. *Tomorrow's tomorrow: The black woman.* Garden City, NY: Doubleday.

Lamanna, Marianne, and Agnes Reidman. 1991. *Marriages and families: Making choices and facing change.* Belmont, CA: Wadsworth.

Lamb, E., and A. Elster. 1986. Parental behavior of adolescent mothers and fathers. In A. Elster and M. Lamb (eds.), *Adolescent fatherhood* (pp. 89–106). Hillsdale, NJ: Lawrence Erlbaum.

Lamb, Michael. 1987. *The father's role: Crosscultural perspectives.* Hillsdale, NJ: Erlbaum.

Lamphere, Louise. 1985. Bringing the family to work: Women's culture on the shop floor. *Feminist Studies* 11 (3):519–540.

Lander, Eric, and Joseph Ellis. 1998. Founding father. *Nature* 396:13–14.

Landner, George. 1999. Laws that protect women should be fully enforced. In J. Torr and K. Swisher (eds.), *Violence against women* (pp. 127–132). San Diego: Greenhaven.

LaPrensa. 2004. Study finds few Latinos on television. San Diego: LaPrensa, Vol 28(14). (April 9).

LaRossa, Ralph. 1992. Fatherhood and social change. In M. Kimmel and M. Messner (eds.), *Men's lives.* 2d ed. (pp. 521–534). New York: Macmillan.

LaRossa, Ralph, and Maureen LaRossa. 1981. *Transition to parenthood.* Beverly Hills, CA: Sage.

Larson, Lyle, and J. Walter Goltz. 1989. Religious participation and marital commitment. *Review of Religious Research* 30 (4):387–400.

Larson, Michael. 1999. Home buyers may be better off sticking with old loan standards. Bankrate.com. (March 25).

Lasch, Christopher. 1977. *Haven in a heartless world: The family besieged.* New York: Basic.

Lauer, Robert, Jeanette Lauer, and Sarah Kerr. 1995. The long-term marriage: Perceptions of stability and satisfaction. In J. Hendricks (ed.), *The ties of later life* (pp. 35–41). Amityville, NY: Baywood Publishing.

Laumann, Edward, John Gagnon, Robert Michael, and Stuart Michaels. 1994. *The social organization of sexuality: Sexual practices in the United States.* Chicago: University of Chicago Press.

Lawson, Annette, and Deborah Thone. 1993. *The politics of pregnancy: Adolescent sexuality and public policy.* New Haven, CT: Yale.

Lawson, Erma Jean. 1999. Black men after divorce: How do they cope? In R. Staples (ed.), *The black family: Essays and studies* (pp. 112–127). Belmont, CA: Wadsworth.

Lawson, Erma, and Aaron Thompson. 1999. *Black men and divorce.* Thousand Oaks, CA: Sage.

Lazarovici, Laureen. 1999. Transforming low pay into a living wage. *America and Work* 4 (5):14.

Lazarre, Jane. 1986. *The mother knot.* New York: McGraw-Hill.

Leacock, Eleanor. 1973. Introduction to *Origins of the family,* by F. Engels. New York: International Publishers.

Lee, Dwight. 1986. Government policy and the distortions in family housing. In J. Peden and F. Glahe (eds.), *American family and the state* (pp. 310–320). San Francisco: Pacific Research Institute.

Lee, John. 1974. *Colours of love.* Toronto: New Press.

Lee, Sharon M. 2005. New marriages: U.S. racial and Hispanic intermarriage. *Population Bulletin* (June).

Lee, Sharon, and Barry Edmonston. 2005. New marriages, new families: U.S. racial and Hispanic intermarriage. Population Reference Bureau, 60 (2) (June).

Leicht, Kevin. 1998. Work (if you can get it) and occupations (if there are any)? *Work and Occupations* 25 (1):36–48.

Lein, Laura, M. Durham, M. Pratt, M. Schudson, R. Thomas, and H. Weiss. 1974. *Work and family life: Final report to the National Institute of Education.* Cambridge, MA: Center for the Study of Public Policy.

Lembcke, Jerry. 1991. New approaches to the problems of labor. In B. Berberoglu (ed.), *Critical perspectives in sociology* (pp. 93–103). Dubuque, IA: Kendall Hunt.

Lempert, Lora. 1999. "Other fathers: An alternative perspective on African American community caring." In R. Staples (ed.), *The black family* (pp. 189–201). Belmont, CA: Wadsworth.

Lengermann, Patricia Madoo, and Jill Niebrugge-Brantley. 1992. Contemporary feminist theory. In G. Ritzer (ed.), *Sociological theory.* 3d ed. (pp. 447–496). New York: McGraw-Hill.

Lengermann, Patricia, and Ruth Wallace. 1985. *Gender in America: Social control and social change.* Englewood Cliffs, NJ: Prentice-Hall.

Leontief, Wassily. 1983. National perspective: The definition of problems and opportunities. Paper presented at the National Academy of Engineering Symposium, June 30.

Leontief, Wassily, and Faye Duchen. 1986. *The future impact of automation on workers.* New York: Oxford University Press.

Lerner, Gerda. 1973. *Black women in white America: A documentary history.* New York: Vintage.

Lerner, Gerda. 1982. *An economic history of women in America: Women's work, the sexual division of labor, and the development of capitalism.* New York: Schocken.

Lerner, Gerda. 1986. *The creation of patriarchy.* New York: Oxford University Press.

Levin, Irene, and Marvin Sussman, eds. 1997. *Stepfamilies: History, research and policy.* New York: Haworth.

Levine, James, and Todd Pettinsky. 1997. *Working fathers: New strategies for balancing work and family.* New York: Addison Wesley Publishers.

Levitan, Sarah, Richard Belous, and Frank Gallo. 1988. *What's happening to the American family? Tensions, hopes, realities.* Baltimore: Johns Hopkins University Press.

Levta, W., J. Capitman, M. MacAdams, and R. Abraham. 1992. *Care for frail elders: Developing community solutions.* Westport, CT: Auburn House.

Lewin, Ellen. 1984. Lesbianism and motherhood: implications for child custody. In T. Darty and S. Potter (eds.), *Women-identified women* (pp. 163–183). Palo Alto, CA: Mayfield.

Lewin, Miriam. 1992. Coping with catastrophe. *Women's Review of Books* 10 (2):16–17.

Lewin, Tamar. 1991. Shadows cloud early optimism about Norplant. *New York Times,* 29 November, A1.

Lewin, Tamar. 1994. Sex in America: Faithfulness in marriage is overwhelming. *New York Times,* 7 November, A1, A18.

Lewin, Tamar. 1998. Debate distant for many having abortions. *New York Times,* 17 January, A1.

Lewontin, Richard, Steven Rose, and Leon Kamin. 1984. *Not in our genes: Ideology and human nature.* New York: Pantheon.

Lichter, D. T., D. McLaughlin, G. Kephart, and D. Landry. 1992. Race and the retreat from marriage: A shortage of marriagable men? *American Sociological Review* 57:781–799.

Lichter, Daniel. 1997. Poverty and inequality among children. In J. Hagan and K. Cook (eds.), *Annual review of sociology*. Vol. 23. (pp. 121–145). Palo Alto, CA: Annual Reviews, Inc.

Liem, Ramsay. 1988. Unemployed workers and their families: Social victims or social critics. In P. Voydanoff and L. Majka (eds.), *Families and economic distress: Coping strategies and social policy* (pp. 135–152). Beverly Hills, CA: Sage.

Lim, In-Sook. 1997. Korean immigrant women's challenge to gender inequality at home: The interplay of economic resources, gender and family. *Gender & Society* 11 (1):52–68.

Lin, J. 1991. Satisfaction and conflict in Asian correspondence marriages. *Focus* 5:1–2.

Link, Bruce. 1995. Lifetime and five year prevalence of homelessness in the United States. *American Journal of Orthopsychiatry* 3:347–354.

Lipman, A. 1961. Role conception and morale in couples in retirement. *Journal of Gerontology* 16:267–271.

Lipman-Blumen, Jean. 1984. *Gender roles and power.* Englewood Cliffs, NJ: Prentice-Hall.

Littlefield, Alice. 1989. The B.I.A. boarding school: Theories of resistance and social reproduction. *Humanity and Society* 13 (4):428–441.

Littman, Mark, ed. 1998. *Statistical portrait of U.S.: Social conditions and trends, 1998.* Lanham, MD: Bernan Press.

Lockery, Shirley. 1998. Caregiving among racial and ethnic minority elders: Family and social supports. In E. Stanford and F. Torres-Gil (eds.), *Diversity: New approaches to ethnic minority aging* (pp. 113–122). Amityville, NY: Baywood.

Longman, Philip. 1999. The cost of children. In K. Gilbert (ed.), *Marriage and family 99/00* (pp. 69–75). Guilford, CT: Dushkin.

Look. 1956. American women at home. October 16, 35.

Lopata, Helena. 1971. *Occupation housewife.* New York: Oxford University Press.

Lopata, Helena. 1973. *Widowhood in an American city.* Cambridge, MA: Schenkman.

Lopata, Helena. 1979. *Women as widows: Support systems.* New York: Elsevier.

Lopata, Helena. 1996. *Current widowhood: Myths and realities.* Thousand Oaks, CA: Sage.

Lopez, Iris. 1997. Agency and constraint: Sterilization and reproductive freedom among Puerto Rican women in New York City. In L. Lamphere, H. Ragone, and P. Zavella (eds.), *Situated lives: Gender and culture in everyday life* (pp. 157–177). New York: Routledge.

Lorber, Judith. 1984. *Women physicians.* New York: Tavistock.

Lorber, Judith. 1996. *Paradoxes of gender.* New Haven: Yale University Press.

Lorber, Judith, Rose Coser, Alice Rossi, and Nancy Chodorow. 1981. On the reproduction of mothering: A methodological debate. *Signs* 6 (3):482–514.

Loseke, Donileen. 1992. *The battered woman and shelters: The social construction of wife abuse.* Albany, NY: SUNY Press.

Loseke, Donileen, and Spencer Cahill. 1984. The social construction of deviance: Experts on battered women. *Social Problems* 31:296–310.

Lotozo, Eils. 2003. Gay, lesbian communities experiencing gayb boom. *Philadelphia Inquirer.* (28 June).

Lott, Bernice. 1987. *Women's lives: Themes and variation in gender learning.* Belmont, CA: Wadsworth.

Lowenberg, Bert, and Ruth Bogin, eds. 1976. *Black women in 19th century American life.* University Park, PA: Pennsylvania State University.

Lowry, Rich. 2005. "The coming battle of New Orleans." *National Review on-line* 9/12/2005. www.nationalreview .com/lowry

Lozada, Marlene. 1997. "Balancing act," *Vocational Education Journal* 97 (January):14.

Luepnitz, Deborah. 1982. *Child custody: A study of families after divorce.* Lexington, MA: Heath.

Luker, Kristin. 1984. *Abortion and the politics of motherhood.* Berkeley: University of California Press.

Luker, Kristin. 1992. Dubious conceptions: The controversy over teen pregnancy. In A. Skolnick and J. Skolnick (eds.), *Family in transition.* 7th ed. (pp. 160–172). New York: Harper Collins.

Luker, Kristin. 1996. *Dubious conceptions: The politics of teenage pregnancy.* Boston: Harvard University Press.

Luker, Kristin. 1999a. Why do they do it? In A. Skolnick and J. Skolnick (eds.), *Family in transition* 10th ed. (pp. 392–407). New York: Addison Wesley.

Luker, Kristin. 1999b. Constructing an epidemic. In C. Albers, *Sociology of families reader* (pp. 13–26). Thousand Oaks, CA: Sage.

Lund, Kristina. 1990. A feminist perspective on divorce therapy for women. *Journal of Divorce* 13 (3):57–67.

Lyle, Jack, and Heidi Hoffman. 1972. Children's use of television and other media. In U.S. Surgeon General's Scientific Advisory Committee on Television and Social Behavior, *Reports and paper.* Vol. 4. *Television in day-to-day life: Patterns of use* (pp. 145–181). Washington, DC: USGPO.

MacBeth, Tannis, ed. 1996. *Tuning in to young viewers: Social science perspectives on television.* Thousand Oaks, CA: Sage.

Maccoby, Eleanor, and Carol Jacklin. 1974. *The psychology of sex differences.* Stanford, CA: Stanford University Press.

MacDermid, Shelley, Ted Huston, and Susan McHale. 1990. Changes in marriage associated with the transition to parenthood: Individual differences as a function of sex-role attitudes and changes in the division of household labor. *Journal of Marriage and the Family* 52:475–486.

Machung, Anne. 1984. Word processing: Forward for business, backward for women. In K. Sacks and D. Remy (eds.), *My troubles are going to have troubles with me* (pp. 124–139). New Brunswick, NJ: Rutgers University Press.

Mack, Delores. 1978. The power relations in black families and white families. In R. Staples (ed.), *The black family* (pp. 144–149). Belmont, CA: Wadsworth.

Mackey, Richard, and Bernard O'Brien. 1995. *Lasting marriages: men and women growing together.* Westport, CT: Praeger.

MacKinnon, Catherine. 1982. Feminism, Marxism, method and the state: An agenda for theory. *Signs* 7 (Spring):515–544.

Maher, Bridget E. 2002. Background on out-of-wedlock births. Family Research Council (April 24).

Mahony, Sarah. 2003. Seeking love. *AARP Magazine.* (November–December).

Mainardi, Pat. 1970. The politics of housework. In D. Scott and B. Wishy (eds.), *America's families: A documentary history* (pp. 516–518). New York: Harper.

Mandell, Nancy. 1988. The child question: Links between women and children in families (pp. 49–84). In N. Mandell and A. Duffy (eds), *Reconstructing the Canadian family: Feminist perspectives.* Toronto: Butterworths.

Mandle, Jay. 1978. *The roots of black poverty: Southern plantation economy after the Civil War.* Durham, NC: Duke University Press.

Mann, Susan Archer. 1986. *Social change and sexual inequality: The impact of the transition from slavery to sharecropping on black women.* Memphis, TN: Memphis State University Center for Research on Women.

Manning, W. 1990. Parenting employed teenagers. *Youth & Society* 22:184–200

Marcuse, Herbert. 1966. *Eros and civilization.* New York: Beacon Press.

Marks, Carole. 1985. Black workers and the great migration north. *Phylon* 46 (2):148–161.

Marmor, Judd, ed. 1980. *Homosexual behavior.* New York: Basic Books.

Marquardt, Elizabeth. 2005. *Between two worlds: The inner lives of children of divorce.* New York: Crown.

Marshall, Sandra. 1996. Feminists and the state: A theoretical exploration. In J. Josephson (ed.), *Gender, family and state* (pp. 95–108). Lanham, MD: Rowman & Littlefield.

Martin, E. 1988. 150 apply for plan permitting tenants to save for homes. *Charlotte Observer,* 8 August, 1.

Martin, Joyce, Brady Hamilton, and Stephanie Ventura. 2001. "Births: Preliminary data for 2000" *National Vital Statistics Reports* 49 (5):1–20.

Martin, Judith. 1983. Maternal and paternal abuse of children: Theoretical and research perspectives. In D. Finkelhor et al. (eds.), *The dark side of families: Current family violence research* (pp. 293–304). Beverly Hills, CA: Sage.

Martin, Teresa, and Larry Bumpass. 1989. Recent trends in marital disruption. *Demography* 26:37–52.

Martineau, Harriet. 1834. *Illustration of political economy, the moral of many fables.* 6 vols. London: Charles Fox.

Marx, Fern. 1985. Child care. In H. McAdoo and T. Parkham (eds.), *Services to young families: Program review and policy recommendations.* Washington, DC: American Public Welfare Association.

Marx, Fern, and Michelle Seligson. 1990. Child care in the U.S. In S. Rix (ed.), *The American woman 1990–1991: A status report* (pp. 132–169). New York: W. W. Norton.

Marx, Karl. 1869/1963. *The 18th Brumaire of Louis Bonaparte.* New York: International Publishers.

Masters, William, Virgina Johnson, and R. Kolodny. 1995. *Human sexuality.* 5th ed. New York: HarperCollins.

Matsumoto, Valerie. 1990. Japanese American women during World War II. In E. Dubois and V. Ruiz (eds.), *Unequal sisters: A multicultural reader in U.S. women's history* (pp. 373–386). New York: Routledge.

Matsuoka, Jon. 1990. Differential acculturation among Vietnamese refugees. *Social Work* 35:341–345.

Mattessich, Paul, and Rueben Hill. 1987. Life cycle and family development. In M. Sussman and S. Steinmetz (eds.), *Handbook of Marriage and the family* (pp. 437–469). New York: Plenum.

Matthaei, Julie. 1982. *An economic history of women in America.* New York: Schocken.

May, Elaine. 1995. *Barren in the promised land: Childless Americans and the pursuit of happiness.* New York: Basic Books.

May, Martha. 1982. The historical problem of the family wage: The Ford Motor Company and the five dollar day. *Feminist Studies* 8 (2):399–424.

May, Rollo. 1969. *Love and will.* New York: W. W. Norton and Company.

Mayer, Susan. 1997. Indicators of economic well being and parental employment. In R. Hauser, B. Brown, and W. Prosser (eds.), *Indicators of children's well-being* (pp. 237–257). New York: Russell Sage.

McAdoo, John. 1988. Roles of black fathers in the socialization of black children. In H. McAdoo (ed.), *Black families.* Newbury Park, CA: Sage.

McChesney, K. 1986. New findings on homeless families. Family *Professional* 1 (2):93–98.

McClennan, Joan. 2005. Domestic violence between same-gender partners. *Journal of Interpersonal Violence,* 20 (2):149–154.

McCloskey, Laura. 1996. Socioeconomic and coercive power in families. *Gender & Society* 10 (4): 449–463.

McCubbin, Hamilton, Constance Joy, A. Cauble, Joan Comeau, Joan Patterson, and Richard Needle. 1980. Family stress and coping: A decade review. *Journal of Marriage and the Family* 42:855–871.

McElroy, Wendy. 2005. Spousal rape case sparks old debate. *Fox News* (16 February).

McGuire, Meredith. 1992. *Religion: The social context.* 3rd ed. Belmont, CA: Wadsworth.

McKinlay, D. 1964. *Social class and family life.* New York: Free Press.

McKintosh, Kenneth. 2006. *Latinos Today.* Philadelphia: Mason Crest.

McLanahan, Sara. 1983. Family structure and stress: A longitudinal study of two-parent and female-headed families. *Journal of Marriage and the Family* 45:347–357.

McLanahan, Sara, and Julia Adams. 1987. Parenthood and psychological well-being. *Annual Review of Sociology* 13:237–257.

McLaurin, Melton. 1992. *Celia: A slave.* Athens, GA: University of Georgia Press.

McNall, Scott, and Sally McNall. 1983. *Plains families: Exploring sociology through social history.* New York: St. Martin's.

Mead, George Herbert. 1934/1962. *Mind, self and society: From the standpoint of a social behaviorist.* Chicago: University of Chicago Press.

Mead, Margaret. 1935. *Sex and temperament in three primitive societies.* New York: Dell.

Mednick, Martha. 1992. Single mothers: A review and critique of current literature. In A. Skolnick and J. Skolnick (eds.), *Family in transition.* 7th ed. (pp. 363–378). New York: Harper Collins.

Medrich, Elliott, Judith Roizan, Victor Rubin, and Stuart Buckley. 1982. *The serious business of growing up.* Berkeley: University of California Press.

Mehl, Lewis, Gail Peterson, Michael Whitt, and Warren Hawes. 1980. Evaluation of outcomes of non-nurse midwives: Matched comparisons with physicians. *Women and Health* 5:17–29.

Meissner, Martin, E. W. Humphries, S. M. Meis, and W. J. Scheu. 1975a. No exit for wives: Sexual division of labour and the cumulation of household demands. *Canadian Review of Sociology and Anthropology* 12:424–439.

Meissner, Martin, E. W. Humphries, S. M. Meis, and W. J. Scheu. 1975b. *The sociology of housework.* New York: Pantheon Books.

Meissner, Martin, E. W. Humphries, S. M. Meis, and W. J. Scheu. 1980. Prologue: Reflections on the study of household labor. In S. Berk (ed.), *Women and household labor* (pp. 7–14). Beverly Hills, CA: Sage.

Mercer, R. 1986. *First time motherhood: Experiences from the teens to the forties.* New York: Springer.

Messner, Michael. 1998. Boyhood, organized sports, and the construction of masculinities. In M. Kimmel (ed.), *Men's lives.* 4th ed. (pp. 109–121). Boston: Allyn and Bacon.

Meyer, Agnes. 1950. Women aren't men. *Atlantic Monthly* 186:32.

Meyer, Daniel, and Judi Barfield. 1996. Compliance with child support orders in divorce cases. *Journal of Marriage and the Family* 58 (1):201–212.

Meyer, H. 1992. The billion dollar epidemic. *American Medical News,* 6 January.

Meyers, Daniel, and Seven Garasky. 1991. *Custodial fathers: Myths, realities and child support policy.* U.S. Department of Health and Human Services. Washington, DC: USGPO.

Meyersohn, Rolf. 1963. Changing work and leisure routines. In E. Smigel (ed.), *Work and leisure: A contemporary social problems* (pp. 97–106). New Haven, CT: College and University Press.

Michael, Robert, John Gagnon, Edward Laumann, and Gina Kolata. 1994. *Sex in America: A definitive survey.* Boston: Little Brown.

Middleton, R., and S. Putney. 1960. Dominance in decisions in the family: Race and class differences. *American Journal of Sociology* 65 (6):605–609.

Mies, Maria. 1983. Toward a methodology for feminist research. In G. Bowles and R. Klein (eds.), *Theories of women's studies* (pp. 117–139). London: Routledge and Kegan Paul.

Mifflin, Larie. 1998. Planned TV channels raise gender stereotype worries. *New York Times,* 2 November.

Milkman, Ruth. 1976. Women's work and economic crisis: Some lessons of the Great Depression. *Radical Review of Political Economy* 8:73–97.

Milkman, Ruth. 1991. Gender at work: The sexual division of labor during World War II. In L. Kerber and J. De Hart (eds.), *Women's America.* 3d ed. (pp. 437–450). New York: Oxford University Press.

Miller, C. 1987. Qualitative differences among gender-stereotyped toys: Implications for cognitive and social development in girls and boys. *Sex Roles* 16:473–488.

Miller, Dorothy. 1990. *Women and social welfare: A feminist analysis.* New York: Praeger.

Miller, JoAnn, and Amy Krull. 1997. Controlling domestic violence: Victim resources and police intervention. In G. Kantor and J. Jasinski (eds.), *Out of the darkness* (pp. 235–252). Thousand Oaks, CA: Sage.

Millett, Kate. 1970. *Sexual politics.* Garden City, NY: Doubleday.

Millman, Marcia. 1991. *Warm hearts and cold cash: The intimate dynamics of families and money.* New York: Free Press.

Mills, C. Wright. 1956. *The power elite.* London: Oxford University Press.

Mills, C. Wright. 1959. *The sociological imagination.* London: Oxford University Press.

Mills, Trudy. 1985. The assault on the self: Stages in coping with battering husbands. *Qualitative Sociology* 8:2.

Mincer, Jacob. 1962. Labor force participation of married women. In *National Bureau of Economic Research, Aspects of Labor Economics* (pp. 63–97). Princeton, NJ: Princeton University Press.

Mink, Gwendolyn. 1990. The lady and the tramp: Gender, race and the origins of the welfare state. In L. Gordon (ed.), *Women, the state and welfare* (pp. 92–122). Madison: University of Wisconsin Press.

Mintz, Stephen, and Susan Kellogg. 1988. *Domestic revolutions: A social history of American family life.* New York: Free Press.

Mirowsky, John, and Catherine Ross. 1989. *Social causes of psychological distress.* New York: Aldine deGruyter.

Mischel, Harriet, and Robert Fuhr. 1988. Maternal employment: Its psychological effects on children and their families. In S. Dorribusch and M. Strober (eds.), *Feminism, children and the new families* (pp. 191–211). New York: Guilford Press.

Mishel, Lawrence, and Jared Bernstein. 1992. *The state of working America, 1992–1993.* Washington, DC: Economic Policy Institute.

Mishel, Lawrence, Jared Bernstein, and Heather Boushey. 2003. *State of Working Poor: 2002–2003.* Ithaca: Cornwell University Press.

Mishel, Lawrence, Jared Bernstein, and John Schmitt. 1997. *The state of working America 1996–1997.* Armonk, NY: Economic Policy Institute.

Mishel, Lawrence, Jared Bernstein, and John Schmitt. 2001. *The state of working America 2000–2001.* Ithaca, NY: Cornell University Press.

Mishel, Lawrence, Jared Bernstein, and Sylvia Allegretto. 2005. *The State of Working America 2004–2005.* Ithaca: Cornwell University Press.

Mitchell, Juliet. 1984. *Women: The longest revolution.* New York: Pantheon.

Mitchell, Juliet. 1986. Reflections on twenty years of feminism. In J. Mitchell and A. Oakley (eds.), *What is feminism: A re-examination* (pp. 34–48). New York: Pantheon.

Moberg, David. 2005. "Class Matters" In These Times. Posted on June 30, 2005. Printed on July 23, 2005. http://www.alternet.org/story/23250/ (accessed May 29, 2006).

Mochizuki, K. 1987. I think Oriental women are just great. *International Examiner,* 7 May, 13.

Modell, John, and Tamara Haraven. 1978. Urbanization and the malleable household: An examination of boarding and lodging in American families. In M. Gordon (ed.), *The American family in social historical perspective* (pp. 51–68). New York: St. Martin's Press.

Moen, Phyllis. 1989. *Working parents: Gender roles and public policies in Sweden.* Madison: University of Wisconsin Press.

Moen, Phyllis. 1992. *Women's two roles.* Westport, CT: Auburn House.

Moen, Phyllis, and Alvin Schorr. 1987. Families and social policies. In M. Sussman and S. Steinmetz (eds.), *Handbook of marriage and the family* (pp. 795–813). New York: Plenum.

Moore, Charles, David Sink, and Patricia Hoban-Moore. 1988. The politics of homelessness. *PS Political Science and Politics* 21:57–63.

Moore, David. 1994. Approval of husband slapping wife continues to decline. *The Gallup Poll Monthly,* February, 2.

Moore, David. 1995. Three million children victims of physical abuse last year. *Gallup Poll Monthly,* December, 4–15.

Moore, David. 1996. Public opposes gay marriages: Major generational, gender gaps on homosexuality issue. *Gallup Poll Monthly,* April, 19–21.

Moore, Kristin, and Isabel Sawhill. 1984. Implications of women's employment for home and family life. In A. Stromberg and S. Harkess (eds.), *Women working: Theories and facts in perspective* (pp. 201–223). Palo Alto, CA: Mayfield.

Moore, Thomas. 1996. *The disposable workforce: Worker displacement and employment instability in America.* New York: Aldine de Gruyter.

Morgan, David. 1975. *Social theory and the family.* Boston: Routledge and Kegan Paul.

Morgan, David. 1985. *The family, politics and social theory.* Boston: Routledge and Kegan Paul.

Morgan, Edmund. 1978. The puritans and sex. In M. Gordon (ed.), *The American family in social-historical perspective.* 2d ed. (pp. 363–373). New York: St. Martin's Press.

Morgan, L. 1965. *Houses and houselife of the American aborigines.* Chicago: University of Chicago Press.

Morr, Mary, and Paul A. Mongeau. 2004. First date expectations: The impact on sex of initiator, alcohol consumption, and relationship type. *Communication Research,* 31 (1):3–35. Sage Publication.

Morris, Betsy. 1998. It's her job too: Lorna Wendt's $20 million divorce case is the shot heard 'round the water cooler. *Fortune* 137 (2):64–73.

Mortimer, J. 1976. Social class, work and the family: Some implications of the father's occupation for familial relationships and son's career decisions. *Journal of Marriage and the Family* 38:241–256.

Mortimer, J., and D. Kumka. 1982. A further examination of the occupational linkage hypothesis. *Sociological Quarterly* 23 (Winter):3–16.

Mortimer, Jeylan, and Michael Finch. 1996. Work, family and adolescent development. In M. Jelan and M. Finch (eds.), *Adolescents, work and family: An intergenerational developmental analysis* (pp. 1–24). Thousand Oaks, CA: Sage.

Mosher, William D., Anjani Chandra, and Jo Jones. 2005. Sexual Behavior and Selected Health Measures: Men and Women 15–44 Years of Age, United States, 2002. Advance Data from Vital and Health Statistics, No. 362, (September 15). Atlanta, GA: CDC.

Moyers, Bill. 2005. Mugging of the American dream. June 6, 2005. www.alternet.org (accessed May 29, 2006).

Moynihan, Daniel. 1965. *The Negro family: The case for national action.* Office of Policy Planning and Research, U.S. Department of Labor. Washington, DC: GPO.

Mulroy, Elizabeth. 1995. *The new uprooted: single mothers in urban life.* San Diego: Greenwood.

Murdock, George. 1949. *Social structure.* New York: Macmillian.

Murray, Charles. 1984. *Losing ground: American social policy, 1950–1980.* New York: Basic.

Murstein, Bernard, and C. Holden. 1979. Sexual behavior and correlates among college students. *Adolescence* 4 (56):625–639.

Musick, Judith. 1993. *Young, poor and pregnant: The psychology of teenage motherhood.* New Haven, CT: Yale.

Myers, Kristin, Cynthia Anderson, and Barabar Risman. 1998. *Feminist foundations: Toward transforming sociology.* Thousand Oaks, CA: Sage.

Myers, S. 1979. Child abuse and the military community. *Military Medicine* 144:23–25.

Nabakov, Peter. 1991. *Native American testimony: A chronicle of Indian-white relations from prophecy to the present, 1492–1992.* New York: Viking.

Nagata, Donna. 1991. Transgenerational impact of the Japanese-American internment: Clinical issues in working with children of former internees. *Psychotherapy* 28:121–128.

Nakano, Mei. 1990. *Japanese American women: Three generations, 1890–1990.* Berkeley: Mina Press.

Naples, Nancy. 1991. Contradictions in the gender subtext of the war on poverty: The community work and resistance of women from low income communities. *Social Problems* 38 (3):316–332.

Naples, Nancy. 1992. Activist mothering: Crossgenerational continuity in the community work of women from low-income urban neighborhoods. *Gender and Society* 6 (3):441–463.

Naples, Nancy. 1996. Activist mothering: Cross-generational continuity in the community work of women from low income urban neighborhoods. In E. Chow, D. Wilkinson, and M. Baca Zinn (eds.), *Race, class and gender: Common bonds, different voices* (pp. 223–246). Thousand Oaks, CA: Sage.

National Adoption Clearinghouse. 2005. How many children have gay parents in the U.S.? www.about.com accessed July 29, 2006.

National Alliance for Caregiving and AARP. 2004. Caregiving in the U.S. caregiving.org

National Asian Pacific American Legal Consortium. 2005. "Report shows mixed results for increased diversity in Primetime TV." www.advancingequality.org accessed May 29, 2006

National Center for Health Statistics. 1995. Advance report of final divorce statistics, 1989 and 1990. *Monthly Vital Statistics Reports* 43 (9):4.

National Center for Health Statistics. 1997. New report documents trends in childbearing. Reproductive Health. Atlanta, GA. (June).

National Center for Housing Policy. 2005. *The housing landscape for America's working families, 2005.* Washington, DC: NCHP.

National Center for Victims of Crime. 1992. Rape in America. Arlington, VA.

National Committee for Pay Equity. 2006. "Gender wage gap by selected occupations." www.infoplease.com

National Council for the Prevention of Child Abuse (NCPCA). 1991. *Current trends in child abuse reporting and fatalities: The results of the 1990 annual fifty state survey.* Chicago: NCPCA.

National Institutes of Health. 2005. *Teen birthrate continues to decline.* National Institute of Child Health and Human Development. (July 20).

National Law Center on Homelessness and Poverty. *Key data concerning homeless person in America.* 2004. (July).

National Urban League. 2005. Sunday morning apartheid: A diversity study of the Sunday morning talk shows. Policy Institute (August).

National Welfare Rights Union. 1988. *Up and out of poverty.* Convention Report, First Annual Convention. Detroit, September 3–5.

Nature. 1998. DNA testing of Thomas Jefferson and Sally Hemings. November 5.

NC NOW. 1992. Sharon Kowalski is home. *Nownews,* Spring, 6.

Nee, Victor, and Herbert Wong. 1985. Asian Americans socioeconomic achievement: The strength of the family bond. *Sociological Perspectives* 28:281–306.

Negrey, Cynthia. 1990. Contingent work and the rhetoric of autonomy. *Humanity and Society* 14 (1):16–33.

New York Times. 1992. Excerpts from vice president's speech on cities and poverty. *New York Times* 20 May, A20.

New York Times. 1993. *Special Report: The downsizing of America.* New York: Random House.

Newman, Elana, Danny Kaloupek, Terence Keane, and Susan Folstein. 1997. Ethical issues in trauma research: The evolution of an empirical model for decision making. In G. Kantor and J. Jasinski (eds.), *Out of the darkness* (pp. 271–281). Thousand Oaks, CA: Sage.

Newman, Katherine. 1988. *Falling from grace: The experience of downward mobility in the American middle class.* New York: Random House.

Newman, Maria. 1992. Lawmaker from riot zone insists on a new role for black politicians. *New York Times* 19 May, A18.

Newport, Frank. 1996. Americans generally happy with their marriages. *The Gallup Poll Monthly,* September, 18–22.

Newsweek. 1997. Parenting and Child Care (29 September).

Nielsen Media Research. 2005. Nielsen Reports Americans watch TV at record levels (September).

Nieves, Evelyn, and Ann Tyson. 2005. Statistics show a near 50% drop in military discharges of homosexuals. *Detroit News,* (12 February).

Nieves, Evelyn. 2006. "S.D. abortion bill takes aim at 'Roe'" *Washington Post.* 12, February A1.

Nock, Stephen. 1987. *Sociology of the family.* Englewood Cliffs, NJ: Prentice-Hall.

Noriega, Jorge. 1992. American Indian education in the U.S.: Indoctrination for subordination to colonialism. In M. Jaimes (ed.), *The state of Native America: Genocide, colonization, and resistance* (pp. 371–402). Boston: Southend Press.

Norlicht, S. 1979. Effects of stress on the police officer and family. *New York State Journal of Medicine* 79:400–401.

Norsigian, Judy. 1990. RU-486. In M. Fried (ed.), *From abortion to reproductive freedom* (pp. 197–203). Boston: South End Press.

NPR. 2002. Housing first, women/children fleeing abuse. NPR Special Report. NPR News.

Nulty, Peter. 1987. Pushed out at 45: Now what? *Fortune* 115 (5):26–30.

Nye, F. Ivan. 1974. Emerging and declining family roles. *Journal of Marriage and the Family* 36: 238–245.

O'Brien, Conor Cruise. 1998. *The long affair: Thomas Jefferson and the French Revolution.* Chicago: University of Chicago Press.

O'Bryant, Shirley, and Robert Hansson. 1995. Widowhood. In R. Blieszner and V. Bedford (eds.), *Handbook of aging and the family* (pp. 440–458). Westport, CT: Greenwood.

O'Connor, James. 1973. *Fiscal crisis of the state.* New York: St. Martin's Press.

O'Sullivan, Chris. 1998. Ladykillers: Similarities and divergences of masculinities in gang rape and wife battery. In

L. Bowker (ed.), *Masculinities and violence* (pp. 82–110). Thousand Oaks, CA: Sage.

O'Toole, Laura and Jessica Schiffman. 1997. *Gender Violence.* New York: NYU Press.

Oakley, Ann. 1974. *The sociology of housework.* New York: Pantheon.

Oakley, Ann. 1981a. Interviewing women: A contradiction in terms. In H. Roberts (ed.), *Doing feminist research* (pp. 30–61). London: Routledge and Kegan Paul.

Oakley, Ann. 1981b. *Subject women.* New York: Pantheon.

OECD. 2004. Social expenditure data base (SOCX) 1980-2001. www.oecd.org. (May 29, 2006).

Off Our Backs. 1992. Child victims of sexual abuse: A bill of rights. *Off Our Backs* 22 (5):1.

Ogbu, John. 1978. *Minority education and caste: The American system in cross cultural perspective.* New York: Academic Press.

Okihiro, G., M. Alquezola, D. Rony, and K. Wong, eds. 1995. *Privileging positions: The state of Asian American studies.* Pullman, WA: Washington State University Press.

Ollman, Bertell. 1976. *Alienation.* 2d ed. Cambridge: Cambridge University Press.

Oppenheimer, Valerie. 1969. *The female labor force in the U.S.: Demographic and economic factors governing its growth and changing composition.* Berkeley: University of California Population Monograph Series 5.

Orenstein, Peggy. 2001. "Will your child suffer if you work?" *Redbook* (August):54–57.

Osmond, Marie. 1987. Radical-critical sociology. In M. Sussman and S. Stienmetz (ed.), *Handbook of marriage and the family* (pp. 103–124). New York: Plenum Press.

Ostrander, Susan. 1984. *Women of the upper class.* Philadelphia: Temple University Press.

Oxford Analytica. 1986. *America in perspective.* Boston: Houghton Mifflin.

Padgug, Robert, ed. 1979. Special issue on sexuality. *Radical History Review,* Spring/Summer.

Pagelow, Mildred. 1981. *Woman battering: Victims and their experience.* Beverly Hills, CA: Sage.

Palmer, John, and Isabel Sawhill. 1984. *The Reagan record.* Cambridge, MA: Ballinger.

Pardo, Mary. 1990. Mexican American women grassroots community activists: The Mothers of East Los Angeles. *Frontiers* 11 (1):1–7.

Pardo, Mary. 1998. *Mexican American women activists: Identity and resistance in two Los Angeles communities.* Philadelphia: Temple University Press.

Parker, Robert. 1991. Urban social problems in the United States: Issues in urban political economy. In B. Berberoglu (ed.), *Critical perspectives in sociology: A reader* (pp. 169–184). Dubuque, IA: Kendall/Hunt.

Parsons, Talcott. 1955. The American family: Its relation to personality and to the social structure. In T. Parsons and R. Bales (eds.), *Family socialization and interaction process* (pp. 3–33). Glencoe, IL: Free Press.

Pascal, Gillian. 1986. *Social policy: A feminist analysis.* New York: Tavistock.

Patterson, C. 1995. Families and the lesbian baby boom: Parents' division of labor and childrens' adjustments. *Developmental Psychology* 31:115–163.

Patterson, Charlotte. 1992. Children of lesbian and gay parents. *Child Development* 63 (October):1025–1942.

Patterson, Charlotte, and Richard Redding. 1996. Lesbian and gay families with children. *Journal of Social Issues* 52 (Fall):29–50.

Patterson, James. 1981. *America's struggle against poverty, 1900–1980.* Cambridge, MA: Harvard University Press.

Patzer Gordon. 1985. *The physical attractiveness phenomenon.* New York: Plenum Press.

Pearce, Diana. 1978. The feminization of poverty: Women, work and welfare. *Urban and Social Change* 2:24–36.

Pearce, Diana. 1989. Farewell to alms. In J. Freeman (ed.), *Women: A feminist perspective.* 4th ed. (pp. 493–506). Mountain View, CA: Mayfield.

Pecora. Norma. 1998. *The business of children's entertainment.* New York: Guilford Press.

Pellman, Julie. 1995. Widowhood in elderly women: Exploring its relationship to community integration, hassles, stress, social support and social support seeking. In J. Hendricks (ed.), *The ties of later life* (pp. 75–85). Amityville, NY: Baywood.

Peplau, Letitia, and Susan Campbell. 1989. The balance of power in dating and marriage. In J. Freeman (ed.), *Woman: A feminist perspective* (pp. 121–137). Mountain View, CA: Mayfield.

Perdue, C., and T. Barden. 1976. *Weevils in the wheat: Interviews with Virginia ex-slaves.* Charlottesville, VA: University of Virginia Press.

Perrin, Ellen C. 2002. Technical report: Coparent or second parent adoption by same-sex parents. *Pediatrics.* 102 (2) (February).

Perry, Charlotte. 1999. Extended family support among older black females. In R. Staples (ed.), *The black family,* 6th ed. (pp. 70–76). Belmont, CA: Wadsworth.

Perucci, Carolyn, and Dena Targ. 1988. Effects of plant closings on marriage and family life. In P. Voydanoff and L. Majka (eds.), *Families and economic distress: Coping strategies and public policy* (pp. 55–72). Beverly Hills, CA: Sage.

Petchesky, Rosalind. 1990. *Abortion and woman's choice: The state, sexuality and reproductive freedom.* Boston: Northeastern University Press.

Peters, Marie. 1985. Racial socialization of young black children. In H. McAdoo and J. McAdoo (eds.), *Black children: Social, educational and parental environments* (pp. 159–173). Newbury Park, CA: Sage.

Peters, Marie. 1988. Parenting in black families with young children: A historical perspective. In H. McAdoo (ed.), *Black families.* 2d ed. (pp. 228–241). Newbury Park, CA: Sage.

Peterson, Paul. 1985. Introduction, technology, race and urban policy. In P. Peterson (ed.), *The new urban reality* (pp. 1–35). Washington, DC: Brookings Institute.

Pew Internet and American Life Project. 2005. May-June 2005 Tracking Survey. Washington, D.C. www.pewinternet.org (accessed May 29, 2006).

Pew Research Center 2003. Religious beliefs underpin opposition to homosexuality: Republicans unified, Democrats split on gay marriage (November 18).

Pew Research Center. 2005. Pew forum on religion and public life (July).

Peyser, Mark. 1997. "Time bind? What time bind?" *Newsweek* (May 12).

Philipson, Ilene. 1982. Heterosexual antagonisms and the politics of mothering. *Socialist Review* 66:55–77.

Phillips, Julie A., and Meagan M. Sweeney. 2005. Premarital cohabitation and marital disruption among White, Black, and Mexican American women. *Journal of Marriage and the Family.* (May) 67 (2):296–314.

Phillips, Kevin. 1990. *The politics of rich and poor: Wealth and the American electorate in the Reagan aftermath.* New York: HarperCollins

Phillips, Randy. 1994. Spiritual purity. In A. Hanssen (ed.), *Seven promises of a promise keeper* (pp. 73–80). Colorado Springs, CO: Focus on the Family.

Phoenix, Ann. 1991. *Young mothers.* Cambridge, MA: Basil Blackwell.

Pilkington, Constance, Whitney Kern, and David Indest. 1994. Is safer sex necessary with a "safe" partner? Condom use and romantic feelings. *Journal of Sex Research* 31:203–210.

Pinson-Milburn, Nancy, Ellen Fabian, Nancy Schlossberg, and Marjorie Pyle. 1999. Grandparents raising grandchildren. In L. Smith (ed.), *Selected readings in marriage and family* (pp. 190–196). San Diego, CA: Greenhaven Press.

Pitzer, Claire G., and Benyam Tsehaye. 2003. Federal budget estimates, fiscal year 2004. *Survey of Current Business.* U.S. Department of Commerce. (March). Washington, DC: USGPO.

Piven, Francis Fox. 1990. Ideology and the state: Women, power and the welfare state. In L. Gordon (ed.), *Women, the state and welfare* (pp. 250–264). Madison: University of Wisconsin Press.

Piven, Francis Fox, and Richard Coward. 1982. *The new class war: Reagan's attack on the welfare state and its consequences.* New York: Pantheon.

Pizzey, Erin. 1974. *Scream quietly or the neighbors will hear you.* New York: Penguin.

Pleck, Elizabeth. 1991. *An historical overview of American gender roles and relations from precolonial times to the present.* Wellesley, MA: Wellesley College Center for Research on Women.

Pleck, Elizabeth, Joseph Pleck, M. Grossman, and Pauline Bart. 1977–1978. The battered data syndrome: A comment on Steinmetz' article. *Victimology: An International Journal* 2:680–684.

Pleck, Joseph. 1983. Husband's paid work and family roles: Current research issues. In H. Lopata and J. Pleck (eds.), *Research in the interweave of social roles.* Vol. 3. Greenwich, CT: JAI Press.

Pleck, Joseph. 1987. The theory of male sex role identity: Its rise and fall, 1936 to the present. In H. Brod (ed.), *The making of masculinities* (pp. 21–38). Boston: Allen and Unwin.

Pleck, Joseph. 1992. *Feminist methods in social research.* New York: Oxford University Press.

Pleck, Joseph, Graham Staines, and Linda Lang. 1980. Conflicts between work and family. *Monthly Labor Review,* March, 29–31.

Pogrebin, Letty. 1983. *Family politics: Love and power on an intimate frontier.* New York: McGraw-Hill.

Pohlman, E. 1969. *The psychology of birth planning.* Cambridge, MA: Shenkman.

Poitier, Linda. 1999. Universal screening for a universal problem. In L. Gerdes (ed.), *Battered women* (pp. 41–48). San Diego: Greenhaven.

Polatnick, Margaret. 1983. Why men don't rear children. In J. Trebilcot (ed.), *Mothering* (pp. 21–40). Totawa, NJ: Rowman and Allanheld.

Polikoff, Nancy. 1983. Gender and child custody determinations: Exploding the myths. In I. Diamond (ed.), *Families, politics and public policy: A feminist dialogue on women and the state* (pp. 183–202). New York: Longman.

Polikoff, Nancy. 1990. Why are mothers losing: A brief analysis of criteria used in child custody determination. *Women's Rights Law Reports.* (Spring/Fall): 175–184.

Pollin, Robert. 1990. Borrowing more, buying less. *Dollars and Sense* 156 (May):7.

Pollin, Robert, and Stephanie Luce. 1998. *The living wage: Building a fair economy.* New York: New Press.

Popple, Philip, and Leslie Leighninger. 1993. *Social work, social welfare, and American society.* Boston: Allyn and Bacon.

Potuchek, J. 1992. Employed wives' orientation to breadwinning: A gender, theory analysis. *Journal of Marriage and the Family* 54:548–558.

Potuchek, Jean. 1997. *Who supports the family? Gender and breadwinning in dual-earner marriages.* Stanford: Stanford University Press.

Powell, Lawrence, Kenneth Branco, and John Williamson. 1996. *The senior rights movement: Framing the policy debate in America.* New York: Twayne Publishers.

President's Commission on Privatization. 1988. *Privatization: Toward more effective government.* Washington, DC: President's Commission on Privatization.

Press, Julie, and Eleanor Townsley. 1998. Wives' and husbands' housework reporting: Gender, class and social desirability. *Gender and Society* 12 (2):188–218

Presser, Harriet. 1998. Toward a 24 hour economy: The U.S. experience and implications for the family. In D. Vannoy and P. Dubeck (eds.), *Challenges for work and family in the twenty first century* (pp. 39–48). New York: Aldine de Gruyter.

Ptacek, James. 1988. Why do men batter wives? In K. Ylto and M. Bograd (eds.), *Feminist perspectives of wife abuse* (pp. 133–157). Beverly Hills, CA: Sage.

Pupo, Norene. 1988. Preserving patriarchy: Women, the family and the state. In N. Mandell and A. Duffy (eds.), *Reconstructing the Canadian family* (pp. 207–238). Toronto: Buttersworth.

Purrington, Beverly. 1980. Effects of children on their parents: Parents' perceptions. Ph.D. dissertation, Michigan State University.

Quadagno, Jill. 1994. *The color of welfare.* New York: Oxford University Press.

Quinn, Michelle. 2005. In it's infancy. *Mercury News,* (1 July).

Raabe, Phyllis. 1998. Being a part-time manager: One way to combine family and career. In D. Vannoy and P. Dubeck (eds.), *Challenges for work and family in the twenty first century* (pp. 81–92). New York: Aldine de Gruyter.

Radhill, Samual. 1968. A history of child abuse and infanticide. In C. Kempe (ed.), *The battered child.* Chicago: University of Chicago Press.

Rainwater, Lee, and William Yancey. 1967. *The Moynihan Report and the politics of the controversy.* Cambridge, MA: MIT Press.

Raman, Paula. 2000. Life's work: Generational attitudes toward work and life integration. Cambridge, MA: Public Policy Center.

Ramey, C., D. Bryant, and T. Suarez. 1985. Preschool compensatory education and the modifiability of intelligence: A critical review. In D. Detterman (ed.), *Current topics in human intelligence* (pp. 247–296). Norwood, NJ: Ablex.

Ramos, Reyes. 1979. The Mexican American: Am I who they say I am? In A. Trejo (ed.), *The Chicanos as we see ourselves* (pp. 49–66). Tucson, AZ: University of Arizona Press.

Randle, M. 1951. Iroquois women, then and now. In W Fenton (ed.), *Symposium on local diversity in Iroquois culture.* Washington, DC: Bureau of American Ethnology, Bulletin 149.

Rank, Mark. 1989. Fertility among women on welfare. *American Sociological Review* 54 (April).

Rapp, Rayna. 1982. Family and class in contemporary America: Notes toward an understanding of ideology. In B. Thorne with M. Yalom (eds.), *Rethinking the family: Some feminist questions* (pp. 168–187). New York: Longman.

Rapp, Rayna, Ellen Ross, and Renate Bridenthal. 1979. Examining family history. *Feminist Studies* 5 (1):172–200.

Red Horse, John. 1980. Family structure and value orientation in American Indians. *Social Casework: The Journal of Contemporary Social Work* 59:462–467.

Reese, Ellen. 1996. Maternalism and political mobilization: How California's postwar child care campaign was won. *Gender & Society* 10 (5):566–589.

Reich, Wilhelm. 1945. *The sexual revolution.* New York: Farrar, Straus and Giroux.

Reinharz, Shulamit. 1992. *Feminist methodology in social research.* New York: Oxford University Press.

Reinisch, June. 1990. *The Kinsey Institute new report on sex: What you must know to be sexually literate.* New York: St. Martin's Press.

Reiss, Ira. 1986. *Journey into sexuality: An exploratory voyage.* Englewood Cliffs, NJ: Prentice-Hall.

Reissman, Catherine. 1991. *Divorce talk: Women and men make sense of personal relationships.* New Brunswick, NJ: Rutgers University Press.

Reiter, Rayna, ed. 1975. *Toward an anthropology of women.* New York: Monthly Review Press.

Renvoize, Jean. 1985. *Going solo: Single mothers by choice.* Boston: Routledge and Kegan Paul.

Renzetti, Claire. 1992. *Violent betrayal: Partner abuse in lesbian relationships.* Newbury Park, CA: Sage.

Renzetti, Claire. 1997. Confessions from a reformed positivist. In M. Schwartz (ed.), *Researching sexual violence: Methodological and personal perspectives* (pp. 131–143). Thousand Oaks, CA: Sage.

Renzetti, Claire, and Daniel Curran. 1992. *Social problems: Society in crisis.* 2d ed. Boston: Allyn and Bacon.

Renzetti, Claire, and Daniel Curran. 1998. *Women, men and society.* 4th ed. Boston: Allyn & Bacon.

Renzetti, Claire, and Daniel Curran. 1999. *Women and men in society.* 4th ed. Boston: Allyn and Bacon.

Reuters. 2005. Bush Pushes Questionable Abstinence Programs (March 22).

Reyes, L., and L. Waxman. 1986. *The continued growth of hunger, homelessness and poverty in America's cities, 1986.* U.S. Conference on Mayors. Washington, DC: USGPO.

Rheingold, H., and K. Cook. 1975. The content of boys' and girls' rooms as an index of parents' behavior. *Child Development* 46:459–463.

Rhode, Deborah. 1989. *Justice and gender, sex discrimination and the law.* Cambridge, MA: Harvard University Press.

Ribbens, Jane. 1994. *Mothers and their children: A feminist sociology of childrearing.* Thousand Oaks, CA: Sage.

Rich, Adrienne. 1976. *Of woman born: Motherhood as experience and institution.* New York: Norton.

Rich, Adrienne. 1980. Compulsory heterosexuality and lesbian existence. *Signs* 5 (Summer):631–660.

Rich, Ruby. 1986. Feminism and sexuality in the 1980s. *Feminist Studies* 12 (3):525–561.

Richardson, B. 1981. *Racism and child-rearing: A study of black mothers.* Ph.D. dissertation, Claremont Graduate School.

Richardson, Diane, ed. 1996. *Theorizing heterosexuality.* Buckingham, UK: Open University Press.

Rideout, Victoria, Donald Roberts, and Ulla Foehr. 2005. *Generation M.* Menlo Park, CA: Kaiser Family Foundation.

Ries, Paula, and Anne Stone. 1992. *The American woman, 1992–1993: A status report.* New York: Norton.

Rifkin, Jeremy. 1995. *End of work: The decline of the global labor force and the dawn of the post-market era.* New York: Putnam Books.

Riley, Glenda. 1991. *Divorce: An American tradition.* New York: Oxford.

Riley, Matilda White. 1999. "The family in an aging society: A matrix of latent relationships" pp. 429–438 in A. Skolnick and J. Skolnick (Eds.) *Family in Transition* (10th ed.). Boston: Allyn & Bacon.

Risman, Barbara. 1987. Intimate relationships from a microstructural perspective: Men and women who mother. *Gender and Society* 1 (1):6–32.

Risman, Barbara. 1998. *Gender vertigo: American families in transition.* New Haven, CT: Yale University Press.

Risman, Barbara, and Myra Marx Ferree. 1995. Making gender visible: Comments on Coleman. *American Sociological Review* 61:231–249.

Ritzer, George. 1992. *Sociological theory.* 3d ed. New York: McGraw-Hill.

Roberts, Dorothy. 1998. The future of reproductive choice for poor women and women of color. In R. Weitz (ed.), *The politics of women's bodies: Sexuality, appearance, and behavior* (pp. 270–277). New York: Oxford University Press.

Roberts, Karen, and Johanna Stroes. 1995. Grandchildren and grandparents: Roles, influences and relationships. In J. Hendricks (ed.), *The ties of later life* (pp. 141–153). Amityville, NY: Baywood.

Robertson, John. 1995. Grandparenting in an era of rapid change. In Ro Blieszern and V. Bedford (eds.), *Handbook of aging and the family* (pp. 243–260). Westport, CT: Greenwood.

Robinson, John. 1985. *American's use of time, 1985 computer file.* College Park: University of Maryland, Survey Research Center (producer, 1992); Ann Arbor, MI: Interuniversity Consortium for Political and Social Research (distributor, 1993).

Robinson, John. 1988. Who's doing the housework? *American Demographics* 10:24–28, 63.

Robson, Ruthann. 1992. *Lesbian (out)law: Survival under the rule of law.* Ithaca, NY: Firebrand Books.

Rodgers, William, and Arland Thornton. 1985. Changing patterns of first marriage in the U.S. *Demography* 22:265–279.

Rodriguez, Julia. 1988. Labor migration and familial responsibilities: Experience of Mexican women. In M. Melville (ed.), *Mexicanas at work in the U.S.* (pp. 47–63). Houston: University of Houston Press.

Rodrique, Jessie. 1990. The black community and the birth control movement. In E. Dubois and V. Ruiz (eds.), *Unequal sisters: A multicultural reader in U.S. women's history* (pp. 333–344). New York: Routledge.

Rogers, Susan. 1978. A woman's place: A critical review of anthropological theory. *Comparative Studies in Society and History* 20:123–162.

Rohrbaugh, J. 1979. Femininity on the line. *Psychology Today,* August, 30.

Rohrbaugh, J. 1992. Lesbian families: Clinical issues and theoretical implications. *Professional Psychological Research and Practice* 23:467–473.

Rollins, Boyd, and Kenneth Cannon. 1974. Marital satisfaction over the family life cycle. *Journal of Marriage and the Family* 36:271–284.

Rollins, Judith. 1985. *Between women: Domestics and their employers.* Philadelphia: Temple University Press.

Romero, Mary. 1988. Sisterhood and domestic service: Race, class and gender in the mistressmaid relationship. *Humanity and Society* 12 (4):318–346.

Romero, Mary. 1992. *Maid in the USA.* New York: Routledge.

Romero, Mary. 1997. Chicanas modernize domestic service. In D. Dunn (ed.), *Workplace/woman's place* (pp. 358–368). Los Angeles: Roxbury.

Roosa, Mark, Antonio Morgan-Lopez, Willa Cree, and Michele Spector. 2002. Ethnic culture, poverty and context. (pp. 27–40) In J. Contreras, K. Kerns, and A. Neal-Bennett (eds.) *Latino children and families in the United States:* Westport, CT: Praeger.

Root, Maria, ed. 1996. *The multiracial experience: Racial borders as the new frontier.* Thousand Oaks, CA: Sage.

Root, Maria. 1998. *Racially mixed people in America.* Newbury Park, CA: Sage.

Rosaldo, Michele, and Louise Lamphere, eds. 1974. *Women, culture and society.* Stanford: Stanford University Press.

Roschelle, Anne. 1997. *No more kin: Exploring race, class and gender in family networks.* Thousand Oaks, CA: Sage.

Rose, Nancy. 1995. Workfare or fair work. New Brunswick, NJ: Rutgers University Press.

Rose, S., and I. Frieze. 1989. Young singles' scripts for a first date. *Gender and Society* 3:258–268.

Rosen, David. 1999. The meaning(s) of family. In A. Skolnick and J. Skolnick (eds.), *Family in transition,* 10th ed. (pp. 53–63). New York: Addison Wesley Longman.

Rosen, Ellen. 1987. *Bitter choices.* Chicago: University of Chicago Press.

Rosen, Ellen. 1991. Beyond the factory gates: Blue collar women at home. In L. Kraem (ed.), *The sociology of gender* (pp. 233–254). New York: St. Martin's Press.

Rosen, Ruth. 2005. "Get hitched young woman" September 26. www.alternet.org/story/26033 (accessed May 29, 2006).

Rosenblatt, Paul, Terri Karis and Richard Powell. 1995. *Multi-racial couples: Black and white voices.* Thousand Oaks, CA: Sage

Rosenblatt, Roger. 1983. The baby in the factory. *Time* 14 (February):72.

Rosenfield, S. 1992. The cost of sharing: wives' employment and husbands' mental health. *Journal of Health and Social Behavior* 33:213–225.

Rosenthal, Andrew. 1992. Quayle says riots sprang from lack of family values. *New York Times,* 20 May, A1, 20.

Rossi, Alice, ed. 1973. *The feminist papers.* New York: Bantam.

Rossi, Alice. 1964. Equality between the sexes: An immodest proposal. *Daedalus,* Spring, 1–19.

Rossi, Alice. 1977. A bio-social perspective on parenting. *Daedalus* 106 (2):1–31.

Rossi, Alice. 1992. Transition to parenthood. In A. Skolnick and J. Skolnick (eds.), *Family in transition.* 7th ed. (pp. 453–463). New York: Harper Collins.

Rothberg, B. 1983. Joint custody: Parental problems and satisfactions. *Family Process* 22:43–52.

Rothman, Barbara Katz. 1982. *In labor: Women and power in the birthplace.* New York: W. W. Norton.

Rothman, Barbara Katz. 1989a. *Recreating motherhood: Ideology and technology in a patriarchal society.* New York: W. W. Norton.

Rothman, Barbara Katz. 1989b. Women, health and medicine. In J. Freeman (ed.), *Women: A feminist perspective.* 4th ed. (pp. 76–86). Mountain View, CA: Mayfield.

Rothman, Robert. 1998. *Inequality and stratification: Race, class and gender.* Upper Saddle River, NJ: Prentice Hall.

Rothman, Sheila, and Emily Marks. 1989. Flexible work schedules and family policy. In F. Getstel and H. Gross (eds), *Families and work* (pp. 469–477). Philadelphia: Temple University Press.

Rotundo, E. 1985. American fatherhood: A historical perspective. *American Behavioral Scientist* 29:7–23.

Rouse, L., R. Breen, and M. Howell. 1988. Abuse in intimate relationships. A comparison of dating and married college students. *Journal of Interpersonal Violence* 3:414–429.

Rubel, Arthur. 1966. *Across the tracks: Mexican Americans in Texas City.* Austin: University of Texas Press.

Rubin, Gayle. 1975. The traffic in women. In R. Reiter (ed.), *Toward an anthropology of women* (pp. 157–211). New York: Monthly Review Press.

Rubin, Gayle. 1984. Thinking sex: Notes for a radical theory of the politics of sexuality. In C. Vance (ed.), *Pleasure and danger: Exploring female sexuality* (pp. 267–319). Boston: Routledge and Kegan Paul.

Rubin, Lillian. 1976. *Worlds of pain: Life in working class families.* New York: Basic Books.

Rubin, Lillian. 1981. *Intimate strangers.* New York: Harper Row.

Rubin, Lillian. 1991. *Erotic wars: What happened to the sexual revolution.* New York: Harper.

Rubin, Lillian. 1994. *Families on the faultline: America's working class speaks about the family, the economy, race and ethnicity.* New York: HarperCollins.

Rubin, Lillian. 1995. *Families on the faultline: American's working class speaks about the family, the economy, race and ethnicity.* New York: Harperperrenial.

Rubin, Zick. 1973. *Liking and loving: An invitation to social psychology.* New York: Holt, Rinehart and Winston.

Ruddick, Sara. 1982. Maternal thinking. In B. Thorne with M. Yalom (eds.), *Rethinking family: Some feminist questions* (pp. 76–94). New York: Longman.

Ruiz, Vicki. 1990. A promise fulfilled: Mexican cannery workers in Southern California. In D. Dubois and V. Ruiz (eds.), *Unequal sisters: A multicultural reader in U.S. women's history* (pp. 264–274). New York: Routledge.

Rupp, Leila, and Verta Taylor. 1987. *Survival in the doldrums: The American women's rights movement, 1945 to the 1960s.* New York: Oxford University Press.

Rush, F. 1980. *Best kept secrets: Sexual abuse of children.* Englewood Cliffs, NJ: Prentice-Hall.

Russell, Diana. 1986. *The secret trauma: Incest in the lives of girls and women.* New York: Basic Books.

Russell, Diane. 1990. *Rape in marriage.* Bloomington, IN: Indiana University Press.

Russell, James. 1994. *After the fifth sun: Class and race in North America.* Englewood Cliff, NJ: Prentice Hall.

Ruth, Sheila. 1998. *Issues in feminism: An introduction to women's studies.* 4th ed. Mountain View, CA: Mayfield.

Rutman, Deborah. 1996. Childcare as women's work: Workers' experience of powerfulness and powerlessness. *Gender & Society* 10 (5):629–649.

Ryan, William. 1971. *Blaming the victim.* New York: Random House.

Ryscavage, P. 1979. More wives in the labor force have husbands with "above average" incomes. *Monthly Labor Review* 102 (6):40–42.

Saad, Lydia. 1996. America's religious commitment affirmed. *Gallup Poll Monthly,* January, 21–23.

Sacks, Karen. 1984. Generations of working-class families. In K. Sacks and D. Remy (eds.), *My troubles are going to have trouble with me: Everyday triumphs of women workers* (pp. 15–38). New Brunswick, NJ: Rutgers.

Safilios-Rothschild, Constantina. 1970. The study of family power structure: A review, 1960–1969. *Journal of Marriage and the Family* 31:539–543.

Safilios-Rothschild, Constantina. 1977. *Love, sex and sex roles.* Englewood Cliffs, NJ: Prentice-Hall.

Salholz, Eloise. 1990. The Future of Gay America. *Newsweek,* 23 (March 12).

Samuelson, Paul, and William Nordhaus. 1989. *Economics.* 13th ed. New York: McGraw Hill.

Samuelson, Robert. 2000. Goodbye, new economy. *Washington Post,* 26 December.

Sanchez, Rene. 1999. Antiabortion web site loses lawsuit. *Washington Post,* 3 February, A1.

Sanger, Margaret. 1931. *An autobiography.* New York: Dover.

Sanik, Margaret Mietus. 1981. Divisions of household work: A decade comparison, 1967–1977. *Home Economics Research Journal* 10:175–180.

Sarmiento, Socorro. 2002. *Making ends meet.* NY: LFB Scholarly Publishing.

Sarvasy, Wendy. 1988. Reagan and low-income mothers: A feminist recasting of the debate. In M. Brown (ed.), *Remaking the welfare state* (pp. 253–276). Philadelphia: Temple University Press.

Sattel, Jack. 1976. The inexpressive male: Tragedy or sexual politics. *Social Problems* 23 (April):469–477.

Saunders, D., A. Lynch, M. Grayson, and D. Linz. 1987. The inventory of beliefs about wife-beating: The construction and initial validation of a measure of beliefs and attitudes. *Violence and Victims* 2:39–57.

Scanzoni, John. 1971. *The black family in modern society.* Boston: Allyn and Bacon.

Scarr, Sandra. 1984. *Mother care/other care.* New York: Basic Books.

Scarr, Sandra, Deborah Phillips, and Kathleen McCartney. 1992. Working mothers and their families. In A. Skolnick and J. Skolnick (eds.), *Family in transition.* 7th ed. (pp. 414–430). New York: HarperCollins.

Schaevetz, Marjorie. 1984. *The superwoman syndrome.* New York: Warner Books.

Schaffer, Dianne. 1996. Mexican American and Anglo single mothers. *Hispanic Journal of Behavioral Sciences* 18 (1):74–87

Schechter, Susan. 1982. *Women and male violence: The visions and struggles of the battered women's movement.* Boston: South End Press.

Schechter, Susan. 1988. Building bridges between activists, professionals and researchers. In K. Yllo and M. Bogard (eds.), *Feminist perspectives on wife abuse* (pp. 299–312). Beverly Hills, CA: Sage.

Schneider, Beth, and Meredith Gould. 1987. Female sexuality: Looking back into the future. In B. Hess and M. Ferree (eds.), *Analyzing gender* (pp. 120–153). Newbury Park, CA: Sage.

Schoen, Robert. 1983. Measuring the tightness of the marriage squeeze. *Demography* 20:61–78.

Schor, Julia. 1991. *The overworked American: The unexpected decline of leisure.* New York: Basic Books.

Schorr, Alvin. 1962. Family policy in the United States. *International Social Science Journal* 14:452–467.

Schwartz, Felice. 1989. Management, women and the new facts of life. *Harvard Business Review* 67 (January-February):65–76.

Schwartz, John. 1983. *America's hidden success: A reassessment of 20 years of public policy.* New York: Norton.

Schwartz, L., and W. Markham. 1985. Sex stereotyping in children's toy advertisements. *Sex Roles* 12:157–170.

Schwartz, Martin. 1987. Gender and injury in spousal assault. *Social Forces* 20 (1):61–75.

Schwartz, Pepper, and Virginia Rutter. 1998. *The gender of sexuality.* Thousand Oaks, CA: Pine Forge Press.

Scott, Anne Firor. 1989. Conclusions, trends and future directions. In C. Little and R. Vaughn (eds.), *A new perspective: Southern women's cultural history from the Civil War to civil rights* (pp. 77–83). Charlottesville, VA: Virginia Foundation for the Humanities.

Scott, Jerome. 1988. Four stages of African American history. Paper presented at Conference for Black History Month, Howard University, Washington, DC.

Scott, Rebecca. 1985. The battle over the child: Child apprenticeship and the Freedman's Bureau in North Carolina. In N. Hiner and J. Hawes (eds.), *Growing up in America: Children in historical perspective* (pp. 193–207). Chicago: University of Chicago Press.

Segal, Elizabeth, and Keith Kilty. 1998. The resurgence of biological determinism. *Race, Class and Gender* 5 (3):61–75.

Segura, Denise. 1999. "Inside the worlds of Chicana and Mexican immigrant women." In J. Kourna et al. (eds.), *Feminist Philosophies* (pp. 180–188). Upper Saddle River, NJ: Prentice Hall.

Seidenberg, R. 1973. *Corporate wives—corporate casualties?* New York: Amacon.

Seligman, Jean. 1990. Variations on a theme. *Newsweek,* Winter/Spring, 38.

Seltzer, Judith. 1994. Consequences of marriage dissolution for children. In J. Hagan and K. Cook (eds.), *Annual review of sociology,* Vol. 20 (pp. 235–358). Palo Alto: Annual Reviews Inc.

Senour, Maria, and Lynda Warren. 1976. Sex and ethnic differences in masculinity, femininity, and anthropology. Paper presented at the annual meeting of the Western Psychological Association, Los Angeles, CA.

Shagall, Johanna. 1999. Federal protection: The Violence Against Women Act. In L. Gerdes (ed.), *Battered women* (pp. 75–81). San Diego: Greenhaven.

Shaiken, Harley. 1984. *Work transformed: Automation and labor in the computer age.* New York: Holt Rinehart and Winston.

Shapiro, Isaac. 2001. *The latest IRS data on after-tax income trends.* Washington, DC: Center on Budget and Policy Priorities.

Shapiro, Isaac, and Robert Greenstein. 1988. *Holes in the safety nets: Poverty programs and policies in the states.* Washington, DC: Center on Budget and Policy Priorities.

Shapiro, Isaac, Robert Greenstein and Wendell Primus. 2000. *Poverty rate hits lowest level since 1979 as unemployment hits 30 year low.* Washington, DC: Center on Budget Priorities.

Shapiro, L. 1990. Guns and dolls. *Newsweek,* 28 May, 56–65.

Shapiro, Laura. 1997. The myth of quality time. *Newsweek,* 12 May, 62–69.

Shaw, Anna Howard. 1915. *Story of a pioneer.*

Shaw, Nancy. 1974. *Forced labor: Maternity care in the United States.* New York: Pergamon.

Sheak, Robert. 1990. Corporate and state attacks on the material conditions of the working class. *Humanity and Society* 14:105–127.

Shelton, Beth Anne, and B. Agger. 1993. Shotgun wedding, unhappy marriage, no fault divorce? In P. England (ed.), *Theory on gender/feminism on theory* (pp. 25–42). New York: Aldine de Gruyter.

Shelton, Beth Anne, and Daphne John. 1993. Does marital status make a difference? *Journal of Family Issues* 14:401–420.

Shelton, Beth Anne, and Daphne John. 1996. The division of household labor. *Annual Review of Sociology* 22:299–322.

Sheppard, Annamary. 1982. Unspoken premises in custody litigation. *Women Rights Law Reporter* 7 (Spring):229–234.

Sherman, Arloc, and Jodi Sandfort. 1998. Fighting child poverty in America: How research can help. *Contemporary Sociology* 27 (6):555–561

Sherman, Lawrence, and Richard Berk. 1984. The specified deterrent effects of arrest for domestic assault. *American Sociological Review* 49:261–272.

Shibley, Mark. 1996. *Resurgent evangelicalism in the United States.* Columbia, SC: USC Press.

Shinn, Marybeth, and Beth Weitzman. 1997. Homeless families are different. In J. Baumohl (ed.), *Homelessness in America* (pp. 109–121). Phoenix: Oryx Press.

Shock, Pamela, Wendy Manning, and Meredith Porter. 2005. Everything's there but the money: How money shapes decisions to marry among cohabitors. *Journal of Marriage and the Family,* 67 (3).

Sidel, Ruth. 1990. *On her own: Growing up in the shadow of the American dream.* New York: Viking.

Sigelman, Lee, and Susan Welch. 1991. *Black Americans' views of racial inequality: The dream deferred.* Cambridge: Cambridge University Press.

Sigmon, Scott, and Rosemary Gainey. 1995. High risk sexual activity and alcohol consumption among college students. *College Student Journal* 29:128.

Simmel, Georg. (1907/1978). *The philosophy of money.* London: Routledge and Kegan Paul.

Simmons, T., and M. O'Connell. 2003. Married couple and unmarried partner households: 2000. U.S. Census Bureau. (February) Washington, DC: USGPO.

Simon, Rita, and Gloria Danziger. 1991. *Women's movements in America: Their successes, disappointments, and aspirations.* New York: Praeger.

Simons, Ronald, and associates. 1996. *Understanding differences between divorced and intact families: Stress, interaction and child outcome.* Thousand Oaks, CA: Sage.

Simons, William. 1996. *Postmodern sexualities.* New York: Routledge.

Singleton, Judy. 1998. The impact of family caregiving to the elderly on the American workplace: Who is affected and what is being done? In D. Vannoy and P. Dubeck (eds.), *Challenges for work and family in the twenty-first century* (pp. 201–216). New York: Aldine de Gruyter.

Skocpol, Theda, and Edwin Amenta. 1986. States and social policies. In R. Turner and J. Short, (eds.), *Annual review of sociology* (pp. 131–157). Vol. 12. Palo Alto, CA: Annual Reviews.

Skolnick, Arlene. 1991. *Embattled paradise: The American family in an age of uncertainty.* New York: Basic Books.

Skolnick, Arlene. 2005. Marriage. Microsoft Encarta Online Encyclopedia.

Skolnick, Arlene and Jerome Skolnick. 1999. "Introduction." In A. Skolnick and J. Skolnick (eds.), *Family in Transition* 10th ed. (pp. 1–13). Boston: Allyn & Bacon.

Smith, Dorothy. 1974. Women's perspective as a radical critique of sociology. *Sociological Inquiry* 44:7–13.

Smith, Dorothy. 1979. A sociology for women. In J. Sherman and E. Beck (eds.), *The prism of sex: Essays in the sociology of knowledge* (pp. 16–35). Madison: University of Wisconsin Press.

Smith, Dorothy. 1987. Women's inequality and the family. In N. Gerstel and H. Gross (eds.), *Families and work* (pp. 23–54). Philadelphia: Temple University Press.

Smith, J., V. Waldorf, and D. Trembath. 1990. Single white male looking for thin very attractive. *Sex Roles,* 23:675–685.

Smith, Steven, and Deborah Stone. 1988. The unexpected consequences of privatization. In M. Brown (ed.), *Remaking the welfare state: Retrenchment and social policy in America and Europe* (pp. 232–252). Philadelphia: Temple University Press.

Smith, Tom. 1990. Adult sexual behavior in 1989. Unpublished paper presented at the annual meetings of the American Association for the Advancement of Science.

Smith-Rosenberg, Carroll. 1985. *Disorderly conduct.* New York: Knopf.

Snell, Marilyn. 1997. Home work time. *Mother Jones* 22 (3):26–31.

Snitow, Ann. 1978. Thinking about the mermaid and the minotaur. *Feminist Studies* 4 (2):190–198.

Sobel, Herman. 1962. Can I help my husband avoid a heart attack? *Reader's Digest,* September, 69.

Sobieraj, Sarah. 1998. Taking control: Toy commercials and the social construction of patriarchy. In L. Bowker (ed.), *Masculinities and violence* (pp. 15–28). Thousand Oaks, CA: Sage.

Sokoloff, Natalie. 1980. *Between money and love: The dialectics of women's home and market work.* New York: Praeger.

Solis, Julie. 1995. The status of Latino children and youth: Challenges and perspectives. In R. Zambrano (ed.), *Understanding Latino families: Scholarship, policy and practice* (pp. 62–81). Thousand Oaks, CA: Sage.

Solomon, Sondra E., Ester D. Rothblum, and Kimberely F. Balsam. 2005. Money, housework, sex and conflict: Same-sex couples in civil unions, those not in civil unions, and heterosexual married siblings. *Sex Roles: A Journal of Research* (May).

Sonfield, Adam, and Rachel Gold. 2005. Conservatives' agenda threatens public funding for family planning. The Guttmacher Report on Public Policy, Vol 8(1) (February).

Song, Young. 1991. Single Asian American women as a result of divorce: Depressive affect and changes in social support. *Journal of Divorce and Remarriage* 14:219–230.

South, S., and Glenna Spitze. 1994. The division of task responsibility in U.S. households: Longitudinal adjustments to change. *Social Forces* 64:689–701.

Spain, Daphne, and Suzanne Bianchi. 1996. *Balancing act: Motherhood, marriage, and employment among American women.* New York: Russell Sage Foundation.

Spanier, Graham. 1983. Married and unmarried cohabitation in the U.S., 1980. *Journal of Marriage and the Family* 45 (May):277–288.

Spanier, Graham, and Paul Glick. 1981. Marital instability in the U.S.: Some correlates and recent changes. *Family Relations* 30 (July):329–338.

Spenner, K. 1981. Occupational role characteristics and intergenerational transmission. *Work and Occupations* 8:89–112.

Sperling, Susan. 1991. Baboons with briefcases vs langurs with lipstick: Feminism and functionalism in primate studies. *Signs* 17 (1):1–27.

Spinetta, J., and Rigler, D. 1972. The child-abusing parent: A psychological review. *Psychological Bulletin* 77:296–304.

Stacey, Judith, and Barrie Thorne. 1985. The missing feminist revolution in sociology. *Social Problems* 32:301–316.

Stacey, Judith, and Susan Gerard. 1998. We are not doormats: The influence of feminists on contemporary evangelicals in the United States. In M. Baca Zinn, P. Hondagneu-Sotelo, and M. Messner (eds.), *Through the prism of difference: Readings on sex and gender,* (pp. 498–508). Boston: Allyn and Bacon.

Stacey, Judith. 1988. Can there be a feminist ethnography? *Women Studies International Forum* 11:21–27.

Stacey, Judith. 1990. *Brave new families: Stories of domestic upheaval in late twentieth century America.* New York: Basic Books.

Stacey, Judith. 1996. *In the name of the family: Rethinking family values in the postmodern age.* Boston: Beacon Press.

Stacey, Judith, and Timothy Biblarz. 2003. (How) Does the sexual orientation of parents matter? *American Sociological Review,* (April) 66:159–183.

Stack, Carol. 1974. *All our kin: Strategies for survival in the black community.* New York: Harper and Row.

Stafford, Frank, and Greg Duncan. 1978. Market hours, real hours and labor productivity. *Economic Outlook USA* 5:103–119.

Stanford Center for the Study of Families, Children, and Youth. 1991. *The Stanford studies of homeless families, children, and youth.* Stanford, CA: Stanford University Press.

Stanton, Elizabeth Cady. 1889/1990. Speech before the legislature 1860. In S. Ruth (ed.), *Issues in feminism* (pp. 465–470). Toronto: Mayfield.

Stanworth, Michelle. 1990. Birth pangs: Conceptive technologies and the threat to motherhood. In M. Hirsch and E. Keller (eds.), *Conflicts in feminism* (pp. 288–304). New York: Routledge.

Staples, Robert. 1973. *The black woman in America: Sex, marriage and the family.* Chicago: Nelson Hall.

Staples, Robert. 1981. The myth of the black matriarchy. *Black Scholar,* December, 32.

Staples, Robert, and T. Jones. 1985. Culture, ideology and black television images. *The Black Scholar* 16:10–20.

Staples, Robert. 1998. Interracial relationships: A convergence of desire and opportunity. In R. Staples (ed.), *The black family: Essays and studies.* 6th ed. (pp. 129–136). Belmont, CA: Wadsworth.

Stark, Evan, and Anne Flitcraft. 1979. Medicine and patriarchal violence: The social construction of a "private" event. *International Journal of Health Services* 98:461–491.

Stark, Evan, and Anne Flitcraft. 1983. Social knowledge, social policy and the abuse of women: The case against patriarchal benevolence. In D. Finkelhor et al. (eds.), *The dark side of families: Current family violence research* (pp. 330–348). Beverly Hills, CA: Sage.

Stark, Evan, and Anne Flitcraft. 1996. *Women at risk.* Thousand Oaks, CA: Sage.

Starr, Paul. 1989. The meaning of privatization. In S. Kamerman and A. Kahn (eds.), *Privatization and the welfare state* (pp. 15–48). Princeton: Princeton University Press.

Stein, Peter, ed. 1981. *Single life: Unmarried adults in social context.* New York: St. Martin's Press.

Steinberg, Lawrence, et al. 1982. Effects of early work experience on adolescent development. *Developmental Psychology* 18:385–395.

Steinberg, Shirley, and Joe Kincheloe. 1997. *Kinderculture: The corporate construction of childhood.* Boulder, CO: Westview Press.

Steiner, Jerome. 1972. What price success? *Harvard Business Review,* March, 69–74.

Steinmetz, Suzanne. 1977–1978. The battered husband syndrome. *Victimology: An International Journal* 2: 499–509.

Steinmetz, Suzanne, Sylvia Clavin, and Karen Stein. 1990. *Marriage and the family.* New York: Harper and Row.

Stetson, Dorothy. 1997. *Women's rights in the U.S. A.: Policy debates and gender roles.* New York: Garland Publishing.

Stewart, Abigail, Anne Copeland, Nia Chester, Janet Malley, and Nicole Barenbau. 1997. *Separating together: How divorce transforms families.* New York: Guilford.

Stier, Haya. 1991. Immigrant women go to work: Analysis of immigrant wives' labor supply for six Asian groups. *Social Science Quarterly* 72:67–82.

Stiffarm, Lenore, and Phil Lane. 1992. The demography of Native North America: A question of American Indian survival. In M. Jaimes (ed.), *The state of Native America: Genocide, colonization and resistance* (pp. 23–54). Boston: South End Press.

Stith, Sandra, and Murray Straus. 1995. *Understanding partner violence: Prevalence, causes, consequences and solutions.* Minneapolis: National Council on Family Relations.

Stockard, Jean, and Miriam Johnson. 1992. *Sex and gender in society.* 2d ed. Englewood Cliffs, NJ: Prentice-Hall.

Stoesz, D. 1987. Privatization: Reforming the welfare state. *Journal of Sociology and Social Welfare* 14:3–20.

Stoltenberg, John. 1997. How men have (a) sex. In E. Disch (ed.), *Reconstructing gender: A multicultural anthology* (pp. 218–227). Mountain View, CA: Mayfield.

Straus, Murray. 1980. Sexual inequality and wife beating. In M. Straus and G. Hotaling (eds.), *The social causes of husband-wife violence* (pp. 86–93). Minneapolis: UM Press.

Straus, Murray. 1986. Societal change and change in family violence from 1975 to 1985 as revealed by two national surveys. *Journal of Marriage and the Family* 48:465–479.

Straus, Murray. 1991. Discipline and deviance: Physical punishment of children and violence and other crimes in adulthood. *Social Problems* 38:133–152.

Straus, Murray. 1994. *Beating the devil out of them: Corporal punishment in American families.* Lexington, MA: Lexington/Macmillian Books.

Straus, Murray, and Anita Mathur. 1996. Social change and trends in approval of corporal punishment by parents from 1968 to 1994. In D. Frehsee, W. Horn, and K. Bussman (eds.), *Violence against children* (pp. 91–105). New York: Walter de Gruyter.

Straus, Murray, Richard Gelles, and Suzanne Steinmetz. 1980. *Behind closed doors: Violence in the American family.* Garden City, NY: Doubleday.

Straus, Murray, Richard Gelles, and Suzanne Steinmetz. 1988. The marriage license as a hitting license. In A. Skolnick and J. Skolnick (eds.), *Family in transition.* 6th ed. (pp. 301–314). Boston: Scott, Foresman.

Strauss, Joseph. 1995. Reframing and refocusing American Indian family strengths. In C. Jacobson (ed.), *American families: Issues in race and ethnicity* (pp. 105–118). New York: Garland.

Street, David, George Martin, and Laura Gordon. 1979. *The welfare industry.* Beverly Hills, CA: Sage.

Strober, Myra. 1988. Two-earner families. In S. Dornbusch and M. Strober (eds.), *Feminism, children and new families* (pp. 161–190). New York: Guilford.

Strober, Myra, and Sanford Dornbusch. 1988. Public policy alternatives. In S. Dombusch and M. Strober (eds.), *Feminism, children and the new families* (pp. 327–356). New York: Guilford.

Sudarkasa, Niara. 1988. Interpreting the African heritage in Afro-American family organization. In H. McAdoo (ed.), *Black families.* 2d ed. (pp. 27–43). Beverly Hills, CA: Sage.

Sudarkasa, Niara. 1998. Interpreting the African heritage in Afro-American family organization. In S. Ferguson (ed.), *Shifting the center: Understanding contemporary families* (pp. 62–77). Mountain View, CA: Mayfield.

Sullivan, Andrew. 1992. Here comes the groom. In G. Bird and M. Sporakowski (eds.), *Taking sides: Clashing views on controversial issues in family and personal relationships* (pp. 76–79). Guilford, CT: Dushkin.

Sullivan, Deborah, and Rose Weitz. 1988. *Labor pains: Modern midwives and home birth.* New Haven: Yale University Press.

Sullivan, Joyce. 1984. Family support systems paychecks can't buy. In P. Voydanoff (ed.), *Work and family: Changing roles of men and women* (pp. 310–319). Palo Alto, CA: Mayfield.

Sullivan, Maureen. 1996. Rozzie and Harriet: Gender and family patterns of lesbian coparents. *Gender and Society* 10 (6):747–767.

Suro, Robert. 1998. *Strangers among us: How Latino immigration is transforming America.* New York: Knopf.

Suro, Roberto. 1992. For women, varied reasons for single motherhood. *New York Times,* 26 May, A12.

Surra, Catherine. 1991. Research and theory on mate selections and premarital relationships in the 1980s. In A. Booth (ed.), *Contemporary families: Looking forward, looking back* (pp. 54–75). Minneapolis: National Council on Family Relations.

Swanstrom, Todd. 1992. Homeless a product of policy. In R. Baker, L. Anderson, and D. Dorn (eds.), *Social problems: A critical thinking approach* (pp. 335–336). Belmont, CA: Wadsworth.

Swart, J. 1979. Flextime's debit and credit option. *Harvard Business Review* 1:10–12.

Sweet, Larry, James Bumpass, and Vaughn Call. 1988. *The design and contact of the survey of families and households.* NSFH Working Paper No. 1. Madison: University of Wisconsin Center for Demography and Ecology.

Sydie, Rosalind. 1987. *Natural woman, cultured men: A feminist perspective on sociological theory.* New York: New York University Press.

Szasz, Margaret. 1985. Federal boarding schools and the Indian child, 1920–1960. In N. Hiner and J. Hawes (eds.),

Growing up in America: Children in historical perspective (pp. 209–218). Chicago: University of Chicago Press.

Tafel, Selma, Paul Placek, and Mary Moien. 1985. One fifth of U.S. births by cesarean section. *American Journal of Public Health* 75:190.

Takaki, Ronald. 1989. *Strangers from a different shore: A history of Asian Americans.* Boston: Little Brown.

Tanzer, Michael. 1974. *The energy crisis: World struggle for power and wealth.* New York: Monthly Review Press.

Taylor, Paul. 1991. Day care: Soaring popularity, stable cost. *Washington Post,* 7 November, A20.

Taylor, Robert, James Jackson, and Linda Chatters. 1996. *Family life in black America.* Thousand Oaks, CA: Sage.

Taylor, Robert, Linda Chatters, M. Belinda Tucker, and Edith Lewis. 1992. Developments in research on black families: A decade review. In A. Skolnick and J. Skolnick (eds.), *Family in transition.* 7th ed. (pp. 439–471). New York: Harper Collins.

Taylor, Verta. 1983. The future of feminism in the 1980s: A social movement analysis. In V. Taylor and L. Richardson (eds.), *Feminist frontiers: Rethinking sex, gender and society* (pp. 434–451). Palo Alto, CA: Mayfield.

Teachman, Jay. 1991. Contributions to children by divorced fathers. *Social Problems* 38 (3):358–371.

TenHouten, W. 1970. The black family: Myth and reality. *Psychiatry* 25:145–173.

Testa, Mark, and Marilyn Krogh. 1995. The effect of employment on marriage among black men in inner city Chicago. In M. Tucker and C. Mitchell-Kernan (eds.), *The decline in marriage among African Americans: Causes, consequences, and policy implications* (pp. 59–101). New York: Russell Sage.

Testa, Mark, N. M. Astone, Marilyn Krogh, and Kathryn Neckerman. 1989. Employment and marriage among inner-city fathers. *Annals of the American Academy of Political and Social Science* 501:79–91.

Thoits, Peggy. 1985. Multiple identities: Examining gender and marital status differences in distress. *American Sociological Review* 51:259–272.

Thompson, Edward. 1992. Older men as invisible men in contemporary society. In M. Kimmel and M. Messner (eds.), *Men's lives* (pp. 68–83). New York: MacMillan.

Thompson, Martie, and J. Kingree. 2004. The Role of Alcohol Use in Intimate Partner Violence. *Violence and Victims,* 19 (1):63–71.

Thompson, Sharon. 1984. Search for tomorrow: On feminism and the construction of teen romance. In C. Vance (ed.), *Pleasure and danger: Exploring female sexuality* (pp. 350–357). Boston: Routledge and Kegan Paul.

Thorne, Barrie. 1987. Revisioning women and social change: Where are the children? *Gender and Society* 1:85–109.

Thorne, Barrie. 1993. *Gender play: Girls and boys in school.* New Brunswick, NJ: Rutgers University Press.

Thorne, Barrie, with Marilyn Yalom. 1992. *Rethinking the family: Some feminist questions.* 2d ed. New York: Longman.

Thornton, Arland. 1988. Cohabitation and marriage in the 1980s. *Demography* 25:497–508.

Thornton, Arland, and Deborah Friedman. 1983. The changing American family. *Population Bulletin.* 38 (4):2–43.

Thornton, Michael. 1997. Strategies of racial socialization among black parents: Mainstreaminig, minority and cultural messages. In R. Taylor, J. Jackson, and L. Chatters (eds.), *Family life in black America* (pp. 201–215). Thousand Oaks, CA: Sage.

Thornton, Philip. 2006. "US Savings Rate Sinks to Lowest Since Great Depression" *Independent / UK,* 31 January.

Thrall, C. 1978. Who does what? Role stereotyping, children's work, and continuity between generations in the household division of labor. *Human Relations* 31:249–265.

Tierney, Kathleen. 1982. The battered women's movement and the creation of the wife beating movement. *Social Problems* 29 (February):207–220.

Tillmon, Johnnie. 1976. Welfare is a woman's issue. In R. Baxandall, L. Gordon, and S. Reverby (eds.), *America's working women: A documented history, 1600 to the present* (pp. 354–356). New York: Vintage Books.

Tilly, Louise, and Joan Scott. 1978. *Women, work and family.* New York: Holt, Rinehart and Winston.

Timmer, Doug, and D. Stanley Eitzen. 1992. The root causes of urban homelessness in the United States. *Humanity and Society* 16 (2):159–175.

Tjaden, Patricia, and Nancy Thoennes. 2000. Full Report on the Prevalence of, Incidence and Consequences of Violence Against Women. National Institute of Justice and CDC. (November).

Tolentina, Roland. 1996. Bodies, letters, catalogs: Filipinas in transnational space. *Social Text* 48 (Fall):49–76.

Trattner, William. 1999. *From poor law to welfare state: A history of social welfare in the U.S.* 6th ed. New York: Free Press.

Traveler's Aid Program and Child Welfare League. 1987. *Study of homeless children and families: Preliminary findings.* Conducted by P. Maza and J. Hall.

Treas, Judith, and Ramon Torrecilha. 1995. The older population. In R. Farley (ed.), *State of the Union* (pp. 47–92). New York: Russell Sage.

Treaster, Joseph, and N. Kleinfield. 2005. "New Orleans is inundated as 2 levees fail" *New York Times,* 31 August.

Trennert, Robert. 1979. Peaceably if they will, forcibly if they must: The Phoenix Indian school, 1890–1901. *Journal of Arizona History* 20 (Autumn): 297–322.

Trennert, Robert. 1990. Educating Indian girls at nonreservation boarding schools, 1878–1920. In E. DuBois and V. Ruiz (eds.), *Unequal sisters: A multicultural reader in U.S. women's history* (pp. 224–237). New York: Routledge.

Tucker, M. Belinda, and Claudia Mitchell-Kernan. 1995. Trends in African American family formation: A theoretical and statistical overview. In M. Tucker and C. Mitchell-Kernan (eds.), *The decline in marriage among African Americans: Causes, consequences and policy* (pp. 3–26). New York: Russell Sage.

Tucker, M. Belinda, and Robert Taylor. 1989. Demographic correlates of relationship status among black Americans. *Journal of Marriage and the Family* 51:655–665.

Turnbull, C. 1972. *The mountain people.* New York: Simon and Schuster.

U.S. Bureau of Census. 1993. "Table 2" *Current Population Reports* P25-1104. Washington, DC: GPO.

U.S. Bureau of Census. 2000. *Poverty in the U.S. 1999.* Washington, DC: GPO.

U.S. Bureau of the Census. 1975. *Historical statistics of the United States, colonial times to 1970.* Washington, DC: USGPO.

U.S. Bureau of the Census. 1983. *Contribution of wives' earnings to family income. Current Population Reports,* Series P-60. Washington, DC: GPO.

U.S. Bureau of the Census. 1985. *Money income and poverty status of families and persons in the U.S.: 1984. Current Population Reports,* Series P-60, No. 149. Washington, DC: GPO.

U.S. Bureau of the Census. 1988. *Households, families, marital status and living arrangements, March 1988. Current Population Reports,* Series P-20, No. 432. Washington, DC: USGPO.

U.S. Bureau of the Census. 1989a. *Child support and alimony, 1985. Current Population Reports,* Series P-23, No. 154. Washington, DC: USPGO.

U.S. Bureau of the Census. 1989b. *Population profile of the United States. Current Population Reports,* Series P-23, No. 129. Washington, DC: USGPO.

U.S. Bureau of the Census. 1989c. *Marital status and living arrangements: March 1988. Current Population Reports,* Series P-20, No. 418. Washington, DC: USGPO.

U.S. Bureau of the Census. 1989d. *Changes in America family life. Current Population Reports* P-23, No. 163.

U.S. Bureau of the Census. 1990a. *Household and family characteristics: 1990 and 1989.* P-20, No. 447. Washington, DC: USGPO.

U.S. Bureau of the Census. 1990c. *Money income and poverty status of families and persons in the U.S.: 1989. Current Population Reports,* Series P-60. Washington, DC: GPO.

U.S. Bureau of the Census. 1991a. *Money income of households, families and persons in the United States, 1991. Current Population Reports,* Series P-60, Washington, DC: USGPO.

U.S. Bureau of the Census. 1991b. *Fertility of American women: June 1990.* Washington, DC: USGPO.

U.S. Bureau of the Census. 1991c. *Marital status and living arrangements: March 1991. Current Population Reports,* Series P-20, No. 450. Washington, DC: USGPO.

U.S. Bureau of the Census. 1991d. *Statistical abstract of the U.S., 1989.* Washington, DC: USGPO.

U.S. Bureau of the Census. 1991e. Studies in household and family formation.

U.S. Bureau of the Census. 1992. *Money income of households, families and persons in the United States: 1991. Current Population Reports.*

U.S. Bureau of the Census. 1992a. *Census and you.* 27.

U.S. Bureau of the Census. 1992b. *Census and you.* May.

U.S. Bureau of the Census. 1992c. *Statistical abstracts of the U.S.* Washington, DC: USGPO.

U.S. Bureau of the Census. 1992d. *Marital status and living arrangements.* Series P20, Number 468. Washington, DC: USGPO.

U.S. Bureau of the Census. 1994a. *Current population reports,* Series P20–475. Washington, DC: USGPO, 1994.

U.S. Bureau of the Census. 1994b. *Statistical abstract of the United States, 1994.* Washington, DC: USGPO.

U.S. Bureau of the Census. 1994c. *Marital status and living arrangements: March 1994. Current Population Reports.*

U.S. Bureau of the Census. 1995. *Statistical abstract of the United States.* Washington, DC: USGPO.

U.S. Bureau of the Census. 1996. *Statistical abstract of the United States: 1996.* Washington, DC: USGPO.

U.S. Bureau of the Census. 1997. *Statistical abstracts of the United States.* Washington DC: USGPO.

U.S. Bureau of the Census. 1998a. *Statistical abstract of the United States, 1998.* Washington, DC: USGPO.

U.S. Bureau of the Census. 1998b. *Poverty in the United States: 1997.* Washington, DC: USGPO.

U.S. Bureau of the Census. 1999. Poverty in the United States, 1998. *Current Population Reports* P60-207. Washington, DC: USGPO.

U.S. Bureau of the Census. 2000a. *American Indian and Alaska native summary file 2000.* Washington, DC: USGPO.

U.S. Bureau of the Census. 2000b. *America's families and living arrangements.* (March). Washington, DC: USGPO.

U.S. Bureau of the Census. 2000c. *Census 2000 summary file 1.* Washington, DC: USGPO.

U.S. Bureau of the Census. 2000d. *Census 2000 summary file 4.* Washington, DC: USGPO.

U.S. Bureau of the Census. 2000e. *Census 2000 supplementary survey, 2000.* Washington, DC: USGPO.

U.S. Bureau of the Census. 2000f. *Marital status of people 15 years and over by age, sex, personal earnings, race and hispanic origin.* (March). Washington, DC: USGPO.

U.S. Bureau of the Census. 2000g. *Poverty in the U.S. 1999.* Washington, DC: USGPO.

U.S. Bureau of the Census. 2001. *Statistical abstracts of the United States, 2001.* Washington, DC: USGPO.

U.S. Bureau of the Census. 2002a. *American community survey.* Summary Tables. Sex by Age. Washington, DC: USGPO.

U.S. Bureau of the Census. 2002b. *Statistical abstracts of the United States, 2002.* Washington, DC: USGPO.

U.S. Bureau of the Census. 2002c. *Statistical abstracts of the United States. Families Below Poverty by Selected Characteristics 2002.* #690. Washington, DC: USGPO.

U.S. Bureau of the Census. 2002d. U.S. Census Bureau News. *Marital Status and Living Arrangements.* (February 8). Washington, DC: USGPO.

U.S. Bureau of the Census. 2003a. *American community survey.* Washington, DC: USGPO.

U.S. Bureau of the Census. 2003b. *Annual social and economic supplement: 2003. Current population survey. Current Population Reports.* Series P20-553. *America's families and living arrangements: 2003,* and earlier reports. Washington, DC: USGPO.

U.S. Bureau of the Census. 2003c. *Custodial mothers and fathers and their child support: 2001. Current Population Reports.* (October). Washington, DC: USGPO.

U.S. Bureau of the Census. 2003d. *Family type by presence and age of own children. American community survey.* Washington, DC: USGPO.

U.S. Bureau of the Census. 2003e. *Grandparents living with grandchildren: 2000.* (October). Washington, DC: USGPO.

U.S. Bureau of the Census. 2003f. *Percentage of childless women 40 to 44 years old increases since 1976.* Census Bureau Reports. (October 23). Washington, DC: USGPO.

U.S. Bureau of the Census. 2003g. *Young adults living at home 1960–2002.* (June 12). Washington, DC: USGPO.

U.S. Bureau of the Census. 2004a. *Age of own children under 18 years in families and subfamilies by living arrangements by employment status of parents.* Washington DC: USGPO.

U.S. Bureau of the Census. 2004b. *American community survey 2004.* Washington, DC: USGPO.

U.S. Bureau of the Census. 2004c. *America's families and living arrangements: 2004.* Washington, DC: USGPO.

U.S. Bureau of the Census. 2004d. *Children and the households they live in: 2000.* (March). Washington, DC: USGPO.

U.S. Bureau of the Census. 2004e. *Current population survey. Annual demographic supplements. Historical income Tables—Families.* (May 12). Washington, DC: USGPO.

U.S. Bureau of the Census. 2004f. *Current population survey, 2003 and 2004.* Annual Social and Economic Supplements. Washington, DC: USGPO.

U.S. Bureau of the Census. 2004g. *Facts for features.* (August 6). Washington, DC: USGPO.

U.S. Bureau of the Census. 2004h. *Facts for features, Fathers' Day; June 20.* (April 29). Washington, DC: USGPO.

U.S. Bureau of the Census. 2004i. *General Demographic Characteristics, 2004. American community survey, race.* Washington, DC: USGPO.

U.S. Bureau of the Census. 2004j. *Housing: Financial characteristics.* (September 17). Washington, DC: USGPO.

U.S. Bureau of the Census. 2004k. *Population division. Current population survey, 2004.* Annual Social and Economic Supplement. Washington, DC: USGPO.

U.S. Bureau of the Census. 2005a. *Current population survey.* Annual Social and Economic Supplement. (accessed May 29, 2006).

U.S. Census Bureau. 2005b. *Current population survey.* Annual Social and Economic Supplements. Historic Poverty Tables. Poverty and Health Statistics Branch. (August 30).

U.S. Census Bureau. 2005c. *Examining American household composition: 1990 and 2000.* Census 2000 Special Report. (August).

U.S. Census Bureau. 2005d. Housing and Household Economic Statistics. (May 13).

U.S. Census Bureau. 2005e. *Participation of mothers in government assistance programs: Survey of income reports and program participation 2001.* (November).

U.S. Census Bureau. 2005f. *Population division.* Fertility and Family Statistics Branch.

U.S. Census Bureau. 2005g. *Poverty Thresholds 2004.* (January 28).

U.S. Census Bureau. 2005h. *Statistical abstract of the United States: 2004–2005.*

U.S. Commission on Civil Rights. 1981. *Child care and equal opportunity for women.* June. Washington, DC: USGPO.

U.S. Conference of Mayors. 2002. Hunger/Homelessness Report.

U.S. Conference of Mayors. 2003. Hunger and Homelessness Survey. (December 18).

U.S. Congress House Committee on Ways and Means. 1987a. *Background material and data on programs within the jurisdiction of the Committee on Ways and Means.* 100th Congress, 1st Session, March 6. Washington, DC: USGPO.

U.S. Congress House Committee on Ways and Means. 1987b. *Stewart P. McKinney Homeless Assistance Act.* Conference Report to accompany H.R. 558. 100th Congress, 1st Session. Washington, DC: USGPO.

U.S. Department of Agriculture. 1991. *The cost of raising a child.* Washington, DC: USGPO.

U.S. Department of Agriculture. 2004. *Expenditures on children by families, 2004 Annual Report.* Center for Nutrition Policy and Promotion. Washington, DC: USGPO.

U.S. Department of Health and Human Services. 1990. *Vital Statistics.* 7–8. (Statistics on teen pregnancy from 1955 to 1990 by race)

U.S. Department of Health and Human Services. 1991. *Cohabitation, marriage, marital dissolution and remarriage in the United States, 1988.* Washington, DC: USGPO.

U.S. Department of Health and Human Services. 2001. *Administration for children and families.* Office of Family Assistance. Fifth Report to Congress. Washington, DC: USGPO.

U.S. Department of Health and Human Services. 2002a. *Child maltreatment 2002.* Administration for Children and Families. Washington, DC: USGPO.

U.S. Department of Health and Human Services. 2002b. *Preventing teenage pregnancy.* Press Office. (June 10). Washington, DC: USGPO.

U.S. Department of Health and Human Services. 2004a. *Child abuse and neglect fatalities: Statistics and interventions.* National Clearinghouse on Child Abuse and Neglect Information. Washington, DC: USGPO.

U.S. Department of Health and Human Services. 2004b. Office of Family Assistance. TANF Sixth Annual Report to Congress. (November). Washington, DC: USGPO.

U.S. Department of Health and Human Services. 2005. *Child maltreatment 2003: Summary of key findings.* National Clearinghouse on Child Abuse and Neglect Information. Washington, DC: USGPO.

U.S. Department of Justice. 1985. *FBI uniform crime reports.* Washington, DC: GPO.

U.S. Department of Justice. 2003. *Criminal victimization in the United States—Statistical tables.* Bureau of Justice Statistics. Washington, DC: USGPO.

U.S. Department of Justice. 2004. Bureau of Justice Statistics. Washington, DC: USGPO.

U.S. Department of Justice. 2005. *Violent victimization rates by Gender 1973–2004.* Bureau of Justice Statistics. Washington, DC: USGPO.

U.S. Department of Labor and Bureau of Labor Statistics. 1997. Occupational employment projections to 2006. *Monthly Labor Review* 120 (11).

U.S. House of Representatives. 2004. *The 2004 green book: Background material and data on programs within the jurisdiction of the committee on ways and means.* (January). Washington, DC: USGPO.

U.S. National Center for Education Statistics. 1995. *Statistics in brief.* October 1995, NCES 95–824.

Udry, J. 1977. The importance of being beautiful: A re-examination and racial comparison. *American Journal of Sociology* 83:154–160.

Uhlenberg, John. 1989. Death and the family. In A. Skolnick and J. Skolnick (eds.), *Family in transition.* 6th ed. (pp. 87–96). Boston: Scott Foresman.

Uhlenberg, Peter. 1998. Mortality decline in the 20th century and supply of kin over the life course. In K. Hansen and A. Garey (eds.), *Families in the U. S: Kinship and domestic politics* (pp. 69–77). Philadelphia: Temple University Press.

Ullmann, Owen. 1993. U.S. future relies on adapting to global economy. *Charlotte Observer,* 25 April, 1e, 4e.

Ulrich, Laurel Thatcher. 1991. *Good wives: Image and reality in northern New England 1650–1750.* New York: Vintage Books.

UNICEF. 2005. Child Poverty in rich countries. www.unicef-icdc.org (accessed May 29, 2006).

United Nations. 2005. *World survey on the role of women in development.* New York: UN.

Upson, Norma. 1974. *How to survive as a corporate wife.* Garden City, NY.: Doubleday & Co.

Uttal, Lynn. 1999. Custodial care, surrogate care, and coordinated care: Employed mothers and the meaning of child care. In S. Ferguson (ed.), *Shifting the center: Understand-*

ing contemporary families (pp. 562–577). Moutain View, CA: Mayfield.

Valman, H. 1980. The first year of life: Mother infant bonding. *British Medical Journal* 280 (6210):308–310.

van den Wijngaard, Marianne. 1997. *Reinventing the sexes: The biomedical construction of femininity and masculinity.* Bloomington, IN: University of Indiana Press.

Van Til, Jon. 1988. *Mapping the third sector: Voluntarism in a changing social economy.* Washington, DC: Foundation Center.

Vance, Carol. 1984. *Pleasure and danger: Exploring female sexuality.* Boston: Routledge and Kegan Paul.

VanEvery, Dale 1976. *The disinherited: The lost birthright of the American Indian.* New York: Morrow.

VanWormer, Katherine, and Robin McKinney. 2003. What Can Schools Do to Help Gay/Lesbian/Bisexual Youth? *Adolesence,* 38 (151);409–420.

Veevers, Jean. 1980. *Childless by choice.* Toronto: Butterworth.

Ventura, S. J., J. A. Martin, S. C. Curtin and J. J. Matthews. 1999. "Births: Final data for 1997" *National Vital Statistics Report* 47, No. 18. Hyattsville, MD: National Center for Health Statistics.

Verne, D. P. 1995. *Sexual love and western morality: A philosophical anthology.* Boston: Jones and Bartlett Publishers.

Veroff, Joseph, Elizabeth Douvan, and Richard Kukla. 1981. *The inner American: A self-portrait from 1957–1976.* New York: Basic Books.

Vickery, C. 1979. Women's economic contribution to the family. In R. Smith (ed.), *The subtle revolution: Women at work* (pp. 159–200). Washington, DC: The Urban Institute.

Vobejda, B. 1997. Abortion rate in U.S. off sharply. *Washington Post,* 5 December, A1

Vobejda, Barbara. 1998. Return back, blacks moving to the South. *Washington Post,* 29 January, A3.

Voydanoff, Patricia. 1963. *The influence of economic security on morale.* Unpublished thesis, Wayne State University.

Voydanoff, Patricia. 1984. Unemployment: Family strategies for adaptation. In P. Voydanoff (ed.), *Work and family: Changing roles of men and women* (pp. 61–72). Palo Alto, CA: Mayfield.

Voydanoff, Patricia, and Brenda Donnelley. 1988. Economic distress, family coping and the quality of life. In P. Voydanoff and L. Majka (eds.), *Families and economic distress: Coping strategies and public policy* (pp. 97–116). Beverly Hills, CA: Sage.

Walby, Sylvia. 1986. *Patriarchy at work: Patriarchal and capitalist relations in employment.* Minneapolis: University of Minnesota Press.

Waldfogel, Jane. 1998. *The future of child protection: How to break the cycle of abuse and neglect.* Cambridge, MA: Harvard University Press.

Waldfogel, Jane. 1998. The family gap for young women in the United States and Britain. *Journal of Labor Economics.* 76 (3):505–545.

Walker, Alice. 1990. The right to life: What can the white man say to the black woman? In M. Fried (ed.), *From abortion to reproductive freedom: Transforming a movement* (pp. 65–70). Boston: South End Press.

Walker, K., and M. Woods. 1976. *Time use: A measure of household production of family goods and services.* Washington, DC: American Home Economics Association.

Walker, Lenore. 1979. *The battered woman.* New York: Harper.

Walker, Lenore. 1983. The battered woman syndrome study. In D. Finkelhor et al. (eds.), *The dark side of families: Current family violence research* (pp. 31–48). Beverly Hills, CA: Sage.

Walker, Nancy, Catherine Brooks, and Lawrence Wrightsman. 1999. *Children's rights in the United States: In search of a national policy.* Thousand Oaks, CA: Sage.

Wall Street Journal Almanac. 1998. World Almanac Education. 710.

Wall Street Journal. 1994. "Retooling lives: Technological gains are cutting costs and jobs in services" (2/24):A1.

Wallerstein, Judith, and Sandra Blakeslee. 1989. *Second chances: Men, women and children a decade after divorce.* New York: Ticknor and Field.

Walzer, Susan. 1998. *Thinking about the baby: Gender transitions into parenthood.* Philadelphia: Temple University Press.

Wang, Penelope. 2005. Four myths about college costs. *Money Magazine.*

Ward, Kelly, and Lisa Wolf-Wendel. 2004. Academic motherhood: Managing complex roles in research. *Review of Higher Education.* 27 (2):233–257.

Warlamount, H. 1993. Visual grammars of gender. *Journal of Communication Inquiry* 17 (1):25.

Warner, Michael, ed. 1993. *Fear of a queer planet: Queer politics and social theory.* Minneapolis: University of Minnesota Press.

Warren, Elizabeth, and Amelia Warren Tyagi. 2003. The two income trap: Why middle class mothers and fathers are going broke. New York: *Basic Books.*

Washburne, Carolyn. 1983. A feminist analysis of child abuse and neglect. In D. Finkelhor et al. (eds.), *The dark side of families: Current family violence research* (pp. 289–292). Beverly Hills, CA: Sage.

Washington Post. 1992. Violence against women. 1 September, 115.

Waxman, Laura, and Remy Tripin. 1997. *A status report on hunger and homelessness in America's cities.* Washington, DC: US Conference of Mayors.

Weber, Max. 1969. *The theory of social and economic organization.* New York: Free Press.

Weeks, Jeffrey. 1985. *Sexuality and its discontents: Meanings, myths and modern sexualities.* London: Routledge and Kegan Paul.

Weeks, John. 1993. *Population: Introduction to concepts and issues.* 5th ed. Belmont, CA: Wadsworth.

Weissman, M., and S. Paykel. 1972. *The depressed woman: A study of social relationships.* Chicago: University of Chicago Press.

Weitz, Rose, and Deborah Sullivan. 1986. The politics of childbirth: The re-emergence of midwifery in Arizona. *Social Problems* 33 (3):163–175.

Weitzman, Lenore. 1981. *The marriage contract: Spouses, lovers and the law.* New York: Free Press.

Weitzman, Lenore. 1985. *The divorce revolution: The unexpected social and economic consequences for women and children in America.* New York: Free Press.

Weitzman, Lenore, and Ruth Dixon. 1992. The transformation of legal marriage through no-fault divorce. In A. Skolnick and J. Skolnick (eds.), *Family in transition.* 7th ed. (pp. 217–230). New York: Harper Collins.

Welfare Mother's Voice. 1992. California moms fight back. Spring, 1.

Wells, Carla. 1993. The role of the church and family support in the lives of older African Americans. In L. Butler (ed.), *Families and Aging* (pp. 67–74).

Welter, Barbara. 1978. The cult of true womanhood, 1820–1860. In M. Gordon (ed.), *The American family in social-historical perspective.* 2d ed. (pp. 313–333). New York: St. Martin's Press.

West, Candace, and Don Zimmerman. 1987. Doing gender. *Gender and Society* 1:125–151.

West, Elliott. 1992. Children on the plains frontier. In E. West and P. Petrik (eds.), *Small worlds: children and adolescents, 1850–1950* (pp. 26–41). Lawrence, KS: University Press of Kansas.

West, Guida. 1981. *The national welfare rights movement: The social protest of poor women.* New York: Praeger.

Weston, Kath. 1991. *Families we choose.* New York: Columbia University Press.

Westwood, Sallie. 1984. *All day, every day: Factory and family in the making of women's lives.* London: Pluto Press.

Wharton, Carol. 1987. Establishing shelters for battered women: Local manifestations of a social movement. *Qualitative Sociology* 10 (2):146–163.

Wharton, Carol. 1994. "Finding time for the second shift" *Gender and Society* 8 (2):189–205.

White, Deborah. 1985. *Aren't I a woman: Female slaves in the plantation South.* New York: W. W. Norton.

White, Lynn. 1991. Determinants of divorce: Review of research in the 1980s. In A. Booth (ed.), *Contemporary families: Looking forward, looking back* (pp. 141–149). Minneapolis: National Council on Family Relations.

White, Lynn. 1994. Coresidence and leaving home: Young adults and their parents. *Annual Review of Sociology* 20:81–102.

White, Lynn, Alan Booth, and John Edwards. 1986. Children and marital happiness: Why the negative relationship? *Journal of Family Issues* 7:131–148.

White, Lynn, and David Brinkerhoff. 1987. Children's work in families: Its significance and meaning. In N. Gerstel and H. Gross (eds.), *Families and work* (pp. 204–219). Philadelphia: Temple University Press.

Whitehead, Barbara Dafoe, and David Popenoe. 2005. *The state of our unions: The social health of marriage in america 2005. The national marriage project.* New Jersey: Rutgers.

Wiggins, David. 1985. The play of slave children in plantation communities in the old South, 1820–1860. In N. Hiner and J. Hawes, *Growing up in America: Children in historical perspectives* (pp. 173–192). Chicago: University of Illinois Press.

Wiley, Norbert. 1979. The rise and fall of dominating theories in sociology. In W. Snizek, E. Fuhrman, and M. Miller (eds.), *Contemporary issues in theory and research* (pp. 47–49). Westport, CT: Greenwood Press.

Wilkinson, Darlene. 1998. A wife's role. In S. Ruth (ed.), *Issues in feminism: An introduction to women's studies,* 4th ed. (pp. 136–148). Mountain View, CA: Mayfield.

Wilkinson, Doris. 1984. Afro-American women and their families. *Marriage and Family Review* 7 (Fall):459–467.

William T. Grant Foundation Commission on Work, Family and Citizenship. 1988. *The forgotten half: Pathways to success for America's youth and young families.* Washington, DC: William T. Grant Foundation Commission on Work, Family and Citizenship.

Williams, Constance. 1990. *Black teenage mothers.* New York: Lexington.

Williams, Linda. 2005. "Repairing the past." Proceedings of the Seventh Annual Gilder Lehmann Center International Conference, Yale University.

Williams, Norma. 1990. Role making among married Mexican American women: Issues of class and ethnicity. In C. Carlson (ed.), *Perspectives on the family: History, class and feminism* (pp. 186–204). Belmont, CA: Wadsworth.

Williams, Terry, and William Kornblum. 1991. Sneaker mothers. In M. Hutter (ed.), *The family experience* (pp. 589–600). New York: MacMillan.

Willie, Charles. 1983. *Race, ethnicity and socioeconomic status: A theoretical analysis of their interrelationship.* Dix Hills, NY: General Hall.

Willie, Charles. 1985. *Black and white families: A study in complementarity.* Bayside, NY: General Hall.

Willie, Charles. 1988. *A new look at black families.* 3d ed. Bayside, NY: General Hall.

Willis, Ellen. 1983. Abortion: Is a woman a person? In A. Snitow, C. Stansell, and S. Thompson (eds.), *Powers of desire: The politics of sexuality* (pp. 471–476). New York: Monthly Review Press.

Wilson, E. O. 1975. *Sociobiology: The new synthesis.* Cambridge, MA: Harvard University Press.

Wilson, M., H. Johnson, and M. Daly. 1995. Lethal and nonlethal violence against wives. *Canadian Journal of Criminology* 37:331–361.

Wilson, Michael. 1977. *Salt of the Earth.* NY: CUNY Feminist Press.

Wilson, William Julius, and Kathryn Neckerman. 1986. Poverty and family structure: The widening gap between evidence and public policy issues. In S. Danziger and D. Weinberg (eds.), *Fighting poverty: What works and what doesn't* (pp. 240–264). Chicago: University of Chicago Press.

Wiltz, Teresa. 2004. The evil sista of reality television: Shows trot out old stereotypes to spice up stagnant story lines. *Washington Post.* (25 February).

Winnick, Andrew. 1988. The changing distribution of income and wealth in the U.S., 1960–1985: An examination of the movement toward two societies separate but equal. In R. Voydanoff and L. Majka (eds.), *Economic distress and families: Coping strategies and public policy* (pp. 232–260). Beverly Hills, CA: Sage.

Witt, Susan D. 2000. The influences of television on children's gender role socialization. *The Journal of Childhood Education: Infancy through adolescence,* 76 (5):322–324.

Wolf, Naomi. 1993. *Fire with fire: The new female power and how it will change the 21st century.* New York: Random House.

Wolf, Wendy, and Neil Fligstein. 1979. Sex and authority in the workplace. *American Sociological Review* 44:235–252.

Wolfe, Christopher. 1998. *The family, civil society and the state.* Boston: Rowman and Littlefield.

Wolff, Edward N. 2000. Recent Trends in Wealth Ownership, 1983–1998. Jerome Levy Economics Institute. (April).

Wolff, Edward. 1995a. *Study of increasing inequality in America.* New York: Twentieth Century Fund.

Wolff, Edward. 1995b. *Top heavy: Increasing inequality of wealth in America.* New York: Twentieth Century Fund.

Women's Institute for Freedom of the Press (WIFP). 1986. 1955 to 1985: Women in prime time TV still traditional, but new treatment of women's rights themes. *Media Report to Women,* November-December, 7.

Women's Institute for Freedom of the Press (WIFP). 1990. TV portrayal of the childless black female: Superficial, unskilled, dependent. *Media Report to Women,* March–April, 4.

Wong, Morrison. 1995. Chinese Americans. In P. Min (ed.), *Asian Americans: Contemporary trends and issues* (pp. 58–94). Thousand Oaks, CA: Sage.

Wood, J. 1996. She says/he says: Communication, caring and conflict. In J. Wood (ed.), *Gendered relationships* (pp. 149–162). Mountain View, CA: Mayfield.

World Almanac and Book of Facts 1997. 1996. Mahwah, NJ: World Almanac Books.

World Almanac and Book of Facts, 1992. 1991. New York: World Almanac Books

Wright, Eric Olin, Karen Shire, Shu-Ling Hwang, Maureen Dolan, and Janeen Baxter. 1992. The non-effects of class on the gender division of labor in the home: A comparative study of Sweden and the U.S. *Gender and Society* 6 (2):252–282.

Wright, Eric Olin. 1985. *Classes.* London: Verso.

Wright, Eric Olin. 1990. *A debate on classes.* London: Verso.

Wright, James, Beth Rubin, and Joel Devine. 1998. *Beside the golden door: Policy, politics and the homeless.* New York: Aldine de Gruyter.

Wrigley, Julia. 1995. *Other people's children: An intimate account of the dilemmas facing middle class parents and the women they hire to raise their children.* New York: Basic Books.

WWW.KWRU.ORG. 2006. Kensington Welfare Rights Union. (accessed May 29, 2006).

WWW.NATIONALWRU.ORG. 2006. National Welfare Rights Union. (accessed May 29, 2006).

WWW.NDVH.ORG. 2005. "Hotline Reports 15% Increase." National Domestic Violence Hotline Press Release.

WWW.PFLAG.ORG. 2006. (accessed May 29, 2006).

WWW.UDWA.ORG. 2006. United Domestic Workers of America. (accessed May 29, 2006).

Wyatt, Gail, Hector Myers, Kimlin Ashing-Giwa, and Ramani Durvasula. 1998. Sociocultural factors affecting sexual risk taking in African American women and men: Results from two empirical studies. In R. Staples (ed.), *The black family* (pp. 45–58). Belmont, CA: Wadsworth.

Yangisako, Sylvia. 1985. *Transforming the past: Tradition and kinship among Japanese Americans.* Stanford: Stanford University Press.

Ybarra, Leonarda. 1977. *Conjugal role relationships in the Chicano family.* Ph.D. dissertation, University of California, Berkeley.

Ybarra, Leonarda. 1982a. Marital decision making and the role of machismo in the Chicano family. *De Colores, Journal of Chicano Expression and Thought* 6:32–47.

Ybarra, Leonarda. 1982b. When wives work: The impact on the Chicano family. *Journal of Marriage and the Family* 44 (1):169–178.

Yllo, Kersti. 1988. Political and methodological debates in wife abuse research. In K. Yllo and M. Bograd (eds.), *Feminist perspectives on wife abuse* (pp. 28–51). Newbury Park, CA: Sage.

Zaretsky, Eli. 1982. *Capitalism, the family and personal life.* New York: Harper.

Zaretsky, Eli. 1987. The place of family in the origins of the welfare state. In B. Thorne with M. Yalom (eds.), *Rethinking the family: Some feminist questions* (pp. 188–224). New York: Longman.

Zavella, Patricia. 1987. *Women's work and Chicano families: Cannery workers of the Santa Clara Valley.* Ithaca: Cornell University Press.

Zelizer, Viviana. 1985. *Pricing the priceless child: The changing social value of children.* New York: Basic Books.

Zelnick, Melvin, John Kanter, and Kathleen Ford. 1981. *Sex and pregnancy in adolescence.* Beverly Hills, CA: Sage.

Zhou, Min, and Carl Bankston. 1998. *Growing up American: How Vietnamese children adapt to life in the U.S.* New York: Russell Sage.

Zhou, Min. 1999. "The Other Half of the Sky: Socioeconomic Adaptation of Immigrant Women." In C. Ellison and W. Martin (eds.), *Race and Ethnic Relations in the United States: Readings for the 21st Century.* (pp. 132–141). Los Angeles: Roxbury Publishing Company.

Zicklin, Gilbert. 1995. Deconstructing legal rationality: the case of lesbian and gay family relationships. In L. McIntyre and M. Sussman (eds.), *Families and law* (pp. 55–76). New York: Hayworth Press.

Zigler, Edward, and Meryl Frank. 1988. *The parental leave crisis.* New Haven: Yale University Press.

Zigler, Edward, and Mary Long. 1991. *Childcare choices: Balancing the needs of children, families and society.* New York: Free Press.

Zimmerman, Shirley. 1992. *Family policies and family well-being: The role of political culture.* Newbury Park, CA: Sage.

Zinn, Howard. 1980. *A people's history of the U.S.* New York: Harper & Row.

Zoroya, Gregg. 2005. Soldiers' divorce rates up sharply. *USA Today.* (8 June).

Zorza, Joan and Laurie Woods. 1994. *Mandatory arrest: problems and possibilities.* New York: National Center on Women and Family Law.

Zuckerman, Diana, and Stacey Friedman. 1998. *Measuring the cost of domestic violence against women: A summary of the findings of the domestic violence project.* Washington, DC: Institute for Women's Policy Research.

INDEX